TRANSLATOR AND SENIOR EDITOR:
Rabbi Israel V. Berman

MANAGING EDITOR:
Baruch Goldberg

EDITORS:
Rabbi Moshe Sober
Rabbi David Strauss

ASSOCIATE EDITOR:
Dr. Jeffrey M. Green

COPY EDITOR:
Alec Israel

BOOK DESIGNER:
Ben Gasner

GRAPHIC ARTIST:
Michael Etkin

TECHNICAL STAFF:
Moshe Greenvald
Inna Schwartzman

Random House Staff

PRODUCTION MANAGER:
Kathy Rosenbloom

ART DIRECTOR:
Bernard Klein

CHIEF COPY EDITOR:
Amy Edelman

The Talmud

The Steinsaltz Edition

Volume XIII

Tractate Ta'anit

Part I

VOLUME XIII
TRACTATE TA'ANIT
PART I

RANDOM HOUSE
NEW YORK

THE TALMUD

תלמוד בבלי

THE STEINSALTZ EDITION

Commentary by Rabbi Adin Steinsaltz (Even Yisrael)

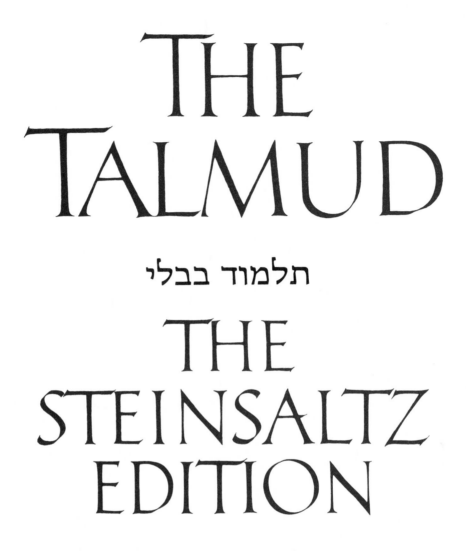

Published in the United States by Random House, Inc., New York,
and simultaneously in Canada by Random House of Canada Limited, Toronto.

Library of Congress Cataloging-in-Publication Data
(Revised for volume XIII)
The Talmud
English, Hebrew, and Aramaic.
Includes bibliographical references.
v.XIII-Tractate Ta'anit, pt.1
Accompanied by a reference guide.
1. Title.
BM499.5.E4 1989 89-842911
ISBN 0-679-42961-1 (v. XIII)
ISBN 0-394-57665-9 (guide)

Manufactured in the United States of America on acid-free paper
9 8 7 6 5 4 3 2
First Edition

״ושננתם לבניך״

"You shall teach them diligently unto your children"
Deuteronomy 6:7

This volume is dedicated by
Frances and Hubert J. Brandt
with love to our children

Sherry and Paul Brandt-Rauf
James and Kathryn Brandt
Karen and Kenan Onel

our grandchildren
Elka, Joshua and Oren Brandt-Rauf
Lindsay, Jennifer and David Brandt

and those who will come after
whom we do not yet know
or may never have the pleasure to meet

to express the joy which has enriched our lives by watching our family grow to become part of the Jewish people we cherish.

We pray that you are blessed as we have been:

״יברכך ה׳ מציון״

"May the Lord bless you out of Zion;
and may you look upon the good of Jerusalem
all the days of your life;
may you see the children of your children.
Peace upon Israel."
Psalm 128:5-6

The Steinsaltz Talmud in English

The English edition of the Steinsaltz Talmud is a translation and adaptation of the Hebrew edition. It includes most of the additions and improvements that characterize the Hebrew version, but it has been adapted and expanded especially for the English reader. This edition has been designed to meet the needs of advanced students capable of studying from standard Talmud editions, as well as of beginners, who know little or no Hebrew and have had no prior training in studying the Talmud.

The overall structure of the page is similar to that of the traditional pages in the standard printed editions. The text is placed in the center of the page, and alongside it are the main auxiliary commentaries. At the bottom of the page and in the margins are additions and supplements.

The original Hebrew-Aramaic text, which is framed in the center of each page, is exactly the same as that in the traditional Talmud (although material that was removed by non-Jewish censors has been restored on the basis of manuscripts and old printed editions). The main innovation is that this Hebrew-Aramaic text has been completely vocalized and punctuated, and all the terms usually abbreviated have been fully spelled out. In order to retain the connection with the page numbers of the standard editions, these are indicated at the head of every page.

We have placed a *Literal Translation* on the right-hand side of the page, and its punctuation has been introduced into the Talmud text, further helping the student to orientate himself. The *Literal Translation* is intended to help the student to learn the meaning of specific Hebrew and Aramaic words. By comparing the original text with this translation, the reader develops an understanding of the Talmudic text and can follow the words and sentences in the original. Occasionally, however, it has not been possible

to present an exact literal translation of the original text, because it is so different in structure from English. Therefore we have added certain auxiliary words, which are indicated in square brackets. In other cases it would make no sense to offer a literal translation of a Talmudic idiom, so we have provided a close English equivalent of the original meaning, while a note, marked "lit.," explaining the literal meaning of the words, appears in parentheses. Our purpose in presenting this literal translation was to give the student an appreciation of the terse and enigmatic nature of the Talmud itself, before the arguments are opened up by interpretation.

Nevertheless, no one can study the Talmud without the assistance of commentaries. The main aid to understanding the Talmud provided by this edition is the *Translation and Commentary,* appearing on the left side of the page. This is Rabbi Adin Steinsaltz's highly regarded Hebrew interpretation of the Talmud, translated into English, adapted and expanded.

This commentary is not merely an explanation of difficult passages. It is an integrated exposition of the entire text. It includes a full translation of the Talmud text, combined with explanatory remarks. Where the translation in the commentary reflects the literal translation, it has been set off in bold type. It has also been given the same reference numbers that are found both in the original text and in the literal translation. Moreover, each section of the commentary begins with a few words of the Hebrew-Aramaic text. These reference numbers and paragraph headings allow the reader to move from one part of the page to another with ease.

There are some slight variations between the literal translation and the words in bold face appearing in the *Translation and Commentary.* These variations are meant to enhance understanding, for a juxtaposition of the literal translation and the sometimes freer translation in the commentary will give the reader a firmer grasp of the meaning.

The expanded *Translation and Commentary* in the left-hand column is intended to provide a conceptual understanding of the arguments of the Talmud, their form, content, context, and significance. The commentary also brings out the logic of the questions asked by the Sages and the assumptions they made.

Rashi's traditional commentary has been included in the right-hand column, under the *Literal Translation.* We have left this commentary in the traditional "Rashi script," but all quotations of the Talmud text appear in standard square type, the abbreviated expressions have all been printed in full, and Rashi's commentary is fully punctuated.

Since the *Translation and Commentary* cannot remain cogent and still encompass all the complex issues that arise in the Talmudic discussion, we have included a number of other features, which are also found in Rabbi Steinsaltz's Hebrew edition.

At the bottom of the page, under the *Translation and Commentary*, is the *Notes* section, containing additional material on issues raised in the text. These notes deepen understanding of the Talmud in various ways. Some provide a deeper and more profound analysis of the issues discussed in the text, with regard to individual points and to the development of the entire discussion. Others explain Halakhic concepts and the terms of Talmudic discourse.

The *Notes* contain brief summaries of the opinions of many of the major commentators on the Talmud, from the period after the completion of the Talmud to the present. Frequently the *Notes* offer interpretations different from that presented in the commentary, illustrating the richness and depth of Rabbinic thought.

The *Halakhah* section appears below the *Notes.* This provides references to the authoritative legal decisions reached over the centuries by the Rabbis in their discussions of the matters dealt with in the Talmud. It explains what reasons led to these Halakhic decisions and the close connection between the Halakhah today and the Talmud and its various interpreters. It should be noted that the summary of the Halakhah presented here is not meant to serve as a reference source for actual religious practice but to introduce the reader to Halakhic conclusions drawn from the Talmudic text.

English commentary and expanded translation of the text, making it readable and comprehensible

Hebrew/Aramaic text of the Talmud, fully vocalized, and punctuated

Literal translation of the Talmud text into English

Marginal notes provide essential background information

Hebrew commentary of Rashi, the classic explanation that accompanies all editions of the Talmud

Numbers link the three main sections of the page and allow readers to refer rapidly from one to the other

Notes highlight points of interest in the text and expand the discussion by quoting other classical commentaries

REALIA

קַלְתָּה **Her basket.** The source of this word is the Greek κάλαθος, kalathos, and it means a basket with a narrow base.

Illustration from a Greek drawing depicting such a basket of fruit.

CONCEPTS

פֵּאָה *Pe'ah.* **One of the presents left for the poor** (מַתְּנוֹת עֲנִיִּים). The Torah forbids harvesting "the corners of your field," so that the produce left standing may be harvested and kept by the poor (Leviticus 19:9).

The Torah did not specify a minimum amount of produce to be left as *pe'ah*. But the Sages stipulated that it must be at least one-sixtieth of the crop.

Pe'ah is set aside only from crops that ripen at one time and are harvested at one time. The poor are allowed to use their own initiative to reap the *pe'ah* left in the fields. But the owner of an orchard must see to it that each of the poor gets a fixed share of the *pe'ah* from places that are difficult to reach. The poor come to collect *pe'ah* three times a day. The laws of *pe'ah* are discussed in detail in tractate *Pe'ah*.

TRANSLATION AND COMMENTARY

[1]**and her husband threw her a bill of divorce into her lap or into her basket**, which she was carrying on her head, [2]would you say **here, too,** that **she would not be divorced**? Surely we know that the law is that she *is* divorced in such a case, as the Mishnah (*Gittin* 77a) states explicitly!

אֲמַר לֵיהּ [3]Rav Ashi **said** in reply to Ravina: The woman's **basket is** considered to be **at rest, and it is she who walks beneath it.** Thus the basket is considered to be a "stationary courtyard," and the woman acquires whatever is thrown into it.

MISHNAH הָיָה רוֹכֵב [4]If a **person was riding on an animal and he saw an ownerless object** lying on the ground, **and he said to another person** standing nearby, **"Give that object to me,"** [5]if **the other person took** the ownerless object **and said, "I have acquired it for myself,"** [6]he has **acquired it** by lifting it up, even though he was not the first to see it, and the rider has no claim to it. [7]But **if, after he gave** the object **to** the rider, the person who picked it up **said, "I acquired** the object **first,"** [8]**he** in fact **said nothing.** His words are of no effect, and the rider may keep it. Since the person walking showed no intention of acquiring the object when he originally picked it up, he is not now believed when he claims that he acquired it first. Indeed, even if we maintain that when a person picks up an ownerless object on behalf of someone else, the latter does *not* acquire it automatically, here, by *giving* the object to the rider, he makes a gift of it to the rider.

GEMARA תְּנַן הָתָם [9]**We have learned elsewhere** in a Mishnah in tractate *Pe'ah* (4:9): **"Someone who gathered** *pe'ah* — produce which by Torah law [Leviticus 23:22] is left unharvested in the corner of a field by the owner of the field, to be gleaned by the poor — **and said, 'Behold, this** *pe'ah* which I have gleaned **is** intended **for so-and-so the poor man,'** [10]**Rabbi Eliezer says:** The person who gathered the *pe'ah* **has acquired it**

בִּרְשׁוּת הָרַבִּים [1]וְזָרַק לָהּ גֵּט לְתוֹךְ חֵיקָהּ אוֹ לְתוֹךְ קַלְתָּהּ — [2]הָכָא נַמִּי דְּלָא מִגָּרְשָׁה? [3]אֲמַר לֵיהּ: קַלְתָּהּ מֵינָח נַיְיחָא, וְאִיהִי דְּקָא מְסַגְּיָא מִתּוּתָהּ.

משנה [4]הָיָה רוֹכֵב עַל גַּבֵּי בְהֵמָה וְרָאָה אֶת הַמְּצִיאָה, וְאָמַר לַחֲבֵירוֹ "תְּנָה לִי", [5]נְטָלָהּ וְאָמַר, "אֲנִי זָכִיתִי בָּהּ", [6]זָכָה בָּהּ. [7]אִם, מִשֶּׁנְּתָנָהּ לוֹ, אָמַר, "אֲנִי זָכִיתִי בָּהּ תְּחִלָּה", [8]לֹא אָמַר כְּלוּם.

גמרא [9]תְּנַן הָתָם: "מִי שֶׁלִּיקֵּט אֶת הַפֵּאָה וְאָמַר, 'הֲרֵי זוֹ לִפְלוֹנִי עָנִי', [10]רַבִּי אֱלִיעֶזֶר

LITERAL TRANSLATION

in a public thoroughfare [1]and [her husband] threw her a bill of divorce into her lap or into her basket, [2]here, too, would she not be divorced?

[3]He said to him: Her basket is at rest, and it is she who walks beneath it.

MISHNAH [4][If a person] was riding on an animal and he saw a found object, and he said to another person, "Give it to me," [5][and the other person] took it and said, "I have acquired it," [6]he has acquired it. [7]If, after he gave it to him, he said, "I acquired it first," [8]he said nothing.

GEMARA [9]We have learned there: "Someone who gathered *pe'ah* and said, 'Behold this is for so-and-so the poor man,' [10]Rabbi Eliezer says:

RASHI

קלתה – סל שעל ראשה, שנותנת בה כלי מלאכתה וטווי שלה. הכי נמי דלא הוי גיטא – והאנן תנן במסכת גיטין (עז,א): זרק לה גיטה לתוך חיקה או לתוך קלתה – הרי זו מגורשת!

משנה לא אמר כלום – דאפילו אמרינן המגביה מציאה לחבירו לא קנה חבירו, כיון דיהבה ליה – קנייה ממה נפשך. אי קנייה קמא דלא מתכוין להקנות לחבירו – הא יהבה ניהליה במתנה. ואי לא קנייה קמא משום דלא היה מתכוין לקנות – הויא ליה הפקר עד דמטא לידיה דהאי, וקנייה האי במאי דעקרה מידיה דקמא לשם קנייה.

גמרא מי שליקט את הפאה – אדם בעלמא שאינו בעל שדה. דאי בבעל שדה – לא אמר רבי אליעזר זכה. דליכא למימר "מגו דזכי לנפשיה", דאפילו הוא עני מוזהר הוא שלא ללקט פאה משדה שלו, כדאמר בשחיטת חולין (קלא,ב): "לא תלקט לעני" – להזהיר עני על שלו.

NOTES

מִי שֶׁלִּיקֵּט אֶת הַפֵּאָה **If a person gathered** ***pe'ah.*** According to *Rashi*, the Mishnah must be referring to someone other than the owner of the field. By Torah law the owner of a field is required to separate part of his field as *pe'ah*, even if he himself is poor, and he may not take the *pe'ah* for himself. Therefore the "since" (מִגּוֹ) argument

HALAKHAH

קַלְתָּהּ **A woman's basket.** "If a man throws a bill of divorce into a container that his wife is holding, she thereby acquires the bill of divorce and the divorce takes effect." (*Shulḥan Arukh, Even HaEzer* 139:10.)

הַמְלַקֵּט פֵּאָה עֲבוּר אַחֵר **A person who gathered** ***pe'ah*** **for someone else.** "If a poor person, who is himself entitled to collect *pe'ah*, gathered *pe'ah* for another poor person, and said, 'This *pe'ah* is for X, the poor person,' he acquires the *pe'ah* on behalf of that other poor person. But if the person who collected the *peah* was wealthy, he does not acquire the *pe'ah* on behalf of the poor person. He must give it instead to the first poor person who appears in the field," following the opinion of the Sages, as explained by Rabbi Yehoshua ben Levi. (*Rambam, Sefer Zeraim, Hilkhot Mattenot Aniyyim* 2:19.)

On the outer margin of the page, factual information clarifying the meaning of the Talmudic discussion is presented. Entries under the heading *Language* explain unusual terms, often borrowed from Greek, Latin, or Persian. *Sages* gives brief biographies of the major figures whose opinions are presented in the Talmud. *Terminology* explains the terms used in the Talmudic discussion. *Concepts* gives information about fundamental Halakhic principles. *Background* provides historical, geographical, and other information needed to understand the text. *Realia* explains the artifacts mentioned in the text. These notes are sometimes accompanied by illustrations.

The best way of studying the Talmud is the way in which the Talmud itself evolved - a combination of frontal teaching and continuous interaction between teacher and pupil, and between pupils themselves.

This edition is meant for a broad spectrum of users, from those who have considerable prior background and who know how to study the Talmud from any standard edition to those who have never studied the Talmud and do not even know Hebrew.

The division of the page into various sections is designed to enable students of every kind to derive the greatest possible benefit from it.

For those who know how to study the Talmud, the book is intended to be a written Gemara lesson, so that, either alone, with partners, or in groups, they can have the sense of studying with a teacher who explains the difficult passages and deepens their understanding both of the development of the dialectic and also of the various approaches that have been taken by the Rabbis over the centuries in interpreting the material. A student of this kind can start with the Hebrew-Aramaic text, examine Rashi's commentary, and pass on from there to the expanded commentary. Afterwards the student can turn to the Notes section. Study of the *Halakhah* section will clarify the conclusions reached in the course of establishing the Halakhah, and the other items in the margins will be helpful whenever the need arises to clarify a concept or a word or to understand the background of the discussion.

For those who do not possess sufficient knowledge to be able to use a standard edition of the Talmud, but who know how to read Hebrew, a different method is proposed. Such students can begin by reading the Hebrew-Aramaic text and comparing it immediately to the *Literal Translation*. They can then move over to the *Translation and Commentary*, which refers both to the original text and to the *Literal Translation*. Such students would also do well to read through the *Notes* and choose those that explain matters at greater length. They will benefit, too, from the terms explained in the side margins.

The beginner who does not know Hebrew well enough to grapple with the original can start with the *Translation and Commentary*. The inclusion of a translation within the commentary permits the student to ignore the *Literal Translation*, since the commentary includes both the Talmudic text and an interpretation of it. The beginner can also benefit from the *Notes*, and it is important for him to go over the marginal notes on the concepts to improve his awareness of the juridical background and the methods of study characteristic of this text.

Apart from its use as study material, this book can also be useful to those well versed in the Talmud, as a source of additional knowledge in various areas, both for understanding the historical and archeological background and also for an explanation of words and concepts. The general reader, too, who might not plan to study the book from beginning to end, can find a great deal of interesting material in it regarding both the spiritual world of Judaism, practical Jewish law, and the life and customs of the Jewish people during the thousand years (500 B.C.E.–500 C.E.) of the Talmudic period.

The Talmud
The Steinsaltz Edition

Volume XIII
Tractate Ta'anit
Part I

Introduction to Ta'anit

T*a'anit* ("fast") is the ninth tractate in the second Order of the Talmud, the Order of *Mo'ed* ("appointed time," "festival"). In the Jerusalem Talmud and in some of the works of the Rishonim, the tractate is called *Ta'aniyyot* ("fasts"). Most of the tractate deals with the laws regulating public fast-days, with special emphasis on those fasts that do not have a fixed date in the calendar but were decreed in periods of severe drought or as a result of some other calamity. The tractate also discusses the fixed public fast-days, as well as fasts observed by individuals.

In the Torah, there is almost no mention of specific fasts or of a commandment to fast. Yom Kippur is designated (Leviticus 16:29) as a day on which "you shall afflict your souls," a concept which among other things includes fasting. The purpose of fasting on Yom Kippur is to purify the soul, and as such it is different from the fasts described in our tractate, though there are certain similarities between that fast and the other fasts, regarding their purpose and conception as well as their regulations. In the Prophets and Writings, however, there are many references to fasting. Much can be learned from those passages about the significance and function of fasting, as well as about the customs observed on the fasts, both public and private, in Israel in ancient times. Thus the discussions in our tractate are based on oral traditions going back to Sinai, which find written expression in the later books of the Bible.

The practice of fasting is based on the principle that nothing occurs in this world by accident. The causes that determine events are not only physical but spiritual. Good deeds are rewarded and evil is punished. Divine providence responds to men's actions,

both those of individuals as well as those of the community or the nation as a whole. Thus the calamities that occur to an individual or to the community all serve a purpose. They may be a warning that the community or the individual has sinned and that remorse and repentance are necessary, or they may be a punishment for sins that have been committed. Thus, whenever a person faces a calamity, he must immerse himself in prayer and repentance, must entreat divine forgiveness, and must offer supplications to elicit God's compassion so that He will avert or terminate the calamity.

The word *ta'anit* (תַּעֲנִית) is associated with the idea of *innui nefesh* (עִינּוּי נֶפֶשׁ — "afflicting the soul"), which, as is explained in the Oral Law and the Books of the Prophets and Writings, includes abstention from eating and drinking, and, on the more severe public fasts, also prohibits wearing shoes, bathing, and engaging in sexual relations. But both the Prophets (see, for example, Isaiah, chapter 58, the prophetic portion read on the morning of Yom Kippur) and the Rabbinic sources emphasize that fasting and afflicting the soul are not ends in themselves. They are the means by which a person can repent for his sins. Thus it is prayer, repentance, charity, remorse for sins committed in the past, and commitment to improved behavior in the future, which constitute the primary goals of fasting.

The most common calamity threatening the community, which should serve as an impetus for communal repentance, is the failure of rain. The Torah itself (Deuteronomy 11:17) sees periods of drought as a sign of God's anger, whether in the form of a warning or as a punishment. Drought is not merely a temporary or local affliction, but a calamity that can cause long-term and nationwide damage. More so than when he is faced with other types of calamity, man has almost no other way to help himself during periods of drought except by turning to God and praying for divine compassion.

Thus the major portion of tractate *Ta'anit* deals with fasts that are decreed in times of drought. Since the difficulties caused by the failure of rain grow more and more serious as the drought continues, the fasts decreed in times of drought become more and more severe with the passage of time. During periods of extended drought, the Rabbis decree three series of fasts, each series more severe than the preceding one. The Rabbis enacted that the public fast-days that do not have a fixed date in the calendar are to be observed on Mondays and Thursdays, the days on which the Torah is read in public and on which the courts are in session. It stands to reason that there should be a certain degree of similarity between the customs associated with fasting and those of mourning, since fasts are decreed in response to unhappy events and are intended to avert the continuation or worsening of those events. The mourning customs prescribed on fast-days are a means of leading people to humble themselves and repent their sins. The public gatherings for prayer and Torah reading, as well as the admonitions delivered by the communal leaders, are also directed to this end.

While drought is the most common reason for proclaiming a fast, any calamity threatening the community — whether a natural disaster such as flooding, a visitation of wild beasts or locusts, an infectious disease, or a human disaster such as war or religious persecution — is cause for communal penance and prayer (see I Kings, chapter 8), and reason for proclaiming a public fast. A public fast is appropriate both as a response to a calamity that has already struck the community, and as a means of eliciting God's compassion in order to avert a potential calamity, as well as a way of participating in the distress of another Jewish community, particularly the community living in Eretz Israel. Individual fasts are similar to those observed by the community as a whole. An individual may undertake a fast as a means of winning divine forgiveness for the sins that led to his being struck by some affliction, or he may undertake a fast as a means of averting an impending calamity, as in the case of a fast accepted in response to a disturbing dream. Individual fasts differ from public fasts, both with respect to their stringency and with respect to the manner in which they must be undertaken.

In addition to the fasts proclaimed in order to avert or bring to an end a disaster facing an individual or the entire community, there are also fixed public fasts which

were instituted to commemorate certain national calamities. But like the fasts decreed in times of trouble, the primary purpose of these commemorative fasts is to stimulate repentance and the desire for salvation in the future. Since these fasts commemorate national calamities, in particular the destruction of the First and Second Temples, they are not merely fast-days but also days of mourning. The Ninth of Av, which commemorates the day of the destruction of the two Temples and numerous other national calamities, serves as a symbol of all the tragedies that have befallen the Jewish people. As a result, the day is governed by most of the obligations and prohibitions that apply to a person who is mourning the death of a close relative.

Public fast-days are instituted by Rabbinic decree. Even though the four fixed public fasts — the Ninth of Av, the Tenth of Tevet, the Seventeenth of Tammuz, and the Third of Tishri — are mentioned in the Book of Zechariah, they too are regarded as Rabbinic decrees, for they are not Pentateuchal in origin. Thus it is clear that they are not to be observed on days that are designated by the Torah as days of pleasure and enjoyment, Shabbat and the Festivals. But a question arises regarding the semi-festivals of Biblical origin, the New Moon and the intermediate days of the Festivals, and also the semi-festivals instituted by the Rabbis to commemorate happy events that occurred during the period of the Second Temple and that were recorded in a work known as *Megillat Ta'anit* ("The Scroll of Fasts"): If a fast or a series of fasts has been proclaimed, and the fast or one of the series of fasts coincides with one of these semi-festivals, is the fast to be observed, put off to another date, or canceled altogether?

The following is a list of the four chapters of tractate *Ta'anit*, each known by the first words of the Mishnah passage which begin it:

1. מֵאֵימָתַי — "From when..." — determines the times of year when rain is expected to fall, discusses the special passages that are inserted in the daily Amidah during the rainy season, and outlines the order of the fasts that are decreed when the rains are late in falling.

2. סֵדֶר תַּעֲנִיּוֹת כֵּיצַד — "What is the order of service on fasts?" — describes in detail the special prayers recited on the communal fast-days decreed in times of drought, and discusses the various customs that accompany the service.

3. סֵדֶר תַּעֲנִיּוֹת אֵלּוּ — "The order of these fasts..." — discusses the fasts that are decreed for reasons other than drought.

4. בִּשְׁלֹשָׁה פְּרָקִים — "On three occasions..." — deals primarily with the groups of priests and non-priests who were responsible for offering the sacrifices or being present in the Temple at the time the sacrifices were being offered. It also deals with the fixed fast-days of the Seventeenth of Tammuz and the Ninth of Av.

Introduction to Chapter One

מֵאֵימָתַי

"But the land into which you are passing to possess it is a land of hills and valleys, and drinks water of the rain of heaven: a land which the Lord your God cares for: the eyes of the Lord your God are always upon it, from the beginning of the year to the end of the year." (Deuteronomy 11:11-12.)

"And the anger of the Lord will be kindled against you, and He will shut up the heavens, and there will be no rain, and the earth will not give its fruit, and you will perish quickly from upon the good land which the Lord gives you." (Deuteronomy 11:17.)

"When heaven is shut up, and there is no rain, because they have sinned against You, if they pray toward this place, and confess Your name, and turn from their sin, when You afflict them, and You, hear in the heavens, and forgive the sin of Your servants and of Your people Israel, that You may teach them the good way in which they should walk, and give rain on Your land, which You have given to Your people as an inheritance." (I Kings 8:35-36.)

The first chapter of tractate *Ta'anit* deals primarily with the dates of the fasts that are decreed during periods of drought. The discussion revolves around two issues — the periods when rain is expected to fall, and the order of the fasts that are decreed when the rain is late.

Before discussing when it is proper to decree a fast because the rain is late in coming, it is necessary to determine the time when rain is expected in an ordinary year. The dates when the rainy season begins and ends must be clearly established. This is accomplished in our chapter through a clarification of the periods during which rain is mentioned and requested in our daily prayers, for the passages mentioning and requesting rain are only inserted into these prayers during or shortly before the rainy season. Since the Mishnah was written in Eretz Israel and the laws recorded in it are intimately bound up with life in that land, the regulations concerning the mention of rain and the prayer for rain apply only in places where the climatic conditions are similar to those found in Israel. It is, therefore, necessary to determine the law regarding these matters in other places, particularly in those places where the rainy season is very different from that of Eretz Israel.

Once it has been determined when rain is expected to fall, a second question may be asked: When should fast-days be declared on account of the rain being late? At what point should the delay of the rain be taken as an indication of drought, so that special prayers should be offered and fasts proclaimed? The longer the dry spell, the worse off are the farmers whose livelihood depends on the rain. As the drought continues and the plight of the community worsens, the fasts to be observed become more and more severe. Our chapter outlines the various series of fasts that are declared during periods of extended drought, each series more stringent that the preceding one.

A detailed analysis of these and other topics constitutes the main subject matter of this chapter.

TRANSLATION AND COMMENTARY

MISHNAH The first Mishnayot in this chapter deal with the prayers that are said for rain during the rainy season. Two additions connected with rain are inserted in the Amidah prayer, otherwise known as the Eighteen Blessings (שְׁמוֹנֶה עֶשְׂרֵה — *shemoneh esreh*), which is the central part of every service and is recited three times every day, morning, afternoon, and night. The second blessing of the Amidah begins: "You are mighty forever, O Lord. You revive the dead, and are great to save." At this point, during the rainy season, the worshiper inserts the words, "Who causes the wind to blow and the rain to fall [מַשִּׁיב הָרוּחַ וּמוֹרִיד הַגֶּשֶׁם]," before continuing the blessing. The ninth blessing of the Amidah begins: "Bless for us, O Lord our God, this year and all the kinds of its produce for good." At this point, during the rainy season, the worshiper inserts the words, "and give dew and rain for a blessing on the face of the earth," before continuing the blessing. These insertions in the Amidah are made only during the rainy season, which in Eretz Israel occurs during late autumn, winter, and early spring. During this period, considerable amounts of rain may fall in a good year. During the dry season, by contrast, it does not normally rain at all. Moreover, agriculture in Eretz Israel is organized around this seasonal pattern, and if substantial rain were to fall during the summer, it would be almost as bad for the crops as a drought during the winter. Accordingly, prayers for rain are recited in Eretz Israel during the rainy season only (the practice outside Eretz Israel is discussed below, 10a).

מֵאֵימָתַי מַזְכִּירִין In the early autumn an occasional rainstorm may occur; so during this period the insertion in the second blessing of the Amidah is made, but not the more explicit request for rain inserted in the ninth blessing. Accordingly, our Mishnah asks: [1]**From when do we make mention of "the power of rain"?** In other words, on what date in the Hebrew calendar do we begin to make the insertion in the second blessing and mention rainfall as one of God's mighty deeds? (The date on which we begin explicitly to entreat God for rain in the ninth blessing is discussed below, 10a.)

רַבִּי אֱלִיעֶזֶר אוֹמֵר [2]**Rabbi Eliezer says:** We begin to insert the words, "who causes the wind to blow and the rain to fall," **from the first holy day of the Festival of Sukkot.** When the term "Festival" (חַג) appears by itself in the Talmud, the reference is always to the Festival of Sukkot ("Tabernacles"), which lasts for eight days, from the fifteenth of the month of Tishri to the twenty-second. The first and eighth days of this Festival are full holy days, on which work is forbidden. Sukkot marks the end of the dry season and also anticipates the rainy season. According to Jewish tradition, it is on Sukkot that God decrees whether the coming rainy

LITERAL TRANSLATION

MISHNAH [1]From when do we mention "the powers of rains"?

[2]Rabbi Eliezer says: From the first holy day of the Festival [of Sukkot].

מֵאֵימָתַי

[1]מַזְכִּירִין "גְּבוּרוֹת גְּשָׁמִים"?

[2]רַבִּי אֱלִיעֶזֶר אוֹמֵר: מִיּוֹם טוֹב הָרִאשׁוֹן שֶׁל חַג.

RASHI

משנה מאימתי מזכירין גבורות גשמים — שאומר "משיב הרוח ומוריד הגשם", ובגמרא מפרש טעמא אמאי קרי ליה "גבורות גשמים" — מפני שיורדין בגבורה, שנאמר "עושה גדולות" וגו'.

NOTES

מֵאֵימָתַי מַזְכִּירִין **From when do we mention?** In most manuscripts and printed editions of the Mishnah and the Talmud, tractate *Ta'anit* is the ninth tractate in the second Order of the Talmud, *Mo'ed*, and follows immediately after tractate *Rosh HaShanah* (see *Meiri,* who possessed a different tradition regarding the arrangement of the tractates). A number of authorities have sought to explain the order of the tractates and the inner connection between them. *Rambam* (in his introduction to his *Commentary to the Mishnah*) suggests that the Order *Mo'ed* opens with the tractates dealing with Shabbat and with the Festivals recorded in the Torah. Tractate *Rosh HaShanah* concludes the discussion of the Torah Festivals, and tractate *Ta'anit* begins the discussion of those special occasions whose sources are found in the Prophets (regarding fasts decreed in times of calamity, see Isaiah chapter 58; regarding fixed fasts commemorating the destruction of the Temple, see Zechariah 8:19).

Melekhet Shlomo adds that tractate *Ta'anit* follows tractate *Rosh HaShanah* because the prayer service conducted on public fast days resembles the prayer service on Rosh HaShanah, both with respect to the sounding of the shofar and the blowing of trumpets, and with respect to the blessings that are inserted in the Amidah prayer on both occasions (see the beginning of chapter 2).

HALAKHAH

מֵאֵימָתַי מַזְכִּירִין "גְּבוּרוֹת גְּשָׁמִים" **From when do we mention "the powers of rains"?** "We begin to insert the expression מַשִּׁיב הָרוּחַ וּמוֹרִיד הַגֶּשֶׁם ('Who causes the wind to blow and the rain to fall') during the musaf Amidah on the last day of the Sukkot Festival, and we stop saying it before the musaf Amidah on the first day of the Pesaḥ Festival," following Rabbi Yehudah. (*Shulḥan Arukh, Oraḥ Ḥayyim* 114:1.)

BACKGROUND

גְּבוּרוֹת גְּשָׁמִים **The powers of rains.** This expression, explained below in the Gemara, links the mention of rain specifically with the second blessing of the Amidah, which is sometimes called בִּרְכַּת גְּבוּרוֹת — "the blessing of powers" — because it speaks of the revelation of God's power in many areas, both in the present and in the future. Since rain is a manifestation of God's power, it is appropriate that it should be mentioned in this blessing.

SAGES

רַבִּי אֱלִיעֶזֶר **Rabbi Eliezer.** When the name "Rabbi Eliezer" occurs in the Talmud without a patronymic, it refers to Rabbi Eliezer ben Hyrcanus (also known as Rabbi Eliezer the Great), who was one of the leading scholars during the period after the destruction of the Second Temple.

Rabbi Eliezer was born to a wealthy family of Levites who traced their descent to Moses. Rabbi Eliezer began studying Torah late in life, but quickly became an outstanding and beloved disciple of Rabban Yoḥanan ben Zakkai. Indeed, Rabban Yoḥanan remarked that "if all the Sages of Israel were on one side of a scale and Eliezer ben Hyrcanus on the other, he would outweigh them all."

Rabbi Eliezer was known for his remarkable memory, and was famed for faithfully reporting and following the traditions of others without altering them. He himself leaned toward the views of Bet Shammai, even though Rabban Yoḥanan ben Zakkai, with whom he studied, was a follower of Bet Hillel. Rabbi Eliezer's principal opponent, Rabbi Yehoshua ben Ḥananyah, generally followed the views of Bet Hillel, and many basic Halakhic disputes between these scholars are recorded in the Mishnah.

Because of his staunch and unflinching adherence to tradition, Rabbi Eliezer was unwilling to accede to the majority view when his own views were based on tradition. Indeed, Rabbi Eliezer's conduct generated so much tension among the Sages that his own brother-in-law, Rabban Gamliel, eventually

placed him under a ban to prevent controversy from proliferating. This ban was lifted only after Rabbi Eliezer's death.

All the Sages of the next generation were Rabbi Eliezer's students. Most prominent among them was Rabbi Akiva. Rabbi Eliezer's son, Hyrcanus, was also a Sage.

SAGES

רַבִּי יְהוֹשֻׁעַ **Rabbi Yehoshua.** This is Rabbi Yehoshua ben Ḥananyah the Levite, one of the leading Sages of the generation following the destruction of the Second Temple. Rabbi Yehoshua had served in the Temple as a singer and, after the destruction, he was one of the students who went to Yavneh with their outstanding teacher, Rabban Yoḥanan ben Zakkai. Unlike his colleague Rabbi Eliezer, Rabbi Yehoshua followed the Halakhic viewpoint of his teacher and of Bet Hillel.

Although Rabbi Yehoshua played an important part in the leadership of the people (he was apparently a senior judge), he earned a meager living from hard and unremunerative work. After renewing his close ties with the House of the Nasi (the president of the Sanhedrin), he was apparently supported by Rabban Gamliel, who used to give him the tithe belonging to the Levites.

Rabbi Yehoshua was famous among both Jews and non-Jews as an extraordinary scholar, possessing wide knowledge not only of Torah but also of secular subjects. He was also a celebrated preacher.

Continuing the method of his teacher, Rabban Yoḥanan ben Zakkai, Rabbi Yehoshua was a moderate person who tried to deter the people from ferment which would lead to rebellion against the Roman regime. For a while he had close relations with the imperial court and was highly regarded there, as he had been sent to Rome as a member of several national delegations.

Although Rabbi Yehoshua was modest and humble, he was very firm in maintaining his opinions and principles, and did not make concessions even when difficult

TRANSLATION AND COMMENTARY

season will be blessed with an abundance of rain or not. Consequently, Rabbi Eliezer rules that the insertion in the second blessing of the Amidah should be recited from the first day of Sukkot.

רַבִּי יְהוֹשֻׁעַ אוֹמֵר [1]**Rabbi Yehoshua says:** The insertion in the second blessing of the Amidah is made only **from the last holy day of the Festival of Sukkot** (the eighth day). Rabbi Yehoshua maintains that the insertion in the second blessing should not be recited during the first seven days of Sukkot, when we are commanded by the Torah to dwell in tabernacles, unprotected from the rain, but only from the eighth day, when we complete the Festival and return to our permanent homes.

אָמַר לוֹ רַבִּי יְהוֹשֻׁעַ [2]**Rabbi Yehoshua explained** his position **to** Rabbi Eliezer: **Rain is nothing but a sign of a curse** during the first seven days of **the Festival of Sukkot,** because it forces us to leave our tabernacles and return to our houses, and makes it impossible for us to fulfill the Torah's commandment. The Mishnah (*Sukkah* 28b) explains that rain on Sukkot is an evil omen, since it indicates that God does not want our service. [3]And **since** we do not want rain during this week, **why should we mention it** in our prayers?

אָמַר לוֹ רַבִּי אֱלִיעֶזֶר [4]**Rabbi Eliezer said to** Rabbi Yehoshua in reply: **I too did not say** that we **ask for rain** during the Festival, as we do explicitly in the ninth blessing of the Amidah ("and give dew and rain for a blessing on the face of the earth"). We do not make that insertion in the Amidah until the rainy season has properly begun. [5]**Rather,** I was referring to the insertion in the second blessing, in which we **mention** among God's other mighty deeds that God **"causes the wind to blow and the rain to fall,"** but we do not explicitly ask for rain. This insertion should not be interpreted as referring to rain falling now during Sukkot, but rather to rain falling later, [6]**in its proper season.**

[1]רַבִּי יְהוֹשֻׁעַ אוֹמֵר: מִיּוֹם טוֹב הָאַחֲרוֹן שֶׁל חַג.
[2]אָמַר לוֹ רַבִּי יְהוֹשֻׁעַ: הוֹאִיל וְאֵין הַגְּשָׁמִים אֶלָּא סִימַן קְלָלָה בֶּחָג, [3]לָמָּה הוּא מַזְכִּיר?
[4]אָמַר לוֹ רַבִּי אֱלִיעֶזֶר: אַף אֲנִי לֹא אָמַרְתִּי לִשְׁאוֹל, [5]אֶלָּא לְהַזְכִּיר "מַשִּׁיב הָרוּחַ וּמוֹרִיד הַגֶּשֶׁם" [6]בְּעוֹנָתוֹ.

LITERAL TRANSLATION

[1]Rabbi Yehoshua says: From the last holy day of the Festival [of Sukkot].

[2]Rabbi Yehoshua said to him: Since rains are nothing but a sign of a curse on the Festival [of Sukkot], [3]why should one mention [them]?

[4]Rabbi Eliezer said to him: I too did not say to ask [for rain], [5]but to mention "Who causes the wind to blow and the rain to fall" [6]in its season.

RASHI

סימן קללה בחג הן – כדאמרינן במסכת סוכה בפרק "הישן" (כח,ב): מאימתי מותר לפנות – משתסרח המקפה. משל לעבד שבא למזוג כוס לרבו ושפך לו קיתון על פניו, ואמר לו אי אפשי בשמושך, כלומר: כשהגשמים יורדין לסוכה הכל יוצאין, ונראה שאין הקדוש ברוך הוא חפץ שנשמש לפניו. ואמאי מתחילין להזכיר גבורות גשמים בחג, ונראה שהוא מתפלל שיבא מטר בחג? **לא אמרתי לשאול** – שיתפלל על הגשמים בחג, כגון "ותן טל ומטר". **אלא להזכיר** – שמתחיל להזכיר בחג גבורות של מקום שמוריד גשמים. **בעונתו** – כלומר: בזמנו.

NOTES

סִימַן קְלָלָה בֶּחָג **A sign of a curse on the Festival.** *Rashi* explains that rain on Sukkot is an ominous sign, for it is regarded as a divine rebuke, indicating that God does not wish His people to dwell in the temporary structures they are commanded to inhabit during the seven days of the Sukkot Festival, but wishes them to return to their permanent homes instead. A Mishnah in tractate *Sukkah* (28b) describes such a situation by making the following analogy: "To what may the matter be compared? To a servant who comes to pour a cup of wine for his master, and the master pours a ladle of water in his face." Here, too, the people wish to serve their Master, but He refuses to accept their service.

Meiri explains that rain on Sukkot is an ominous sign, because rain makes it impossible for people to fulfill their obligation to dwell in a sukkah.

Rabbenu Efrayim (cited by *Ritva* and others) maintains that it is only on the first night of Sukkot that rain is a sign of a curse, for according to the Sages it is only on the first night of Sukkot that one is obligated to eat in the sukkah, whereas during the rest of the week one may eat elsewhere, provided that the eating is limited to casual meals. (See *Sukkah* 25a.) According to Rabbi Eliezer, who maintains that a person is obligated to eat fourteen meals in the sukkah, one meal each day and one meal each night, rain is certainly a sign of a curse all seven days. By contrast, Rabbi Yehoshua argues that rain should not be mentioned throughout the week of Sukkot, for even if rain is not a sign of a curse after the first day of the Festival, it is certainly not a sign of a blessing, for it makes it difficult for a person to eat in the sukkah, even if he desires to do so. (See *Rif, Ritva* and others who read in the Mishnah: "Since rains are not a sign of a blessing, etc.")

"מַשִּׁיב הָרוּחַ וּמוֹרִיד הַגֶּשֶׁם" בְּעוֹנָתוֹ **"Who causes the wind to blow and the rain to fall" in its season.** *Ra'ah* maintains that according to Rabbi Eliezer the text of the insertion is: "Who causes the wind to blow and the rain to fall in its season." However, most Rishonim understand that "in its season" is not part of the text inserted into the Amidah prayer, but is Rabbi Eliezer's interpretation of that insertion. According to Rabbi Eliezer, rain may be mentioned from the first day of Sukkot, for the reference is to rain that falls in its season after the conclusion of the Festival, when it is appropriate for rain to fall.

TRANSLATION AND COMMENTARY

אָמַר לוֹ [1]Rabbi Yehoshua **said to him** in reply: **If** the insertion in the second blessing is not to be interpreted as referring to rain falling now but rather to the general concept of rain falling when it is appropriate, the worshiper **should always mention it!** Why is it not recited during the dry season as well? Rather, says Rabbi Yehoshua, it is clear that although this prayer is not an explicit request for rain, it is inappropriate to insert it when rain is not desired at all.

אֵין שׁוֹאֲלִין אֶת הַגְּשָׁמִים [2]The Mishnah notes that Rabbi Eliezer and Rabbi Yehoshua disagree only about the "mention" of rain in the second blessing of the Amidah during the first seven days of Sukkot, but according to both opinions **we only ask for rain close to the rainy season.**

רַבִּי יְהוּדָה אוֹמֵר [3]The Mishnah now cites a third opinion, attributed to Rabbi Yehudah, on this matter. **Rabbi Yehudah** agrees with Rabbi Yehoshua that the mention of rain in the second blessing should not be made until the eighth day of the Festival. But Rabbi Yehoshua is of the opinion that rain is mentioned from the beginning of the eighth day of the Festival, on the evening of the twenty-second of Tishri. According to Rabbi Yehudah, however, rain is not mentioned during the evening Amidah on the eighth day, nor during the first Amidah recited on the morning of the eighth day. Rather, it is mentioned for the first time during the musaf or "additional" Amidah, which is recited on Sabbaths and Festivals after the morning Amidah, in commemoration of the additional sacrifices that were offered in the Temple on these occasions. [4]Rabbi Yehudah explains: **Whoever** leads the service in the synagogue, which is called **"passing before the ark," on the last holy day of the Festival of Sukkot,** [5]**the last one,** who recites the musaf Amidah aloud, **mentions** rain in the second blessing, [6]whereas **the first one,** who recites the morning Amidah aloud, **does not mention** it. [7]Rabbi Yehudah goes on to explain that a similar procedure is followed **on the first holy day of Pesaḥ,** when the dry season officially begins and we cease to mention rain in our prayers. Here, too, Rabbi Yehudah maintains that the change is made in the middle of the morning service of the first day of Pesaḥ during the musaf Amidah. [8]Rabbi Yehudah explains: Whoever leads the service on the first day of Pesaḥ, **the first one,** who recites the morning Amidah aloud, continues to **mention** rain in the second blessing, [9]whereas **the last one,** who recites the musaf Amidah aloud, **does not mention** it.

GEMARA תַּנָּא הֵיכָא קָאֵי דְּקָתָנֵי [10]The Gemara begins its analysis of the Mishnah by considering the first clause, which asked from when we begin to make the insertion about rain in the second blessing of the Amidah, making mention of rainfall together with God's other mighty deeds. The Mishnah has not yet described this prayer at all, but assumes that the reader knows that there is an obligation to make mention of rain in the Amidah when it asks: "From when is this prayer recited?" On this point the Gemara asks: **On what does the Tanna base himself when he teaches: "From when"?** How do we know that this prayer is recited at all?

[1]אָמַר לוֹ: אִם כֵּן לְעוֹלָם יְהֵא מַזְכִּיר!

[2]אֵין שׁוֹאֲלִין אֶת הַגְּשָׁמִים אֶלָּא סָמוּךְ לַגְּשָׁמִים.

[3]רַבִּי יְהוּדָה אוֹמֵר: [4]הָעוֹבֵר לִפְנֵי הַתֵּיבָה בְּיוֹם טוֹב הָאַחֲרוֹן שֶׁל חַג — [5]הָאַחֲרוֹן מַזְכִּיר; [6]הָרִאשׁוֹן אֵינוֹ מַזְכִּיר. [7]בְּיוֹם טוֹב רִאשׁוֹן שֶׁל פֶּסַח, [8]הָרִאשׁוֹן מַזְכִּיר; [9]הָאַחֲרוֹן אֵינוֹ מַזְכִּיר.

גמרא [10]תַּנָּא הֵיכָא קָאֵי דְּקָתָנֵי: "מֵאֵימָתַי"?

LITERAL TRANSLATION

[1]He said to him: If so, one should always mention [it]!

[2]We do not ask for rains except close to the [season of] rains.

[3]Rabbi Yehudah says: [4]He who passes before the ark on the last holy day of the Festival [of Sukkot] — [5]the last mentions; [6]the first does not mention. [7]On the first holy day of Pesaḥ, [8]the first mentions; [9]the last does not mention.

GEMARA [10]On what is the Tanna basing himself (lit., "where does the Tanna stand") when he teaches: "From when"?

RASHI

אם כן — ואמאי פוסק בפסח מלהזכיר?

גמרא תנא היכא קאי — כלומר, מדקתני "מאימתי" מכלל דפשיטא ליה להאי תנא דחייבים להזכיר, והיכא חזינן דמחייב להזכיר?

NOTES

הָעוֹבֵר לִפְנֵי הַתֵּיבָה בְּיוֹם טוֹב הָאַחֲרוֹן שֶׁל חַג **He who passes before the ark on the last holy day of the Festival of Sukkot.** The Jerusalem Talmud explains Rabbi Yehudah's position as follows: Rain is first mentioned in the musaf Amidah on the last day of the Sukkot Festival, and last mentioned in the morning Amidah on the first day of the Pesaḥ Festival, so that dew should be mentioned alone in the Amidah prayer on all the days of the year that are full Festivals. Although there is no obligation to praise God for causing the dew to fall, the mention of dew is appropriate all year long, for dew is regarded as a blessing throughout the year, during both summer and winter.

personal controversies developed. However, in other matters he accepted authority, and in general had a humorous, realistic temperament. All the Sages of the following generation were his students, and in most of the controversies with the Sages of his own generation the Halakhah followed his view, and his system became the path taken by the Halakhah. Ḥananyah, his nephew, was his outstanding student.

BACKGROUND

סָמוּךְ לַגְּשָׁמִים **Close to the season of rains.** Everything in this Mishnah and most of the matters associated with it relate to the climatic conditions in Eretz Israel, and the main themes of communal prayer always refer to Eretz Israel, the heart of the Jewish people.

As will be explained at length below in this tractate, the rainy season normally begins in Eretz Israel in the month of Marḥeshvan, which falls according to the Gregorian calendar during the months of October or November. If Marḥeshvan comes relatively early according to the solar calendar, the rain may begin even later. Nevertheless it is quite common for scattered showers to fall even during the previous month of Tishri. As in the other lands of the Mediterranean region, the rainy season lasts throughout the winter from Marḥeshvan until Nisan. During the summer no rain falls at all, and summer rain is liable to bring significant damage to plants and fruit.

SAGES

רַבִּי יְהוּדָה **Rabbi Yehudah.** When the Mishnah speaks of Rabbi Yehudah without any further details, it is referring to Rabbi Yehudah son of Rabbi Il'ai, one of the greatest Tannaim of the fourth generation. He was one of the last five of Rabbi Akiva's disciples, and his father, Rabbi Il'ai, had been a disciple of Rabbi Eliezer. Rabbi Yehudah learned Rabbi Eliezer's teachings from his father. In his youth he studied with Rabbi Tarfon, and he transmits teachings in his name as well as in the names of the other Sages of

TRANSLATION AND COMMENTARY

תַּנָּא הָתָם קָאֵי [1]The Gemara answers: Although the discussion of this topic in this tractate begins with "when...," this prayer was properly introduced elsewhere in the Mishnah. In fact, **the Tanna** who wrote our Mishnah **is basing** his question **on** what was taught in **a Mishnah elsewhere** (*Berakhot* 33a), [2]where the mention of rain in the second blessing of the Amidah was introduced **as follows: "We mention 'the power of rain'** by inserting the words 'Who causes the wind to blow and the rain to fall' **in the blessing that refers to the resurrection of the dead** (the second blessing of the Amidah, which describes God's mighty deeds and emphasizes His power to resurrect the dead), [3]**and we ask for rain** by inserting the words 'and give dew and rain for a blessing on the face of the earth' **in the blessing of the years,** the ninth blessing of the Amidah. [4]Furthermore, during the service on Saturday evening after Shabbat the prayer called **havdalah** (which literally means 'distinction') **is recited in** the fourth blessing of the Amidah, **the blessing** that concludes: 'Blessed are you, O Lord, **who favors with knowledge.'** [5]**And here,** since the mention of rain in the second blessing of the Amidah was introduced in the Mishnah in *Berakhot*, our Mishnah continues the topic by **teaching** the regulations concerning this prayer, beginning with the first line of our Mishnah: **"From when do we mention 'the power of rain'?"**

וְלִיתְנֵי הָתָם [6]The Gemara is not satisfied with this explanation and objects: If the introduction to this topic was in *Berakhot*, the Mishnah **should have introduced** the difference of opinion over the date when **it** is recited **there,** in *Berakhot*, where it was introduced. [7]**Why did** the Mishnah **leave it until** tractate *Ta'anit*, one of the last tractates of the second Order of the Mishnah, *Mo'ed*, rather than discuss it in tractate *Berakhot*, the first tractate in the first Order of the Mishnah, *Zeraim*?

LITERAL TRANSLATION

[1]The Tanna is basing himself on [the Mishnah] there, [2]which teaches: "We mention 'the powers of rains' in [the blessing of] the resurrection of the dead, [3]and we ask [for rain] in the blessing of the years, [4]and havdalah [is recited] in [the blessing of] 'who favors with knowledge.' " [5]And [here] he teaches: "From when do we mention 'the powers of rains'?"

[6]But let him teach [it] there! [7]For what reason did he leave it until here?

תַּנָּא הָתָם קָאֵי, [2]דִּקְתָנֵי: "מַזְכִּירִין 'גְּבוּרוֹת גְּשָׁמִים' בִּתְחִיַּית הַמֵּתִים, [3]וְשׁוֹאֲלִין בְּבִרְכַּת הַשָּׁנִים, [4]וְהַבְדָּלָה בְּ'חוֹנֵן הַדַּעַת'". [5]וְקָתָנֵי: "מֵאֵימָתַי מַזְכִּירִין 'גְּבוּרוֹת גְּשָׁמִים'?"

[6]וְלִיתְנֵי הָתָם! [7]מַאי שְׁנָא דִּשְׁבַקֵיהּ עַד הָכָא?

RASHI

הָתָם קָאֵי — "מַזְכִּירִין גְּבוּרוֹת גְּשָׁמִים כו'" בְּמַסֶּכֶת בְּרָכוֹת. **וְלִיתְנֵי הָתָם** — בְּמַסֶּכֶת בְּרָכוֹת. סָמוּךְ דְּתָנֵי "מַזְכִּירִין", "לֵיתְנֵי מֵאֵימָתַי". **מַאי שְׁנָא דִּשְׁבַקֵיהּ עַד הָכָא** — כְּלוֹמַר, הַאי דְּקָתָנֵי הָכָא בְּסֵדֶר מוֹעֵד "מֵאֵימָתַי" — לֵיתְנֵי הָתָם, דְּקָתָנֵי "מַזְכִּירִין", בְּמַסֶּכֶת בְּרָכוֹת הַיְינוּ סֵדֶר זְרָעִים. **עַד הָכָא** — עַד סֵדֶר מוֹעֵד.

Yavneh: Rabbi Eliezer, Rabbi Yehoshua, Rabban Gamliel, Rabbi Elazar ben Azaryah, Rabbi Yishmael, and Rabbi Yose HaGelili. But Rabbi Yehudah's main teacher was Rabbi Akiva, according to whose teachings he laid the foundations for the Halakhic exegesis of Leviticus in a work known as the *Sifra* (or *Torat Kohanim*). According to tradition, an unattributed statement in the *Sifra* is the teaching of Rabbi Yehudah. He was ordained by Rabbi Yehudah ben Bava and is frequently quoted in Aggadic exegesis together with Rabbi Neḥemyah. In differences of opinion between Rabbi Yehudah and Rabbi Meir, or between Rabbi Yehudah and Rabbi Shimon, the Halakhah follows Rabbi Yehudah. Among his disciples were Rabbi Elazar son of Rabbi Shimon, Rabbi Yishmael son of Rabbi Yose, and Rabbi Yehudah HaNasi. His son, Rabbi Yose son of Rabbi Yehudah, was also a famous Sage.

BACKGROUND

מַזְכִּירִין... וְשׁוֹאֲלִין **We mention...and we ask for.** The Halakhah distinguishes between the time when it is appropriate to mention rain and the time when it is appropriate to ask for it. Naturally, we ask for rain only when we indeed want it to fall. But sometime before then we begin to think about the coming year's rain, and, as noted in the Gemara, "on Sukkot, we are judged with regard to rain." Thus the appropriate time to mention rain is the Sukkot season. And even Rabbi Eliezer agrees that we should not mention something at an inappropriate time, even when the mention is praise of God and not a request.

NOTES

During the winter months rain must be mentioned, but during the rest of the year dew can be mentioned by itself. Delaying the mention of rain until the musaf Amidah of the last day of Sukkot, and mentioning rain for the last time in the morning Amidah of the first day of Pesaḥ, allows dew to be mentioned by itself on all the days that are full Festivals — the first and last days of Sukkot, the first and last days of Pesaḥ, and Shavuot.

גְּבוּרוֹת גְּשָׁמִים **The powers of rains.** Many commentators have mentioned the relationship between rain and the resurrection of the dead, the main theme of the second blessing of the Amidah prayer, into which the mention of

HALAKHAH

מַזְכִּירִין 'גְּבוּרוֹת גְּשָׁמִים' בִּתְחִיַּית הַמֵּתִים **We mention "the powers of rains" in the blessing of the resurrection of the dead.** "We mention rain — by reciting: 'Who causes the wind to blow and the rain to fall' — in the second blessing of the Amidah throughout the winter. During the summer there are different customs. The practice of Sephardi communities [and those Ashkenazi communities that follow Ḥassidic customs] is to recite: 'Who causes the dew to come down' [מוֹרִיד הַטָּל] during the summer. But Ashkenazi communities outside Israel do not recite it." (*Shulḥan Arukh, Oraḥ Ḥayyim* 114:1-2.)

וְשׁוֹאֲלִין בְּבִרְכַּת הַשָּׁנִים **And we ask for rain in the blessing of the years.** "During the winter, a prayer for rain is inserted in the ninth blessing of the Amidah. [The date from which we begin to insert this prayer is discussed in the Gemara below.] According to the Ashkenazi custom, the text of the blessing remains essentially the same throughout the year, except that during the summer the text uses the expression "and give a blessing" [וְתֵן בְּרָכָה], whereas during the winter it reads: "And give dew and rain for a blessing [וְתֵן טַל וּמָטָר לִבְרָכָה]." According to the Sephardic custom, the text of the ninth blessing recited during the winter is significantly different from that recited during the summer (*Tur*). (*Shulḥan Arukh, Oraḥ Ḥayyim* 117:1.)

וְהַבְדָּלָה בְּ'חוֹנֵן הַדַּעַת' **And Havdalah is recited in the blessing of "who favors with knowledge."** "During the evening service at the conclusion of Shabbat or of a Festival, the havdalah prayer is inserted in the fourth blessing of the Amidah, 'who favors with knowledge.' " (*Shulḥan Arukh, Oraḥ Ḥayyim* 117:1.)

TRANSLATION AND COMMENTARY

אֶלָּא [1]Rather, explains the Gemara, the Tanna of our Mishnah continued from tractate *Rosh HaShanah*, the tractate immediately preceding *Ta'anit* in the second Order, *Moed*. [2]For we have learned in a Mishnah in tractate *Rosh HaShanah* (16a): "At four times during the course of the year the world is judged... **and on the Festival of Sukkot we are judged concerning water,**" since Sukkot immediately precedes the rainy season. And the rituals of Sukkot reflect this fact. [3]Thus our Mishnah should be read as a continuation of the principle **taught by the Mishnah** in *Rosh HaShanah*: **"And on the Festival of Sukkot we are judged concerning water."** The Mishnah in *Berakhot* does not tell us that there is a particular season when prayers for rain are especially appropriate. But the Mishnah in *Rosh HaShanah* informs us that the Festival of Sukkot is intimately connected with God's judgment as to whether there will be ample rain during the coming winter season. Hence it is the right time to pray to God for rain. Since the mention of rain in the second blessing of the Amidah was introduced in the Mishnah in *Berakhot*, and the significance of Sukkot was introduced in the Mishnah in *Rosh HaShanah*, [4]**the Mishnah** in *Ta'anit* can now continue the topic by **teaching** us **"from when** precisely on Sukkot **we mention 'the power of rain'."**

וְלִיתְנֵי [5]The Gemara now considers another problem concerning the first clause of our Mishnah, which ruled that we make mention of "the power of rain" from the first or the last day of the Sukkot Festival. **But,** suggests the Gemara, **let** the Mishnah **teach** this law as follows: **"From when do we mention rain?"** [6]**What is** meant by: **"the power of rain"?** Why does the Mishnah describe the mention of rain in the second blessing of the Amidah as "the power of rain" instead of simply "rain"?

אָמַר רַבִּי יוֹחָנָן [7]**Rabbi Yoḥanan said:** The Mishnah describes rain as "power" **because it comes down through** the **power** of God, [8]**as the** following **verse** (Job 5:9) **says: "He does great things and there is no comprehension, wonders without number."** [9]**And it is** further **written** in the next verse: **"Who gives rain on the face of the earth, and sends water on the face of the fields."** Thus we see that the "great things" and "wonders" refer to rain.

מַאי מַשְׁמַע [10]The Gemara asks: **What proof is provided** by these verses? The word "power" does not appear in either of them. How, then, does Rabbi Yoḥanan infer from these two verses that rain comes down through the power of God?

[1]אֶלָּא, תַּנָּא מֵרֹאשׁ הַשָּׁנָה סְלֵיק. [2]דִּתְנַן: "וּבֶחָג נִידּוֹנִין עַל הַמַּיִם". [3]וְאַיְּידֵי דִּתְנָא: "וּבֶחָג נִידּוֹנִין עַל הַמַּיִם", [4]תָּנָא: "מֵאֵימָתַי מַזְכִּירִין 'גְּבוּרוֹת גְּשָׁמִים'?"

[5]וְלִיתְנֵי: "מֵאֵימָתַי מַזְכִּירִין עַל הַגְּשָׁמִים?" [6]מַאי "גְּבוּרוֹת גְּשָׁמִים"?

[7]אָמַר רַבִּי יוֹחָנָן: מִפְּנֵי שֶׁיּוֹרְדִין בִּגְבוּרָה, [8]שֶׁנֶּאֱמַר: "עֹשֶׂה גְדֹלוֹת וְאֵין חֵקֶר, נִפְלָאוֹת עַד אֵין מִסְפָּר". [9]וּכְתִיב: "הַנֹּתֵן מָטָר עַל פְּנֵי אָרֶץ, וְשֹׁלֵחַ מַיִם עַל פְּנֵי חוּצוֹת".

[10]מַאי מַשְׁמַע?

LITERAL TRANSLATION

[1]Rather, the Tanna continued (lit., "went up") from *Rosh HaShanah*. [2]For we have learned [there]: "And on the Festival [of Sukkot] we are judged concerning water." [3]And since he taught [there]: "And on the Festival [of Sukkot] we are judged concerning water," [4]he taught [here]: "From when do we mention 'the powers of rains'?"

[5]But let him teach: "From when do we mention the rains?"! [6]What is "the powers of rains"?

[7]Rabbi Yoḥanan said: Because they come down with power, [8]as it is said: "He does great things and there is no comprehension, wonders without number." [9]And it is written: "Who gives rain on the face of the earth, and sends water on the face of the fields."

[10]What does it teach [us]?

RASHI

אלא — לא תימא דהא דקתני "מאימתי" דהתם קאי, דתנא מראש השנה סליק, ששניהן בסדר אחד הן, להכי לא מצי למימר: מאי שנא דשבקיה עד הכא. **בחג** — הוי דין על המים, ומשום דתני מאימתי הוי דין על המים — קתני נמי אימתי זמן הזכרה. **ואיידי דתני בחג נידונין** — כלומר, אגב דתנא "בחג נידונין על המים", קסבר בנפשיה הואיל ונידונין בחג על המים — שמע מינה בעינן להזכיר עניינא דמיא, לרצויי על המים דליתו לברכה, להכי קתני "מאימתי מזכירין". **כתיב עושה גדולות עד אין חקר** — אלמא דכתיב "חקר" בגשמים, וכתיב "חקר" בברייתו של עולם. מה ברייתו של עולם כתיב ביה גבורה — אף גשמים הוי כמאן דכתיב ביה גבורה.

NOTES

rain is inserted. *Ritva* writes that rain "resurrects" the seeds, for the seeds lie buried in the ground and begin to sprout after rain. Moreover, those who suffer from famine during times of drought are "resurrected" by God when He sends rain. Causing the rain to fall is also similar to the resurrection of the dead that will take place at the end of days, for they are both revelations of God's might in this world and His ability to alter the laws of Nature.

BACKGROUND

מִפְּנֵי שֶׁיּוֹרְדִין בִּגְבוּרוֹת **Because they come down with power.** Our tractate speaks a great deal about rainfall, explaining that the "power" of God is revealed especially in rain, both in the power of the rain, and also in the well-defined and controlled way in which it falls, for power and definition are characteristics of might.

Today we have the means to measure the force of rainfall, and it is estimated that the energy freed in any large rainstorm exceeds that of an atomic bomb.

SAGES

רַבִּי יוֹחָנָן **Rabbi Yoḥanan.** This is Rabbi Yoḥanan bar Nappaḥa, one of the greatest Amoraim, whose teachings are of primary importance both in the Babylonian and in the Jerusalem Talmud. He lived in Tiberias and survived to a great age. Almost nothing is known of his family origins. He became an orphan at an early age and, although his family apparently owned considerable property, he spent most of his wealth in pursuit of constant Torah studies, so that he actually became poor. He was just old enough to study under Rabbi Yehudah HaNasi, the editor of the Mishnah. But most of his Torah knowledge was gained from Rabbi Yehudah HaNasi's students, from Ḥizkiyah ben Ḥiyya and from Rabbi Oshaya, from Rabbi Ḥanina and from Rabbi Yannai, who greatly praised him. In time he became the head of a yeshivah in Tiberias, marking the beginning of a period when his fame and influence constantly increased. For a long time Rabbi Yoḥanan was the leading Rabbinic scholar of the entire Jewish world, not only in Eretz Israel but also in Babylonia, whose Sages respected him greatly. Many of them came to Eretz Israel and became his outstanding students. He was a master of both Halakhah and Aggadah. His teachings in both areas are found in many places, and serve as a basis for both of the Talmuds. In recognition of his intellectual and spiritual greatness, the Halakhah is decided according to

[1]אָמַר רַבָּה בַּר שֵׁילָא: אָתְיָא "חֵקֶר", "חֵקֶר", מִבְּרִיָּיתוֹ שֶׁל עוֹלָם. [2]כְּתִיב הָכָא: "עֹשֶׂה גְדֹלוֹת וְאֵין חֵקֶר", [3]וּכְתִיב הָתָם: "הֲלוֹא יָדַעְתָּ? אִם לֹא שָׁמַעְתָּ? אֱלֹהֵי עוֹלָם, ה׳, בּוֹרֵא קְצוֹת הָאָרֶץ, לֹא יִיעַף וְלֹא יִיגָע. אֵין חֵקֶר לִתְבוּנָתוֹ". [4]וּכְתִיב: "מֵכִין הָרִים בְּכֹחוֹ; נֶאְזָר בִּגְבוּרָה".

[5]וּמְנָא לָן דִּבְתְפִלָּה?

[6]דְּתַנְיָא: "'לְאַהֲבָה אֶת ה׳ אֱלֹהֵיכֶם, וּלְעָבְדוֹ בְּכָל לְבַבְכֶם'. [7]אֵיזוֹ הִיא עֲבוֹדָה שֶׁהִיא בַּלֵּב? [8]הֱוֵי אוֹמֵר זוֹ תְּפִלָּה. [9]וּכְתִיב בַּתְרֵיהּ: 'וְנָתַתִּי מְטַר אַרְצְכֶם בְּעִתּוֹ, יוֹרֶה וּמַלְקוֹשׁ'".

LITERAL TRANSLATION

[1]Rabbah bar Shela said: It is derived (lit., "it comes") [through the word] "comprehension," "comprehension," from the creation of the world. [2]It is written here: "He does great things and there is no comprehension," [3]and it is written there: "Did you not know? Have you not heard? The God of the world, the Lord, the Creator of the ends of the earth, does not faint and is not weary. There is no comprehension of His wisdom." [4]And it is written: "He sets firm the mountains with His strength; He is girded with power."

[5]And from where do we [know] that it is [mentioned] in the [Amidah] prayer?

[6]For it is written: "'To love the Lord your God, and to serve Him with all your heart.' [7]What is service that is in the heart? [8]You have to say [that] this is prayer. [9]And it is written after it: 'And I will give the rain of your land in its time, the early rain and the late rain.'"

TRANSLATION AND COMMENTARY

אָמַר רַבָּה בַּר שֵׁילָא [1]**Rabbah bar Shela said:** Rabbi Yoḥanan's **inference** is based on a *gezerah shavah*. According to this hermeneutical rule, when the Torah uses the same word in two otherwise unconnected verses, it intends these verses to be compared and information to be transferred from one to the other. Thus in this case the idea that rain reflects the power of God is inferred **from the creation of the world through the** use of the **word "comprehension"** in two contexts, once in connection with the creation, and the other in connection with rain. [2]**It is written** in the verse from Job cited by Rabbi Yoḥanan: **"He does great things and there is no comprehension,"** [3]**and it is written** in a verse in Isaiah (40:28) dealing with the creation of the world: **"Did you not know? Have you not heard? The God of the world, the Lord, the Creator of the ends of the earth, does not faint and is not weary. There is no comprehension of His wisdom."** Thus we see that the word "comprehension" appears both in connection with the creation of the world and in connection with rain. [4]**And,** continues Rabbah bar Shela, we know that the creation of the world is a reflection of God's power, as **it is written** (Psalms 65:7): **"He sets firm the mountains with His strength; He is girded with power."** Thus we can infer that rain, like the creation of the world, is a reflection of God's power.

וּמְנָא לָן דִּבְתְפִלָּה [5]The Gemara now asks: **From where do we know that the mention** of rain **is** included **in the Amidah prayer,** which is recited three times each day?

דְּתַנְיָא [6]The Gemara answers: We know this from what **is written** in a Baraita commenting on the verse (Deuteronomy 11:13) that commands us **"to love the Lord your God, and to serve Him with all your heart."** The Baraita asks: "What is meant by serving God with our hearts? The term 'serving' usually refers to the sacrificial service in the Temple. [7]**What service is** performed **in the heart** rather than by sacrificing an animal in the Temple? [8]**We must say that** the Torah **is** referring to **prayer.** Thus we see that in this verse the Torah is commanding us to offer prayers to God. [9]**And it is written** in the verse immediately **after this** one (Deuteronomy 11:14): **'And I will give the rain of your land in its time, the early rain and the late rain.'"** The

NOTES

וּמְנָא לָן דִּבְתְפִלָּה And from where do we know that it is mentioned in the Amidah prayer? *Maharsha* asks: Why does the Gemara search for a source that prayers for rain should be recited? Surely we can derive this from the prayer offered by King Solomon when the Temple was dedicated (I Kings 8:35-36): "When heaven is shut up and there is no rain because they have sinned against You, if they pray toward this place, and confess Your name, and turn from their sin when you afflict them, then may You hear in heaven and forgive the sin of Your servants and of Your people Israel, that You may teach them the good way in which they should walk, and give rain upon Your land which You have given to Your people for an inheritance."

Maharsha answers (and his explanation is reflected in our translation and commentary) that Solomon's prayer teaches that prayers for rain are to be recited in times of drought, "when heaven is shut up." Here, however, the Gemara is seeking a source for the obligation to petition for rain on a regular basis in one's daily prayers throughout the rainy season.

It has also been suggested that Solomon's prayer serves as a source for the obligation to entreat for rain when rain is necessary. But here the Gemara wishes to find Biblical support for the obligation to mention among the rest of God's praises His ability to cause the rain to fall (*Keren Orah*).

וּכְתִיב בַּתְרֵיהּ: "וְנָתַתִּי מְטַר אַרְצְכֶם" And it is written after it: "And I will give the rain of your land." It has been

his opinion in almost every case, even when Rav or Shmuel, the great Amoraim of Babylonia (whom he himself regarded as his superiors), disagree with him. Only when he disagrees with his teachers in Eretz Israel (such as Rabbi Yannai and Rabbi Yehoshua ben Levi) does the Halakhah not follow his opinion.

Rabbi Yoḥanan was renowned for being handsome, and much was said in praise of his good looks. By nature he was excitable, so that occasionally he was too severe with his friends and students, but immediately afterwards was stricken with remorse. We know that his life was full of suffering. Ten of his sons died in his lifetime. There is a Geonic tradition that one of his sons, Rabbi Matena, an Amora of Babylonia, did not predecease him. The death of Rabbi Yoḥanan's student, friend and brother-in-law, Resh Lakish, for which he considered himself responsible, brought his own death closer.

Rabbi Yoḥanan had many students. In fact, all the Amoraim of Eretz Israel in succeeding generations were his students and benefited from his teachings — so much so that he is said to be the author of the Jerusalem Talmud. His greatest students were his brother-in-law Resh Lakish, Rabbi Elazar, Rabbi Ḥiyya bar Abba, Rabbi Abbahu, Rabbi Yose bar Ḥanina, Rabbi Ammi, and Rabbi Assi.

רַבָּה בַּר שֵׁילָא Rabbah bar Shela. A Babylonian Amora of the third and fourth generations, Rabbah bar Shela was a disciple of Rav Ḥisda, whose teachings he frequently cites. He seems to have lived near Meḥoza, and is usually associated with Rava, who came from Meḥoza. Rabbah bar Shela apparently served as a Rabbinic judge where he lived, and he may have had a small academy of his own there.

BACKGROUND

עֲבוֹדָה שֶׁהִיא בַּלֵּב Service that is in the heart. The Hebrew word עֲבוֹדָה, meaning "work" or "service," also means "worship" or "prayer" to God. It is the act by which a person expresses his

[1]אָמַר רַבִּי יוֹחָנָן: שְׁלֹשָׁה מַפְתְּחוֹת בְּיָדוֹ שֶׁל הַקָּדוֹשׁ בָּרוּךְ הוּא שֶׁלֹּא נִמְסְרוּ בְּיַד שָׁלִיחַ, [2]וְאֵלּוּ הֵן: מַפְתֵּחַ שֶׁל גְּשָׁמִים, מַפְתֵּחַ שֶׁל חַיָּה, וּמַפְתֵּחַ שֶׁל תְּחִיַּית הַמֵּתִים. [3]מַפְתֵּחַ שֶׁל גְּשָׁמִים, [4]דִּכְתִיב: ״יִפְתַּח ה׳ לְךָ אֶת אוֹצָרוֹ הַטּוֹב, אֶת הַשָּׁמַיִם, לָתֵת מְטַר אַרְצְךָ בְּעִתּוֹ״. [5]מַפְתֵּחַ שֶׁל חַיָּה מִנַּיִן? [6]דִּכְתִיב: ״וַיִּזְכֹּר אֱלֹהִים אֶת רָחֵל, וַיִּשְׁמַע [2B] אֵלֶיהָ אֱלֹהִים וַיִּפְתַּח אֶת רַחְמָהּ״. [7]מַפְתֵּחַ שֶׁל תְּחִיַּית הַמֵּתִים

LITERAL TRANSLATION

[1]Rabbi Yoḥanan said: There are three keys in the hand of the Holy One, blessed be He, that were not entrusted to the hand of an agent, [2]and these are they: The key of rains, the key of a woman giving birth, and the key of the resurrection of the dead.

[3]The key of rains, [4]as it is written: "The Lord will open for you His good treasure house, the heavens, to give the rain of your land in its time."

[5]From where [do we derive] the key of a woman giving birth? [6]As it is written: "And God remembered Rachel, and [2B] God listened to her and opened her womb."

[7]From where [do we derive] the key of the resurrection

RASHI

ואמר רבי יוחנן שלש מפתחות — היינו שלא נמסרו לשליח אחד ביחד.

TRANSLATION AND COMMENTARY

Baraita concludes that the Torah particularly wants us to offer prayers in connection with rain, and these prayers are to be included in the regular Amidah prayer.

אָמַר רַבִּי יוֹחָנָן [1]Having mentioned Rabbi Yoḥanan's statement about rain reflecting the power of God, the Gemara considers another statement by Rabbi Yoḥanan on a related topic. **Rabbi Yoḥanan said: There are three keys in the hand of the Holy One, blessed be He, that were not entrusted to the hands of an intermediary.** After God created the world, He refrained from intervening directly in its functioning. Even miracles were usually performed through an Angel or a Prophet. But there are three events — two of them natural and one miraculous — that remain dependent on God's will in a direct way, [2]**and they are these: The key of rain, the key of a woman giving birth, and the key of the resurrection of the dead.**

מַפְתֵּחַ שֶׁל גְּשָׁמִים [3]Rabbi Yoḥanan goes on to cite Scriptural sources for his claim that these particular events remain directly dependent on God's will. All the sources cited contain expressions in which the Hebrew root פתח ("to open") is used in various forms, and this constitutes a linguistic link with the noun מַפְתֵּחַ ("key"), which is based on the same root. We know that **the key of rain** is not entrusted to an intermediary, [4]**as it is written** (Deuteronomy 28:12): **"The Lord will open** [יִפְתַּח] **for you His good treasure house, the heavens, to give the rain of your land in its time."** In this verse God is portrayed as opening His treasure house himself, rather than acting through an intermediary.

מַפְתֵּחַ שֶׁל חַיָּה מִנַּיִן [5]Rabbi Yoḥanan continues: **From where do we know** that **the key of a woman giving birth** is also not entrusted to an intermediary? [6]**For it is written** regarding Rachel, Jacob's wife, who was initially unable to bear children (Genesis 30:22): **"And God remembered Rachel, and** [2B] **God listened to her and opened** [וַיִּפְתַּח] **her womb."** We see from this verse that God opened Rachel's womb Himself and not through an intermediary.

מַפְתֵּחַ שֶׁל תְּחִיַּית הַמֵּתִים מִנַּיִן [7]Rabbi Yoḥanan continues: **From where do we know** that **the key of the**

NOTES

noted that the very same verse continues: "And you will gather in your grain and your wine and your oil," alluding to the fact that it is on the "Festival of Ingathering," on Sukkot, that the prayers for rain begin (*Rosh Yosef*).

שֶׁלֹּא נִמְסְרוּ בְּיַד שָׁלִיחַ That were not entrusted to the hand of an agent. The Rishonim object: Elsewhere (*Sanhedrin* 113a), it is stated that the keys of rain and of resurrection were indeed entrusted to Elijah the Prophet. *Rashi* (following *Rabbenu Gershom*) explains that Rabbi Yoḥanan means to say that the three keys — of rain, of a woman giving birth, and of resurrection — were not entrusted together to a single intermediary. *Tosafot* (see also *Ra'avad*, cited by *Shittah*) explains that these three keys could indeed be entrusted to an intermediary for a limited period of time, but not permanently.

וַיִּפְתַּח אֶת רַחְמָהּ And opened her womb. *Maharsha* asks: Why does the Gemara not cite the earlier verse (Genesis 29:31): "And when the Lord saw that Leah was hated, he opened her womb"? *Maharsha* explains that the Gemara cites the verse referring to Rachel, because in that verse the name of God immediately precedes the expression "and opened her womb." This emphasizes that it was God Himself, and not an intermediary, who was responsible for opening Rachel's womb. But in the verse referring to Leah the name of God does not directly precede the expression "He opened her womb." Thus it is possible to interpret the verse as follows: And when the Lord saw that Leah was hated, He into whose hand the key to childbirth had been entrusted opened her womb.

veneration for the Creator. Therefore, when the term עֲבוֹדָה appears without qualification in Rabbinic literature, it refers to worship in the Temple, specifically the offering of sacrifices. Regarding the expression in Deuteronomy, "and to serve Him with all your heart," the Sages say that this means prayer, the essence of which is directing one's heart to one's Creator. This, too, is a form of worship, and is regarded as one of the most natural ways of serving God.

שְׁלֹשָׁה מַפְתְּחוֹת Three keys. These three keys, each in its own way, refer to significant changes that take place in reality. Although rainfall and childbirth seem like natural events to us, they are defined here, no less than the resurrection of the dead, as departures from the normal course of nature which effect a change and create a new reality. Therefore control over them is not entrusted to an emissary, and God Himself is responsible for them.

CONCEPTS

תְּחִיַּית הַמֵּתִים The resurrection of the dead. This is hinted at in various places in the Torah and in the Prophets, and is mentioned explicitly in Daniel (12,2).

According to *Rambam*, the resurrection of the dead will take place after the coming of the Messiah, and it is the opinion of many authorities (see *Ramban*, *Sha'ar HaGemul*) that this will mark the beginning of a new era of life on earth.

The resurrection of the dead is therefore a unique development that will occur in the future. Nevertheless, we pray for it and expect it at all times.

מִנַּיִן? [1]דִּכְתִיב: "וִידַעְתֶּם כִּי אֲנִי ה', בְּפִתְחִי אֶת קִבְרוֹתֵיכֶם".
[2]בְּמַעַרְבָא אָמְרִי: [3]אַף מַפְתֵּחַ שֶׁל פַּרְנָסָה, [4]דִּכְתִיב: "פּוֹתֵחַ אֶת יָדֶךָ, וגו'".
[5]וְרַבִּי יוֹחָנָן מַאי טַעֲמָא לָא קָא חָשֵׁיב לְהָא?
[6]אָמַר לָךְ: גְּשָׁמִים הַיְינוּ פַּרְנָסָה.
[7]"רַבִּי אֱלִיעֶזֶר אוֹמֵר: מִיּוֹם טוֹב הָרִאשׁוֹן שֶׁל חַג, כו'". [8]אִיבַּעְיָא לְהוּ: [9]רַבִּי אֱלִיעֶזֶר מֵהֵיכָא גָּמֵיר לַהּ? מִלּוּלָב גָּמַר לַהּ,

LITERAL TRANSLATION

of the dead? [1]As it is written: "And you will know that I am the Lord, when I open your graves." [2]In Eretz Israel (lit., "in the West") they said: [3]Also the key of sustenance, [4]as it is written: "You open Your hand, etc." [5]And what is the reason that Rabbi Yoḥanan did not count this? [6]He can say to you: Rains are the same as sustenance. [7]"Rabbi Eliezer says: From the first holy day of the Festival [of Sukkot], etc." [8]It was asked of them: [9]From where did Rabbi Eliezer derive this? Did he derive it from the lulav,

RASHI

יפתח ה' – ולא שליח. **כי אני ה'** – ולא שליח. **פותח את ידך** – ולא שליח. **גשמים נמי היינו פרנסה** – וככר חשבנא ליה. **מלולב גמר ליה** – שדומה ללולב, שכשם שאי אפשר לאלו ארבע מינין בלא גשמים, ובאין לרצות על המים, כדאמרינן בסוכה, כך אי אפשר לעולם בלא מים.

TRANSLATION AND COMMENTARY

resurrection of the dead is also not entrusted to an intermediary? [1]**For it is written** regarding Ezekiel's vision of the dry bones coming to life (Ezekiel 37:13): **"And you will know that I am the Lord, when I open** [בְּפִתְחִי] **your graves."** We see from this verse that God is portrayed as opening the graves Himself and not as acting through an intermediary.

בְּמַעַרְבָא אָמְרִי [2]**In Eretz Israel they** made the same inferences about rain, childbirth, and resurrection from these three verses. [3]But they **added** that a fourth key, **the key of sustenance, is also** not entrusted to an intermediary, [4]**for it is written** (Psalms 145:16): **"You open** [פּוֹתֵחַ] **Your Hand** and satisfy the desire of every living thing," by giving all creatures enough to eat. We see from this verse that God is portrayed as opening His Hand Himself and not as acting through an intermediary. Hence sustenance is a fourth key and should be added to Rabbi Yoḥanan's list.

וְרַבִּי יוֹחָנָן מַאי טַעֲמָא [5]The Gemara asks: **And what is the reason that Rabbi Yoḥanan did not count** sustenance as one of the keys?

אָמַר לָךְ [6]The Gemara explains: Rabbi Yoḥanan **can answer you** that in fact there are only three keys, because **rain is the same as sustenance.** Since earning a livelihood is ultimately dependent on the success of the harvest, which in turn is dependent on rain, Rabbi Yoḥanan considered these two "keys" to be one and the same, and therefore the two verses are teaching us the same point.

רַבִּי אֱלִיעֶזֶר אוֹמֵר [7]The Gemara now turns to the next clause of the Mishnah, which stated: **"Rabbi Eliezer says:** We begin to insert the words 'who causes the wind to blow and the rain to fall' **from the first holy day of the Festival of Sukkot**, because God decides on Sukkot about the coming rainy season," as the Gemara explained above (2a). [8]**A problem was raised** concerning Rabbi Eliezer's view. Granted that we must begin to mention rain in our prayers at some point during Sukkot; but why does Rabbi Eliezer assume that we should begin mentioning rain on the first day of the Festival? [9]**From where did Rabbi Eliezer derive this** law? There are two water-related rituals prescribed for Sukkot, the lulav and the water libation, both of which apply from the first day. The Torah commands (Leviticus 23:40) that on the first day of Sukkot we take in our hands the fruit of the *hadar* tree (an etrog) together with the branches of three green trees: the date palm (called lulav in the Talmud, and from which the name of the entire ritual is derived), the myrtle, and the willow. We are enjoined to "rejoice" with these plants before God for the first seven days of the Festival. This rejoicing takes the form of holding these plants in our hands, and waving them during prayers and during the Temple service (the ritual to be followed is described in detail in the third and fourth chapters of tractate *Sukkah*). As the Gemara explains below, these fresh green plants symbolize the need for rain, and the waving symbolizes the winds that bring the rain. Thus the use of the lulav during

NOTES

"פּוֹתֵחַ אֶת יָדֶךָ" **"You open Your hand."** It has been suggested that the inference regarding the key to sustenance is based on a grammatical difficulty in the verse, "You open Your hand." The verse begins with the word פּוֹתֵחַ, which would ordinarily be understood as "He opens," but continues with יָדֶךָ, meaning "Your hand," so that the whole expression must be taken to mean: "You open Your hand." The change from third person to second person teaches that it is the hand of God Himself and not that of an intermediary which opens and satisfies the desires of every living thing (*Maharsha*).

TRANSLATION AND COMMENTARY

prayer physically emphasizes the importance of rain. Similarly, there is a tradition transmitted by Moses as part of the Oral Law, that a measure of water is poured on the altar in the Temple as a libation as part of the morning sacrifice during Sukkot, in addition to the regular libation of wine poured on the altar every day, as prescribed by the Torah (Exodus 29:40). The water libation is not explicitly commanded in the Torah, although the Talmudic Sages found several Scriptural hints about it (as the Gemara explains below). This ritual is also a prayer that God grant ample rain during the coming year. Both the taking of the lulav and the water libation are performed during the seven days of Sukkot, starting from the first day, and either of them could have served as a precedent for Rabbi Eliezer's ruling that we begin to make mention of rain from the first day of Sukkot. But this presents a problem: Which ritual actually served as Rabbi Eliezer's source? **Did** Rabbi Eliezer **derive this** ruling **from the lulav,** [1]**or did he derive it from the water libation?**

מִלּוּלָב [2]The Gemara now explains why this problem is significant. If we say that Rabbi Eliezer **derived this** ruling **from** the ceremony of the taking of **the lulav**, then it does indeed follow that rain should be mentioned from the first day of Sukkot, just as the lulav is taken from the first day. [3]But if so, we can argue that **just as the lulav is taken** only **in the daytime,** [4]**so too is** rain **to be mentioned** only **in the daytime.** The Mishnah (*Megillah* 20b; *Sukkah* 38a) rules that a person may fulfill the commandment to take the four plants of the lulav in his hand any time during the day (although it should ideally be done during the morning service), but may not do so at night. Thus, if the lulav is the source of Rabbi Eliezer's ruling, the first mention of rain in the Amidah prayer should take place during the morning service on the first day of Sukkot, when the lulav is first taken. [5]On the other hand, **it is possible that** Rabbi Eliezer **derived this** ruling **from the water libation** that is offered every morning of the Sukkot Festival. If so, it does indeed follow that rain should be mentioned from the first day, just as the water libation is performed from the first day. [6]But if so, we can argue that rain should be mentioned from the service on the first evening of Sukkot, **just as the water libation**

[1]אוֹ מִנִּיסּוּךְ הַמַּיִם גָּמַר לָהּ? [2]מִלּוּלָב גָּמַר לָהּ: [3]מַה לּוּלָב בַּיּוֹם, [4]אַף הַזְכָּרָה בַּיּוֹם. [5]אוֹ דִּלְמָא מִנִּיסּוּךְ הַמַּיִם גָּמַר לָהּ? [6]מַה נִּיסּוּךְ הַמַּיִם מֵאוּרְתָּא —

LITERAL TRANSLATION

[1]or did he derive it from the water libation? [2]He derived it from the lulav: [3]Just as the lulav is [taken] in the daytime, [4]so too is the mention [made] in the daytime. [5]Or did he perhaps derive it from the water libation? [6]Just as the water libation can be [performed] from the evening —

RASHI

מה לולב ביום – שמתחילין ליטול ביום ראשון, אף הזכרה נמי ביום. כלומר, שאין מזכירין בלילי יום טוב הראשון, עד למחר. **מה ניסוך המים מאורתא** – כדאשכחן במסכת סוכה (נא,ב): שממלאין הכלי מים לניסוך המים בלילה. ויש ספרים דכתיב בהו: דאמר מר ומנחתם ונסכיהם בלילה, שמקריבין הקרבנות ביום יכולין להביא המנחות והנסכים בלילה. אף האי, ניסוך המים, נמי יכול לנסך בלילה.

CONCEPTS

לוּלָב Lulav, palm branch. Referred to in the Torah as "branches of palm trees" (Leviticus 23:40), the lulav must be held in the hand together with three other plants (the etrog, the myrtle, and the willow) on the Festival of Sukkot. The lulav is a young branch of a date palm, with the leaves still pressed tightly against the branch. All four plants must be of high quality. Therefore the lulav may not be crooked, nor may its top be damaged or broken. It must be at least four handbreadths (about 35 cm.) long.

נִיסּוּךְ הַמַּיִם The water libation. During the Festival of Sukkot, in addition to the other special sacrifices offered in the Temple, a water libation was poured over the altar. This libation is not mentioned explicitly in the Torah, its source being an oral tradition transmitted to Moses on Mount Sinai (הֲלָכָה לְמֹשֶׁה מִסִּינַי). The water libation was accompanied by great festivity and ceremony, from the time that the water was drawn from the Siloam Spring until it was poured over the altar. The water libation was offered on all seven days of Sukkot, including Shabbat, even though it was not permitted to draw water for this offering on Shabbat.

NOTES

נִיסּוּךְ הַמַּיִם מֵאוּרְתָּא The water libation can be performed from the evening. According to the plain reading of the standard text of the Gemara it would seem that the water libation poured on the altar during Sukkot may be offered even at night. But this presents a difficulty, for it is stated elsewhere (*Temurah* 14b) that libations brought independently of a sacrifice may be offered even at night, but libations that accompany a sacrifice may be offered only during the day. And it is also stated (*Yoma* 26b) that the water libation on Sukkot is offered together with the daily sacrifice brought in the morning. The difficulty is mitigated according to the texts of the Talmud used by some of the Rishonim which omit the words: "For the Master said: 'And their meal-offerings and their libations,' means even at night." But even according to these texts, the Gemara states that the water libation can be performed from the evening, implying that at least some part of the water-libation ceremony can be performed at night!

In his first explanation, *Rashi* suggests that, although the water libation may be offered only during the day, the water to be used for the ceremony may be prepared the night before (see also *Rabbenu Elyakim* and *Tosefot Rid*). *Ra'avad* and *Shittah* offer a similar explanation: The water-libation ceremony may be performed only during the day, but the water to be used for the libation may be consecrated the night before.

Other Rishonim maintain that the water-libation may indeed be performed at night. According to *Rambam* (*Hilkhot Temidim* 10:7), the water-libation ceremony should be performed during the day; but if it is performed at night,

HALAKHAH

נִיסּוּךְ הַמַּיִם The water libation at night. "The wine libations offered together with sacrifices are valid only if performed during the day. However, the water libation (offered only during the Sukkot Festival) is considered a different type of libation — and even though the proper time to perform it is with the continual burnt-offering (*tamid*) in the morning, nevertheless, if the water libation is performed at night, it is valid, as stated in the Gemara here and in tractate *Sukkah* (*Maggid Mishneh*)." (*Rambam, Sefer Avodah, Hilkhot Ma'aseh HaKorbanot* 4:5; *ibid., Hilkhot Temidin* 10:7.)

[1]דְּאָמַר מָר: ״וּמִנְחָתָם וְנִסְכֵּיהֶם״ אֲפִילּוּ בַּלַּיְלָה — [2]אַף הַזְכָּרָה מֵאוּרְתָּא? [3]תָּא שְׁמַע, דְּאָמַר רַבִּי אַבָּהוּ: [4]לֹא לְמָדָהּ רַבִּי אֱלִיעֶזֶר אֶלָּא מִלּוּלָב.

[5]אִיכָּא דְּאָמְרִי רַבִּי אַבָּהוּ גְּמָרָא גְּמִיר לַהּ, [6]וְאִיכָּא דְּאָמְרִי מַתְנִיתָא שְׁמִיעַ לֵיהּ.

[7]מַאי הִיא?

[8]דְּתַנְיָא: [9]״מֵאֵימָתַי מַזְכִּירִין עַל הַגְּשָׁמִים? [10]רַבִּי אֱלִיעֶזֶר אוֹמֵר: מִשְּׁעַת נְטִילַת לוּלָב. [11]רַבִּי יְהוֹשֻׁעַ אוֹמֵר: מִשְּׁעַת הַנָּחָתוֹ.

LITERAL TRANSLATION

[1]for the Master said: "And their meal-offerings and their libations" [means] even at night — [2]so too can the mention be [made] from the evening?

[3]Come [and] hear, for Rabbi Abbahu said: [4]Rabbi Eliezer learned it only from the lulav.

[5]There are [some] who say [that] Rabbi Abbahu derived it [from] a tradition, [6]and there are [some] who say [that] he learned it from a Baraita.

[7]Which is it?

[8]For it was taught: [9]"From when do we make mention of rain? [10]Rabbi Eliezer says: From the time of the taking of the lulav. [11]Rabbi Yehoshua says: From the time of putting it down.

TRANSLATION AND COMMENTARY

can be performed from the evening. [1]**For** although the proper procedure is to perform the water libation in the morning, **the Master said** (in other words, there is an authoritative source) that it may be performed at night as well. There is a Baraita (*Temurah* 14a) which explains the verse (Numbers 29:18) dealing with the additional sacrifices offered during the Sukkot Festival: **"And their meal-offerings and their libations."** From this expression the Baraita infers that meal-offerings and libations may be brought separately, even when they are associated with a particular animal sacrifice. [2]And the Baraita concludes that the meal-offering or the libation may be brought **even at night,** when it is forbidden to offer an animal sacrifice. Thus it follows that although the water libation is supposed to be offered together with the morning sacrifice, it can in fact be brought separately, even at night. And just as the water libation begins theoretically from the first night of Sukkot, **so too is** rain to be **mentioned from the evening** service that ushers in the Festival of Sukkot.

תָּא שְׁמַע [3]The Gemara replies: **Come and hear** a resolution of your problem from what **Rabbi Abbahu said:** [4]**Rabbi Eliezer learned only from the lulav** that prayers for rain are appropriate from the first day of Sukkot. Hence it follows that Rabbi Eliezer is of the opinion that we do not mention rain until the morning service on the first day of Sukkot, but not during the evening service that ushers in the Festival.

אִיכָּא דְּאָמְרִי [5]It is clear that Rabbi Abbahu maintained that Rabbi Eliezer's precedent was the lulav, but it is not entirely clear why Rabbi Abbahu's opinion should be so authoritative. **There are those who say that Rabbi Abbahu had a tradition** about this matter, passed down to him through the generations from Rabbi Eliezer himself. [6]**And there are those who say that** Rabbi Abbahu **derived** Rabbi Eliezer's opinion **from a Baraita,** which explicitly states that Rabbi Eliezer's precedent was the lulav. Thus, according to this view, it was not the Rabbi Abbahu's statement that was so authoritative, but rather the Baraita that he was able to cite as proof.

מַאי הִיא [7]The Gemara asks: **Which is** the Baraita from which Rabbi Abbahu derives his proof?

דְּתַנְיָא [8]The Gemara answers: The following Baraita **was taught,** elaborating on the dispute between Rabbi Eliezer and Rabbi Yehoshua in our Mishnah, and also citing additional Tannaim who disagree with both opinions: [9]**"From when do we make mention of rain** in the second blessing of the Amidah? [10]**Rabbi Eliezer says: From the time of the taking of the lulav** — from the morning of the first day of Sukkot. [11]**Rabbi Yehoshua says: From the time of putting** the lulav **down** — from the morning of the seventh day of Sukkot, when we take the **lulav** for the last time, and put it away." It should be noted that in our Mishnah Rabbi Yehoshua maintains that this prayer should not be recited until the eighth day, but according to the Baraita

RASHI

אף הזכרה נמי מאורתא — שבלילי יום טוב הראשון קאמר רבי אליעזר שמתחילין להזכיר גבורות גשמים. **גמרא גמיר לה** — רבי אבהו, דרבי אליעזר לא למדה אלא מלולב. **מתניתין שמיע ליה** — דרבי אליעזר גמר מלולב. **משעת הנחתו** — מיום שמברכין בו באחרונה, דהיינו בשביעי.

SAGES

רַבִּי אֲבָהוּ Rabbi Abbahu. A Palestinian Amora of the third generation, Rabbi Abbahu was the most important of Rabbi Yoḥanan's disciples. He was the head of a yeshivah and a judge in Caesarea, as well as the representative of the Jewish people to the Romans. He also transmitted teachings in the name of Resh Lakish, Rabbi Elazar, Rabbi Yose bar Ḥanina, and others. Rabbi Zera was a student and colleague of his. His other colleagues were Rabbi Ḥiyya bar Abba, and Rabbi Ammi and Rabbi Assi, the heads of the Tiberias Yeshivah. Among his students were Rabbi Yonah, Rabbi Yose, and Rabbi Yirmeyah. Sages gathered around him, and they became known as the "Rabbis of Caesarea." He was prolific in Aggadah and was an excellent preacher. He spoke Greek well, and taught that language to his daughter. His father-in-law was Rabbi Taḥlifa of Caesarea, and his sons were the Sages Ḥanina, Avimi, and Zera.

TERMINOLOGY

גְּמָרָא גְּמִיר לַהּ He derived it from a tradition. In other words, this matter was derived from tradition, rather than from a Biblical verse.

BACKGROUND

מִשְּׁעַת נְטִילַת לוּלָב.... מִשְּׁעַת הַנָּחָתוֹ From the time of the taking of the lulav....From the time of putting it down. From the text of the Baraita it seems that both Rabbi Eliezer and Rabbi Yehoshua connect the mention of rain with the taking of the lulav. However, in Rabbi Eliezer's opinion, all the things meant to recall rain should be connected — the taking of the lulav, the water libation, and the mention of rain in the second blessing of the Amidah. By contrast, Rabbi Yehoshua maintains that we must first conclude the symbolic deeds meant to recall rain, and only afterwards mention rain explicitly in prayer.

NOTES

it is still valid. According to *Tosafot* (and, possibly, the second explanation of *Rashi*), there may not even be a preference that the ceremony be performed during the day.

Ritva resolves the difficulty raised above by arguing that the water libation brought on Sukkot is not considered a libation that accompanies a sacrifice but rather an independent obligation imposed on account of the Festival.

רַבִּי אֱלִיעֶזֶר וְרַבִּי יְהוֹשֻׁעַ Rabbi Eliezer and Rabbi Yehoshua. The Jerusalem Talmud expands on the reasoning of Rabbi Eliezer and Rabbi Yehoshua. Rabbi Eliezer argues that it is

LITERAL TRANSLATION

[1] Rabbi Eliezer said: Since these four species come only to intercede for water, [2] and just as these four species cannot exist without water, so too the world cannot exist without water. [3] Rabbi Yehoshua said to him: But are not rains on the Festival [of Sukkot] nothing but a sign of a curse? [4] Rabbi Eliezer said to him: I too did not say 'to ask for,' but 'to mention.' [5] And just as one mentions the resurrection of the dead throughout the entire year, but it [will take place] only in its [proper] time, [6] so too may we mention the powers of rains throughout the year, but they [occur] only in their [proper] time.

[1] אָמַר רַבִּי אֱלִיעֶזֶר: הוֹאִיל וְאַרְבַּעַת מִינִין הַלָּלוּ אֵינָן בָּאִין אֶלָּא לְרַצּוֹת עַל הַמַּיִם, [2] וּכְשֵׁם שֶׁאַרְבַּע מִינִין הַלָּלוּ אִי אֶפְשָׁר בָּהֶם בְּלֹא מַיִם, כָּךְ אִי אֶפְשָׁר לָעוֹלָם בְּלֹא מַיִם. [3] אָמַר לוֹ רַבִּי יְהוֹשֻׁעַ: וַהֲלֹא גְּשָׁמִים בֶּחָג אֵינוֹ אֶלָּא סִימַן קְלָלָה? [4] אָמַר לוֹ רַבִּי אֱלִיעֶזֶר: אַף אֲנִי לֹא אָמַרְתִּי ׳לִשְׁאוֹל׳, אֶלָּא ׳לְהַזְכִּיר׳. [5] וּכְשֵׁם שֶׁתְּחִיַּית הַמֵּתִים מַזְכִּיר כָּל הַשָּׁנָה כּוּלָּהּ, וְאֵינָהּ אֶלָּא בִּזְמַנָּהּ, [6] כָּךְ מַזְכִּירִים גְּבוּרוֹת גְּשָׁמִים כָּל הַשָּׁנָה, וְאֵינָן אֶלָּא בִּזְמַנָּן.

RASHI

ארבעה מינין הללו – שבלולב ואתרוג. כך גשמים – יהא מזכיר כל השנה, אפילו בימות החמה, אם הוא רוצה – יהא מזכיר.

TRANSLATION AND COMMENTARY

he maintains that it should be recited from the morning service of the seventh day. [1] The Baraita continues: "**Rabbi Eliezer said:** We should mention rain in our prayers from the time when we begin to perform the lulav ritual, **because the four species** of plants used in the lulav ritual **come to intercede** with God **for water** (as a prayer for rain). [2] The taking of the lulav is a symbolic way of saying to God that **just as these four species** of plants **cannot survive without water, so too the world cannot survive without water.** [This clause of the Baraita is the source of Rabbi Abbahu's statement that Rabbi Eliezer based his ruling on the lulav and not the water libation.] [3] But **Rabbi Yehoshua said to** Rabbi Eliezer in reply: **But surely rain on the Festival of Sukkot is nothing but a sign of a curse?** Rain makes it impossible to fulfill the commandment to dwell in a sukkah, and is thus an indication that God does not desire our service. How, then, can you rule that we should pray for rain during Sukkot, when we do not want rain during this week? [4] **Rabbi Eliezer said to** Rabbi Yehoshua in reply: **I did not say that we ask for** rain during Sukkot. Prayers for rain are not included in the Amidah until the rainy season has begun. **Rather,** I was referring **to** making **mention** of rain in the second blessing of the Amidah, which also refers to the resurrection of the dead as well as to God's other mighty deeds. This blessing is not to be interpreted as a request but rather as a declaration of praise. [5] **And just as** the worshiper **mentions the resurrection of the dead** and God's other powers **throughout the entire year, although** each of these powers **will be manifested only in its appointed time,** [6] **so too may we mention the gift of rain throughout the year, even though** rain actually **falls only in**

NOTES

appropriate to begin mentioning rain on the first day of Sukkot because it is on that day that the four species — the lulav, the etrog, the myrtle, and the willow — are first taken. These four species, which are dependent upon water, are intended to act as "intercessors for rain," and so we begin to mention rain in our prayers from the beginning of Sukkot, when these species are first taken. Moreover, when a servant sees that he has served his master faithfully, he takes advantage of the first opportunity to ask for his reward, even if he only wishes to receive it later. It is therefore fitting to begin mentioning rain on the first day of Sukkot when God's commandments are fulfilled and the four species are first taken. Rabbi Yehoshua counters that a servant does not ask for his reward, even if he has served his master faithfully, unless it is clear to him that his master is pleased with his service. Thus we should not mention rain until the end of Sukkot, for rain during the Festival is seen as an indication that God is not pleased with our service. Moreover, even if a servant has served his master faithfully and even if he has received an indication that his master is pleased with his service, it is inappropriate for him to ask for his reward before he actually wishes to receive it.

מִשְּׁעַת הַנָּחָתוֹ From the time of putting it down. Our commentary follows *Rashi*, who explains that according to Rabbi Yehoshua in the Baraita we begin to mention rain on the day when the lulav is taken for the last time — on the seventh day of Sukkot. *Tosafot*, however, explains that, according to Rabbi Yehoshua, we begin to mention rain on the night following the seventh day of Sukkot, after the lulav has been put down for the last time.

The Jerusalem Talmud discusses the precise meaning of the term "from the time of putting it down." This expression may refer to the morning of the seventh day of Sukkot, the time when the lulav is ordinarily taken and put down for the last time, in which case the viewpoint of Rabbi Yehoshua as reported in the Baraita contradicts his viewpoint as reported in the Mishnah that the mention of rain begins on the eighth day of Sukkot. On the other hand, since the obligation of taking the lulav can be fulfilled throughout the day, the lulav is sometimes not put down until the end of the seventh day of Sukkot; and so, even according to Rabbi Yehoshua's view as reported in the Baraita, the mention of rain begins only on the eighth day of Sukkot.

[1]לְפִיכָךְ, אִם בָּא לְהַזְכִּיר כָּל הַשָּׁנָה כּוּלָּהּ — מַזְכִּיר. [2]רַבִּי אוֹמֵר: אֲנִי מִשָּׁעָה שֶׁמַּפְסִיק לִשְׁאֵלָה כָּךְ מַפְסִיק לְהַזְכָּרָה. [3]רַבִּי יְהוּדָה בֶּן בְּתֵירָה אוֹמֵר: בַּשֵּׁנִי בֶּחָג הוּא מַזְכִּיר. [4]רַבִּי עֲקִיבָא אוֹמֵר: בַּשִּׁשִּׁי בֶּחָג הוּא מַזְכִּיר. [5]רַבִּי יְהוּדָה מִשּׁוּם רַבִּי יְהוֹשֻׁעַ אוֹמֵר: [6]הָעוֹבֵר לִפְנֵי הַתֵּיבָה בְּיוֹם טוֹב הָאַחֲרוֹן שֶׁל חַג — [7]הָאַחֲרוֹן מַזְכִּיר; [8]הָרִאשׁוֹן אֵינוֹ מַזְכִּיר. [9]בְּיוֹם טוֹב רִאשׁוֹן שֶׁל פֶּסַח, [10]הָרִאשׁוֹן מַזְכִּיר; [11]הָאַחֲרוֹן אֵינוֹ מַזְכִּיר״.
[12]שַׁפִּיר קָאָמַר לֵיהּ רַבִּי אֱלִיעֶזֶר לְרַבִּי יְהוֹשֻׁעַ!

LITERAL TRANSLATION

[1]Therefore, if one comes to mention [rain] throughout the entire year, one may mention [it]. [2]Rabbi [Yehudah HaNasi] says: I say [that] from the time when one ceases to ask [for rain] one likewise ceases to mention [it]. [3]Rabbi Yehudah ben Beterah says: On the second [day] of the [Sukkot] Festival one mentions [rain]. [4]Rabbi Akiva says: On the sixth [day] of the [Sukkot] Festival one mentions [it]. [5]Rabbi Yehudah says in the name of Rabbi Yehoshua: [6]He who passes before the ark on the last holy day of the Festival [of Sukkot] — [7]the last mentions; [8]the first does not mention. [9]On the first holy day of Pesaḥ, [10]the first mentions; [11]the last does not mention." [12]Rabbi Eliezer replied (lit., "said") well to Rabbi Yehoshua!

TRANSLATION AND COMMENTARY

its proper time, during the winter. [1]**Therefore,** even though it is not necessary to mention rain in the second blessing of the Amidah during the summer, **if someone happens to mention** it at any time **during the entire year, he is permitted to mention it** in the second blessing, and it is not considered an inappropriate prayer. And during Sukkot, when we mention rain, as it were, by taking the lulav in our hands, it is not only permitted but obligatory to mention rain in our prayers as well." The Baraita goes on to cite additional Tannaitic views on this matter. [2]**"Rabbi Yehudah HaNasi says: I maintain that from the time when we cease to ask for rain** in the ninth blessing, **we likewise cease to mention** rain in the second blessing. For just as it is forbidden explicitly to ask for rain during the summer, so too is it forbidden to make mention of it." [3]The Baraita now cites yet another view: **"Rabbi Yehudah ben Beterah** takes an intermediate position between that of Rabbi Eliezer and that of Rabbi Yehoshua and **says: We mention rain from the second day of the Sukkot Festival** onwards in the second blessing of the Amidah." [4]The Baraita continues: **"Rabbi Akiva,** too, takes an intermediate position between that of Rabbi Eliezer and that of Rabbi Yehoshua and **says: We mention rain from the sixth day of the Sukkot Festival** onwards in the second blessing." [5]The Baraita concludes: **"Rabbi Yehudah said in the name of Rabbi Yehoshua:** Rain should not be mentioned in our prayers until we leave the sukkah and return to our houses on the eighth day of the Festival. Moreover, we do not begin to mention rain in the evening service that ushers in the eighth day, nor in the first Amidah recited on the morning of the eighth day. Rather, we mention rain for the first time during the musaf Amidah, which is recited on Sabbath and Festivals after the morning Amidah. [6]Thus, according to Rabbi Yehudah, **whoever** leads the morning service by **'passing before the ark'** in the synagogue **on the last holy day of the Festival of Sukkot,** [7]**the last one,** who recites the musaf Amidah aloud, **mentions** rain in the second blessing, [8]whereas **the first one,** who recites the morning Amidah aloud, **does not mention** it. [9]Rabbi Yehudah goes on to explain, in the name of Rabbi Yehoshua, that a similar procedure is followed **on the first holy day of Pesaḥ,** when the dry season officially begins and we cease to mention rain in our prayers. Here, too, Rabbi Yehudah rules, in the name of Rabbi Yehoshua, that the change is made in the middle of the morning service on the first day of Pesaḥ, during the musaf Amidah. [10]Whoever leads the service on that day, **the first one,** who recites the morning Amidah aloud, continues to **mention** rain in the second blessing, [11]whereas **the last one,** who recites the musaf Amidah aloud, **does not mention** it."

שַׁפִּיר קָאָמַר לֵיהּ [12]Having cited this Baraita in connection with Rabbi Abbahu's explanation of Rabbi Eliezer's viewpoint, the Gemara now proceeds to discuss it in detail and, through it, to explain our Mishnah. The Gemara objects: **Did not Rabbi Eliezer answer Rabbi Yehoshua well?** We see from the Baraita that Rabbi Eliezer dismisses Rabbi Yehoshua's argument that rain during Sukkot is an evil omen. Rabbi Eliezer

RASHI

משעה שפוסק מלשאול — שכפסח פוסק מלומר ״ותן טל ומטר״ פוסק מלהזכיר גבורות גשמים. והשתא לא מלית למימר אם בא להזכיר כל השנה כולה מזכיר, אלא בימות החמה אינו מזכיר — הואיל ואין זמנו, אף בחג אינו מזכיר — הואיל ולא סימן ברכה הן. **הראשון** — המתפלל תפלת יוצר. **אינו מזכיר** — ושוב אין מזכירין. **שפיר קאמר ליה ר׳ אליעזר לרבי יהושע** — דאמר: כי היכי דמזכירין תחיית המתים כל השנה, אף על גב דלא מטא זימנייהו — כך מזכירין גבורות גשמים, אם רוצה, כל השנה, ובחג נמי, אף על גב דלאו סימן ברכה הן — מזכירין, הואיל ואין שואלין.

SAGES

רַבִּי יְהוּדָה בֶּן בְּתֵירָה Rabbi Yehudah ben Beterah. The Bnei Beterah family produced renowned Sages over a number of generations. Some members of the family served as Nasi during the time of Hillel, but transferred the position to him.

It is almost certain that there were two Sages named Yehudah ben Beterah. The second may have been the grandson of the first. Both lived in the city of Netzivin (Nisibis) in Babylonia — one while the Temple was still standing, and the second at the end of the Tannaitic period. The Rabbi Yehudah ben Beterah whose teaching is cited here is probably the second one. He was one of the greatest Torah scholars of his age, and organized the study of Torah throughout Babylonia before the great yeshivot were established. He was held in great veneration by the Sages of Eretz Israel.

TRANSLATION AND COMMENTARY

maintains that mention of the resurrection of the dead in the second blessing of the Amidah, even though this resurrection will not take place until the coming of the Messiah, makes it clear that this blessing deals not only with current manifestations of God's power, but also with potential manifestations. Why, then, does Rabbi Yehoshua not permit the mention of rain during Sukkot — or even during the summer, for that matter — as Rabbi Eliezer argued, since this blessing is not an explicit request for rain, but praise of God for causing rain to fall in its season?

אָמַר לָךְ רַבִּי יְהוֹשֻׁעַ [1]The Gemara answers: **Rabbi Yehoshua can say to you: It is correct to mention the resurrection of the dead** daily, even though the resurrection is not expected until the coming of the Messiah, [2]**because every day is the right time** for the resurrection. There is no special season that is suitable for resurrecting the dead, and whenever God chooses to do it, it will be an equally positive manifestation of His power and His kindness. [3]**But** regarding rain, is it true that **whenever** the **rains come, it is their proper time?** [4]**Surely** rain out of season is not a manifestation of God's kindness at all, but of His anger, as **we have learned** in the following Mishnah (below, 12b): **"If** the month of **Nisan** [corresponding approximately to April in the Gregorian calendar] **has ended and** then **rains fall, they are a sign of a curse,** [5]**as the verse says** (I Samuel 12:17): **'Is it not the wheat harvest today?** I will call unto the Lord and He will send thunder and rain, and you will know and you will see that your evil is great, which you have done in the sight of the Lord." The wheat harvest occurs at the beginning of the summer, about a month after the end of Nisan. Thus we see that rain during the dry season is considered a clear sign of God's displeasure, because it is contrary to the natural order in Eretz Israel and causes considerable damage to the crops.

רַבִּי יְהוּדָה בֶּן בְּתֵירָה אוֹמֵר [6]The Gemara now considers the next clause of the Baraita: **"Rabbi Yehudah ben Beterah** takes an intermediate position between that of Rabbi Eliezer and that of Rabbi Yehoshua and **says:** [7]We do not mention rain on the first day of Sukkot, as Rabbi Eliezer claimed, but **from the second day of the Sukkot Festival** onwards **we do mention it** in the second blessing." [8]The Gemara asks: **What is the reasoning of Rabbi Yehudah ben Beterah?** His position appears inconsistent. If he agrees with Rabbi Eliezer that rain may be mentioned even when we do not wish it to fall, why does he not rule that rain should be mentioned on the first day as well? And if he agrees with Rabbi Yehoshua that rain should not be mentioned on Sukkot because it is an evil omen, why does he permit it to be mentioned after the first day? Why does he not wait until the eighth day, when we leave the sukkah and return to our houses?

דְּתַנְיָא [9]The Gemara answers: Rabbi Yehudah ben Beterah's precedent for mentioning rain on Sukkot is not the lulav ritual, but rather the water libation. And his viewpoint in this Baraita is based on another statement of his, which **was taught** in the following Baraita: **"Rabbi Yehudah ben Beterah says:** Although the water libation is not mentioned explicitly in the Torah itself, the passage in the Torah that describes the sacrifices to be offered on each day of Sukkot hints at this practice. On each of the days of Sukkot, from the second to the seventh, the Torah says (Numbers 29:17-34): 'And on the [second, third, etc.] day so-and-so many young bullocks [the number depends on the day], two rams, and fourteen yearling lambs without blemish. And their meal-offerings and their libations, for the bullocks, the rams, and the lambs, shall be according to their number, according to the law. And one kid of the goats as a sin-offering, besides the daily burnt-offering and its meal offering and its libation.' The Torah's choice of words in this passage is almost identical for each day. Even the spelling is the same, with three notable exceptions: [10]**It says about the second**

[1]אָמַר לָךְ רַבִּי יְהוֹשֻׁעַ: בִּשְׁלָמָא תְּחִיַּית הַמֵּתִים מַזְכִּיר, [2]דְּכוּלֵּי יוֹמָא זִמְנֵיהּ הוּא. [3]אֶלָּא גְּשָׁמִים כָּל אֵימַת דְּאָתְיָין, זִמְנַיְיהוּ הִיא? [4]וְהָתְנַן: "יָצָא נִיסָן וְיָרְדוּ גְּשָׁמִים, סִימַן קְלָלָה הֵם, [5]שֶׁנֶּאֱמַר: 'הֲלוֹא קְצִיר חִטִּים הַיּוֹם', וגו'".

[6]"רַבִּי יְהוּדָה בֶּן בְּתֵירָה אוֹמֵר: [7]בַּשֵּׁנִי בֶּחָג הוּא מַזְכִּיר". [8]מַאי טַעֲמָא דְּרַבִּי יְהוּדָה בֶּן בְּתֵירָה? [9]דְּתַנְיָא: "רַבִּי יְהוּדָה בֶּן בְּתֵירָה אוֹמֵר: [10]נֶאֱמַר בַּשֵּׁנִי:

LITERAL TRANSLATION

[1]Rabbi Yehoshua can say to you: Granted that one [always] mentions the resurrection of the dead, [2]because every day is its [proper] time. [3]But whenever rains come, is it their [proper] time? [4]But surely we have learned: "[If] Nisan has ended (lit., 'has gone out') and rains fall, they are a sign of a curse, [5]for it is said: 'Is it not the wheat harvest today, etc.'"

[6]"Rabbi Yehudah ben Beterah says: [7]On the second [day] of the [Sukkot] Festival one mentions [rain]." [8]What is the reason of Rabbi Yehudah ben Beterah?

[9]For it was taught: "Rabbi Yehudah ben Beterah says: [10]It is said about the second [day]:

RASHI

כל אימת דאתיין זימנייהו הוא — וכיון דלאו זימניה הוא — אין מזכירין, והוא הדין בחג.

TRANSLATION AND COMMENTARY

day [1]**'and their libations,'** instead of 'and its libation.' The difference in Hebrew between 'their' and 'its' is conveyed by the letter mem [מ] taking the place of the letter heh [ה] at the end of the Hebrew word for 'libation.' [2]Likewise, **it says about the sixth day 'and its libations,'** instead of 'and its libation.' The difference between these two expressions is conveyed in Hebrew by the additional letter yod [י] before the letter heh [ה] at the end of the Hebrew word for 'libation.' [3]Likewise, **it says about the seventh day 'according to their laws,'** instead of 'according to the law.' The difference between these two expressions is conveyed in Hebrew by adding the letter mem [מ] to the end of the Hebrew word for 'law.' [4]**As a result** of adding these letters in these three words we have **the** three additional **letters mem, yod, and mem.** And if we put these three letters together, [5]**we have the word** *mayyim* [מַיִם], which means **'water'** in Hebrew. [6]From this oblique reference to water in connection with the sacrifices brought during Sukkot we see **a hint** in the written text of **the Torah regarding the water libation."**

וּמַאי שְׁנָא בַּשֵּׁנִי דְּנָקַט [7]But, the Gemara objects, granted that Rabbi Yehudah ben Beterah derives the ruling that we mention rain in our prayers from the water libation, **what is special about the second day** of Sukkot **that he chose it** as the starting date? Why did he not rule that we mention rain from the first day, when the libation is first brought?

דְּכִי רְמִיזִי לְהוּ בִּקְרָא [8]The Gemara answers: According to Rabbi Yehudah ben Beterah, the water libation is not offered until the second day, **because** the first time **the water libation is hinted at in the Torah is in connection with the second day,** since the three additional letters appear in the verses describing the offerings of the second, sixth, and seventh days. [9]**Therefore we mention rain** for the first time **on the second day,** because we interpret the oblique reference to water on the second day of Sukkot as teaching us that we should begin to bring the water libation and to mention rain in our prayers from that day.

רַבִּי עֲקִיבָא אוֹמֵר [10]The Gemara now considers the next clause of the Baraita: **"Rabbi Akiva says:** We do not mention rain on the first day of Sukkot, as Rabbi Eliezer claimed, but **from the sixth day of the Sukkot Festival** onwards **we do mention it** in the second blessing of the Amidah." The Gemara explains that Rabbi Akiva, like Rabbi Yehudah ben Beterah, bases his ruling that rain should be mentioned on Sukkot on the precedent of the water libation. However, Rabbi Akiva found a different hint of the water libation in the passage in the Torah that details the sacrifices to be offered on each day of Sukkot. Rabbi Akiva's derivation is quoted in the following Baraita: [11]"When **the verse** [Numbers 29:31] **refers to** the sacrifice offered on **the sixth day** of Sukkot, it uses the plural form **'and its libations,'** instead of 'and its libation.' [12]From this linguistic change we learn that **the verse is speaking about two libations:** [13]**One is the water libation** that is poured on the altar on Sukkot, **and one is the wine libation** that is poured on the altar every

[1]'וְנִסְכֵּיהֶם', [2]וְנֶאֱמַר בַּשִּׁשִּׁי: 'וּנְסָכֶיהָ', [3]וְנֶאֱמַר בַּשְּׁבִיעִי: 'כְּמִשְׁפָּטָם'. [4]הֲרֵי מ"ם יו"ד מ"ם. [5]הֲרֵי כָּאן 'מַיִם'. [6]מִכָּאן רֶמֶז לְנִיסּוּךְ הַמַּיִם מִן הַתּוֹרָה". [7]וּמַאי שְׁנָא בַּשֵּׁנִי דְּנָקַט? [8]דְּכִי רְמִיזִי לְהוּ בִּקְרָא, בַּשֵּׁנִי הוּא דִּרְמִיזִי. [9]הִלְכָּךְ בַּשֵּׁנִי מַדְכְּרִינַן.
[10]"רַבִּי עֲקִיבָא אוֹמֵר: בַּשִּׁשִּׁי בֶּחָג הוּא מַזְכִּיר". [11]שֶׁנֶּאֱמַר בַּשִּׁשִּׁי: 'וּנְסָכֶיהָ'. [12]בִּשְׁנֵי נִיסּוּכִין הַכָּתוּב מְדַבֵּר, [13]אֶחָד נִיסּוּךְ הַמַּיִם וְאֶחָד נִיסּוּךְ הַיַּיִן.

LITERAL TRANSLATION

[1]'And their libations,' [2]and it said about the sixth [day]: 'And its libations,' [3]and it is said about the seventh [day]: 'According to their laws.' [4]Here [are the letters] mem (מ) [and] yod (י) [and] mem (מ). [5]Behold here is [the word] 'water' (מים). [6]From here is a hint regarding the water libation from the Torah."

[7]And what is different about the second [day] that he chose [it]?

[8]Because when they [the water libations] are hinted at in the Torah it is [in connection] with the second [day] that they are hinted at. [9]Therefore we mention [rain] on the second [day].

[10]"Rabbi Akiva says: On the sixth [day] of the [Sukkot] Festival one mentions [it]." [11]For it is said about the sixth [day]: "And its libations." [12]The verse is speaking about two libations, [13]one the water libation and one the wine libation.

RASHI

בשני ונסכיהם — דסגי "בנסכה", וכיון דבשני איתר מ"ם לדרשה — להכי מתחילין להזכיר בשני. **בשני ניסוכין הכתוב מדבר** — שני ניסוכין על קרבן אחד. אבל "ונסכיהם" משמע הרבה, דבקרבנות הרבה. לכן לא הוה דריש רבי עקיבא מ"ונסכיהם".

NOTES

שֶׁנֶּאֱמַר בַּשִּׁשִּׁי: 'וּנְסָכֶיהָ' For it is said about the sixth day: "And its libations." The Rishonim ask: Why does Rabbi Akiva maintain that an allusion to the water libation can only be found in the verse dealing with the sixth day of Sukkot (verse 31) — "and its libations" (וּנְסָכֶיהָ) — and not in the verse dealing with the second day of the Festival (verse 19), which says "and their libations" (וְנִסְכֵּיהֶם). Surely both verses use the plural form, "libations," which can be

BACKGROUND

הֲרֵי מ"ם יו"ד מ"ם Here are the letters "mem, yod, mem." This method of exegesis is similar to techniques of secret coding. Many codes are constructed from a basic text (which sometimes has no special significance in itself) in which slight discrepancies or variations are incorporated. These variations serve as hints of the key for deciphering the code.

This method of singling out particular letters was frequently used when people wished to incorporate their names within a text. The Samaritans, for example, would emphasize certain letters in a Torah scroll, and this would indicate the name of the scribe who had written it.

רֶמֶז A hint. The proof offered by Rabbi Yehudah ben Beterah is not regarded as absolute, since this method of combining superfluous letters is not included in the hermeneutic principles for interpreting the Torah. Although the proof may not be absolute, nevertheless it provides a hint that the water libation does have a basis in the Torah, though it is not mentioned explicitly.

The Sages of the Mishnah and the Talmud found similar "hints" for various Halakhot elsewhere, and they coined the following expression: "Even though there is no proof of the matter, there is a hint of the matter," meaning that although the proof from the text is insufficient from the point of view of the Halakhah, it is nevertheless an indication supporting the established Halakhah.

SAGES

רַבִּי עֲקִיבָא Rabbi Akiva. The greatest of the Tannaim, Rabbi Akiva (ben Yosef) belonged to the fourth generation. He began his Torah education when already an adult, and studied under Rabbi Eliezer and Rabbi Yehoshua for many years. Many stories are told in Rabbinic literature of his devotion to Torah study, of the loyalty of his wife, and of the financial difficulties they had to overcome.

Rabbi Akiva was responsible for the first systematic arrangement and division of the Oral Law. This work was

[1]וְאֵימָא תַּרְוַיְיהוּ דְּחַמְרָא! [2]סָבַר לָהּ כְּרַבִּי יְהוּדָה בֶּן בְּתֵירָה, [3]דַּאֲמַר: רְמִיזִי מַיָּא. [3A] [4]אִי סָבַר לָהּ כְּרַבִּי יְהוּדָה בֶּן בְּתֵירָה, נֵימָא כְּוָותֵיהּ! [5]קָסָבַר רַבִּי עֲקִיבָא כִּי כְּתִיב נִיסּוּךְ יְתֵירָא, בַּשִּׁשִּׁי הוּא דִּכְתִיב.

[6]תַּנְיָא: ״רַבִּי נָתָן אוֹמֵר: [7]׳בַּקֹּדֶשׁ הַסֵּךְ נֶסֶךְ שֵׁכָר לַה׳׳. [8]בִּשְׁנֵי נִיסּוּכִין הַכָּתוּב מְדַבֵּר, [9]אֶחָד נִיסּוּךְ הַמַּיִם וְאֶחָד נִיסּוּךְ הַיַּיִן״.

LITERAL TRANSLATION

[1]But say [that] both of them are of wine!

[2]He is of the same opinion about it as Rabbi Yehudah ben Beterah, [3]who said: Water is hinted at.

[3A] [4]If he is of the same opinion about it as Rabbi Yehudah ben Beterah, let him say as he [does]!

[5]Rabbi Akiva is of the opinion [that] when the additional libation was written, it was [in connection] with the sixth [day] that it was written.

[6]It was taught: "Rabbi Natan says: [7]'In the holy place pour a libation of strong drink to the Lord.' [8]The verse is speaking about two libations, [9]one the water libation and one the wine libation."

TRANSLATION AND COMMENTARY

day of the year." Since this allusion to the water libation appears in connection with the sixth day, Rabbi Akiva argues that it should not be brought — and we should not mention rain — until the sixth day.

וְאֵימָא תַּרְוַיְיהוּ דְּחַמְרָא [1]**But,** the Gemara objects, from Rabbi Akiva's derivation we see only that an additional libation must be brought on Sukkot. Why do we not **say** that the Torah requires a double libation on Sukkot, but **that both of the** libations **are of wine?**

סָבַר לָהּ [2]The Gemara answers: Rabbi Akiva did not intend his exegesis to stand on its own. Rather, **he is of the same opinion about this** matter **as Rabbi Yehudah ben Beterah,** [3]**who said: Water is hinted at** through the superfluous letters mem, yod, and mem used by the Torah in describing the sacrifices of the second, sixth, and seventh days. Rabbi Akiva feels the need for both allusions — one to show that two libations are to be brought, and the other to show that the additional libation is of water, rather than of wine.

אִי סָבַר לָהּ [3A] [4]The Gemara objects: But **if** Rabbi Akiva **is of the same opinion about this** matter **as Rabbi Yehudah ben Beterah, let him give the same ruling!** If Rabbi Akiva applies Rabbi Yehudah ben Beterah's exegesis in addition to his own, why does he not rule that we should begin to mention rain from the second day, when the first superfluous letter appears in the Torah hinting at the water libation?

קָסָבַר רַבִּי עֲקִיבָא [5]The Gemara answers: **Rabbi Akiva is of the opinion that the additional libation was written** specifically **in connection with the sixth day.** Even though the Torah begins to hint at the Hebrew word for water (מַיִם — *mayim*) from the second day, the main place where the Torah hints at the water libation is in its description of the sacrifices offered on the sixth day, where the Torah explicitly mentions a double libation. Hence Rabbi Akiva maintains that we begin to bring the water libation and to mention rain in our prayers from the sixth day onward.

תַּנְיָא [6]The Gemara notes that an additional Scriptural hint with regard to the water libation **was taught in** the following Baraita: **"Rabbi Natan says:** The following verse (Numbers 28:7), dealing with the daily morning sacrifice in the Temple, says: [7]**'In the holy place pour a libation of strong drink to the Lord.'** This verse uses a double verb form — הַסֵּךְ נֶסֶךְ [which we have translated as 'pour a libation']. [8]From this double verb, Rabbi Natan infers that **the verse is speaking about two libations** that are poured on the altar in the Temple together with the morning sacrifice. [9]**One is the water libation** that is brought during the week of Sukkot, **and the other is the wine libation** that is brought every day of the year."

RASHI

סבר לה כרבי יהודה — דמ״ס יו״ד מ״ס מרבה ניסוך המים. **אי סבר לה כרבי יהודה. לימא כרבי יהודה** — שיזכיר בשני. **ניסוך יתירא בששי כתיב** — כלומר "ונסכיה" דמרבי תרי ניסוכין כתיב בששי, להכי אמר: בששי מתחיל להזכיר. ואהני מ״ס יו״ד מ״ס — מים, דלא מצינו למימר תרוייהו דיין.

carried on by his disciple Rabbi Meir, and formed the basis of the Mishnah as finally edited by Rabbi Yehudah HaNasi. Rabbi Akiva was also the founder of a new school of Biblical interpretation, according to which almost all the regulations of the Oral Law are found to have their basis in the text of the Bible. Rabbi Akiva was active in the period between the destruction of the Second Temple and the Bar Kokhba revolt, in the preparations for which he took an active part. He met his death as a martyr at the hands of the Romans.

CONCEPTS

נִיסּוּךְ הַיַּיִן The wine libation. Wine libations were offered together with burnt-offerings of animals (עוֹלָה) and with peace-offerings (שְׁלָמִים), as well as with the sin- and guilt-offerings of the leper. Different quantities of wine were offered, depending on the animal that was sacrificed: a fourth of a *hin* (i.e., three *lugin*) was offered for any sheep other than a ram, a third of a *hin* (four *lugin*) was offered for a ram, and half a *hin* (six *lugin*) was offered for a bullock. Libations of wine could also be brought as independent, voluntary offerings.

NOTES

understood as a hint that in addition to the wine libation offered daily, a second libation of water must also be brought!

Rashi and *Shittah* suggest that the expression used with reference to the second day — "and *their* libations" — can be understood as referring to the libations that accompany the bullocks, rams, and lambs, which constitute additional sacrifices of the day. But the expression used with reference to the sixth day — "and *its* libations" — can be understood only as referring to the libations that accompany the daily morning sacrifice, and it therefore follows that the verse is referring to two libations, the ordinary wine libation and the special water libation, which are offered together with the morning sacrifice brought on that day.

״בַּקֹּדֶשׁ הַסֵּךְ נֶסֶךְ שֵׁכָר לַה׳״ **"In the holy place pour a libation of strong drink to the Lord."** Rabbi Natan's

TRANSLATION AND COMMENTARY

אֵימָא תַּרְוַיְיהוּ דְּחַמְרָא [1]The Gemara objects: From Rabbi Natan's exegesis we can see only that an additional libation must occasionally be brought together with the daily morning sacrifice. Why do we not **say that** the Torah requires a double libation on Sukkot, but that **both of the** libations **are of wine!**

אִם כֵּן [2]The Gemara answers: **If** this were the case, **the** expression used in this **verse should have been either** ***"hassekh hessekh*** [הַסֵּךְ הֶסֵּךְ]," [3]**or** ***"nassekh nesekh*** [נַסֵּךְ נֶסֶךְ]" — doubling the verb and using the same letters in each case. [4]**Why** did the verse both double the verb and change the letters, writing ***"hassekh nesekh*** [הַסֵּךְ נֶסֶךְ]?" These two deviations from standard linguistic practice are intended as a hint that the two libations are different, [5]**so that we may infer from** the Hebrew forms adopted that **one** of the two libations is **of water and the other is of wine.**

אֶלָּא הָא דִּתְנַן [6]We have seen from our Mishnah and from the Baraita quoted above (2b) that the Tannaim differ as to whether we begin mentioning rain in our prayers from the first, second, sixth, seventh, or eighth day of Sukkot. Rabbi Yehoshua as quoted in our Mishnah is the only Tanna who says that we do not mention rain until the eighth day (according to the Baraita's version of his opinion, we begin from the morning of the seventh day). Rabbi Eliezer, the Tanna who maintains that we mention rain on the first day, bases his opinion on the precedent of the lulav. Rabbi Yehudah ben Beterah and Rabbi Akiva, on the other hand, base their opinions on the precedent of the water libation, and they infer from Scriptural hints that this libation is not brought until the second or the sixth day of the Festival (each Tanna according to his own exegesis). At this stage in the argument, the Gemara assumes that none of these Tannaim maintains that we refrain from mentioning rain in our prayers even after the bringing of the water libation. Therefore, like Rabbi Yehudah ben Beterah and Rabbi Akiva, who maintain that we first mention rain on the second or the sixth day and also maintain that the water libation is not brought until the second or the sixth day, Rabbi Yehoshua too should maintain that the water libation is not brought until the eighth day (or the seventh according to the Baraita). Likewise Rabbi Eliezer, who does not accept the precedent of the water libation and bases his ruling that we mention rain on the first day on the lulav, should maintain that the water libation is not brought on the first day. **But consider what we have learned** in the following Mishnah (*Sukkah* 42b): **"The water libation is** performed for **seven days** out of the eight days of Sukkot." This Mishnah does not stipulate to which seven days it is referring, but it is presumably referring to the first seven days of the Festival, when the other commandments relating to Sukkot apply. [7]**Whose opinion is** reflected in **this** Mishnah? [8]**If it is** that of **Rabbi Yehoshua,** who maintains (according to the Baraita) that we do not mention rain until the seventh day of Sukkot, **let** the Mishnah **say** that the water libation is brought on only **one day** of

[1]אֵימָא תַּרְוַיְיהוּ דְּחַמְרָא! [2]אִם כֵּן, לִכְתּוֹב קְרָא אוֹ "הַסֵּךְ, הֶסֵּךְ" [3]אוֹ "נַסֵּךְ נֶסֶךְ". [4]מַאי "הַסֵּךְ נֶסֶךְ"? [5]שְׁמַעַתְּ מִינָּהּ: חַד דְּמַיָּא וְחַד דְּחַמְרָא.
[6]אֶלָּא הָא דִּתְנַן: "נִיסּוּךְ הַמַּיִם כָּל שִׁבְעָה". [7]מַנִּי? [8]אִי רַבִּי יְהוֹשֻׁעַ, נֵימָא חַד יוֹמָא.

LITERAL TRANSLATION

[1]Say [that] both of them are of wine!
[2]If so, let the verse write either *"hassekh hessekh,"* [3]or *"nassekh nesekh."* [4]What is *"hassekh nesekh"*? [5]Conclude from it: One is of water and one is of wine.
[6]But [consider] what we have learned: "The water libation is all seven [days]." [7]Whose [opinion] is it? [8]If it is Rabbi Yehoshua, let it say one day.

RASHI

או הסך הסך או נסך נסך — מדסני קרא בדיבוריה — שמע מינה תרתי.

NOTES

citation of this verse as a Scriptural hint at the water libation offered on Sukkot poses a certain difficulty, for the verse does not deal with Sukkot, but rather with the daily morning sacrifice. How, then, does Rabbi Natan infer from this verse that the water libation is offered only on Sukkot? Perhaps the two libations, one of wine and one of water, must be poured on the altar every day!

It has been suggested that Rabbi Natan derives the law that a special libation must be offered on Sukkot from the verse cited above by Rabbi Akiva: "and its libations." He needs the expression "pour a libation" only to establish that it is not a double libation of wine that must be poured on the altar on Sukkot, but two separate libations, one of wine and one of water (*Shittah, Gevurat Ari*).

HALAKHAH

נִיסּוּךְ הַמַּיִם The water libation. "On each of the seven days of Sukkot, a water libation was poured on the altar, the source of this practice being an oral tradition transmitted to Moses on Mount Sinai." (*Rambam, Sefer Avodah, Hilkhot Temidin U'Musafin* 10:6.)

[1] אִי רַבִּי עֲקִיבָא, תְּרֵי יוֹמֵי. [2] אִי רַבִּי יְהוּדָה בֶּן בְּתֵירָה, שִׁיתָּא יוֹמֵי!

[3] לְעוֹלָם רַבִּי יְהוּדָה בֶּן בְּתֵירָה הִיא, [4] וּסְבִירָא לֵיהּ כְּרַבִּי יְהוּדָה דְּמַתְנִיתִין. [5] דִּתְנַן: ״רַבִּי יְהוּדָה אוֹמֵר: [6] בְּלוֹג הָיָה מְנַסֵּךְ כָּל שְׁמוֹנָה״. [7] וּמַפִּיק רִאשׁוֹן וּמְעַיֵּיל שְׁמִינִי.

[8] וּמַאי שְׁנָא רִאשׁוֹן דְּלָא? [9] דְּכִי רְמִיזִי מַיִם, בַּשֵּׁנִי הוּא דִּרְמִיזִי? [10] שְׁמִינִי נַמִי, כִּי רְמִיזִי מַיִם, [11] בַּשְּׁבִיעִי הוּא דִּרְמִיזִי!

LITERAL TRANSLATION

[1] If it is Rabbi Akiva, two days. [2] If it is Rabbi Yehudah ben Beterah, six days!

[3] In fact, it is Rabbi Yehudah ben Beterah, [4] and he is of the same opinion as Rabbi Yehudah of the [following] Mishnah. [5] For we have learned: "Rabbi Yehudah says: [6] He would pour with [a utensil containing] a *log* all eight [days]." [7] But he takes away the first [day] and includes the eighth.

[8] But what is different about the first day that [the libation] is not [made]? [9] Is it because when the water [libations] are hinted at, it is [in connection] with the second [day] that they are hinted at? [10] [Then on] the eighth [day] too, when the water [libations] are hinted at, [11] it is [in connection] with the seventh [day] that they are hinted at!

RASHI

אי רבי עקיבא תרי יומי הוו — ותו לא, דהא אמר ״ונסכיה״ דהיינו בששי מרבה ניסוך המים. **וסבר לה כרבי יהודה דמתניתין** — דאמר: בלוג הוה מנסך כל שמנה, לא סבר כוותיה במה דאמר ״כל שמונה מנסך״, אלא במה דאמר ״בשמיני מנסך״, וכיון דבשמיני מנסך — משכחת לה לרבי יהודה [בן בתירה] דאמר: בשני מתחילין לניסוך המים כל שבעה. **דמפיק ראשון ומעייל שמיני** — משיב בעל הגמרא: מי מצי אמר רבי יהודה דבשמיני מנסך? **מאי שנא** — דקאמר דבראשון אינו מזכיר, דכי רמיזי מיא — בשני הוא דרמיזי דמ״ונסכיהם״ מרבה ניסוך המים, שמיני נמי, מי מצי אמר דמנסך הא שביעי אמר רחמנא, דמ״ם יו״ד מ״ם מים כתיב בשביעי, דסיום קראי דניסוך המים בשביעי כתיב ״כמשפטם״, ולא בשמיני.

TRANSLATION AND COMMENTARY

Sukkot — the seventh day. [1] **If it is Rabbi Akiva,** who maintains that we do not mention rain until the sixth day of Sukkot, let the Mishnah say that the water libation is brought on only **two days** of Sukkot — the sixth and the seventh days. [2] **If it is Rabbi Yehudah ben Beterah,** who maintains that we begin to mention rain from the second day of Sukkot, let the Mishnah say that the water libation is poured on **six days** of Sukkot — from the second day onward. None of the Tannaim have ruled that we mention rain from the first day, except Rabbi Eliezer, and he bases his ruling on the lulav, not the water libation — presumably because he agrees with the other Tannaim that the water libation is not performed on the first day. How, then, can the Mishnah rule that the water libation is performed from the first day?

לְעוֹלָם רַבִּי יְהוּדָה בֶּן בְּתֵירָה הִיא [3] The Gemara answers: **In fact,** the Mishnah in *Sukkah* reflects the viewpoint of **Rabbi Yehudah ben Beterah,** who maintains that we begin to mention rain and to pour the water libation on the second day of Sukkot. However, when the Mishnah rules that the water libation is performed for seven out of the eight days of Sukkot, it is not referring to the first seven days of Sukkot but to the last seven — from the second to the eighth days, those days on which Rabbi Yehudah ben Beterah maintains that we mention rain in our prayers. The Gemara explains: There is a Tannaitic dispute in a later Mishnah in tractate *Sukkah* (48a) as to whether the water libation is performed on the eighth day as well, [4] **and** Rabbi Yehudah ben Beterah **is of the same opinion** in principle **as Rabbi Yehudah of** that **Mishnah,** who rules that the water libation is brought on the eighth day. [5] **For we have learned** in that Mishnah: **"Rabbi Yehudah says:** [6] The priest bringing the water libation **would pour a *log*** measure of water **all eight days** of the Festival." Thus Rabbi Yehudah ben Beterah agrees with Rabbi Yehudah that the water libation is performed on the eighth day, but disagrees with Rabbi Yehudah's statement that it is performed for eight days, because Rabbi Yehudah ben Beterah maintains that the libation is not brought on the first day. [7] Thus Rabbi Yehudah ben Beterah **takes away the first day and includes the eighth** to make a total of seven days of water libation, as recorded in the earlier Mishnah in *Sukkah*.

וּמַאי שְׁנָא רִאשׁוֹן דְּלָא [8] **But,** the Gemara objects, **what is different about the first day,** in the opinion of Rabbi Yehudah ben Beterah, which results in the fact **that** the water libation is **not** performed on that day? [9] **Is it because** the first time the water libation **is hinted at** in the Torah, **it is in connection with the second day,** and that is why we pour the libation for the first time on the second day? [10] But the same argument applies to **the eighth** day **as well.** [11] For the last time the water libation **is hinted at** in the Torah, **it is in connection with the seventh day!** If Rabbi Yehudah ben Beterah infers from the three superfluous letters used in the text that the libation is not performed on the first day, he should also infer that it is not performed on the eighth day. Hence we are forced to conclude that, when the first Mishnah quoted from *Sukkah* ruled that the libation is performed for seven days, it was indeed referring to the first seven days of the Festival, and our original

TRANSLATION AND COMMENTARY

question remains: Who is the Tanna who maintains that the libation is performed from the first day?

אֶלָּא רַבִּי יְהוֹשֻׁעַ הִיא [1]**Rather,** concludes the Gemara, we must say that the Mishnah in *Sukkah* reflects the viewpoint of **Rabbi Yehoshua,** who maintains that rain is not mentioned at all until the eighth day (according to the Mishnah), or until the seventh day (according to the Baraita). Rabbi Yehoshua made no statement about the water libation. Until now we have assumed that Rabbi Yehoshua agrees that we mention rain in our prayers on the day that we bring the water libation. But this is not the case. According to Rabbi Yehoshua, rain is not mentioned until the seventh or eighth days, whereas the water libation is performed from the first day, because the water libation and the laws governing it, [2]including the rule that **the water libation** is performed **all seven days, are a Halakhah we have as a tradition.** The term "a Halakhah we have as a tradition" refers to "a Halakhah of Moses from Sinai" — a law which enjoys full Torah status, but is neither mentioned explicitly in the Torah nor inferred by applying the regular hermeneutical rules. [3]**For Rabbi Ammi said in the name of Rabbi Yohanan in the name of Rabbi Neḥunya of the valley of Bet Ḥortan:** The following three laws found in the Oral Law — [4]**the law of ten saplings** (see notes),

[1]אֶלָּא רַבִּי יְהוֹשֻׁעַ הִיא, [2]וְנִיסּוּךְ הַמַּיִם כָּל שִׁבְעָה הִלְכְתָא גְּמִירִי לָהּ. [3]דְּאָמַר רַבִּי אַמִּי אָמַר רַבִּי יוֹחָנָן מִשּׁוּם רַבִּי נְחוּנְיָא אִישׁ בִּקְעַת בֵּית חוֹרְתָן: [4]עֶשֶׂר נְטִיעוֹת,

LITERAL TRANSLATION

[1]Rather, it is Rabbi Yehoshua, [2]and the water libation all seven [days] is a Halakhah we have as a tradition. [3]For Rabbi Ammi said in the name of Rabbi Yoḥanan in the name of Rabbi Neḥunya of the valley of Bet Ḥortan: [4][The laws of] ten saplings,

RASHI

אלא רבי יהושע היא — דאמר משעת הנחתו [דהיינו בשביעי] מזכיר, ואף על פי כן סבר דניסוך המים כל שבעה, דגמרא גמיר לה הלכה למשה מסיני דניסוך המים כל שבעה. ודאי כרבי אליעזר אתי שפיר, אבל כרבי יהודה בן בתירה וכרבי עקיבא לא מיתוקמא. אלא להכי לא מוקי לה כרבי אליעזר — דהא לא מיבעי אי רבי אליעזר סבירא ליה הכי, דודאי לרבי אליעזר אתי שפיר, והא דקא מוקים כרבי יהושע — רבותא קמשמע לן. אבל כרבי יהודה בן בתירה וכרבי עקיבא — לא מיתוקמא, דרבי יהודה יליף מונאמר בשני "ונסכיהם" כו', אלמא דסבר דניסוך המים לא הוו אלא ששה ימים, דאיהו לא מפיק ראשון ומעייל שמיני, משום הני פירכא דפריך לעיל — לא אתי כרבי יהודה. ורבי עקיבא יליף מ"נסכיה" שנאמר בששי, אלמא דסבר דניסוך המים לא הוו אלא תרי יומי. אבל כרבי יהושע מיתוקמא. לפיכך אין מזכירין אלא ביום טוב האחרון, דגשמים בחג סימן קללה, אבל ניסוך המים — הוי כל שבעה, דגמרא גמיר לה. **עשר נטיעות** — המפוזרות בתוך בת סאה, חורשין כל בית סאה ערב שביעית עד ראש השנה. אף על גב דשאר שדות אין חורשין לפני שביעית שלשים יום — זה חורשין, שהואיל אם אין חורשין סביבן — מפסידין.

NOTES

אֶלָּא רַבִּי יְהוֹשֻׁעַ הִיא **Rather, it is Rabbi Yehoshua.** According to *Rashi,* the Gemara concludes that the Mishnah's ruling that the water libation is performed all seven days of Sukkot follows the viewpoint of Rabbi Yehoshua. Even though we do not mention rain in our prayers until the seventh or eighth day of the Festival, the water libation is performed from the first day of Sukkot, because that regulation is derived from an oral tradition transmitted to Moses on Mount Sinai. This is not to say that Rabbi Eliezer, who maintains that we begin to mention rain in our prayers from the first day of Sukkot, would disagree with the Mishnah's ruling that the water libation is performed all seven days of Sukkot, for it is obvious that the Mishnah's ruling can be reconciled with Rabbi Eliezer's view. The Gemara means only to exclude the viewpoints of Rabbi Yehudah ben Beterah and Rabbi Akiva, who infer from the Torah text that the water libation begins on the second or the sixth day of Sukkot, and so they cannot maintain that the libation is performed for seven days.

Others (see *Rabbenu Elyakim, Sfat Emet* and others), however, explain that according to the Gemara's conclusion all agree about the oral tradition transmitted to Moses on Mount Sinai that the water libation is performed on all seven days of Sukkot. The verses cited by Rabbi Yehudah ben Beterah and Rabbi Akiva are merely Scriptural supports for a regulation whose true source is the Oral Law. Thus, writes *Rambam* (*Commentary to Mishnah, Sukkah* 4:8), "The water libation on Sukkot is an oral tradition transmitted to Moses on Mount Sinai, and there are hidden allusions to it in Scripture." This second approach is supported by the following manuscript reading, according to which the Gemara concludes: "Rather, the water libation all seven [days] is derived from tradition," omitting all reference to Rabbi Yehoshua. See also *Dikdukei Soferim,* who argues at great length that all the Tannaim agree that the water libation is poured on the altar all seven days of Sukkot.

עֶשֶׂר נְטִיעוֹת **Ten saplings.** Working the land is forbidden not only during the Sabbatical Year but also during the last days of the sixth year. The source of this prohibition is an oral tradition transmitted to Moses on Mount Sinai. By Rabbinic decree this prohibition begins even earlier — on

HALAKHAH

עֶשֶׂר נְטִיעוֹת **Ten saplings.** "If ten saplings were planted in the area of a *bet se'ah* [2,500 square cubits], the entire area may be plowed on account of them until Rosh HaShanah of the Sabbatical Year. The source of this regulation is an oral tradition transmitted to Moses on Mount Sinai." (*Rambam, Sefer Zeraim, Hilkhot Shemittah VeYovel* 3:5.)

SAGES

רַבִּי אַמִּי **Rabbi Ammi.** A Palestinian Amora of the third generation, Rabbi Ammi (bar Natan) was a priest and a close friend of Rabbi Assi. They studied with the greatest Sages of Eretz Israel and were especially close disciples of Rabbi Yoḥanan. Rabbi Ammi also studied with Rabbi Yoḥanan's greatest students. In the Jerusalem Talmud he is commonly known as Rabbi Immi.

After Rabbi Yoḥanan's death Rabbi Ammi was appointed head of the Tiberias Yeshivah in his place. The Sages of Babylonia also consulted him about Halakhic problems. He is widely quoted in both the Babylonian and the Jerusalem Talmud, not only in transmitting statements from his teachers, but also in debate with Rabbi Assi and with other Sages of the generation. Most of the Palestinian Amoraim of the following generation received and transmitted his teachings. He and Rabbi Assi were known as "the distinguished priests of Eretz Israel," and stories are told of their righteousness and holiness. Rabbi Ammi seems to have lived to a great age, and even the Sages of the fourth generation in Babylonia used to send him their questions.

רַבִּי נְחוּנְיָא אִישׁ בִּקְעַת בֵּית חוֹרְתָן **Rabbi Neḥunya of the valley of Bet Ḥortan.** This Sage is called Rabbi Ḥunya in various sources, especially the Jerusalem Talmud, and there are also differing versions of the name of the place where he lived. He belonged to the transitional generation between the Tannaim and the Amoraim. Various traditions were delivered by Rabbi Neḥunya to the great Palestinian Amoraim of the second and third generations. Rabbi Neḥunya was highly respected and belonged to the special tribunal that decided when to lengthen the year by adding an intercalary month. A number of tales are also told about wonders which he performed or which occurred in his honor. His son, Rabbi Uziel, was also an important Sage.

BACKGROUND

בִּקְעַת בֵּית חוֹרְתָן **The valley of Bet Ḥortan.** According

עֲרָבָה, וְנִיסּוּךְ הַמַּיִם [1]הֲלָכָה לְמֹשֶׁה מִסִּינַי.
[2]"רַבִּי יְהוּדָה אוֹמֵר מִשּׁוּם רַבִּי יְהוֹשֻׁעַ: [3]הָעוֹבֵר לִפְנֵי הַתֵּיבָה בְּיוֹם טוֹב הָאַחֲרוֹן שֶׁל חַג — הָ[4]אַחֲרוֹן מַזְכִּיר; [5]הָרִאשׁוֹן אֵינוֹ מַזְכִּיר. [6]בְּיוֹם טוֹב הָרִאשׁוֹן שֶׁל פֶּסַח, [7]הָרִאשׁוֹן מַזְכִּיר; [8]הָאַחֲרוֹן אֵינוֹ מַזְכִּיר".
[9]הֵי רַבִּי יְהוֹשֻׁעַ?
[10]אִילֵימָא רַבִּי יְהוֹשֻׁעַ

LITERAL TRANSLATION

the willow, and the water libation are [1]a Halakhah of Moses from Sinai.

[2]"Rabbi Yehudah says in the name of Rabbi Yehoshua: [3]He who passes before the ark on the last holy day of the Festival [of Sukkot] — [4]the last mentions; [5]the first does not mention. [6]On the first holy day of Pesaḥ, [7]the first mentions; [8]the last does not mention."

[9]Which Rabbi Yehoshua is [meant]?

[10]If we say it is Rabbi Yehoshua

TRANSLATION AND COMMENTARY

the willow (see notes), **and** the law of **the water libation** — [1]**are** all **Halakhot of Moses from Sinai.**

רַבִּי יְהוּדָה אוֹמֵר [2]The Gemara now turns to the last clause of the Baraita quoted above (2b) as an elaboration on our Mishnah: **"Rabbi Yehudah says in the name of Rabbi Yehoshua:** [3]**Whoever** leads the service by **passing before the ark** in the synagogue **on the last holy day of the Festival of Sukkot** — [4]**the last one,** who recites the musaf Amidah aloud, **mentions** rain in the second blessing, [5]whereas **the first one,** who recites the morning Amidah aloud, **does not mention** it. [6]A similar procedure is followed **on the first holy day of Pesaḥ.** Here, too, the change is made in the middle of the morning service on the first day of Pesaḥ, during the musaf Amidah. [7]Whoever leads the service on that day, **the first one,** who recites the morning Amidah aloud, continues to **mention** rain in the second blessing, [8]whereas **the last one,** who recites the Musaf Amidah aloud, **does not mention** it."

הֵי רַבִּי יְהוֹשֻׁעַ [9]This viewpoint was also cited in our Mishnah. But in the Mishnah this opinion was presented as Rabbi Yehudah's, whereas in the Baraita it is quoted in the name of Rabbi Yehoshua. The Gemara asks: To **which Rabbi Yehoshua is** the Baraita referring?

אִילֵימָא רַבִּי יְהוֹשֻׁעַ [10]The Gemara explains the difficulty involved: **If we say** that the Baraita **is** referring

RASHI

וניסוך המים — כל שבעה. **רבי יהודה אומר משום רבי יהושע העובר לפני התיבה ביום טוב האחרון של חג כו'** — כעין אמר מר הוא. כלומר אמרינן לעיל רבי יהודה אומר. **הי רבי יהושוע אילימא רבי יהושע** דמתניתין מיום טוב האחרון הוא

NOTES

Shavuot of the sixth year in the case of orchards, and on Pesaḥ in the case of grain fields. These prohibitions applied only in the time of the Temple, but after the Temple was destroyed working the land was permitted until Rosh HaShanah of the Sabbatical Year.

There is a second oral tradition transmitted to Moses on Mount Sinai according to which a special allowance is granted in the case of saplings. If ten saplings are dispersed in an orchard of 2,500-square cubits (approximately 600 square meters) the entire orchard may be plowed until Rosh HaShanah of the Sabbatical Year. This special allowance was granted because the saplings would wither if the prohibition against plowing that applies throughout the Sabbatical Year were to begin on Shavuot of the sixth year. This dispensation does not apply if there are less than ten saplings planted in the 2,500-square-cubit orchard, or if the ten saplings were planted in a row or in a circle. In such cases, plowing is permitted only in the areas immediately surrounding each of the saplings.

עֲרָבָה The willow. In addition to the willow that must be taken in the hand on Sukkot as one of the "four species" — the other three being the palm branch, the myrtle, and the etrog — a separate willow must be taken to the Temple and placed against the altar on each of the seven days of Sukkot. The Tannaim disagree about the source of this law (see *Sukkah* 34a). Abba Shaul maintains that it is derived from the words עַרְבֵי נַחַל — "willows of the river" — in the verse in Leviticus (23:40) which deals with the law of the four species, the plural form "willows" indicating that there are two separate obligations regarding the willow. According to the Sages, the source of the law is an oral tradition transmitted to Moses on Mount Sinai. Elsewhere, the Mishnah (*Sukkah* 45a) gives a vivid description of the ceremony of placing the willow against the altar, as well as of the ceremony of circling the altar (according to some authorities, with the willow; according to others, with the four species) once on each of the first six days of Sukkot, and seven times on the seventh day, Hoshanah Rabbah. The practice observed today, of taking a willow on Hoshanah Rabbah and beating it on the ground, was instituted as a reminder of the ceremony that used to take place in the Temple.

HALAKHAH

עֲרָבָה The willow. "According to an oral tradition transmitted to Moses on Mount Sinai, each person must bring a willow branch to the Temple and place it against the altar on each of the seven days of Sukkot, in addition to the willow branch taken as part of the commandment of the lulav." (*Rambam, Sefer Zemanim, Hilkhot Shofar VeSukkah VeLulav* 7:20.)

to parallel sources, Rabbi Neḥunya's home was in Ḥauran, which is also called Havran, an area partially corresponding to the Biblical land of Bashan — the fertile region in the northern part of eastern Transjordan. In this area there are plains and hills (extinct volcanoes) with valleys between them. At one time many Jewish settlements existed there.

CONCEPTS

הֲלָכָה לְמֹשֶׁה מִסִּינַי A Halakhah of Moses from Sinai. The Halakhot described as having been given to Moses on Mount Sinai occupy a special place in the tradition of the Oral Law. These Halakhot were transmitted from Sage to Sage, going back to Moses. What they have in common is that they are individual rulings, sometimes clarifying basic definitions of the Halakhah and sometimes dealing with specific laws.

In practice, the authority of the rulings given to Moses on Mount Sinai is equal to that of the Torah itself, although these Halakhot do not appear in the Torah. While the Sages often find allusions to these Halakhot, they emphasize that they are merely allusions, and not Halakhic sources. These Halakhot differ from those explicitly written or derived through the process of Halakhic Midrash, in that they are isolated. In other words, they cannot be used to infer other rulings from them, even by the most logical and straightforward methods such as *a fortiori* arguments. Indeed, this was the reason why they were not written down — so that they would remain separate units, from which nothing can be learned except what they explicitly say.

דְּמַתְנִיתִין, [1]הָא אָמַר בְּיוֹם טוֹב הָאַחֲרוֹן שֶׁל חַג הוּא מַזְכִּיר.
[2]אֶלָּא רַבִּי יְהוֹשֻׁעַ דְּבָרַיְיתָא?
[3]הָאָמַר: ״מִשְּׁעַת הַנָּחָתוֹ״!
[4]וְתוּ, הָא דְּתַנְיָא: ״רַבִּי יְהוּדָה אוֹמֵר מִשּׁוּם בֶּן בְּתֵירָה:
[5]הָעוֹבֵר לִפְנֵי הַתֵּיבָה בְּיוֹם טוֹב הָאַחֲרוֹן שֶׁל חַג — [6]הָאַחֲרוֹן מַזְכִּיר״.
[7]הֵי בֶּן בְּתֵירָה?
[8]אִילֵימָא רַבִּי יְהוּדָה בֶּן בְּתֵירָה, הָא אָמַר: [9]״בַּשֵּׁנִי בֶּחָג הוּא מַזְכִּיר״!
[10]אָמַר רַב נַחְמָן בַּר יִצְחָק: תְּהֵא בְּרַבִּי יְהוֹשֻׁעַ בֶּן בְּתֵירָה.
[11]זִמְנִין דְּקָרֵי לֵיהּ בִּשְׁמֵיהּ וְזִימְנִין דְּקָרֵי לֵיהּ בִּשְׁמֵיהּ

LITERAL TRANSLATION

of our Mishnah, [1]surely he said [that] on the last holy day of the Festival [of Sukkot] he mentions [it]. [2]Or is it Rabbi Yehoshua of the Baraita? [3]Surely he said: "From the time of putting it down"!

[4]And furthermore, [consider what] was taught: "Rabbi Yehudah says in the name of Ben Beterah: [5]He who passes before the ark on the last holy day of the Festival [of Sukkot] — [6]the last mentions." [7]Which Ben Beterah is meant? [8]If we say it is Rabbi Yehudah ben Beterah, surely he said: [9]"On the second [day] of the [Sukkot] Festival one mentions [rain]"!

[10]Rav Naḥman bar Yitzḥak said: Let it be referring to Rabbi Yehoshua ben Beterah. [11]Sometimes it calls him by his name and sometimes it calls him by his father's name.

TRANSLATION AND COMMENTARY

to Rabbi Yehoshua ben Ḥananyah, the **Rabbi Yehoshua** mentioned in **the Mishnah,** [1]**surely** this is untenable, because Rabbi Yehoshua **said** in the Mishnah **that** we **mention** rain **on the last holy day of the Festival of Sukkot.** Since Rabbi Yehoshua does not mention any particular time to begin to mention rain, we can assume that he is referring to the first Amidah prayer recited on the eighth day — the evening prayer. We must conclude from this that the Rabbi Yehoshua cited by Rabbi Yehudah in the Baraita is not the Rabbi Yehoshua who appears in the Mishnah.

אֶלָּא ר׳ יְהוֹשֻׁעַ דְּבָרַיְיתָא [2]**On the other hand,** the Gemara continues, **is** Rabbi Yehudah citing the opinion of **Rabbi Yehoshua** that appears earlier **in the** same **Baraita** elaborating on our Mishnah? The Baraita presents a different version of Rabbi Yehoshua's viewpoint, and it is possible that Rabbi Yehudah is referring to this ruling by Rabbi Yehoshua. [3]But **surely** this too is untenable, because Rabbi Yehoshua **said** in the Baraita that we mention rain **"from the time** we **put** the lulav **down** on the seventh day of Sukkot," and not from the musaf Amidah of the eighth day, as Rabbi Yehudah ruled in his name. We must conclude from this that the Rabbi Yehoshua cited by Rabbi Yehudah in the Baraita is not the same Rabbi Yehoshua who appears earlier in the Baraita itself.

וְתוּ, הָא דְּתַנְיָא [4]**And furthermore,** the Gemara continues, **consider what was taught** in the following Baraita: **"Rabbi Yehudah says in the name of Ben Beterah:** [5]**Whoever passes before the ark on the last holy day of the Festival of Sukkot,** [6]**the last one,** who recites the musaf Amidah aloud, **mentions** rain in the second blessing, whereas the first one, who recites the morning Amidah aloud, does not mention it." In this Baraita the ruling is not issued in Rabbi Yehudah's own name, as in our Mishnah, or in Rabbi Yehoshua's name, as in the other Baraita, but is ascribed to a Sage called Ben Beterah. [7]To **which Ben Beterah is** Rabbi Yehudah referring? [8]**If we say** that he **is** referring to the well-known Tanna, **Rabbi Yehudah ben Beterah, surely** this is untenable, because Rabbi Yehudah ben Beterah **said** in the first Baraita quoted above (2b) [9]that **we mention** rain in our prayers **from the second day of the Sukkot Festival onwards,** not from the musaf Amidah of the eighth day, as Rabbi Yehudah rules in the name of Ben Beterah. Thus the Ben Beterah cited by Rabbi Yehudah in this Baraita is not to be identified with Rabbi Yehudah ben Beterah who appears in the previous Baraita.

אָמַר רַב נַחְמָן בַּר יִצְחָק [10]Accordingly, **Rav Naḥman bar Yitzḥak said:** Rabbi Yehudah **must be referring** in both Baraitot **to** another Tanna, **Rabbi Yehoshua ben Beterah.** As for the reason why this Tanna was called "Rabbi Yehoshua" in the first Baraita, and "Ben Beterah" in the second Baraita, Rav Naḥman bar Yitzḥak explains: [11]**Sometimes** Rabbi Yehoshua ben Beterah is called **by his** full **name and sometimes** he is **called by his father's name**, but in fact both Baraitot are to be understood as referring to the same Tanna.

RASHI

מזכיר — דראשון נמי המתפלל תפלת יוצר מזכיר. ואילו הכא תני: הראשון אינו מזכיר. **האמר משעת הנחתו** — דהיינו בשביעי. והכא קתני ״יום טוב האחרון של חג״, דהיינו בשמיני. **ותו הא דתניא** — במכילתא אחריתי: רבי יהודה אומר משום בן בתירה: העובר לפני התיבה ביום טוב האחרון של חג — האחרון מזכיר, הראשון אינו מזכיר. (אלא) **אמר רב נחמן בר יצחק תהא** — תרוייהו, הא דבעית הי רבי יהושע, והא דבעית הי בן בתירה — רבי יהושע בן בתירה היא. דהאי דקאמר רבי יהודה לעיל משום רבי יהושע, והדר קאמר משום בן בתירה — תהא תרוייהו רבי יהושע בן בתירה, ולא קשיא: זמנין קרו ליה בשמיה דאבוה — בן בתירה, וזמנין דקרו ליה בשמיה דידיה — רבי יהושע.

SAGES

בְּנֵי בְּתֵירָה **The sons of Beterah.** The Beterah family produced renowned Sages over a number of generations. Some members of the family served as Nasi during the time of Hillel, but transferred the position to him. The two most famous Sages of the family were Rabbi Yehudah and Yehoshua Bnei Beterah.

רַב נַחְמָן בַּר יִצְחָק **Rav Naḥman bar Yitzḥak.** One of the leading Babylonian Amoraim of the fourth generation. Rav Naḥman bar Yitzḥak was born in Sura. His mother was the sister of Rav Aḥa bar Yosef. His principal teacher was Rav Naḥman bar Ya'akov, but he also studied under Rav Ḥisda. After the death of Rava, Rav Naḥman bar Yitzḥak was appointed head of the Pumbedita Yeshivah.

BACKGROUND

זִמְנִין דְּקָרֵי לֵיהּ בִּשְׁמֵיהּ **Sometimes it calls him by his name.** The custom of giving a person his father's name is found in many places in the world. Generally in the Jewish cultural tradition, a person is known as "the son of So-and-so," especially when he is young or not well-known. Only after he becomes older and achieves fame does everyone call him by his given name. Therefore a distinction was made between young scholars (who were sometimes known by their fathers' names) and Sages who had achieved importance and were known by their own names (with or without the addition of the father's name). Certain Sages who were never officially ordained and given the title of "Rabbi" were called by their fathers' names alone, although some of them were themselves important Sages. Occasionally we find that a Sage is sometimes called by his father's name and is sometimes called by his own name. Usually, when he is called by his father's name, the reference is to the time when he was a young scholar, for it was only later that he was ordained and merited being called by his full name.

דְּאַבָּא. [1]וְהָא מִקַּמֵּי דְּלִיסְמְכוּהוּ, [2]וְהָא לְבָתַר דְּלִיסְמְכוּהוּ.

[3]תָּנָא: "בְּטַל וּבְרוּחוֹת לֹא חִיְּיבוּ חֲכָמִים לְהַזְכִּיר, [4]וְאִם בָּא לְהַזְכִּיר, מַזְכִּיר".

[5]מַאי טַעֲמָא?

[6]אֲמַר רַבִּי חֲנִינָא: לְפִי שֶׁאֵין נֶעֱצָרִין.

[7]וְטַל מְנָלַן דְּלָא מִיעֲצַר?

LITERAL TRANSLATION

[1]And this [was] before they ordained him, [2]and that [was] after they ordained him.

[3]It was taught: "The Sages did not obligate [a person] to mention dew and winds, [4]but if he comes to mention [them], he may mention [them].

[5]What is the reason?

[6]Rabbi Ḥanina said: Because they are not withheld.

[7]And from where [do we know] that dew is not withheld?

RASHI

מקמי דליסמכהו – לא הוה חשוב, וקרו ליה בשמיה דאבוה. והאי דקרו ליה בשמיה דנפשיה, רבי יהושע – היינו לבתר דסמכוהו. **בטל וברוחות** – "משיב הרוח ומוריד הטל" לא חייבוהו חכמים להזכיר, אפילו בימות הגשמים. **לפי שאינן נעצרין** – שאלמלא הן אין העולם מתקיים. והאי דאמרינן בתפלה "משיב הרוח ומוריד הגשם" – לאו משום חיוב, אלא חוק גשם הוא מזכיר, דטל ורוחות מועילות לארץ לתקנה ולנגבה, כדבסמוך: זיקא דבתר מיטרא כמיטרא.

TRANSLATION AND COMMENTARY

[1]However, **the second** Baraita is referring to Yehoshua ben Beterah **before he was ordained** and given the title "Rabbi." [2]By contrast, **the first** Baraita is referring to him **after he was ordained** and given the title "Rabbi." Hence it describes him as "Rabbi Yehoshua," in his own right.

תָּנָא [3]The Gemara now cites another Baraita, in which the following **was taught: "The Sages did not obligate a person to mention dew and winds** in the second blessing of the Amidah, even during the winter, [4]**but if** a person **does actually mention them** [i.e., for some personal reason, he feels inspired to mention dew or wind in his prayers], **he may mention them** in the second blessing, and such an insertion is not considered an inappropriate prayer."

מַאי טַעֲמָא [5]The Gemara asks: **What is the reason?** Why should mention not be made of God's power as demonstrated through wind and dew as well as through rain?

אֲמַר רַבִּי חֲנִינָא [6]**Rabbi Ḥanina said** in reply: **Because** winds and dew **are not withheld** but come regularly. Hence it is not necessary to ask God for them explicitly, although a person who feels the need to mention them together with rain may do so.

וְטַל מְנָלַן דְּלָא מִיעֲצַר [7]The Gemara asks: **From where** in the Bible **do we know that dew is not withheld** even in an especially dry year?

NOTES

וְהָא מִקַּמֵּי דְּלִיסְמְכוּהוּ **And the one was before they ordained him.** A young man or a man of little importance is often called by his father's name, the son of So-and-so. Describing a distinguished person as the son of his father is also a way of minimizing his importance (see I Samuel 20:27, where King Saul mockingly refers to David as "the son of Jesse"). Talmudic Sages who were never ordained and were not given the title "Rabbi" are frequently referred to as the sons of their fathers (for example, Ben Azzai, Ben Zoma, and others), but this is no reflection on their Halakhic stature.

בְּטַל וּבְרוּחוֹת לֹא חִיְּיבוּ חֲכָמִים לְהַזְכִּיר **The Sages did not obligate a person to mention dew and winds.** *Rashi* and others explain the Baraita's ruling as follows: The Sages did not impose an obligation to mention dew and winds in the second blessing of the Amidah prayer, either during the summer or even during the winter when there is an obligation to mention rain. But if a person wishes to mention dew or winds, he may indeed mention them at any time of the year.

Ritva explains that the Baraita is saying that the Sages did not impose an obligation to mention dew or winds, even when people customarily mention them — the dew during the summer and winds during the winter. But if a person wishes to mention dew or winds, even at a time when they are not customarily mentioned (dew during the winter and winds during the summer), he may indeed mention them then as well.

Ran observes that the Sages did not make the mention of dew or winds obligatory, even during the appropriate season; but if a person wishes to mention them at the appropriate time, he may indeed do so and his action is deemed praiseworthy.

דְּלָא מִיעֲצַר **Because they are not withheld.** *Tosafot* considers the argument put forward in our Gemara, that dew is never withheld in the light of the series of miracles

HALAKHAH

בְּטַל וּבְרוּחוֹת **Of dew and of winds.** "If someone mentions dew in the second blessing of the Amidah prayer during the winter, or if he fails to mention it during the summer, he is not required to correct his mistake (even if he has not yet finished saying the blessing, for there is no obligation to mention dew at all; *Magen Avraham*). *Rema* notes that, according to the Ashkenazi custom, no mention is made of dew either in the winter or in the summer. According to the Sephardi custom (and similarly that of Ashkenazi Ḥasidim in the Diaspora and of all Jews living in Eretz Israel), the expression 'Who causes the dew to fall [מוֹרִיד הַטָּל]' is inserted in the blessing during the summer." (*Shulḥan Arukh, Oraḥ Ḥayyim* 114:3.)

SAGES

רַבִּי חֲנִינָא **Rabbi Ḥanina.** When the name of the Amora Rabbi Ḥanina is used without a patronymic in the Talmud, the reference is to Rabbi Ḥanina bar Ḥama, a first-generation Amora from Eretz Israel. Rabbi Ḥanina originally came from Babylonia, although he immigrated to Eretz Israel at a relatively early age, and studied there with Rabbi Yehudah HaNasi, who was very fond of him (and indeed remarked that Rabbi Ḥanina was "not a human being, but an angel"). Rabbi Ḥanina also studied with Rabbi Yehudah HaNasi's most distinguished students, in particular with Rabbi Ḥiyya. On his deathbed, Rabbi Yehudah HaNasi designated Rabbi Ḥanina as the new head of his yeshivah, although the latter, in his great modesty, refused to accept the position as long as his older colleague, Rabbi Efes, was still alive.

Rabbi Ḥanina lived in Sepphoris, where he earned a living as a honey dealer, from which he became wealthy and established a large academy. He was renowned for his acuity, as well as for his righteousness and piety.

Numerous Halakhic and Aggadic teachings of Rabbi Ḥanina appear in the Babylonian and the Jerusalem Talmud. He lived to a great age, and had many students over an extended period, among them Rabbi Yehoshua ben Levi, a student-colleague of his, and Rabbi Yoḥanan, who studied with him for many years.

His son was the Amora Rabbi Ḥama the son of Rabbi Ḥanina.

BACKGROUND

טַל **Dew.** Dew is formed by the condensation of water vapor from the air and from the ground. Most objects (including plants) radiate and lose more heat than does the air, and they therefore cool more than the air. On clear nights and when the atmosphere is sufficiently humid, droplets of dew are formed on the ground. Although various factors can reduce the formation of dew (low clouds, strong winds, etc.), it is very seldom that there is no dew at all. The amount

TRANSLATION AND COMMENTARY

דִּכְתִיב [1]The Gemara replies that we know this from the story of Elijah the Prophet, who punished King Ahab by decreeing a drought, **as it is written** (I Kings 17:1): **"And Elijah the Tishbite, of the inhabitants of Gilead, said to Ahab: As the Lord God of Israel lives, before whom I stand, there will not be these years dew and rain except by my word."** In the third year, God told Elijah that He intended to end the drought, in order not to prolong the suffering of the people. [2]**And it is written** (ibid., 18:1) that God said to Elijah: **"Go, show yourself to Ahab, and I will give rain on the face of the earth."** [3]God mentioned rain, **but as for** giving **dew** at the end of the drought **He said nothing to** Elijah. [4]**What is the reason** that God did not mention dew? [5]It is **because** [3B] the dew **was not withheld** during the drought, despite Elijah's decree.

וְכִי מֵאַחַר דְּלָא מִיעֲצַר [6]**But,** the Gemara objects, according to this explanation, God did not mention dew when the drought ended, **because** dew **was not withheld** during the drought. [7]But if so, **why did Elijah take an oath** when the drought began that dew as well as rain would be withheld?

הָכִי קָאָמַר לֵיהּ [8]The Gemara answers: **This is what** Elijah **said to** Ahab: **"Even** the dew that does **come will not be dew of blessing."** Although dew of some kind will still fall during the years of drought, it will not be of the kind that helps the crops to grow.

[1]דִּכְתִיב: "וַיֹּאמֶר אֵלִיָּהוּ הַתִּשְׁבִּי, מִתֹּשָׁבֵי גִלְעָד, אֶל אַחְאָב: חַי ה' אֱלֹהֵי יִשְׂרָאֵל, אֲשֶׁר עָמַדְתִּי לְפָנָיו, אִם יִהְיֶה הַשָּׁנִים הָאֵלֶּה טַל וּמָטָר כִּי אִם לְפִי דְבָרִי". [2]וּכְתִיב: "לֵךְ הֵרָאֵה אֶל אַחְאָב, וְאֶתְּנָה מָטָר עַל פְּנֵי הָאֲדָמָה". [3]וְאִילּוּ טַל, לֹא קָאָמַר לֵיהּ. [4]מַאי טַעֲמָא? [5]מִשּׁוּם [3B] דְּלָא מִיעֲצַר. [6]וְכִי מֵאַחַר דְּלָא מִיעֲצַר, [7]אֵלִיָּהוּ אִשְׁתַּבּוּעֵי לָמָּה לֵיהּ? [8]הָכִי קָאָמַר לֵיהּ: "אֲפִילּוּ טַל דִּבְרָכָה נַמִּי לָא אָתֵי".

LITERAL TRANSLATION

[1]For it is written: "And Elijah the Tishbite, of the inhabitants of Gilead, said to Ahab: As the Lord God of Israel lives, before whom I stand, there will not be these years dew and rain except by my word." [2]And it is written: "Go, show yourself to Ahab, and I will give rain on the face of the earth." [3]But as for dew, He did not say to him. [4]What is the reason? [5]Because [3B] it is not withheld.

[6]But since it is not withheld, [7]why did Elijah swear?

[8]This is what he said to him: "Even dew of blessing too will not come."

RASHI

ואילו טל לא קאמר — ואתנה טל ומטר, אלא מטר בלבד. **ולא מיעצר** — לעולם, אפילו באותן שנים. **אישתבועי למה ליה** — "אם יהיה השנים האלה טל ומטר כי אם לפי דברי" — הא לא נעצר. **אפילו טל דברכה** — שיצמיח שום צמח.

of dew varies according to weather and location. In many areas in Eretz Israel the overall quantity of dew is almost equal to that of rain, and it is only by means of dew that agriculture is possible in these areas.

An excess of dew can damage crops during certain times of the year, and this is called "dew that is not a blessing." Usually, however, dew is a blessing, not only in summer when it is a source of additional water, but also in winter when it serves as a defence against frost at night.

BACKGROUND

טַל דִּבְרָכָה Dew of blessing. Usually dew is greatly beneficial to plants in many ways. However, it can sometimes happen that dew is not a blessing — for example, when there is dew on plants and the temperature falls below freezing point. In such cases the droplets of frozen dew cause considerable damage to the plants.

NOTES

that were performed for Gideon. Regarding the divine signs requested by Gideon, the Bible states (Judges 6:37-40): "Behold, I will put a fleece of wool on the threshing floor; and if there is dew on the fleece only and it is dry on all the ground elsewhere, then I shall know.... And it was so.... Let it now be dry only upon the fleece, and upon all the ground let there be dew. And God did so that night." *Tosafot* notes that, regarding the first sign, the verse says, "And it was so," whereas regarding the second sign, it says, "And God did so that night." When Gideon asked that dew be on the fleece but not on the ground, "it was so." His request was fulfilled in part, for there was dew on the fleece, as the verse continues: "And he pressed the fleece together and wrung the dew out of the fleece." But the second half of his request was not fulfilled, for dew is never withheld, and so there was dew on the ground as well. But when Gideon asked that dew be on the ground but not on the fleece, "God did so that night," fulfilling Gideon's request in its entirety. Alternatively, both requests were fulfilled in their entirety. When Gideon asked that dew be on the ground, "God did so that night," but when he asked that the ground be dry, "it was so." The verse refrains from associating God's name with the cessation of dew, so as not to mention God's name in connection with a calamity. *Rishon LeTzion* suggests that the miracle performed for Gideon does not contradict the Gemara's argument that dew is never withheld, for if dew fails to fall for no more than a day or two, it is not yet regarded as having ceased.

"אִם יִהְיֶה הַשָּׁנִים הָאֵלֶּה טַל וּמָטָר" **"There will not be these years dew and rain."** Our Gemara explains that Elijah the Prophet did not ask that dew be withheld entirely, but only that there should be no dew of blessing, and therefore there was no need for Elijah to inform King Ahab that the dew would resume forming. The Jerusalem Talmud and the Midrashim written in Eretz Israel argue that Elijah did in fact ask that the dew cease entirely. Opinions differ as to whether God heeded Elijah's request even with respect to dew, or only with respect to rain (see the Jerusalem Talmud and *Aggadat Bereshit*).

אִשְׁתַּבּוּעֵי לָמָּה לֵיהּ? **Why did Elijah swear?** Some commentators ask why the Gemara does not raise a different question: If dew is never withheld, how could Elijah the Prophet have taken a false oath, swearing that there would be no dew? (See *Ein Ya'akov;* see also *Shittah,* who understood that this is indeed the Gemara's question.

Maharasha suggests that when the world follows its natural course, dew is never withheld even in times of drought. But a righteous man has the ability to change the laws of Nature by the power of his word.

TRANSLATION AND COMMENTARY

וְלִיהַדְרֵיהּ לְטַל דִּבְרָכָה [1]The Gemara objects: **But** if so, why did God not command Elijah to tell Ahab that He was **restoring the dew of blessing** when the drought ended?

מִשּׁוּם דְּלָא מִינְכְּרָא מִילְּתָא [2]The Gemara answers: There was no point in mentioning dew when the drought ended, **because** dew fell all the time and only its quality changed. Hence **the matter was not distinguishable.** Elijah did not mention dew at the end of the drought, since stubborn people like Ahab could pretend that no miracle had occurred, and that God's warning had not been fulfilled.

אֶלָּא [3]The Gemara continues: It is clear that dew is never completely withheld, which is why we are not obliged to mention it in our prayers. **But** the Baraita also ruled that we need not mention the wind in our prayers, since it too is not withheld. **From where** in the Bible **do we know that the wind is not withheld?**

אָמַר רַבִּי יְהוֹשֻׁעַ בֶּן לֵוִי [4]**Rabbi Yehoshua ben Levi said:** We know this **because the verse says** (Zechariah 2:10): **"For I have spread you about like the four winds of heaven, says the Lord."** The word "wind" in Hebrew (רוּחַ) also means "direction" (north, south, east, or west), and Rabbi Yehoshua ben Levi's exegesis is based on this double meaning of the word. According to the plain meaning of the verse, Zechariah is referring to the exile of the Jewish people, who are spread out over the world in all four directions. But this straightforward explanation poses linguistic difficulties, as Rabbi Yehoshua ben Levi goes on to explain: [5]**What** was God **telling** the Israelites in this prophecy? [6]**If we say that the Holy One Blessed be He said to Israel: "I have scattered you to the four winds** [i.e., directions] **of the world,"** north, south, east, and west, in accordance with the plain meaning of the verse, [7]why did God say in that case that He had scattered them ***"like* the four** winds of heaven"? [8]To convey the plain meaning, the verse **should have said** that God had scattered them ***"to* the four** winds of the world"! Why did the verse use the preposition "like" if no comparison was being made? [9]**Rather,** says Rabbi Yehoshua ben Levi, **this is what** God **was telling** Israel in this prophecy: The Jewish people, who are scattered all over the world, are like the winds. [10]**Just as the world cannot exist without winds, so too can the world not exist without Israel.** And conversely we may infer that the existence of winds is a permanent feature of the world. Hence we see that winds are never withheld, so it is not necessary to mention them in our prayers.

[1]וְלִיהַדְרֵיהּ לְטַל דִּבְרָכָה!

[2]מִשּׁוּם דְּלָא מִינְכְּרָא מִילְּתָא.

[3]אֶלָּא רוּחוֹת מְנָא לָן דְּלָא מִיעַצְרִי?

[4]אֲמַר רַבִּי יְהוֹשֻׁעַ בֶּן לֵוִי: דַּאֲמַר קְרָא: ״כִּי כְּאַרְבַּע רוּחוֹת הַשָּׁמַיִם פֵּרַשְׂתִּי אֶתְכֶם, נְאֻם ה׳״. [5]מַאי קָאָמַר לְהוּ? [6]אִילֵימָא הָכִי קָאָמַר לְהוּ הַקָּדוֹשׁ בָּרוּךְ הוּא לְיִשְׂרָאֵל: ״דִּבְדַרְתִּינְכוּ בְּאַרְבַּע רוּחֵי דְּעָלְמָא״, [7]אִי הָכִי, ״כְּאַרְבַּע״? [8]״בְּאַרְבַּע״ מִיבָּעֵי לֵיהּ! [9]אֶלָּא הָכִי קָאָמַר: [10]״כְּשֵׁם שֶׁאִי אֶפְשָׁר לָעוֹלָם בְּלֹא רוּחוֹת, כָּךְ אִי אֶפְשָׁר לָעוֹלָם בְּלֹא יִשְׂרָאֵל״.

LITERAL TRANSLATION

[1]But let Him restore the dew of blessing!

[2]Because the matter is not distinguishable.

[3]But from where [do we know] that the winds are not withheld?

[4]Rabbi Yehoshua ben Levi said: Because the verse said: "For I have spread you about like the four winds of heaven, says the Lord." [5]What did He say to them? [6]If we say this is what the Holy One Blessed be He said to Israel: "That I have scattered you to the four winds of the world," [7]if so, [why] "like the four"? [8]He should have said "to the four"! [9]Rather, this is what He said: [10]"Just as the world cannot exist without winds, so too can the world not exist without Israel."

RASHI

וליהדריה לטל דברכה — ולימא: ואתנה טל ומטר. **דלא מינכרא מילתא** — דהא טל הוה מעיקרא, ולא היה אחאב הרשע מודה בחזירה דטל של ברכה, דאי הוה אומר "ואתנה טל ומטר" — היה אחאב מקנטרו, ואומר לו שלא נעצר. **אלא דמכניפנא לכו מארבע רוחי עלמא** — לא גרסינן, דהא "פרשתי אתכם" כתיב בקרא, ואיכא למימר דגרס ליה, והכי משתמע קרא: כי מארבע רוחות השמים שפרשתי אתכם — משם אקבצכם. ואריכות לשון בעלמא הוא, דלא כתיב קיבוץ בקרא. **כשם שאי אפשר לעולם בלא רוחות** — שלא יתקיים מרוב הבל וחמימות. **בלא ישראל** — שאין העולם מתקיים אלא בשביל ישראל, והכי אמר קרא: כי כארבע רוחות השמים פרשתי אתכם לרוחות העולם, כדי שיתקיים, שנאמר (ירמיהו לג) "אם לא בריתי יומם ולילה חקות שמים וארץ לא שמתי".

NOTES

לָא מִינְכְּרָא מִילְּתָא **Because the matter is not distinguishable.** Some commentators explain that Elijah mentioned dew in the oath he took that brought about the drought, because he knew that Ahab would be forced to admit that Elijah's curse on the dew of blessing was being fulfilled when he saw that nothing was growing even though the

BACKGROUND

רוחות **Winds.** Many factors cause winds: differences in temperature between the ground and the air, between the land and the sea, between the polar regions and the equator, and the atmospheric layers around the earth.

While the winds that bring rain are connected to complex meteorological systems, the factors that cause winds in general are constant and determined, and therefore some wind there is always blowing; in other words, winds are never totally "withheld."

SAGES

רַבִּי יְהוֹשֻׁעַ בֶּן לֵוִי **Rabbi Yehoshua ben Levi.** One of the greatest Amoraim of the first generation in Eretz Israel. Rabbi Yehoshua ben Levi was, according to some opinions, the son of Levi ben Sisi, one of the outstanding students of Rabbi Yehudah HaNasi; and it seems that Rabbi Yehoshua ben Levi was himself one of Rabbi Yehudah HaNasi's younger students. Many Halakhic disputes are recorded between him and Rabbi Yoḥanan, who was apparently the younger and a student and colleague of his. In general, the Halakhah follows Rabbi Yehoshua ben Levi, even against Rabbi Yoḥanan, whose authority was very great.

Rabbi Yehoshua ben Levi was also a renowned teacher of Aggadah. Because of the great respect in which he was held, Aggadic statements in his name are presented at the end of the six orders of the Mishnah.

A great deal is told of his piety and sanctity, and he is regarded as one of the most righteous men who ever lived. Among other things, it is told that he would sit with the most dangerously infected lepers and study Torah. He was famous as a worker of miracles, to whom Elijah the Prophet appeared, and his prayers were always answered. According to tradition he was one of those over whom the Angel of Death had no dominion, and he entered the Garden of Eden alive.

He taught many students. All the Sages of the succeeding generation were his students to some degree, and quote Torah teachings in his name. His son, Rabbi Yosef, was also a Sage, and married into the Nasi's family.

TERMINOLOGY

תָּנָא (occasionally **תָּאנָא**) **A Tanna taught.** A term used to introduce Baraitot and Toseftot. Usually the Baraitot introduced by this expression are very short (one or two sentences), and they clarify, supplement or limit statements in the Mishnah.

TRANSLATION AND COMMENTARY

אָמַר רַבִּי חֲנִינָא [1]The Gemara now returns to Rabbi Ḥanina, who explained above (3a) that we do not mention dew and wind in our prayers because they are never withheld. **Rabbi Ḥanina** also **said**: Since we know that dew and wind are never withheld, **therefore in the summer if** a worshiper **inserts** in the second blessing of the Amidah the expression, **"Who causes the wind to blow," we do not make him go back** and repeat the blessing from the beginning, as we would if he had uttered a completely inappropriate prayer, because the winds blow both in summer and in winter. [2]But **if he inserts** the expression, **"Who causes the rain to fall," we** do **make him go back** and repeat the blessing from the beginning, because he has uttered a completely inappropriate prayer, as we do not want rain to fall in the summer. [3]Rabbi Ḥanina continued: Regarding the recitation of the Amidah **in the winter, if** a worshiper **does not insert** the expression, **"Who causes the wind to blow," we do not make him go back** and repeat the blessing from the beginning, because the winds blow in any case, and it is not absolutely necessary to pray for them. [4]**But if he does not insert** the expression, **"Who causes the rain to fall," we** do **make him go back** and repeat the blessing from the beginning, because he has omitted an essential prayer. [5]**Moreover,** concludes Rabbi Ḥanina, wind and dew occur so regularly that **even if** the worshiper prays to God to stop them, **saying, "Who takes the wind away and causes the dew to fly away," we do not make him go back** and repeat the blessing, because such a prayer will not be answered.

תָּנָא [6]The Gemara now cites another Baraita on a similar topic. **It was taught** in the following Baraita: "The worshiper need mention only rain in the second blessing of the Amidah. [7]**The Sages did not obligate a person to mention clouds and winds** in the second blessing, even during the winter, [8]**but if he does wish to mention them, he may mention them** and it is not considered an inappropriate prayer.

[1]אָמַר רַבִּי חֲנִינָא: הִלְכָּךְ, בִּימוֹת הַחַמָּה אָמַר: "מַשִּׁיב הָרוּחַ", אֵין מַחֲזִירִין אוֹתוֹ. [2]אָמַר: "מוֹרִיד הַגֶּשֶׁם", מַחֲזִירִין אוֹתוֹ. [3]בִּימוֹת הַגְּשָׁמִים לֹא אָמַר: "מַשִּׁיב הָרוּחַ", אֵין מַחֲזִירִין אוֹתוֹ. [4]לֹא אָמַר: "מוֹרִיד הַגֶּשֶׁם", מַחֲזִירִין אוֹתוֹ. [5]וְלֹא עוֹד אֶלָּא אֲפִילּוּ אָמַר: "מַעֲבִיר הָרוּחַ וּמַפְרִיחַ הַטַּל", אֵין מַחֲזִירִין אוֹתוֹ. [6]תָּנָא: [7]"בְּעָבִים וּבְרוּחוֹת לֹא חִיְּיבוּ חֲכָמִים לְהַזְכִּיר, [8]וְאִם בָּא לְהַזְכִּיר, מַזְכִּיר".

LITERAL TRANSLATION

[1]Rabbi Ḥanina said: Therefore, in the summer (lit., "in the days of the sun") [if] he said: "Who causes the wind to blow," we do not make him go back. [2][But if] he said: "Who causes the rain to fall," we make him go back. [3]In the winter (lit., "in the days of the rains") [if] he did not say: "Who causes the wind to blow," we do not make him go back. [4][But if] he did not say: "Who causes the rain to fall," we make him go back. [5]And not only that, but even [if] he said: "Who takes the wind away and causes the dew to fly away," we do not make him go back. [6][A Tanna] taught: [7]"The Sages did not obligate [a person] to mention clouds and winds, [8]but if he comes to mention [them], he may mention [them]."

RASHI

בימות החמה — מניסן עד החג. **משיב הרוח אין מחזירין אותו** — דבלאו הכי לא מיעצר. **מוריד הגשם מחזירין אותו** — דמיעצר, וכיון דבעא אמיטרא — לא התפלל תפלתו כהוגן, וחוזר לראש הברכה, ואומרה בלא "מוריד הגשם", לפי שהגשמים בקיץ סימן קללה הן, מפני הקציר. **מעביר הרוח** — שלא ינשב. **ומפריח הטל** — שלא ירד. **אין מחזירין אותו** — דלא מיעצרי. **בעבים** — מקשר עבים.

NOTES

dew was forming. But no mention of dew was made when God brought the drought to an end and the dew of blessing resumed, for Ahab might have argued that the crops had begun to grow not because of the dew but because of the rain that was once again falling (*Riaf*).

HALAKHAH

בִּימוֹת הַחַמָּה אָמַר, "מַשִּׁיב הָרוּחַ" In the summer, if he said, "Who causes the wind to blow." If someone inserts 'Who causes the wind to blow' (without mentioning rain) into the second blessing of the Amidah prayer during the summer, or if he fails to mention the wind during the winter, he is not required to correct his mistake. But if he says 'Who causes the rain to fall' during the summer, he must correct his mistake and go back to the beginning of the blessing, and if he has already completed the blessing, he must go back to the beginning of the Amidah. (The authorities disagree about whether or not he must also repeat the verse, 'O Lord, open my lips, and my mouth will declare your praise,' with which the Amidah opens; see *Sha'arei Teshuvah* and *Arukh HaShulḥan*.) This mistake must be corrected even if the prayer was recited in a place where rain is needed during the summer months, and even if he mentioned both dew and rain (*Rema*). If someone fails to mention 'Who causes the rain to fall' during the winter, he must correct his mistake, provided that he did not mention dew. But if he mentioned dew, he is not required to go back and correct the mistake (following the Jerusalem Talmud)." (*Shulḥan Arukh, Oraḥ Ḥayyim* 114:3-5.)

TRANSLATION AND COMMENTARY

מַאי טַעֲמָא [1]The Gemara asks: **What is the reason?** Why should we not mention winds and clouds as well as rain?

מִשּׁוּם דְּלָא מִיעַצְרִי [2]The Gemara answers: **Because** winds and clouds, like dew, **are not withheld,** but come regularly, year after year.

וְלָא מִיעַצְרִי [3]**But,** the Gemara objects, granted that dew is not withheld, even during a year of drought, but **are** clouds and winds **not withheld?** [4]**But surely Rav Yosef taught** the following Baraita, which declares that God does sometimes withhold both clouds and winds in order to punish people for their sins: "The verse states [Deuteronomy 11:17]: [5]'And the anger of the Lord will be kindled against you, **and He will shut up the heavens.'** The expression 'shut up the heavens' **means** that God will withhold **the clouds and the winds."** [6]The Baraita continues: **"You say** that the verse refers to God withholding **the clouds and the winds.** [7]**But might it not mean** that the clouds and the winds will continue and that God will **only** withhold **the rain?"** [8]The Baraita explains: "This cannot be the meaning, for the verse **goes on to say** that after God shuts up the heavens, **'there will be no rain.'** [9]The withholding of the **rain is mentioned** specifically. [10]**So what do we learn from** the first part of the verse which says: **'And He will shut up the heavens'?** Clearly, the first part of the verse **teaches** us that not only will there be no rain, [11]but also that God will withhold **the clouds and the winds."**

קַשְׁיָא רוּחוֹת אַרוּחוֹת [12]How, asks the Gemara, can the first Baraita rule that we need not mention clouds and winds in our prayers, because they are never withheld, whereas the second Baraita declares that they are indeed sometimes withheld? Surely **there is a contradiction** between the first Baraita's ruling about **winds and** the second Baraita's ruling about **winds,** [13]and **there is** also **a contradiction** between the first Baraita's ruling about **clouds and** the second Baraita's ruling about **clouds!**

עָבִים אַעָבִים לָא קַשְׁיָא [14]The Gemara answers: **There is no contradiction between** the first Baraita's ruling about **clouds and** the second Baraita's ruling about **clouds.** [15]**The first Baraita refers to early clouds,** the clouds that make the sky overcast in anticipation of rain. These clouds never disappear altogether, even in a year in which no rain actually falls. [16]**The second Baraita refers to late clouds,** that appear after rainfall. These clouds may sometimes not appear. They are very beneficial to the crops, as the Gemara explains below, and the verse in Deuteronomy threatens that God may withhold these beneficial clouds if our sins kindle His anger.

[1]מַאי טַעֲמָא?
[2]מִשּׁוּם דְּלָא מִיעַצְרִי.
[3]וְלָא מִיעַצְרִי? [4]וְהָתָנֵי רַב יוֹסֵף: [5]"'וְעָצַר אֶת הַשָּׁמַיִם' מִן הֶעָבִים וּמִן הָרוּחוֹת. [6]אַתָּה אוֹמֵר מִן הֶעָבִים וּמִן הָרוּחוֹת. [7]אוֹ אֵינוֹ אֶלָּא מִן הַמָּטָר? [8]כְּשֶׁהוּא אוֹמֵר: 'וְלֹא יִהְיֶה מָטָר', [9]הֲרֵי מָטָר אָמוּר. [10]הָא מָה אֲנִי מְקַיֵּים 'וְעָצַר אֶת הַשָּׁמַיִם'? [11]מִן הֶעָבִים וּמִן הָרוּחוֹת".
[12]קַשְׁיָא רוּחוֹת אַרוּחוֹת;
[13]קַשְׁיָא עָבִים אַעָבִים!
[14]עָבִים אַעָבִים לָא קַשְׁיָא.
[15]הָא בְּחָרְפֵי, [16]הָא בְּאַפְלֵי.

LITERAL TRANSLATION

[1]What is the reason?
[2]Because they are not withheld.
[3]But are they not withheld? [4]But surely Rav Yosef taught: [5]"'And He will shut up the heavens' [means] from the clouds and from the winds. [6]You say [it means] from the clouds and from the winds. [7]But might it not [mean] from the rain? [8]When it says: 'And there will not be rain,' [9]rain is mentioned. [10]So what do I learn from (lit., 'establish') 'and He will shut up the heavens'? [11][It means] from the clouds and from the winds."
[12]There is a contradiction between winds and winds; [13]there is a contradiction between clouds and clouds!
[14]There is no contradiction between clouds and clouds. [15]This [Baraita refers] to early [clouds], [16]that [Baraita refers] to late [clouds].

RASHI

למימרא דלא מיעצרי — לפיכך לא חייבוהו להזכיר.

SAGES

רַב יוֹסֵף **Rav Yosef.** The son of Ḥiyya, Rav Yosef was one of the greatest Amoraim of Babylonia during the third generation. He was a disciple of Rav Yehudah and a colleague of Rabbah, and was head of the Pumbedita Yeshivah for two-and-a-half years. He was known as "Sinai" because of his expert knowledge of Baraitot and the oral traditions of the Bible, as well as its translation. His most important students were Abaye and Rava. An illness caused him to forget all his learning, but Abaye helped him to acquire it again. Rav Yosef also became blind. After Rav Yosef's death, Abaye succeeded him as head of the Pumbedita Yeshivah.

NOTES

הָא בְּחָרְפֵי, הָא בְּאַפְלֵי **This Baraita refers to early clouds, that Baraita refers to late clouds.** Our commentary follows *Rashi* and most Rishonim in explaining that "early" and "late" refer to two types of clouds — the clouds that come before rain and the clouds that appear in the sky after rain has fallen. The clouds that come before rain do not disappear altogether, but sometimes clouds do not form after rain has fallen. *Shittah* accepts this interpretation of "early" and "late" as referring to clouds, but he explains that sometimes there are no clouds before rain, although there are always clouds after rain. But some authorities explain that the terms "early" and "late" do not refer to two types of clouds, but rather to two types of crops — crops that ripen early and crops that ripen late (see *Tosafot* and *Ra'avad*).

TRANSLATION AND COMMENTARY

רוּחוֹת אַרוּחוֹת לָא קַשְׁיָא [1] Likewise, continues the Gemara, **there is no contradiction between** the first Baraita's ruling about **winds and** the second Baraita's ruling about **winds.** [2] **The first Baraita refers to normal winds.** These winds never disappear altogether, even in a year of drought. [3] The second Baraita **refers to abnormally strong winds.** The verse in Deuteronomy threatens that God may withhold these strong winds if our sins kindle His anger. Both kinds of winds are beneficial to the crops, but the normal winds are sufficient for the world to survive.

רוּחַ שֶׁאֵינָהּ מְצוּיָה [4] But, the Gemara objects, how can you say that abnormally strong winds are not essential? **Abnormally strong winds are** the only winds that are **suitable for the threshing floor!** Ordinary winds are not sufficient to winnow grain after it has been threshed. Why, then, do we not pray for strong winds as well as for rain, since it is possible for them to be withheld?

אֶפְשָׁר בְּנַפְוָותָא [5] The Gemara answers: **It is possible to winnow** grain **by means of sieves.** While abnormally strong winds can be a blessing, they are not really a necessity, but merely a convenience. Therefore, since ordinary winds are never withheld, the Sages did not require a person to pray for wind as well as for rain.

תָּנָא [6] The Gemara now cites another Tannaitic statement on the subject of wind and clouds. **It was taught** in a Baraita: **"Clouds and winds are second only to rain** itself in the benefits they bring."

הֵיכִי דָּמֵי [7] The Gemara asks: **How do we visualize the case** to which the Baraita is referring?

אָמַר עוּלָּא [8] **Ulla, and some say Rav Yehudah, said** in reply: The Baraita is referring to **those** winds and clouds **that** come **after rain.** They complete the work of the rain, and do almost as much good as the rain itself.

לְמֵימְרָא דְּמַעַלְיוּתָא הִיא [9] The Gemara objects: **Is this to say that** winds that blow after a rainfall **are beneficial?** [10] **But surely it is written** (Deuteronomy 28:24): **"The Lord will make the rain of your land powder and dust."** [11] **And Ulla** himself, **and some say Rav Yehudah, said** that **this** verse **is referring** to **winds that** blow **after rain.** Thus we see that winds that blow after a rainfall are harmful.

[1] רוּחוֹת אַרוּחוֹת לָא קַשְׁיָא. [2] הָא בְּרוּחַ מְצוּיָה, [3] הָא בְּרוּחַ שֶׁאֵינָהּ מְצוּיָה. [4] רוּחַ שֶׁאֵינָהּ מְצוּיָה חֲזְיָא לְבֵי דָרֵי! [5] אֶפְשָׁר בְּנַפְוָותָא. [6] תָּנָא: "הֶעָבִים וְהָרוּחוֹת שְׁנִיּוֹת לְמָטָר". [7] הֵיכִי דָּמֵי? [8] אָמַר עוּלָּא וְאִיתֵּימָא רַב יְהוּדָה: דְּבָתַר מִיטְרָא. [9] לְמֵימְרָא דְּמַעַלְיוּתָא הִיא? [10] וְהָכְתִיב: "יִתֵּן ה׳ אֶת מְטַר אַרְצְךָ אָבָק וְעָפָר". [11] וְאָמַר עוּלָּא וְאִיתֵּימָא רַב יְהוּדָה: זִיקָא דְּבָתַר מִטְרָא!

LITERAL TRANSLATION

[1] There is no contradiction between winds and winds. [2] This [Baraita refers] to normal wind, [3] that [Baraita refers] to abnormal wind.

[4] Abnormal wind is suitable for the threshing floor!

[5] It is possible [to winnow] with sieves.

[6] [A Tanna] taught: "The clouds and the winds are second [only] to rain."

[7] How do we visualize the case (lit., "how is it like")?

[8] Ulla, and some say Rav Yehudah, said: [Those] that are after rain.

[9] [Is this] to say that it is a benefit? [10] But surely it is written: "The Lord will make the rain of your land powder and dust." [11] And Ulla, and some say Rav Yehudah, said: [This refers to] wind that is after rain!

RASHI

בחרפי — עבים בכירות, הבאים לפני המטר, אינן עצורות. **באפלי** — הבאות מאוחרות לאחר המטר, דשניות למטר הן, כדלקמן. ובהנהו כתיב "ועצר", וכיון דאין כולם נעצרות — לא חייבו להזכיר. **שאינה מצויה** — כתיב "ועצר", ואפילו הכי לא חייבוהו להזכיר, דסגי ליה במצויה, רוחות לא מצי לתרוצי: הא בחרפי הא באפלי, דרוח בין במטר בין בלא מטר לא מיעצר, כגון רוח מצויה. **רוח שאינה מצויה נמי חזיא לבי דרי** — לגורן, לזרות הקשין מן התבואה, ואחייב להזכיר. **אפשר בנפוותא** — *וו"ן בלעז, בנפה וכברה. **שניות** — כמעט שמועילות כמטר עצמו. **מאי היא** — אי זה עבים ורוחות קאמר דשניות למטר? **אמר עולא ואיתימא רב יהודה דבתר מיטרא** — עבים ורוחות שלאחר המטר. **זיקא** — לא גרסינן הכא. **יתן ה׳** — את מטר ארצך אבק ועפר וגו׳. **זיקא דבתר מיטרא** — שהרוח מעלה אבק אחר הגשמים, ונדבק בתבואה.

LANGUAGE (RASHI)

וו"ן* From the Old French *van,* meaning "a fan" or "a sieve."

BACKGROUND

הֶעָבִים וְהָרוּחוֹת שְׁנִיּוֹת לְמָטָר The clouds and the winds are second only to rain. The benefit to the soil and crops caused by rainfall depends to some degree on the ambient temperature afterwards. If there is a sudden rise in temperature after the rain, this can cause desiccation and hardening of the upper layers of the soil, resulting in much damage to the roots of plants. By contrast, gentle winds and rain allow the upper layer to evaporate slowly, so that the water is well absorbed by the earth and by the roots. The water seeps down to a lower level and creates a reservoir for the future.

SAGES

עוּלָּא Ulla. A Palestinian Amora of the second and third generations. Ulla was the most important of those scholars who transmitted information and Halakhic rulings from Eretz Israel to the Diaspora. His full name seems to have been Ulla the son of Yishmael. Ulla was one of the disciples of Rabbi Yoḥanan, and was responsible for conveying to Babylonia the Torah rulings laid down in Eretz Israel. He would likewise transmit the Halakhic teachings of the Babylonian scholars to Eretz Israel.

It seems that Ulla made frequent journeys, and would travel from place to place teaching Torah. (For this reason Yalta, the wife of Rav Naḥman, described him as a "peddler" [*Berakhot* 51b].) In the eyes of the Babylonian scholars, Ulla was particularly important, and the scholars of the second generation of Amoraim there treated him with great respect. Thus Rav Ḥisda referred to him as "our teacher who comes from Eretz Israel," and Rav Yehudah sent his son to learn Halakhic practice from Ulla's conduct.

In the Jerusalem Talmud, in which he is generally referred to as Rabbi Ulla the son of

NOTES

שְׁנִיּוֹת לְמָטָר Second only to the rain. *Rabbenu Ḥananel* explains this in a slightly different manner. The clouds and the winds that follow rain benefit the crops in the same measure as would a second rainfall.

TRANSLATION AND COMMENTARY

לָא קַשְׁיָא [1]The Gemara answers: **There is no difficulty** in reconciling Ulla's two statements. [2]Ulla's first statement **refers to** a case **where** the wind **comes gently.** A light wind after a rainfall enhances the effect of the rainfall. [3]But Ulla's second statement **refers to** a case **where** the wind **comes forcefully.** Strong winds can cause more damage after rainfall than they do before it.

וְאִי בָּעֵית אֵימָא [4]**And,** continues the Gemara, **if you wish** you can **say** that Ulla's second statement **refers to** a case **where** the wind **raises dust.** In such a case, the combination of wind, rain, and dust produces a harmful storm. [5]But Ulla's first statement **refers to** a case **where** the wind **does not raise dust.** If the wind does not raise any dust, it is beneficial, even if it is strong.

וַאֲמַר רַב יְהוּדָה [6]The Gemara now cites another statement of Rav Yehudah on a similar topic. **Rav Yehudah said: Wind** that blows **after rain is like rain** in the benefits it brings, because it adds to the effect of the rain. [7]**Clouds** that appear **after rain are** also **like rain** in the benefits they bring. [8]And if the **sun** comes out **after rain,** the benefits it brings **are like two rainfalls,** because it adds significantly to the effects of the rain. Thus we see that wind, clouds, and sun are all beneficial after a rainstorm.

לְמַעוּטֵי מַאי [9]The Gemara asks: **What** then is **excluded?** What can happen after a rainstorm that is not beneficial?

לְמַעוּטֵי גִּילְהֵי דְלֵילְיָא [10]The Gemara answers: Rav Yehuda's statement **excludes the glow of** the rising moon at **night and** when the **sun** appears **between the clouds** (i.e., if the weather is partly cloudy in the daytime). These two situations are not beneficial if they occur after rain.

אֲמַר רָבָא [11]The Gemara now cites a statement of Rava on the same topic. **Rava said: Snow is as beneficial to mountains,** where it normally falls, **as five rainfalls** are to **the soil** of the valleys and plains where snow

LITERAL TRANSLATION

[1]There is no difficulty. [2]This [refers to wind] which comes gently, [3]that [refers to wind] which comes forcefully.

[4]And if you wish, say: This [refers to wind] which raises dust, [5]that [refers to wind] which does not raise dust.

[6]And Rav Yehudah said: Wind that is after rain is like rain. [7]Cloud that is after rain is like rain. [8]Sun that is after rain is like two rainfalls.

[9]To exclude what?

[10]To exclude the glow of night, and sun that is between the clouds.

[11]Rava said: Snow is as beneficial to mountains as five rainfalls to the ground,

[1]לָא קַשְׁיָא. [2]הָא דַּאֲתָא נִיחָא,
[3]הָא דַּאֲתָא רַזְיָא.
[4]וְאִי בָּעֵית אֵימָא: הָא דְּמַעֲלֶה
אָבָק, [5]הָא דְּלָא מַעֲלֶה אָבָק.
[6]וַאֲמַר רַב יְהוּדָה: זִיקָא דְּבָתַר
מִיטְרָא כְּמִיטְרָא. [7]עִיבָא דְּבָתַר
מִיטְרָא כְּמִיטְרָא. [8]שִׁימְשָׁא
דְּבָתַר מִיטְרָא כִּתְרֵי מִטְרֵי.
[9]לְמַעוּטֵי מַאי?
[10]לְמַעוּטֵי גִּילְהֵי דְלֵילְיָא,
וְשִׁמְשָׁא דְּבֵינֵי קָרְחֵי.
[11]אֲמַר רָבָא: מַעֲלֵי תַּלְגָּא
לְטוּרֵי כְּחַמְשָׁה מִטְרֵי לְאַרְעָא,

RASHI

רזיא — בכח, ולא גרסינן ואי בעית אימא הא והא כו׳, אלא הכי גרסינן: הא דמעלה אבק הא דלא מעלה אבק, והיינו הך. **כמיטרא** — שניות למטר, כדקתני בתוספתא. **למעוטי מאי** — מאחר דכולהו כמיטרא, מאי קמעטינן דהוי בתריה, ולא הוי כמיטרא? **ילהי דליליא** — *אישלושטר״א בלעז. בגילהי הוה קאי במסכת (פסחים יג,א), ורוב גילהי בלילה שכיח. **וביומא שמשא דביני קרחי** — שבין העבים שנראה במקום אחד אורה ובמקום אחר מעונן, כקרחת שיש לו שערות במקום אחד וקרחה במקום אחר. **מעלי תלגא לטורי** — וכל שכן לבקעה, אלא הרים אין להם גשמים אלא שלג, שהגשמים יורדין למטה ואין ההר שותה מהן. ועוד, שלג שבעמקים נמס והולך מפני החום ששולט שם — כמים הוא, אבל בהרים קרוי שלג. **בחמשה מיטרי לארעא** — דהכי משמע קרא ״כי לשלג יאמר הוא ארץ״ כשיאמר לשלג הוה ארץ — הרי הוא כגשם מטר וגשם מטרות, והרי יש כאן חמשה.

NOTES

הָא דַּאֲתָא נִיחָא **This refers to wind that comes gently.** Our commentary follows *Rabbenu Ḥananel* and others, who explain that the Gemara is referring here to the wind, which may blow gently or with great force. A gentle wind after rain is beneficial, but a strong wind after rain can cause considerable damage. This explanation fits in well with the reading found in the standard texts of our Gemara, according to which this distinction is followed by: "And if you wish say, etc.," which implies that a second distinction will now be offered.

Rashi understands the matter differently. He explains that the Gemara is referring here to rain, which may fall lightly or heavily. Wind that follows light rain is beneficial, because light rain does not raise dust, but wind that follows heavy rain is detrimental, because the wind will carry the dust raised by the rain and deposit it upon the crops. According to *Rashi,* the words, "And if you wish say," must be omitted, because what follows is merely an explanation of what came before.

גִּילְהֵי דְלֵילְיָא **The glow of night.** Our commentary follows *Tosafot,* who explains this expression as a reference to moonrise (see also *Rashi* and *Arukh*). *Rabbenu Elyakim* explains that the word גִּילְהֵי is derived from the root גלה, meaning "to uncover." Thus the expression refers to a situation in which the clouds have scattered and the sky has become clear after rain at night.

Yishmael (or "Ulla, the traveler down to Babylonia"), Torah rulings are recorded in his name. Many scholars of the next generation were his pupils.

Of his private life we know nothing. It is possible that the Amora Rabbah the son of Ulla was his son.

We know that Ulla died in Babylonia on one of his journeys, and that he was brought back to Eretz Israel to be buried.

רַב יְהוּדָה **Rav Yehudah.** The name of Rav Yehudah without any patronymic in the Gemara refers to Rav Yehudah bar Yeḥezkel, one of the greatest Babylonian Amoraim of the second generation. He was the founder of the Pumbedita Yeshivah. According to tradition he was born on the day Rabbi Yehudah HaNasi died (*Kiddushin* 72b). His father, Rav Yeḥezkel, was an Amora of the first generation, and Rami bar Yeḥezkel was his brother. He studied under Rav and Shmuel, and Shmuel used to call him שִׁינְנָא — "the sharp-witted one." Rav Sheshet was his colleague, and among his students were Rabbah, Rav Yosef, Rabbi Zera and others. Eretz Israel was very dear to him, but he nevertheless strongly opposed the emigration from Babylonia of his students who wanted to live in Eretz Israel. The Hebrew language was also very dear to him, and he used it frequently.

LANGUAGE

רַזְיָא **Forcefully.** This word has the connotation of "strength," or "forcefulness." Some authorities believe that it is derived from the Greek word ῥῶσις, *rhosis,* meaning "strength" or "violence."

LANGUAGE (RASHI)

אישלושטר״א* A word similar to the Old French *lustre,* meaning "sparkle" or "glitter."

BACKGROUND

שִׁימְשָׁא דְּבָתַר מִיטְרָא **Sun that is after rain.** After a considerable amount of rain has fallen, the sun's heat causes the water to evaporate and to be absorbed by the fine fibers of the roots of plants. The combination of water and bright sunlight

hastens the growth of the plants' leaves.

LANGUAGE

פַּרְצִידָא A seed. This word means "a seed," or "a kernel," and is similar to the Arabic word فرصد with the same meaning.

צוֹרְבָא מֵרַבָּנַן A Rabbinic scholar. This is a common term for a scholar (usually a young scholar) in the Talmud, though its source and precise significance are not clear. Some suggest that it derives from the root צרב — something hot, burning with the fire of Torah. Others suggest that it is derived from the Arabic word ضرب meaning "hard," or "strong," for indeed a צוֹרְבָא מֵרַבָּנַן has a sharp and powerful mind (*Rav Hai Gaon*).

BACKGROUND

מַעֲלֵי תַּלְגָּא לְטוּרֵי Snow is as beneficial to mountains. Snow is mentioned in connection with mountains not only because in the Middle East it is rare for snow to fall on low ground, but also because snow is especially good for mountain plants. On the one hand, the snow creates a ventilated stratum isolated from heat, so that the plants can continue developing beneath it; also, the snow melts slowly, and almost all of it is absorbed by the soil and by the roots of the plants. On the other hand, even if the snow melts too fast, the fact that this occurs in the mountains means that the excess water does not collect and create a marsh, but flows down without causing damage.

עוּרְפִּילָא Drizzle. This term refers to the finest rain, consisting of drops of mist that have condensed slightly but fall softly and slowly. The earth absorbs such drizzle well. Since this kind of rain fills the air, even places that ordinary rain does not reach are moistened by it.

צוֹרְבָא מֵרַבָּנַן A Rabbinic scholar. Such a person is expected to serve as an example of pious conduct, and not just be learned in the Torah. Hence, Rabbinic scholars are often expected to act more strictly than ordinary people, particularly

TRANSLATION AND COMMENTARY

does not fall. [1]Rava infers this **from the** following **verse** (Job 37:6), **which says: "For He says to the snow, 'Be on the earth,' and to the small rain, and to the great rain of His strength."** This verse describes the different kinds of rain that God sends to the world at different times. The word "rain" (גֶּשֶׁם or מָטָר in Hebrew) appears four times in this verse, and in one case it appears in the plural (מִטְרוֹת), to make a total of five. Hence Rava argues that the verse compares snow on the one hand to five references to rain on the other. Thus we see that snow can be as beneficial as five rainfalls.

וַאֲמַר רָבָא [2]The Gemara continues with another statement of Rava on the same topic. **Rava said:** Different forms of precipitation have different effects. **Snow is good for mountains;** [3]**heavy rain is good for trees,** for trees are strong enough to withstand it, and it penetrates to their roots; [4]**light rain is good for produce** such as grain, providing needed water without causing damage; [4A] and **drizzle** helps seed to germinate, for although it is not as strong as even light rain, it moistens the topsoil where it is cracked, so that [5]**even a seed beneath a clod of earth** benefits from it.

מַאי עוּרְפִּילָא [6]The Gemara notes that Rava's insight may be connected to a play on words involving the Aramaic word *urpila* (עוּרְפִּילָא — "drizzle") itself. **What,** asks the Gemara, **is** the meaning of the word *urpila?*

עוּרוּ, פִּילֵי [7]The Gemara answers: It is a combination of two words, *uru pilei* (עוּרוּ פִּילֵי), which mean: **"Wake up, you furrows,"** and cause the seeds that are in the cracks of the topsoil to germinate.

וַאֲמַר רָבָא [8]Having mentioned Rava's statement about the seed that germinates under the clod of earth, the Gemara cites another statement of Rava which makes use of the same concept. **Rava said: A** young **Rabbinic scholar is like a seed beneath a clod of earth.** [9]**For** although his progress may initially be slow, **when he does sprout, he goes on sprouting,** and does not stop until he becomes a full-fledged Torah scholar.

וַאֲמַר רָבָא [10]The Gemara cites another statement by Rava about young Torah scholars. **Rava said: When** a young **Rabbinic scholar is angry,** judge him sympathetically, for [11]**it is the Torah** that he has learned

[1]שֶׁנֶּאֱמַר: ״כִּי לַשֶּׁלֶג יֹאמַר, ׳הֱוֵא אָרֶץ׳, וְגֶשֶׁם מָטָר, וְגֶשֶׁם מִטְרוֹת עֻזּוֹ״.
[2]וַאֲמַר רָבָא: תַּלְגָּא לְטוּרֵי; [3]מִטְרָא רַזְיָא לְאִילָנֵי; [4]מִטְרָא נִיחָא לְפֵירֵי; [4A] עוּרְפִּילָא [5]אֲפִילּוּ לְפַרְצִידָא דְּתוּתֵי קָלָא מְהַנְיָא לֵיהּ.
[6]מַאי עוּרְפִּילָא?
[7]״עוּרוּ, פִּילֵי״.
[8]וַאֲמַר רָבָא: הַאי צוֹרְבָא מֵרַבָּנַן דָּמֵי לְפַרְצִידָא דְּתוּתֵי קָלָא, [9]דְּכֵיוָן דְּנָבַט, נָבַט.
[10]וַאֲמַר רָבָא: הַאי צוֹרְבָא מֵרַבָּנַן דְּרָתַח, [11]אוֹרַיְיתָא הוּא

LITERAL TRANSLATION

[1]as it is said: "For He says to the snow, 'Be on the earth,' and to the small rain, and to the great rain of His strength."

[2]And Rava said: Snow is [good] for mountains; [3]heavy rain is [good] for trees; [4]light rain is [good] for produce; [4A] drizzle is of benefit [5]even to a seed that is under a clod [of earth].

[6]What is *urpila* ("drizzle")?

[7]"Wake up, furrows."

[8]And Rava said: A Rabbinic scholar is similar to a seed that is under a clod [of earth], [9]for when he sprouts, he sprouts.

[10]And Rava said: When a Rabbinic scholar is angry, [11]it is the Torah

RASHI

מיטרא ניחא — שיורד בנחת יפה לפירות התבואה. **עורפילא** — גשמים דקים, כך שמן כדלקמן. **אפילו לפרצידא דתותי קלא** — הגרעין שתחת גושה של קרקע. **מהניא** — שמתחיל לצבץ ולעלות מיד. **עורו פילי** — שסותם סדקי הארץ, לשון אחר: שמגדלת ומצמחת הגרעינין העומדין בסדקי הקרקע. **צורבא מרבנן** — בחור חריף, כמו ביעי דצרינן במסכת ביצה (ז, א), תלמיד חכם זקן לא קרי צורבא, אלא ״ההוא מרבנן״ קרי ליה. **כיון דנבט נבט** — שמתחיל לצבץ ולעלות — עולה למעלה, כך תלמיד חכם, כיון שיצא שמו — הולך וגדל למעלה.

NOTES

דָּמֵי לְפַרְצִידָא דְּתוּתֵי קָלָא Is similar to a seed that is under a clod of earth. Most commentators explain that a young Torah scholar is compared here to a seed under a clod of earth because they are both hidden from the eye — the seed because it is still buried in the ground, and the Torah scholar because he has not yet earned a reputation and become the focus of public attention. But just as the seed sprouts, breaks through the ground, and grows into a plant that is visible to all, so too does a young Torah scholar begin to sprout, and he continues to grow in scholarship until one day he is recognized as a famous Sage. Others suggest that the analogy is to be understood differently: Just as a seed buried in the ground is protected from the elements, so too is a young Torah scholar protected from danger, for the Torah he studies shields him from all harm (*Rabbenu Elyakim*).

TRANSLATION AND COMMENTARY

that makes him angry. Rava demonstrates this point with a play on words, based on the Aramaic word for being angry (רתח), which literally means "to boil water over fire." [1]Now **the verse** says (Jeremiah 23:29): **"Is not my word like fire, says the Lord."** Since the Torah is compared to fire, we should not be surprised at the fiery temper of a young Torah scholar.

וְאָמַר רַב אַשִׁי [2]The Gemara now cites a similar statement by Rav Ashi about Torah scholars, based on the same verse. **Rav Ashi said: Any Torah scholar who is not as hard as iron is not a Torah scholar,** [3]**as** we see from the end of this **verse** in Jeremiah, which **says:** "Is not my word like fire, says the Lord, **and like a hammer that smashes a rock."** We see from this verse that the word of God is compared to an iron hammer that smashes rocks. Torah scholars, too, must have the characteristics of iron.

אֲמַר לֵיהּ [4]**Rabbi Abba said to Rav Ashi: You learn** the idea that Torah scholars must be as hard as iron **from** the verse **there,** in Jeremiah. [5]**We learn** the same idea **from here,** a verse in the Torah itself, **as it is written** (Deuteronomy 8:9): **"A land whose stones are iron."** Literally, the verse is referring to Eretz Israel, where iron ore is found on the surface of the ground. But Rabbi Abba finds another meaning in the verse, by making a play on words: [6]**Do not read** the Hebrew word ***"avaneha"*** (אֲבָנֶיהָ — "**its stones**") **but *"boneha"*** (בּוֹנֶיהָ — "**its builders**"). By replacing the expression "its stones" with the very similarly spelled expression "its builders," Rabbi Abba makes the verse read: "A land whose builders are iron." Rabbi Abba argues that the builders of the world, who are made of iron, are the Torah scholars. Thus the verse in Deuteronomy teaches us that Torah scholars must be as hard as iron, just as Rav Ashi inferred from the verse in Jeremiah.

אֲמַר רָבִינָא [7]Having cited Rav Ashi and Rabbi Abba on the strong convictions and unyielding principles that must guide Torah scholars, the Gemara concludes with a statement of **Ravina,** who **said: Even** though it is true that a Torah scholar must have these characteristics, nevertheless every **person must train himself to act with gentleness,** [8]**as it is said** (Ecclesiastes 11:10): **"And remove anger from your heart,** and put away evil from your flesh." Thus we see that a person who wishes to serve God must not surrender to his anger, but must train himself to develop a more understanding character.

דְּקָא מַרְתַּחָא לֵיהּ, [1]שֶׁנֶּאֱמַר: "הֲלוֹא כֹה דְבָרִי כָּאֵשׁ, נְאֻם ה׳".

[2]וְאָמַר רַב אַשִׁי: כָּל תַּלְמִיד חָכָם שֶׁאֵינוֹ קָשֶׁה כַּבַּרְזֶל אֵינוֹ תַּלְמִיד חָכָם, [3]שֶׁנֶּאֱמַר: "וּכְפַטִּישׁ יְפֹצֵץ סָלַע".

[4]אֲמַר לֵיהּ רַבִּי אַבָּא לְרַב אַשִׁי: אַתּוּן מֵהָתָם מַתְנִיתוּ לָהּ. [5]אֲנַן מֵהָכָא מַתְנִינַן לָהּ, דִּכְתִיב: "אֶרֶץ אֲשֶׁר אֲבָנֶיהָ בַרְזֶל". [6]אַל תִּקְרֵי "אֲבָנֶיהָ" אֶלָּא "בּוֹנֶיהָ".

[7]אֲמַר רָבִינָא: אֲפִילּוּ הָכִי, מִיבָּעֵי לֵיהּ לְאִינִישׁ לְמֵילַף נַפְשֵׁיהּ בְּנִיחוּתָא, [8]שֶׁנֶּאֱמַר: "וְהָסֵר כַּעַס מִלִּבֶּךָ, וגו׳".

LITERAL TRANSLATION

that makes him angry, [1]as it is said: "Is not my word like fire, says the Lord."

[2]And Rav Ashi said: Any Torah scholar who is not as hard as iron is not a Torah scholar, [3]as it is said: "And like a hammer that smashes a rock."

[4]Rabbi Abba said to Rav Ashi: You learn it from there. [5]We learn it from here, as it is written: "A land whose stones are iron." [6]Do not read *"avaneha"* ["its stones"] but *"boneha"* ["its builders"].

[7]Ravina said: Even so, a person must teach himself [to act] with gentleness, [8]as it is said: "And remove anger from your heart, etc."

RASHI

אורייתא מרתחא ליה – שיש לו רוחב לב מתוך תורתו, ומשים ללבו יותר משאר בני אדם, וקא משמע לן דחייבין לדונו לכף זכות. **באש** – שמחמם כל גופו. **בוניה** – תלמידי חכמים מקיימי עולם בבנייניהו. **ברזל** – קפדנים וקשים כברזל.

NOTES

אוֹרַיְיתָא הוּא דְּקָא מַרְתַּחָא לֵיהּ It is the Torah that makes him angry. Many commentators have expressed astonishment at some of the statements made in our passage, for it follows from what Rava says that anger — which is elsewhere likened to idolatry — is actually a quality that a person who devotes himself to Torah study acquires together with his Torah scholarship. Some Rishonim explain that, as a person devotes himself increasingly to Torah study and to the spiritual world, he becomes sensitive to evil and injustice. Thus Rava offers a defense for those

HALAKHAH

לְמֵילַף נַפְשֵׁיהּ בְּנִיחוּתָא To train himself in gentleness. Anger is an exceedingly bad quality, from which one should distance oneself to the far extreme. A person should train himself not to be angry, even in cases where anger would be appropriate. If he wishes to instill fear in his household or in the community over which he is a head so that they improve their ways, he may make a show of being angry with them, but inside he must remain composed. (*Rambam, Sefer Mada, Hilkhot De'ot* 2:3.)

where others might suspect that they have done something forbidden. Indeed, an unwitting transgression committed by a Rabbinic scholar is regarded as having been committed intentionally (שִׁגְגַת תַּלְמִיד חָכָם עוֹלָה זָדוֹן) Nevertheless, Rabbinic scholars are sometimes permitted to do things forbidden to ordinary people, since the latter, being less knowledgeable in the law, are more likely to fall unwittingly into transgression.

BACKGROUND

שֶׁאֵינוֹ קָשֶׁה כַּבַּרְזֶל Who is not as hard as iron. These words apply not only to the uncompromising character of a Torah scholar, but also to his manner of studying and arguing. "A man as hard as iron" is a man who insists on the greatest precision in citing rulings and in drawing conclusions from them, one who makes no concessions regarding any flaw in an argument or proof. This quality of his in study helps to make him a figure of uncompromising intellectual honesty.

לְמֵילַף נַפְשֵׁיהּ בְּנִיחוּתָא Teach himself to act with gentleness. Ravina comments that, despite the many advantages of a hot and uncompromising temperament, nevertheless in the larger scheme of moral improvement it is better for a person to act pleasantly and gently. Anger and firmness are liable to expand to undesirable proportions and to corrupt the soul of a their possessor. By contrast, pleasant conduct leads not only to better relations with people but also to self-control against unchecked outbursts.

SAGES

רָבִינָא Ravina. A Babylonian Amora of the fifth and sixth generations, Ravina apparently came from Mata Meḥasya, though some authorities claim that he came from Eretz Israel. He was among Rava's students. The Gemara records Halakhic discussions between the two and, more frequently, between Ravina and various other students of Rava. Although Ravina was older than Rav Ashi, he accepted him as his teacher and became his student and colleague. Ravina was apparently also actively

¹אָמַר רַבִּי שְׁמוּאֵל בַּר נַחְמָנִי אָמַר רַבִּי יוֹנָתָן: שְׁלֹשָׁה שָׁאֲלוּ שֶׁלֹּא כַּהוֹגֶן. ²לִשְׁנַיִם הֱשִׁיבוּהוּ כַּהוֹגֶן; לְאֶחָד הֱשִׁיבוּהוּ שֶׁלֹּא כַּהוֹגֶן. ³וְאֵלּוּ הֵן: אֱלִיעֶזֶר עֶבֶד אַבְרָהָם, וְשָׁאוּל בֶּן קִישׁ, וְיִפְתָּח הַגִּלְעָדִי.

⁴אֱלִיעֶזֶר עֶבֶד אַבְרָהָם, ⁵דִּכְתִיב: "וְהָיָה הַנַּעֲרָה אֲשֶׁר אֹמַר אֵלֶיהָ, 'הַטִּי נָא כַדֵּךְ', וגו'". ⁶יָכוֹל אֲפִילּוּ חִיגֶּרֶת, אֲפִילּוּ סוּמָא. ⁷הֱשִׁיבוֹ כַּהוֹגֶן, וְנִזְדַּמְּנָה לוֹ רִבְקָה.

LITERAL TRANSLATION

¹Rabbi Shmuel bar Nahmani said in the name of Rabbi Yonatan: Three [people] entreated [God] improperly. ²To two He responded properly; to one He responded improperly. ³And these are they: Eliezer the servant of Abraham, and Saul the son of Kish, and Jephthah the Gileadite.

⁴Eliezer the servant of Abraham, ⁵as it is written: "And let it come to pass that the maiden to whom I shall say, 'Let down your pitcher, I pray you,' etc." ⁶She could even have been lame, [or] even blind. ⁷[Nevertheless] He responded to him properly, and Rebecca chanced to meet him.

TRANSLATION AND COMMENTARY

אָמַר רַבִּי שְׁמוּאֵל בַּר נַחְמָנִי ¹The Gemara now returns to the topic of dew and rain. It begins by citing a Midrashic analysis of hasty vows described in the Bible, and uses this as an introduction to an Amoraic statement comparing the benefits of dew and of rain. **Rabbi Shmuel bar Nahmani said in the name of Rabbi Yonatan: Three people** in the Bible **entreated God improperly.** Three Scriptural personalities vowed to do something to whoever accomplished a certain task. All three personalities behaved improperly in their vows, in that they made their vows in haste and did not consider all the implications carefully. ²Nevertheless, **to two** of them God **responded properly,** and selected the perfect subject; but **to one** of the three personalities, God **responded improperly,** and punished the person who had made the vow by selecting a subject who technically fulfilled the stipulated condition but was otherwise disastrously unsuitable. ³**And these are the** three personalities: **Eliezer the servant of Abraham, Saul the son of Kish, and Jephthah the Gileadite.**

אֱלִיעֶזֶר עֶבֶד אַבְרָהָם ⁴Rabbi Shmuel bar Nahmani in the name of Rabbi Yonatan now explains each of these cases in turn. **Eliezer the servant of Abraham** was entrusted by his master with a mission — to travel to Haran and to find a wife suitable for Abraham's son, Isaac. When Eliezer reached Haran, he prayed to God to help him in his search. He set a task for the girls of the town to fulfill that would demonstrate their kindheartedness, and asked God to select a girl who would pass the test, ⁵**as it is written** (Genesis 24:14): **"And let it come to pass that the maiden to whom I shall say, 'Let down your pitcher, I pray you,** that I may drink,' and she shall say, 'Drink, and I will give your camels drink also,' let her be the one that You have appointed for your servant Isaac." Eliezer's vow was improper and hasty, for while it was important for Isaac's wife to be kindhearted, Eliezer was obliged to consider other factors as well and not leave them to chance. The first girl who passed the test might have been unsuitable. ⁶**She could even have been lame or blind.** ⁷**Nevertheless,** God did not punish Eliezer for his lack of caution, but **responded to him properly** and generously, **and** the girl who **chanced to meet him** was none other than **Rebecca,** Isaac's cousin, who was perfectly suited for Isaac in every way.

RASHI

שלשה שאלו כו' — משום דרבי ברכיה מיירי בגשמים לקמן, נקט לה. **ובנות אנשי העיר יוצאות והיה הנערה** — משמע: הנערה היוצאה תחילה מן העיר, ויאמר לה השקיני, לה היה מנחש. **אפילו חיגרת אפילו סומא** — לפי שלא פירש בשאילתו, ואפשר שתהיה בעלת מום, ולא יכין בה אליעזר ויקחנה. **(אלא) השיבוהו כהוגן** — וזימנו לו רבקה.

NOTES

young Torah scholars who react with anger to what most people would consider relatively minor infractions. This anger, argues Rava, is not a sign of defective moral character, but rather the mark of unusual sensitivity (see *Rashi, Meiri,* and *Shittah*).

The statements of Rav Ashi and Rabbi Abba pose an even greater difficulty, for they argue that a person who is not as hard as iron cannot be a true Torah scholar, thus implying that susceptibility to anger is not only a necessary by-product of a Torah scholar's immersion in his spiritual life, but rather a quality that a true Torah scholar must nourish and develop. This is particularly difficult to understand in the light of statements made elsewhere in the Talmud that a Sage or Prophet who allows himself to become angry loses his wisdom or power of prophecy, as is evidenced from incidents involving Moses and Elisha. *Gevurat Ari* concludes from this that, although a Torah scholar must in fact train himself to show gentleness, as argued by Ravina, it is sometimes proper for him to express his anger in the most forceful way. If a Torah scholar sees injustice, and he knows that there is no other way to right the wrong without expressing his anger, and he is also sure that the wrong will be righted if he indeed admonishes the wrongdoer, it is proper for him to administer the rebuke in the strongest terms.

לְאֶחָד הֱשִׁיבוּהוּ שֶׁלֹּא כַּהוֹגֶן To one He responded improperly. Many commentators ask why God responded properly to Eliezer and to Saul, whereas Jephthah received an

---

involved in the editing of the Babylonian Talmud, which was accomplished by Rav Ashi. We have little information about his private life, though the Talmud implies that he had children. Rav Ashi's sons were students of Ravina. He also had many other students, the most important of whom was Ravina the Younger (רְבִינָא זוּטֵי), his sister's son, who completed the main task of the final editing of the Talmud.

SAGES

רַבִּי שְׁמוּאֵל בַּר נַחְמָנִי Rabbi Shmuel bar Nahmani. A Palestinian Amora of the second and third generations, Rabbi Shmuel bar Nahmani was an important teacher of Aggadah. He was a disciple of Rabbi Yonatan and transmitted many teachings in his name. He also studied with Rabbi Yehoshua ben Levi. He lived in Lydda in central Palestine.

BACKGROUND

שְׁלֹשָׁה שָׁאֲלוּ שֶׁלֹּא כַּהוֹגֶן Three people entreated God improperly. Although the oaths that a person may take in a time of distress are not regarded as inherently improper, the Gemara emphasizes here how important it is for a person to be cautious and to avoid saying anything liable to have adverse effects. Jephthah's oath is an example of the terrible consequences that can result from an improperly sworn oath, and the Gemara explains that in the other cases, where such an oath did not lead to disastrous results, it was because of heavenly mercy and the merit of righteous people. But Jephthah, who is described in the Bible as a coarse and harsh man, was punished for the improper oath he took.

[1]שָׁאוּל בֶּן קִישׁ, [2]דִּכְתִיב: ״וְהָיָה הָאִישׁ אֲשֶׁר יַכֶּנּוּ, יַעְשְׁרֶנּוּ הַמֶּלֶךְ עֹשֶׁר גָּדוֹל, וְאֶת בִּתּוֹ יִתֶּן לוֹ״. [3]יָכוֹל אֲפִילּוּ עֶבֶד, אֲפִילּוּ מַמְזֵר. [4]הֱשִׁיבוֹ כַּהוֹגֶן, וְנִזְדַּמֵּן לוֹ דָּוִד.

[5]יִפְתָּח הַגִּלְעָדִי, [6]דִּכְתִיב: ״וְהָיָה הַיּוֹצֵא אֲשֶׁר יֵצֵא מִדַּלְתֵי בֵיתִי, וגו׳״. [7]יָכוֹל אֲפִילּוּ דָּבָר טָמֵא. [8]הֱשִׁיבוֹ שֶׁלֹּא כַּהוֹגֶן, [9]נִזְדַּמְּנָה לוֹ בִּתּוֹ.

[10]וְהַיְינוּ דְּקָאָמַר לְהוּ נָבִיא לְיִשְׂרָאֵל: [11]״הַצֳּרִי אֵין בְּגִלְעָד? אִם רוֹפֵא אֵין שָׁם?״.

LITERAL TRANSLATION

[1]Saul the son of Kish, [2]as it is written: "And it shall be that the man who kills him, the king will enrich him with great wealth, and will give him his daughter." [3]He could even have been a slave, [or] even a *mamzer*. [4][Nevertheless] He responded to him properly, and David chanced to come to him.

[5]Jephthah the Gileadite, [6]as it is written: "And it shall be that whatever comes out of the doors of my house, etc." [7]It could even have been an unclean thing. [8]He responded to him improperly, [9][and] his daughter chanced to come [out] to him.

[10]And this is what the Prophet said to Israel: [11]"Is there no balm in Gilead? Is there no physician there?"

RASHI

דבר טמא — כלב או חזיר. **והיינו דאמר להו נביא כו׳** — מדגלי ביה קרא ואמר ״הצרי אין בגלעד״ [אלמא דלא הוי ניחא קמי שמיא, כדאמרינן ״הצרי אין בגלעד״] פנחס היה שם, והיה יכול להתיר נדרו. אלא שלא רצה יפתח לילך אצלו, והוא לא רצה לבוא אצל יפתח, בבראשית רבה.

TRANSLATION AND COMMENTARY

שָׁאוּל בֶּן קִישׁ [1]Similarly, King **Saul the son of Kish** faced a grave challenge in his struggle with the Philistines, when Goliath challenged the Israelites to produce a champion to fight him in single combat. Nobody volunteered, so King Saul made a vow, promising to favor whoever successfully fought and killed Goliath, [2]**as it is written** (I Samuel 17:25): **"And it shall be that the man who kills him, the king will enrich him with great wealth, and will give him his daughter."** Saul's vow was improper and hasty, for he was promising to give this champion to his daughter in marriage, and the man who passed the test might have been unsuitable. [3]**He could even have been a slave or a mamzer** (the offspring of an incestuous or adulterous union) — both of whom are forbidden to marry any Jewish woman. [4]**Nevertheless,** God did not punish King Saul for his lack of caution, but **responded to him properly** and generously, **and** the champion who **chanced to come to him** was none other than **David,** who became the supreme example of Jewish royalty.

יִפְתָּח הַגִּלְעָדִי [5]Similarly, **Jephthah the Gileadite** fought a war against the Ammonites. He called upon God to help him, and vowed to sacrifice the first creature that came out of his house, if he was victorious, [6]**as it is written** (Judges 11:31): **"And it shall be that whatever comes out of the doors of my house** to meet me, when I return in peace from the children of Ammon, shall surely be the Lord's, and I will offer it up as a burnt-offering." Jephthah's vow was improper and hasty, for even assuming that the first creature that came out of his house was an animal, it might still have been unsuitable for a sacrifice. [7]**It could even have been an unclean thing** such as a dog or a pig, which may not be eaten by Jews, let alone be offered as a sacrifice. [8]In this case, God punished Jephthah for his lack of caution, and **responded to him improperly.** [9]God selected the worst possible subject for his vow, **and** the one who **chanced to come out to him** was none other than **his** own **daughter.**

וְהַיְינוּ דְּקָאָמַר לְהוּ [10]The Gemara pauses briefly in its discussion of vows made in haste, to dwell on the sacrifice of Jephthah's daughter: **And this is what the Prophet** Jeremiah was referring to, when he **said to Israel** (Jeremiah 8:22): [11]**"Is there no balm in Gilead? Is there no physician there?** Why then has the health of the daughter of my people not recovered?" Literally, Jeremiah is referring to the decline of the Kingdom of Judah as the destruction of the Temple approached. But the mention of Gilead suggests Jephthah the Gileadite, and according to this homiletic interpretation Jeremiah is decrying Jephthah's failure to escape his impetuous vow, although there is an accepted Torah procedure for annulling vows that turn out to have unanticipated consequences (see note).

NOTES

improper response. *Iyyun Ya'akov* explains that both Eliezer and Saul asked for a sign from God: Eliezer assumed that a girl who was ready to give his camels to drink would be appropriate for Isaac, and Saul assumed that a man who could defeat the Philistines would be a fitting husband for his daughter. But Jephthah wished to offer a sacrifice to God. Why, then, did he formulate his vow in such an irresponsible way, not allowing for the possibility that the first thing to emerge from the door of his house might not be suitable for the altar? It would have been better had he not taken a vow at all. Consequently God responded to him improperly, causing his daughter to be the first to leave his house to greet him.

״הַצֳּרִי אֵין בְּגִלְעָד?״ **"Is there no balm in Gilead?"** The mention of Gilead seems to have been understood by the Midrash as a double allusion — to Jephthah the Gileadite

BACKGROUND

"אֲשֶׁר לֹא צִוִּיתִי" "Which I did not command." Human sacrifice was widespread in many cultures and also penetrated Jewish society of the Biblical period through the cult of Moloch. Doubtless there were people who viewed human sacrifice, especially that of their children, as the highest level of self-sacrifice. But the Torah expresses deep revulsion against all human sacrifice (see Deuteronomy 12:31), and this verse from Jeremiah is interpreted as an allusion to the three instances of human sacrifice mentioned in the Bible. It says "which I did not command," in reference to Mesha the King of Moab, who, since he was not Jewish, was not commanded to make a sacrifice, and certainly not any human sacrifice. "And I did not speak" refers to Jephthah, whom God certainly did not tell what to do, for he himself spoke and took the oath. "And did not come into my heart" refers to what seemed to have been an explicit command to sacrifice Isaac, which the Torah prefaces and explains with the remark, "And the Lord tested Abraham."

כְּנֶסֶת יִשְׂרָאֵל The community of Israel. This passage teaches us that not only a private individual is liable to err in petitioning God, but also the Jewish people as a whole are liable to do so. Therefore we preface the Amidah prayer with the words, "Lord, open my lips," requesting that God grant us the ability to pray and petition in a fit manner. Such requests are also found in many prayers recited by prayer leaders during Rosh HaShanah and Yom Kippur.

SAGES

רַבִּי בֶּרֶכְיָה Rabbi Berekhyah. A Palestinian Amora of the fourth generation, Rabbi Berekhyah received and transmitted teachings in the names of Sages of previous generations; in particular, he seems to have been the student of Rabbi Ḥelbo.

He is seldom quoted in the Babylonian Talmud, but his teachings are found often in the Jerusalem Talmud and

TRANSLATION AND COMMENTARY

וּכְתִיב [1] **And** the following **is written** in Jeremiah (19:5) concerning human sacrifice: Jeremiah declares that God abominates this practice, **"which I did not command, and I did not speak, and did not come into My heart."** Since Jeremiah uses three expressions, the Gemara assumes that he is referring to three cases of human sacrifice, which may have been thought to have God's approval. [2] The first expression, **"which I did not command,"** refers to **the son of Mesha the King of Moab,** who was offered as a sacrifice to the God of Israel, in the hope that He would spare the Moabites from being destroyed by the Israelites. [3] This episode is described **in the following verse** (II Kings 3:27): **"And he took his firstborn son, who would reign after him, and he offered him as a burnt-offering."** Even though God later became angry with Israel, and Moab was saved, nevertheless the human sacrifice was not in accordance with God's command. [4] The second expression, **"and I did not speak,"** refers to **Jephthah** who (according to some opinions) sacrificed his daughter in fulfillment of an impetuous vow. Even though the verse states that Jephthah felt obliged to fulfill his vow, it was not in accordance with God's command. [5] The third expression, **"and did not come into My heart,"** refers to **Isaac the son of Abraham,** who was prepared as a sacrifice and bound on the altar at the command of God (Genesis 22:1-19). At the last moment, God commanded Abraham not to sacrifice Isaac and explained that the entire episode had been no more than a test. Thus, even though this particular human sacrifice had indeed been commanded and was indeed in accordance with the will of God, it had not in fact entered God's heart, as it was never intended to be carried out in practice.

אָמַר רַבִּי בֶּרֶכְיָה [6] The Gemara now returns to the subject of improper entreaties, citing an Amoraic statement in which the benefits of rain and of dew are compared. **Rabbi Berekhyah said: The community of Israel also entreated God improperly,**

[1] וּכְתִיב: "אֲשֶׁר לֹא צִוִּיתִי, וְלֹא דִבַּרְתִּי, וְלֹא עָלְתָה עַל לִבִּי". [2] "אֲשֶׁר לֹא צִוִּיתִי" — זֶה בְּנוֹ שֶׁל מֵישַׁע מֶלֶךְ מוֹאָב, [3] שֶׁנֶּאֱמַר: "וַיִּקַּח אֶת בְּנוֹ הַבְּכוֹר, אֲשֶׁר יִמְלֹךְ תַּחְתָּיו, וַיַּעֲלֵהוּ עֹלָה". [4] "וְלֹא דִבַּרְתִּי" — זֶה יִפְתָּח. [5] "וְלֹא עָלְתָה עַל לִבִּי" — זֶה יִצְחָק בֶּן אַבְרָהָם. [6] אָמַר רַבִּי בֶּרֶכְיָה: אַף כְּנֶסֶת יִשְׂרָאֵל שָׁאֲלָה שֶׁלֹּא כַּהוֹגֶן,

LITERAL TRANSLATION

[1] And it is written: "Which I did not command, and I did not speak, and did not come into My heart." [2] "Which I did not command" — this is the son of Mesha the King of Moab, [3] as it is said: "And he took his firstborn son, who would reign after him, and he offered him as a burnt-offering." [4] "And I did not speak" — this is Jephthah. [5] "And did not come into My heart" — this is Isaac the son of Abraham.

[6] Rabbi Berekhyah said: The community of Israel also entreated [God] improperly,

RASHI

וכתיב אשר לא צויתי — בירמיה כתיב בפרשת בקבוק [פרק יט]: "ובנו את במות (התופת אשר בגיא בן הנם) לשרוף את (בנותיהם ואת) בניהם באש אשר לא [צויתי ולא] דברתי ולא עלתה על לבי". שלא תאמרו: הלא צוה כמו כן הקדוש ברוך הוא ליפתח ומישע ואברהם, כי מעולם לא צויתי למישע לשרוף את בנו באש, דכתיב "ויקח את בנו הבכור אשר ימלך תחתיו ויעלהו עולה על החומה", ולשמים נתכוון, כסבור היה לרצות להקדוש ברוך הוא, והאי דכתיב "על שרפו עצמות מלך אדום לשיד" — מילתא אחרינא הוא. "ולא דברתי" — ליפתח, "מימים ימימה ותהי חק בישראל". ובתרגום מזכיר פנחס לגנאי ויפתח לגנאי, אלמא: לא היה הקדוש ברוך הוא רוצה בבתו, שהרי מזכירם לגנאי, לפי שלא הלכו זה אצל זה לבטל הנדר. הכי גרסינן: "ולא עלתה על לבי" — זה יצחק בן אברהם, כלומר, שאף על פי שצויתי לו — מעולם לא עלתה על לבי לשחוט בנו, אלא לנסותו, מפני קטיגורו היינו שטן, כדאמר בסנהדרין ב"הנחנקין" (פט,ב): "ויהי אחר הדברים האלה" — אחר דבריו של שטן וכו'. ואית דלא גרסינן האי "ולא עלתה על לבי" בקרא אחרינא, דלא כתב אלא "אשר לא צויתי ולא דברתי" (ירמיהו ז, לא), ובפרשת בקבוק כתיב כל הני שלשה "אשר לא צויתי ולא דברתי ולא עלתה על לבי". בתנחומא: "אשר לא צויתי" — זו בתו של יפתח, אף על פי שצויתי לו תורה ומצות — מצוה זו לא צויתי עליו. "ולא דברתי" זה בנו של מישע מלך מואב, והלא מישע נכרי הוא, ולא חולין הוא לי לדבר עמו אפילו דיבור בעלמא. ובאגדה קא חשיב כָּלֵב בהדייהו "אשר יכה את קרית ספר ולכדָה" וגו'. ורבי יונתן דלא חשיב ליה, דבגמרא פשיט ליה להאי קרא בהלכות שנשתכחו בימי אבלו של משה, כדאמרינן בתמורה (טז, א), ואין לחוש שתשרה רוח הקדש על עבד ועל ממזר, כדאמרינן בנדרים (לח,א): שאין שכינה שורה כו', מפי רבי. וגדעון ששאל למנוע טל מעל הארץ ובגזה לבדה יהיה — אין זה שלא כהוגן, ומה תקלה יש אם יחסר העולם טל לילה אחת לבדו? מפי רבי.

NOTES

and to the Prophet Elijah (whom the Midrash identifies with Phinehas the grandson of Aaron), who was also a Gileadite. Phinehas could have annulled the vow taken by Jephthah, but each of the two thought that it was beneath his dignity to approach the other to dissolve the vow — the one because he was the High Priest, and the other because he was the Judge of Israel. In the end, both Jephthah and Phinehas were punished for their haughtiness, which forced Jephthah's daughter either to live a life of misery (according to *Rashi* and *Tosafot;* see also *Bereshit Rabbah* 60:3) or actually to be sacrificed (*Ramban*).

[1]וְהַקָּדוֹשׁ בָּרוּךְ הוּא הֱשִׁיבָהּ כַּהוֹגֶן, [2]שֶׁנֶּאֱמַר: "וְנֵדְעָה, נִרְדְּפָה לָדַעַת אֶת ה׳. כְּשַׁחַר נָכוֹן מֹצָאוֹ, וְיָבוֹא כַגֶּשֶׁם לָנוּ". [3]אָמַר לָהּ הַקָּדוֹשׁ בָּרוּךְ הוּא: "בִּתִּי, אַתְּ שׁוֹאֶלֶת דָּבָר שֶׁפְּעָמִים מִתְבַּקֵּשׁ וּפְעָמִים אֵינוֹ מִתְבַּקֵּשׁ. [4]אֲבָל אֲנִי אֶהְיֶה לָךְ דָּבָר הַמִּתְבַּקֵּשׁ לְעוֹלָם", [5]שֶׁנֶּאֱמַר: "אֶהְיֶה כַטַּל לְיִשְׂרָאֵל".

[6]וְעוֹד שָׁאֲלָה שֶׁלֹּא כַּהוֹגֶן. [7]אָמְרָה לְפָנָיו: "רִבּוֹנוֹ שֶׁל עוֹלָם, 'שִׂימֵנִי כַחוֹתָם עַל לִבֶּךָ, כַּחוֹתָם עַל זְרוֹעֶךָ'". [8]אָמַר לָהּ הַקָּדוֹשׁ בָּרוּךְ הוּא: "בִּתִּי, אַתְּ שׁוֹאֶלֶת דָּבָר שֶׁפְּעָמִים נִרְאֶה וּפְעָמִים אֵינוֹ נִרְאֶה. [9]אֲבָל אֲנִי אֶעֱשֶׂה לָךְ דָּבָר שֶׁנִּרְאֶה לְעוֹלָם", [10]שֶׁנֶּאֱמַר: "הֵן עַל כַּפַּיִם חַקֹּתִיךְ".

LITERAL TRANSLATION

[1]but the Holy One blessed be He responded to her properly, [2]as it is said: "And let us know, let us pursue so as to know the Lord. His going forth is as sure as morning, and He will come to us like the rain." [3]The Holy One blessed be He said to her: "My daughter, you are asking for something that is sometimes wanted and is sometimes not wanted. [4]But I will be for you something that is always wanted," [5]as it is said: "I will be as the dew to Israel."

[6]And she again entreated [God] improperly. [7]She said before Him: "Master of the world, 'set me as a seal upon your heart, as a seal upon your arm.'" [8]The Holy One blessed be He said to her: "My daughter, you are asking for something that is sometimes seen and is sometimes not seen. [9]But I will make for you something that is always seen," [10]as it is said: "Behold, I have engraved you on the palms of My hands."

TRANSLATION AND COMMENTARY

[1]**but the Holy One blessed be He responded to her properly,** by fulfilling her wish more completely than she had asked. The Prophet Hosea calls upon Israel to return to God, and promises that He will heal Israel's wounds in return, [2]**as it is said** (Hosea 6:3): **"And let us know, let us pursue so as to know the Lord. His going forth is as sure as morning, and He will come to us like the rain."** The Prophet promises that when God heals Israel's wounds, He will be to us as the rain is to the parched ground. Thus the community of Israel has implicitly requested God to be as good to them as rain. [3]But **the Holy One Blessed be He said to her: "My daughter, you are asking** Me to be like rain, **something that is sometimes wanted and is sometimes not wanted.** [4]**But** I will respond to you in a generous spirit and give you more than you asked. **I will be for you something that is always wanted,"** [5]**as it is said** in another verse in Hosea (14:6): **"I will be as the dew to Israel,"** if she repents. Just as dew is always beneficial, regardless of the season, so too will God always be beneficent to a repentant Israel.

וְעוֹד שָׁאֲלָה שֶׁלֹּא כַּהוֹגֶן [6]The Gemara continues: **And** the community of Israel **again entreated God improperly,** on yet another occasion. [7]**She said before Him: "Master of the world, 'set me as a seal upon your heart, as a seal upon your arm'** [Song of Songs 8:6]." The Song of Songs is traditionally interpreted as an allegory symbolizing the love between God and the people of Israel. Thus, in this verse, the shepherdess, symbolizing the community of Israel, asks her lover, symbolizing God, to keep her close to him, like a person keeps his personal seal on a chain over his heart, or on a bracelet upon his arm. [8]**The Holy One blessed be He said to her: "My daughter, you are asking** me to keep you as close as a personal seal, **something that is sometimes seen and is sometimes not seen.** [9]**But** I will respond to you generously and give you more than you asked. **I will do something for you** that will demonstrate our closeness in a way **that is always seen,"** [10]**as it is said** (Isaiah 49:16): **"Behold, I have engraved you on the palms of My hands."** Just as the palms of the hands are always visible, so too will the closeness of God and Israel always be manifest.

RASHI

ויבוא כגשם לנו – פעמים אינו מתבקש, שהוא סימן קללה בקיץ. **דבר המתבקש לעולם** – טל אפילו בימות החמה. **פעמים נראה** – כשהוא ערום נראה זרועו וכנגד לבו, ואינו נראה כשהוא לבוש, והכף נראית כל שעה שהיד נראית לעינים. ויש לומר: "על כפים" – על השמים – צורת אדם שהוא בכסא וכן "נשא לבבנו אל כפים" (איכה ג), מפי רבי.

the Midrashim. Though there are a few Halakhic teachings in his name, most of his statements are Aggadic. The collections of Aggadic Midrash collected in Eretz Israel present many of his homiletic interpretations.

We possess almost no information about his personal life. The Jerusalem Talmud states that his daughter's son, Rabbi Ḥiyya, was also a Torah Sage.

NOTES

וּפְעָמִים אֵינוֹ מִתְבַּקֵּשׁ And is sometimes not wanted. *Riaf* explains that there are times when rain is not wanted even during the rainy season, for too much rain can cause considerable damage. But dew is always wanted, for there can be no such thing as too much dew.

TERMINOLOGY

סְבָרוּהָ **They assumed [that]....** This term introduces an assumption proposed at the beginning of a discussion, but later found to be erroneous.

TRANSLATION AND COMMENTARY

אֵין שׁוֹאֲלִין אֶת הַגְּשָׁמִים [1]The Gemara now considers the next clause of the Mishnah, which reads: **"We only entreat God for rain close to the rainy season."** [2]The Gemara notes that when the Amoraim studied this Mishnah, **they assumed that "entreaty" and "making mention" are one matter** in this Mishnah. Although the Mishnah refers specifically to "entreating God for rain" in the ninth blessing of the Amidah, the Amoraim assumed that the same law would also apply to making mention of rain in the second blessing. But if so, it follows that the author of this line of the Mishnah is of the opinion that we do not even make mention of rain in the second blessing until we are ready to pray for it explicitly in the ninth blessing — at the earliest on the seventh day of Sukkot, when we are about to leave the sukkah. For it is inconceivable that we would pray for rain earlier in the Festival, since rain during Sukkot is an evil omen. [3]**Who, then, is the Tanna** whose viewpoint is reflected in this line of the Mishnah?

אֲמַר רָבָא [4]**Rava said** in reply: **It must be Rabbi Yehoshua, who said** in the Baraita quoted above (2b): "We begin to mention rain in the second blessing of the Amidah **from the time of putting** the lulav **down** on the seventh day of the Sukkot Festival." The author of this line of the Mishnah cannot be Rabbi Yehoshua of the Mishnah or Rabbi Yehudah, because they maintain that we begin to mention rain in the second blessing on the eighth day, and we cannot pray for rain on the eighth day because the ninth blessing of the Amidah (and all the other blessings of petition in the central section of the Amidah) is not recited on full Festivals. Thus the Mishnah must be ruling in favor of the viewpoint of Rabbi Yehoshua in the Baraita. Moreover, by implication, it is also informing us that Rabbi Yehoshua maintains that we begin to pray for rain in the ninth blessing of the Amidah on the seventh day of Sukkot, when we begin to mention rain in the second blessing, and we do not wait until the third or seventh day of the month of Marḥeshvan, as the Mishnah rules below (10a).

אֲמַר לֵיהּ אַבַּיֵי [5]**Abaye said to** Rava: **You may even say that** this line of the Mishnah reflects the viewpoint of **Rabbi Eliezer,** because your basic assumption is mistaken. [6]The term **"entreaty" is** a term **by itself, and** the term **"making mention" is** a term **by itself.** Thus, when the Mishnah ruled that "we only entreat God for rain close to the rainy season," it was referring specifically to the explicit entreaty in the ninth blessing, and everyone agrees that this entreaty is not made until well after Sukkot. The Mishnah here has no bearing

[1]"אֵין שׁוֹאֲלִין אֶת הַגְּשָׁמִים, כו'". [2]סְבָרוּהָ שְׁאֵלָה וְהַזְכָּרָה חֲדָא מִילְּתָא הִיא. [3]מַאן תַּנָּא? [4]אֲמַר רָבָא: רַבִּי יְהוֹשֻׁעַ הִיא, דְּאָמַר: "מִשְּׁעַת הַנָּחָתוֹ". [5]אֲמַר לֵיהּ אַבַּיֵי: אֲפִילּוּ תֵּימָא רַבִּי אֱלִיעֶזֶר. [6]שְׁאֵלָה לְחוּד וְהַזְכָּרָה לְחוּד.

LITERAL TRANSLATION

[1]"We do not pray for rains, etc." [2]They assumed [that] praying and making mention are one thing. [3]Who is the Tanna? [4]Rava said: It is Rabbi Yehoshua, who said: "From the time of putting it down." [5]Abaye said to him: You may even say [that] it is Rabbi Eliezer. [6]Praying is by itself, and making mention is by itself.

RASHI

הכי גרסינן: סברוה שאלה והזכרה חדא מילתא היא – כלומר הא דקתני "אין שואלין את הגשמים" היינו אין מזכירין את הגשמים. **ומאן תנא** – דאמר: סמוך לימות הגשמים מזכירין אבל לא קודם לכן. **רבי יהושע היא** – דאמר: משעת הנחת לולב הוא מזכיר, דהיינו יום שמיני וזהו סמוך לגשמים, דמן החג ואילך הוא זמן גשמים.

NOTES

שְׁאֵלָה וְהַזְכָּרָה חֲדָא מִילְּתָא **Praying and making mention are one thing.** This assumption poses a certain difficulty, for the Mishnah clearly distinguishes between praying for rain and making mention of it, as Rabbi Eliezer says to Rabbi Yehoshua: "I too did not say to pray for but to mention 'Who causes the wind to blow and the rain to fall.'" Why, then, should the Gemara have even considered the possibility that the two terms refer to one and the same thing?

Gevurat Ari suggests that the Gemara assumed that the Mishnah's statement, "We do not pray for rains except close to the season of rains," refers to making mention of rain, because both the previous line in the Mishnah and also the following line refer to the mention of rain, and not to praying for it. Had the Mishnah's middle ruling been referring to praying for rain, it should have appeared after the third ruling, which concludes the discussion regarding the mention of rain.

Rambam (*Commentary to the Mishnah*) explains that the Mishnah's statement, "We do not pray for rain except close to the season of rains," is in accordance with the viewpoint of Rabbi Yehudah, who says in the next line that the mention of rain is first made during the musaf service of the last day of Sukkot. Thus he too understands that praying for rain and mentioning it are one and the same thing — they both refer to the mention of rain in the insertion, "Who causes the wind to blow and the rain to fall."

מַאן תַּנָּא **Who is the Tanna.** The Rishonim offer two basic explanations of the Gemara's question, if we assume that praying for rain is the same as mentioning it. *Rashi* and others explain that the Gemara is looking for a Tanna who

[1]וְאִיכָּא דְּאָמְרִי: [2]לֵימָא [4B] רַבִּי יְהוֹשֻׁעַ הִיא, [3]דְּאָמַר: "מִשְּׁעַת הַנָּחָתוֹ"? [4]אֲמַר רָבָא: אֲפִילּוּ תֵּימָא רַבִּי אֱלִיעֶזֶר. [5]שְׁאֵלָה לְחוּד וְהַזְכָּרָה לְחוּד.

[6]"רַבִּי יְהוּדָה אוֹמֵר: הָעוֹבֵר

LITERAL TRANSLATION

[1]And there are [some] who say: [2]Shall we say [that] [4B] it is Rabbi Yehoshua, [3]who said: "From the time of putting it down"?

[4]Rava said: You may even say [that] it is Rabbi Eliezer. [5]Praying (lit., "asking") is by itself, and mentioning by itself.

[6]"Rabbi Yehudah says: He who passes

RASHI

הכי גרסינן: ואיכא דאמרי לימא רבי יהושע היא אפילו תימא רבי אליעזר כו' — ולא גרסינן סברוה שאלה לחוד והזכרה לחוד, דהא לא משתמע ממתניתין.

TRANSLATION AND COMMENTARY

on the dispute in the Baraita between Rabbi Eliezer and Rabbi Yehoshua regarding "making mention" of rain in the second blessing. Thus this clause of the Mishnah is valid both according to Rabbi Eliezer and according to Rabbi Yehoshua.

וְאִיכָּא דְּאָמְרִי [1]The Gemara now records a variant version of the preceding discussion. **There are some who say** that it was not Rava who made the original erroneous assumption but his students, and that it was Rava rather than Abaye who corrected their understanding of the Mishnah. The students asked Rava: [2]**Shall we say that** this line of the Mishnah [4B] reflects the viewpoint of **Rabbi Yehoshua,** [3]**who said** in the Baraita: "We begin to mention rain in the second blessing of the Amidah **from the time of putting** the lulav **down** at the end of the Sukkot Festival"? For even though the Mishnah referred only to praying for rain (in the ninth blessing), it would appear that the same law should apply to mentioning rain in the second blessing, since this clause appears in the middle of a Mishnah referring to making mention of rain in the second blessing. By the logic of his ruling, the author of this line of the Mishnah should maintain that we do not mention rain until we are ready to pray for it explicitly in the ninth blessing — which means (at the earliest) on the seventh day of Sukkot, when we are about to leave the sukkah. For it is inconceivable that we should pray for rain earlier in the Festival, since rain during Sukkot is an evil omen. Yet it is clear that we begin to mention rain at some point during Sukkot, because God judges the world during Sukkot concerning water. Thus the Mishnah must agree with the viewpoint of Rabbi Yehoshua in the Baraita. Moreover, by implication, it is also informing us that Rabbi Yehoshua maintains that we begin to pray for rain in the ninth blessing of the Amidah on the seventh day of Sukkot, when we begin to mention rain in the second blessing, and we do not wait until the third or seventh day of the month of Marḥeshvan, as the Mishnah rules below (10a).

אֲמַר רָבָא [4]**Rava said** to them: **You may even say that** this line of the Mishnah reflects the viewpoint of **Rabbi Eliezer,** because your assumption is mistaken. [5]The term **"entreaty" is** a term **by itself, and** the term **"making mention" is** a term **by itself**. Thus, when the Mishnah ruled that "we only entreat God for rain close to the rainy season," it was referring specifically to the explicit entreaty in the ninth blessing, and everyone agrees that this insertion is not made until well after Sukkot. The Mishnah was not referring to the dispute between Rabbi Eliezer and Rabbi Yehoshua regarding "making mention" of rain in the second blessing. It is simply ruling that in spite of the difference of opinion regarding the second blessing, everyone agrees that we do not pray for rain in the ninth blessing until the rainy season itself — until the third or the seventh day of the month of Marḥeshvan, as the Mishnah rules below (10a). Thus this clause of the Mishnah is valid according to both Rabbi Eliezer and Rabbi Yehoshua.

רַבִּי יְהוּדָה אוֹמֵר [6]The Gemara now turns to the next clause of the Mishnah: **"Rabbi Yehudah says:** Rain is mentioned for the first time during the musaf Amidah on the eighth day of Sukkot. **Whoever** leads the service in the synagogue, which is called **"passing before the ark,"** on the last holy day of the Festival of Sukkot, the last one, who recites the musaf Amidah aloud, mentions rain in the second blessing, whereas the first one, who recites the morning Amidah aloud, does not mention it. And similarly, on the first holy day of Pesaḥ, when the dry season officially begins and we cease to mention rain in our prayers, the change

NOTES

maintains that we only insert the prayer for rain close to the rainy season and not before. Rava argues that the Tanna must be Rabbi Yehoshua, because according to Rabbi Eliezer rain is mentioned from the first day of Sukkot. *Rabbenu Ḥananel* and others explain that the Gemara is looking for a Tanna who may possibly maintain that we begin to pray for rain on the same day that we begin to mention it. Rava argues that the Tanna must be Rabbi Yehoshua, because according to Rabbi Eliezer we begin to mention rain on the first day of Sukkot, and on that day the prayer for rain cannot be inserted into the Amidah, since the ninth blessing into which the prayer is inserted is not recited on a Festival.

TRANSLATION AND COMMENTARY

is made during the musaf Amidah. Whoever leads the service on the first day of Pesah, the first one, who recites the morning Amidah aloud, continues to mention rain in the second blessing, whereas the last one, who recites the musaf Amidah aloud, does not mention it." From Rabbi Yehudah's statement it would appear that we stop mentioning rain from the middle of the morning service on the first day of Pesah. [1]**But a contradiction can be raised** against this representation of Rabbi Yehudah's view. The next Mishnah (below, 5a) records a Tannaitic dispute about when we stop praying for rain at the beginning of the dry season. According to our Mishnah, we would assume that Rabbi Yehudah maintains that we stop when the congregation recites the musaf Amidah on the first day of Pesah. [2]But the next Mishnah states as follows: **"Until when do we pray for rain** in the ninth blessing of the Amidah? [3]**Rabbi Yehudah says: Until Pesah is over.** [4]**Rabbi Meir says: Until the month of Nisan is over** [about a week after Pesah is over]." Thus we see that Rabbi Yehudah is of the opinion that we continue to pray for rain until the end of Pesah, and it is only in the first Amidah after Pesah, the evening Amidah of the twenty-second of Nisan, that we omit the prayer for rain from the ninth blessing.

אָמַר רַב חִסְדָּא [5]**Rav Hisda said: There is no difficulty** in resolving the contradiction between the viewpoint attributed to Rabbi Yehudah in our Mishnah and that attributed to him in the next Mishnah. [6]**There,** in the next Mishnah, Rabbi Yehudah **is referring** to the explicit **entreaty** for rain inserted in the ninth blessing of the Amidah. That prayer is inserted until the end of Pesah. [7]**Here,** in our Mishnah, he **is referring** to the **mention** of rain in the second blessing. That insertion is no longer made after musaf on the first day of Pesah. [8]Thus, during the week of Pesah we **go on praying for rain** in the ninth blessing, [9]but **we stop making mention** of rain in the second blessing **on the first holy day** of Pesah during the musaf prayer.

לִפְנֵי הַתֵּיבָה, כו׳". [1]וּרְמִינְהוּ: [2]"עַד מָתַי שׁוֹאֲלִין אֶת הַגְּשָׁמִים? [3]רַבִּי יְהוּדָה אוֹמֵר: עַד שֶׁיַּעֲבוֹר הַפֶּסַח. [4]רַבִּי מֵאִיר אוֹמֵר: עַד שֶׁיַּעֲבוֹר נִיסָן"! [5]אֲמַר רַב חִסְדָּא: לָא קַשְׁיָא. [6]כָּאן לִשְׁאוֹל. [7]כָּאן לְהַזְכִּיר. [8]מִישְׁאַל שָׁאֵיל וְאָזֵיל; [9]לְהַזְכִּיר בְּיוֹם טוֹב הָרִאשׁוֹן פָּסֵיק.

LITERAL TRANSLATION

before the ark, etc." [1]A contradiction was raised (lit., "cast them together"): [2]"Until when do we pray for rains? [3]Rabbi Yehudah says: Until Pesah has passed. [4]Rabbi Meir says: Until Nisan has passed"! [5]Rav Hisda said: There is no difficulty. [6]Here [it means] to pray for. [7]Here [it means] to mention. [8]He goes on praying for [rain]; [9]he stops making mention on the first holy day.

RASHI

עד אימתי שואלין את הגשמים — בסוף ימות הגשמים. **עד שיעבור הפסח** — דאמרינן כל כולו של מועד "תן טל ומטר". **עד שיצא ניסן** — וכדמפיק טעמא במתניתין. הכי גרסינן: **אמר רב חסדא כאן לשאול כאן להזכיר מישאיל שאיל ואזיל והזכרה ביום טוב ראשון פוסק** — לשאול שואל והולך עד שיעבור הפסח, כדקתני "עד מתי שואלין כו'", להזכיר — אינו מזכיר אלא בתפלת יוצר של יום טוב ראשון.

TERMINOLOGY

וּרְמִינְהוּ **A contradiction was raised.** An expression used by the Gemara to introduce a contradiction between the source about to be cited and the source that has just been cited, where both sources are of equal authority.

BACKGROUND

עַד שֶׁיַּעֲבוֹר הַפֶּסַח....עַד שֶׁיַּעֲבוֹר נִיסָן **Until Pesah has passed.... Until Nisan has passed.** This dispute concerns how late in the growing season rain is necessary and useful in Eretz Israel. On the one hand, we know that the time of harvesting the Omer, which is the beginning of the barley harvest, is immediately after the first day of Pesah. Hence it can be said that the harvest starts then, and, after that, rain can only be damaging. On the other hand, most people's staple food is wheat, and the wheat harvest begins some time later, from the month of Iyar on.

SAGES

רַב חִסְדָּא **Rav Hisda.** Considered among the greatest Babylonian Amoraim of the second generation, Rav Hisda, a priest, was one of Rav's younger students. After Rav's death he remained a colleague and a student of Rav's student, Rav Huna. Throughout his life Rav Hisda showed great affection for Rav's words, and tried to add to his knowledge of Rav's teachings. Though he was poor as a youth, he became wealthy and lived most of his life in comfort. He was affable toward his fellowmen, and devoted to his students, to his sons, and to his daughters, guiding them along the right path in both spiritual and worldly matters.

Rav Hisda is regarded as one of the most sharp-witted and profound thinkers of his generation, while his friend and colleague, Rav Sheshet, was known for his extensive knowledge.

Rav Hisda served as a judge in Sura for many years, together with Rav Huna, and both of them continued the tradition of Rav's School. After Rav Huna's death, Rav Hisda took his place as head

NOTES

רַבִּי יְהוּדָה אוֹמֵר **Rabbi Yehudah says.** The Jerusalem Talmud analyzes the viewpoint of Rabbi Yehudah that rain is first mentioned in the musaf Amidah on the last day of Sukkot and is first omitted in the musaf Amidah on the first day of Pesah. The Jerusalem Talmud asks: If Rabbi Yehudah is in basic agreement with Rabbi Yehoshua that rain is mentioned for the first time on the last day of Sukkot, why do we not mention it first in the evening Amidah of that day? And similarly, why do we wait until the musaf Amidah on the first day of Pesah to omit mention of rain, when it can already be omitted in the previous evening's Amidah?

The Jerusalem Talmud (cited by *Rif* and many Rishonim) answers that rain is mentioned for the first time in the musaf Amidah on the last day of Sukkot, in order to allow dew to be mentioned in the evening and morning services of that day. In this way dew, which is always a propitious sign, is mentioned on every full Festival. For this reason the mention of rain ceases on the first day of Pesah, but the question remains as to why the mention of rain is first omitted only in the musaf Amidah of that day. The Jerusalem Talmud explains that the change is not made in the evening service, because not everybody attends the evening service. Such a change should only be made in a service which everybody attends, so as not to create a situation in which some people are still mentioning rain and others have already stopped. The change is also not made in the morning service, so that a person should not think that the change was already made the night before (when he was not present), and he may come to omit the mention of rain in future years in the evening service on the first day of Pesah. When he sees that the rain is mentioned in the morning service, but omitted from the musaf service, he will understand that it must also have been mentioned the night before.

Another explanation is found in *Pesikta DeRav Kahana* (cited by *Ba'al HaMa'or, Ritva,* and others). The change is made in the musaf service because it is only in that Amidah, after a person has already recited the Shema and the morning Amidah, that he can fully concentrate on his prayers.

[1]אֲמַר עוּלָּא: הָא דְּרַב חִסְדָּא קַשְׁיָא ״כַּחֹמֶץ לַשִּׁנַּיִם וְכֶעָשָׁן לָעֵינָיִם״. [2]וּמַה בְּמָקוֹם שֶׁאֵינוֹ שׁוֹאֵל, מַזְכִּיר, [3]בְּמָקוֹם שֶׁשּׁוֹאֵל, אֵינוֹ דִּין שֶׁיְּהֵא מַזְכִּיר!

[4]אֶלָּא [5]אֲמַר עוּלָּא: תְּרֵי תַּנָּאֵי אַלִּיבָּא דְּרַבִּי יְהוּדָה.

[6]רַב יוֹסֵף אֲמַר: מַאי ״עַד שֶׁיַּעֲבוֹר הַפֶּסַח״? [7]עַד שֶׁיַּעֲבוֹר שְׁלִיחַ צִבּוּר רִאשׁוֹן הַיּוֹרֵד בְּיוֹם טוֹב רִאשׁוֹן שֶׁל פֶּסַח.

LITERAL TRANSLATION

[1]Ulla said: This [explanation] of Rav Ḥisda is as hard "as vinegar to the teeth and as smoke to the eyes." [2]For if when he does not pray for [rain], he does mention [it], [3]when he does pray for [it], how much more so should he mention [it]!

[4]Rather, [5]Ulla said: Two Tannaim [disagree] about [the viewpoint of] Rabbi Yehudah.

[6]Rav Yosef said: What is "until Pesaḥ has passed"? [7]Until the first prayer leader (lit., "agent of the community") who goes down [before the ark] on the first holy day of Pesaḥ has walked away.

RASHI

במקום שאינו שואל — ביום טוב האחרון של חג, שאינו מתפלל תפלתו תפלת חול, דאין שאלה אלא בברכת השנים. **מזכיר** — גבורות גשמים, כדאמר רבי יהודה: האחרון מזכיר. **במקום שהוא שואל** — בחולו של מועד של פסח. **תרי תנאי** — חד אמר: עד שיעבור הפסח שואלין — כל שכן שמזכירין, וחד אמר: שאלה עד הפסח, והזכרה, שיכול להזכיר ביום טוב — מזכיר ביום טוב הראשון של פסח בתפלת יוצר, ובמוספין פוסק. **רב יוסף אמר** — האי דקתני עד אימתי שואלין "עד שיעבור כו'" — הכי קאמר: עד שיעבור שליח צבור כו', והיינו כאידך רבי יהודה דמתניתין, דאמר: הראשון מזכיר האחרון אינו מזכיר.

TRANSLATION AND COMMENTARY

אֲמַר עוּלָּא [1]Ulla said: **This explanation of Rav Ḥisda is as hard** to accept **"as vinegar to the teeth and as smoke to the eyes"** (a simile borrowed from Proverbs 10:26). All agree that we begin to mention rain in the second blessing of the Amidah by the last day of Sukkot at the latest, before we begin praying for rain in the ninth blessing. [2]But **if when** a person **is not** permitted to **pray** explicitly for rain, such as between the last day of Sukkot and the beginning of the rainy season, **he** is nevertheless required to **make mention** of rain in the second blessing, [3]**how much more so should he** be required to **make mention** of rain in the second blessing **when he** *is* **required to pray** for rain, such as on Pesaḥ according to Rabbi Yehudah?

אֶלָּא [4]**Rather,** says the Gemara, we must reject Rav Ḥisda's distinction between the prayer for rain in the ninth blessing and the mention of rain in the second blessing, and we must conclude that in the next Mishnah Rabbi Yehudah does indeed rule that we continue to mention rain until the end of Pesaḥ. [5]Accordingly, **Ulla said: There are two Tannaim who disagree as to the viewpoint of Rabbi Yehudah.** We are forced to admit that there is indeed a contradiction here, and the two rulings attributed to Rabbi Yehudah represent conflicting versions of his viewpoint, reported by different disciples of his. According to the Tanna whose viewpoint is represented in our Mishnah, Rabbi Yehudah maintains that we stop mentioning rain in the second blessing, and stop praying for rain in the ninth blessing, on the first day of Pesaḥ, whereas according to the Tanna whose viewpoint is represented in the next Mishnah, we continue to make these insertions until the end of Pesaḥ.

רַב יוֹסֵף אֲמַר [6]Although Ulla's solution is acceptable, the Gemara seeks additional solutions to this problem. **Rav Yosef said:** There is no contradiction between the two rulings attributed to Rabbi Yehudah. In fact they mean the same thing. **What** did Rabbi Yehudah mean when he said that we pray for rain in the ninth blessing **"until Pesaḥ has passed"?** [7]He meant that we recite this prayer **until the first** member of the congregation who **leads the prayers by passing before the ark** in the synagogue **on** the morning of **the first holy day of Pesaḥ has walked away** from his position in front of the ark to make room for the second member of the congregation to recite the musaf Amidah. In other words, we stop mentioning rain in our prayers before the musaf Amidah of the first day of Pesaḥ, as our Mishnah ruled.

of the Sura Yeshivah. Much is told of his deeds of charity. He lived to the age of ninety-two. Many of the Sages of the following generation were his students, and he had many sons who became Sages: Rav Ḥanan bar Rav Ḥisda, Mar Yenuka and Mar Keshisha, Rav Mari, Rav Pineḥas and Rav Taḥlifa. However, Rav Ḥisda used to say that he preferred his daughters to his sons because they married the greatest Sages of the generation, Mar Ukva bar Ḥama and his brother, Rami bar Ḥama. The daughter referred to as "the daughter of Rav Ḥisda," who married Rami bar Ḥama, later married Rava.

BACKGROUND

כַּחֹמֶץ לַשִּׁנַּיִם וְכֶעָשָׁן לָעֵינָיִם **"As vinegar to the teeth and as smoke to the eyes."** This Biblical image refers to something that causes an unpleasant, even painful, sensation. In both cases, the sensation becomes harder to bear, the longer it continues. Therefore Ulla said that Rav Ḥisda's words aroused these reactions in him, for the longer he thought about them, the harder and less understandable they became.

TERMINOLOGY

תְּרֵי תַּנָּאֵי וְאַלִּיבָּא דְּרַבִּי פְּלוֹנִי **Two Tannaim disagree about the viewpoint of Rabbi X.** Sometimes a contradiction between two statements made by the same Tanna is resolved by suggesting that his original statement was reported differently by two other scholars: "Two later Tannaim reported the view of Rabbi X differently."

NOTES

תְּרֵי תַּנָּאֵי אַלִּיבָּא דְּרַבִּי יְהוּדָה **Two Tannaim disagree about the viewpoint of Rabbi Yehudah.** This expression usually means that the Gemara wishes to resolve an apparent contradiction between two statements made by the same Tanna by suggesting that two later Tannaim reported the view of the earlier Tanna in different ways. *Rashi, Rambam* (*Commentary to the Mishnah*) and others explain that this is the meaning of the expression in our Gemara as well, and that the two rulings attributed to Rabbi Yehudah represent two versions of his viewpoint as reported by two different disciples.

Ritva suggests that the expression is used here in a different sense: The viewpoint found in our Mishnah is the viewpoint reported by Rabbi Yehudah in the name of Rabbi Yehoshua ben Beterah (as was established above, 3a), whereas the viewpoint found in the next Mishnah is that maintained by Rabbi Yehudah himself (see also *Gevurat Ari*).

BACKGROUND

שׁוֹאֵל מְתוּרְגְּמָן The interpreter prays for rain. From the context as well as from the explanations of the commentators, it appears that the interpreter had an additional function in the synagogue — to explain the prayers. In Talmudic times there were already many worshipers who did not understand Hebrew. They spoke various dialects of Aramaic in Eretz Israel and in Babylonia, whereas in Egypt they spoke Greek. Thus they needed an explanation of what they were saying in their prayers. In various places in Eastern Europe there were women who provided a similar translation and explanation in Yiddish for the other women who came to pray.

TRANSLATION AND COMMENTARY

אֲמַר לֵיהּ אַבַּיֵי [1]But Rav Yosef's explanation is flawed, as **Abaye said to him:** According to you, the next Mishnah is referring to the musaf Amidah on the first day of Pesaḥ. But that Mishnah mentions "praying for rain," and this implies that the reference is to the insertion in the ninth blessing of the Amidah. Thus, according to you, Rabbi Yehudah is saying that we pray for rain in the ninth blessing in the morning service of the first day of Pesaḥ and stop in the musaf service. [2]But **is there** such an insertion, **praying for rain, on a holy day?** On full Festivals, such as the first day of Pesaḥ, a special Amidah is recited, which includes the second blessing but not the ninth. Thus, while it is possible to change the insertion in the second blessing during the musaf Amidah of the first day of Pesaḥ, as Rabbi Yehudah ruled in our Mishnah, it is impossible to change the insertion in the ninth blessing until (at the earliest) the second day of Pesaḥ, when the regular weekday Amidah is once again recited. How can we omit the prayer in the musaf Amidah on the first day of Pesaḥ if the ninth blessing is not recited at all on this day?

אֲמַר לֵיהּ [3]Rav Yosef **said to** Abaye in reply: There is **indeed** a prayer for rain on a full Festival, [4]because **the interpreter prays for rain.** On Festivals in Talmudic times, it was customary for a functionary in the synagogue to expand in Aramaic on the discourse of the Rabbi and to pray for the needs of the community. Thus it is possible that Rabbi Yehudah is of the opinion that the interpreter who spoke during the evening and morning services on the first day of Pesaḥ would include a prayer for rain in his explanation of the Rabbi's discourse.

וְכִי מְתוּרְגְּמָן [5]**But** Abaye rejects this explanation: **Does the interpreter pray for something that the congregation does not need?** If the congregation does not pray for rain in the morning service on the first day of Pesaḥ, why should the interpreter insert such a prayer on his own initiative?

אֶלָּא [6]**Rather,** says the Gemara, **it is clear that** there is no convincing resolution of the contradiction between the two Mishnayot, and we are forced to say that there are conflicting versions of Rabbi Yehudah's viewpoint, [7]**as Ulla explained.**

רַבָּה אֲמַר [8]The Gemara offers yet another explanation. **Rabbah said:** There is no contradiction between the two rulings attributed to Rabbi Yehudah. Our Mishnah refers to the mention of rain in the second blessing of the Amidah, whereas the next Mishnah refers to the prayer for rain inserted in the ninth blessing. Rav Ḥisda gave a similar explanation above, but it was rejected because Rabbi Yehudah could not conceivably maintain that we stop mentioning rain in the second blessing *before* we stop inserting the prayer for rain in the ninth blessing. But, says Rabbah, the opposite is in fact the case: Rabbi Yehudah is of the opinion that we stop mentioning rain in the second blessing *after* we stop praying for rain in the ninth blessing. [9]For **what** did Rabbi Yehudah mean when he said that we pray for rain **"until Pesaḥ has**

[1]אֲמַר לֵיהּ אַבַּיֵי: [2]שְׁאֵלָה בְּיוֹם טוֹב מִי אִיכָּא? [3]אֲמַר לֵיהּ: אִין. [4]שׁוֹאֵל מְתוּרְגְּמָן. [5]וְכִי מְתוּרְגְּמָן שׁוֹאֵל דָּבָר שֶׁאֵינוֹ צָרִיךְ לַצִּבּוּר? [6]אֶלָּא, מְחַוַּורְתָּא [7]כִּדְעוּלָּא. [8]רַבָּה אֲמַר: [9]מַאי "עַד שֶׁיַּעֲבוֹר

LITERAL TRANSLATION

[1]Abaye said to him: [2]Is there praying for [rain] on a holy day?

[3]He said to him: Yes. [4]The interpreter prays for [rain].

[5]But does the interpreter pray for something that the community does not need?

[6]Rather, it is clear that it is [7]as Ulla [explained].

[8]Rabbah said: [9]What is "until Pesaḥ has passed"?

RASHI

שאלה ביום טוב מי איכא — וכי מתפלל הוא תפלת חול, שאתה אומר "עד שיעבור הפסח" דהיינו זמן שליח צבור של תפלת יום טוב הראשון של פסח. **אמר ליה אין שאלה דמתורגמן** — בדרשה שהוא דורש אומר ברכת שאלה לבדה. **דבר שאינו צריך לצבור** — דכיון דזמן הפסקה הוא — לאו אורח ארעא למישאל בצבור דבר שאינו צריך.

NOTES

שׁוֹאֵל מְתוּרְגְּמָן The interpreter prays for rain. Most commentators explain that reference is being made here to the "interpreter" whose function it was to convey the Rabbi's lecture to the congregation. Such a spokesman was needed either because it was difficult for the entire congregation to hear the lecture, or because they did not understand the Hebrew in which the lecture was delivered. The interpreter was given considerable leeway when communicating the lecture, so that he was even able to insert supplications into his interpretation. Thus the Gemara argues that, while there is no prayer for rain in the official prayers recited on a Festival, a prayer for rain could indeed have been inserted into the interpreter's rendition of the Rabbi's lecture. Others suggest that the Gemara is referring here to a *piyyut*, a poetic embellishment that was customarily added to the obligatory prayers. While there is no prayer for rain in the obligatory prayers recited on a Festival, such a supplication may be inserted by the interpreter into the *piyyut* added on that day (*Shittah*).

LITERAL TRANSLATION

הַפֶּסַח"? [1]עַד שֶׁיַּעֲבוֹר זְמַן שְׁחִיטַת הַפֶּסַח. [2]וְכִתְחִילָּתוֹ, כֵּן סוֹפוֹ. [3]מַה תְּחִילָּתוֹ מַזְכִּיר אַף עַל פִּי שֶׁאֵינוֹ שׁוֹאֵל, [4]אַף סוֹפוֹ מַזְכִּיר אַף עַל פִּי שֶׁאֵינוֹ שׁוֹאֵל. [5]אָמַר לֵיהּ אַבַּיֵי: בִּשְׁלָמָא תְּחִילָּתוֹ מַזְכִּיר, [6]הַזְכָּרָה נָמֵי רִיצּוּי שְׁאֵלָה הִיא. [7]אֶלָּא סוֹפוֹ [8]מַאי רִיצּוּי שְׁאֵלָה אִיכָּא? [9]אֶלָּא מְחַוַּורְתָּא כִּדְעוּלָּא.

[1]Until the time for the slaughtering of the Pesah [sacrifice] has passed. [2]And as its beginning is, so is its end. [3]Just as [at] its beginning he mentions [rain] even though he does not pray for [it], [4]so too [at] its end he mentions [rain] even though he does not pray for [it].

[5]Abaye said to him: Granted that he mentions [rain at] its beginning, [6][for] mentioning is also seeking acceptance of praying. [7]But [at] its end [8]what seeking acceptance of praying is there?

[9]Rather, it is clear that it is as Ulla [explained].

RASHI

עד שיעבור זמן שחיטת פסח — צלות יום דארבעה עשר. עד שיעבור צלות — דהיינו כל תפלת יוצר. ואשמעינן רבי יהודה דבמנחה דערבי פסחים, אף על גב דמצלינן תפלת חול מפסיקינן, ולא יאמר "ותן טל ומטר". ואף על גב דמדכרינן עד למחר במוספין — פוסק השאלה בתפלת מנחה של ערב יום טוב הראשון. והזכרה, שיכול להזכיר ביום טוב — מזכיר עד תפלת מוסף של יום טוב הראשון. **כתחילתו** — שהוא מזכיר תחלה ביום טוב אחרון של חג, ואינו שואל עד לאחר החג — כך בסופו אינו שואל במנחה ערב יום טוב הראשון, ומזכיר עד מוסף של יום טוב ראשון, והכא ליכא למיפרך: שאלה ביום טוב מי איכא. **דהזכרה נמי צורך שאלה היא** — שמרצה תחילה, לפי שאי אפשר לו לשאול ביום טוב, וכיון דאיכא שאלה אבתריה מזכיר הוא לרצויי בעלמא. **אבל סופו** — למה הוא מזכיר הואיל ואינו צריך לשאול מכאן ואילך, הא כיון דאפסקת מאתמול — גלית אדעתך דלא ניחא לך בהו, ואמאי מזכיר?

TRANSLATION AND COMMENTARY

passed"? [1]He meant that we recite this prayer **until the time for the slaughtering of the Paschal sacrifice has passed.** For although the word "Pesaḥ" can refer to the week-long Passover Festival (as we have assumed until now), it can also refer to the Paschal sacrifice, which is slaughtered on the fourteenth of Nisan and eaten that evening, the first night of Pesaḥ. Thus Rabbi Yehudah is ruling that we stop praying for rain in the ninth blessing during the day before Pesaḥ, whereas we continue mentioning rain in the second blessing until the musaf Amidah on the following day. Rabbah explains: We should not be surprised that Rabbi Yehudah rules that we continue to mention rain in the second blessing for one day after we have stopped praying for rain in the ninth blessing. [2]For **as its beginning is, so is its end.** Rabbi Yehudah maintains that the proper practice at the end of the winter should be the same as that followed at its beginning. [3]**Just as we mention** rain **at the beginning** of the rainy season, **even though we do not pray for it,** [4]**so too do we** continue **to mention rain** for one more day **at the end** of the rainy season, **even though we do not pray for it** any longer.

אָמַר לֵיהּ אַבַּיֵי [5]But **Abaye said to** Rabbah: Your explanation is not acceptable, because there is no comparison between the beginning of the rainy season and its end. **Granted that we mention rain at the beginning** of the rainy season, even before the time has come to pray for rain. [6]**For mentioning** something **is also** an appropriate way of **seeking acceptance of a prayer**. It is perfectly natural to introduce a request in an indirect way, before making the request explicitly. [7]**But** to mention rain **at the end** of the rainy season makes no sense, because no explicit request for rain is going to follow the mention of it. [8]For **what prayer is there** for which the supplicant needs to **seek acceptance?**

אֶלָּא מְחַוַּורְתָּא כִּדְעוּלָּא [9]Rather, concludes the Gemara, **it is clear** that the only resolution of the contradiction between the two Mishnayot is to say that they reflect conflicting versions of Rabbi Yehudah's viewpoint, **as Ulla explained.**

BACKGROUND

זְמַן שְׁחִיטַת הַפֶּסַח The time for the slaughtering of the Pesaḥ sacrifice. The Paschal lamb was sacrificed in the afternoon (בֵּין הָעַרְבַּיִם) of the fourteenth of Nisan, the day before Pesaḥ. Although the afternoon, as defined in the Halakhah, begins after the sun has turned toward the west, a little after noon, and lasts until sunset, the Paschal lamb was usually slaughtered in the late afternoon. Sometimes, however, such as when the eve of Pesaḥ fell on the eve of Shabbat, the sacrifice would be offered closer to noon so as not to lead people to violate Shabbat by roasting the meat.

רִיצּוּי שְׁאֵלָה Seeking acceptance of praying. This refers to the way a person asks a favor from someone. One does not enter and immediately make one's request. Rather, one first prepares the ground by touching on the subject in a general way, mentioning it but not yet making the explicit request. Similarly, the mention of rain is like a polite beginning, an entry into the subject, and only later comes the explicit request that God give us rain.

NOTES

עַד שֶׁיַּעֲבוֹר זְמַן שְׁחִיטַת הַפֶּסַח Until the time for the slaughtering of the Pesaḥ sacrifice has passed. Our commentary follows *Rashi* and *Rabbenu Yehonatan*, who explain that, according to Rabbah, the prayer for rain is recited until noon on the fourteenth of Nisan when the beginning of the time for slaughtering the Paschal lamb has passed. Thus the prayer is included in the morning Amidah on the fourteenth of Nisan but omitted in the afternoon Amidah. The mention of rain continues until the musaf Amidah the next day.

Rabbenu Ḥananel and *Rabbenu Gershom* explain that the prayer for rain is recited until the end of the fourteenth of Nisan, when the time for slaughtering the Paschal lamb is entirely over. Thus the prayer for rain is included in every Amidah recited on the fourteenth of Nisan, even in the afternoon service. On the fifteenth of Nisan there is no prayer for rain, but the mention of rain continues until the musaf Amidah.

LITERAL TRANSLATION

[1] Rabbi Assi said in the name of Rabbi Yoḥanan: The Halakhah is in accordance with Rabbi Yehudah. [2] Rabbi Zera said to Rabbi Assi: But did Rabbi Yoḥanan say this? [3] But surely we have learned: "On the third of Marḥeshvan we pray (lit., 'ask') for rains. [4] Rabban Gamliel says: On the seventh of it." [5] And Rabbi Elazar said: The Halakhah is in accordance with Rabban Gamliel! [6] He said to him: Are you contradicting (lit., "casting") one man with another man?

[1] אָמַר רַבִּי אַסִּי אֲמַר רַבִּי יוֹחָנָן: הֲלָכָה כְּרַבִּי יְהוּדָה. [2] אֲמַר לֵיהּ רַבִּי זֵירָא לְרַבִּי אַסִּי: וּמִי אֲמַר רַבִּי יוֹחָנָן הָכִי? [3] וְהָתְנַן: "בִּשְׁלֹשָׁה בְּמַרְחֶשְׁוָן שׁוֹאֲלִין אֶת הַגְּשָׁמִים. [4] רַבָּן גַּמְלִיאֵל אוֹמֵר: בְּשִׁבְעָה בּוֹ". [5] וְאָמַר רַבִּי אֶלְעָזָר: הֲלָכָה כְּרַבָּן גַּמְלִיאֵל! [6] אֲמַר לֵיהּ: גַּבְרָא אַגַּבְרָא קָא רָמֵית?

TRANSLATION AND COMMENTARY

אָמַר רַבִּי אַסִּי [1] **Rabbi Assi said in the name of Rabbi Yoḥanan: The Halakhah is in accordance with Rabbi Yehudah,** who ruled that we do not mention rain in the second blessing of the Amidah until the musaf service on the eighth day of Sukkot.

אֲמַר לֵיהּ רַבִּי זֵירָא [2] The Gemara assumes at this stage that Rabbi Yehudah — and by implication Rabbi Yoḥanan — maintains that we begin to pray for rain in the ninth blessing of the Amidah at the same time as we begin to mention rain in the second blessing. This would mean in practice that the first time we pray for rain is in the first weekday Amidah immediately after Sukkot. **Rabbi Zera said to Rabbi Assi: Did Rabbi Yoḥanan** really **say this?** [3] **Surely we have learned** the following in a Mishnah (below, 10a): **"On the third** day **of** the month of **Marḥeshvan,** eleven days after the last day of Sukkot, **we** begin to **pray for rain** by including the words, 'and give dew and rain for a blessing on the face of the earth' in the ninth blessing of the weekday Amidah. [4] **Rabban Gamliel says:** We begin reciting this prayer **on the seventh of** Marḥeshvan, fifteen days after Sukkot." [5] **And,** continues Rabbi Zera, we know that **Rabbi Elazar said: The Halakhah is in accordance with Rabban Gamliel,** and we do not recite this prayer until fifteen days after Sukkot. How, then, could Rabbi Yoḥanan rule that the Halakhah is in accordance with Rabbi Yehudah, who maintains that we recite this prayer immediately after Sukkot?

אֲמַר לֵיהּ [6] Rabbi Assi **said to** Rabbi Zera in reply: What kind of objection is this? **Are you seeking to point out a contradiction between one man's ruling and another's?** It was Rabbi Elazar who ruled that the Halakhah is in accordance with Rabban Gamliel, and it was Rabbi Yoḥanan who ruled that the Halakhah is in accordance with Rabbi Yehudah. Perhaps Rabbi Yoḥanan simply disagrees with his disciple, Rabbi Elazar, about this matter!

RASHI

הלכה כרבי יהודה — דאמר: העובר לפני התיבה וכו׳. **מי אמר רבי יוחנן הכי** — דהלכה כרבי יהודה, דמזכיר ביום טוב האחרון. **בשלשה במרחשון** — הכי קים להו דהוה זמן גשמים וכו׳. **הלכה כרבן גמליאל** — דאינו שואל עד שבעה במרחשון, וקא סלקא דעתך דבמקום שהוא שואל מזכיר, עד דמשני לקמן.

NOTES

הֲלָכָה כְּרַבִּי יְהוּדָה....הֲלָכָה כְּרַבָּן גַּמְלִיאֵל **The Halakhah is in accordance with Rabbi Yehudah....The Halakhah is in accordance with Rabban Gamliel.** The law regarding the proper time at which to begin inserting the prayer for rain into the Amidah is the subject of a dispute among Rishonim. According to the plain sense of our passage, the Gemara's conclusion seems to be that in Eretz Israel when the Temple is not in existence the prayer is inserted in the Amidah immediately after Sukkot, whereas outside Eretz Israel it is first inserted in the Amidah on the seventh of Marḥeshvan. But there is another passage (below, 10a) that must be considered before a final decision on the matter can be reached. A Baraita is cited there according to which Ḥananyah ruled that in the Diaspora the prayer for rain is first inserted into the Amidah sixty days after the autumn equinox. And Shmuel is reported to have ruled in accordance with this view of Ḥananyah's. If we are to accept both passages, it follows that in Eretz Israel we pray for rain immediately after Sukkot; outside Eretz Israel, the prayer is first recited on the seventh of Marḥeshvan; and in Babylonia, the prayer is not inserted into the Amidah until sixty days after the autumn equinox (*Meiri*).

According to *Rambam* (*Hilkhot Tefillah* 2:16), the discussion in our passage is set aside in the light of the Gemara's rulings that appear below. Thus the law in Eretz Israel is in accordance with the ruling of Rabban Gamliel that we begin to pray for rain on the seventh of Marḥeshvan even today when the Temple is no longer standing. In Babylonia and everywhere else outside Eretz Israel, the prayer for rain is first inserted sixty days after the autumn equinox.

גַּבְרָא אַגַּבְרָא קָא רָמֵית **Are you contradicting one man with another man?** An objection cannot be raised against one Amora's ruling by citing that of another. Here it is surprising that the Gemara objects to Rabbi Yoḥanan's

HALAKHAH

בְּשִׁבְעָה בּוֹ **On the seventh of it.** "Those living in Eretz Israel begin to insert the prayer for rain in the ninth blessing of the Amidah on the night of the seventh of Marḥeshvan," following Rabban Gamliel. (*Shulḥan Arukh, Oraḥ Ḥayyim* 117:1.)

TERMINOLOGY

גַּבְרָא אַגַּבְרָא קָא רָמֵית **Are you contradicting one man with another man?** Sometimes, after an objection has been raised to the view of one Amora based on the statement of another Amora, the Talmud asks this question, meaning: "Why do you raise an objection to Rabbi A's viewpoint from a statement by Rabbi B? Surely both have the same authority and are entitled to differ!"

SAGES

רַבִּי אַסִּי **Rabbi Assi.** A leading Amora of the third generation, Rabbi Assi was born and brought up in Babylonia, and studied there under Shmuel and Rav Yehudah. He immigrated to Eretz Israel, where his principal teacher was Rabbi Yoḥanan. He was a close colleague and friend of Rabbi Ammi.

רַבִּי זֵירָא **Rabbi Zera.** One of the greatest of the third generation of Babylonian Amoraim, he belonged essentially to the Babylonian tradition and studied mainly with the disciples of Rav and Shmuel. After some time he immigrated to Eretz Israel, where he studied under Rabbi Yoḥanan and was a colleague of Rabbi Yoḥanan's greatest disciples. When Rabbi Zera reached Eretz Israel he was extremely impressed by the method of learning used there and decided to accept it in full. Accordingly, he undertook 100 fasts in order to forget the Babylonian method of learning. He also fasted so that the fire of Gehinnom should not rule over him, and as he did so the calves of his legs were burned. Because of this he became known as the "short man with the scorched calves." Rabbi Zera was famous for his great piety, for his modesty, and for being affable and accommodating, and the members of his generation greatly loved and honored him. He had many disciples throughout Eretz Israel, and quotations of his teachings are numerous in both the Babylonian and the Jerusalem Talmud. He had a son who was also a Sage, Rabbi Ahavah.

רַבָּן גַּמְלִיאֵל **Rabban Gamliel II (of Yavneh).** Rabban

TRANSLATION AND COMMENTARY

אִיבָּעֵית אֵימָא [1]And, continues Rabbi Assi, **if you wish** you can **say** that **there is no difficulty** in resolving the seeming contradiction you have pointed out, even on the assumption that Rabbi Yoḥanan agrees with Rabbi Elazar. Rabban Gamliel's ruling that we do not recite the prayer for rain until fifteen days after Sukkot refers to the insertion in the ninth blessing of the Amidah, [2]in which we **pray** explicitly for rain. On the other hand, Rabbi Yehudah's ruling that we pray for rain from the musaf Amidah of the eighth day of Sukkot refers to the insertion in the second blessing, [3]in which we **mention** rain but do not explicitly ask for it. Thus it is possible that Rabbi Yehudah agrees that we do not pray for rain in the ninth blessing of the weekday Amidah until the seventh day of Marḥeshvan, as Rabban Gamliel ruled. Hence there is not necessarily a contradiction between the rulings of Rabbi Yoḥanan and Rabbi Elazar.

וְהָאָמַר רַבִּי יוֹחָנָן [4]**But,** the Gemara objects, **surely** this latter solution is untenable. For **Rabbi Yoḥanan** himself **said: Whenever one prays for rain** in the ninth blessing, **one mentions it** in the second blessing. Thus we see that Rabbi Yoḥanan is of the opinion that we begin to make both insertions at the same time. How, then, could he rule in favor of Rabbi Yehudah, who maintains that we begin to mention rain on the eighth day of Sukkot, and also rule in favor of Rabban Gamliel, who maintains that we begin to pray for rain fifteen days later, on the seventh of Marḥeshvan?

הַהוּא לְהַפְסָקָה אִיתְּמַר [5]The Gemara answers: In **that** statement Rabbi Yoḥanan **was speaking** specifically **about** the end of winter, when we **stop** reciting these prayers. Rabbi Yoḥanan was saying that we do not go on mentioning rain in the second blessing after we have stopped praying for rain in the ninth blessing. But Rabbi Yoḥanan would agree that we begin mentioning rain in the second blessing fifteen days before we begin praying for rain in the ninth blessing.

וְהָאָמַר רַבִּי יוֹחָנָן [6]**But,** the Gemara objects, **surely** this explanation, too, is untenable, because Rabbi Yoḥanan explicitly ruled that the two insertions are linked, both at the beginning and at the end of the winter. For **Rabbi Yoḥanan said:** [7]**Once one has begun to mention** rain in the second blessing, **one** also **begins to pray** for it in the ninth blessing. [8]And **once one has stopped praying** for rain in the ninth blessing on the eve of Pesaḥ, **one also stops mentioning it** in the second blessing.

LITERAL TRANSLATION

[1]If you wish, say: There is no difficulty. [2]Here [it means] to pray for. [3]Here [it means] to mention.

[4]But surely Rabbi Yoḥanan said: Whenever one prays for [rain] one mentions [it]!

[5]That was said about stopping.

[6]But surely Rabbi Yoḥanan said: [7][Once] one has begun to mention [rain], one begins to pray for [it]. [8][Once] one has stopped praying for [it], one stops mentioning [it]!

[1]אִיבָּעֵית אֵימָא: לָא קַשְׁיָא. [2]כָּאן לִשְׁאוֹל. [3]כָּאן לְהַזְכִּיר. [4]וְהָאָמַר רַבִּי יוֹחָנָן: בְּמָקוֹם שֶׁשּׁוֹאֵל מַזְכִּיר!

[5]הַהוּא לְהַפְסָקָה אִיתְּמַר.

[6]וְהָאָמַר רַבִּי יוֹחָנָן: [7]הִתְחִיל לְהַזְכִּיר, מַתְחִיל לִשְׁאוֹל. [8]פָּסַק מִלִּשְׁאוֹל, פּוֹסֵק מִלְּהַזְכִּיר!

RASHI

כאן לשאול — בשבעה במרחשון. **כאן להזכיר** — מיום טוב האחרון, ורבי יוחנן אית ליה דרבי אלעזר. **והא אמר רבי יוחנן במקום ששואל מזכיר** — במקום שאינו שואל — אינו מזכיר. והיכי אמר רבי יוחנן דהלכה כרבי יהודה שמזכיר ביום טוב האחרון הא ליכא שאלה, דאין אומר ברכת השנים ביום טוב. **להפסקה איתמר** — דכשהוא מפסיק לשאלה בערב הפסח — פוסק נמי להזכרה, דהכי משמע "במקום ששואל מזכיר". **והא תרווייהו איתמר** — התחלה והפסקה. **יתחיל לשאול** — דהיינו בחול, שיכול לשאול. **פסק מלשאול** — בערב הפסח, פוסק מלהזכיר, אלמא לא סבירא ליה כרבי יהודה, והיכי אמר: הלכה כמותו?

NOTES

ruling in favor of Rabbi Yehudah on the basis of Rabbi Elazar's ruling in favor of Rabbi Gamliel. The objection becomes more understandable when we consider the special relationship that existed between Rabbi Yoḥanan and his disciple Rabbi Elazar. Though Rabbi Elazar also studied with the leading Babylonian scholars, there is a general assumption in the Talmud that whatever Rabbi Elazar said was based on the teachings of Rabbi Yoḥanan. If we assume that Rabbi Elazar's ruling does reflect Rabbi Yoḥanan's own view, then there is indeed an internal contradiction between the rulings issued by Rabbi Yoḥanan and by his disciple Rabbi Elazar. Accordingly, Rabbi Assi answers Rabbi Zera's objection by saying that on this matter Rabbi Elazar does indeed disagree with his teacher Rabbi Yoḥanan, and therefore no objection can be raised from the one ruling to the other. *Rabbenu Elyakim* maintains that even according to the Gemara's conclusion Rabbi Elazar does not disagree with Rabbi Yoḥanan. He disagrees with Rabbi Assi about what Rabbi Yoḥanan said.

Gamliel was president of the Sanhedrin and one of the most important Tannaim in the period following the destruction of the Second Temple. His father, Rabban Shimon ben Gamliel (the Elder) had also been president of the Sanhedrin, and one of the leaders of the nation during the rebellion against Rome. Rabban Gamliel was taken to Yavneh by Rabban Yoḥanan ben Zakkai after the destruction of the Temple, so that he became known as Rabban Gamliel of Yavneh. After Rabban Yoḥanan ben Zakkai's death, Rabban Gamliel presided over the Sanhedrin.

During Rabban Gamliel's presidency, Yavneh became an important spiritual center. The greatest of the Sages gathered around him: Rabbi Eliezer (Rabban Gamliel's brother-in-law), Rabbi Yehoshua, Rabbi Akiva, Rabbi Elazar ben Azaryah, and others. Rabban Gamliel wished to create a spiritual center for the Jews which would unite the entire people, as the Temple had done until that time. For this reason he strove to enhance the honor and the central authority of the Sanhedrin and its president. His strict and vigorous leadership eventually led his colleagues to remove him from his post for a short period, replacing him with Rabbi Elazar ben Azaryah. However, since all knew that his motives and actions were for the good of the people and were not based on personal ambition, they soon restored him to his position.

We do not possess many Halakhic rulings explicitly given in the name of Rabban Gamliel. However, in his time, and under his influence, some of the most important decisions in the history of Jewish spiritual life were made. These included the decision to follow the School of Hillel; the rejection of the Halakhic system of Rabbi Eliezer; and the establishment of fixed formulae for prayers. In those Halakhic decisions attributed to Rabban Gamliel, we find an uncompromising approach to the Halakhah; in reaching his conclusions he was faithful to his

¹אֶלָּא, לָא קַשְׁיָא. ²הָא לָן. ³הָא לְהוּ.
⁴מַאי שְׁנָא לְדִידַן? ⁵דְּאִית לָן פֵּירֵי בְּדַבְרָא? ⁶לְדִידְהוּ נַמִי אִית לְהוּ עוֹלֵי רְגָלִים!
⁷כִּי קָאָמַר רַבִּי יוֹחָנָן, בִּזְמַן שֶׁאֵין בֵּית הַמִּקְדָּשׁ קַיָּים.
⁸הָשְׁתָּא דְּאָתֵית לְהָכִי, ⁹הָא וְהָא לְדִידְהוּ, ¹⁰וְלָא קַשְׁיָא. ¹¹כָּאן, בִּזְמַן שֶׁבֵּית הַמִּקְדָּשׁ

LITERAL TRANSLATION

¹Rather, there is no difficulty. ²This [applies] to us. ³That [applies] to them.

⁴What is different for us? ⁵That we have produce in the field? ⁶They too have pilgrims!

⁷When Rabbi Yoḥanan said [this, it referred] to the time when the Temple does not exist.

⁸Now that you have come to this, ⁹this and that [apply] to them, ¹⁰and there is no difficulty. ¹¹Here, it is in the time when the Temple exists,

TRANSLATION AND COMMENTARY

אֶלָּא ¹**Rather,** says the Gemara, we must concede that Rabbi Yoḥanan was indeed ruling that we begin to pray for rain immediately after the eighth day of Sukkot, when we begin to mention rain in the Amidah, and not on the seventh day of Marḥeshvan, as is the accepted Halakhah as decided by Rabbi Elazar. Nevertheless, **there is no difficulty** in resolving the seeming contradiction between the two rulings. ²For Rabbi Elazar's ruling that we begin to pray for rain on the seventh of Marḥeshvan **was** intended **for us,** the residents of Babylonia, ³whereas Rabbi Yoḥanan's ruling that we begin to pray for rain at the same time as we begin to mention it in the second blessing **was** intended **for them,** the residents of Eretz Israel. Rabbi Yoḥanan and Rabbi Elazar agree that in both countries we begin mentioning rain in the second blessing of the musaf Amidah on the eighth day of Sukkot, as Rabbi Yehudah ruled in our Mishnah. But the residents of Eretz Israel begin praying for rain at the same time, whereas the residents of Babylonia wait until the seventh of Marḥeshvan, in accordance with Rabban Gamliel's ruling in the next Mishnah.

מַאי שְׁנָא לְדִידַן ⁴The Gemara rejects this suggestion. **What is different about us,** in Babylonia, that we wait two weeks after Sukkot before praying for rain? Why do we not pray for rain as soon as we leave the Sukkah? ⁵Is the reason **that,** in Babylonia, where the rainy season begins a little later than in Eretz Israel, ⁶**we still have produce in the fields** that needs to be gathered before the rains come, so that rain is not desirable until the seventh of Marḥeshvan, whereas in Eretz Israel, where the rainy season comes a little earlier, they have already gathered their produce before Sukkot? If so, the people living in Eretz Israel should **also** wait until the seventh of Marḥeshvan, because **they have pilgrims!** Rabban Gamliel selected the seventh of Marḥeshvan as the date to begin praying for rain so that pilgrims who have traveled to the Temple in Jerusalem to celebrate Sukkot should have two full weeks after the Festival ends to return home before the rains begin. Thus it would be absurd to explain that Rabban Gamliel's ruling applies only to the Jews of Babylonia, who are concerned about their produce, and not to the Jews of Eretz Israel, who are concerned about the pilgrims returning home after their visit to the Temple.

כִּי קָאָמַר רַבִּי יוֹחָנָן ⁷The Gemara answers: **When Rabbi Yoḥanan** said that the Jews of Eretz Israel begin praying for rain immediately after Sukkot, **he had in mind the period when the Temple was no longer standing.** But following the destruction of the Temple, the residents of Eretz Israel began to pray for rain immediately after Sukkot, whereas the residents of Babylonia waited until the seventh of Marḥeshvan, in order to give them time to gather their crops.

הָשְׁתָּא דְּאָתֵית לְהָכִי ⁸This explanation is acceptable, says the Gemara. But **now that we have come to this** idea of distinguishing between the period before and after the destruction of the Temple, our original solution can be simplified, because we no longer need to introduce the residents of Babylonia at all. We can say instead that both Rabbi Elazar's ruling, that we begin to pray for rain on the seventh of Marḥeshvan, ⁹**and** Rabbi Yoḥanan's ruling, that we begin to pray for rain immediately after we begin to mention it, **were** intended **for** the residents of Eretz Israel, ¹⁰**and there is no difficulty** in resolving the contradiction between the two rulings. ¹¹For Rabbi Elazar's ruling **was** directed to the period **when the Temple was** still **standing.** At that time, the residents of Eretz Israel would wait until the seventh of Marḥeshvan before beginning to pray for rain, in order not to cause inconvenience to the pilgrims returning home from Jerusalem.

RASHI

הא לן והא להו — לבני בבל, שיש לנו תבואה ופירות בשדה כל תשרי — אין מזכירין עד שבעה במרחשון, והם שואלים, כדאמר רבי יוחנן: מתחיל להזכיר מתחיל לשאול. **והא להו** — לבני ארץ ישראל דקוצרין בניסן ואוספין בתשרי — מזכירין ביום טוב האחרון, כרבי יהודה, דאמר רב אסי הלכה כמותו. **בדברא** — מדבר, כלומר בשדות. **אית להו עולי רגלים** — ואם ירדו להן גשמים — קשה להן בחזרתן. **אלא כי אמר רבי יוחנן** — הלכה כרבי יהודה, דמזכיר מיום טוב האחרון כו׳, בזמן שאין בית המקדש קיים, וליכא עולי רגלים — מזכיר. **כאן בזמן שבית המקדש קיים** — דאיכא עולי רגלים, אינו מזכיר עד שביעי במרחשון.

principles. We know that two of his sons were Sages: Rabban Shimon ben Gamliel, who served as president of the Sanhedrin after him, and Rabbi Ḥanina ben Gamliel.

TERMINOLOGY

הָא לָן, הָא לְהוּ This applies to us. That applies to them. Sometimes the Talmud resolves a contradiction between two Halakhot by suggesting that one reflects the Babylonian practice ("this applies to us"), and the other reflects the practice followed in Eretz Israel ("that applies to them"). The difference between the two Halakhot reflects the different Halakhic traditions or the different circumstances in the two countries.

הָשְׁתָּא דְּאָתֵית לְהָכִי Now that you have come to this. Sometimes the Rabbis raise a series of objections to a certain viewpoint, and each objection is given a different answer; then a new objection is raised, and someone suggests an answer which resolves not only the new objection but also the previous ones. At that point the Talmud uses this expression, proposing a revision of the solutions first advanced.

TRANSLATION AND COMMENTARY

[1]Rabbi Yoḥanan's ruling, on the other hand, **was** intended for the period **when the Temple was no** longer **standing,** when pilgrims no longer traveled to Jerusalem, and it became appropriate to pray for rain from the eighth day of Sukkot, when we mention rain for the first time in the Amidah. The residents of Babylonia were not discussed by Rabbi Yoḥanan or by Rabbi Elazar, who both lived in Eretz Israel, and in fact the Gemara rules below (10a) that the prayer for rain is not recited there until a much later date. Thus we have resolved the contradiction between the rulings of Rabbi Yoḥanan and of Rabbi Elazar. Both agree that we begin to mention rain in the second blessing of the musaf Amidah on the eighth day of Sukkot, as Rabbi Yehudah ruled in our Mishnah. Rabbi Yoḥanan's ruling that we pray for rain in the ninth blessing at the same time as we begin to mention rain in the second blessing applies only to the period after the destruction of the Temple. But as long as the Temple was standing, the Halakhah was in accordance with Rabban Gamliel, who ruled that we wait until the seventh of Marḥeshvan to pray for rain in the ninth blessing, as Rabbi Elazar ruled.

קַיָּים. [1]כָּאן, בִּזְמַן שֶׁאֵין בֵּית הַמִּקְדָּשׁ קַיָּים.

[2]וַאֲנַן דְּאִית לָן תְּרֵי יוֹמֵי, הֵיכִי עָבְדִינַן?

[3]אָמַר רַב: מַתְחִיל בְּמוּסָפִין, [4]וּפוֹסֵק בְּמִנְחָה, [5]עַרְבִית, וְשַׁחֲרִית, [6]וְחוֹזֵר בְּמוּסָפִין.

[7]אֲמַר לְהוּ שְׁמוּאֵל: פּוּקוּ וְאִמְרוּ לֵיהּ לְאַבָּא: [8]אַחַר שֶׁעֲשִׂיתוֹ קוֹדֶשׁ, תַּעֲשֵׂהוּ חוֹל? [9]אֶלָּא אָמַר שְׁמוּאֵל: [10]מַתְחִיל

LITERAL TRANSLATION

[1]There, it is in the time when the Temple does not exist.

[2]And we who have two days, how do we act?

[3]Rav said: He begins [to mention rain] in musaf, [4]and stops in the afternoon service, [5]the evening service, and the morning service, [6]and starts again in musaf.

[7]Shmuel said to them: Go out and say to Abba: [8]After you have made it [the day] holy, will you make it a weekday?

[9]Rather, Shmuel said: [10]He begins

RASHI

ואנן דאית לן תרי יומי — שני ימים טובים אחרונים, שמיני ספק שביעי, ותשיעי ספק שמיני, לרבי יהודה דאמר: מיום טוב האחרון, באיזה מהן מזכיר? **מתחיל במוסף** — של שמיני ספק שביעי, דשמא יום טוב האחרון הוא. **ופוסק במנחה** — שמא שביעי חול הוא, ואין זמן הזכרה עד מוסף של מחר. **ופוסק נמי בערבית ושחרית** — של תשיעי ספק שמיני. **לאבא** — חברי. **לאחר שעשיתו קודש** — לשמיני ספק שביעי, שהזכרת בו גבורות גשמים כרבי יהודה מיום טוב האחרון. **תעשהו חול** — בתמיה: שמפסיק במנחה של אותו היום. **ופוסק ערבית ושחרית** — דלאו היינו תפלה של אותו היום.

וַאֲנַן דְּאִית לָן תְּרֵי יוֹמֵי [2]The Gemara now considers another problem regarding the Jews living in Babylonia. Rabbi Yehudah ruled in our Mishnah that we begin to mention rain in the second blessing of the musaf Amidah of the eighth day of Sukkot. But in Babylonia and everywhere else outside Eretz Israel, all the full holy days mentioned in the Torah (with the exception of Yom Kippur) are celebrated for two days and not one, as in Eretz Israel. Thus the last holy day of Sukkot is celebrated on the eighth and ninth days of the Festival rather than on the eighth day alone. So **how do we,** the residents of Babylonia, **who have two** holy **days** to celebrate at the end of Sukkot, make the change during the musaf Amidah, as prescribed by Rabbi Yehudah in our Mishnah? On other Festivals we simply repeat on the second day all the commandments and prayers that apply to the first day. But how can we repeat the change from the prayers recited in the morning Amidah to the prayers recited in the musaf Amidah?

אָמַר רַב [3]**Rav said** in reply: In Babylonia, **we begin to mention rain in** the **musaf** Amidah on the eighth day, as described in the Mishnah. [4]But **we** then **stop** mentioning rain **in the afternoon service** later on the same day, [5]and we continue not to mention rain in **the evening service and the morning service** of the ninth day. [6]We then **start** to mention rain **again in** the **musaf** Amidah of the ninth day, and continue to mention rain in every Amidah from then until Pesaḥ.

אֲמַר לְהוּ שְׁמוּאֵל [7]**Shmuel said to** his students: **Go and say to Abba** (sc., Rav, whose real name was Abba ben Aivo, and who was also known as Abba Arikha): Your solution to this problem is unacceptable. According to you, rain is not mentioned in the afternoon Amidah on the eighth day of Sukkot. Thus the afternoon of the eighth day is being treated as though it were the day before the final holy day of Sukkot and not the holy day itself. But in the musaf Amidah of the eighth day, rain was already mentioned, as if that day were the full Festival. [8]Can it be that **after you have made the** eighth **day holy, you will** then reverse yourself and **make it a weekday,** as if it were merely the day before the Festival and not the Festival itself?

אֶלָּא אָמַר שְׁמוּאֵל [9]**Rather, said Shmuel,** we must seek a different solution for the problem of the two-day Festival in Babylonia. [10]**We begin** to mention rain **in** the **musaf** Amidah on the eighth day, as described in

BACKGROUND

וְאִמְרוּ לֵיהּ לְאַבָּא **And say to Abba.** According to a Geonic tradition, Rav's given name was Abba. Usually people called him by his title, "Rav," but Shmuel was his friend and used his given name. Moreover, the name "Abba" means father, and was used as an honorable epithet in addressing older people. Thus Shmuel could have called Rav by name even before strangers without giving the impression that he was being disrespectful.

בְּמוּסָפִין וּבְמִנְחָה, [1]וּפוֹסֵק עַרְבִית וְשַׁחֲרִית, [2]וְחוֹזֵר וּמַתְחִיל בְּמוּסָפִין. [5A] [3]רָבָא אָמַר: כֵּיוָן שֶׁהִתְחִיל, שׁוּב אֵינוֹ פּוֹסֵק.

[4]וְכֵן אָמַר רַב שֵׁשֶׁת: [5]כֵּיוָן שֶׁהִתְחִיל, שׁוּב אֵינוֹ פּוֹסֵק.

[6]וְאַף רַב הֲדַר בֵּיהּ, [7]דְּאָמַר רַב חֲנַנְאֵל אָמַר רַב: [8]מוֹנֶה עֶשְׂרִים וְאֶחָד יוֹם, כְּדֶרֶךְ שֶׁמּוֹנֶה עֲשָׂרָה יָמִים מֵראשׁ הַשָּׁנָה עַד יוֹם הַכִּפּוּרִים, [9]וּמַתְחִיל. [10]וְכֵיוָן שֶׁהִתְחִיל, שׁוּב אֵינוֹ פּוֹסֵק.

LITERAL TRANSLATION

in musaf and [continues] in the afternoon service, [1]and stops [in] the evening service and the morning service, [2]and starts again and begins in musaf. [5A] [3]Rava said: Once he has begun, he does not stop again.

[4]And Rav Sheshet said the same: [5]Once he has begun, he does not stop again.

[6]And Rav too retracted [his opinion], [7]for Rav Ḥananel said in the name of Rav: [8]He counts twenty-one days, in the way in which he counts ten days from Rosh HaShanah to Yom Kippur, [9]and he begins. [10]And once he has begun, he does not stop again.

TRANSLATION AND COMMENTARY

the Mishnah, **and we continue** to mention rain in **the afternoon service** later on the same day. [1]However, **we** then **stop** mentioning rain **in the evening service and the morning service** of the ninth day. [2]**We then start** to mention rain **again in** the **musaf** Amidah of the ninth day, and we continue to mention rain in every Amidah from then until Pesaḥ. [5A] [3]**Rava** disagreed with Shmuel's solution and **said: Once a person has begun** to mention rain in his prayers, **he does not stop** until the end of the rainy season. Hence the law in Babylonia is the same as in Eretz Israel: We begin to mention rain in the musaf Amidah of the eighth day of Sukkot and continue mentioning it in the Amidah from then on.

וְכֵן אָמַר רַב שֵׁשֶׁת [4]The Gemara notes that **Rav Sheshet said the same** thing: [5]**Once a person has begun** to mention rain in his prayers, **he does not stop** making the insertion until the end of the rainy season.

וְאַף רַב הֲדַר בֵּיהּ [6]**And** the Gemara notes that **Rav too retracted his opinion.** [7]**For Rav Ḥananel said in the name of Rav:** The day on which we begin to mention rain in our prayers can be determined by the following rule: [8]**We count twenty-one days, in the same way as we count ten days from** the first day of **Rosh HaShanah to Yom Kippur** (see note), [9]**and** we then **begin** to mention rain on the following day, the twenty-second of the month, which is the eighth day of Sukkot. [10]**And once we begin** to mention rain in our prayers, **we do not stop** making the insertion until the end of the rainy season.

RASHI

רבא אמר כיון שהתחיל — בשמיני ספק שביעי שוב אינו פוסק. **הדר ביה** — ממאי דאמר: פוסק. **מונה עשרים ואחד יום** — מראש השנה עד שמיני ספק שביעי של חג, כדרך שמונה מראש השנה ועד יום הכפורים עשרה ימים, שמתחיל למנות מיום ראשון של ראש השנה, ומזכיר מכאן ואילך. וזהו שמזכיר בשמיני ספק שביעי שהוא עשרים ושתים — שוב אינו פוסק. והא דמתחילין אנו למנות מיום ראשון — דהא דאנו עושין שני ימים לאו משום ספק דשמא עיברו לאלול, דהא אנן בקיאין בקביעא דירחא. אלא משום דמנהג אבותינו בידינו, לשון אחר: מונה עשרים ואחד יום כדרך שמונה כו׳, כלומר, אם עיברו אלול — לא יחשוב מיום ראשון של ראש השנה עשרים ואחד יום — שאם כן לא ימצאו בידו אלא עשרים, וכלים ביום טוב שביעי, יום נטילת ערבה, אלא מיום שמתחילין למנות עשרה ימים, לעשות בעשירי יום הכפורים — יתחיל למנות באלו, שבכך לא יטעה, שיום הכפורים יום אחד לבד, וידע מהיכן התחילו למנות לו. וביום שכלין עשרים ואחד, דהיינו ביום טוב אחרון — מתחיל להזכיר, וכיון שהתחיל — שוב אינו פוסק.

NOTES

כְּדֶרֶךְ שֶׁמּוֹנֶה עֲשָׂרָה יָמִים In the way in which he counts ten days. The Rishonim suggest several different explanations of this comparison. In his first explanation, *Rashi* argues that we count the twenty-one days from Rosh HaShanah in the same way that we count the ten days from Rosh HaShanah to Yom Kippur — from the first day of Rosh HaShanah. We count from the first day of Rosh HaShanah because today we celebrate Rosh HaShanah for two days, not on account of any real doubt as to which of the two days is the first of Tishri, but because we continue to observe the Festival in the way it was observed by our forefathers. In his second explanation, *Rashi* maintains that we count the twenty-one days from Rosh HaShanah in the same way that we count the ten days from Rosh HaShanah to Yom Kippur — from the first day of Tishri, the first day of Rosh HaShanah if Elul is a month of twenty-nine days, or the second day of Rosh HaShanah if Elul is a month of thirty days. After twenty-one days have passed from the first of Tishri, we begin to mention rain in the Amidah.

Gevurat Ari suggests (see also *Shittah*) that we count twenty-one days from Rosh HaShanah in the same way that we count the ten days from Rosh HaShanah to Yom Kippur — from the first day of Rosh HaShanah. Just as with respect to setting the date for Yom Kippur we rely on the fact that in the vast majority of years Elul has twenty-nine days — and we observe Yom Kippur ten days after the first day of Rosh HaShanah even if word has not yet been received from Jerusalem that the month of Elul was indeed twenty-nine days — so too with respect to the date on which we begin to mention rain we assume that Elul had twenty-nine days.

SAGES

רָבָא Rava. A great Babylonian Amora of the fourth generation, Rava was a colleague of Abaye. His father, Rav Yosef bar Ḥama, was also a famous Sage. Rava's outstanding teacher was Rav Naḥman bar Ya'akov, and Rava was also a student of Rav Ḥisda, with whom he studied together with his colleague Rami bar Ḥama. Rav Ḥisda's daughter married Rami bar Ḥama, and when Rami bar Ḥama died she married Rava. Rava also studied with Rav Yosef. He founded a yeshivah in Meḥoza. In all the many Halakhic controversies between him and Abaye the Halakhah follows him, except for six cases (יע״ל קג״ם). After Abaye's death, Rava was appointed head of the Pumbedita Yeshivah, which he transferred to his home city of Meḥoza. Among his students were Rav Pappa and Rav Huna the son of Rav Yehoshua. A great number of Sages transmit teachings in his name: Rav Zevid, Mar the son of Rav Yosef, Rav Mesharshiya, Rav Pappi, Ravina, and others. After his death the yeshivah of Meḥoza split in two, and Rav Naḥman bar Yitzḥak took his place as the head of the Pumbedita Yeshivah, while Rav Pappa established a yeshivah of his own in Neresh.

רַב חֲנַנְאֵל Rav Ḥananel. A Babylonian Amora of the second generation, Rav Ḥananel was a disciple of Rav, and most of his teachings are transmitted in the name of his great teacher. He was apparently one of Rav's more important students, for his successor, Rav Huna, treated Rav Ḥananel with great respect. By profession he seems to have been a scribe, writing Torah scrolls. It is said of him that he could write the entire Torah by heart.

TRANSLATION AND COMMENTARY

וְהִלְכְתָא [1] **And** the Gemara concludes that **the Halakhah is** indeed in accordance with the rulings of these Amoraim: [2] **Once a person has begun** to mention rain in his prayers, **he does not stop** until the end of the rainy season.

MISHNAH עַד מָתַי שׁוֹאֲלִין [3] We have seen that during the winter we insert in the ninth blessing of the Amidah an explicit prayer for rain: "And give dew and rain for a blessing on the face of the earth." But during the summer we do not pray for rain. Accordingly, our Mishnah asks: **Until when do we pray for rain** in this way? When does the winter end, and the dry season begin? [4] **Rabbi Yehudah says:** We continue to pray for rain in the ninth blessing **until Pesaḥ is over.** [5] **Rabbi Meir says:** We continue praying for rain **until the end of the month of Nisan,** just over a week after Pesaḥ. [6] **For it is said** (Joel 2:23), in a verse dealing with a long famine that ended when God miraculously caused a year's rainfall to fall at the very end of the rainy season: **"And He made rain fall for you, the former rain and the latter rain, in the first month."** Thus we see that rain is considered to be a blessing throughout the month of Nisan, which the Torah calls "the first month."

GEMARA אֲמַר לֵיהּ רַב נַחְמָן [7] The Gemara begins its analysis of the Mishnah by considering the verse cited at the end of the Mishnah. **Rav Naḥman said to Rabbi Yitzḥak:** The verse states that God caused the former rain and the latter rain to fall in Nisan. The rainy season in Eretz Israel usually begins with a series of heavy downpours, called *yoreh* (יוֹרֶה — translated as "the former rain"), followed by alternating wet and dry spells, and concluding with a gentle, steady rainfall called *malkosh* (מַלְקוֹשׁ — translated as "the latter rain"). The heavy, early rain moistens the ground and causes seeds to germinate; and the gentle, late rain gives the already developed plants the water necessary for them to ripen properly. [8] But, asks the Gemara, **does the former**

[1] וְהִלְכְתָא: [2] כֵּיוָן שֶׁהִתְחִיל, שׁוּב אֵינוֹ פּוֹסֵק.

מִשְׁנָה [3] עַד מָתַי שׁוֹאֲלִין אֶת הַגְּשָׁמִים? [4] רַבִּי יְהוּדָה אוֹמֵר: עַד שֶׁיַּעֲבוֹר הַפֶּסַח. [5] רַבִּי מֵאִיר אוֹמֵר: עַד שֶׁיֵּצֵא נִיסָן, [6] שֶׁנֶּאֱמַר: "וַיּוֹרֶד לָכֶם גֶּשֶׁם, יוֹרֶה וּמַלְקוֹשׁ, בָּרִאשׁוֹן".

גְּמָרָא [7] אֲמַר לֵיהּ רַב נַחְמָן לְרַבִּי יִצְחָק: [8] יוֹרֶה בְּנִיסָן?

LITERAL TRANSLATION

[1] And the Halakhah is: [2] Once he has begun, he does not stop again.

MISHNAH [3] Until when do we pray for rains? [4] Rabbi Yehudah says: Until Pesaḥ has passed. [5] Rabbi Meir says: Until Nisan has passed, [6] as it is said: "And He made rain fall for you, the former rain and the latter rain, in the first month."

GEMARA [7] Rav Naḥman said to Rabbi Yitzḥak: [8] Is the former rain in Nisan?

RASHI

אמר ליה רב נחמן לר׳ יצחק יורה בניסן הוא — דכתיב "ויורד לכם גשם מורה ומלקוש בראשון" בתמיה.

TERMINOLOGY

וְהִלְכְתָא **And the Halakhah is....** An expression used to introduce the Talmud's decision about a Halakhic issue left unresolved in the previous discussion.

NOTES

עַד מָתַי שׁוֹאֲלִין **Until when do we pray?** Since the first Mishnah in the tractate dealt with the issue of when to begin praying for rain, the second Mishnah now addresses the question of when to stop, even though the discussion regarding when to begin adding the prayer for rain is completed only in the third Mishnah (below, 10a) (*Meiri*).

עַד שֶׁיַּעֲבוֹר הַפֶּסַח **Until Pesaḥ has passed.** When the Talmud mentions "Pesaḥ," the reference is almost always to the seven-day Festival from the fifteenth to the twenty-first of the Hebrew month of Nisan (see Leviticus 23:5-14). In the Bible this Festival is called "the festival of unleavened bread [חַג הַמַּצּוֹת]," whereas "Pesaḥ" always refers to the Paschal lamb that was offered as a sacrifice in the Temple on the fourteenth of Nisan. According to the Gregorian calendar, the fifteenth of Nisan falls on different dates from year to year, in late March or early April. The first and last days of Pesaḥ are full holidays in Eretz Israel (in the Diaspora, the first two days and the seventh and eighth days are full holidays). Pesaḥ marks the beginning of the dry season in Eretz Israel, when the crops that have grown during the rainy season ripen and are harvested. Accordingly, the Torah commands us to offer the Omer sacrifice on the second day of Pesaḥ. This sacrifice consists of a measure of barley — the first crop to ripen — from the new harvest. Once the Omer has been sacrificed, the harvest season officially begins, and new grain that is harvested may be eaten. Accordingly, the previous Mishnah ruled that we cease mentioning rain in the second blessing of the Amidah on the first day of Pesaḥ. In this Mishnah, however, Rabbi Yehudah rules that we continue praying for rain until the end of Pesaḥ and stop when Pesaḥ is over — during the evening service after the twenty-first of Nisan.

שֶׁנֶּאֱמַר: "וַיּוֹרֶד לָכֶם גֶּשֶׁם" **As it is said: "And He made rain fall for you."** Our commentary follows the straightforward understanding of the Mishnah that this verse was cited by Rabbi Meir, and that he infers from it that rain is considered a blessing throughout "the first month" the month of Nisan, and this is why the prayer for rain is recited until the end of the month (see *Tosefot Yom Tov* and *Tiferet Yisrael*). *Melekhet Shlomo* suggests that the verse is

HALAKHAH

כֵּיוָן שֶׁהִתְחִיל, שׁוּב אֵינוֹ פּוֹסֵק **Once he has begun, he does not stop again.** "Even in the Diaspora, where two days of each Festival are observed, we begin to insert the expression 'Who causes the wind to blow and the rain to fall' in the musaf Amidah on the eighth day of Sukkot, and we do not stop mentioning rain until the musaf Amidah on the first day of Pesaḥ." (*Shulḥan Arukh, Oraḥ Ḥayyim* 114:1.)

BACKGROUND

וּמַלְקוֹשׁ בְּנִיסָן And the latter rain is in Nisan. According to weather observations, only a small amount of rain (one percent of the annual precipitation) falls in Eretz Israel in May. Weather observations in the Coastal Plain, covering a period of many years, show that the last rain usually falls no later than April 28, approximately at the end of the Hebrew month of Nisan.

TRANSLATION AND COMMENTARY

rain ever fall **in Nisan?** [1]Surely **the former rain** falls **in Marheshvan,** [2]**as it was taught** in the following Baraita (below, 6a): **"The former rain falls in Marheshvan and the latter rain falls in Nisan."**

[3]Rabbi Yitzhak **said to** Rav Nahman in reply: **This is what Rabbi Yohanan said** about this verse: [4]In regular times, the early rain does not fall in Nisan, but **in the days of Joel the son of Pethuel this verse was fulfilled.** The verse is referring to a miraculous event that occurred only at the time of the prophecy, when the early and the late rains fell in the same month. Rabbi Yohanan now gives a graphic description of the events surrounding the prophecy of Joel. [5]**For it is written about** the period preceding this miracle (Joel 1:4): **"What was left by the grasshopper the locust ate."** Eretz Israel was strucked by an unprecedented plague, which itself followed several years of drought. The Prophet describes the devastation caused by the plague (Joel 1:1-20), and calls on the people to repent their sins (2:1-17). He then promises (2:18-27) that God will hear their prayers and restore the fertility of the land with miraculous rapidity, including a full year's rainfall in the first month, Nisan. Rabbi Yohanan describes the transformation from devastation to celebration: [6]**That year the month of Adar,** the month preceding Nisan, **ended and the rains** had still **not fallen.** The rainy season was almost over, when the Prophet proclaimed that God had heard their prayers. [7]**The first** heavy **rainfall fell on the first of Nisan,** moistening the ground and making it fit to grow crops. But this rain did not cause seeds to germinate, because there were no seeds in the ground. [8]**The Prophet said to** the people of **Israel: "Go out** and take whatever grain you have left in your houses **and sow** it." [9]**They said to him** in reply: **"Someone who has a *kav*** [a measure] **of wheat or two *kabbim* of barley — should he eat it and live, or sow it and die?"** We cannot afford to sow our last remnants of grain, for we have nothing else to eat. [10]The Prophet **said to them: "Even so, go out and sow,** for God has promised to bestow His blessing upon you." [11]As soon as they had sown the grain, **a miracle was performed for them, and they discovered** grain stored by mice **in the walls** of their houses, **and** grain stored by ants **in ant holes,** so that

[1]יוֹרֶה בְּמַרְחֶשְׁוָן הוּא! [2]דְּתַנְיָא: "יוֹרֶה בְּמַרְחֶשְׁוָן וּמַלְקוֹשׁ בְּנִיסָן". [3]אֲמַר לֵיהּ: הָכִי אָמַר רַבִּי יוֹחָנָן: [4]בִּימֵי יוֹאֵל בֶּן פְּתוּאֵל נִתְקַיֵּים מִקְרָא זֶה. [5]דִּכְתִיב בֵּיהּ: "יֶתֶר הַגָּזָם אָכַל הָאַרְבֶּה, וגו'". [6]אוֹתָהּ שָׁנָה יָצָא אֲדָר וְלֹא יָרְדוּ גְּשָׁמִים. [7]יָרְדָה לָהֶם רְבִיעָה רִאשׁוֹנָה בְּאֶחָד בְּנִיסָן. [8]אָמַר לָהֶם נָבִיא לְיִשְׂרָאֵל: "צְאוּ וְזִרְעוּ". [9]אָמְרוּ לוֹ: "מִי שֶׁיֵּשׁ לוֹ קַב חִטִּים אוֹ קַבַּיִם שְׂעוֹרִין, יֹאכְלֶנּוּ וְיִחְיֶה, אוֹ יִזְרָעֶנּוּ וְיָמוּת"? [10]אָמַר לָהֶם: "אַף עַל פִּי כֵן, צְאוּ וְזִרְעוּ". [11]נַעֲשָׂה לָהֶם נֵס, וְנִתְגַּלָּה לָהֶם מַה שֶּׁבַּכְּתָלִין וּמַה שֶּׁבְּחוֹרֵי

LITERAL TRANSLATION

[1]The former rain is in Marheshvan! [2]For it was taught: "The former rain is in Marheshvan and the latter rain is in Nisan."

[3]He said to him: This is what Rabbi Yohanan said: [4]In the days of Joel the son of Pethuel this verse was fulfilled. [5]For it is written about it: "What was left by the grasshopper the locust ate, etc." [6]That year [the month of] Adar went out but the rains had not fallen. [7]The first rainfall fell for them on the first of Nisan. [8]The Prophet said to Israel: "Go out and sow." [9]They said to him: "He who has a *kav* of wheat or two *kabbim* of barley, should he eat it and live, or sow it and die?" [10]He said to them: "Even so, go out and sow." [11]A miracle was performed for them, and they discovered whatever [grain] was in the walls and whatever [grain] was in the ant

RASHI

והא במרחשון הוא — כדתניא לקמן, ובספרי הוא. **יורה ומלקוש** — מפרש לקמן. **אמר ליה** — ודאי במרחשון הוא, ומקרא זה בימי יואל בן פתואל נתקיים, שיורה ומלקוש היה בראשון על ידי נס, שהיה רעב שבע שנים, דכתיב "כי קרא ה' לרעב וגם בא אל הארץ שבע שנים" וכתיב "יתר הגזם אכל הארבה" וגו'. **הכי גרסינן: יצא אדר ולא ירדו גשמים** — ולא זרעו רוב אדר לא גרסינן. **רביעה ראשונה** — התחלת גשמים, ולקמן (תענית ו,ב) מפרש: רביעה — שמרביע את הארץ. **או יזרענו וימיות** — ברעב, קודם שתגדל התבואה החדשה, שלא יהיה לו מה יאכל. **נעשה להם נס כו'** — והיינו דכתיב "ושלמתי לכם את השנים אשר אכל הארבה" וגו'. **נתגלה להם תבואה שבחורי נמלים ומה שבבתלים** — שאגרו העכברים.

NOTES

cited not by Rabbi Meir but by the anonymous author of the Mishnah. The verse speaks of rain in the month of Nisan as being a blessing, and Rabbi Yehudah and Rabbi Meir disagree about whether this refers only to rain that falls before the end of Pesah or whether it refers even to rain that falls during the last week of the month.

TRANSLATION AND COMMENTARY

people had something to eat. [1]**They then went out and sowed** their grain **on the second and third and fourth** of Nisan, [2]**and a second** heavy **rainfall fell on the fifth of Nisan,** causing the seeds to germinate and the grain to sprout. [3]The grain grew miraculously fast, so that the first crop was harvested in time for the people to **offer up the omer** sacrifice from the first barley **on the sixteenth of Nisan,** the second day of Pesaḥ, as commanded by the Torah. [4]**The result was that grain that** normally takes about **six months to grow,** from the beginning of Marḥeshvan, when the first rains normally fall, until Nisan, miraculously **grew** that year **in eleven days,** from the fifth of Nisan to the sixteenth. [5]And **the result was that the omer that is** normally **offered up from grain** that has already grown for **six months, was offered up** that year **from grain** that took just **eleven days** to grow. [6]Rabbi Yoḥanan concludes his description of the miracle by saying: It was **about that generation,** the generation of the Prophet Joel, that **it says** in Psalms (126:5-6): [7]**"They that sow in tears shall reap in joy. He that goes on his way weeping, bearing the measure of seed,** shall surely come with joy, bearing his sheaves." This psalm refers to the miraculous transformation of the people of Israel's fortunes when they were redeemed from exile. The Psalmist employs the metaphor of people who sow their seed in tears, having little expectation of a good outcome, and who see a rapid reversal of their fortunes, so that they reap the crop with joy. Rabbi Yoḥanan explains that the Psalmist had the story of Joel in mind when he selected this metaphor, for on this occasion the people literally sowed in tears and reaped in joy.

מַאי [8]The Gemara now asks: **What is** the meaning of the verse (Psalms 126:6): **"He that goes on his way weeping, bearing the measure** of seed, shall surely come with joy, bearing his sheaves"? The previous verse has already described the people as sowing in tears and reaping in joy. What is added by this verse?

אָמַר רַב יְהוּדָה [9]**Rav Yehudah said** in reply: This verse teaches us that even **when an ox plowed** the earth during the first days of Nisan, **it went on its way weeping from hunger.** [10]**But on its return** from plowing the field, the same ox **ate young shoots from the furrow** it had plowed. The crops grew so quickly that by the time the ox had finished plowing the field, grain was already growing in the furrow. [11]**And that is** what is meant by the latter part of the verse: **"He shall surely come with joy."**

מַאי [12]The Gemara now asks: **What is** the meaning of the last expression in this verse: **"Bearing his sheaves"?** The previous verse has already described the people of Joel's generation as sowing in tears and reaping in

נְמָלִים. [1]יָצְאוּ וְזָרְעוּ שֵׁנִי וּשְׁלִישִׁי וּרְבִיעִי, [2]וְיָרְדָה לָהֶם רְבִיעָה שְׁנִיָּה בַּחֲמִשָּׁה בְּנִיסָן. [3]הִקְרִיבוּ עוֹמֶר בְּשִׁשָּׁה עָשָׂר בְּנִיסָן. [4]נִמְצֵאת תְּבוּאָה הַגְּדֵילָה בְּשִׁשָּׁה חֳדָשִׁים גְּדֵילָה בְּאַחַד עָשָׂר יוֹם. [5]נִמְצָא עוֹמֶר הַקָּרֵב מִתְּבוּאָה שֶׁל שִׁשָּׁה חֳדָשִׁים קָרֵב מִתְּבוּאָה שֶׁל אַחַד עָשָׂר יוֹם. [6]וְעַל אוֹתוֹ הַדּוֹר הוּא אוֹמֵר: [7]״הַזֹּרְעִים בְּדִמְעָה בְּרִנָּה יִקְצֹרוּ. הָלוֹךְ יֵלֵךְ וּבָכֹה, נֹשֵׂא מֶשֶׁךְ הַזָּרַע, וגו׳״.

[8]מַאי: ״הָלוֹךְ יֵלֵךְ וּבָכֹה, נֹשֵׂא מֶשֶׁךְ, וגו׳״?

[9]אָמַר רַב יְהוּדָה: שׁוֹר כְּשֶׁהוּא חוֹרֵשׁ, הוֹלֵךְ וּבוֹכֶה, [10]וּבַחֲזִירָתוֹ אוֹכֵל חָזִיז מִן הַתֶּלֶם. [11]וְזֶהוּ: ״בֹּא יָבֹא בְרִנָּה״.

[12]מַאי: ״נֹשֵׂא אֲלֻמֹּתָיו״?

LITERAL TRANSLATION

holes. [1]They went out and sowed [on] the second and third and fourth, [2]and the second rainfall fell for them on the fifth of Nisan. [3]They offered up the omer on the sixteenth of Nisan. [4]It turned out [that] grain that grows in six months grew in eleven days. [5]It turned out that the omer that is offered up from the grain of six months was offered up from the grain of eleven days. [6]And about that generation, it says: [7]"They that sow in tears shall reap in joy. He that goes on his way weeping, bearing the measure of seed, etc."

[8]What is [meant by]: "He that goes on his way weeping, bearing the measure, etc."?

[9]Rav Yehudah said: When an ox plows, it goes on its way weeping, [10]but on its return it eats young grain from the furrow. [11]And that is: "He shall surely come with joy."

[12]What is [meant by]: "Bearing his sheaves"?

RASHI

יצאו וזרעו – וזרעו מה שבידם. **שני** – בניסן, ושלישי ורביעי, ומה שנשאר אכלו. **ולאחר שזרעו** – ירדו להם גשמים בחמישה בניסן, והקריבו עומר בששה עשר בניסן, מאותה תבואה חדשה. **הגדילה בששה חדשים** – מתשרי ועד ניסן. **באחד עשר יום** – מחמשה בניסן עד ששה עשר בו. **הזורעים בדמעה ברנה יקצורו** – שלא היה להן מה לאכול. **מאי הלך ילך ובכה** – אם לבני אדם – כבר נאמר ״הזורעים בדמעה ברנה יקצורו״, אלא על השור הכתוב אומר. **בהליכתו** – לחרוש התלם. **ובחזירתו אוכל חזיז** – שחת, מן התלם שזרעו בהליכתן. **שכשהוא זורע** – אם מפני התבואה שיש להם לאכול – הרי כבר אמור ״ברנה יקצורו״.

LANGUAGE

חָזִיז Young shoots. *Arukh* and the Geonim have the reading חִזִּין. Both terms are explained as meaning tender shoots, such as very green stalks of grain.

[1] אָמַר רַב חִסְדָּא, וְאָמְרִי לַהּ בְּמַתְנִיתָא תָּנָא: [2] ״קָנֶה זֶרֶת, שִׁיבּוֹלֶת זְרָתַיִם״.
[3] אֲמַר לֵיהּ רַב נַחְמָן לְרַבִּי יִצְחָק: מַאי דִּכְתִיב: [4] ״כִּי קָרָא ה׳ לָרָעָב, וְגַם בָּא אֶל הָאָרֶץ שֶׁבַע שָׁנִים״? [5] בְּהָנָךְ שֶׁבַע שָׁנִים מַאי אֲכוּל?
[6] אֲמַר לֵיהּ: הָכִי אָמַר רַבִּי יוֹחָנָן: [7] שָׁנָה רִאשׁוֹנָה, אָכְלוּ מַה שֶּׁבַּבָּתִּים. [8] שְׁנִיָּה, אָכְלוּ מַה שֶּׁבַּשָּׂדוֹת. [9] שְׁלִישִׁית, בְּשַׂר בְּהֵמָה טְהוֹרָה. [10] רְבִיעִית, בְּשַׂר בְּהֵמָה טְמֵאָה. [11] חֲמִישִׁית, בְּשַׂר שְׁקָצִים וּרְמָשִׂים. [12] שִׁשִּׁית, בְּשַׂר בְּנֵיהֶם וּבְנוֹתֵיהֶם. [13] שְׁבִיעִית, בְּשַׂר זְרוֹעוֹתֵיהֶם, [14] לְקַיֵּים מַה שֶּׁנֶּאֱמַר: ״אִישׁ בְּשַׂר זְרֹעוֹ יֹאכֵלוּ״.
[15] וַאֲמַר לֵיהּ רַב נַחְמָן לְרַבִּי יִצְחָק: מַאי דִּכְתִיב: ״בְּקִרְבְּךָ

LITERAL TRANSLATION

[1] Rav Ḥisda said, and some say [that] it was taught in a Baraita: [2] "The stalk was a span, [and] the ear was two spans."

[3] Rav Naḥman said to Rabbi Yitzḥak: What is [the meaning of] what is written: [4] "For the Lord has called for a famine, and it will also come upon the land for seven years"? [5] In those seven years what did they eat?

[6] He said to him: This is what Rabbi Yoḥanan said: [7] The first year, they ate what was in the houses. [8] The second [year], they ate what was in the fields. [9] The third [year], the meat of clean animals. [10] The fourth [year], the meat of unclean animals. [11] The fifth [year] the flesh of abominable things and creeping things. [12] The sixth [year], the flesh of their sons and their daughters. [13] The seventh [year], the flesh of their arms, [14] to fulfill what was said: "Each man will eat the flesh of his arm."

[15] And Rav Naḥman said to Rabbi Yitzḥak: What is [the meaning of] what is written: "In

TRANSLATION AND COMMENTARY

joy, and we have already learned that the rejoicing spread even to the animals. What is added by this phrase?

אָמַר רַב חִסְדָּא [1] **Rav Ḥisda said, and some say that it was taught in a Baraita:** [2] "The crop in the days of the Prophet Joel grew so fast and was of such quality that **the stalk** on each ear of wheat **was** the length of the **span** of a man's hand, **and the ear** itself **was** the length of **two spans.** Two-thirds of the ear of wheat consisted of grain, and only one-third consisted of straw, whereas normally the reverse is true.

אֲמַר לֵיהּ רַב נַחְמָן [3] Having cited the explanation of the verse in Joel given by Rabbi Yitzḥak in the name of Rabbi Yoḥanan in response to a question by Rav Naḥman, the Gemara now cites a series of explanations of other verses, involving the same three Amoraim. **Rav Naḥman said to Rabbi Yitzḥak: What is the meaning of the following verse** (II Kings 8:1) also dealing with famine: [4] **"For the Lord has called for a famine, and it will also come upon the land for seven years"?** [5] **What did they eat during those seven years?**

אֲמַר לֵיהּ [6] Rabbi Yitzḥak **said to** Rav Naḥman in reply: **This is what Rabbi Yoḥanan said** about this verse: [7] **The first year, they ate what was** left **in** their **houses** from previous years. [8] **The second year, they ate what** they could find **in the fields.** [9] **The third year,** they ate **the meat of** their **kosher animals.** [10] **The fourth year,** they were forced to save their lives by eating **the meat of** their **non-kosher animals** — their horses and camels. [11] **The fifth year,** they were reduced to eating **the flesh of abominable and creeping things** — rats and mice, and lizards and insects. [12] **The sixth year,** they were reduced to eating **the flesh of their sons and daughters** who had died in the famine. [13] **The seventh year,** they ate **the flesh of their** own **arms** and legs, [14] and in this way **they fulfilled what was prophesied by** Isaiah (9:19): **"Each man will eat the flesh of his arm."**

וַאֲמַר לֵיהּ [15] The Gemara now cites an explanation, involving the same three Amoraim, of another verse. **And Rav Naḥman said to Rabbi Yitzḥak: What is the meaning of what was written** in the following verse (Hosea 11:9): "I will not execute the fierceness of My anger. I will not return to destroy Ephraim, for I am

RASHI

שבולת זרתים — זהו נס גדול, מה שאין כן דרך כל תבואה, שהקנה פי שלשה וארבעה בשבולת. **כי קרא ה׳ לרעב** — בימי יהורם בן אחאב נאמר. **מה שבשדות** — ספיחים, ומה שנשתייר בשדות. **אכלו בשר בניהם** — מקלאס.

BACKGROUND

קָנֶה זֶרֶת, שִׁיבּוֹלֶת זְרָתַיִם **The stalk was a span, and the ear was two spans.** Usually, when grain is growing well, both the stalk and the ear develop fully. This can cause the grain to "lie down," creating difficulties in harvesting it. Today, by means of spraying with various chemicals and by developing dwarf strains of wheat, an effort is made to produce grain with a very short stalk. In these strains, the ear grows relatively larger than in the strains with long stalks.

SAGES

רַבִּי יִצְחָק **Rabbi Yitzḥak.** A prominent Palestinian Amora of the second and third generations. Rabbi Yitzḥak's full name was Rabbi Yitzḥak Nappaḥa. He was a disciple of Rabbi Yoḥanan, and often presents teachings in the latter's name. He spent part of his life in Babylonia, where he was an important source of information about the teachings and customs of Eretz Israel. In our passage here, Rabbi Yitzḥak was Rav Naḥman's guest, and his host used the opportunity to ask Rabbi Yitzḥak for explanations of various verses that he found difficult. This entire passage in the Gemara is a description of an extended meeting between these two Sages.

NOTES

בְּהָנָךְ שֶׁבַע שָׁנִים מַאי אֲכוּל **In those seven years what did they eat?** Even though we find numerous other instances of famine in the Bible, Rav Naḥman singled out the famine that afflicted the people in the days of Jehoram, King of Israel, to ask what it was that the people ate during that period of scarcity. *Maharsha* explains that the divine decree regarding this famine was carried out in full severity and for as long as was originally intended, for the verse says: "For the Lord has called for a famine, and it will also come upon the land for seven years."

TRANSLATION AND COMMENTARY

God and not man. **In your midst is the Holy One, and I will not come into the city"?** The last clause of this verse is unclear, and has been given various interpretations by the commentators. But the Talmud interprets it to mean "into the city of Jerusalem." Hence, Rav Nahman says: The Prophet Hosea is promising that God will respond to Israel's repentance. [1]But **because the Holy One is in your midst** — since God has accepted your repentance, and has returned to dwell among you — [2]is that a reason why God **will not come into the city** of Jerusalem? Surely, this should be a reason for Him to return to the city, not to avoid it!

אֲמַר לֵיהּ [3]Rabbi Yitzḥak **said to** Rav Naḥman in reply: **This is what Rabbi Yoḥanan said** about this verse: The "city" in the verse is not the earthly Jerusalem, where the Temple was built, but the spiritual city of Jerusalem in Heaven. [4]**The Holy One Blessed be He said:** I promise to restore the Divine Presence to the earthly Jerusalem, and **I will not enter the heavenly Jerusalem until I have entered the earthly Jerusalem.**

וּמִי אִיכָּא [5]But, Rav Naḥman objected, **is there a heavenly Jerusalem?**

אִין [6]Rabbi Yitzḥak answered: **Yes,** there is a heavenly Jerusalem as well, **as it is written** (Psalms 122:3): [7]**"Jerusalem the built is like the city that is joined together with it."** This verse, too, is somewhat unclear, and has been given different interpretations by the commentators. Rabbi Yitzḥak explains it as meaning: "Jerusalem is built like the other city that is attached to it," suggesting that Jerusalem's physical form is modeled on another, spiritual city in the heavens.

וַאֲמַר לֵיהּ רַב נַחְמָן [8]The Gemara now cites another explanation of a verse, involving the same three Amoraim. **And Rav Naḥman said to Rabbi Yitzḥak: What is the meaning of what is written** in the following verse (Jeremiah 10:8): [9]**"And about one they are stupid and foolish, the teaching of vanity is wood"?** In the

קָדוֹשׁ, וְלֹא אָבוֹא בְּעִיר״? [1]מִשּׁוּם דִּבְקִרְבְּךָ קָדוֹשׁ, [2]לֹא אָבוֹא בָּעִיר? [3]אֲמַר לֵיהּ: הָכִי אָמַר רַבִּי יוֹחָנָן: [4]אָמַר הַקָּדוֹשׁ בָּרוּךְ הוּא: לֹא אָבוֹא בִּירוּשָׁלַיִם שֶׁל מַעְלָה עַד שֶׁאָבוֹא לִירוּשָׁלַיִם שֶׁל מַטָּה. [5]וּמִי אִיכָּא יְרוּשָׁלַיִם לְמַעְלָה? [6]אִין, דִּכְתִיב: [7]״יְרוּשָׁלַיִם הַבְּנוּיָה כְּעִיר שֶׁחֻבְּרָה לָּהּ יַחְדָּו״. [8]וַאֲמַר לֵיהּ רַב נַחְמָן לְרַבִּי יִצְחָק: מַאי דִּכְתִיב: [9]״וּבְאַחַת יִבְעֲרוּ וְיִכְסָלוּ, מוּסַר הֲבָלִים עֵץ הוּא״?

LITERAL TRANSLATION

your midst is the Holy One, and I will not come into the city"? [1]Because the Holy One is in your midst, [2]I will not come into the city?

[3]He said to him: This is what Rabbi Yoḥanan said: [4]The Holy One blessed be He said: I will not come into the Jerusalem on high until I come into the Jerusalem below.

[5]But is there a Jerusalem on high?

[6]Yes, as it is written: [7]"Jerusalem the built is like the city that is joined together with it."

[8]And Rav Naḥman said to Rabbi Yitzḥak: What is [the meaning of] what is written: [9]"And about one they are stupid and foolish, the teaching of vanity is wood"?

RASHI

משום דבקרבך קדוש — שאתה מטיב מעשיך — לא יבא הקדוש ברוך הוא בעיר?! **לא אבא בירושלים כו׳** — והכי קאמר: עד שיהא בקרבך קדוש למטה, דהיינו ירושלים, לא אבוא בעיר שלמעלה. **ירושלים הבנויה כעיר שחוברה לה יחדיו** — ירושלים שלמטה תהא בנויה כעיר שחוברה לה, שהיא כיוצא בה, חבירתה ודוגמתה. מכלל דאיכא ירושלים אחריתי, והיכן אם לא למעלה? **ובאחת יבערו ויכסלו מוסר הבלים עץ הוא** — אילאו גזרה שוה היה משמע: אטומים כעץ לקבל מוסר, ולשוא היו לוקין. **באחת** — עבירה שהן עושין יתבערו הכסילים = רשעים.

BACKGROUND

יְרוּשָׁלַיִם שֶׁל מַעְלָה Jerusalem on high. The heavenly city of Jerusalem and the celestial Temple and altar are mentioned in several passages in the Talmud. The central concept here is not a Platonic idea of Jerusalem that exists in a spiritual world, but an explanation of the special sanctity of Jerusalem. The earthly city of Jerusalem is a special place in the world because it is intrinsically connected (חוּבְּרָה לָּהּ יַחְדָּו) to a supreme spiritual essence. The connection with the celestial Jerusalem is what makes the material city holy. The teaching cited here is connected to the general idea of the exile of the Divine Presence (גָּלוּת הַשְּׁכִינָה), for the exile of the Jews and the destruction of the Temple were not merely mundane events. Rather they must be seen as parallel to events of universal significance. As long as the earthly city of Jerusalem has not been fully reconstructed, so too does the celestial Jerusalem remain incomplete.

NOTES

לֹא אָבוֹא בִּירוּשָׁלַיִם שֶׁל מַעְלָה I will not come into the Jerusalem on high. *Rashi* explains that, according to the Midrash quoted here, the verse in Hosea should be understood as follows: *Until* the Holy One is in your midst, in the earthly Jerusalem, I will not go into the city, the heavenly Jerusalem. *Maharsha* argues that if we supply the word "until," then there is no reason to explain the verse as referring to the heavenly Jerusalem, for it can be explained as follows: Until the Holy One is in your midst because you have repented, I will not go into the earthly Jerusalem. Hence the verse should be understood as a question: If the Holy One is in your midst, if He sets His Divine Presence in the earthly Jerusalem, will I not go into the city, will I not also set My Divine Presence in the heavenly Jerusalem? Since the verse speaks first of the Divine Presence in the earthly Jerusalem, and only afterwards speaks about the Divine Presence in the heavenly Jerusalem, Rabbi Yoḥanan concludes that God will not enter the heavenly Jerusalem until He has first entered the earthly Jerusalem.

Iyyun Ya'akov notes that this Midrash treats the verse in Hosea as a message of comfort to the people of Israel while they are in exile — that even God is in exile and will not return to the heavenly Jerusalem until His people return to the earthly Jerusalem.

TRANSLATION AND COMMENTARY

preceding verses of this passage in Jeremiah, the Prophet notes that all over the world everyone shows signs of fear of God. Jeremiah tells us that in their stupidity the people of the world teach themselves to direct these feelings toward idols of wood. Rav Naḥman asks if there is any deeper meaning contained in this verse.

אֲמַר לֵיהּ [1]Rabbi Yitzḥak **said to** Rav Naḥman in reply: **This is what Rabbi Yoḥanan said** about this verse: [2]**There is one sin that destroys the wicked in Gehenna.** The word יִבְעֲרוּ, which we have translated as "they are stupid," can also be translated as "they will be destroyed." Rabbi Yoḥanan explains that Jeremiah is saying that the wicked of the world will be destroyed because of one sin. [3]**What is** this sin? [4]**Idol worship,** the "wood" of the verse. How do we know that the word "wood" in the verse refers to idol worship? We know it from the similarity between this verse and a verse later in the same chapter (10:15). [5]**It is written here** in verse 8: **"The teaching of vanity is wood."** [6]**And it is written there,** in verse 15, which deals explicitly with the folly of idol worship: **"They are vanity, a work of delusions."** Thus, from the use of the same word, "vanity," in verses 8 and 15, we may infer that the sin described in verse 8 is idol worship.

וַאֲמַר לֵיהּ רַב נַחְמָן [7]The Gemara now cites another explanation of a verse, involving the same three Amoraim: **And Rav Naḥman said to Rabbi Yitzḥak:** [8]**What is the meaning of what is written** in the following verse (Jeremiah 2:13): **"For My people has done two evils"?** [9]**Were there only two** evil deeds done by Israel before the destruction of the Temple? [10]**Did** God **pardon them for the twenty-four** sins of which they are accused in the Book of Ezekiel (chapter 22), which deals with the same period?

אֲמַר לֵיהּ [11]Rabbi Yitzḥak **said to** Rav Naḥman in reply: **This is what Rabbi Yoḥanan said** about this verse: The other sins were counted individually, [12]but **there was one** sin committed by Israel before the destruction of the Temple **that** [5B] **weighed** against them **like two** sins. [13]**And what was** this sin?

[1]אֲמַר לֵיהּ: הָכִי אָמַר רַבִּי יוֹחָנָן: [2]אַחַת הִיא שֶׁמְּבַעֶרֶת רְשָׁעִים בַּגֵּיהִנָּם. [3]מַאי הִיא? [4]עֲבוֹדָה זָרָה. [5]כְּתִיב הָכָא: ״מוּסַר הֲבָלִים עֵץ הוּא״. [6]וּכְתִיב הָתָם: ״הֶבֶל הֵמָּה, מַעֲשֵׂה תַּעְתֻּעִים״.

[7]וַאֲמַר לֵיהּ רַב נַחְמָן לְרַבִּי יִצְחָק: [8]מַאי דִּכְתִיב: ״כִּי שְׁתַּיִם רָעוֹת עָשָׂה עַמִּי״? [9]תַּרְתֵּין הוּא דַּהֲווּ? [10]עֶשְׂרִין וְאַרְבַּע שְׁבִיקָא לְהוּ?

[11]אֲמַר לֵיהּ: הָכִי אָמַר רַבִּי יוֹחָנָן: [12]אַחַת שֶׁהִיא [5B] שְׁקוּלָה כִּשְׁתַּיִם. [13]וּמַאי נִיהוּ?

LITERAL TRANSLATION

[1]He said to him: This is what Rabbi Yoḥanan said: [2]There is one [sin] that destroys the wicked in Gehenna. [3]What is it? [4]Idol worship. [5]It is written here: "The teaching of vanity is wood." [6]And it is written there: "They are vanity, a work of delusions."

[7]And Rav Naḥman said to Rabbi Yitzḥak: [8]What is [the meaning of] what is written: "For My people has done two evils"? [9]Were there [only] two? [10]Were twenty-four pardoned for them?

[11]He said to him: This is what Rabbi Yoḥanan said: [12][There is] one that is [5B] weighed like two. [13]And what is it?

RASHI

עשרים וארבע שביקא להו — בתמיה, בפרשת "התשפוט" (יחזקאל כב) עשרים וארבע עבירות שעברו. לשון אחר: שעברו על עשרים וארבעה ספרים. **ששקולה בשתים** — דכותיים וקדריים, כדמפרש שהרעו משניהן, לא הבינו מהן, דכותיים וקדרים אף על פי שיראתם פחותה לא רצו להמיר — ועמי המירו באחר, ולא עוד אלא בלא יועיל.

NOTES

עֶשְׂרִין וְאַרְבַּע שְׁבִיקָא לְהוּ Were twenty-four pardoned for them? Some manuscripts and sources read "twenty-two" instead of "twenty-four." This reading makes it clearer that reference is being made to the twenty-four charges God brought against Israel, as recounted in the twenty-second chapter of Ezekiel. Rav Naḥman asks: If the people will be punished for only two evils, what happened to the other twenty-two offenses? *Maharsha* suggests that an allusion is being made here to the entire Torah, which was written with twenty-two letters. Some Rishonim (*Rabbenu Gershom, Shittah*) have the reading "twenty-six." This is also taken as an allusion to the offenses mentioned in Ezekiel, using a slightly different way of counting them.

As for the twenty-four offenses, most commentators explain that the reference is to the twenty-four offenses listed in the Book of Ezekiel (chapter 22) as the sins of Jerusalem. Some Geonim suggest that twenty-four transgressions can also be found in the continuation of the passage in Jeremiah cited here, which speaks of the two evils of which the people of Israel are guilty (Jeremiah 2:13). *Rabbenu Ḥananel* cites a tradition that reference is being made here to the twenty-four offenses mentioned in the eleventh chapter of tractate *Sanhedrin* in the Jerusalem Talmud (see also *Rambam, Hilkhot Teshuvah,* chapter 4) as transgressions for which repentance is particularly difficult. *Rashi* and others maintain that Rav Naḥman is referring here to the twenty-four books of the Bible that Israel violated. *Rav Hai Gaon* suggests that there is no particular significance to the number twenty-four, and that it is being used here, as it is used elsewhere in the Gemara, as an expression meaning "many."

אַחַת שֶׁהִיא שְׁקוּלָה כִּשְׁתַּיִם There is one that is weighed like two. Our commentary follows *Rashi* and *Rabbenu Gershom,* who explain that the people of Israel were guilty

TRANSLATION AND COMMENTARY

[1] **Idol worship, as it is written** in this verse (Jeremiah 2:13): [2] **"For My people has done two evils. They have forsaken Me, the fountain of living waters, to dig for themselves cisterns, broken cisterns."** Thus we see that the Prophet is referring to the sin of idol worship, which he metaphorically compares to abandoning a spring of flowing water in exchange for an empty pit. [3] **And** as for the reason why this is considered a double sin, the following **is written about** idol worshipers in the same chapter (Jeremiah 2:10-11): **"For pass over the isles of the Kittites and see; and send to Kedar and consider well,** and see if there has been such a thing. [4] **Has a nation exchanged its gods, and they are no gods?** [5] **But My people has exchanged its glory for that which does not profit."** The Prophet illustrates the folly of exchanging God for an idol with two examples, one from the isles of the Kittites and one from Kedar, both of which remained loyal to their idolatrous national cults. Hence the sin of Israel in exchanging the true God for an empty idol is worse than the combined sins of the Kittites and the Kedarites, who worshipped idols but were not disloyal to them.

תָּנָא [6] The Gemara now explains the lesson to be learned from the Kittites and from Kedar. **It was taught** in a Baraita: **"The Kutites** [a variant of 'Kittites'] **worship fire, whereas the Kedarites worship water.** [7] **And even though** the Kutites **know that water extinguishes fire, they have not exchanged their** national **god,** [8] **'but My people has exchanged its glory,'** its uniquely pure national religion, which is its pride among the nations, **'for that which does not profit,'** idols of wood or stone."

וַאֲמַר לֵיהּ [9] The Gemara now cites the explanation of another verse, involving the same three Amoraim. **And Rav Naḥman said to Rabbi Yitzḥak:** [10] **What is the meaning of what is written** in the following verse (I Samuel 8:1): **"And it came to pass when Samuel became old,** that he made his sons judges over Israel"? The following verses relate that the people complained to Samuel that since he was old and his sons were not worthy, the time had come to anoint a king. [11] **But was Samuel** really **so old?** [12] **Surely he was only**

[1] עֲבוֹדָה זָרָה, דִּכְתִיב: [2] ״כִּי שְׁתַּיִם רָעוֹת עָשָׂה עַמִּי. אֹתִי עָזְבוּ, מְקוֹר מַיִם חַיִּים, לַחְצֹב לָהֶם בֹּארוֹת, בֹּארוֹת נִשְׁבָּרִים״. [3] וּכְתִיב בְּהוּ: ״כִּי עִבְרוּ אִיֵּי כִתִּיִּים וּרְאוּ; וְקֵדָר שִׁלְחוּ וְהִתְבּוֹנְנוּ מְאֹד, וגו׳. [4] הַהֵימִיר גּוֹי אֱלֹהִים, וְהֵמָּה לֹא אֱלֹהִים? [5] וְעַמִּי הֵמִיר כְּבוֹדוֹ בְּלוֹא יוֹעִיל״.

[6] תָּנָא: ״כּוּתִיִּים עוֹבְדִים לָאֵשׁ, וְקֵדָרִיִּים עוֹבְדִין לַמַּיִם. [7] וְאַף עַל פִּי שֶׁיּוֹדְעִים שֶׁהַמַּיִם מְכַבִּין אֶת הָאֵשׁ, לֹא הֵמִירוּ אֱלֹהֵיהֶם, [8] ׳וְעַמִּי הֵמִיר כְּבוֹדוֹ בְּלוֹא יוֹעִיל׳״.

[9] וַאֲמַר לֵיהּ רַב נַחְמָן לְרַבִּי יִצְחָק: [10] מַאי דִּכְתִיב: ״וַיְהִי כַּאֲשֶׁר זָקֵן שְׁמוּאֵל״? [11] וּמִי סִיב שְׁמוּאֵל כּוּלֵּי הַאי? [12] וְהָא בַּר

LITERAL TRANSLATION

[1] Idol worship, as it is written: [2] "For My people has done two evils; They have forsaken Me, the fountain of living waters, to dig for themselves cisterns, broken cisterns." [3] And it is written about them: "For pass over the isles of the Kittites and see; and send to Kedar and consider well, etc. [4] Has a nation exchanged its gods, and they are no gods? [5] But My people has exchanged its glory for that which does not profit."

[6] It was taught: "The Kutites worship fire, and the Kedarites worship water. [7] And even though they know that the waters extinguish the fire, they have not exchanged their gods, [8] 'but my people has exchanged its glory for that which does not profit.'"

[9] And Rav Naḥman said to Rabbi Yitzḥak: [10] What is [the meaning of] what is written: "And it came to pass when Samuel became old"? [11] But did Samuel become so old? [12] But surely he was [only]

BACKGROUND

עֲבוֹדָה זָרָה **Idol worship.** Although this term has many meanings in the Halakhah, here it is to be understood in its most extreme form — abandoning belief in God for belief in idols. Though the prohibition against idol worship is one of the 613 commandments of the Torah, by its nature it has special importance. Thus the Rabbis said that anyone who subscribes to idol worship denies the authenticity of the entire Torah. For the Torah is the theoretical and practical expression of pure faith in God, and the abandonment of that faith means complete departure from any connection with Judaism.

כּוּתִיִּים עוֹבְדִים לָאֵשׁ, וְקֵדָרִיִּים עוֹבְדִין לַמַּיִם **The Kutites worship fire, and the Kedarites worship water.** It is not clear who the "Kittites" were who are mentioned in the verse quoted here and also elsewhere in the Bible. The Sages identified them as the "Kutites," people who came from the land of Kuta (apparently in the area of the Caucasus mountains). The Kedarites were the ancient Arabs. We know little about their religions, but fire and water cults were common in various pagan religions, and sometimes a single god, such as the god of fire, was the central figure in their pantheon.

The words of the Gemara emphasize that although these two nations know by experience that the things they worship are not omnipotent, for water can extinguish fire, nevertheless these two nations remain faithful to their cults. By contrast, the Jews, who should have recognized the unlimited greatness of God both from their religious faith and from history, go astray after foreign cults.

NOTES

of two evils — in other words, their idol worship was worse than the combined sins of the Kittites and the Kedarites — because those nations at least remained loyal to their religion, the former to fire and the latter to water, whereas the people of Israel exchanged their true God for an idol.

Rabbenu Ḥananel explains that there are two elements involved in the sin of idol worship: the abandonment of the true God, and the acceptance of a powerless idol. Others suggest that idolatry is the equivalent of two sins because it is the subject of one of the three most severe prohibitions in the Torah (idolatry, murder and incest), the violation of which must be avoided even at the cost of one's life, and as such the prohibition against idol worship is equal in severity to the other two prohibitions (*Rabbenu Elyakim*). Still others argue that an idol worshipper is regarded as having committed two transgressions because idolatry involves the violation of the positive commandment, "I am the Lord your God," as well as the negative commandment, "You shall have no other gods beside me" (*Ahavat Eitan*).

BACKGROUND

וְהָא בַּר חֲמִישִׁים וּשְׁתַּיִם הֲוָה But surely he was only fifty-two. In the Talmud it is said that death at an early age is a sign of heavenly punishment. If someone dies at fifty, this is a sign of the punishment of "excision" (כרת), and if someone dies at sixty, this is a sign of "death at the hands of heaven." It is explained that death at the specific age of fifty-two is not a bad sign, because the great Prophet Samuel also died at that age. There is a voluminous Rabbinic literature dealing with the relationship between a person's deeds and the length of his life.

LANGUAGE (RASHI)

דשיבירי״ר* From the Old French *desseverer,* meaning "to wean."

חֲמִישִׁים וּשְׁתַּיִם הֲוָה, דְּאָמַר מָר: [1]״מֵת בַּחֲמִישִׁים וּשְׁתַּיִם שָׁנָה, זֶהוּ מִיתָתוֹ שֶׁל שְׁמוּאֵל הָרָמָתִי״.

[2]אֲמַר לֵיהּ: הָכִי אָמַר רַבִּי יוֹחָנָן: [3]זִקְנָה קָפְצָה עָלָיו, [4]דִּכְתִיב: ״נִחַמְתִּי כִּי הִמְלַכְתִּי אֶת שָׁאוּל״. [5]אָמַר לְפָנָיו: רִבּוֹנוֹ שֶׁל עוֹלָם, שְׁקַלְתַּנִי כְּמשֶׁה וְאַהֲרֹן, [6]דִּכְתִיב: ״משֶׁה וְאַהֲרֹן בְּכֹהֲנָיו, וּשְׁמוּאֵל בְּקֹרְאֵי שְׁמוֹ״. [7]מַה משֶׁה וְאַהֲרוֹן, לֹא בָּטְלוּ מַעֲשֵׂה יְדֵיהֶם בְּחַיֵּיהֶם, [8]אַף אֲנִי לֹא יִתְבַּטֵּל מַעֲשֵׂה יָדַי בְּחַיַּי. [9]אָמַר הַקָּדוֹשׁ בָּרוּךְ הוּא:

LITERAL TRANSLATION

fifty-two, for the Master said: [1]"He who dies at [the age of] fifty-two years, that is the death of Samuel of Ramah."

[2]He said to him: This is what Rabbi Yoḥanan said: [3]Old age came prematurely (lit., "jumped") upon him, [4]as it is written: "I have repented that I made Saul king." [5]He [Samuel] said before Him: Master of the World, You have compared me to Moses and Aaron, [6]as it is written: "Moses and Aaron among His priests, and Samuel among those that call upon His Name." [7]Just as [in the case of] Moses and Aaron, the work of their hands was not annulled in their lifetime, [8]I too [wish that] the work of my hands may not be annulled in my lifetime. [9]The Holy One blessed be He said:

TRANSLATION AND COMMENTARY

fifty-two years old at most, **for the Master said** in a Baraita discussing the significance of the age at which a person dies (*Moed Katan* 28a): [1]**"He who dies at the age of fifty-two years, that is the death of Samuel of Ramah,"** the Prophet Samuel, who was a native of the town of Ramah in the mountains of Ephraim. A careful examination of the verses in the Book of Samuel indicates that Samuel died at the age of fifty-two. Thus he must have been even younger — forty-eight or forty-nine — when he handed over his authority to his sons.

אֲמַר לֵיהּ [2]Rabbi Yitzḥak **said to** Rav Naḥman in reply: **This is what Rabbi Yoḥanan said** about this verse: [3]Samuel was not old in years, but **old age came upon him prematurely.** Rabbi Yoḥanan goes on to explain that this was the result of divine intervention, [4]**for it is written** (I Samuel 15:11) that God told Samuel: **"'I have repented that I made Saul king,** for he has turned away from Me and has not fulfilled My words.' And it grieved Samuel, and he cried to the Lord all night." [5]Rabbi Yoḥanan explains that **Samuel said to God: "Master of the World, You have compared me to Moses and Aaron,** [6]**as it is written** [Psalms 99:6]: **'Moses and Aaron among His priests, and Samuel among those that call upon His Name,** call upon the Lord and He answers them.'" Thus we see that Samuel's status in the eyes of God was as great as that of Moses and Aaron together. Accordingly, Samuel expected that God would show him as much consideration as He had shown Moses and Aaron: [7]**"Just as the deeds of Moses and Aaron were not annulled in their lifetime,** [8]**I too wish that my deeds may not be annulled in my lifetime."** Moses and Aaron, like Samuel, appointed their successors in their lifetime, and their successors survived them. By contrast, Samuel, who had anointed Saul under very similar circumstances (I Samuel 9:17), was now forced to see his achievement taken away from him before his very eyes. [9]**The Holy One blessed be He said:**

RASHI

והאמר מר — במועד קטן (כח,א): זו מיתתו של שמואל הרמתי. ולא כרת היא. במסכת שמחות (פרק ג) מפרש: מת בכך שנים — זו היא מיתת כרת, בכך וכך — זו היא מיתת אסכרה. **ימיו של שמואל חמישים ושתים שנה** — דכתיב "עד יגמל הנער" וגו' = *דשיבירי"ר בלעז. ועשרים וארבעה חדשים נקרא תינוק, וכתיב (שמואל א א) "וישב שם עד עולם" עולמו של לוי חמשים שנה, שנאמר (במדבר ח) "ומבן חמשים שנה ישוב מצבא העבודה". [בבכורים] ירושלמי ובסדר עולם תמצא כשני דפין תוספת על זה. **קפצה** — הלבין שערו. **נחמתי** — ורצה הקדוש ברוך הוא להורגו מיד. **שקלתני כמשה ואהרן דכתיב משה ואהרן בכהניו ושמואל בקוראי שמו וגו'** — שוין הן. **מעשה ידיהן** — יהושע אף הוא היה תלמידו של אהרן, כדאמרינן בעירובין (נד,ב): יצא משה ושנה להן אהרן פירקו.

NOTES

זִקְנָה קָפְצָה עָלָיו Old age came prematurely upon him. *Maharsha* and others point out that the verse (I Samuel 8:1), "And it came to pass when Samuel became old," comes before the verse (I Samuel 15:11), "I have repented that I made Saul king." How, then, can it be argued that old age came prematurely upon Samuel following God's rejection of King Saul? Some explain that God foresaw that Saul's monarchy would come to an untimely end, and this is why he caused Samuel to become old prematurely, even before Saul was crowned king (*Riaf, Ramat Shmuel*).

מְרַנְּנֵי אַבַּתְרֵיהּ They will speak ill of him. *Rashi* explains that the concern was that the people would speak ill of Samuel, for they would assume that he had been guilty of a serious sin if he died so young. Others suggest that the problem was that the people would express resentment toward God, for they would question the justice of God's striking down a man as righteous as Samuel before his time (*Shittah*).

[1]הֵיכִי אַעֲבִיד? לֵימוּת שָׁאוּל? [2]לָא קָא שָׁבֵיק שְׁמוּאֵל. [3]לֵימוּת שְׁמוּאֵל אַדְזוּטָר? [4]מְרַנְּנֵי אַבַּתְרֵיהּ. [5]לָא לֵימוּת שָׁאוּל וְלָא לֵימוּת שְׁמוּאֵל? [6]כְּבָר הִגִּיעָה מַלְכוּת דָּוִד, [7]וְאֵין מַלְכוּת נוֹגַעַת בַּחֲבֶרְתָּהּ אֲפִילּוּ כִּמְלֹא נִימָא. [8]אָמַר הַקָּדוֹשׁ בָּרוּךְ הוּא: אַקְפִּיץ עָלָיו זִקְנָה. [9]הַיְינוּ דִּכְתִיב: [10]״וְשָׁאוּל יוֹשֵׁב בַּגִּבְעָה תַּחַת הָאֵשֶׁל בָּרָמָה״. [11]וְכִי מָה עִנְיַן גִּבְעָה אֵצֶל רָמָה? [12]אֶלָּא לוֹמַר לְךָ: מִי גָּרַם לְשָׁאוּל שֶׁיֵּשֵׁב בַּגִּבְעָה שְׁתֵּי שָׁנִים וּמֶחֱצָה? [13]תְּפִלָּתוֹ שֶׁל שְׁמוּאֵל הָרָמָתִי.

[14]וּמִי מִידְחֵי גַּבְרָא מִקַּמֵּי גַּבְרָא?

[15]אִין, דְּאָמַר רַבִּי שְׁמוּאֵל בַּר נַחְמָנִי אָמַר רַבִּי יוֹנָתָן: [16]מַאי דִּכְתִיב: ״עַל כֵּן חָצַבְתִּי בַּנְּבִיאִים; הֲרַגְתִּים בְּאִמְרֵי פִי״? [17]״בְּמַעֲשֵׂיהֶם״ לֹא נֶאֱמַר, [18]אֶלָּא: ״בְּאִמְרֵי פִי״. [19]אַלְמָא מִידְחֵי גַּבְרָא מִקַּמֵּי גַּבְרָא.

LITERAL TRANSLATION

[1]How should I act? Let Saul die? [2]Samuel will not allow [it]. [3]Let Samuel die young? [4]They will speak ill of (lit., "murmur after") him. [5]Let Saul not die and let Samuel not die? [6]The reign of David has already arrived, [7]and one reign may not touch its fellow even by a hairsbreadth. [8]The Holy One blessed be He said: I will cause old age to come prematurely upon him. [9]This is what is written: [10]"And Saul was dwelling in Gibeah under the tree in Ramah." [11]But what connection does Gibeah have with Ramah? [12]Rather, [it is] to say to you: Who caused Saul to dwell in Gibeah two-and-a-half years? [13]The prayer of Samuel of Ramah.

[14]But is [one] man superseded by [another] man?

[15]Yes, as Rabbi Shmuel bar Naḥmani said in the name of Rabbi Yonatan: [16]What is [the meaning of] what is written: "Therefore I have hewed by the Prophets; I have slain them by the words of My mouth"? [17]"By their deeds" is not said, [18]but rather: "By the words of My mouth." [19]It follows that [one] man is superseded by [another].

TRANSLATION AND COMMENTARY

[1]**"How should I act?** Should I **let Saul die** now? [2]This is impossible, for **Samuel will not allow** Me to do this, as his complaint is just. [3]Shall I **let Samuel die young** before his time, to spare him the sight of Saul's downfall? [4]This too is impossible, because as a result the people **will speak ill of him."** If God's Prophet dies a sudden death while still young, people will wonder why God struck him down, and assume that he was disobedient in some way. [5]"Shall I **let Saul not die and Samuel not die?** Shall I allow Saul to remain on the throne until after Samuel has lived a full life? [6]This too is impossible, because **the reign of David has already arrived.** Having decided to replace Saul with David, [7]I have set the course of history and cannot delay it, since **one reign may not impinge on another, even by a hairsbreadth."** [8]Accordingly, **the Holy One blessed be He said:** "I will cause Samuel to die while Saul is still on the throne, but **I will cause old age to come prematurely upon him."** [9]**This is** the meaning of **what is written** in another verse (I Samuel 22:6), which describes the events that took place shortly before the death of Samuel: [10]**"And Saul was dwelling in** the town of **Gibeah, under the tree in Ramah."** [11]The verse identifies Gibeah with Ramah. **But what connection does Gibeah have with Ramah?** Gibeah, Saul's native town and capital city, was in the territory of the tribe of Benjamin, whereas Ramah, Samuel's native town, was in the territory of the tribe of Ephraim! [12]**Rather,** the purpose of this verse **is to say to you: Who caused Saul to dwell in Gibeah** and reign for an additional **two-and-a-half years** after God had decided to depose him? [13]**Samuel of Ramah, through his prayer.**

וּמִי מִידְחֵי גַּבְרָא [14]**But,** the Gemara objects, **is one man superseded by another?** Does God cause an innocent man to die prematurely so as not to interfere with His divine plan for another?

אִין [15]**Yes,** answers the Gemara, **as Rabbi Shmuel bar Naḥmani said in the name of Rabbi Yonatan:** [16]**What is the meaning of what is written** in the following verse (Hosea 6:5): **"Therefore I have hewed by the Prophets, I have slain them by the words of My mouth"?** This verse informs us that God sometimes kills Prophets in the course of their mission. [17]But **it does not say** that God kills them **"because of their deeds,"** [18]**but rather** that He does so **"by the words of My mouth,"** for some reason connected to God's plans and independent of the Prophet himself. [19]**Thus we see that one man is** sometimes **superseded by another.**

LANGUAGE

נִימָא **Hairsbreadth.** This word is derived from the Greek νῆμα, *nima*, meaning "thread."

RASHI

כי זוטר — בחור. **מרנני כולי עלמא אבתריה** — דאמרי: מדמית זוטר — שמא חטא ועבירה היתה בו. **וכי מה ענין גבעת בנימין אצל רמה** — בהר אפרים. **שישב שתי שנים ומחצה** — כדמפרש בסדר עולם: שמלך מתחילת שנת עשתי עשרה ושנים עשרה ושלשה עשר, ושמואל מת בתוך שנת שלש עשרה לסוף שמונה חדשים. **מי מידחי גברא כו׳** — דאידחי שמואל מקמי דוד. **במעשיהם לא נאמר** — דמשמע בעבור חטא. **אלא באמרי פי** — מפני דבר שגזרתי, כגון האי מעשה דשמואל.

[1]רַב נַחְמָן וְרַבִּי יִצְחָק הֲווּ יָתְבִי בִּסְעוּדְתָא. [2]אָמַר לֵיהּ רַב נַחְמָן לְרַבִּי יִצְחָק: ״לֵימָא מָר מִילְּתָא!״

[3]אֲמַר לֵיהּ: ״הָכִי אָמַר רַבִּי יוֹחָנָן: [4]אֵין מְסִיחִין בִּסְעוּדָה, שֶׁמָּא יַקְדִּים קָנֶה לַוֵּשֶׁט, [5]וְיָבֹא לִידֵי סַכָּנָה״.

[6]בָּתַר דִּסְעוּד, אֲמַר לֵיהּ: [7]״הָכִי אָמַר רַבִּי יוֹחָנָן: יַעֲקֹב אָבִינוּ לֹא מֵת״.

[8]אֲמַר לֵיהּ: ״וְכִי בִּכְדִי סָפְדוּ סַפְדָּנַיָּא וְחָנְטוּ חַנָּטַיָּא וְקָבְרוּ קַבְּרַיָּא״?

TRANSLATION AND COMMENTARY

רַב נַחְמָן [1]The Gemara now relates a story about Rav Naḥman, and about Rabbi Yitzḥak's interpretations of Scripture in the name of Rabbi Yoḥanan. **Rav Naḥman and Rabbi Yitzḥak were sitting** together **at dinner.** [2]**Rav Naḥman said to Rabbi Yitzḥak: "Say a word of Torah, Sir!"**

אֲמַר לֵיהּ [3]Rabbi Yitzḥak **said to** Rav Naḥman in reply: **"This is what Rabbi Yoḥanan said:** [4]**One should not make conversation while dining, lest one's windpipe come before one's esophagus** [lest food get into the windpipe], [5]causing one to choke **and come to danger."**

בָּתַר דִּסְעוּד [6]After **they had finished dinner,** Rabbi Yitzḥak responded to Rav Naḥman's previous request, and **said to him:** [7]**"This is what Rabbi Yoḥanan said: Our father Jacob,** whose death is described in Genesis [49:33], **did not** in fact **die,** but lives forever, for the verse describing his death does not explicitly say that he died."

אֲמַר לֵיהּ [8]Rav Naḥman reacted strongly to this astonishing statement and **said to** Rabbi Yitzḥak: **"But** surely the Torah describes Jacob's sons and the Egyptians **eulogizing** Jacob, **and embalming him, and burying him! Was it for nothing that they** did all this?"

LITERAL TRANSLATION

[1]Rav Naḥman and Rabbi Yitzḥak were sitting at dinner. [2]Rav Naḥman said to Rabbi Yitzḥak: "Say something [of Torah], Sir!"

[3]He said to him: "This is what Rabbi Yoḥanan said: [4]We do not converse during a meal, lest one's windpipe come before one's esophagus, [5]and one come to danger."

[6]After they had dined, he said to him: [7]"This is what Rabbi Yoḥanan said: Jacob our father did not die."

[8]He said to him: "But was it for nothing that the eulogizers eulogized [him] and the embalmers embalmed [him] and the buriers buried [him]?"

RASHI

שמא יקדים קנה – כשיוצא הקול נפתח אותו כובע שעל פי הקנה, ונכנס בו המאכל ומסתכן. ולפיכך לא אומר לך כלום. מאכל ומשתה הולך דרך הושט. **הכי גרסינן: לימא לן מר מידי** – ולא גרסינן חד לחבריה. **לא מת** – אלא חי הוא לעולם. **בבדי** – וכי בחנם ספדו ספידא וחנטו חנטיא? דכתיב ביה (בראשית נ) ״ויחנטו (אותו) ויספדו (לו)״.

BACKGROUND

יַעֲקֹב אָבִינוּ לֹא מֵת Jacob our father did not die. In a slightly different way, when *Rambam* speaks of the death of Moses he says: "When that thing happened to our teacher Moses which regarding other people is called death."

Indeed, from the Talmudic period onward, in Aggadic and esoteric literature, death is treated not only as the end of the life of the body in this world but as a phenomenon that has meaning for the soul of the deceased. Death is a transition to another form of existence, which also includes the destruction of the soul itself in various ways. Therefore, when it is said of certain righteous people that they did not die, or that they entered the Garden of Eden alive, the meaning is that these people did not undergo the normal process of death but passed on to a higher reality without impediment, and in some sense they are still living as they were.

NOTES

יַעֲקֹב אָבִינוּ לֹא מֵת Jacob our father did not die. Many commentators have addressed themselves to this strange statement. Some have suggested that Rabbi Yoḥanan meant to say that the Patriarch Jacob did not die in Egypt — he became unconscious in Egypt and appeared to have died, but he did not actually die until after he was taken to Eretz Israel (*Riaf, Ḥokhmat Manoah*). The problem with this explanation is that there does not seem to be even the slightest hint in the passage in our Gemara that the issue under discussion concerns Jacob's place of death. The issue is clearly whether or not Jacob actually died.

Rabbi Yitzḥak reported as a metaphor Rabbi Yoḥanan's statement that Jacob did not die. When Rav Naḥman took the statement literally, Rav Yitzḥak cited a verse from which Rav Naḥman was meant to understand that Rabbi Yoḥanan's statement was an allusion to some deeper truth. Rav Naḥman accepted this metaphoric interpretation of Rabbi Yoḥanan's statement, which when taken literally is contradicted by explicit verses in the Torah (see *Rashba* and *Riaf*).

As for the deeper meaning of Rabbi Yoḥanan's statement, some commentators suggest that the other patriarchs, Abraham and Isaac, are not regarded as still living, because each of them had a son who went astray (Ishmael and Esau, respectively). But Jacob, whose descendants continue in his path until this day and will continue in it until the final redemption, may be spoken of as being alive through his children. In that sense he has never died (*Rashba*). Alternatively, it has been suggested that Jacob did not die, because he did not have to pass through the various stages of the afterlife through which most other people have to go. The souls of those who must struggle with their evil inclination throughout their lives and who sometimes fail in the contest must be purged from sin before they are permitted to enjoy the World to Come. But when Jacob died, his soul went directly to the World to Come, for he had lived a perfect life (*Otzar HaKavod*).

HALAKHAH

אֵין מְסִיחִין בִּסְעוּדָה We do not converse during a meal. "A person should not talk during a meal, lest food get into his windpipe and cause him to choke. Even Torah matters may not be discussed (*Magen Avraham,* in accordance with our Gemara). According to some authorities (*Arukh HaShulḥan, Mishnah Berurah*), conversations may be conducted between courses; according to others (*Perishah*), even this is forbidden. Nowadays, this precaution is not observed, apparently because the prohibition was understood to apply only where meals were eaten in a reclining position (*Eliya Rabbah, Sha'arei Teshuvah*)." (*Shulḥan Arukh, Oraḥ Ḥayyim* 170:1.)

TRANSLATION AND COMMENTARY

אֲמַר לֵיהּ [1]Rabbi Yitzḥak **said to** Rav Naḥman in reply: **"I am interpreting a Biblical verse.** My statement in the name of Rabbi Yoḥanan can be proved from the Bible, [2]**as it is said** [Jeremiah 30:10]: **'And you, my servant Jacob, do not fear, says the Lord, and do not be dismayed, O Israel, for behold I will save you from afar, and your seed from the land of their captivity.'** In this verse, Jeremiah is addressing the Patriarch Jacob himself, because he refers to the people of Israel as 'your seed.' Moreover, it is not merely a poetic form of address to a dead Patriarch who is described as showing concern for the fate of his children, because it declares that God will save Jacob as well as his descendants. [3]Thus we see that **the verse compares** Jacob **himself with his seed,** and declares that both will be taken to Eretz Israel from the lands of their captivity. [4]And **just as his seed must be alive** in order to be redeemed, **so too must** Jacob **himself be alive.** Thus we see that Jacob did not actually die, but will remain alive until the time of redemption."

אָמַר רַבִּי יִצְחָק [5]Rabbi Yitzḥak made another unusual statement, concerning Rahab the prostitute (Joshua 2:1), who assisted Joshua's spies in obtaining information about the land of Canaan. There is a Baraita in tractate *Megillah* (15a), which singles out four beautiful women — among them Rahab the prostitute — whom the Bible describes as having used their charms on behalf of the Jews. The Baraita informs us that all these women had the power to arouse irresistible desire in men who saw them. Rahab, for example, was able to excite desire in a man by her name alone. Commenting on this Baraita, **Rabbi Yitzḥak said:** The Baraita is to be understood literally. [6]**Anyone who says, "Rahab, Rahab," will immediately have a seminal emission,** for her very name is sufficient to arouse a man in this way.

אֲמַר לֵיהּ [7]**Rav Naḥman said to** Rabbi Yitzḥak: [8]"It is not so! **I say** the name **'Rahab,' and it makes no difference to me!** What possible power of arousal can there be in a mere name?"

אֲמַר לֵיהּ [9]Rabbi Yitzḥak **said to** Rav Naḥman in reply: "I do not mean that this name has such power inherently, or that it is still effective today. [10]**When do I say** that the name 'Rahab' had such power? [11]Only in the days of Joshua, and only for a man who **knew her and was familiar with her.** When such a person would **mention her name,** the very memory of her would cause his sexual feelings to be aroused. But for those who never saw Rahab, her name is a name and nothing more.

כִּי הָווּ מִיפַּטְרִי מֵהֲדָדֵי [12]The Gemara now relates that **when** Rabbi Yitzḥak and Rav Naḥman **were taking**

[1]אֲמַר לֵיהּ: ״מִקְרָא אֲנִי דּוֹרֵשׁ, [2]שֶׁנֶּאֱמַר: ׳וְאַתָּה, אַל תִּירָא, עַבְדִּי יַעֲקֹב, נְאֻם ה׳, וְאַל תֵּחַת, יִשְׂרָאֵל, כִּי הִנְנִי מוֹשִׁיעֲךָ מֵרָחוֹק, וְאֶת זַרְעֲךָ מֵאֶרֶץ שִׁבְיָם׳. [3]מַקִּישׁ הוּא לְזַרְעוֹ. [4]מַה זַּרְעוֹ בַּחַיִּים, אַף הוּא בַּחַיִּים״.
[5]אָמַר רַבִּי יִצְחָק: [6]כָּל הָאוֹמֵר, ״רָחָב, רָחָב״, מִיָּד נִקְרֵי.
[7]אֲמַר לֵיהּ רַב נַחְמָן: [8]״אֲנָא אָמִינָא, וְלָא אִיכְפַּת לִי!״
[9]אֲמַר לֵיהּ: [10]״כִּי קָאָמִינָא, [11]בְּיוֹדְעָהּ וּבְמַכִּירָהּ וּבְמַזְכִּיר אֶת שְׁמָהּ״.
[12]כִּי הָווּ מִיפַּטְרִי מֵהֲדָדֵי,

LITERAL TRANSLATION

[1]He said to him: "I am interpreting a Biblical verse, [2]as it is said: 'And you, my servant Jacob, do not fear, says the Lord, and do not be dismayed, O Israel, for behold I will save you from afar, and your seed from the land of their captivity.' [3][The verse] compares him with his seed. [4]Just as his seed is alive, so too is he alive."

[5]Rabbi Yitzḥak said: [6]Anyone who says, "Rahab, Rahab," will immediately have a seminal emission.

[7]Rav Naḥman said to him: [8]"I say it, and it makes no difference to me!"

[9]He said to him: [10]"When I say [this, I mean] [11]when he knows her and is familiar with her and mentions her name."

[12]When they were taking leave of each other,

RASHI

מקרא אני דורש — והאי דחנטו חנטיא — סבורים היו שמת. **מה זרעו בחיים** — כשהוא מקבץ את ישראל מארץ שִׁבְיָם — החיים הוא מקבץ, שהן בשבי, שהמתים אינן בשבי. **אף הוא בחיים** — שיביאנו בגולה כדי לגאול את בניו לעיניו, כמו שמצינו במצרים: וירא ישראל וגו׳, ודרשינן: ישראל סבא. ודחנטו חנטיא — נדמה להם שמת, אבל חי היה. **כל האומר רחב רחב מידי נקרי** — נעשה בעל קרי. **לא איכפת לי** — איני חושש. **ביודעה** — היינו נמי מכירה. **כי הוה מיפטר** — רב נחמן מרב יצחק.

BACKGROUND

מִקְרָא אֲנִי דּוֹרֵשׁ I am interpreting a Biblical verse. Rabbi Yitzḥak's words were apparently based on a precise reading of the language of the Bible, for the word "death" is not mentioned explicitly in connection with Jacob. Rabbi Yitzḥak's interpretation seemed strange to Rav Naḥman. Therefore, Rabbi Yitzḥak said that it was not based solely on the absence of a single word. Instead, it was connected with the understanding of various verses, which speak of "Jacob" or of "Israel" in such a way that the personal, individual meaning of the name and its general, national meaning are not distinguished from each other, but Israel the man and Israel the nation are regarded as a single entity.

NOTES

בְּיוֹדְעָהּ וּבְמַכִּירָהּ When he knows her and is familiar with her. *Tosafot* suggests that the term "he knows her" should be understood in its Biblical sense (see, for example, Genesis 24:16: "And no man had known her") as referring to someone who had had sexual intercourse with Rahab. Such a person would be overcome by irresistible desire upon the mere mention of her name.

TRANSLATION AND COMMENTARY

leave of each other, [1]**Rav Naḥman said to** Rabbi Yitzḥak: "Please, **Sir,** give **me a blessing** before we part!"

אֲמַר לֵיהּ [2]Rabbi Yitzḥak **said to** Rav Naḥman in reply: **"I will tell you a parable.** [3]**To what may the matter** of your blessing **be compared?** [4]**It may be compared to** the case of **a person who was walking in the desert, hungry and tired and thirsty.** [5]The wanderer **found a tree whose fruit was sweet and whose shade was pleasant, and** which had **a stream of water flowing beneath it.** [6]**He ate of its fruits, and he drank of its waters, and he sat in its shade,** until he had fully recovered. [7]**When he decided to go,** he showed his gratitude for all that the tree had done for him by giving it a blessing. **He said: O tree, O tree, with what shall I bless you?** [8]**If I say to you, May your fruits be sweet, behold your fruits are** already **sweet.** [9]If I say to you, **May your shade be pleasant, behold your shade is** already **pleasant.** [10]If I say to you, **May a stream of water flow beneath you, behold a stream of water** already **flows beneath you.** [11]**Rather,** there is only one blessing that I can give to you: **May it be God's will that all the shoots that are planted from** cuttings taken from **you** [6A] **will** have sweet fruits and pleasant shade and a stream of water, **like you.** [12]**So it is with you,** Rav Naḥman. **With what shall I bless you** that you do not already have? [13]**If** I bless you **with Torah, behold you** already **have Torah.** [14]**If** I bless you **with wealth, behold you** already **have wealth.** [15]**If** I bless you **with children, behold you** already **have children.** [16]**Rather,** there is only one blessing that I can give to you: **May it be God's will that your descendants will be like you."**

תָּנוּ רַבָּנַן [17]The Gemara returns to the verse (Joel 2:23) cited at end of our Mishnah, which refers to "the former rain," the *yoreh* or *moreh*, and "the latter rain," the *malkosh*. These two types of rainfall are mentioned in other places in the Bible as well, in particular Deuteronomy 11:14: "And I will give the rain of your land in its due time, the *yoreh* and the *malkosh*, and you will gather in your grain and your wine and your oil." The Gemara now finds hints of the characteristics of these two types of rainfall in the etymologies of the words themselves. **Our Rabbis taught** the following Baraita: **"The former rain is called** ***yoreh*** [יוֹרֶה — from the Hebrew root ירה, meaning 'to teach'] **because it teaches people**

[1]אֲמַר לֵיהּ: ״לִיבָרְכָן מָר״!
[2]אֲמַר לֵיהּ: ״אֶמְשׁוֹל לְךָ מָשָׁל.
[3]לְמָה הַדָּבָר דּוֹמֶה? [4]לְאָדָם שֶׁהָיָה הוֹלֵךְ בַּמִּדְבָּר, וְהָיָה רָעֵב וְעָיֵף וְצָמֵא, [5]וּמָצָא אִילָן שֶׁפֵּירוֹתָיו מְתוּקִין, וְצִלּוֹ נָאֶה, וְאַמַּת הַמַּיִם עוֹבֶרֶת תַּחְתָּיו. [6]אָכַל מִפֵּירוֹתָיו, וְשָׁתָה מִמֵּימָיו, וְיָשַׁב בְּצִילּוֹ. [7]וּכְשֶׁבִּיקֵּשׁ לֵילֵךְ, אָמַר: אִילָן, אִילָן, בַּמָּה אֲבָרֶכְךָ? [8]אִם אוֹמַר לְךָ שֶׁיְּהוּ פֵּירוֹתֶיךָ מְתוּקִין, הֲרֵי פֵּירוֹתֶיךָ מְתוּקִין. [9]שֶׁיְּהֵא צִילְּךָ נָאֶה, הֲרֵי צִילְּךָ נָאֶה. [10]שֶׁתְּהֵא אַמַּת הַמַּיִם עוֹבֶרֶת תַּחְתֶּיךָ, הֲרֵי אַמַּת הַמַּיִם עוֹבֶרֶת תַּחְתֶּיךָ. [11]אֶלָּא, יְהִי רָצוֹן שֶׁכָּל נְטִיעוֹת שֶׁנּוֹטְעִין מִמְּךָ [6A] [12]יִהְיוּ כְּמוֹתְךָ. אַף אַתָּה, בַּמֶּה אֲבָרֶכְךָ? [13]אִם בְּתוֹרָה, הֲרֵי תּוֹרָה. [14]אִם בְּעוֹשֶׁר, הֲרֵי עוֹשֶׁר. [15]אִם בְּבָנִים, הֲרֵי בָּנִים. [16]אֶלָּא, יְהִי רָצוֹן שֶׁיִּהְיוּ צֶאֱצָאֵי מֵעֶיךָ כְּמוֹתְךָ״.
[17]תָּנוּ רַבָּנַן: ״יוֹרֶה שֶׁמּוֹרֶה אֶת

LITERAL TRANSLATION

[1]he [Rav Naḥman] said to him: "Bless me, Sir!" [2]He said to him: "I will tell you a parable. [3]What is the matter like? [4][It is like] a person who was walking in the desert, and was hungry and tired and thirsty, [5]and he found a tree whose fruits were sweet, and its shade was pleasant, and a stream of water was flowing beneath it. [6]He ate of its fruits, and he drank of its waters, and he sat in its shade. [7]And when he wished to go, he said: O tree, O tree, with what shall I bless you? [8]If I say to you that your fruits should be sweet, behold your fruits are sweet. [9]That your shade should be pleasant, behold your shade is pleasant. [10]That a stream of water should flow beneath you, behold a stream of water flows beneath you. [11]Rather, may it be [God's] will that all shoots that they plant from you [6A] will be like you. [12]Similarly, with what shall I bless you? [13]If with Torah, behold [you have] Torah. [14]If with wealth, behold [you have] wealth. [15]If with children, behold [you have] children. [16]Rather, may it be [God's] will that the offspring of your loins will be like you." [17]Our Rabbis taught: "[The former rain is called] *yoreh* (יורה) because it teaches

RASHI

והיה צילו נאה — שזה צריך לאדם עייף לנוח תחתיו. **ופירותיו מתוקין** — לרעב. **ואמת המים** — לצמא. **יהיו כמותך** — בתורה, ולעושר וכבוד. **יורה** — ״ונתתי מטר ארצכם בעתו יורה ומלקוש״ (דברים יא). **יורה** — רביעה ראשונה היורדת במרחשון, כדלקמן: למה נקרא יורה — שמורה להן להטיח גגותיהן בטיח של טיט, שלא יטפו גשמים בבית.

TRANSLATION AND COMMENTARY

to plaster their roofs and to bring in their produce and to attend to all their needs." Since the *yoreh* is the first rainfall of the season, it stimulates the people to make their final preparations for the winter. [1]The Baraita continues: "There is **another explanation** of the etymology of the word *yoreh*: It has this name **because it saturates** [from the Hebrew root, רוה, meaning 'to quench' or 'to saturate'] **the earth and waters it to the depths,** [2]**as it is said** [Psalms 65:11]: **'You water its ridges abundantly; You settle its furrows; You make it soft with showers; You bless its growth.'"** [3]The Baraita continues: "There is **another explanation:** The former rain is called *yoreh* **because it comes down gently and does not come down heavily."** Gentle rain can be compared to gentle instruction by a sympathetic teacher, and thus the word *yoreh* can be derived from the Hebrew root ירה, meaning "to teach." Until now we have assumed that *yoreh* displays only positive qualities. [4]**"But,"** continues the Baraita, **"perhaps** this is not so. Perhaps the former rain **is called *yoreh*** [from the Hebrew root ירה, meaning 'to shoot'] **because of** the negative qualities that such rain sometimes displays, in that **it makes the fruit** on the trees **fall** to the ground, **and it washes away the seeds** that have just been sown, **and it** even **washes away the trees."** [5]The Baraita rejects this explanation: **"The verse states** [Deuteronomy 11:14]: ***'Malkosh,'*** the latter rain. The word *malkosh* appears immediately after the word *yoreh* in this verse in Deuteronomy. [6]Thus both rainfalls are similar, and **just as** the word ***malkosh*** refers only to a kind of rain that **is a blessing, so too must** the word ***yoreh*** refer to a kind of rain that **is a blessing.** [7]**But,"** continues the Baraita,

הַבְּרִיּוֹת לְהַטִּיחַ גַּגּוֹתֵיהֶן, וּלְהַכְנִיס אֶת פֵּירוֹתֵיהֶן, וְלַעֲשׂוֹת כָּל צָרְכֵיהֶן. [1]דָּבָר אַחֵר: שֶׁמַּרְוֶה אֶת הָאָרֶץ וּמַשְׁקֶה עַד תְּהוֹם, [2]שֶׁנֶּאֱמַר: ׳תְּלָמֶיהָ רַוֵּה; נַחֵת גְּדוּדֶהָ; בִּרְבִיבִים תְּמֹגְגֶנָּה; צִמְחָהּ תְּבָרֵךְ׳. [3]דָּבָר אַחֵר: יוֹרֶה שֶׁיּוֹרֵד בְּנַחַת, וְאֵינוֹ יוֹרֵד בְּזַעַף. [4]אוֹ אֵינוֹ יוֹרֶה אֶלָּא שֶׁמַּשִּׁיר אֶת הַפֵּירוֹת, וּמַשְׁטִיף אֶת הַזְּרָעִים, וּמַשְׁטִיף אֶת הָאִילָנוֹת? [5]תַּלְמוּד לוֹמַר: ׳מַלְקוֹשׁ׳. [6]מַה מַּלְקוֹשׁ לִבְרָכָה, אַף יוֹרֶה לִבְרָכָה. [7]אוֹ

LITERAL TRANSLATION

people to plaster their roofs and to bring in their produce and attend to all their needs. [1]Another explanation (lit., 'thing'): Because it saturates the earth and waters [it] to the depths, [2]as it is said: 'You water its ridges abundantly; You settle its furrows; You make it soft with showers; You bless its growth.' [3]Another explanation: [It is called] *yoreh* because it comes down gently, and it does not come down heavily. [4]Or perhaps [it is called] *yoreh* only because it makes the fruits fall, and it washes away the seeds, and it washes away the trees? [5]The verse states: *'Malkosh.'* [6]Just as *malkosh* is for a blessing, so too is *yoreh* for a blessing. [7]Or

RASHI

ולהכניס פירותיהן — שהניחו בשדות לייבשן עד עכשיו. **כל צרכיהן** — שאר דברים הצריכים לימות הגשמים. **תלמיה רוה** — כשאתה מרוה תלמי חרישה של ארץ ישראל. **נחת הוא לגדודיה** — בני אדם, היינו פשט המקרא. ולקמיה דריש שאפילו גייסות פוסקות בו. **שיורד בנחת** — והכי משמע: יורה — כאדם שמורה לתלמידיו בנחת, דכתיב (קהלת ט): דברי חכמים בנחת נשמעים. אי נמי: לשון חץ יורה, ההולך ביושר ואינו נוטה לכאן ולכאן. לשון אחר: שמתכוין לארץ, ואינו יורד בזעף, בספרי. הכי גרסינן: **או אינו אלא ששוטף את הזרעים** — כלומר, דעד השתא אמרינן יורה לברכה, או נו אלא יורה לשון קללה כמו ״ירה יירה״ (שמות יט) — ששובר הכל, או לשון חץ היורה, והכי משמע קרא: ״והיה אם שמוע תשמעו אל מצותי״ וגו׳ ואם לאו — ונתתי מטר ארצכם יורה לרעה. מלתא בעלמא הוא, ואורחא דברייתא למתני כי האי גוונא. **משיר פירותיהן** — שעודן באילן, כגון אתרוגים או רמונים, או סופי תאנים. ולא גרסינן שוטף את הגרנות — דגרנות במרחשון ליכא. **מה מלקוש לברכה** — שאי אפשר לדורשו לשבר גרנות ולהשיר פירות, שאינם מצויים באותו הפרק. ואי אתה יכול לדורשו אלא לטובה, שיורד על המלילות ועל הקשין, וממלא את התבואה בקשיה. הדר אמר: דלמא מלקוש קללה הוא, והכי משמע: שמל וקשה, כלומר: מל את הבתים והאילנות, שמפילן ומשברן, וקשה לתבואה.

BACKGROUND

יוֹרֶה וּמַלְקוֹשׁ The former rain and the latter rain. The first and last rains of the season are important not only in themselves but also because they mark the opening and closing of the rainy season. Usually the first rain is short and not light. Sometimes it arrives before the onset of steady rains. When the *yoreh*, the first rain, falls on time and in the normal way, it brings a double blessing — on the one hand, everyone knows that it is time to prepare for the rainy season, and the rain itself lowers the temperature and settles the dirt and dust on the ground. By contrast, and this is another possibility mentioned in the Baraita, if the *yoreh* comes as a rainstorm, as sometimes happens following a sharp atmospheric change, it can cause great damage since people are not prepared for it.

Similarly, the final rains of the year, the *malkosh*, are usually beneficial. They generally fall when the weather is quite warm. The wheat in the fields is already ripe. The additional water at this time serves to fill out the ears of grain, to strengthen the straw, and to increase the growth of fruit. Nevertheless, a *malkosh* that comes too late can cause damage. If it arrives as a storm, it damages the grain that has already somewhat dried (see Exodus 9:31-32); it can also sometimes soak and ruin the sheaves of grain that have already been harvested.

NOTES

יוֹרֶה *Yoreh.* Very different etymologies are suggested here for the word *yoreh* because it may be derived from several Hebrew roots, each of which has more than one meaning. According to the simplest etymology, *yoreh* is derived from the root ירה which can mean "to teach," and hence *yoreh* is the rain that instructs the people to plaster their roofs, or the rain that comes down as gently as that a master teaches his students. But the root ירה can also mean "to shoot," or "to hurl," and hence *yoreh* is also rain that comes down straight, like an arrow shot by an archer, or it is rain that is hurled down violently and causes damage. The word *yoreh* may also be derived from the root רוה which means "to saturate," and hence *yoreh* is rain that saturates the earth.

מַלְקוֹשׁ *Malkosh.* The word *malkosh* appears to be derived from the relatively rare Biblical root לקש meaning "to be late," and hence *malkosh* is the last rain of the season. *Rashi* suggests that the word לֶקֶשׁ (Amos 7:1) is a synonym for locusts, and thus *malkosh* is also the rain that brings forth locusts.

אֵינוֹ מַלְקוֹשׁ אֶלָּא שֶׁמַּפִּיל אֶת הַבָּתִּים, [1]וּמְשַׁבֵּר אֶת הָאִילָנוֹת, וּמַעֲלֶה אֶת הַסַּקָּאִין? [2]תַּלְמוּד לוֹמַר: ׳יוֹרֶה׳. [3]מַה יּוֹרֶה לִבְרָכָה, אַף מַלְקוֹשׁ לִבְרָכָה. וְיוֹרֶה גּוּפֵיהּ מְנָלַן? [4]דִּכְתִיב: ׳וּבְנֵי צִיּוֹן, גִּילוּ וְשִׂמְחוּ בַּה׳ אֱלֹהֵיכֶם, כִּי נָתַן לָכֶם אֶת הַמּוֹרֶה לִצְדָקָה, וַיּוֹרֶד לָכֶם גֶּשֶׁם, מוֹרֶה וּמַלְקוֹשׁ, בָּרִאשׁוֹן׳״.

[5]תָּנוּ רַבָּנַן: ״יוֹרֶה בְּמַרְחֶשְׁוָן וּמַלְקוֹשׁ בְּנִיסָן. [6]אַתָּה אוֹמֵר יוֹרֶה בְּמַרְחֶשְׁוָן וּמַלְקוֹשׁ בְּנִיסָן. [7]אוֹ אֵינוֹ אֶלָּא יוֹרֶה בְּתִשְׁרֵי וּמַלְקוֹשׁ בְּאִיָּיר? [8]תַּלְמוּד לוֹמַר: ׳בְּעִתּוֹ׳״.

[9]מַלְקוֹשׁ? [10]אָמַר רַב נְהִילַאי בַּר

LITERAL TRANSLATION

perhaps [it is called] *malkosh* only because it knocks down the houses, [1]and it shatters the trees, and it brings up the locusts? [2]The verse states: *'Yoreh.'* [3]Just as *yoreh* is for a blessing, so too is *malkosh* for a blessing. And from where [do we know that] *yoreh* itself [is for a blessing]? [4]For it is written: 'And you children of Zion, be glad and rejoice in the Lord your God, for He has given you the former rain for charity, and He has made rain fall for you, the former rain and the latter rain, in the first month.'"

[5]Our Rabbis taught: "The former rain is in Marḥeshvan and the latter rain is in Nisan. [6]You say the former rain is in Marḥeshvan and the latter rain is in Nisan. [7]But might not the former rain be only in Tishri and the latter rain in Iyyar? [8]The verse states: 'In its due time.'"

[9][What is the meaning of] *malkosh*? [10]Rav Nehilai bar Idi

TRANSLATION AND COMMENTARY

"perhaps the latter rain **is called *malkosh* because** of its negative qualities, [1]in that **it knocks down houses, shatters trees, and brings up locusts."** The etymology on which this explanation of *malkosh* is based derives the meaning of the word from two Hebrew words, *mal* (מַל), meaning "to cut," and *kasheh* (קָשֶׁה) meaning "hard." But the Baraita also rejects this explanation: [2]**"The verse states: *'Yoreh,'*** the former rain. The word *yoreh* appears immediately before the word *malkosh* in the verse in Deuteronomy. [3]Thus both rainfalls are similar, and **just as *yoreh*** refers only to a kind of rain that **is a blessing, so too must** the word ***malkosh*** refer to a kind of rain that **is a blessing. But from where do we know** that the word ***yoreh* itself is a blessing**, so that we can compare *malkosh* to it?" [4]The Baraita answers: "We know that *yoreh* is a blessing because the following **is written** in the verse cited in our Mishnah [Joel 2:23]: **'And you children of Zion, be glad and rejoice in the Lord your God, for He has given you the former rain** [*moreh*] **for charity, and He has made rain fall for you, the former rain and the latter rain, in the first month.'"** Thus we see that the former rain, in particular, is described as falling charitably. Hence it is clear that each kind of rain is essentially positive, and this is implied in the etymology of the words used.

תָּנוּ רַבָּנַן [5]The Gemara now cites another Baraita about *yoreh* and *malkosh*. **Our Rabbis taught** the following Baraita: **"The former rain falls in Marḥeshvan and the latter rain falls in Nisan."** But if the rainy season begins earlier than Marḥeshvan, or ends later than Nisan, the season is considered abnormal, and the additional rain is at best a mixed blessing. [6]The Baraita continues: **"You say** that **the former rain falls in Marḥeshvan and the latter rain in Nisan.** [7]**But might not the former rain fall as early as Tishri,** a month before Marḥeshvan, **and the latter rain in Iyyar,** a month after Nisan? [8]To set aside this suggestion **the verse** [Deuteronomy 11:14] **states:** 'And I will give the rain of your land **in its due time,** the former rain and the latter rain.'" Rain is not supposed to fall early or to continue to fall after its due time.

מַלְקוֹשׁ [9]The Gemara now discusses the etymology of the word *malkosh* — the latter rain — and offers three suggestions as to its derivation. **What,** it asks, **is the meaning of *malkosh*?** (1) [10]**Rav Nehilai**

RASHI

שמעלה סקאים — וברכה דקרא למילוי מים בורות שיחין ומערות, גימגוס. **שמפיל את הבתים** — ומשמעו כדלקמן, שמל קשיותן של ישראל, אי נמי: שמל דבר הקשה — חותך ומשבר את הבתים. כלומר, אין בו תקלת גרנות והשרת פירות, לפי שאי אפשר לו. **סקאי** — מין ארבה, כדמתרגם ״הצלצל״ (דברים כח) — סקאה. ומלקוש לשון ארבה, כמו ״והנה לקש אחר גזי המלך״ (עמוס ז). **את המורה לצדקה** — אלמא: יורה לטובה. **הכי גרסינן: או אינו אלא יורה בתשרי ומלקוש באייר** — שיש עדין מלילות וקשין. **תלמוד לומר בעתו** — יורה במרחשון ומלקוש בניסן, שכך היא העת והזמן, ויפה הוא, כדלקמן דזמן רביעה ראשונה במרחשון הוא. אית ספרים דכתוב בהו: או אינו אלא בכסליו דזמן יורה בכסליו הוא. וכרבנן דפליגי עליה דרבי מאיר לקמן, תלמוד לומר ״בעתו״ יורה ומלקוש, מה מלקוש בעתו — אף יורה בעתו, דמלקוש זהו שיורד על המלילות ועל הקשין, וזהו ניסן שיש בו קשין ומלילות.

BACKGROUND

וּמַעֲלֶה אֶת הַסַּקָּאִין And it brings up the locusts. Locusts (*Schistocerca gregaria*) generally exist in small swarms and do not pose any danger. Occasionally, because of a combination of rain toward the end of the winter and high temperatures, locusts begin to reproduce suddenly and to multiply quickly. Then, aided by southern or southeastern winds, locusts can reach Eretz Israel and can cause much damage to vegetation.

יוֹרֶה בְּמַרְחֶשְׁוָן וּמַלְקוֹשׁ בְּנִיסָן The former rain is in Marḥeshvan and the latter rain is in Nisan. Determining the time of rainfall according to the Hebrew calendar is complicated because the lunar months do not always fall at the same time according to the solar calendar. The first rains (called *yoreh*) occasionally fall in the middle of October (which could still be in the month of Tishri), and the last rains (*malkosh*) sometimes fall as late as the end of April or the beginning of May (which sometimes could be in the middle of Iyyar).

SAGES

רַב נְהִילַאי בַּר אִידִי Rav Nihilai bar Idi. A Babylonian Amora of the second generation. His name is seldom mentioned, but when he appears, it is to transmit teachings in the name of Shmuel, whose disciple he apparently was.

NOTES

הַסַּקָּאִין The locusts. Most commentators explain that סַקָּאִין are a type of locust, but some suggest that they are a type of worm (*Rabbenu Elyakim*). *Targum Onkelos* translates the word צְלָצַל (Deuteronomy 28:42), which *Rashi* and others understand as referring to a type of locust, by using the word סַקָּאָה.

TRANSLATION AND COMMENTARY

bar Idi said in the name of Shmuel: The word *malkosh* (מַלְקֹשׁ) is a combination of *mal* (מָל) meaning "to circumcise" and *kasheh* (קָשֶׁה) meaning "hard." [1]Thus *malkosh* is **something that removes** (lit., "circumcises") **the hardness of Israel's** heart, because the need for *malkosh* is so great that even hardhearted people repent and learn to pray for it. (2) [2]**In the School of Rabbi Yishmael** the following Baraita **was taught:** "The first part of the word *malkosh* suggests the Hebrew word *malei,* meaning 'to fill,' and the last part of the word suggests the Hebrew word *kash*, meaning 'stalks.' [3]Thus *malkosh* is **something that fills the grain in its stalks."** In other words, the latter rain gives the already developed plants the necessary moisture to ripen fully. (3) [4]**In** another **Baraita** a similar idea **was taught:** "The first part of the word *malkosh* suggests the Hebrew word *melilah*, meaning 'ear of grain,' and the last part of the word suggests *kash*, meaning 'stalks.' Thus *malkosh* is **something that comes down on the ears and on the stalks** of the already developed grain."

תָּנוּ רַבָּנַן [5]The Gemara now cites another source about the former and the latter rain. **Our Rabbis taught** the following Baraita: **"The former rain falls in Marḥeshvan and the latter rain falls in Nisan."** But if the rainy season begins later than Marḥeshvan, even if rains do subsequently fall, the impact of the initial drought will still be felt. [6]The Baraita continues: **"You say** that **the former rain falls in Marḥeshvan and the latter rain in Nisan.** [7]**But might not the former rain fall** as late as **the month of Kislev**, a month after Marḥeshvan? [8]To make this point clear **the verse** [Deuteronomy 11:14] **states:** 'And I will give the rain of your land **in its due time, the former rain and the latter rain.'** [9]**Just as the latter rain falls** only **in its due time, so too does the former rain fall in its due time.** [10]And we know that the latter rain is supposed to fall only in its due time, because if **rains fall once Nisan is over, it is not a sign of blessing."** Thus we see that in order to have the best effect the former rain should fall at the very beginning of the rainy season.

תַּנְיָא אִידָךְ [11]Although all opinions agree that in order to have the best effect the rains should fall on time, there is a Tannaitic dispute about the precise time when the former rain should fall, as **was taught in another Baraita: "The former rain falls in Marḥeshvan and the latter rain** falls **in Nisan.** [12]**This is the opinion of Rabbi Meir,** whose viewpoint was also reflected in the previous Baraitot. [13]**But the Sages say: The former rain falls in Kislev."**

מַאן חֲכָמִים [14]The Gemara asks: **Who are the Sages** mentioned in this Baraita? Whose viewpoint do they represent?

אָמַר רַב חִסְדָּא [15]**Rav Ḥisda said** in reply: **It is** the viewpoint of **Rabbi Yose, as was**

אִידִי אָמַר שְׁמוּאֵל: [1]דָּבָר שֶׁמָּל קַשְׁיוּתֵיהֶן שֶׁל יִשְׂרָאֵל. [2]דְּבֵי רַבִּי יִשְׁמָעֵאל תָּנָא: [3]"דָּבָר שֶׁמְּמַלֵּא תְּבוּאָה בְּקַשֶּׁיהָ". [4]בְּמַתְנִיתָא תָּנָא: "דָּבָר שֶׁיּוֹרֵד עַל הַמְּלִילוֹת וְעַל הַקַּשִּׁין". [5]תָּנוּ רַבָּנַן: "יוֹרֶה בְּמַרְחֶשְׁוָן וּמַלְקוֹשׁ בְּנִיסָן. [6]אַתָּה אוֹמֵר יוֹרֶה בְּמַרְחֶשְׁוָן. [7]אוֹ אֵינוֹ אֶלָּא בְּחֹדֶשׁ כִּסְלֵיו? [8]תַּלְמוּד לוֹמַר: 'בְּעִתּוֹ יוֹרֶה וּמַלְקוֹשׁ'. [9]מַה מַּלְקוֹשׁ בְּעִתּוֹ, אַף יוֹרֶה בְּעִתּוֹ. [10]כֵּיוָן שֶׁיָּצָא נִיסָן וְיָרְדוּ גְּשָׁמִים, אֵינוֹ סִימַן בְּרָכָה". [11]תַּנְיָא אִידָךְ: "יוֹרֶה בְּמַרְחֶשְׁוָן וּמַלְקוֹשׁ בְּנִיסָן. [12]דִּבְרֵי רַבִּי מֵאִיר. [13]וַחֲכָמִים אוֹמְרִים: יוֹרֶה בְּכִסְלֵיו". [14]מַאן חֲכָמִים? [15]אָמַר רַב חִסְדָּא: רַבִּי יוֹסֵי

LITERAL TRANSLATION

said in the name of Shmuel: [1]Something that removes (lit., "circumcises") the hardness of Israel. [2]In the School of Rabbi Yishmael it was taught: [3]"Something that fills the grain in its stalks." [4]In a Baraita it was taught: "Something that comes down on the ears and on the stalks."

[5]Our Rabbis taught: "The former rain is in Marḥeshvan and the latter rain is in Nisan. [6]You say the former rain is in Marḥeshvan. [7]But might it not be only in the month of Kislev? [8]The verse states: 'In its due time, the former rain and the latter rain.' [9]Just as the latter rain is in its due time, so too is the former rain in its due time. [10]Once Nisan has passed and rains fall, it is not a sign of blessing."

[11]Another [Baraita] was taught: "The former rain is in Marḥeshvan and the latter rain is in Nisan. [12][These are] the words of Rabbi Meir. [13]But the Sages say: The former rain is in Kislev."

[14]Who are the Sages?

[15]Rav Ḥisda said: It is Rabbi

RASHI

דבר שמל קשיותן של ישראל — שבשבילו יורד חוזרין ישראל בתשובה, ומתענין ועושין צדקות. **מלילות** — ראשי שיבולות שאדם מולל בידו, כדכתיב (דברים כג) "וקטפת מלילות בידך". **וקשין** — קנה. **שממלא תבואה בקשיה** — ומשלימה.

SAGES

דְּבֵי רַבִּי יִשְׁמָעֵאל תָּנָא In the School of Rabbi Yishmael it was taught. Rabbi Yishmael ben Elisha was both a colleague of Rabbi Akiva and a scholar who challenged his views. Though they seldom disagreed about the practical implementation of the Halakhah, they did have very different approaches regarding Halakhic Midrash, in which each established his own school. Some authorities view this difference of opinion broadly — as the basis of distinct general principles of legislation — while others restrict it. However, even the more limited approach notes major differences between the schools in the principles of Halakhic Midrash. Most extant Halakhic works of that period follow Rabbi Akiva's approach, for it was his disciples and, in turn, their disciples who composed the basic works of Halakhah — the Mishnah, the Tosefta, and others. It is only in the collections of Halakhic Midrashim (such as the Mekhilta and part of Sifrei) that we find entire works or parts of works written in the spirit of Rabbi Yishmael's School. Moreover, Rabbi Yishmael's disciples are not so well known, and their names are cited only occasionally in the Talmud. Nonetheless, the Talmud contains many rulings transmitted by the School of Rabbi Yishmael, though they are not attributed to a specific Sage. Among these teachings, a large number are Halakhic teachings or Halakhic Midrashim presented in the name of "a Tanna from the School of Rabbi Yishmael" — an anonymous Sage from the School of Rabbi Yishmael.

רַבִּי יוֹסֵי Rabbi Yose. This is Rabbi Yose ben Ḥalafta, one of the greatest Tannaim. He lived in the generation before the completion of the Mishnah, and the imprint of his teachings is evident throughout Tannaitic literature.
His father, known as Abba Ḥalafta, was also considered one of the Sages of his generation, and his family, according to one tradition, was descended from Jehonadab

הִיא, דְּתַנְיָא: [1]"אֵיזוֹ הִיא רְבִיעָה רִאשׁוֹנָה? [2]הַבַּכִּירָה בִּשְׁלֹשָׁה בְּמַרְחֶשְׁוָן. בֵּינוֹנִית בְּשִׁבְעָה בּוֹ. אֲפִילָה בְּשִׁבְעָה עָשָׂר בּוֹ. [3]דִּבְרֵי רַבִּי מֵאִיר. [4]רַבִּי יְהוּדָה אוֹמֵר: בְּשִׁבְעָה, וּבְשִׁבְעָה עָשָׂר, וּבְעֶשְׂרִים וּשְׁלֹשָׁה. [5]רַבִּי יוֹסֵי אוֹמֵר: בְּשִׁבְעָה עָשָׂר, וּבְעֶשְׂרִים וּשְׁלֹשָׁה, וּבְרֹאשׁ חֹדֶשׁ כִּסְלֵיו. [6]וְכֵן הָיָה רַבִּי יוֹסֵי אוֹמֵר: אֵין הַיְּחִידִים מִתְעַנִּין עַד שֶׁיַּגִּיעַ רֹאשׁ חֹדֶשׁ כִּסְלֵיו".

[7]אָמַר רַב חִסְדָּא: הֲלָכָה כְּרַבִּי יוֹסֵי.

[8]אֲמֵימָר מַתְנֵי לְהָא דְּרַב חִסְדָּא בְּהָא לִישָּׁנָא: [9]"בִּשְׁלֹשָׁה בְּמַרְחֶשְׁוָן שׁוֹאֲלִין אֶת הַגְּשָׁמִים.

LITERAL TRANSLATION

Yose, for it was taught: [1]"What is the first rainfall? [2]The earliest is on the third of Marḥeshvan. The average is on the seventh. The latest is on the seventeenth. [3][These are] the words of Rabbi Meir. [4]Rabbi Yehudah says: On the seventh, and on the seventeenth, and on the twenty-third. [5]Rabbi Yose says: On the seventeenth, and on the twenty-third, and on the first of the month of Kislev. [6]And so did Rabbi Yose say: [Pious] individuals do not fast until the first of the month of Kislev arrives."

[7]Rav Ḥisda said: The Halakhah is in accordance with Rabbi Yose.

[8]Amemar taught this [ruling] of Rav Ḥisda in the following language: [9]"On the third of Marḥeshvan we pray for rains.

TRANSLATION AND COMMENTARY

taught in the following Baraita (Tosefta 1:3): [1]**"When is the first rainfall** of the winter supposed to occur?" [2]The Baraita explains: "It varies slightly from year to year, but **the earliest** time **is on the third of Marḥeshvan, the average is on the seventh,** and **the latest is on the seventeenth** of Marḥeshvan. Within this range, the rainfall can be considered normal. After the seventeenth, however, the former rain is definitely late, and a drought has begun. [3]**These are the words of Rabbi Meir.** [4]**Rabbi Yehudah says:** The earliest time is **on the seventh** of Marḥeshvan, the average is **on the seventeenth, and** the latest is **on the twenty-third** of Marḥeshvan. [5]**Rabbi Yose says:** The earliest time is **on the seventeenth** of Marḥeshvan, the average is **on the twenty-third, and** the latest is **on the first** day **of the month of Kislev.** [6]**And in accordance with this** principle **Rabbi Yose said** that if the former rain has not fallen by the dates mentioned above, a general fast is not decreed until a few weeks have passed, and even **pious individuals do not fast until the beginning of the month of Kislev arrives,** because there is nothing unusual about rain being delayed until then, according to Rabbi Yose."

אָמַר רַב חִסְדָּא [7]**Rav Ḥisda said: The Halakhah is in accordance with Rabbi Yose,** and there is no need for anyone to fast until after the first of Kislev.

אֲמֵימָר מַתְנֵי לְהָא [8]**Amemar** had a different version of **this ruling of Rav Ḥisda,** which he **transmitted in the following language:** According to Amemar, Rav Ḥisda issued two rulings, one of which appears to support Rabbi Yehudah, while the other supports Rabbi Yose. The first ruling was given in connection with the following Mishnah (below, 10a): [9]**"From the third of Marḥeshvan we** begin to **pray for rain** by inserting the prayer, 'and give dew and rain for a blessing upon the face of the earth,' in the

RASHI

הי רביעה — איזה זמן רביעה. **בכירה** — ראשונה, ולקמן מפרש מאי הלכתא ניהו. יורה יש בו שלשה זמני גשמים. **אפילה** — אחרונה, כמו "כי אפילות הנה" (שמות ט). **רבי יהודה אומר** — בכירה בשבעה במרחשון, ובינונית בשבעה עשר, ואפילה בעשרים ושלשה, וכולהו הני תלתא "יורה" קרי להו. **אין היחידים מתענין כו'** — דאמרינן בסמוך: שלישית להתענות, והואיל וזמן שלישית בראש חדש הוא — אין ליחידים להתענות. **יחידים** — חסידים, והכי אמרינן במתניתין לקמן (י,א): הגיע שבעה עשר במרחשון ולא ירדו גשמים — התחילו היחידים להתענות, שמכאן ואילך זמן רביעה אפילה לרבי מאיר, דסתם מתניתין רבי מאיר. והכי נמי אמר רבי יוסי דאין מתענין עד ראש חדש כסליו — דהיינו רביעה אפילה, והיינו כחכמים דאמרי יורה בכסליו. **אמר רב חסדא הלכה כרבי יוסי** — ואמימר תני להא דאמר רב חסדא הלכה כרבן גמליאל, דאינו שואל עד שבעה במרחשון.

the son of Rachab (see II Kings 10:15 ff.).

In addition to studying with his father, Rabbi Yose was an outstanding student of Rabbi Akiva. Rabbi Yose and his contemporaries, the other students of Rabbi Akiva — Rabbi Meir, Rabbi Yehudah, and Rabbi Shimon bar Yoḥai — formed the center of Talmudic creativity of that entire generation. In his Halakhic method, as in his way of life, Rabbi Yose was moderate; he refrained from taking an extreme position on Halakhic issues. Because of his moderation and the logic of his teachings, the Halakhah follows him in every instance, against all his colleagues. A well-known principle in the Halakhah is that "Rabbi Yose's views are based on sound reasoning" (רַבִּי יוֹסֵי נִימּוּקוֹ עִמּוֹ), and therefore the Halakhah is always in accordance with his view.

Just as Rabbi Yose was a great master of the Halakhah, so too was he famous for his piety. The Talmud tells many stories about his modesty, his humility, and his sanctity. It is related that Elijah the Prophet would reveal himself to him every day, and several conversations between him and Elijah are recorded in the Talmud. Rabbi Yose was apparently the main editor of a series of Baraitot on the history of the Jewish people known as Seder Olam. For many years he lived in Tzipori (Sepphoris) in Galilee, and earned his living as a leather worker.

Many of the Sages of the following generation, including Rabbi Yehudah HaNasi, the editor of the Mishnah, were his students. But the students to whom he was closest were his five sons, all of whom were Sages in their generation. The most famous of them were Rabbi Eliezer ben Rabbi Yose, one of the great masters of Aggadah, and Rabbi Yishmael ben Rabbi Yose.

BACKGROUND

הַבַּכִּירָה בֵּינוֹנִית וַאֲפִילָה The earliest, the average, and the latest. We do not know whether the amounts of rain and the seasons of rainfall in Talmudic times were like

NOTES

הַבַּכִּירָה...בֵּינוֹנִית...אֲפִילָה.... The earliest...The average...The latest.... There is a major difference of opinion among the commentators regarding these terms. *Rashi*, *Ran*, and others explain that they refer to three separate rainfalls that together constitute the first period of rain in the autumn. But *Rambam*, whom we have followed in our commentary, is of the opinion that these terms refer to the possible dates on which the rains are liable to begin, in accordance with the solar calendar. The earlier Rosh HaShanah falls according to the solar calendar, the later will the rains begin according to the lunar calendar. The later Rosh HaShanah falls according to the solar calendar, the earlier will the rains begin according to the lunar calendar. Thus, according to *Rambam*, these three terms are to be understood as statistical predictions as to the start of the rainy season.

TRANSLATION AND COMMENTARY

ninth blessing of the Amidah. [1]**Rabban Gamliel says:** We do not begin to say this prayer **until the seventh** of Marḥeshvan." [2]Concerning this Mishnah, **Rav Ḥisda said** that **the Halakhah is in accordance with Rabban Gamliel.** Thus it would appear that Rav Ḥisda is of the opinion that the first rain falls on the seventh of Marḥeshvan, the viewpoint attributed to Rabbi Yehudah above.

כְּמַאן אָזְלָא הָא דְּתַנְיָא [3]But according to Amemar, Rav Ḥisda issued another ruling in which he made it clear that he supported the viewpoint of Rabbi Yose in principle, and that his ruling in favor of Rabban Gamliel was exceptional. The ruling was issued in connection with the following question: **In accordance with which Tanna is** the ruling of Rabban Shimon ben Gamliel that **was taught in the following Baraita** (Tosefta 1:4)? The Tannaim discuss three rainfalls that are expected during the first part of the rainy season, corresponding to the early, average, and late dates for the first rainfall mentioned in the Tosefta considered above. The Tosefta that is about to be quoted discusses a case in which rain falls early, stops, and does not resume for some time. There is a Tannaitic dispute as to whether the second rainfall is considered to have arrived on the average date, even though it did not do so, or if it is not considered to have arrived until rain actually falls again. [4]Addressing this dispute, the Tosefta states: **"Rabban Shimon ben Gamliel says:** Even the Tanna who maintains that rain must actually fall again would agree that **if rain falls** on **seven days one after the other,** from the early date to the average date, such rain may be considered two separate rainfalls, [5]so that **we may consider it as** a combination of **the first and the second** rainfalls. **Similarly** if rain falls for seven days from the average date to the third date, we may consider it as a combination of **the second and the third** rainfalls."

כְּמַאן [6]Since Rabban Shimon ben Gamliel describes the rain as falling for seven consecutive days, it is clear that he must maintain that the early, average, and late dates are respectively seven days apart, and that the late date is seven days after the average date. **According to which** set of dates is this possible? [7]It is possible only **according to Rabbi Yose's** set of dates, because he maintains that the first rainfall is on the seventeenth of Marḥeshvan, the second on the twenty-third of Marḥeshvan, and the third on the first of Kislev, which is the day after the twenty-ninth of Marḥeshvan, at intervals of seven days. By contrast, according to Rabbi Meir the intervals are four days and ten days, and according to Rabbi Yehudah, the second rain comes ten days after the first.

[1]רַבָּן גַּמְלִיאֵל אוֹמֵר: בְּשִׁבְעָה בּוֹ". [2]אָמַר רַב חִסְדָּא: הֲלָכָה כְּרַבָּן גַּמְלִיאֵל.

[3]כְּמַאן אָזְלָא הָא דְּתַנְיָא, [4]"רַבָּן שִׁמְעוֹן בֶּן גַּמְלִיאֵל אוֹמֵר: גְּשָׁמִים שֶׁיָּרְדוּ שִׁבְעָה יָמִים זֶה אַחַר זֶה, [5]אַתָּה מוֹנֶה בָּהֶן רְבִיעָה רִאשׁוֹנָה וּשְׁנִיָּה וּשְׁלִישִׁית"? [6]כְּמַאן? [7]כְּרַבִּי יוֹסֵי.

LITERAL TRANSLATION

[1]Rabban Gamliel says: On the seventh of it." [2]Rav Ḥisda said: The Halakhah is in accordance with Rabban Gamliel.

[3]In accordance with whom is (lit., "goes") what was taught in the following [Baraita]: [4]"Rabban Shimon ben Gamliel says: [If] rains fell seven days one after the other, [5]you may consider them the first rainfall and the second, [or the second] and the third"? [6]In accordance with whom? [7]In accordance with Rabbi Yose.

RASHI

שבעה ימים בזה אחר זה — שירדו גשמים עכשיו, ופסקו עד יום שביעי, וירדו שבעה ימים זה אחר זה — אתה מונה בהן ראשונה ושניה ושלישית. **כרבי יוסי** — דאליבא דרבי יוסי הכי הוו בין רביעה ראשונה ושניה, או שניה ושלישית. דראשונה בשבעה עשר, ושניה בעשרים ושלשה — דהיינו שבעה ימים עם שנים ימי רביעה. ומעשרים ושלשה עד שלשים — שבעה ימים בלא יום רביעה אחרונה. דלכולהו תנאי לא הוי הכי, דלרבי מאיר דאמר ראשונה בשלשה ושניה בשבעה — ליכא בין זו לזו אלא ארבעה ימים, בין שניה לשלישית יש עשרה ימים. ולרבי יהודה בין ראשונה לשניה עשרה ימים, אבל בין שניה לשלישית יש יותר. נראה לרבי דהכי גרסינן: אמר רב חסדא הלכה כרבי יהודה דאמר בכירה בשבעה במרחשון, ואז מתחילין לשאול כדלקמן (י,א).

those today. Taking into account the climate in the entire world and changes in the vegetation and forestation of the Middle East, there is reason to believe that in the past the rains were somewhat more plentiful, and perhaps came somewhat earlier.

However, the rainy season did not begin on a precise date. Because of the lunar calendar, it is clear that a given date in the Hebrew year can vary with respect to the length of the day and the temperature.

The differences of opinion between the Sages are to some degree statistical: What are the average dates for the start of the rainy season? On the basis of these data, predictions can be made regarding the future.

NOTES

רְבִיעָה רִאשׁוֹנָה וּשְׁנִיָּה וּשְׁלִישִׁית **The first rainfall and the second, or the second and the third.** The reading found in the standard printed text of the Talmud presents a certain difficulty, because there is no Tanna who maintains that all three rainfalls occur within a seven-day period. *Rashi* explains that when the Baraita speaks of rain that falls for seven consecutive days, it is actually referring to a case in which the rain fell one day, and then stopped for a period of a week, and then fell again for seven consecutive days. Thus the Baraita can be understood as following the viewpoint of Rabbi Yose, who maintains that seven days separate the first and second rainfalls, and likewise seven days separate the second and third rainfalls. A number of Rishonim have different readings in our passage. *Tosafot* omits mention of the third rainfall, whereas the Sages of Narbonne (cited by *Tosafot*) omit mention of the first rainfall. Some Talmudic manuscripts, followed by our translation, preserve yet another reading: "You may consider them the first rainfall and the second, *or* the second and the third."

LITERAL TRANSLATION

[1]Rav Ḥisda said: The Halakhah is in accordance with Rabbi Yose.

[2]Granted that the first rainfall is to pray, [3][and] the third is to fast, [4]for what [purpose] is the second?

[5]Rabbi Zera said: For vows, [6]as we have learned: [6B] [7]"[If] someone takes a vow 'until the rains,' [8][or] 'from when the rains fall,' [9][it is] until the second rainfall falls."

[1]אָמַר רַב חִסְדָּא: הֲלָכָה כְּרַבִּי יוֹסֵי.

[2]בִּשְׁלָמָא רְבִיעָה רִאשׁוֹנָה לִשְׁאוֹל, [3]שְׁלִישִׁית לְהִתְעַנּוֹת, [4]שְׁנִיָּה לְמַאי?

[5]אָמַר רַבִּי זֵירָא: לִנְדָרִים, [6]דִּתְנַן: [6B] [7]"הַנּוֹדֵר 'עַד הַגְּשָׁמִים', [8]'מִשֶּׁיֵּרְדוּ גְּשָׁמִים', [9]עַד שֶׁתֵּרֵד רְבִיעָה שְׁנִיָּה".

RASHI

ראשונה לשאול — מכאן ואילך "ותן טל ומטר". **שלישית להתענות** — שאם לא ירדו גשמים עד זמן רביעה שלישית אפילו פעם אחת — מתענין היחידים שני וחמישי ושני. **הנודר עד הגשמים** — לאמר: קונם אם אהנה מדבר זה עד הגשמים. **עד שתרד רביעה שניה** — בנדרים הולכין אחר לשון בני אדם, ואין קורין גשמים לראשונה, עד שתרד שניה, שמכאן ואילך מקולקלות הדרכים ומאוסות מפני הגשמים, לשון אחר: עד הגשמים משמע תרי, דהיינו רביעה שניה.

TRANSLATION AND COMMENTARY

אָמַר רַב חִסְדָּא [1]It was concerning this Tosefta that **Rav Ḥisda said,** in Amemar's version of his ruling, that **the Halakhah is in accordance** with **Rabbi Yose,** because his viewpoint is supported by that of Rabban Shimon ben Gamliel. Thus the early date for the first rainfall is the seventeenth of Marḥeshvan, even though we begin to pray for rain on the seventh.

בִּשְׁלָמָא [2]The Gemara notes that the Tosefta mentioned three rainfalls. Presumably, this means that each of them has Halakhic significance. The significance of **the** date of the **first rainfall is clear** — it informs us when to begin **to pray** for rain in the ninth blessing of the Amidah. Rabbi Meir rules in favor of the first Tanna of the Mishnah, who maintains that we first pray for rain in the ninth blessing on the third of Marḥeshvan, when the first rainfall is supposed to occur, whereas Rabbi Yehudah rules in favor of Rabban Gamliel, who maintains that we do so only on the seventh of Marḥeshvan. [3]The Halakhic significance of **the** date of the **third** rainfall is also clear — it informs us when to begin **fasting** if a drought appears to be imminent. According to Rabbi Meir, pious individuals begin fasting if no rain at all has fallen by the seventeenth of Marḥeshvan, when the third rainfall is supposed to occur; according to Rabbi Yehudah, they begin fasting after the twenty-third; and according to Rabbi Yose, after the first of Kislev. [4]But, asks the Gemara, **what is** the Halakhic significance of **the** date of the **second** rainfall?

אָמַר רַבִּי זֵירָא [5]The Gemara gives four answers to this question. (1) **Rabbi Zera said:** The second rainfall has Halakhic significance **in connection with vows,** [6]**as we have learned** in the following Mishnah (*Nedarim* 62b): [6B] [7]**"If someone takes a vow** and stipulates in his vow that it should be in effect **'until the rains,'** [8]**or** that it should take effect **'from when the rains fall,'** [9]it is still in force (in the first case) or it does not take effect (in the second case) **until the second rainfall."** We interpret vows in accordance with the commonly accepted meaning of the words used, and in common parlance "the rains" (in plural) have not yet arrived until the first two rainfalls have fallen. Thus it is important to know the date when the second rainfall is expected to fall.

BACKGROUND

הַנּוֹדֵר עַד הַגְּשָׁמִים **If someone takes a vow "until the rains."** A vow is an obligation that a person takes upon himself. A vow can be limited to a certain event, to a set time, or be eternal. When a person utters a vow, he does not always define the exact meaning of the words to himself. Therefore the Sages have to define matters, and they follow the common meaning of the expressions in ordinary speech.

NOTES

הֲלָכָה כְּרַבִּי יוֹסֵי **The Halakhah is in accordance with Rabbi Yose.** *Rashi* suggests that the text be emended here to read: "The Halakhah is in accordance with Rabbi Yehudah." According to *Rashi*'s reading, this ruling can easily be reconciled with Amemar's version of Rav Ḥisda's first ruling, in which Amemar states that Rav Ḥisda ruled in accordance with the viewpoint of Rabban Gamliel that we begin to pray for rain on the seventh of Marḥeshvan. That ruling can best be understood if we assume that Rav Ḥisda agreed with Rabbi Yehudah that the earliest time for the first rainfall is the seventh of Marḥeshvan. For it would stand to reason that this is also the appropriate time to begin praying for rain. If we are to accept the reading found in the standard text of the Talmud, that Rav Ḥisda ruled in accordance with the viewpoint of Rabbi Yose that the earliest time for the first rainfall is the seventeenth of

HALAKHAH

הַנּוֹדֵר עַד הַגְּשָׁמִים **If someone takes a vow "until the rains."** "If someone takes a vow forbidding something upon himself, and stipulates that the vow is to be in effect 'until the rain,' the vow is in effect until the time of the rains, which in Eretz Israel is the first of Kislev, following Rabbi Yose. Once the time of the rains has arrived, the vow is no longer in effect, whether or not any rain has actually fallen. If it rains at any time after the seventeenth of Marḥeshvan, the vow is also no longer in effect. If he stipulates that the vow is to be in effect 'until the rains,' the vow is in effect until it rains after the time of the second rainfall, which in Eretz Israel is the twenty-third of Marḥeshvan. *Rema* adds that in the Diaspora the time of the rains is sixty days after the equinox, when the prayer for rain is first recited, and the time of the second rainfall is seventy days after the equinox." (*Shulḥan Arukh, Yoreh De'ah* 220:18.)

רַב זְבִיד אָמַר: לְזֵיתִים. [1] דִּתְנַן: [2] "מֵאֵימָתַי כָּל אָדָם מוּתָּרִין בְּלֶקֶט, בְּשִׁכְחָה, וּבְפֵאָה? [3] מִשֶּׁיֵּלְכוּ הַנָּמוֹשׁוֹת. [4] בְּפֶרֶט וּבְעוֹלֵלוֹת? [5] מִשֶּׁיֵּלְכוּ עֲנִיִּים בַּכֶּרֶם וְיָבוֹאוּ. [6] בְּזֵיתִים? [7] מִשֶּׁתֵּרֵד רְבִיעָה שְׁנִיָּה". [8]

TRANSLATION AND COMMENTARY

רַב זְבִיד אָמַר (2) [1] **Rav Zevid said: It is** important to know the expected date of the second rainfall, in order to determine a Halakhah **regarding olives.** [2] **We have learned** this Halakhah in the following Mishnah (*Pe'ah* 8:1), regarding those parts of the harvest that the farmer is required by Torah law to leave for the poor. Sheaves or other produce forgotten in the field by their owner during the harvest must be left for the poor (Deuteronomy 24:19). Similarly, the farmer must leave for the poor one unharvested corner in each field (Leviticus 19:9 and 23:22). These laws apply to all forms of produce. There is one additional law that applies to grain only: Gleanings of individual stalks of grain left in the field after the harvest belong only to the poor (ibid.). There are two further laws that apply specifically to grapes: When a cluster of three or more grapes falls from the grape harvest, the harvester may pick it up, but if a single grape or a pair of grapes should fall in this way, that is called *peret* and must be left for the poor. In addition, malformed clusters of grapes are called *olelot*, and must be left on the vine for the poor to pick (Leviticus 19:10). None of these gleanings may be taken by the owner or by anyone who is not poor. But once the poor have lost interest in gleaning, or have given up hope of finding anything worth gleaning, whatever is left in the field or on the tree is considered ownerless and may be taken by anyone, rich or poor. [3] In relation to such a situation, the Mishnah asks: **"From what stage is anyone,** and not just someone poor, **permitted to collect** for himself **gleanings** of grain left over in the field after the harvest, or **forgotten sheaves, or the corner of the field** that the farmer must leave for the poor?" [4] The Mishnah answers: **"After the *namoshot*** [נָמוֹשׁוֹת; see below] **have passed through** the field, at which point we may assume that the poor have taken everything that they wish, and the rest of the grain is ownerless." [5] Similarly, the Mishnah asks: "From when may anyone **collect *peret*** and ***olelot*** from a vineyard? [6] **After the poor have passed through the vineyard and come back.** After the poor have passed through the vineyard twice, we may assume that they have taken everything that they wish, and the rest of the grapes are ownerless." [7] Similarly, the Mishnah asks: "From when may anyone collect the **olives** left by the farmer for the poor? [8] **After the second rainfall has occurred."** Olives must be harvested before the rains fall. Accordingly, when the time of the second rainfall has arrived, the poor assume that the olives have long since been harvested, and any gleanings have already been picked up by previous visitors. Hence, any remaining olives are of no further interest to the poor. Thus we see from this Mishnah that it is important to know when the second rainfall is expected to occur, in order to determine when leftover olives may be taken by anyone.

LITERAL TRANSLATION

[1] Rav Zevid said: It is for olives, [2] as we have learned: [3] "From when is every man permitted [to collect] gleanings, forgotten [sheaves], and the corner [of the field]? [4] After the *namoshot* have passed [through it]. [5] [To collect] *peret* and *olelot*? [6] After the poor have passed through the vineyard and come back. [7] [To collect] olives? [8] After the second rainfall has fallen."

RASHI

כל אדם — אפילו העשירים. **פרט** — "לא תפאר אחריך" (דברים כד) — לא תטול תפארתו ממנו. **משילכו הנמושות** — בשדה, דמכאן ואילך נתייאשו שאר העניים. לפי שיודעין אם נשאר לקט שכחה ופאה — נמושות נטלום. **נמושות** — לשון ממשש. **משילכו עניים בכרם ויבאו** — כלומר: שלקטו וחזרו ובאו פעם שניה, והשתא מסחי דעתייהו עניים. **משתרד רביעה שניה** — דעד ההיא שעתא לקטו הכל.

NOTES

Marḥeshvan, it must be argued that Rav Ḥisda ruled that it is proper to begin praying for rain several days before the time for the first rainfall, just as we begin to mention rain in the second blessing of the Amidah before the time of the rains (see *Rabbenu Yehonatan*).

HALAKHAH

מֵאֵימָתַי כָּל אָדָם מוּתָּרִין בְּלֶקֶט, בְּשִׁכְחָה, וּבְפֵאָה From when is every man permitted to collect gleanings, forgotten sheaves, and the corner of the field. "From what stage is anyone permitted to collect gleanings of grain left over in the field after the harvest? From when the first and second set of gleaners have finished their gleaning. According to *Rambam,* there is no practical difference between Rabbi Yoḥanan and Resh Lakish, but merely a disagreement over the meaning of the word *namoshot* (*Kesef Mishneh* in the name of *Rashba*)." (*Rambam, Sefer Zeraim, Hilkhot Mattenot Aniyyim* 1:11.)

בְּפֶרֶט וּבְעוֹלֵלוֹת To collect *peret* and *olelot*. "From what stage is anyone permitted to collect for himself *peret* and *olelot* left in the vineyard? From when the poor have passed through the vineyard and come back. From what stage is anyone permitted to collect olives forgotten on the tree? In Eretz Israel, such olives are permitted from the first of Kislev, which is the time of the second rainfall in a year when the rain is late. (*Rambam, Sefer Zeraim, Hilkhot Mattenot Aniyyim* 1:11.)

CONCEPTS

לֶקֶט Gleanings. One of the obligatory agricultural gifts given to the poor. The Torah prohibits the owner of a field from gleaning individual stalks that have fallen during the harvest (Leviticus 19:9). Less than three stalks that have fallen in one place are deemed לֶקֶט and considered the property of the poor. The owner of the field is forbidden to take them for his own use.

שִׁכְחָה Forgotten sheaves. One of the agricultural gifts to which the poor are entitled. A farmer who has forgotten a sheaf in the field while harvesting his grain may not return to collect it. It must be left instead for the poor (Deuteronomy 24:19).

פֵּאָה *Pe'ah*. One of the agricultural gifts left for the poor (מַתְּנוֹת עֲנִיִּים). The Torah forbids harvesting "the corners of your field," so that the produce left standing may be harvested and kept by the poor (Leviticus 19:9).

The Torah does not specify a minimum amount of produce to be left as *pe'ah*. But the Sages stipulated that it must be at least one-sixtieth of the crop.

Pe'ah is set aside only from crops that ripen at one time and are harvested at one time. The poor are allowed to use their own initiative to reap the *pe'ah* left in the fields. But the owner of an orchard must see to it that each of the poor gets a fixed share of the *pe'ah* from places that are difficult to reach. The poor come to collect *pe'ah* three times a day. The laws of *pe'ah* are discussed in detail in tractate *Pe'ah*.

פֶּרֶט *Peret*. Single grapes. The owner of a vineyard is forbidden to collect individual fallen grapes at the time of the harvest. Such grapes must be left for the poor.

עוֹלֵלוֹת *Olelot*. Small, incompletely formed clusters of grapes. These are clusters of grapes lacking a central stalk, or ones in which the grapes do not hang down one upon the other. The Torah prohibits the harvesting of these incompletely formed clusters of grapes (Leviticus 19:20; see also Deuteronomy 24:21). They must be left for

TRANSLATION AND COMMENTARY

מַאי נְמוֹשׁוֹת **[1]Having mentioned this Mishnah, the** Gemara now explains one of its terms. **What is meant by** the term **"namoshot"?**

אָמַר רַבִּי יוֹחָנָן **[2]Rabbi Yoḥanan said:** The word *"namoshot"* means **"old men who walk leaning on a staff."** Such people walk slowly, and whatever they miss is not worth taking. **[3]Resh Lakish said:** The word *"namoshot"* means **"people who glean after the first gleaners have finished."** According to both interpretations, the Mishnah is teaching us that after these *namoshot* have finished gleaning, we may assume that there is hardly any produce left.

(3) רַב פַּפָּא אָמַר **[4]Rav Pappa said: It is** important to know the expected date of the second rainfall, **in order** to determine a Halakhah regarding a person who wishes **to walk on the permitted paths.** Generally, it is forbidden to take a shortcut through private property. There is a tradition, however, that when the Israelites first entered Eretz Israel, Joshua stipulated that the people accept ten legally enforceable limitations on their private-property rights for the benefit of the general public. One of the ten conditions was to permit the public to walk through privately owned agricultural fields, provided that nothing was growing there that could be trampled on and damaged. **[5]For the Master has said** in a Baraita (*Bava Kamma* 81a), listing the ten conditions of Joshua, **"Everyone may walk on the permitted paths until the second rainfall.** By then we assume that seed sown in the field has sprouted, and there is a danger of causing damage to the crops." Thus we see from this Baraita that it is important to know when the second rainfall is expected, in order to determine when using paths through private property is no longer permitted.

(4) רַב נַחְמָן בַּר יִצְחָק **[6]Rav Naḥman bar Yitzḥak said: It is** important to know the expected date of the second rainfall, in order to determine a Halakhah **regarding the removal of the produce of the seventh year.** The produce of the Sabbatical Year is what grows in fields and orchards without being planted or tended. It may be picked and eaten by anyone, and it may not be harvested in its entirety by the owner of the land and kept in storage to be sold. But it is permitted to keep an unlimited amount of produce at home for personal use, provided that the field is not completely emptied of produce. Accordingly, once the last of the produce has been taken from the field, all produce must be removed from storage and made available for anyone to take. The time for removing the produce of the Sabbatical Year varies from crop to crop, **[7]as we have learned** in a Mishnah (*Shevi'it* 9:7): **"Until when may we derive benefit from the stubble**

LITERAL TRANSLATION

[1]What is [meant by] *"namoshot"*?

[2]Rabbi Yoḥanan said: Old men who walk [leaning] on a staff. [3]Resh Lakish said: Gleaners after gleaners.

[4]Rav Pappa said: It is in order to walk on the permitted paths, [5]as the master said: "Everyone may walk on the permitted paths until the second rainfall falls."

[6]Rav Naḥman bar Yitzḥak said: It is to dispose of the produce of the seventh [year], [7]as we have learned: "Until when may we derive benefit from or burn

מַאי "נְמוֹשׁוֹת"?

[2]אָמַר רַבִּי יוֹחָנָן: סָבֵי דְּאָזְלִי אַתִּיגְרָא. [3]רֵישׁ לָקִישׁ אָמַר: לָקוֹטֵי בָּתַר לָקוֹטֵי.

[4]רַב פַּפָּא אָמַר: כְּדֵי לְהַלֵּךְ בִּשְׁבִילֵי הָרְשׁוּת, [5]דְּאָמַר מָר: "מְהַלְּכִין כָּל אָדָם בִּשְׁבִילֵי הָרְשׁוּת עַד שֶׁתֵּרֵד רְבִיעָה שְׁנִיָּה".

[6]רַב נַחְמָן בַּר יִצְחָק אָמַר: לְבַעֵר פֵּירוֹת שְׁבִיעִית, [7]דִּתְנַן: "עַד מָתַי נֶהֱנִין וְשׂוֹרְפִין בְּתֶבֶן

RASHI

דאזלי אתיגרא — הולכין בנחת, ומעייני טפי. "מחזיק בפלך" (שמואל ב ג) מתרגמא: אתיגרא. לקוטי בתר לקוטי — עני מוליך בנו אחריו, שמכאן ואילך פוסקים שאר עניים מללקוט. הכי גרסינן: רב פפא אמר לשבילי הרשות — כלומר, שיש רשות מבית דין לעוברי דרכים לקצר שבילן לילך בשדות. עד שתרד רביעה שניה — שמכאן ואילך גדלה התבואה, וקשה לה דישת הרגל. דאמר מר בפרק "מרובה" בתמניא שהתנה יהושע: מהלכין בשבילי הרשות וכו'.

---

the poor. The Sages differed as to whether this law applies if a person's entire vineyard grew in this manner.

LANGUAGE

נְמוֹשׁוֹת *Namoshot.* Scholars of Hebrew etymology have debated the source of this word. Some maintain that there is a verb *namash* (נמש) similar in meaning to *emesh* (אֶמֶשׁ) — "yesterday evening" — and that it means "to be late." Therefore the *namoshot* would be latecomers. Other authorities maintain that the real root of the word is *mashash* — to grope — and that, in a common exchange of consonants, a letter *nun* (נ) has replaced the letter *mem* (מ). Others have connected this word with various words in Arabic and other ancient Semitic languages.

אַתִּיגְרָא **On a staff.** Most manuscripts of the Talmud read אַתִּיגְדָּא, which is the Aramaic word for a staff or a rod. The word derives from the root גדר, meaning "to cut," hence a branch cut from a tree and used as a staff.

NOTES

לָקוֹטֵי בָּתַר לָקוֹטֵי **Gleaners after gleaners.** From *Rashi* in *Bava Metzia* (21b) it would appear that Resh Lakish is referring to a second set of gleaners who come to collect whatever is left after the first set of gleaners have finished (see *Gevurat Ari*). Here *Rashi* explains that Resh Lakish is referring to the gleaners' children, who follow immediately after their parents, gathering up whatever they have missed.

HALAKHAH

מְהַלְּכִין כָּל אָדָם בִּשְׁבִילֵי הָרְשׁוּת **Everyone may walk on the permitted paths.** "Everyone is permitted to walk on the paths that go through privately owned agricultural fields from the time of the grain harvest until the seventeenth of Marḥeshvan, which is the time of the second rainfall (following Rabbi Yehudah, against Rabbi Yose). After that time, entry into privately owned fields is forbidden, because damage to the crops may result." (*Tur, Ḥoshen Mishpat* 274.)

TRANSLATION AND COMMENTARY

and the straw of the seventh year or burn it for fuel? [1] **Until the second rainfall** at the beginning of the rainy season in the eighth year. At that point, the last of the stubble and the straw from the Sabbatical Year has gone from the fields, and any stubble or straw stored away must be removed from the house and made available to all. Thus we see from this Mishnah that it is important to know the expected date of the second rainfall, in order to determine when straw and stubble may no longer be kept in storage.

מַאי טַעֲמָא [2] The Gemara asks: **What is the reason** for removing the straw and the stubble of the Sabbatical Year from storage when it has gone from the fields? Admittedly, regular crops must be removed from storage in this way, but stubble and straw are not food!

דִּכְתִיב [3] The Gemara explains: **Because it is written** in the Torah (Leviticus 25:7): **"And** all its produce will be food for you and **for your cattle and for the beast that is in your land."** We see from this verse that the Torah permits us to eat the Sabbatical Year produce together with our domestic animals and wild animals, but does not permit us to take any unfair advantage by storing the crops away. From the inclusion of domestic animals ("cattle") in the verse, we see that this law also applies to animal fodder, such as straw and stubble. [4] Thus the legal principle here is as follows: **All the time that a nondomesticated animal can** find straw and stubble to **eat in the field, we** too may **feed our domesticated animals** from straw and stubble stored **at home.** [5] But **once** the supply of straw and stubble **has ended for nondomesticated animals from the field,** we must **end it for domesticated animals at home** as well, by removing it from storage and making it available to everyone.

אָמַר רַבִּי אַבָּהוּ [6] The Gemara now returns to the subject of the etymology of words connected with rain. **Rabbi Abbahu said: What is the meaning of the word *reviah*** [רְבִיעָה — "rainfall"]? [7] It means **something**

וּבְקַשׁ שֶׁל שְׁבִיעִית? [1] עַד שֶׁתֵּרֵד רְבִיעָה שְׁנִיָּה״.

[2] מַאי טַעֲמָא?

[3] דִּכְתִיב: ״וְלִבְהֶמְתְּךָ וְלַחַיָּה אֲשֶׁר בְּאַרְצֶךָ״. [4] כָּל זְמַן שֶׁחַיָּה אוֹכֶלֶת בַּשָּׂדֶה, הַאֲכֵל לִבְהֶמְתְּךָ בַּבַּיִת. [5] כָּלָה לַחַיָּה מִן הַשָּׂדֶה, כַּלֵּה לִבְהֶמְתְּךָ מִן הַבַּיִת.

[6] אָמַר רַבִּי אַבָּהוּ: מַאי לְשׁוֹן רְבִיעָה? [7] דָּבָר שֶׁרוֹבֵעַ אֶת

LITERAL TRANSLATION

stubble and straw of the seventh [year]? [1] Until the second rainfall falls."

[2] What is the reason?

[3] Because it is written: "And for your cattle and for the beast that is in your land." [4] All the time that a beast eats in the field, feed your cattle in the house. [5] [Once] it has ended for the beast from the field, end [it] for your cattle from the house.

[6] Rabbi Abbahu said: What is [the meaning of] the word *revi'ah*? [7] Something that copulates with the

RASHI

בתבן וקש של שביעית – ספיחים שגדלו בשביעית, דיש בהן איסור שביעית, או תבואה שגדלה בשביעית לאחר שנכנסה. **כלה לחיה מן השדה** – לשון זכר, כמו (בראשית יח) ״עשו כָּלָה״ כלומר: כלה האוכל. **כלה לבהמתך** – כמו ״כַּלֵּה בחימה כלה ואיכמו״ (תהלים נט) ומשירדה רביעה שניה מכאן ואילך אין תבן וקש בשדות, שהגשמים עושין אותן זבל.

NOTES

בְּתֶבֶן וּבְקַשׁ שֶׁל שְׁבִיעִית **Stubble and straw of the seventh year.** Our translation and commentary follow the reading found in the standard Talmudic text, according to which the Mishnah asks: "*Until when* may we derive benefit from or burn stubble and straw of the seventh year?" *Meiri* explains this passage on the basis of a variant reading, which parallels the reading found in the Mishnah (*Shevi'it* 9:7): "*From when* may we derive benefit from or burn stubble and straw of the seventh year?" As long as straw and stubble are fit for animal consumption, they may not be burned or used in such a way that they are destroyed. But once they are no longer fit even for animals, they may be burned as fuel or used in any other way. Thus the Mishnah is informing us that once the second rainfall occurs at the beginning of the rainy season in the eighth year, the last of the straw and the stubble may be burned or used for any other purpose, because after the second rainfall they are no longer fit for animal consumption. (See *Rash* and *Rosh, Shevi'it* 9:7; see also Halakhah.)

HALAKHAH

בְּתֶבֶן וּבְקַשׁ שֶׁל שְׁבִיעִית **Stubble and straw of the seventh year.** "After the second rainfall in the year following the Sabbatical Year, one is permitted to benefit from and to burn the straw and the stubble of the Sabbatical Year, for the straw and the stubble are then no longer fit for animals to eat (following the reading in the Mishnah in *Shevi'it*: 'From when are we permitted, etc.')." (*Rambam, Sefer Zeraim, Hilkhot Shemittah* 5:23.)

כָּל זְמַן שֶׁחַיָּה אוֹכֶלֶת בַּשָּׂדֶה **All the time that a beast eats in the field.** "Produce of the Sabbatical Year that has already been brought into the house may be eaten only as long as there is still produce of that same kind in the fields. But if such produce has disappeared from the fields, the produce that has already been brought into the house must be taken out and made available to all." (*Rambam, Sefer Zeraim, Hilkhot Shemittah* 7:1.)

LITERAL TRANSLATION

ground, [1]in accordance with [the statement] of Rav Yehudah. [2]For Rav Yehudah said: Rain is the husband of the ground, [3]as it is said: "For as the rain and the snow comes down from the heavens, and does not return there, but waters the earth, and causes it to give birth and causes it to sprout."

[4]And Rabbi Abbahu said: The first rainfall [must be] enough to go down into the ground [one] handbreadth. [5]The second [must be] enough to seal with it the opening of a barrel.

[6]Rav Ḥisda said: Rains that have come down [in sufficient quantities] to seal with them the opening of a barrel do not come into the category of "and He will shut up."

[7]And Rav Ḥisda said: Rains that have come down before "and He will shut up" [8]do not come into the category of "and He will shut up."

הַקַּרְקַע, [1]כִּדְרַב יְהוּדָה. [2]דְּאָמַר רַב יְהוּדָה: מִיטְרָא בַּעְלָהּ דְּאַרְעָא הוּא, [3]שֶׁנֶּאֱמַר: "כִּי כַּאֲשֶׁר יֵרֵד הַגֶּשֶׁם וְהַשֶּׁלֶג מִן הַשָּׁמַיִם, וְשָׁמָּה לֹא יָשׁוּב, כִּי אִם הִרְוָה אֶת הָאָרֶץ, וְהוֹלִידָהּ וְהִצְמִיחָהּ".

[4]וְאָמַר רַבִּי אַבָּהוּ: רְבִיעָה רִאשׁוֹנָה כְּדֵי שֶׁתֵּרֵד בְּקַרְקַע טֶפַח. [5]שְׁנִיָּה כְּדֵי לָגוּף בָּהּ פִּי חָבִית.

[6]אָמַר רַב חִסְדָּא: גְּשָׁמִים שֶׁיָּרְדוּ כְּדֵי לָגוּף בָּהֶן פִּי חָבִית אֵין בָּהֶן מִשּׁוּם "וְעָצַר".

[7]וְאָמַר רַב חִסְדָּא: גְּשָׁמִים שֶׁיָּרְדוּ קוֹדֶם "וְעָצַר" [8]אֵין בָּהֶן מִשּׁוּם "וְעָצַר".

TRANSLATION AND COMMENTARY

that penetrates the ground [from the Hebrew root רבע, meaning "to copulate"]. The effect of the rain falling on the dry soil is comparable to sexual intercourse, which causes new life to develop. [1]The Gemara notes that Rabbi Abbahu's metaphor is **in accordance with the** following **statement by Rav Yehudah,** in which the same idea was inferred from a Biblical verse. [2]**For Rav Yehudah said: Rain is the husband of the ground,** [3]**as it is said** (Isaiah 55:10): **"For as the rain and the snow comes down from the heavens, and does not return there, but waters the earth and causes it to give birth and causes it to sprout,** so shall My word be that goes forth from My mouth." The Hebrew word וְהוֹלִידָהּ, meaning "and causes it to give birth," suggests sexual intercourse, in which the earth plays the female role and the rain and the snow play the male role.

וְאָמַר רַבִּי אַבָּהוּ [4]Having cited one statement by Rabbi Abbahu about rain, the Gemara notes that **Rabbi Abbahu also said:** To be effective **the first rainfall must be** heavy **enough to penetrate the ground** to a depth of **one handbreadth** (about three-and-a-half inches). [5]**The second** rainfall **must be** heavy **enough to** saturate the soil and turn it into malleable clay that can be used to **seal the opening of a barrel** without further mixing.

אָמַר רַב חִסְדָּא [6]The Gemara now cites a similar statement by **Rav Ḥisda,** who **said:** Only **rains that have come down in sufficient quantities to** saturate the soil and turn it into malleable clay that can be used to **seal the opening of a barrel do not come into the category of** the expression **"and He will shut up"** used in the following verse (Deuteronomy 11:17): "And the anger of the Lord will be kindled against you, and He will shut up the heavens, so that there will be no rain." In other words, even if the rains fall, an inadequate quantity is a reflection of God's anger.

אָמַר רַב חִסְדָּא [7]The Gemara now cites another, similar, statement by Rav Ḥisda. **Rav Ḥisda said:** Even if the amounts are substandard, nevertheless **rain that comes down** just **before** we recite the verse in Deuteronomy containing the words **"and He will shut up"** [8]**does not come into the category of** the expression in the verse: **"And He will shut up."** This verse is recited twice every day, morning and evening, in the *Shema*. Thus Rav Ḥisda is informing us that even if the rainfall is meager, nevertheless if God causes rain to fall just before we recite this verse, we may interpret it as divine reassurance that God is not shutting up the heavens.

BACKGROUND

לָגוּף בָּהּ פִּי חָבִית To seal with it the opening of a barrel. In Talmudic times, earthenware casks were commonly used to store wine. The casks were sealed with a special cover called a מְגוּפָה. In order to preserve the wine, the opening was hermetically sealed by smearing mud around it.

RASHI

והולידה — כאדם שמוליד. **גשמים ברביעה ראשונה** — אם באין כל כך שנימס הקרקע — יפין הן, ואין צריך להתענות. **לגוף בה פי חבית** — ששותת מן המים עד שנעשה תיחוח כל כך שיכול לעשות מגופת חבית בלא תוספת מים. **אין בהם משום ועצר** — אין זו קללה של "ועצר את השמים". **קודם ועצר** — קודם זמן קריאת שמע, דכתיב ביה "ועצר את השמים", אף על פי שלא יהיה רוב גשמים.

NOTES

גְּשָׁמִים שֶׁיָּרְדוּ קוֹדֶם וְעָצַר Rains that have come down before "and He will shut up." The Geonim reverse the reading in our passage: "Abaye said: We said [this] only [if rains fell] before the 'and He will shut up' of the morning, but before the 'and He will shut up' of the evening they do come into the category of 'and He will shut up.'" If it began to rain at the end of the night before the recitation of the morning *Shema,* it will continue to rain, and so the

TRANSLATION AND COMMENTARY

אָמַר אַבָּיֵי [1]**Abaye said:** Rav Ḥisda **made this statement only concerning rain that** falls **just before the evening** recitation of the *Shema* prayer containing the expression **"and He will shut up."** [2]**But** if the rainfall is less than required and it falls just **before the morning** recitation of the *Shema* prayer containing the expression **"and He will shut up,"** the insufficient rainfall **does come into the category of** the absence of rain contained in the expression **"and He will shut up."** [3]**For Rav Yehudah bar Yitzḥak said: Morning clouds have no substance** and usually pass quickly as the sun rises higher in the sky. Thus a small amount of rain in the morning cannot be seen as a good sign. [4]Rav Yehudah bar Yitzḥak notes that we can learn that morning clouds are insubstantial from what **is written** in the following verse (Hosea 6:4): **"What shall I do for you, Ephraim? What shall I do for you, Judah? For your kindness is like a morning cloud."** The Prophet uses a morning cloud as a metaphor for something insubstantial. Hence we can infer that morning clouds have no substance, and that the rain that falls in the early morning is of little value.

אָמַר לֵיהּ רַב פַּפָּא [5]In connection with Rav Ḥisda's statement, **Rav Pappa said to Abaye:** [6]**But surely** it is common knowledge that heavy rain often falls in the early morning. For **people say** the following proverb: **"If there is rain when people open their doors** in the early morning, [7]**fold your sack, ass-driver, and go to sleep."** Ass-drivers used to transport produce from town to town. When food was relatively scarce, they had much work to do, because produce available only in one town would be in high demand in another. But when food was relatively abundant, they had little work to do, because each town was self-sufficient. The popular proverb is informing us that when it rains in the early morning, it is a clear sign that the year will be a good one for the farmers, and a bad one for the ass-drivers. Thus we see that substantial rain does often fall in the early morning, and this contradicts the statement of Rav Ḥisda.

לָא קַשְׁיָא [8]Abaye replied: **There is no contradiction.** [9]The proverb is referring to a situation **when** the sky **is overcast with heavy clouds,** [10]whereas Rav Ḥisda was referring to a situation **when** the sky **is overcast with light clouds.** Light clouds do not last if they appear in the early morning. Heavy clouds, however, can be expected to give substantial rain.

[1]אָמַר אַבָּיֵי: לָא אֲמָרַן אֶלָּא קוֹדֶם "וְעָצַר" דְּאוּרְתָּא, [2]אֲבָל קוֹדֶם "וְעָצַר" דְּצַפְרָא יֵשׁ בָּהֶן מִשּׁוּם "וְעָצַר". [3]דְּאָמַר רַב יְהוּדָה בַּר יִצְחָק: הָנֵי עֲנָנֵי דְּצַפְרָא לֵית בְּהוּ מְשָׁשָׁא, [4]דִּכְתִיב: "מָה אֶעֱשֶׂה לְּךָ, אֶפְרַיִם? מָה אֶעֱשֶׂה לְּךָ, יְהוּדָה? וְחַסְדְּכֶם כַּעֲנַן בֹּקֶר, וגו'".

[5]אָמַר לֵיהּ רַב פַּפָּא לְאַבָּיֵי: [6]וְהָא אָמְרֵי אֱינָשֵׁי: "בְּמִפְתַּח בָּבֵי מִיטְרָא, [7]בַּר חַמָּרָא, מוֹךְ שַׂקָּךְ וּגְנֵי"! [8]לָא קַשְׁיָא. [9]הָא דְּקָטִיר בְּעִיבָא; [10]הָא דְּקָטִיר בַּעֲנָנֵי.

LITERAL TRANSLATION

[1]Abaye said: We said [this] only [if rains fell] before the "and He will shut up" of the evening, [2]but before the "and He will shut up" of the morning they do come into the category of "and He will shut up." [3]For Rav Yehudah bar Yitzḥak said: These morning clouds have no substance, [4]as it is written: "What shall I do for you, Ephraim? What shall I do for you, Judah? For your kindness is like a morning cloud, etc."

[5]Rav Pappa said to Abaye: [6]But surely people say: "[If there is] rain when they open the doors, [7]ass-driver, fold your sack and go to sleep"!

[8]There is no difficulty. [9]This is when it was overcast (lit., "tied") with heavy clouds; [10]that is when it was overcast with light clouds.

RASHI

אבל ירדו קודם ועצר דצפרא יש בהן משום ועצר — הואיל ולא ירדו ביום, ואין יפין לעולם. **לית בהו משׁשא** — ואין שנתן מתברכת. **וחסדכם כענן בקר** — שאין בו ממש. **מיטרא במיפתח בבי** — אם יורדין בבקר, כשפותחין הפתחים — יקפל החמר שמוכר תבואה את שקו ליכנס לישן, מפני שהשנה מתברכת, ויהיה שובע בעולם ולא ישתכר במכירת תבואתו. אלמא: יפין הן. **דקטיר בעיבא** — אם נתקשרו שמים בעננים עבים, ולא קלושים — אין בהם משום ועצר. **דקטיר בעננא** — שהיא קלושה מעט — אין בו ממש.

BACKGROUND

עֲנָנֵי דְּצַפְרָא **Morning clouds.** The clouds that form over land during the early hours of the morning are usually thin and light, and they produce only a small amount of rain, if rain falls at all and the clouds do not scatter as morning mist. Heavy rain clouds (עִיבָא) are mainly produced in the afternoon or evening.

NOTES

expression "and He will shut up" does not apply. But if it began to rain at the end of the day before the evening *Shema,* more rain is unlikely, and therefore the expression "and He will shut up" applies. The Geonim also have a different reading of the popular proverb cited later in the passage: "If there is rain from when they shut the doors [at the end of the day] until they open the doors [the next morning], etc." According to this reading, the proverb implies that substantial rain often falls during the evening.

בַּר חַמָּרָא, מוֹךְ שַׂקָּךְ **Ass-driver, fold your sack.** Our commentary follows *Rashi,* who explains that rain in the early morning is a sign that the current year will be a year of plenty, and therefore there will be little work for the ass-drivers who transport grain from place to place. But

LANGUAGE

תַּרְבִּיצֵי Gardens. The meaning of this word in Aramaic is "garden." The root is "רבץ," meaning the pouring of liquid. Thus the word reflects the fact that plants needing constant watering are commonly grown in a garden. In Rabbinic usage, the same term is often used as a poetic epithet for the House of Study, which is like a garden in which much water (Torah) is poured and in which plants (Torah scholars) grow.

BACKGROUND

שׁוּדְפָנָא Blight. This term apparently refers to blight (*ustilago*), a disease affecting grain. Blight is caused by a fungus that attacks the seeds of the grain, so that instead of an ear of corn, a pouch of black spores is formed. These spores are scattered by the wind and infect the plants in the vicinity. The disease can spread over large distances and cause significant damage to harvests.

TRANSLATION AND COMMENTARY

אָמַר רַב יְהוּדָה [1]**Rav Yehudah said: It is good for** the entire **year when** the month of **Tevet** in the middle of the rainy season (corresponding to December-January in the Gregorian calendar) **is a "widow,"** and no rain falls. Rav Yehudah is referring to the metaphor he employed above, in which he called the rain "the husband of the earth." Thus Rav Yehudah is saying that it is best for the entire year if the rains stop during the month of Tevet, even though the earth then appears to have been abandoned by her "husband."

אִיכָּא דְּאָמְרִי [2]The reason why Rav Yehudah favored a pause of a month in the rainy season is explained in different ways by the later Sages. **There are some who say** that the advantage of the interval without rain is **that gardens should not be desolated.** Rain in Tevet can damage newly sprouted vegetables in gardens. [3]**But there are others who say** that the advantage of the interval without rain is **to prevent blight from destroying the crops.** Heavy rains in midwinter make the crops susceptible to blight.

אִינִי [4]But, the Gemara objects, **is this true?** Is a rainless Tevet beneficial? [5]**Surely Rav Ḥisda said** that **it is good for** the entire **year when** the roads during the month of **Tevet are muddy,** as a result of heavy rain!

לָא קַשְׁיָא [6]The Gemara answers: **There is no contradiction** between the statements of Rav Yehudah and Rav Ḥisda. [7]Rav Yehudah is referring to a year **when the rain came from the beginning,** during the month of Marḥeshvan. In such a case, it is good to have a rainless interval during the month of Tevet. [8]Rav Ḥisda is referring to a year **when the rain did not come from the beginning.** In such a year, a wet Tevet can almost compensate for a dry Marḥeshvan.

וְאָמַר רַב חִסְדָּא [9]The Gemara now cites another statement of Rav Ḥisda on the same topic. **Rav Ḥisda said: Rains that fall on** one **part of a country but do not fall on another part of the country** [10]**do not come into the category of** the expression **"and He will shut up** the heavens" used in the verse in Deuteronomy. If enough rain falls to grow sufficient crops to feed the entire country, there is no need to interpret this phenomenon as an indication of divine displeasure.

[1]אֲמַר רַב יְהוּדָה: טָבָא לְשַׁתָּא דְּטֵבֵת אַרְמַלְתָּא. [2]אִיכָּא דְּאָמְרִי: דְּלָא בַּיְירִי תַּרְבִּיצֵי. [3]וְאִיכָּא דְּאָמְרִי: דְּלָא שָׁקֵיל שׁוּדְפָנָא. [4]אִינִי? [5]וְהָאֲמַר רַב חִסְדָּא: טָבָא לְשַׁתָּא דְּטֵבֵת מְנַוּוּלְתָּא! [6]לָא קַשְׁיָא. [7]הָא דַּאֲתָא מִיטְרָא מֵעִיקָּרָא; [8]הָא דְּלָא אֲתָא מִיטְרָא מֵעִיקָּרָא. [9]וְאָמַר רַב חִסְדָּא: גְּשָׁמִים שֶׁיָּרְדוּ עַל מִקְצָת מְדִינָה וְעַל מִקְצָת מְדִינָה לֹא יָרְדוּ [10]אֵין בָּהֶן מִשּׁוּם "וְעָצַר".

LITERAL TRANSLATION

[1]Rav Yehudah said: It is good for a year when Tevet is a widow.

[2]There are [some] who say: So that the gardens should not be desolate. [3]And there are [others] who say: So that blight should not take [crops] away.

[4]Is this so? [5]But surely Rav Ḥisda said: It is good for a year when Tevet is muddy!

[6]There is no difficulty. [7]This is when the rain came from the beginning; [8]that is when rain did not come from the beginning.

[9]And Rav Ḥisda said: Rains that fell on part of a country but did not fall on [another] part of a country [10]do not come into the category of "and He will shut up."

RASHI

טבא לשתא — אשריה. כלומר, טובה יש לשנה דטבת ארמלתא — שאין גשמים יורדין בה להרביע את הארץ. **איכא דאמרי דלא ביירי תרביצי** — אותן מקומות שמרבילין בהן תורה אינן בורות, מפני שהדרכים יפין הן, והולכין התלמידים ממקום למקום ללמוד תורה. לשון אחר: לא ביירי תרביצי — גנות, שאינן גדלין על רוב מים, כגון כרשינין. **לא שקיל שודפנא** — אין השדפון נאחז ומתדבק בתבואה. **מנוולתא** — שהדרכים מנוולים בטיט מפני הגשמים. **הא דאתא מיטרא מעיקרא** — שירדו הגשמים בזמנן במרחשון, וירדו אף בטבת — רעים הן, שכבר די לעולם בגשמים של מרחשון. **דלא אתא מיטרא מעיקרא** — טבא לשתא, דטבת מנוולתא, לשון אחר: הא דאתא מיטרא מעיקרא — טבא דמנוולתא. **אין בהם משום "ועצר"** — דאותן של קצת מדינה שירדו להן גשמים מוכרין לאחרים.

NOTES

Rabbenu Ḥananel and others explain that rain in the early morning foretells nothing about the year as a whole. Such rain should be taken as a sign that the ass-drivers should not go out to work on that day, for it is likely that the rain will continue all day.

דְּלָא בַּיְירִי תַּרְבִּיצֵי So that gardens should not be desolate. A number of different explanations of this expression have been proposed. *Rashi* suggests that a break in the winter rain ensures that the Talmud academies will be well attended, because the roads will remain passable and the students will be able to travel. Alternatively, a pause in the rain is beneficial because the gardens will not be flooded. The Geonim suggest that a break in the rain during the month of Tevet is beneficial, allowing farmers to plow and sow. *Arukh* explains that the pause in the rain allows the people to carry on their business outside as usual, and to frequent courtyards rather than sheltering in their homes.

[1]אִינִי? [2]וְהָכְתִיב: ״וְגַם אָנֹכִי מָנַעְתִּי מִכֶּם אֶת הַגֶּשֶׁם בְּעוֹד שְׁלֹשָׁה חֳדָשִׁים לַקָּצִיר, וְהִמְטַרְתִּי עַל עִיר אֶחָת, וְעַל עִיר אַחַת לֹא אַמְטִיר, חֶלְקָה אַחַת תִּמָּטֵר, וגו׳״. [3]וְאָמַר רַב יְהוּדָה אָמַר רַב: שְׁתֵּיהֶן לִקְלָלָה!

[4]לָא קַשְׁיָא. [5]הָא דַּאֲתָא טוּבָא; [6]הָא דַּאֲתָא כִּדְמִבָּעֵי לֵיהּ.

[7]אֲמַר רַב אַשִׁי: דַּיְקָא נַמִי, דִּכְתִיב: ״תִּמָּטֵר״, [8]תְּהֵא מְקוֹם מָטָר. [9]שְׁמַע מִינָּהּ.

TRANSLATION AND COMMENTARY

אִינִי [1]But, the Gemara objects, **is this** really **so?** [2]**Surely** we can see that the opposite is true, and that both the part of the country that has received rain and the part that has not received rain should see themselves as being under a curse, as **it is written** (Amos 4:7): **"And I have** also withheld **the rain from you, when there are still three months until the harvest, and I will cause it to rain on one city, but on one city I will not cause it to rain; one portion will be rained upon,** and one portion on which it will not rain will dry up." The Prophet Amos is decrying the fact that several calamities have already befallen the Kingdom of Israel because of God's anger without inspiring the people to repent. Among the calamities, he lists the fact that the rainy season has been cut short, and that rain has fallen in one part of the country and not in another. Thus we see that the Prophet Amos describes such selective rainfall as a manifestation of God's anger. [3]**And** furthermore **Rav Yehudah** gave an interpretation of the verse in Amos **in the name of Rav, saying: Both** parts of the country mentioned in this verse **are** mentioned **for a curse!** Amos is saying that God will show anger to both parts, by bringing excessive and damaging rain to one part and drought to the other. Thus we see that when rain falls in one part of a country and not in another, both parts should see themselves as under a curse. How, then, could Rav Ḥisda claim that such selective rainfall is not a sign of divine displeasure?

לָא קַשְׁיָא [4]The Gemara answers that **there is no difficulty** in explaining Rav Ḥisda's statement. [5]The verse in Amos, as we have seen, **is** referring to a case **where a large quantity** of rain **came down** on one part of the country and flooded it, while another part suffered drought. In such a case, both parts of the country should consider themselves cursed. [6]By contrast, Rav Ḥisda is referring to a case **where** the rain **came down as it should have** done on one part of the country, while the other part went dry. In such a case, both parts of the country may be confident that they are not the victims of God's anger, because if part of a country receives rain, it can then grow sufficient crops to feed the entire country.

אֲמַר רַב אַשִׁי [7]**Rav Ashi said:** The Gemara's interpretation of the verse in Amos as referring to a flood **is also indicated** in the verse itself. **For** in the verse it is **written** concerning the area that will receive rain: "One portion **will be rained upon."** The Prophet employs an unusual construction of the verb "to rain" — תִּמָּטֵר — with a dot in the letter mem indicating a double letter. [8]Thus we can view this word as a contraction of the Hebrew phrase תְּהֵא מְקוֹם מָטָר, **which means: "Let it be a place of rain."** In other words, so much rain will fall on this place that there will be nothing left but rainwater. [9]Thus we can **infer from this** hint in the verse that the Prophet is indeed referring to a situation where both parts of the country were cursed, one with a flood and the other with a drought.

LITERAL TRANSLATION

[1]Is this so? [2]But surely it is written: "And I have also withheld the rain from you when there are still three months until the harvest, and I will cause it to rain on one city, but on one city I will not cause it to rain, one portion will be rained upon, etc." [3]And Rav Yehudah said in the name of Rav: Both of them are for a curse!

[4]There is no difficulty. [5]This is where a large quantity came [down]; [6]that is where it came [down] as it should have.

[7]Rav Ashi said: It is also precise, for it is written: "Will be rained upon," [8][meaning] let it be a place of rain. [9]Conclude from this.

RASHI

ואמר רב יהודה אמר רב שתיהן לקללה — אותן שירדו ואותן שלא ירדו, מפני שרוב גשמים קלקלו את תבואתם. **הא דאיכא מיטרא טובא** — יותר מדאי, שתיהן לקללה. **כדמבעי ליה** — אין בהם משום "ועצר" שקצת מדינה תספק לקצת מדינה. **תמטר תהא מקום מטר** — כלומר יותר מדאי.

NOTES

הָא דַּאֲתָא כִּדְמִבָּעֵי לֵיהּ **That is where it came down as it should have.** Our commentary follows *Rashi* and most Rishonim, who explain that if there is too much rain in one part of the country, and no rain in another part, the people living in both places should see themselves as cursed. But if an appropriate amount of rain falls in one part of the country, and no rain falls in another, then the inhabitants of both areas need not worry that they have been cursed by God, for the area that has received the rain can support the area that has remained dry.

Rabbenu Gershom explains the distinction in just the opposite manner. If an overabundance of rain falls in one

BACKGROUND

דִּכְתִיב: ״תִּמָּטֵר״ **For it is written: "Will be rained upon."** This Midrashic interpretation of the verse is based on its unusual linguistic form. Usually the Bible speaks of the sky or of clouds that pour out water (מַמְטִירִים). But here it says that the earth itself will be watered, which can mean that the earth will become rain — that it will contain much water, as in a flood.

[1] אָמַר רַבִּי אַבָּהוּ: מֵאֵימָתַי מְבָרְכִין עַל הַגְּשָׁמִים? [2] מִשֶּׁיֵּצֵא חָתָן לִקְרַאת כַּלָּה.
[3] מַאי מְבָרֵךְ?
[4] אָמַר רַב יְהוּדָה אָמַר רַב: [5] ״מוֹדִים אֲנַחְנוּ לָךְ, ה׳ אֱלֹהֵינוּ, עַל כָּל טִפָּה וְטִפָּה שֶׁהוֹרַדְתָּ לָנוּ״.
[6] וְרַבִּי יוֹחָנָן מְסַיֵּים בָּהּ הָכִי: [7] ״אִילּוּ פִּינוּ מָלֵא שִׁירָה כַּיָּם, וּלְשׁוֹנֵנוּ רִנָּה כַּהֲמוֹן גַּלָּיו, כו׳״, [8] עַד: ״אַל יַעַזְבוּנוּ רַחֲמֶיךָ,

LITERAL TRANSLATION

[1] Rabbi Abbahu said: From when does one make the blessing on the rains? [2] From when the bridegroom goes out to meet the bride.

[3] What blessing does one make?

[4] Rav Yehudah said in the name of Rav: [5] "We thank you, O Lord our God, for every single drop that you have brought down for us."

[6] And Rabbi Yoḥanan completes it as follows: [7] "Were our mouth filled with song like the sea, and our tongue with celebration like the multitude of its waves, etc.," [8] until: "Let Your mercies not forsake us,

TRANSLATION AND COMMENTARY

אָמַר רַבִּי אַבָּהוּ The Gemara now cites another statement of Rabbi Abbahu on the subject of rain. The Mishnah (*Berakhot* 54a) rules that when a person witnesses certain impressive events or objects, he should recite the appropriate blessing. One of the occasions that calls for a blessing is a major rainfall after a period of drought. Concerning this blessing, [1] **Rabbi Abbahu said: From when do we make the blessing on the rains?** At what point is the rainfall sufficiently significant to require a special blessing? [2] Rabbi Abbahu replies with a metaphor: The blessing is required **when the bridegroom goes out to meet the bride.** When drops of rain falling on puddles cause other drops to splash up to greet them, the rainfall is sufficient to warrant a blessing.

מַאי מְבָרֵךְ [3] The Gemara asks: **What** is the precise wording of the **blessing** that **we make** when the rain falls "like a bridegroom going to meet his bride"?

אָמַר רַב יְהוּדָה [4] **Rav Yehudah said in the name of Rav:** We say as follows: [5] **"We thank you, O Lord our God, for every single drop that you have brought down for us."**

וְרַבִּי יוֹחָנָן [6] The Gemara notes that **Rabbi Yoḥanan would** begin the blessing with the words prescribed by Rav, but he would **complete it** with a passage taken from the well-known Shabbat prayer called *Nishmat*, **as follows:** [7] **"Were our mouth filled with song like the sea, and our tongue with celebration like the multitude of its waves,** and our lips with praise like the expanses of the firmament, and were our eyes as bright as the sun and the moon, and our hands outstretched as the eagles of the heavens, and our feet as swift as gazelles, we would still not be able to thank You, O Lord our God and God of our fathers, and to bless Your name for even one of the thousands upon thousands and myriads upon myriads of kindnesses that You have done for our fathers and for us." Later in the prayer Rabbi Yoḥanan's blessing begins to depart slightly from the regular formulation and he concludes as follows: [8] "Until now Your mercies have helped us and **let Your mercies**

RASHI

מאימתי מברכין על הגשמים — בפרק ״הרואה״ (ברכות נד,א) אמרינן: על הגשמים אומר ״הטוב והמטיב״, והתם (נט,א) פרכינן הך ברכה דתקון לה רבנן, ומשנינן לה: הא — דחזא מיחזא, והא — דשמע משמע. **חתן לקראת כלה** — שירדו כל כך שכשהטפה נופלת יוצאה אחרת ובולטת כנגדה, מפי מורי. לשון אחר: שהשווקין מקלחין מים, שוק מקלח וזה מקלח כנגדו.

NOTES

part of the country, it is a blessing, for enough can be grown there to provide for the rest of the country where there is no rain. But if rain falls in only one part of the country, and in an amount that suffices for that part of the country alone, then the inhabitants of the entire country should see themselves as under a divine curse.

מִשֶּׁיֵּצֵא חָתָן לִקְרַאת כַּלָּה From when the bridegroom goes out to meet the bride. *Rashi* and *Rav Hai Gaon* explain that the blessing for the rain is recited when the ground is so saturated that falling rain ("the bride") lands on puddles and causes the rain on the ground ("the bridegroom") to splash up as if to meet it. Some commentators point out that there is a difficulty with this explanation, for it was stated above that the falling rain is likened to a husband who inseminates his wife, the earth.

Ritva explains that the rain itself may be seen as having both male and female components, the rain already on the ground playing the role of the bridegroom who goes out to meet his bride — the falling rain.

Rambam (*Hilkhot Berakhot* 10:6; see also *Ritva, Shittah*) understands the metaphor used in our Gemara differently. The bridegroom goes out to meet the bride when the puddles expand and begin to approach one another.

HALAKHAH

מֵאֵימָתַי מְבָרְכִין עַל הַגְּשָׁמִים From when does one make the blessing on the rains? "If people have been suffering from a drought, and then it rains, a blessing is recited for the rain. The blessing is recited even if no heavy rainfall has occurred, provided that puddles form and drops of water from them splash up as if to meet the falling rain. *Rema* (in the name of *Smag*) notes that in those places where there is always abundant rain, it is customary not to recite this blessing. *Taz* (in the name of *Bet Yosef*) adds that, even in such places, if a period of drought is followed by rain, the blessing over rain must be recited." (*Shulḥan Arukh, Oraḥ Ḥayyim* 221:1.)

ה׳ אֱלֹהֵינוּ, וְלֹא עֲזָבוּנוּ. בָּרוּךְ רוֹב הַהוֹדָאוֹת״.
[1] ״רוֹב הַהוֹדָאוֹת״ וְלֹא ״כָּל הַהוֹדָאוֹת״?
[2] אֲמַר רָבָא: אֵימָא: ״אֵל הַהוֹדָאוֹת״.
[3] אֲמַר רַב פַּפָּא: הִלְכָּךְ [7A] נֵימְרִינְהוּ לְתַרְוַיְיהוּ: [4] ״אֵל הַהוֹדָאוֹת״ וְ״רוֹב הַהוֹדָאוֹת״.
[5] אָמַר רַבִּי אַבָּהוּ: גָּדוֹל יוֹם הַגְּשָׁמִים מִתְּחִיַּית הַמֵּתִים.
[6] דְּאִילּוּ תְּחִיַּית הַמֵּתִים

LITERAL TRANSLATION

O Lord our God, as they have not forsaken us. Blessed with most thanks."

[1] "Most thanks" and not "all the thanks"?

[2] Rava said: Say: "The God of thanks."

[3] Rav Pappa said: Therefore [7A] we should say them both: [4] "The God of thanks" and "most thanks."

[5] Rabbi Abbahu said: The day of rains is greater than the resurrection of the dead. [6] For whereas the resurrection of the dead

TRANSLATION AND COMMENTARY

not forsake us, O Lord our God, as they have not forsaken us. Blessed are You, O Lord, **with most thanks."**

רוֹב הַהוֹדָאוֹת [1] The Gemara interjects: Rabbi Yoḥanan's blessing ends by giving God **"most thanks."** But the use of the word "most" (רוֹב) can be misleading. It can mean "immense quantities" (and this is the meaning that Rabbi Yoḥanan intended), but it can also mean "a majority," which could easily lead to the improper impression that God is entitled to most of the thanks, **but not to "all the thanks."** Obviously, this impression must be avoided.

אֲמַר רָבָא [2] Accordingly, **Rava said**: We must amend Rabbi Yoḥanan's blessing and **say**: "Blessed are You, O Lord, **the God of thanks."**

אֲמַר רַב פַּפָּא [3] **Rav Pappa said**: Although Rava's version avoids the misleading language of Rabbi Yoḥanan's original version, it lacks some of its details. For in Rabbi Yoḥanan's version it is clear that very many thanks indeed are due, whereas in Rava's version it is not clear how much gratitude is in order. **Therefore** [7A] **we must** combine the two versions and **say them both:** [4] **"The God of thanks," and "most thanks."**

אָמַר רַבִּי אַבָּהוּ [5] The Gemara now cites another statement of Rabbi Abbahu on the subject of rain. **Rabbi Abbahu said: The day** when **the rains** fall **is greater than** the day when **the dead will be resurrected.** [6] **For**

RASHI

רוב ההודאות — כלומר: רוב ההודאות אתה קורא להקדוש ברוך הוא, ולא כל ההודאות, והכי משמע: ברוך אתה ברוב ההודאות, ולא בכל, אלא כך חותם: ברוך אתה ה׳ אלהינו מלך העולם אל ההודאות, דמשמע כל ההודאות. **למימרינהו לתרווייהו** — ״ברוך אתה ברוב ההודאות״ — במרבית ההודאות, האל של כל ההודאות משמע, ומתחלה היה משמע רוב ממש, ולא מרובות. וכמו כן בישתבח ״אל מלך גדול בתשבחות אל ההודאות״. מפי רבי. רשעי עובדי כוכבים אינן חיין ״כי תולעתם לא תמות ואשם לא תכבה״ (ישעיה סו).

NOTES

רוֹב הַהוֹדָאוֹת **Most thanks.** When Rabbi Yoḥanan said that the blessing for rain should conclude with the words רוֹב הַהוֹדָאוֹת, he intended that the word רוֹב be understood in the sense of "immense quantities," so that the phrase means "multiple thanks." Indeed, we find that the word is used in this sense in Scripture: "And plenty of [רוֹב] corn and wine [Genesis 27:28]"; "And the multitude of [רוֹב] his children [Esther 5:11]." But the Gemara is concerned that if this formula is used, the word רוֹב may be understood in the sense of "a majority," as in Esther 10:3: "And accepted by most of [רוֹב] his brethren." The Rabbis should not have formulated the blessing using an ambiguous term that may lead to the very serious error that it is only the majority of our thanks that we offer to God (*Ritva*).

Rid suggests that, even according to Rabbi Yoḥanan, the word רוֹב is to be understood in the sense of "a majority." Man is not able to thank God for all the kindness that God bestows upon him, but only for most of the kindness that God shows him.

אֵל הַהוֹדָאוֹת **The God of thanks.** *Ritva* notes that the word אֵל is used here not only as a name of God, but also in the sense of strength and might, so that the phrase is to be understood to mean: "Mighty in thanks."

נֵימְרִינְהוּ לְתַרְוַיְיהוּ **We should say them both.** Some Rishonim (*Ba'al HaMa'or, Rabbenu Yehonatan of Lunel*) have a reading according to which Rav Pappa said we must say them both, without specifying what must be said. They explain that Rav Pappa was referring to the formulations put forward by Rav Yehudah in the name of Rav, and by Rabbi Yoḥanan, that we must say: "We thank You, O Lord, our God, for every single drop that You have brought down for us. And were our mouth filled with song like the sea, and our tongue with celebration like the multitude of its waves, etc." *Ramban* and most other Rishonim reject this explanation, arguing that what Rav Pappa meant was that we must recite both the conclusions suggested by Rabbi Yoḥanan and by Rav, "the God of thanks," and "most thanks."

It has been noted that in this passage Rav Pappa follows

HALAKHAH

נֵימְרִינְהוּ לְתַרְוַיְיהוּ **We should say them both.** "The blessing recited over rain (according to the wording established by the Geonim and by *Rambam*) concludes with the formula: 'Blessed are you, O Lord, the God of most thanks,'" following Rav Pappa. (*Shulḥan Arukh, Oraḥ Ḥayyim* 221:2.)

TRANSLATION AND COMMENTARY

whereas the resurrection of the dead brings blessing **to the righteous** alone, [1]**yet rain** brings blessing **both to the righteous and to the wicked.**

וּפְלִיגָא דְּרַב יוֹסֵף [2]The Gemara notes that Rabbi Abbahu **disagrees with Rav Yosef** about this matter. [3]**For** Rabbi Abbahu said that the day of rains is greater than the day of the resurrection of the dead, whereas **Rav Yosef said** that rain is merely **equivalent to the resurrection of the dead,** [4]and **because** of this the Rabbis **established** the mention of rain **in the** second **blessing of** the Amidah, whose primary topic is **the resurrection of the dead.**

אָמַר רַב יְהוּדָה [5]The Gemara now cites a similar statement by **Rav Yehudah,** who **said: The day** when **the rains** fall **is as great as the day on which the Torah was given,** both being gifts of God that came down from the heavens, [6]**as it is said** (Deuteronomy 32:2): **"My doctrine will drop as the rain,"** and the word **"doctrine" has no** other meaning **except Torah,** [7]**as it is said** (Proverbs 4:2): **"For I have given you a good doctrine; do not forsake My Torah."**

רָבָא אָמַר [8]Here, too, there is an opinion that rain is even more important, as **Rava said:** The day when the rains fall **is more** important **than the day on which the Torah was given,** [9]**as it is said** (Deuteronomy 32:2): **"My doctrine will drop as the rain,"** which refers to the Torah, as we have seen above. Moses compares the Torah to rain. [10]But when comparisons are made, **which** object **is dependent on which?** [11]Surely **we must say** that **the small** object **is** always **dependent on the great** and not vice versa. Hence we may conclude that the grandeur of the giving of the Torah is merely comparable to the grandeur of rain but not its equal.

רָבָא רָמֵי [12]The Gemara now cites additional interpretations of the same verse in Deuteronomy (32:2). **Rava raised a contradiction** between two parts of this verse: [13]At the beginning of the verse **it is written: "My doctrine will drop as the rain,"** and the Torah is compared to rain, [14]**whereas** later in the verse **it is**

לַצַּדִּיקִים, [1]וְאִילּוּ גְּשָׁמִים בֵּין לַצַּדִּיקִים בֵּין לָרְשָׁעִים.

[2]וּפְלִיגָא דְּרַב יוֹסֵף. [3]דְּאָמַר רַב יוֹסֵף: מִתּוֹךְ שֶׁהִיא שְׁקוּלָה כִּתְחִיַּית הַמֵּתִים, [4]קְבָעוּהָ בִּתְחִיַּית הַמֵּתִים.

[5]אָמַר רַב יְהוּדָה: גָּדוֹל יוֹם הַגְּשָׁמִים כַּיּוֹם שֶׁנִּיתְּנָה בּוֹ תּוֹרָה, [6]שֶׁנֶּאֱמַר: "יַעֲרֹף כַּמָּטָר לִקְחִי", וְאֵין לֶקַח אֶלָּא תּוֹרָה, [7]שֶׁנֶּאֱמַר: "כִּי לֶקַח טוֹב נָתַתִּי לָכֶם; תּוֹרָתִי אַל תַּעֲזֹבוּ".

[8]רָבָא אָמַר: יוֹתֵר מִיּוֹם שֶׁנִּיתְּנָה בּוֹ תּוֹרָה, [9]שֶׁנֶּאֱמַר: "יַעֲרֹף כַּמָּטָר לִקְחִי". [10]מִי נִתְלָה בְּמִי? [11]הֱוֵי אוֹמֵר: קָטָן נִתְלָה בְּגָדוֹל.

[12]רָבָא רָמֵי: [13]כְּתִיב: "יַעֲרֹף כַּמָּטָר לִקְחִי", [14]וּכְתִיב: "תִּזַּל

LITERAL TRANSLATION

is for the righteous, [1]yet rains are both for the righteous and for the wicked.

[2]And he disagrees with Rav Yosef. [3]For Rav Yosef said: Because it is equivalent to the resurrection of the dead, [4]they established it in [the blessing for] the resurrection of the dead.

[5]Rav Yehudah said: The day of rains is as great as the day on which the Torah was given, [6]as it is said: "My doctrine will drop as the rain," and there is no doctrine except Torah, [7]as it is said: "For I have given you a good doctrine; do not forsake My Torah."

[8]Rava said: It is more than the day on which the Torah was given, [9]as it is said: "My doctrine will drop as the rain." [10]Who is dependent on whom? [11]You must say: The small is dependent on the great.

[12]Rava raised a contradiction (lit., "cast"): [13]It is written: "My doctrine will drop as the rain," [14]and it is written: "My speech

RASHI

ופליגא דרב יוסף – דאיהו אמר כתחיית המתים ולא יותר, שבה חיים בני אדם, שהתבואה גדילה בו. **כמטר לקחי** – השוה לקח למטר. **יערף** – כמו "אף שמיו יערפו טל" (דברים לג) "ושחקים ירעפו טל" (משלי ג) – שהיא מרבה הפירות.

NOTES

his general principle that it is preferable to combine two conflicting opinions, provided that there is no internal contradiction between the two, rather than to decide in favor of the one or the other (*Eshel Avraham*).

תְּחִיַּית הַמֵּתִים לַצַּדִּיקִים **The resurrection of the dead is for the righteous.** *Rabbi Ya'akov Emden* notes that Rabbi Abbahu's statement should not be taken as implying that it is only the righteous who will be resurrected, for the wicked will also participate in the resurrection of the dead. Rather, Rabbi Abbahu meant that whereas both the righteous and the wicked benefit from the rain, it is only the righteous who will benefit from the resurrection of the dead, as the verse states (Daniel 12:2): "And many of those who sleep in the dust of the earth shall awake, some to everlasting life, and some to shame and everlasting contempt."

יוֹתֵר מִיּוֹם שֶׁנִּיתְּנָה בּוֹ תּוֹרָה **More than the day on which the Torah was given.** *Keren Orah* explains that the day on which the rain falls is greater than the day on which the Torah was given, for the Torah brings benefit only to the righteous, whereas the rain benefits the wicked as well. According to *Midrash Shoḥer Tov,* rainfall is greater than the revelation of the Torah, for the Torah was given only to the Jewish people, whereas rain is God's gift to all the peoples of the world.

TRANSLATION AND COMMENTARY

written: "My speech will flow as the dew," and the Torah is compared to dew! How can the Torah be compared both to rain and to dew? Rava resolves the contradiction by explaining that the two comparisons apply to two different types of Torah scholar. [1]**If a Torah scholar is a worthy person,** his Torah **is like dew.** [2]**But if** a Torah scholar **is not** a worthy person, the Torah he has learned **will break his neck** and kill him, **like** heavy **rain** which can cause devastation and ruin. Rava's explanation is based on a play on the word יַעֲרֹף, which we have translated as "will drop." However, this word also suggests the verb ערף, which means "to break the neck."

תַּנְיָא [3]A similar explanation, employing the same interpretation of the word יַעֲרֹף, **was taught** in the following Baraita: **"Rabbi Bena'ah used to say: Whoever occupies himself with Torah for its own sake** out of a love of truth and a desire to understand God's will, **his Torah becomes an elixir of life for him,** [4]**as it is said** (Proverbs 3:18): **'It is a tree of life to those who hold on to it.'** [5]**And it also says** in another verse (Proverbs 3:8): **'It will be a healing for your navel** and marrow for your bones.' [6]**And it also says** in another verse (Proverbs 8:35): **'For he who finds Me finds life.'** [7]The healing quality of Torah manifests itself only when Torah is studied for the right reasons; **but whoever occupies himself with Torah not for its own sake,** but in order to make use of it for his own ends, **his Torah becomes a deadly poison for him,** [8]**as it is said** (Deuteronomy 32:2): **'My doctrine will drop as the rain.'** This verse uses the word יַעֲרֹף, which means **'will drop'** in the context, but the Hebrew root ערף **has no** other literal **meaning except killing** by breaking the neck, [9]**as it is said** (Deuteronomy 21:4): **'And they shall break the heifer's neck** [וְעָרְפוּ] **there in the valley.'"** Thus, if we translate the verse in Deuteronomy literally ("My doctrine will break the neck as the rain"), we see that the Torah can be fatal when it is studied for the wrong reasons.

כַּטַּל אִמְרָתִי"! [1]אִם תַּלְמִיד חָכָם הָגוּן הוּא, כַּטַּל, [2]וְאִם לָאו, עוֹרְפֵהוּ כַּמָּטָר.

[3]תַּנְיָא: "הָיָה רַבִּי בְּנָאָה אוֹמֵר: כָּל הָעוֹסֵק בַּתּוֹרָה לִשְׁמָהּ, תּוֹרָתוֹ נַעֲשֵׂית לוֹ סַם חַיִּים, [4]שֶׁנֶּאֱמַר: 'עֵץ חַיִּים הִיא לַמַּחֲזִיקִים בָּהּ'. [5]וְאוֹמֵר: 'רִפְאוּת תְּהִי לְשָׁרֶּךָ'. [6]וְאוֹמֵר: 'כִּי מֹצְאִי מָצָא חַיִּים'. [7]וְכָל הָעוֹסֵק בַּתּוֹרָה שֶׁלֹּא לִשְׁמָהּ, נַעֲשֵׂית לוֹ סַם הַמָּוֶת, [8]שֶׁנֶּאֱמַר: 'יַעֲרֹף כַּמָּטָר לִקְחִי', וְאֵין 'עֲרִיפָה' אֶלָּא הֲרִיגָה, [9]שֶׁנֶּאֱמַר: 'וְעָרְפוּ שָׁם אֶת הָעֶגְלָה בַּנָּחַל'".

LITERAL TRANSLATION

will flow as the dew"! [1]If a Torah scholar is worthy, it is like dew, [2]but if not, it breaks his neck like rain.

[3]It was taught: "Rabbi Bena'ah used to say: Whoever occupies himself with Torah for its own sake, his Torah becomes an elixir of life for him, [4]as it is said: 'It is a tree of life to those who hold on to it.' [5]And it [also] says: 'It will be a healing for your navel.' [6]And it [also] says: 'For he who finds Me finds life.' [7]But whoever occupies himself with Torah not for its own sake, his Torah becomes a deadly poison for him, [8]as it is said: 'My doctrine will drop as the rain,' and there is no 'dropping' except killing, [9]as it is said: 'And they shall break the heifer's neck there in the valley.'"

RASHI

כתיב תזל כטל – דמשמע נחת.
ערפיהו כמטר – הרגהו. **לשמה** – משום "כאשר צוני ה' אלהי" ולא כדי להקרות רבי.

BACKGROUND

אִם תַּלְמִיד חָכָם הָגוּן הוּא If a Torah scholar is worthy. Although the study of Torah demands intellectual capacity, it is not like the study of other disciplines. A Torah scholar must have an exemplary character and behave appropriately. Therefore the Sages were very careful to choose students who were honest and decent, and they kept unsuitable students at a distance, sometimes by imposing fines and bans on them.

כָּל הָעוֹסֵק בַּתּוֹרָה לִשְׁמָהּ Whoever occupies himself with Torah for its own sake. One characteristic of a worthy Torah scholar is that he studies Torah for its own sake, for the sake of Heaven, and in order to achieve a moral way of life. But in all periods there were people who did not study Torah for its own sake. The Sages distinguished between those who studied Torah in order to obtain honor and social status, and the more serious cases in which people studied Torah in order to cause other people to suffer, or in order to falsify the words of the Torah. Of such corrupt scholars, the Sages said: The Torah they teach not only does them no credit, but it also becomes poisonous for them; and the more they study, the more they harm themselves.

SAGES

רַבִּי בְּנָאָה Rabbi Bena'ah. One of the last of the Tannaim, Rabbi Bena'ah was not born in Eretz Israel but came from abroad. We do not know his profession, but in Eretz Israel he took care to mark graves so that priests would not become ritually impure. His permanent place of residence was Tiberias, where he founded a large academy. The great Amora, Rabbi Yoḥanan, studied Torah from him and transmitted most of Rabbi Bena'ah's teachings that have survived. Rabbi Bena'ah was famed for his wisdom, and also attained important status with the non-Jewish authorities.

NOTES

עוֹרְפֵהוּ כַּמָּטָר It breaks his neck like rain. Various explanations have been suggested for this statement. *Meiri* and *Maharsha* explain that Rava's comment is based on a play of words, according to which the word יַעֲרֹף has the meaning "to turn one's back." Thus Rava advises that if a Torah scholar is an unfit person, it is best to turn one's back on him and to seek Torah elsewhere. *Rashi*, followed by our commentary, maintains that Rava takes the word יַעֲרֹף to mean "kill" (as does Rabbi Bena'ah in the Baraita cited immediately below). *Shittah* suggests that Rava's remark is directed to the Rabbinic student himself: If he is fit, the fine distinctions (comparable to dew) which are found in the Halakhah should be explained to him, but if he is unfit, he should first be taught large quantities of Halakhot (comparable to rain), and only later should they be explained to him. *Keren Orah* explains that Rava's statement refers not to the Rabbinic student's teacher, but to the Torah itself: To a worthy student the Torah is as pleasing as dew, but to an unworthy student it is as hard as rain.

HALAKHAH

אִם תַּלְמִיד חָכָם הָגוּן הוּא If a Torah scholar is worthy. "One should not teach Torah to an unworthy student. Such a student should be helped to mend his ways, and only afterwards should he be brought into the academy to begin actual study." (*Shulḥan Arukh, Yoreh De'ah* 246:7.)

אֲמַר לֵיהּ רַבִּי יִרְמְיָה לְרַבִּי זֵירָא: "לֵיתֵי מָר לִיתְנֵי"! [1]

אֲמַר לֵיהּ: "חֲלַשׁ לִבָּאִי, וְלָא יָכֵילְנָא". [2]

"לֵימָא מָר מִילְּתָא דְּאַגַּדְתָּא". [3]

אֲמַר לֵיהּ: "הָכִי אֲמַר רַבִּי יוֹחָנָן: [4] מַאי דִּכְתִיב: 'כִּי הָאָדָם עֵץ הַשָּׂדֶה'? [5] וְכִי אָדָם עֵץ שָׂדֶה הוּא? [6] אֶלָּא מִשּׁוּם דִּכְתִיב: 'כִּי מִמֶּנּוּ תֹאכֵל, וְאֹתוֹ לֹא תִכְרֹת', [7] וּכְתִיב: 'אֹתוֹ תַשְׁחִית וְכָרָתָּ'. [8] הָא כֵּיצַד? [9] אִם תַּלְמִיד חָכָם הָגוּן הוּא, 'מִמֶּנּוּ תֹאכֵל, וְאֹתוֹ לֹא תִכְרֹת', וְאִם לָאו, 'אֹתוֹ תַשְׁחִית וְכָרָתָּ'". [10]

אֲמַר רַבִּי חָמָא בְּרַבִּי חֲנִינָא: [11] מַאי דִּכְתִיב: "בַּרְזֶל בְּבַרְזֶל יָחַד"? [12] לוֹמַר לְךָ: מַה בַּרְזֶל זֶה, אֶחָד מְחַדֵּד אֶת חֲבֵירוֹ, [13] אַף שְׁנֵי תַלְמִידֵי חֲכָמִים מְחַדְּדִין זֶה אֶת זֶה בַּהֲלָכָה. [14]

LITERAL TRANSLATION

[1] Rabbi Yirmeyah said to Rabbi Zera: "Come, Sir, [and] teach."

[2] He said to him: "My heart is weak, and I cannot."

[3] "Say to us, Sir, something of Aggadah."

[4] He said to him: "This is what Rabbi Yoḥanan said: [5] What is [the meaning of] what is written: 'For man is a tree of the field'? [6] But is a man a tree of the field? [7] Rather, it is because it is written: 'For you may eat from it, but you may not cut it down,' [8] and it is written: 'You may destroy it and cut it down.' [9] How so? If a Torah scholar is worthy, 'you may eat from him, but you may not cut him down,' [10] but if not, 'you may destroy him and cut him down.'"

[11] Rabbi Ḥama the son of Rabbi Ḥanina said: What is [the meaning of] what is written: [12] "Iron sharpens iron"? [13] To say to you: Just as [in the case of] iron, one sharpens its fellow, [14] so too do two Torah scholars sharpen each other in Halakhah.

TRANSLATION AND COMMENTARY

אֲמַר לֵיהּ [1] The Gemara now relates that **Rabbi Yirmeyah** once **said to Rabbi Zera: "Come, Sir, and give us a Halakhic discourse."**

אֲמַר לֵיהּ [2] Rabbi Zera **said to** Rabbi Yirmeyah in reply: **"I am not feeling well, and I cannot** find the strength to convey the subtleties of a Halakhic discourse."

לֵימָא [3] Rabbi Yirmeyah said: "Even if you do not have the strength to teach us a complicated Halakhic matter, **tell us something** in the sphere of **Aggadah."** This term refers to all the nonlegalistic parts of the Talmud, including homilies, theological and philosophical discussions, stories about individuals, ethical guidance, and interpretations of Biblical verses. Generally, Aggadah requires less concentration than Halakhah.

אֲמַר לֵיהּ [4] Rabbi Zera acquiesced and **said** the following **to** Rabbi Yirmeyah: **"This is what Rabbi Yoḥanan said: [5] What is the meaning of what is written** in the following verse (Deuteronomy 20:19): **'For man is a tree of the field'? [6] But is a man** really **a tree of the field? [7] Rather,** the meaning of the verse is that there is a close comparison between a human being and a tree, so that the other verses in this passage, which discuss trees, may be applied to human beings as well. **For it is written** in the same verse, concerning fruit trees: **'For you may eat from it, but you may not cut it down,' [8] and it is written** in the next verse, concerning trees that do not bear fruit: **'You may destroy it and cut it down.'** There are two kinds of trees, and, by implication, two kinds of people. [9] **How so? If a Torah scholar is a worthy** human being, he is like a fruit tree and **'you may eat from him'** by studying his wisdom, **'but you may not cut him down'** by abandoning him. [10] On the other hand, **if** a Torah scholar is **not** a worthy person, he is like a tree that does not bear fruit, and **'you may destroy him and cut him down'** by keeping far away from him."

אֲמַר רַבִּי חָמָא בְּרַבִּי חֲנִינָא [11] The Gemara now cites a series of Amoraic teachings on Torah study. **Rabbi Ḥama the son of Rabbi Ḥanina said: What is the meaning of what is written** in the following verse (Proverbs 27:17): [12] **"Iron sharpens iron,** and a man sharpens the face of his friend"? Rabbi Ḥama bar Ḥanina explains: [13] The intention of the verse is **to say to you: Just as in the case of iron,** when **one** implement **sharpens another,** [14] **so too do two Torah scholars sharpen each other** when they discuss questions of **Halakhah** together.

RASHI

יכילנא — למיגמר. **וכי אדם עץ השדה** — אלא מקיש אדם לעץ השדה: מה עץ השדה, אם עץ מאכל הוא — ממנו תאכל ואותו לא תכרות, כך תלמידי חכמים: אם הגון הוא — ממנו תאכל, למוד הימנו, ואם לאו — אותו תשחית, סור מעליו. **ברזל בברזל יחד** "ואיש יחד פני רעהו" מה ברזל זה, אחד מחדד את חבירו, כגון סכין על גבי חבירתה.

NOTES

וְכִי אָדָם עֵץ שָׂדֶה הוּא? But is a man a tree of the field? Rabbi Yoḥanan maintains that it is the Rabbinic scholar whom the verse is comparing to a tree of the field, for we find such a comparison elsewhere — in Psalms 92:13, for example: "The righteous man shall flourish like the palm tree; he shall grow like a cedar in Lebanon."

SAGES

רַבִּי יִרְמְיָה Rabbi Yirmeyah. Born in Babylonia, Rabbi Yirmeyah was one of the leading Amoraim of the third and fourth generations. He studied in Babylonia in his youth, but soon thereafter immigrated to Eretz Israel. There, he was a disciple of the greatest Sages of the generation, the students of Rabbi Yoḥanan (Rabbi Zera and Rabbi Abbahu). Rabbi Yirmeyah had a special dialectical method of great acuity, and he used to ask provocative questions of his teachers and colleagues. Since these questions may have given the impression that Rabbi Yirmeyah was seeking to undermine the accepted rules of Halakhic dialectic, he was even punished and removed from the House of Study for a limited period. Rabbi Yirmeyah's teachings are quoted extensively in both the Babylonian and the Jerusalem Talmud, so much so that in Babylonia his teachings are often introduced by the expression "They say in the West" (i.e., in Eretz Israel).

רַבִּי חָמָא בְּרַבִּי חֲנִינָא Rabbi Ḥama the son of Rabbi Ḥanina. A Palestinian Amora of the second generation, Rabbi Ḥama was the son of Rabbi Ḥanina bar Ḥama. Like his father, he lived in Sepphoris. He was a colleague of Rabbi Yoḥanan and Resh Lakish, and was famous for his Aggadic teachings, which are transmitted by Rabbi Levi and Rabbi Shmuel bar Natan.

[1]אָמַר רַבָּה בַּר בַּר חָנָה: לָמָּה נִמְשְׁלוּ דִּבְרֵי תוֹרָה כָּאֵשׁ, [2]שֶׁנֶּאֱמַר: ״הֲלֹא כֹה דְבָרִי כָּאֵשׁ? נְאֻם ה׳״? [3]לוֹמַר לְךָ: מָה אֵשׁ אֵינוֹ דּוֹלֵק יָחִיד, [4]אַף דִּבְרֵי תוֹרָה אֵין מִתְקַיְּימִין בְּיְחִידִי.

[5]וְהַיְינוּ דַּאֲמַר רַבִּי יוֹסֵי בַּר חֲנִינָא: [6]מַאי דִּכְתִיב: ״חֶרֶב אֶל הַבַּדִּים וְנֹאָלוּ״? [7]חֶרֶב עַל שׂוֹנְאֵיהֶן שֶׁל תַּלְמִידֵי חֲכָמִים שֶׁעוֹסְקִין בַּד בְּבַד בַּתּוֹרָה. [8]וְלֹא עוֹד אֶלָּא שֶׁמִּטַּפְּשִׁין, שֶׁנֶּאֱמַר: ״וְנֹאָלוּ״. [9]וְלֹא עוֹד אֶלָּא שֶׁחוֹטְאִין. [10]כְּתִיב הָכָא: ״וְנֹאָלוּ״, [11]וּכְתִיב הָתָם: ״אֲשֶׁר נוֹאַלְנוּ וַאֲשֶׁר חָטָאנוּ״. [12]וְאִיבָּעֵית אֵימָא מֵהָכָא: [13]״נוֹאֲלוּ שָׂרֵי צֹעַן, [וגו׳,] הִתְעוּ אֶת מִצְרַיִם״.

[14]אָמַר רַב נַחְמָן בַּר יִצְחָק: לָמָּה נִמְשְׁלוּ דִּבְרֵי תוֹרָה כָּעֵץ,

LITERAL TRANSLATION

[1]Rabbah bar Bar Ḥanah said: Why are the words of Torah likened to fire, [2]as it is said: "Is not my word like fire? says the Lord"? [3]To say to you: Just as fire does not burn on its own, [4]so too are the words of Torah not retained by one [who studies] on his own.

[5]And this is what Rabbi Yose bar Ḥanina said: [6]What is [the meaning of] what is written: "A sword is on the lonely and they shall be fools"? [7]A sword is on the enemies of Torah scholars who occupy themselves with the Torah by themselves. [8]And not only this but they grow foolish, as it is said [in the verse]: "And they shall be fools." [9]And not only this but they sin. [10]It is written here: "And they shall be fools," [11]and it is written there: "Because we have been foolish and because we have sinned." [12]And if you wish, say [this] from here: [13]"The princes of Zoan have been fools, etc., they have caused Egypt to go astray."

[14]Rav Naḥman bar Yitzḥak said: Why are the words of Torah likened to a tree,

TRANSLATION AND COMMENTARY

אָמַר רַבָּה בַּר בַּר חָנָה [1]Along the same lines, **Rabbah bar Bar Ḥanah said: Why are the words of Torah likened to fire?** For we find in the Bible that Torah is compared to fire, [2]**as it is said** (Jeremiah 23:29): **"Is not my word like fire? says the Lord."** Rabbah bar Bar Ḥanah explains: [3]The intention of the verse is **to say to you: Just as fire cannot** be made to **burn** with one piece of wood **alone**, [4]**so too the words of Torah cannot be retained by someone who studies alone.**

וְהַיְינוּ [5]The Gemara notes that the idea underlying these two teachings **is the same as** that underlying **what Rabbi Yose bar Ḥanina said** in the following statement: [6]**What is the meaning of what is written** in the verse (Jeremiah 50:36): **"A sword is on the lonely and they shall be fools"?** Jeremiah is referring to the Babylonians, against whom he is prophesying in this chapter. In the context, the word הַבַּדִּים, which we have translated as "the lonely" for the purpose of conveying the meaning of Rabbi Yose bar Ḥanina's statement, refers to people who fabricate stories to impress their listeners, and is presumably a reference to the Babylonian magicians, who will be seen by all to be fools when their "magic powers" fail to save Babylon. Rabbi Yose bar Ḥanina gives a nonliteral interpretation of the verse as cursing Torah scholars who are concerned only with themselves: [7]**A sword is on the enemies of Torah scholars, who occupy themselves with the Torah by themselves.** (It is a Talmudic convention to use a euphemism whenever a basically good person is cursed, directing the curse against the good person's enemies. Thus "the enemies of Torah scholars" is to be understood as a euphemism for Torah scholars themselves.) Rabbi Yose bar Ḥanina continues his nonliteral exposition of this verse by saying: [8]**Not only** are such Torah scholars cursed, **but they** also **grow foolish, as it is said** at the end of the same verse: **"And they shall be fools."** [9]**And not only** are such Torah scholars doomed to become foolish, **but they** will also fall into **sin.** [10]For **it is written here** in this verse: **"And they shall be fools,"** [11]**and it is written** in another verse (Numbers 12:11): **"Because we have been foolish and because we have sinned."** The same Hebrew word for foolish (נוֹאַל) is used in both verses, and this indicates that the kind of foolishness to which these scholars are prone also leads to sin. [12]The Gemara adds that, **if you wish, you can prove from** the following verse (Isaiah 19:13), in which the Prophet proclaims God's retribution against Egypt and her main cities, Zoan and Noph, that the word נוֹאַל does indeed mean both "foolish" and "sinful": [13]**"The princes of Zoan have been fools** [the same word נוֹאַל is used], the princes of Noph have been deceived, **they have caused Egypt to go astray."**

אָמַר רַב נַחְמָן בַּר יִצְחָק [14]The Gemara continues the theme of the importance of collaboration between Torah scholars by citing a statement of **Rav Naḥman bar Yitzḥak,** who **said: Why are the words of Torah likened**

RASHI

אינה דולקת יחידי — עץ אחד אינה דולקת, אלא שנים או שלשה ביחד. **יחידי** — בלא חבר שיחדדנו. **שמוסיפין טפשות דכתיב "נואלנו"** — "אשר נואלנו" מתרגם: דאיטפשנא. **שחוטאין** — דכתיב "נואלו" גבי חטאנו. **ואיבעית אימא מהכא נואלו שרי צוען וגו׳ והתעו את מצרים** — ותועה היינו חוטא. **תורה כעץ** — דכתיב "עץ חיים היא למחזיקים בה", כשמדליק את האור מניח את העצים דקין תחלה.

SAGES

רַבָּה בַּר בַּר חָנָה Rabbah bar Bar Ḥanah. An Amora of the third generation, he was a student of Rabbi Yoḥanan. He was apparently born in Babylonia, emigrated to study Torah in Eretz Israel, and wandered in many lands. He transmitted teachings in the name of Rabbi Yoḥanan, his teacher, as well as in the name of Rabbi Yehoshua ben Levi, Resh Lakish, and Rabbi Elazar; he was also a student of Rabbi Yoshiyah of Usha. One of his sons, Rabbi Yitzḥak, was a Sage. Rabbah bar Bar Ḥanah tells many stories of the wonders he saw in his travels.

BACKGROUND

שֶׁעוֹסְקִין בַּד בְּבַד בַּתּוֹרָה Who occupy themselves with the Torah by themselves. The Sages often spoke of the vital need to study Torah in company, so that at least two people should sit together and study it. The Sages assumed that a single person studying Torah by himself was liable to commit many errors, and, through lack of criticism from others, would continue to maintain his error without realizing that it had to be corrected. The harsh things said against anyone studying Torah alone were meant to prevent people from isolating themselves in a world of their own creation. This causes not only misunderstanding, but also a lack of self-criticism and a loss of the ability to study effectively. If such a person later teaches publicly, not only does he himself err, but he also causes others to err.

TRANSLATION AND COMMENTARY

to a tree, [1]as it is said in the following verse (Proverbs 3:18): **"It is a tree of life to those who hold on to it"?** [2]Rav Naḥman bar Yitzḥak explains: The intention of the verse is **to say to you** that a Torah scholar should appreciate the value of studying with people who are not his equal in scholarship. [3]For **just as a small piece of wood can set light to a large piece,** [4]**so too can younger Torah scholars sharpen the** minds of **older ones** with their questions.

וְהַיְינוּ דַּאֲמַר רַבִּי חֲנִינָא [5]The Gemara notes that the idea underlying Rav Naḥman bar Yitzḥak's interpretation of the Biblical verse **is the same as** that underlying **the** following **statement by Rabbi Ḥanina:** [6]**I have learned much from my teachers, and from my colleagues** I have learned **more than from my teachers;** [7]**but from my students** I have learned **more than from all of them.**

רַבִּי חֲנִינָא בַּר פַּפָּא [8]The Gemara now returns to the topic of good and bad Torah scholars. **Rabbi Ḥanina bar Pappa raised a contradiction** between two verses. [9]In one verse (Isaiah 21:14) **it is written: "Bring water to the thirsty,"** implying that a teacher should go out of his way to find a student, [10]**and** in another verse (Isaiah 55:1) **it is written: "O, whoever is thirsty, go to the water,"** implying that it is the student who is obligated to seek out the teacher and not vice versa. Which approach is correct? Rabbi Ḥanina bar Pappa replies that the two verses apply to two different types of Torah student. [11]**If the student is worthy**, the teacher should seek him out, in fulfillment of the verse: **"Bring water to the thirsty."** [12]**But if** the student is **not** worthy, the teacher should be reluctant to teach him until he seeks the teacher out, in fulfillment of the verse: [13]**"O, whoever is thirsty, go to the water."**

רַבִּי חֲנִינָא בַּר חָמָא [14]The Gemara continues with this subject. **Rabbi Ḥanina bar Ḥama raised a contradiction** between two verses. [15]In one verse (Proverbs 5:16) **it is written: "Let your springs be dispersed outwards;** let rivers of water be in the streets," implying that Torah scholars should spread their learning as widely as possible, [16]**and** in the next verse **it is written: "Let them be for you alone,** and not for strangers with you," implying that Torah scholars should withdraw from public exposure. Which approach is correct? Rabbi Ḥanina bar Ḥama answers that the two verses apply to two different situations. [17]**If the students** who wish to study from the Torah scholar **are worthy,** the teacher should teach them everything he knows, in fulfillment of the verse: **"Let your springs be dispersed outwards."** [18]**But if** the students are **not** worthy, the teacher should avoid them altogether, in fulfillment of the verse: **"Let them be for you alone."**

[1]שֶׁנֶּאֱמַר: ״עֵץ חַיִּים הִיא לַמַּחֲזִיקִים בָּהּ״? [2]לוֹמַר לְךָ: [3]מָה עֵץ קָטָן מַדְלִיק אֶת הַגָּדוֹל, [4]אַף תַּלְמִידֵי חֲכָמִים קְטַנִּים מְחַדְּדִים אֶת הַגְּדוֹלִים. [5]וְהַיְינוּ דַּאֲמַר רַבִּי חֲנִינָא: [6]הַרְבֵּה לָמַדְתִּי מֵרַבּוֹתַי, וּמֵחֲבֵירַי יוֹתֵר מֵרַבּוֹתַי, [7]וּמִתַּלְמִידַי יוֹתֵר מִכּוּלָּן.

[8]רַבִּי חֲנִינָא בַּר פַּפָּא רָמֵי: [9]כְּתִיב: ״לִקְרַאת צָמֵא הֵתָיוּ מָיִם״, [10]וּכְתִיב: ״הוֹי, כָּל צָמֵא, לְכוּ לַמַּיִם״! [11]אִם תַּלְמִיד הָגוּן הוּא, ״לִקְרַאת צָמֵא הֵתָיוּ מָיִם״, [12]וְאִי לֹא, [13]״הוֹי, כָּל צָמֵא, לְכוּ לַמַּיִם״.

[14]רַבִּי חֲנִינָא בַּר חָמָא רָמֵי: [15]כְּתִיב: ״יָפוּצוּ מַעְיְנֹתֶיךָ חוּצָה״, [16]וּכְתִיב: ״יִהְיוּ לְךָ לְבַדֶּךָ״! [17]אִם תַּלְמִיד הָגוּן הוּא, ״יָפוּצוּ מַעְיְנֹתֶיךָ חוּצָה״, [18]וְאִם לָאו, ״יִהְיוּ לְךָ לְבַדֶּךָ״.

LITERAL TRANSLATION

[1]as it is said: "It is a tree of life to those who hold on to it"? [2]To say to you: [3]Just as a small [piece of] wood sets light to a large [piece], [4]so too do younger (lit., "small") Torah scholars sharpen the older (lit., "the great") ones.

[5]And this is what Rabbi Ḥanina said: [6]I have learned much from my teachers, and from my colleagues more than from my teachers [7]and from my students more than from all of them.

[8]Rabbi Ḥanina bar Pappa raised a contradiction: [9]It is written: "Bring water to the thirsty," [10]and it is written: "O, whoever is thirsty, go to the water"! [11]If he is a worthy student, "bring water to the thirsty," [12]but if not, [13]"O, whoever is thirsty, go to the water."

[14]Rabbi Ḥanina bar Ḥama raised a contradiction: [15]It is written: "Let your springs be dispersed outwards," [16]and it is written: "Let them be for you alone"! [17]If he is a worthy student, "let your springs be dispersed outwards," [18]but if not, "let them be for you alone."

RASHI

קטנים מחדדין – ששואלין כל שעה. **התיו** – משמע: להוליך לו מים. **וכתיב לכו למים** – ילך הוא עצמו. **אם תלמיד (חכם) הגון** – שרוצה ללמוד ממך – מלוה לרב לילך אצלו במקומו. **ואם לאו** – ילך הוא אצל הרב. **יפוצו מעינותיך חוצה** – אם הגון הוא – אמור לו סתרי תורה. **ואם לאו יהיו לך לבדך** – ״ואין לזרים אתך״.

BACKGROUND

הַרְבֵּה לָמַדְתִּי מֵרַבּוֹתַי **I have learned much from my teachers.** These words of Rabbi Ḥanina are general instructions as to how to study. Someone who learns only from those who teach him, studies in a passive manner. Therefore a person learns more from his contemporaries, by shared discussion, which clarifies matters, raises different points of view, and gives rise to mutual criticism. Rabbi Ḥanina adds that someone who teaches others learns most of all, both because the need to teach forces one to bring what one knows to maximum clarity, and also because the students' questions raise new ideas in the teacher and cause him to achieve greater spiritual creativity.

SAGES

רַבִּי חֲנִינָא **Rabbi Ḥanina.** When the name of the Amora Rabbi Ḥanina is used without a patronymic in the Talmud, the reference is to Rabbi Ḥanina bar Ḥama, a first-generation Amora from Eretz Israel. Rabbi Ḥanina originally came from Babylonia, although he immigrated to Eretz Israel at a relatively early age and studied there with Rabbi Yehudah HaNasi, who was very fond of him (and indeed remarked that Rabbi Ḥanina was "not a human being, but an angel"). Rabbi Ḥanina also studied with Rabbi Yehudah HaNasi's most distinguished students, in particular with Rabbi Ḥiyya. On his deathbed, Rabbi Yehudah HaNasi designated Rabbi Ḥanina as the new head of his yeshivah, although the latter, in his great modesty, refused to accept the position as long as his older colleague, Rabbi Efes, was still alive.

Rabbi Ḥanina lived in Sepphoris, where he became wealthy as a honey dealer and established a large academy. He was renowned for his acuity, as well as for his uprightness and piety.

The Amora Rabbi Ḥama the son of Rabbi Ḥanina was his son.

רַבִּי חֲנִינָא בַּר פַּפָּא **Rabbi Ḥanina bar Pappa.** A Palestinian Amora of the third

TRANSLATION AND COMMENTARY

וְאָמַר רַבִּי חֲנִינָא בַּר אִידִי [1]The Gemara continues with the theme of metaphorical references to Torah in the Bible. **Rabbi Ḥanina bar Idi said: Why are the words of Torah likened to water,** [2]**as it is written** (Isaiah 55:1): **"O, whoever is thirsty, go to the water"?** [3]Rabbi Ḥanina bar Idi explains: The intention of the verse is **to say to you** that Torah can only be studied properly by people who have mastered the virtue of humility. For **just as water flows from a high place to a low place,** [4]**so too are the words of Torah retained only by someone of humble spirit.**

וְאָמַר רַבִּי אוֹשַׁעְיָא [5]The Gemara now cites another statement along the same lines. **Rabbi Oshaya said: Why are the words of Torah likened to the following three liquids, to water, and to wine, and to milk?** [6]For we see that the Torah is compared to water, **as it is written** (Isaiah 55:1): **"O, whoever is thirsty, go to the water."** [7]**And** we see that the Torah is compared to wine and to milk, **as it says** at the end of the same verse: **"Go, buy, and eat; and go, buy wine and milk without money and without price."** [8]Rabbi Oshaya explains: The intention of the verse is **to tell you** that Torah can only be studied properly by modest people. For **just as these three liquids are preserved only in the least of vessels,** such as those made of baked clay, since expensive metal vessels will spoil them, [9]**so too are the words of Torah preserved only in someone of humble spirit.**

כִּדְאָמְרָה לֵיהּ [10]The Gemara explains that the idea underlying Rabbi Oshaya's Scriptural interpretation is **like** the idea underlying the famous story about **the daughter of the** Roman **Emperor** and **Rabbi Yehoshua ben Ḥananyah,** who was one of the foremost Torah scholars of the period immediately following the destruction of the Second Temple but was ugly. It happened that the princess met Rabbi Yehoshua and was struck by the apparent contradiction between the beauty of his words and the ugliness of his appearance. [11]She **said to** him: **"Alas, such glorious wisdom** is contained **in** so **ugly a vessel!"** Rabbi Yehoshua

[1]וְאָמַר רַבִּי חֲנִינָא בַּר אִידִי: לָמָּה נִמְשְׁלוּ דִּבְרֵי תוֹרָה לַמַּיִם, [2]דִּכְתִיב: ״הוֹי, כָּל צָמֵא, לְכוּ לַמַּיִם״? [3]לוֹמַר לְךָ: מַה מַּיִם מַנִּיחִין מָקוֹם גָּבוֹהַּ וְהוֹלְכִין לְמָקוֹם נָמוּךְ, [4]אַף דִּבְרֵי תוֹרָה אֵין מִתְקַיְּימִין אֶלָּא בְּמִי שֶׁדַּעְתּוֹ שְׁפֵלָה.

[5]וְאָמַר רַבִּי אוֹשַׁעְיָא: לָמָּה נִמְשְׁלוּ דִּבְרֵי תוֹרָה לִשְׁלֹשָׁה מַשְׁקִין הַלָּלוּ, בַּמַּיִם, וּבַיַּיִן, וּבֶחָלָב, [6]דִּכְתִיב: ״הוֹי, כָּל צָמֵא, לְכוּ לַמַּיִם״, [7]וּכְתִיב: ״לְכוּ, שִׁבְרוּ, וֶאֱכֹלוּ; וּלְכוּ, שִׁבְרוּ בְּלוֹא כֶסֶף וּבְלוֹא מְחִיר יַיִן וְחָלָב״? [8]לוֹמַר לְךָ: מַה שְׁלֹשָׁה מַשְׁקִין הַלָּלוּ אֵין מִתְקַיְּימִין אֶלָּא בַּפָּחוּת שֶׁבַּכֵּלִים, [9]אַף דִּבְרֵי תוֹרָה אֵין מִתְקַיְּימִין אֶלָּא בְּמִי שֶׁדַּעְתּוֹ שְׁפֵלָה.

[10]כִּדְאָמְרָה לֵיהּ בְּרַתֵּיהּ דְּקֵיסָר לְרַבִּי יְהוֹשֻׁעַ בֶּן חֲנַנְיָה: [11]״אִי, חָכְמָה מְפוֹאָרָה בִּכְלִי מְכוֹעָר״!

LITERAL TRANSLATION

[1]And Rabbi Ḥanina bar Idi said: Why are the words of Torah likened to water, [2]as it is said: "O, whoever is thirsty, go to the water"? [3]To say to you: Just as water leaves a high place and goes to a low place, [4]so too are the words of Torah not retained except by someone whose mind is humble.

[5]And Rabbi Oshaya said: Why are the words of Torah likened to the following three liquids, to water, and to wine, and to milk, [6]as it is written: "O, whoever is thirsty, go to the water," [7]and it is written: "Go, buy, and eat; and go, buy wine and milk without money and without price"? [8]To say to you: Just as these three liquids are not preserved except in the least of vessels, [9]so too are the words of Torah not preserved except in someone whose mind is humble.

[10]It is as the daughter of the Emperor said to Rabbi Yehoshua ben Ḥananyah: [11]"Alas, glorious wisdom in an ugly vessel!"

RASHI

שלשה משקים הללו — מים יין וחלב, זו התורה שאינו נותן בה כלום ויודעה ולומדה. **בפחות שבכלים** — במאני דפחרא.

NOTES

בַּמַּיִם, וּבַיַּיִן, וּבֶחָלָב To water, and to wine, and to milk. The Midrash explains that the three different drinks to which the Torah is compared allude to the three principal bodies of Torah literature — the Bible, the Mishnah, and the Talmud (see *Iyyun Ya'akov*).

HALAKHAH

אֶלָּא בְּמִי שֶׁדַּעְתּוֹ שְׁפֵלָה Except by someone whose mind is humble. "The words of the Torah are found only among people who are humble in spirit and who sit in the dust of the feet of Sages." (*Rambam, Sefer Mada, Hilkhot Talmud Torah* 3:9.)

generation, Rabbi Ḥanina bar Pappa was a colleague of the most important students of Rabbi Yoḥanan. It is frequently related in the Talmud how Rabbi Ḥanina bar Pappa and his colleagues used to sit together and suggest innovative Torah teachings. He seems to have been a judge in his city, since several Halakhic decisions that he issued are recorded as actual judgments in civil suits. Despite his greatness as a Torah scholar, his Aggadic teachings are more numerous, and in this area he transmitted many teachings that he had received from Rabbi Shmuel bar Naḥmani.

His great righteousness in personal matters and his great piety in relations between God and man were famous in his time, and they became a symbol of a great man who submits to death in order to observe the Torah. It is told that upon his death a pillar of fire stood behind his bed.

SAGES

רַבִּי חֲנִינָא בַּר אִידִי Rabbi Ḥanina bar Idi. A Palestinian Amora of the fourth generation, Rabbi Ḥanina bar Idi is mentioned infrequently in the Talmud and the Midrashim. His statements are of an Aggadic nature and he transmitted teachings in the name of Rabbi Yitzḥak and Rabbi Tanḥum bar Ḥiyya.

BACKGROUND

בְּמִי שֶׁדַּעְתּוֹ שְׁפֵלָה By someone whose mind is humble. Pride is not only considered a contemptible quality, but also a sin. With respect to Torah study, pride is regarded as an obstacle to success. A proud person is not willing to accept anything, nor is he capable of studying the truth. Moreover, he is incapable of correcting judgments that he erroneously holds to be true. Pride also involves an inability to criticize oneself or to accept criticism from friends. Therefore if one is not humble, not only does one have a bad character trait, but one's spiritual capacities are also impaired by it.

בְּרַתֵּיהּ דְּקֵיסָר The daughter of the Emperor. In the first century C.E. there was great interest in other religions — including Judaism — among

TRANSLATION AND COMMENTARY

replied to the princess with a parable. [1]**He said to her: "Does your father,** the Emperor, **put** expensive **wine in** plain **earthenware vessels?"** [2]**She said to him: "In what else should we put** our wine?" [3]Rabbi Yehoshua **said to her:** "Ordinary people may perhaps put their wine in earthenware vessels, but **your** father, the Emperor, **who is** so **important, should put** his wine **in vessels of gold and silver,** as is appropriate to his lofty status." [4]The princess **went and said to her father** that it was not fitting for an Emperor to keep his wine in plain earthenware vessels. [5]The Emperor then **put** his best **wine in vessels of gold and silver,** as his daughter had advised, **and** all the wine **turned sour.** [6]The Emperor's servants **came and told him that the wine had gone sour.** [7]The Emperor **said to his daughter: "Who told you to do this?"** [8]**She said to** her father: "It was **Rabbi Yehoshua ben Ḥananyah."** [9]The Emperor sent his servants **to call** Rabbi Yehoshua to appear before him. When Rabbi Yehoshua came, the Emperor **said to him: "Why did you say this to** my daughter?" [10]**He said to** the Emperor: "What **I said to her was just like** what **she said to me."** It is just as absurd to expect wisdom to be found in a handsome person, as to expect wine to be found in a gold or silver vessel. For a handsome person will inevitably take pride in his physical appearance, and this will spoil his learning, in the same way as the gold and silver vessels spoiled the wine. [11]**"But surely,"** said the Emperor's daughter, **"there are handsome people who are learned!"**

אִי הָווּ סְנוּ [7B] [12]Rabbi Yehoshua replied: "Admittedly, some handsome people have become great scholars. But **if they had been ugly, they would have** been even **more learned."**

דָּבָר אַחֵר [13]The Gemara now returns to the statement of Rabbi Oshaya (above, 7a), in which he explains that the Torah is likened to water, milk, and wine because these three liquids tend to spoil if stored in vessels of gold and silver, and are best kept in plain earthenware vessels. [14]The Gemara now offers **another explanation** of the comparison: **Just as these three liquids can be spoiled through inattention,** [14]**so too can the words of Torah be forgotten through inattention.** Water, milk, and wine have a low viscosity, spill easily, and if left uncovered can become contaminated. They therefore require careful attention. Similarly, a Torah scholar's wisdom can easily be lost or spoiled if he does not guard it carefully.

[1]אֲמַר לָהּ: ״אָבִיךְ רָמֵי חַמְרָא בְּמָנֵי דְּפַחְרָא״? [2]אֲמָרָה לֵיהּ: ״אֶלָּא בְּמַאי נִירְמֵי״? [3]אֲמַר לָהּ: ״אַתּוּן דַּחֲשְׁבִיתוּ רְמוּ בְּמָאנֵי דַּהֲבָא וְכַסְפָּא״. [4]אָזְלָה וַאֲמָרָה לֵיהּ לַאֲבוּהָ. [5]רַמְיָיא לְחַמְרָא בְּמָנֵי דַּהֲבָא וְכַסְפָּא, וּתְקִיף. [6]אֲתוּ וַאֲמָרוּ לֵיהּ. [7]אֲמַר לָהּ לִבְרַתֵּיהּ: ״מַאן אֲמַר לָךְ הָכִי״? [8]אֲמָרָה לֵיהּ: ״רַבִּי יְהוֹשֻׁעַ בֶּן חֲנַנְיָה״. [9]קַרְיוּהוּ. אֲמַר לֵיהּ: ״אַמַּאי אָמְרַתְּ לָהּ הָכִי״? [10]אֲמַר לֵיהּ: ״כִּי הֵיכִי דַּאֲמָרָה לִי, אֲמַרִי לָהּ״. [11]״וְהָא אִיכָּא שַׁפִּירֵי דִּגְמִירִי״!
[7B] [12]״אִי הָווּ סְנוּ, טְפֵי הָווּ גְּמִירִי״.
[13]דָּבָר אַחֵר: מַה שְּׁלֹשָׁה מַשְׁקִין הַלָּלוּ אֵין נִפְסָלִין אֶלָּא בְּהֶיסַּח הַדַּעַת, [14]אַף דִּבְרֵי תוֹרָה אֵין מִשְׁתַּכְּחִין אֶלָּא בְּהֶיסַּח הַדַּעַת.

LITERAL TRANSLATION

[1]He said to her: "Does your father put wine in earthenware vessels?" [2]She said to him: "In what else should we put it?" [3]He said to her: "You who are important should put [it] in vessels of gold and silver." [4]She went and said [this] to her father. [5]He put the wine in vessels of gold and silver, and it turned sour. [6]They came and told him. [7]He said to his daughter: "Who said this to you?" [8]She said to him: "Rabbi Yehoshua ben Ḥananyah." [9]They called him. He said to him: "Why did you say this to her?" [10]He said to him: "Just as she said to me, I said to her." [11]"But surely there are handsome men who are learned!"

[7B] [12]"If they had been ugly, they would have learned more."

[13]Another explanation (lit., "something else"): Just as these three liquids are not spoiled except through inattention (lit., "removal of the mind"), [14]so too are the words of Torah not forgotten except through inattention.

RASHI

במאני דפחרא — בדרך שחוק אמר, ומרמז: מה את אומרת לי? והלא אביך נותן יין בכלים מכוערין של חרס. **ואלא במאי נירמיה** — אם לא בשל חרס, הא כולי עבדי הכי! **ותקיף** = החמיץ. **כי היכי דאמרה לי** — אי חכמה מפוארה בכלי מכוער, הכי אמרי לה כיין משתמר בכלי מכוער — אף התורה מתקיימת בי יותר משאילו הייתי נאה. **אי הוו סנו** — אותם נאים שהם חכמים. **טפי הוו גמירי** — שאי אפשר לנאה להשפיל דעתו, ובא לידי שכחה. **בהיסח הדעת** — שאם לא ישמרם יפה יהו נשפכין או נופל לתוכן דבר מאום, ונפסלים מלשתות בדבר קל, יותר משמן ודבש שמתוך שהן עבים צפה הפסולת למעלה, ואפשר אדם טל העליון וזורקו לחוץ, והתחתון בר ונקי. מה שאין כן במשקה צלול, שאינו עב = *קליי״ר בלעז. **בהיסח הדעת** — אם אינו מחזירם תמיד.

the leaders of Roman society. Not only were their philosophers interested in comparing their doctrines with those of the Rabbis, but people from the highest level of Roman society were eager to enter into spiritual discussion with these Sages. Many high-ranking women became interested in Judaism not only intellectually but also as a personal way of life. Some women actually converted, while a larger number showed an interest in Jewish thought and customs. A whole class of "those who feared the Lord" were to be found in Rome, and these people were very much influenced by everything Jewish, including the Torah.

LANGUAGE (RASHI)

קליי״ר* From the Old French *cler*, which means "clear" or "transparent."

BACKGROUND

וּתְקִיף And it turned sour. The reason why wine is not stored in metal vessels is that the acid in the wine attacks almost all types of metal, including copper and silver, to some degree. Moreover, many compounds of these metals are poisonous, so that not only is the taste of the wine spoiled but the drinker's health is also put at risk.

אִי הָווּ סְנוּ If they had been ugly. Rabbi Yehoshua maintains that external ugliness, like other bodily flaws, makes people turn to spiritual pursuits with greater fervor. Therefore, if handsome people do gain wisdom, it is despite their beauty. And if they are forced to study only spiritual matters, they will certainly reach a higher level.

הֶיסַּח הַדַּעַת Inattention. This trait leads to carelessness. In some areas of the Halakhah, inattention itself is regarded as a cause of ritual impurity or as a sin. Regarding the liquids mentioned here, each of them is liable to be spoiled if it is left without supervision, either because one is not careful and it spills, or because of dirt that may fall into it, or because of damage caused by bacteria. This is also true of the study of Torah. A person must

TRANSLATION AND COMMENTARY

אָמַר רַבִּי חָמָא בְּרַבִּי חֲנִינָא [1]The Gemara now returns to the topic of the importance of rain. **Rabbi Ḥama the son of Rabbi Ḥanina said: The day** when **the rain** falls **is as great as the day when Heaven and Earth were created,** [2]**as it is said** (Isaiah 45:8): **"Drip down, heavens, from above, and let the skies pour down justice; let the earth open and let them bring forth salvation, and let righteousness spring up together."** [3]The Prophet then states, **"I, the Lord have created it"** — the phenomenon of rainfall, and, by implication, the salvation that is being compared to it. The Prophet refers to God taking pride in His creation, in a verse mentioning the heavens and the earth, [4]and yet **he does not say: "I have created *them*"** (the heavens and the earth), **but rather "I have created it"** (the rainfall). Thus we see that rainfall is as great a demonstration of God's creative power as was the creation of the heavens and the earth.

אָמַר רַב אוֹשַׁעְיָא [5]The Gemara now cites a related exposition of the same verse by **Rav Oshaya,** who **said: The greatness of the day of rain** is manifested in the Prophet's declaration **that even** the abstract concept of **salvation is fruitful and multiplies** like a plant **on this day,** [6]**as it is said: "Let the earth open and let them bring forth salvation."** For God is more responsive to Israel's prayers, even concerning matters unrelated to agriculture, on a day when He blesses the earth with rain.

אָמַר רַבִּי תַּנְחוּם בַּר חֲנִילָאי [7]**Rabbi Tanḥum bar Ḥanilai said: Rain does not fall unless Israel's iniquities have been forgiven,** [8]**as it is said** (Psalms 85:2): **"O Lord, You have favored Your land; You have brought back the captivity of Jacob."** According to the plain meaning of the verse, when the Psalmist states that God has "favored His land," he is referring to the return of the Jewish people to Eretz Israel after their captivity. But Rabbi Tanḥum bar Ḥanilai interprets "land" in the sense of "earth," and understands the Psalmist to be referring to the day when God favors the earth with rain. [9]And the next verse says: **"You have forgiven the iniquity of Your people; You have covered all their sin. Selah,"** which teaches us that the events of this day prove that God has forgiven Israel's sins.

[1]אָמַר רַבִּי חָמָא בְּרַבִּי חֲנִינָא: גָּדוֹל יוֹם הַגְּשָׁמִים כַּיּוֹם שֶׁנִּבְרְאוּ שָׁמַיִם וָאָרֶץ, [2]שֶׁנֶּאֱמַר: ״הַרְעִיפוּ שָׁמַיִם מִמַּעַל, וּשְׁחָקִים יִזְּלוּ צֶדֶק; תִּפְתַּח אֶרֶץ וְיִפְרוּ יֶשַׁע, וּצְדָקָה תַצְמִיחַ יַחַד; [3]אֲנִי ה׳ בְּרָאתִיו״. [4]״בְּרָאתִים״ לֹא נֶאֱמַר, אֶלָּא ״בְּרָאתִיו״.

[5]אָמַר רַב אוֹשַׁעְיָא: גָּדוֹל יוֹם הַגְּשָׁמִים, שֶׁאֲפִילּוּ יְשׁוּעָה פָּרָה וְרָבָה בּוֹ, [6]שֶׁנֶּאֱמַר: ״תִּפְתַּח אֶרֶץ וְיִפְרוּ יֶשַׁע״.

[7]אָמַר רַבִּי תַּנְחוּם בַּר חֲנִילָאי: אֵין הַגְּשָׁמִים יוֹרְדִים אֶלָּא אִם כֵּן נִמְחֲלוּ עֲוֹנוֹתֵיהֶן שֶׁל יִשְׂרָאֵל, [8]שֶׁנֶּאֱמַר: ״רָצִיתָ ה׳ אַרְצֶךָ; שַׁבְתָּ שְׁבִית יַעֲקֹב. [9]נָשָׂאתָ עֲוֹן עַמֶּךָ; כִּסִּיתָ כָל חַטָּאתָם. סֶלָה״.

LITERAL TRANSLATION

[1]Rabbi Ḥama the son of Rabbi Ḥanina said: The day of rains is as great as the day when Heaven and Earth were created, [2]as it is said: "Drip down, heavens, from above, and let the skies pour down justice; let the earth open and let them bring forth salvation, and let righteousness spring up together; [3]I, the Lord, have created it." [4]"I have created them" is not said, but rather "I have created it."

[5]Rav Oshaya said: The day of rains is great, for even salvation is fruitful and multiplies on it, [6]as it is said: "Let the earth open and let them bring forth salvation."

[7]Rabbi Tanḥum bar Ḥanilai said: The rains do not fall unless Israel's iniquities have been forgiven, [8]as it is said: "O Lord, You have favored Your land; You have brought back the captivity of Jacob. [9]You have forgiven the iniquity of Your people; You have covered all their sin. Selah."

RASHI

שנאמר הרעיפו שמים ממעל ושחקים יזלו צדק תפתח ארץ ויפרו ישע וצדקה תצמיח יחד אני ה׳ בראתיו בראתים לא נאמר — דמשמע אשחקים יזלו קאי, אלא ״אני ה׳ בראתיו״ לטל ומטר, שמע מינה שמשתבח ומתפאר הקדוש ברוך הוא במטר השמים. **ישועה פרה ורבה בו** — מליצי זכות נכנסין לפניו ביום הגשמים, שנזכר לישועה מתוך שעת רצון, הוא לישנא דקרא ״ויפרו ישע״ ואימתי — בזמן שהשחקים יזלו צדק. **רצית ה׳ ארצך** — במים. **נשאת עון עמך** — מיד.

review what he has studied and consider it carefully, otherwise he will forget it or become confused.

SAGES

רַבִּי תַּנְחוּם בַּר חֲנִילָאי **Rabbi Tanḥum bar Ḥanilai.** A Palestinian Amora of the second and third generations, Rabbi Tanḥum was a student of Rabbi Yehoshua ben Levi, from whom he seems to have learned mostly Aggadah. Rabbi Tanḥum's own teachings are mainly Aggadic. They were transmitted by the Sages of Eretz Israel in the following generation.

NOTES

גָּדוֹל יוֹם הַגְּשָׁמִים **The day of rains is as great.** *Rabbi Ya'akov Emden* points out that Rabbi Ḥama the son of Rabbi Ḥanina and the other Amoraim whose statements about the greatness of "the day of rains" are cited in our passage refer not to any day on which there is rainfall, but rather to the day of rain following an extended period of drought.

אֶלָּא אִם כֵּן נִמְחֲלוּ עֲוֹנוֹתֵיהֶן **Unless Israel's iniquities have been forgiven.** Some commentators note that this may be the reason why we do not begin to pray for rain until Sukkot, which is celebrated a few days after Yom Kippur, the day of pardon and forgiveness for all the sins of Israel (*Sfat Emet*).

LITERAL TRANSLATION

[1]Zeiri from Dihavat said to Ravina: You derive (lit., "teach") it from here. [2]We derive it from here: "And You, hear in the heavens, and forgive the sin of, etc." [3]Rabbi Tanhum the son of Rabbi Ḥiyya from Kfar Akko said: The rains are not withheld except if the enemies of Israel have been condemned to destruction, [4]as it is said: "Drought and heat will steal the snow waters; to the grave they have sinned."

[5]Zeiri from Dihavat said to Ravina: You derive it from here. [6]We derive it from here: "And He will shut up the heavens...and you will perish quickly."

[7]Rav Ḥisda said: The rains are not withheld except because of neglect of terumot and tithes, as it is said:

[1]אֲמַר לֵיהּ זְעִירִי מִדִּיהֲבַת לְרָבִינָא: אַתּוּן מֵהָכָא מַתְנִיתוּ לָהּ. [2]אֲנַן מֵהָכָא מַתְנִינַן לָהּ: ״וְאַתָּה, תִּשְׁמַע הַשָּׁמַיִם, וְסָלַחְתָּ לְחַטַּאת, וגו׳״.

[3]אָמַר רַבִּי תַּנְחוּם בְּרֵיהּ דְּרַבִּי חִיָּיא אִישׁ כְּפַר עַכּוֹ: אֵין הַגְּשָׁמִים נֶעֱצָרִין אֶלָּא אִם כֵּן נִתְחַיְּיבוּ שׂוֹנְאֵיהֶן שֶׁל יִשְׂרָאֵל כְּלָיָה, [4]שֶׁנֶּאֱמַר: ״צִיָּה גַם חֹם יִגְזְלוּ מֵימֵי שֶׁלֶג; שְׁאוֹל חָטָאוּ״.

[5]אֲמַר לֵיהּ זְעִירִי מִדִּיהֲבַת לְרָבִינָא: אַתּוּן מֵהָכָא מַתְנִיתוּ לָהּ. [6]אֲנַן מֵהָכָא מַתְנִינַן לָהּ: ״וְעָצַר אֶת הַשָּׁמַיִם...וַאֲבַדְתֶּם מְהֵרָה״.

[7]אָמַר רַב חִסְדָּא: אֵין הַגְּשָׁמִים נֶעֱצָרִין אֶלָּא בִּשְׁבִיל בִּיטּוּל תְּרוּמוֹת וּמַעַשְׂרוֹת, שֶׁנֶּאֱמַר:

RASHI

הכי גרסינן: אמר ליה מר זעירי מדיהבת לרבינא כו׳ — זעירי סתם היה מן הראשונים, ורבינא סוף הוראה, לא ראו זה את זה. **ואתה תשמע השמים וגו׳** — ואומר ״ונתת מטר על ארצך״ בתפלה דשלמה. **ציה גם חום יגזלו מימי שלג** — כשציה גם חום גוזלין מימות השלג, שאין יורדין מטר כמשפטם — בידוע ששאול חטאו. **ולא יהיה מטר** — וסמיך ליה ״ואבדתם״.

TRANSLATION AND COMMENTARY

אֲמַר לֵיהּ זְעִירִי מִדִּיהֲבַת [1]**Zeiri from** the town of **Dihavat said to Ravina: You have derived** the idea that rainfall is an indication that Israel's sins have been forgiven **from** a figurative interpretation of the verse in Psalms. [2]**We have derived** the same idea **from** the plain meaning of the following verse (I Kings 8:36): **"And You, hear in the heavens, and forgive the sin of** Your servants and of Your people Israel, that You may teach them the good way in which they should walk, and give rain on Your land, which You have given to Your people as an inheritance." This verse forms part of the prayer of King Solomon when dedicating the Temple. The previous verse states that if Israel sins, and God withholds rain in response, the people will come to the Temple to pray to God and to confess their sins. And this verse asks God to respond by forgiving Israel's sins, and causing it to rain. Thus we see that rain is a clear sign that God has forgiven Israel's sins.

אָמַר רַבִּי תַּנְחוּם בְּרֵיהּ דְּרַבִּי חִיָּיא [3]Having established that rain is a clear sign of God's forgiveness, the Gemara now considers the opposite situation. **Rabbi Tanhum the son of Rabbi Ḥiyya from Kfar Akko said: The rains are withheld only if the enemies of Israel** (a euphemism for Israel itself) **have been condemned to be destroyed** for their sins, [4]**as it is said** (Job 24:19): **"Drought and heat will steal the snow waters; to the grave they have sinned."** According to the plain meaning of this verse, the words "snow waters" are a metaphor: Job is saying that just as the snow waters disappear as a result of heat and drought, so too will sinners die and disappear into the grave. But Rabbi Tanḥum interprets "snow waters" literally, and explains that Job is saying that drought and heat steal the snow waters when people have sinned to the point of deserving destruction.

אֲמַר לֵיהּ זְעִירִי מִדִּיהֲבַת [5]Here, too, **Zeiri from Dihavat said to Ravina: You have derived** this idea **from** a figurative interpretation of a verse in Job. [6]**We have derived** the same idea **from** the plain meaning of the following verse (Deuteronomy 11:17): "And the anger of the Lord will be kindled against you, **and He will shut up the heavens,** and there will be no rain, and the earth will not give its fruit, **and you will perish quickly** from upon the good land which the Lord gives you." Thus we see that if rain is withheld, it is a clear sign that the people of Israel are in danger of being destroyed for their sins.

אָמַר רַב חִסְדָּא [7]The Gemara now cites another interpretation of the verse from Job (24:19) quoted above. **Rav Ḥisda said: The rains are withheld only because** people have **neglected** their obligation to separate **terumah** (the portion of one's produce that one is obliged to give to the priests) **and** other **tithes** from their

SAGES

זְעִירִי מִדִּיהֲבַת Zeiri from Dihavat. This Sage is mentioned only here. He seems to have been a Babylonian Amora of the sixth generation.

רַבִּי תַּנְחוּם בְּרֵיהּ דְּרַבִּי חִיָּיא אִישׁ כְּפַר עַכּוֹ Rabbi Tanḥum the son of Rabbi Ḥiyya from Kfar Acco. A Palestinian Amora of the third and fourth generations, he seems to have resided in Tiberias and to have been a student of Rabbi Ammi. Several Aggadic teachings are transmitted in his name elsewhere in the Talmud.

BACKGROUND

בִּיטּוּל תְּרוּמוֹת וּמַעַשְׂרוֹת Neglect of terumot and tithes. There is a kind of poetic justice here, since if people do not act correctly with the harvest given to them, and fail to set aside a portion for the needy as they are required to, God denies them rain for their crops the following year.

NOTES

אֶלָּא אִם כֵּן נִתְחַיְּיבוּ שׂוֹנְאֵיהֶן שֶׁל יִשְׂרָאֵל כְּלָיָה Except if the enemies of Israel have been condemned to destruction. When the people of Israel are condemned to be destroyed, God does not immediately carry out the sentence, but first withholds rain in the hope that the people will understand that if they do not repent and forsake their evil ways, they will be destroyed (*Iyyun Ya'akov*).

¹״צִיָּה גַּם חֹם יִגְזְלוּ מֵימֵי שֶׁלֶג״.
²מַאי מַשְׁמַע?
³תָּנָא דְּבֵי רַבִּי יִשְׁמָעֵאל:
⁴״בִּשְׁבִיל דְּבָרִים שֶׁצִּוִּיתִי אֶתְכֶם בִּימוֹת הַחַמָּה וְלֹא עֲשִׂיתֶם, יִגָּזְלוּ מִכֶּם מֵימֵי שֶׁלֶג בִּימוֹת הַגְּשָׁמִים״.
⁵אָמַר רַבִּי שִׁמְעוֹן בֶּן פָּזִי: אֵין הַגְּשָׁמִים נֶעֱצָרִין אֶלָּא בִּשְׁבִיל מְסַפְּרֵי לְשׁוֹן הָרָע, ⁶שֶׁנֶּאֱמַר: ״רוּחַ צָפוֹן תְּחוֹלֵל גָּשֶׁם, וּפָנִים נִזְעָמִים לְשׁוֹן סָתֶר״.
⁷אָמַר רַב סַלָּא אָמַר רַב הַמְנוּנָא: אֵין הַגְּשָׁמִים נֶעֱצָרִין אֶלָּא בִּשְׁבִיל עַזֵּי פָנִים, ⁸שֶׁנֶּאֱמַר: ״וַיִּמָּנְעוּ רְבִבִים, וּמַלְקוֹשׁ לוֹא הָיָה, וּמֵצַח אִשָּׁה זוֹנָה הָיָה לָךְ, וגו׳״.

LITERAL TRANSLATION

[1] "Drought and heat will steal the snow waters."
[2] What is the proof?
[3] [A Tanna] of the School of Rabbi Yishmael taught:
[4] "Because of things that I commanded you [to do] in the days of the sun and you did not do, the snow waters will be stolen from you in the days of the rains."
[5] Rabbi Shimon ben Pazi said: The rains are not withheld except because of those who speak slander (lit., "relate evil speech"), [6] as it is said: "The north wind halts rain, and a deceptive tongue causes an angry face."
[7] Rav Salla said in the name of Rav Hamnuna: The rains are not withheld except because of the brazen-faced, [8] as it is said: "And the showers were held back, and there was no latter rain, and you had the forehead of a harlot, etc."

TRANSLATION AND COMMENTARY

produce, as required by the Torah. Rav Ḥisda derives this **from what is said** in the verse in Job: [1] **"Drought and heat will steal the snow waters."** Thus we see that, according to Rav Ḥisda, neglect of terumah and tithes is the sin that leads to drought.

מַאי מַשְׁמַע [2] Rav Ḥisda did not explain how this verse leads to this conclusion. Accordingly, the Gemara asks: **What is the inference** on which Rav Ḥisda's interpretation is based.

תָּנָא דְּבֵי רַבִּי יִשְׁמָעֵאל [3] The Gemara answers that Rav Ḥisda is interpreting the verse as **it was taught by a Tanna of the School of Rabbi Yishmael.** According to this interpretation, the words "drought and heat" are to be understood as referring to the summer season, when the crops are harvested. Thus Job is saying that "the dry season will steal the snow waters," and we understand this to mean the following: [4] **"Because of the** tithes **that I commanded you** to separate **in the sunny** season, when you harvested your crops, **but you did not** separate, **the snow waters will be stolen from you in the rainy season,** and no **rain will fall."**

אָמַר רַבִּי שִׁמְעוֹן בֶּן פָּזִי [5] The Gemara now cites a series of other opinions concerning the sins that can lead to a lack of rain. **Rabbi Shimon ben Pazi said: The rains are withheld only because of those who speak slander,** [6] **as it is said** (Proverbs 25:23): **"The north wind halts the rain, and a deceptive tongue causes an angry face."** According to the plain meaning of this verse, the rain is a metaphor: Just as a sudden north wind can dramatically stop what appears to be an imminent cloudburst, so too does a deceptive tongue turn friendship into anger. But Rabbi Shimon ben Pazi interprets "rain" literally, and interprets "face" as "the face of God." Thus the verse is saying that when the north wind halts the rain, we should interpret this as a sign that God is angry with us because of the slanderous language used by those with deceptive tongues.

אָמַר רַב סַלָּא [7] Similarly, **Rav Salla said in the name of Rav Hamnuna: The rains are withheld only because of brazen-faced people,** [8] **as it is said** (Jeremiah 3:3): **"And the showers were held back, and there was no latter rain, and you had the forehead** [i.e., the unabashed direct stare] **of a harlot;** you refused to be ashamed."

RASHI

ציה — דרש לשון צוי, דברים שצויתי אתכם בימות החמה — תרומות ומעשרות, גזלו מימי שלג את המטר. **רוח צפון תחולל גשם ופנים נזעמים לשון שקר** — תחולל = תבטל, כמו "לא יחל דברו" (במדבר ל), כדאמרינן ביבמות (עב, א) דרום צפון ברור הוא, ומביא אורה לעולם. מה שגשמים נעצרין ופנים זועמין שמראה הקדוש ברוך הוא, שאינו מביא מטר לעולם, מפני לשון שקר — רכילות. ופשט המקרא: כשם שרוח צפון תחולל גשם כך פנים זועמים מפני לשון שקר. **וימנעו רביבים** — משום ד"מאנת הכלם", שהיה בך עזות. **היה** — משמע כבר נכשל.

SAGES

רַבִּי שִׁמְעוֹן בֶּן פָּזִי Rabbi Shimon ben Pazi. A Palestinian Amora of the third generation, Rabbi Shimon ben Pazi was the closest disciple of Rabbi Yehoshua ben Levi, and he presents many teachings in the latter's name. Most of Rabbi Shimon ben Pazi's teachings are Aggadic, though some Halakhic teachings are also presented in his name. Rabbi Shimon ben Pazi was a colleague of Rabbi Abbahu, of Rabbi Yitzḥak Nappaḥa, and of Rabbi Yitzḥak bar Naḥmani. Rabbi Shimon ben Pazi's son was Rabbi Yehudah the son of Rabbi Shimon ben Pazi, and was one of the Sages of the following generation.

רַב סַלָּא Rav Salla. A Babylonian Amora of the third generation, Rav Salla was apparently a disciple of Rav's disciples, and he reports various teachings in their name, both in Halakhah and in Aggadah.

רַב הַמְנוּנָא Rav Hamnuna. A Babylonian Amora of the second generation, Rav Hamnuna was a student of Rav. Another Amora of the same name lived in the next generation and was a student of Rav Ḥisda.
The Rav Hamnuna referred to here was one of the students of Rav who remained in his House of Study and continued the tradition of "the School of Rav," so that it is said that the expression "the School of Rav" (בֵּי רַב) refers to Rav Hamnuna.

NOTES

וּפָנִים נִזְעָמִים לְשׁוֹן סָתֶר And a deceptive tongue causes an angry face. Our commentary follows *Rashi* and *Tosafot,* who explain that Rabbi Shimon ben Pazi interprets the angry face mentioned in this verse as meaning the countenance of God. When the north wind halts the rain, it is not by chance, but is a sign that God is angry with His people on account of their slanderous language. *Maharsha* suggests that, even according to Rabbi Shimon ben Pazi, the angry face can be understood as referring to the faces of those who are distressed by the slander spoken against them. God causes the north wind to halt the rain when He sees that relations between people are being strained on account of the slander that is being circulated.

BACKGROUND

עַזּוּת פָּנִים Brazenness. The Sages repeatedly stress the virtues of bashfulness and diffidence, saying that bashfulness is one of the virtues stamped on the heart of all Jews. Bashfulness prevents a person from committing many transgressions, both because one is ashamed of the public gaze and also because one is ashamed of oneself.

By contrast, brazenness and impertinence lead one to commit transgressions without fearing them. This is especially true regarding transgressions of a sexual nature, which sometimes depend on a man's impudence in seducing a woman into sin. Brazenness is considered not only a vice but also a sin (which one confesses on Yom Kippur), because it entails a lack of consideration both for the rule of God in His world and for His constant providence. For that reason the Sages went so far as to say that a brazen man may be shamed and hated for this vice and for the results that will doubtless follow from it.

TRANSLATION AND COMMENTARY

וְאָמַר רַב סַלָּא [1]**And Rav Salla said in the name of Rav Hamnuna** on the same topic: **Everyone who is brazen-faced ultimately stumbles into** serious sexual **transgression,** [2]**as it is said** in the verse just quoted from Jeremiah: **"And you had the forehead of a harlot"** — implying that brazenness is associated with prostitution. [3]**Rav Naḥman** went further, **saying:** If you see a person who is brazen-faced, you **know that he has already stumbled into** serious sexual **transgression,** [4]**for it says** in this verse: **"You had** the forehead of a harlot," in the past tense, **but it does not say: "You will have** the forehead of a harlot," in the future tense.

אָמַר רַבָּה בַּר רַב הוּנָא [5]On the same topic, **Rabbah bar Rav Huna said: If a person is brazen-faced, it is permitted to call him wicked** to his face, even if you have no evidence of misdeeds that he has committed. Normally, it is strictly forbidden to call another person wicked without proper evidence of crime, and the Talmud (*Kiddushin* 28a) prescribes penalties for anyone who does so. But a brazen person is an exception to this rule, [6]**as it is said** (Proverbs 21:29): **"A wicked man makes his face brazen."** Thus we see that brazenness is a sign of wickedness. [7]**Rav Naḥman bar Yitzḥak** went further, **saying:** Not only is it permitted to call him wicked, **it is** even **permitted to hate him,** although hatred of one's fellow Jews is ordinarily forbidden (Leviticus 19:17), [8]**as it is said** (Ecclesiastes 8:1): **"And the brazenness of his face will be changed."** The first part of this verse reads: "Who is like the wise, and who knows the interpretation of a thing? A man's wisdom will make his face shine." Rav Naḥman bar Yitzḥak takes the last part of the verse in isolation from the rest, and since the Hebrew word עֹז is written defectively without the letter vav (ו), he attaches it to the next word, פָּנָיו, and interprets the two words together as referring to brazenness. [9]Moreover, Rav Naḥman bar Yitzḥak also suggests a play on words. **Instead of reading** the last word as יְשֻׁנֶּא, **"will be changed,"** he suggests that **instead** we read it **as** יִשָּׂנֵא, meaning "will be hated." The two words are spelled the same way in Hebrew, even though their vocalization and pronunciation are different. Thus the verse can be interpreted as saying: "He who brazens his face will be hated."

אָמַר רַב קְטִינָא [10]The Gemara now cites another opinion concerning the sins that cause rain to be withheld. **Rav Ketina said: The rains are withheld only because** people have **neglected** their obligation to study **Torah,** [11]**as it is said** (Ecclesiastes 10:18): **"Because of laziness the roof will collapse,** and through idleness of the hands the house will leak." [12]Rav Ketina regards this verse as a metaphor for neglect of the study of Torah: **Because of the laziness that there has been in Israel, that they have not occupied themselves with** the study

[1]וְאָמַר רַב סַלָּא אָמַר רַב הַמְנוּנָא: כָּל אָדָם שֶׁיֵּשׁ לוֹ עַזּוּת פָּנִים סוֹף נִכְשָׁל בַּעֲבֵירָה, [2]שֶׁנֶּאֱמַר: "וּמֵצַח אִשָּׁה זוֹנָה הָיָה לָךְ". [3]רַב נַחְמָן אָמַר: בְּיָדוּעַ שֶׁנִּכְשָׁל בַּעֲבֵירָה, [4]שֶׁנֶּאֱמַר: "הָיָה לָךְ", וְלֹא נֶאֱמַר: "יִהְיֶה לָךְ".

[5]אָמַר רַבָּה בַּר רַב הוּנָא: כָּל אָדָם שֶׁיֵּשׁ לוֹ עַזּוּת פָּנִים, מוּתָּר לִקְרוֹתוֹ רָשָׁע, [6]שֶׁנֶּאֱמַר: "הֵעֵז אִישׁ רָשָׁע בְּפָנָיו". [7]רַב נַחְמָן בַּר יִצְחָק אָמַר: מוּתָּר לְשׂוֹנְאוֹתוֹ, [8]שֶׁנֶּאֱמַר: "וְעֹז פָּנָיו יְשֻׁנֶּא". [9]אַל תִּקְרִי "יְשֻׁנֶּא" אֶלָּא "יִשָּׂנֵא".

[10]אָמַר רַב קְטִינָא: אֵין הַגְּשָׁמִים נֶעֱצָרִין אֶלָּא בִּשְׁבִיל בִּיטּוּל תּוֹרָה, [11]שֶׁנֶּאֱמַר: "בַּעֲצַלְתַּיִם יִמַּךְ הַמְּקָרֶה". [12]בִּשְׁבִיל עַצְלוּת שֶׁהָיָה בְּיִשְׂרָאֵל, שֶׁלֹּא עָסְקוּ בַּתּוֹרָה, נַעֲשָׂה שׂוֹנְאוֹ שֶׁל

LITERAL TRANSLATION

[1]And Rav Salla said in the name of Rav Hamnuna: Every man who has brazenness ultimately stumbles into transgression, [2]as it is said: "And you had the forehead of a harlot." [3]Rav Naḥman said: It is known that he has already stumbled into transgression, [4]for it is said: "You had," and it is not said: "You will have."

[5]Rabbah bar Rav Huna said: Every man who has brazenness, it is permitted to call him wicked, [6]as it is said: "A wicked man makes his face brazen." [7]Rav Naḥman bar Yitzḥak said: It is permitted to hate him, [8]as it is said: "And the brazenness of his face will be changed." [9]Do not read "will be changed" but rather "will be hated."

[10]Rav Ketina said: The rains are not withheld except because of neglect of Torah, [11]as it is said: "Because of laziness the roof will collapse." [12]Because of the laziness that there has been in Israel, that they have not occupied themselves with Torah, the enemy of

RASHI

העז איש — שיש בו עזות פנים, אמור לו "רשע" בפניו, ואין בו משום מלקות, כדאמרינן במסכת קדושין (כח,א), ומשום דבר זה בלבד מותר לקרותו רשע. מותר לשנאותו — אף על גב דכתיב "ואהבת לרעך כמוך". ועז פניו ישונא — "ועז" כתיב חסר ו', מי שהוא עז פנים — ישנא בשין ואלף. ימך — כמי שאין בו כח להוריד טל ומטר.

TRANSLATION AND COMMENTARY

of **Torah, the enemy of the Holy One blessed be He** [a euphemism for "the Holy One blessed be He"] **has collapsed,** as it were, losing His power to make the rain fall. Rav Ketina's explanation is based on an identification of "roof" with "God," and "collapsed" with "powerlessness." [1]Rav Ketina now justifies these identifications: The word **"collapsed" has no other meaning except "poor,"** [2]**as it is said** (Leviticus 27:8): **"But if he is too poor for your estimation,"** in which the same word "collapsed" (מָךְ) is used in the context of poverty. [3]**And** the word **"roof" has no other meaning except "the Holy One blessed be He,"** [4]**as it is said** (Psalms 104:3): **"He who makes a roof with water in His upper chambers."** The Hebrew word for "he who makes a roof" is identical with the word used by Ecclesiastes for "roof."

רַב יוֹסֵף [5]**Rav Yosef derived** the same idea **from** the following verse (Job 37:21): **"And now that they have not seen light, it is bright in the skies, and a wind has passed by and purified them."** Rav Yosef gives this verse a figurative interpretation and explains it as referring to the light of Torah. [6]For the word **"light" has no other meaning except "the Torah," as it is said** (Proverbs 6:23): **"For a commandment is a lamp and the Torah is a light."** Thus the verse can be interpreted as saying that when people do not see the light of Torah, the wind passes by and purifies the sky of clouds, preventing the rain from falling.

בָּהִיר הוּא בַּשְּׁחָקִים [7]In his interpretation of the verse in Job (37:21), Rav Yosef does not explain the words, **"it is bright in the skies,"** that appear in the middle of the verse. The Gemara now cites an explanation of these words that is consistent with Rav Yosef's interpretation of the verse. [8]**A Tanna of the School of Rabbi Yishmael taught:** "The word בָּהִיר [which we have translated as 'bright'] is closely related to the word בְּהוֹר, which means 'a white spot.' [9]Thus the verse is saying: **Even when the sky is made up of bright clouds** about **to bring down dew and rain, 'a wind has passed by and purified them.'"** Thus neglect of the study of Torah, which is compared to light, can cause the rain to be withheld.

אָמַר רַבִּי אַמִי [10]The Gemara now cites yet another opinion concerning the sins that cause rain to be withheld. **Rabbi Ammi said: The rains are withheld only because of the sin of robbery,** [11]**as it is said** (Job 36:32): **"Because of hands He has covered the light,** and He has commanded about it because of imploring." This verse appears in a passage describing the manifestation of God's greatness in rainfall. The plain

הַקָּדוֹשׁ בָּרוּךְ הוּא מָךְ. [1]וְאֵין "מָךְ" אֶלָּא "עָנִי", [2]שֶׁנֶּאֱמַר: "וְאִם מָךְ הוּא מֵעֶרְכֶּךָ". [3]וְאֵין "מְקָרֶה" אֶלָּא "הַקָּדוֹשׁ בָּרוּךְ הוּא", [4]שֶׁנֶּאֱמַר: "הַמְקָרֶה בַמַּיִם עֲלִיּוֹתָיו".

[5]רַב יוֹסֵף אָמַר מֵהָכָא: "וְעַתָּה לֹא רָאוּ אוֹר, בָּהִיר הוּא בַּשְּׁחָקִים, וְרוּחַ עָבְרָה וַתְּטַהֲרֵם". [6]וְאֵין "אוֹר" אֶלָּא תּוֹרָה, שֶׁנֶּאֱמַר: "כִּי נֵר מִצְוָה וְתוֹרָה אוֹר".

[7]"בָּהִיר הוּא בַּשְּׁחָקִים". [8]תָּנָא דְּבֵי רַבִּי יִשְׁמָעֵאל: [9]"אֲפִילּוּ בְּשָׁעָה שֶׁרָקִיעַ נַעֲשָׂה בְּהוֹרִין בְּהוֹרִין לְהוֹרִיד טַל וּמָטָר, 'רוּחַ עָבְרָה וַתְּטַהֲרֵם'".

[10]אָמַר רַבִּי אַמִי: אֵין הַגְּשָׁמִים נֶעֱצָרִין אֶלָּא בַּעֲוֹן גָּזֵל, [11]שֶׁנֶּאֱמַר: "עַל כַּפַּיִם כִּסָּה

LITERAL TRANSLATION

the Holy One blessed be He has collapsed. [1]And there is no [meaning of] "collapsed" except "poor," [2]as it is said: "But if he is too poor for your estimation." [3]And there is no [meaning of] "roof" except "the Holy One blessed be He," [4]as it is said: "He who makes a roof with water in His upper chambers."

[5]Rav Yosef derived (lit., "said") [it] from here: "And now that they have not seen light, it is bright in the skies, and a wind has passed by and purified them." [6]And there is no "light" except the Torah, as it is said: "For a commandment is a lamp and the Torah is a light."

[7]"It is bright in the skies." [8][A Tanna] of the School of Rabbi Yishmael taught: [9]"Even when the sky is made [up of] bright [clouds] to bring down dew and rain, 'a wind has passed by and purified them.'"

[10]Rabbi Ammi said: The rains are not withheld except because of the sin of robbery, [11]as it is said: "Because of hands He has covered the

RASHI

ועתה לא ראו אור – מפני שלא ראו אור של תורה. **אפילו כשהשמים בהורין** – כמו בהרת, מנומר בעבים, ורוצה להוריד גשמים – רוח עברה ותטהרם, מפזרת העבים. המלאך אף ברי שמו – "יפיץ ענן אורו" = גשם שלו.

SAGES

רַבִּי אַמִי **Rabbi Ammi.** A Palestinian Amora of the third generation, Rabbi Ammi (bar Natan) was a priest and a close friend of Rabbi Assi. They studied with the greatest Sages of Eretz Israel and were especially close disciples of Rabbi Yoḥanan. Rabbi Ammi also studied with Rabbi Yoḥanan's greatest students. In the Jerusalem Talmud he is commonly known as Rabbi Immi.

After Rabbi Yoḥanan's death Rabbi Ammi was appointed head of the Tiberias Yeshivah in his place. The Sages of Babylonia also consulted him about Halakhic problems. He is widely quoted in both the Babylonian and the Jerusalem Talmud, not only in transmitting statements from his teachers, but also in debate with Rabbi Assi and with other Sages of the generation. Most of the Palestinian Amoraim of the following generation received and transmitted his teachings. He and Rabbi Assi were known as "the distinguished priests of Eretz Israel," and stories are told of their righteousness and holiness. Rabbi Ammi seems to have lived to a great age, and even the Sages of the fourth generation in Babylonia used to send him their questions.

NOTES

נַעֲשָׂה שׂוֹנְאוֹ שֶׁל הַקָּדוֹשׁ בָּרוּךְ הוּא מָךְ **The enemy of the Holy One blessed be He has collapsed.** *Rashi* explains that when the people of Israel become lazy and fail to study the Torah sufficiently, God Himself becomes weak, as it were, and is unable to make the rain fall. *Rabbenu Elyakim* argues that when the Jewish people do not pay sufficient attention to Torah study, God becomes poor in the sense that He is unable to find among them any merits that would justify bestowing His bounty upon them.

TRANSLATION AND COMMENTARY

meaning of this verse is not entirely clear. Most commentators explain the word כַּפַּיִם, which we have translated as "hands," to mean "clouds," and understand the verse to be saying that God causes the light of the sun to be covered over by clouds. But Rabbi Ammi takes the word "hands" literally, and the verse as a whole is understood to refer to the sin that causes the rain to stop. [1]Thus the verse reads: **"Because of the sin of hands He has covered the light."** [2]**And** the word **"hands,"** when used to refer to a sin, **has no other meaning except "violence,"** [3]**as it is said** (Jonah 3:8): "And let them turn away, each man from his evil way, **and from the violence that is in their hands."** [4]**And** the word **"light" has no other meaning except "rain,"** [5]**as it is said** (Job 37:11): **"He** [the Angel called Af Bri] **spreads the cloud of his light."** Thus the verse is teaching us that violence and robbery prevent rain from falling. Rabbi Ammi goes on to explain the latter part of the verse. If the rain is withheld in this way, and someone suspects that the country is being punished for his own personal misdeeds, [6]**what is his remedy?** How should he act in order that the rain may fall again? [7]**He should pray more, as it is said** in the same verse (Job 36:32): **"And He has commanded about it because of imploring."** [8]**And** the word **"imploring" has no other meaning except "prayer,"** [9]**as it is said** (Jeremiah 7:16): **"And you, do not pray for this nation,** and do not raise a cry or a prayer for them, **and do not implore Me,** for I do not hear you." Thus the verse as interpreted by Rabbi Ammi reads: "Because of robbery committed by man's hands, the light of rain is covered, but He has commanded that it should return, when He has been implored to do so in prayer."

וַאֲמַר רַבִּי אַמִי [10]On a similar topic, **Rabbi Ammi said: What is the meaning of what is written** in the following verse (Ecclesiastes 10:10): **"If the iron is dull, and he has not whetted the surface,** then soldiers must make a greater effort, but it is advantageous to prepare with wisdom"? This verse appears among a series of proverbs dealing with the unanticipated problems that can arise in the performance of ordinary tasks. The previous verse states that someone chopping wood with a sharp iron ax can easily hurt himself. According to the plain meaning of the verse quoted by Rabbi Ammi, one can chop the wood with a dull ax, but this makes for harder work. Hence it is better to use a sharp ax and prepare with wisdom for all eventualities. But Rabbi Ammi gives this verse a figurative interpretation, and explains it as referring to rain: [11]**If you see a sky that is like iron, in that it does not cause dew and rain to come down, it is because of the deeds of the generation, which are corrupt,** [12]**as it is said** in this same verse:

אוֹר״. [1]בַּעֲוֹן כַּפַּיִם כִּסָּה אוֹר.
[2]וְאֵין ״כַּפַּיִם״ אֶלָּא ״חָמָס״,
[3]שֶׁנֶּאֱמַר: ״וּמִן הֶחָמָס אֲשֶׁר
בְּכַפֵּיהֶם״. [4]וְאֵין ״אוֹר״ אֶלָּא
״מָטָר״, [5]שֶׁנֶּאֱמַר: ״יָפִיץ עֲנַן
אוֹרוֹ״. [6]מַאי תַּקַּנְתֵּיהּ? [7]יַרְבֶּה
בִּתְפִלָּה, שֶׁנֶּאֱמַר: ״וַיְצַו עָלֶיהָ
בְמַפְגִּיעַ״. [8]וְאֵין ״פְּגִיעָה״ אֶלָּא
״תְּפִלָּה״, [9]שֶׁנֶּאֱמַר: ״וְאַתָּה, אַל
תִּתְפַּלֵּל בְּעַד הָעָם הַזֶּה, וגו׳,
וְאַל תִּפְגַּע בִּי״.
[10]וַאֲמַר רַבִּי אַמִי: מַאי דִּכְתִיב:
״אִם קֵהָה הַבַּרְזֶל, וְהוּא לֹא
פָנִים קִלְקַל״? [11]אִם רָאִיתָ רָקִיעַ
שֶׁקֵּיהָה כְּבַרְזֶל מִלְּהוֹרִיד טַל
וּמָטָר, בִּשְׁבִיל מַעֲשֵׂה הַדּוֹר
שֶׁהֵן מְקוּלְקָלִין, [12]שֶׁנֶּאֱמַר:

LITERAL TRANSLATION

light." [1]Because of the sin of hands He has covered the light. [2]And there are no "hands" except "violence," [3]as it is said: "And from the violence that is in their hands." [4]And there is no "light" except "rain," [5]as it is said: "He spreads the cloud of his light." [6]What is his remedy? [7]He should pray more, as it is said: "And He has commanded about it because of imploring." [8]And there is no "imploring" except "prayer," [9]as it is said: "And you, do not pray for this nation, etc., and do not implore Me."

[10]And Rabbi Ammi said: What is [the meaning] of what is written: "If the iron is dull, and he has not whetted the surface"? [11]If you have seen a sky that is dull like iron, in that it does not cause dew and rain to come down, it is because of the deeds of the generation which are corrupt, [12]as it is said:

RASHI

ויצו – הקדוש ברוך הוא. **עליה** – על הגשם שתרד. **במפגיע** – כשיתפלל עליה, כמו ״ואל תפגע בי״. **קהה הברזל** – כמו ״הקהה את שיניו״, ״ושיני בנים תקהינה״ (ירמיהו לא). **והוא לא פנים קלקל** – שקלקלו הדור.

NOTES

מַאי תַּקַּנְתֵּיהּ? יַרְבֶּה בִּתְפִלָּה What is his remedy? He should pray more. Rabbi Ammi means to say that the robber must pray for forgiveness after returning to its rightful owner what he took from him by violence. But if he does not first return what he took, all of his repentance and prayers will be to no avail, for the Gemara states elsewhere (below, 16a) that a person who confesses to a robbery while the object he took is still in his possession may be compared to a person who undergoes ritual immersion while holding an unclean reptile in his hand and therefore remains ritually impure (*Gevurat Ari*).

TRANSLATION AND COMMENTARY

[1]**"And he has not whetted the surface."** The word פָּנִים, which we have translated as "surface," is sometimes used to refer to the leadership of a generation, and the word קִלְקַל, which we have translated as "whetted," generally means "to be corrupt." Thus the verse as interpreted by Rabbi Ammi is saying: "When the sky shows no sign of rain, it is because of the corruption of the generation." Here, too, Rabbi Ammi explains the latter part of the verse as providing the solution to the problem posed by the first part. [2]If rain is withheld in this way, **what is** the generation's **remedy?** [3]**They should make increased efforts** to pray **for mercy, as it is said** later in the same verse: **"Then soldiers must make a greater effort."** [4]And what is the meaning of the last part of the verse: **"But it is advantageous to prepare with wisdom"?** The word הַכְשֵׁיר, which we have translated as "prepare," is closely related to the word כָּשֵׁר, which means "fitting." [5]Thus the verse teaches us that a wise generation, **whose deeds were fitting from the outset,** will **all the more** readily have their prayers for rain answered, even without making special efforts.

רֵישׁ לָקִישׁ אָמַר [6]The Gemara now cites a series of additional explanations of this verse in Ecclesiastes. All of them are similar in structure, although they differ in content. **Resh Lakish said:** We may explain this verse as referring to a student of Torah. **If you see a student [8A] who finds his studies to be as hard for him as iron,** [7]**it is because he has not reviewed his learning in an organized,** systematic **manner,** [8]**as it is said: "And he has not whetted the surface."** Resh Lakish explains the latter part of the verse as providing the solution to the problem posed by the first part. [9]If a student has this problem, **what is his remedy?** [10]**He should increase** the time he spends **sitting** and listening to other students who have a clearer grasp of the material, [11]**as it is said** later in the same verse: **"Then soldiers must make a greater effort."** And what is the meaning of the last part of the verse: **"But it is advantageous to prepare with wisdom"?** [12]The verse teaches us that a wise student should see to it that he reviews **his learning** in an **organized** manner **from the outset,** since his understanding of the discussions in the Academy will be **all the more** enhanced, and he will not need to make special efforts.

[1]"וְהוּא לֹא פָנִים קִלְקַל". [2]מַה תַּקָּנָתָן? [3]יִתְגַּבְּרוּ בְּרַחֲמִים, שֶׁנֶּאֱמַר: "וַחֲיָלִים יְגַבֵּר, [4]וְיִתְרוֹן הַכְשֵׁיר חָכְמָה". [5]כָּל שֶׁכֵּן, אִם הוּכְשְׁרוּ מַעֲשֵׂיהֶן מֵעִיקָּרָא.

[6]רֵישׁ לָקִישׁ אָמַר: אִם רָאִיתָ תַּלְמִיד [8A] שֶׁלִּמּוּדוֹ קָשֶׁה עָלָיו כְּבַרְזֶל, [7]בִּשְׁבִיל מִשְׁנָתוֹ שֶׁאֵינָהּ סְדוּרָה עָלָיו, [8]שֶׁנֶּאֱמַר: "וְהוּא לֹא פָנִים קִלְקַל". [9]מַאי תַּקַּנְתֵּיהּ? [10]יַרְבֶּה בִּישִׁיבָה, [11]שֶׁנֶּאֱמַר: "וַחֲיָלִים יְגַבֵּר, וְיִתְרוֹן הַכְשֵׁיר חָכְמָה". [12]כָּל שֶׁכֵּן אִם מִשְׁנָתוֹ סְדוּרָה לוֹ מֵעִיקָּרָא.

LITERAL TRANSLATION

[1]"And he has not whetted the surface." [2]What is their remedy? [3]They should make increased efforts [to pray] for mercy, as it is said: "Then soldiers must make a greater effort, [4]but it is advantageous to prepare with wisdom." [5]All the more so, if their deeds had been fitting from the outset.

[6]Resh Lakish said: If you see a student [8A] whose study is as hard for him as iron, [7][it is] because of his learning, which is not organized for him, [8]as it is said: "And he has not whetted the surface." [9]What is his remedy? [10]He should increase sitting [and studying], [11]as it is said: "Then soldiers must make a greater effort, but it is advantageous to prepare with wisdom." [12]All the more so, if his learning was organized for him from the outset.

RASHI

וכל שכן אם הוכשרו מעשיהן — קודם לכן, והכי משמע: "ויתרון הכשיר" — ויתרון שהכשיר לחכמה, אם הכשירו מעשיהן מתחילה, שיבואו הגשמים — יותר מ"בחיילים יגבר", שהן מגבירין חיילים ועומדין בתפלה בזמן שקלקלו. **שלמודו קשה עליו כברזל** — שקשה לו מרוב קושיות — בשביל משנתו שאינה סדורה לו, ואינו זוכר מה כתיב בה. ולפיכך אינו יודע לפרק. אי נמי שגורסה בטעות, פוטר על החיוב ומחייב על הפטור, ומקשי עלה מדוכתא אחריתי. והכי משמע קרא: "והוא לא", שאינו יודע שמועתו — מפני ש"פנים קלקל", שקלקל במשנה שהיא קודם לגמרא. **ירבה בישיבה** — שיסדירו בני הישיבה משנתם, שנאמר "וחיילים" — בין תלמידים, שהן חיילות חיילות. **ויתרון הכשיר** — כשסידר משנתו מתחילה.

BACKGROUND

שֶׁלִּמּוּדוֹ קָשֶׁה עָלָיו כְּבַרְזֶל Whose study is as hard for him as iron. *Rashi* explains that this refers to someone who has a great many difficulties while studying, because he has not organized efficiently the memorization of Mishnayot, which are the basic texts on which the study of Gemara is organized. In more general terms, difficulties in study are liable to arise because the student does not know the basic material — which the teacher assumes that everyone knows — and therefore fails to understand, or misunderstands, new material.

NOTES

יַרְבֶּה בִּישִׁיבָה He should increase sitting. *Rashi* explains that Resh Lakish's advice to the student who finds his studies as hard as iron is that he should spend a great deal of time with the other students in the yeshivah and review with them the material that he has not fully mastered on his own. *Meiri* suggests that Resh Lakish means that the student having difficulty with his studies should spend a great deal of time sitting by himself, revising the difficult material in an organized manner until he is confident that he knows it well.

[1]כִּי הָא דְּרֵישׁ לָקִישׁ הֲוָה מְסַדֵּר מַתְנִיתֵיהּ אַרְבְּעִין זִמְנִין [2]כְּנֶגֶד אַרְבָּעִים יוֹם שֶׁנִּיתְּנָה תּוֹרָה, [3]וְעָיֵיל לְקַמֵּיהּ דְּרַבִּי יוֹחָנָן.

[4]רַב אַדָּא בַּר אַהֲבָה מְסַדֵּר מַתְנִיתֵיהּ עֶשְׂרִין וְאַרְבַּע זִמְנִין [5]כְּנֶגֶד תּוֹרָה נְבִיאִים וּכְתוּבִים, [6]וְעָיֵיל לְקַמֵּיהּ דְּרָבָא.

[7]רָבָא אָמַר: אִם רָאִיתָ תַּלְמִיד שֶׁלִּמּוּדוֹ קָשֶׁה עָלָיו כְּבַרְזֶל, בִּשְׁבִיל רַבּוֹ, שֶׁאֵינוֹ מַסְבִּיר לוֹ פָּנִים, [8]שֶׁנֶּאֱמַר: ״וְהוּא לֹא פָנִים קִלְקַל״. [9]מַאי תַּקַּנְתֵּיהּ? [10]יַרְבֶּה עָלָיו רֵעִים, [11]שֶׁנֶּאֱמַר: ״וַחֲיָלִים יְגַבֵּר, וְיִתְרוֹן הַכְשֵׁיר חָכְמָה״. [12]כָּל שֶׁכֵּן אִם הוּכְשְׁרוּ מַעֲשָׂיו בִּפְנֵי רַבּוֹ מֵעִיקָּרָא.

[13]וְאָמַר רַבִּי אַמִי: מַאי דִּכְתִיב: [14]״אִם יִשֹּׁךְ הַנָּחָשׁ בְּלוֹא לָחַשׁ, וְאֵין יִתְרוֹן לְבַעַל הַלָּשׁוֹן״?

LITERAL TRANSLATION

[1][It is] like the case of Resh Lakish, [who] would review (lit., "organize") his learning forty times, [2]corresponding to the forty days on which the Torah was given, [3]and would go up before Rabbi Yoḥanan.

[4]Rav Adda bar Ahavah would review his learning twenty-four times, [5]corresponding to the Torah, Prophets, and Writings, [6]and would go up before Rava.

[7]Rava said: If you see a student whose study is as hard for him as iron, [it is] because of his teacher, who does not show him a friendly face, [8]as it is said: "And he has not whetted the surface." [9]What is his remedy? [10]He should bring before him many colleagues, [11]as it is said: "Then soldiers must make a greater effort, but it is advantageous to prepare with wisdom." [12]All the more so, if his deeds were prepared properly before his teacher from the outset.

[13]And Rabbi Ammi said: What is [the meaning of] what is written: [14]"If the snake bites without enchantment, then there is no advantage to the one with a tongue"?

TRANSLATION AND COMMENTARY

כִּי הָא דְּרֵישׁ לָקִישׁ [1]The Gemara notes that this emphasis on reviewing one's studies **is reminiscent of the case of Resh Lakish** himself, **who would review his learning forty times** before listening to the analysis of his teacher, Rabbi Yoḥanan. [2]The forty times **corresponded to the forty days during which the Torah was given** to Moses on Mount Sinai (Exodus 24:18). [3]Only after this preparation **would** Resh Lakish **go before Rabbi Yoḥanan** to study.

רַב אַדָּא בַּר אַהֲבָה [4]The Gemara notes that **Rav Adda bar Ahavah would review his learning twenty-four times** before listening to the analysis of his teacher, Rava. [5]The twenty-four times **corresponded to** the twenty-four books of the Bible — **the Torah, the Prophets, and the Writings.** [6]Only after this preparation **would Rav Adda bar Ahavah go before Rava** to study.

רָבָא אָמַר [7]The Gemara now cites another explanation of the verse in Ecclesiastes (10:10). Like Resh Lakish, **Rava** explains this verse as referring to a dull student, **saying: If you see a student who finds his studies to be as hard for him as iron, it is because his teacher does not encourage him,** [8]**as it said: "And he has not whetted the surface."** The verse as interpreted by Rava is saying: When a student is dull and his studies are as hard for him as iron, it is because his teacher shows him a "bad face," and fails to encourage him in his studies. Like Resh Lakish, Rava explains the latter part of the verse as providing the solution to the problem posed by the first part. [9]If a student has this problem, **what is his remedy?** [10]**He should bring before his** teacher **many colleagues to intercede for him,** [11]**as it is said: "Then soldiers must make a greater effort."** And what is the meaning of the last part of the verse: **"But it is advantageous to prepare with wisdom"?** [12]According to Rava, the verse teaches us that a wise student should see to it that **he prepares himself well before he presents himself to his teacher,** since he will then profit **all the more** from his teacher's encouragement, without having to make special efforts.

וְאָמַר רַבִּי אַמִי [13]Having considered Rabbi Ammi's interpretations of two verses, Job 36:32 and Ecclesiastes 10:10, the Gemara now cites another statement of Rabbi Ammi, referring to the verses immediately following these. **And Rabbi Ammi said** further: **What is the meaning of what is written** in the following verse (Ecclesiastes 10:11): [14]**"If the snake bites without enchantment, then there is no advantage to the one with a tongue"?** Rabbi Ammi gives the verse a nonliteral interpretation, and explains it as referring to rain. According to Rabbi Ammi's explanation, the Hebrew word נָחָשׁ, which we have translated as "snake," is replaced by the similarly spelled word נְחֹשֶׁת, which means "copper"; the

RASHI

כנגד ארבעים יום שניתנה התורה — שתתקיים בידו, והדר עייל קמיה דרבי יוחנן, למיגמר גמרא. **כנגד תורה, נביאים, כתובים** — שהן עשרים וארבעה ספרים. **שפנים קלקל** — שהראה לו פנים רעות. **ירבה עליו רעים** — לפייס הימנו, שיסבור לו פנים.

BACKGROUND

הֲוָה מְסַדֵּר מַתְנִיתֵיהּ Would review his learning. In other words, he reviewed what he had studied in the yeshivah, going over it frequently until he was thoroughly familiar with the material, whether it be a Mishnah, a Baraita, or the teachings of the Amoraim connected with this Talmudic passage.

עֶשְׂרִין וְאַרְבַּע זִמְנִין כְּנֶגֶד תּוֹרָה Twenty-four times, corresponding to the Torah, Prophets and Writings. The number of books in the Bible is twenty-four, according to Jewish tradition, and at times the Bible was called "The Twenty-Four." To understand how the Sages arrived at this number, it must be recalled that each of the paired books of Samuel, Kings, and Chronicles was counted as a single book, that all the Minor Prophets were counted as a single book ("The Twelve"), and that the books of Ezra and Nehemiah were also treated as one book.

רַבּוֹ שֶׁאֵינוֹ מַסְבִּיר לוֹ פָּנִים Who does not show him a friendly face. People with psychological insight know that the personal relations between teacher and student influence success in studies. When a teacher is not cordial toward his student, this can cause great difficulties in study, even if in other respects instruction is given in a regular manner.

As can be understood from the context, the Gemara here is referring to a student whose performance or character needs correction. Because he does not behave properly, his teacher, too, does not give him a cordial reception. Therefore he must make an effort to convince his teacher that he has improved his ways, and then he will be greeted amicably.

SAGES

רַב אַדָּא בַּר אַהֲבָה Rav Adda bar Ahavah. A famous Babylonian Amora of the first and second generations. He was born (or was circumcised) on the day Rabbi Yehudah HaNasi died. Rav Adda was a disciple of Rav, and transmitted several teachings in his name. Among his colleagues were

אִם[1] רָאִיתָ דּוֹר שֶׁהַשָּׁמַיִם מִשְׁתַּכִּין כִּנְחֹשֶׁת מִלְּהוֹרִיד טַל וּמָטָר, [2]בִּשְׁבִיל לוֹחֲשֵׁי לְחִישׁוֹת שֶׁאֵין בְּדוֹר. [3]מַאי תַּקַּנְתָּן? [4]יֵלְכוּ אֵצֶל מִי שֶׁיּוֹדֵעַ לִלְחוֹשׁ, [5]דִּכְתִיב: ״יַגִּיד עָלָיו רֵעוֹ״. [6]״וְאֵין יִתְרוֹן לְבַעַל הַלָּשׁוֹן״. [7]וּמִי שֶׁאֶפְשָׁר לוֹ לִלְחוֹשׁ וְאֵינוֹ לוֹחֵשׁ, [8]מָה הֲנָאָה יֵשׁ לוֹ? [9]וְאִם לָחַשׁ וְלֹא נַעֲנָה, [10]מַאי תַּקַּנְתֵּיהּ? [11]יֵלֵךְ אֵצֶל חָסִיד שֶׁבַּדּוֹר, וְיַרְבֶּה עָלָיו בִּתְפִלָּה, [12]שֶׁנֶּאֱמַר: ״וַיְצַו עָלֶיהָ בְמַפְגִּיעַ״. [13]וְאֵין פְּגִיעָה אֶלָּא תְּפִילָּה, [14]שֶׁנֶּאֱמַר: ״וְאַתָּה, אַל תִּתְפַּלֵּל בְּעַד הָעָם הַזֶּה, וְאַל תִּשָּׂא בַעֲדָם רִנָּה וּתְפִלָּה, וְאַל תִּפְגַּע בִּי״. [15]וְאִם לָחַשׁ, וְעָלְתָה בְּיָדוֹ,

LITERAL TRANSLATION

[1]If you see a generation in which the heavens are rusty like copper from [failing to] bring down dew and rain, [2]it is because of those who pray softly (lit., the "whisperers of whispers") who are not in the generation. [3]What is their remedy? [4]They should go to [someone] who knows [how] to pray softly, [5]as it is written: "Its noise will tell about Him." [6]"Then there is no advantage to the one with a tongue." [7]And he who is able to pray softly but does not pray softly, [8]what benefit does he have? [9]And if he prayed softly but was not answered, [10]what is his remedy? [11]He should go to the [most] pious man of the generation, and let him do much praying for him, [12]as it is said: "And He has commanded about it because of imploring." [13]And there is no "imploring" except "prayer," [14]as it is said: "And you, do not pray for this nation, and do not lift up a cry or a prayer for them, and do not implore Me." [15]But if he prayed softly, and it was successful (lit., "it came up in his hand"),

TRANSLATION AND COMMENTARY

Hebrew word יִשַּׁךְ, which we have translated as "bites," is replaced by the word יִשְׁתַּךְ, which means "corrode"; and the Hebrew word לָחַשׁ, which we have translated as "enchantment," is understood in its more general sense as "whispering." Thus the first part of the verse reads: "If copper corrodes without a whisper," and it means: [1]**If you see a generation in which the heavens are rusty and corroded like copper from failing to bring down dew and rain,** [2]you may be sure that **it is because that generation lacks** pious **people who pray quietly** in private with great fervor. The prayers of humble and unassuming saints are effective precisely because they are not uttered in public. Continuing with his interpretation, Rabbi Ammi asks: [3]**What is their remedy?** How can the generation cause the rain to fall again? The answer can be found in a verse in Job immediately following the one quoted above. [4]**They should go to someone who knows how to pray softly,** and beg him to do so, [5]**as it is written** (Job 36:33): **"Its noise will tell about Him,** the jealous anger of the storm." Rabbi Ammi explains the word רֵעוֹ, which we have translated as "its noise," as "His friend," which is spelled the same way. Thus the first part of the verse in Job, as explained by Rabbi Ammi, teaches us that when a generation are in need of rain, they should go to God's friend, to a person who knows how to pray softly, and he will be able to tell God about the situation through his prayers.

וְאֵין יִתְרוֹן לְבַעַל הַלָּשׁוֹן [6]Continuing with his interpretation, Rabbi Ammi turns to the last part of the verse in Ecclesiastes: **"Then there is no advantage to the one with a tongue."** Rabbi Ammi explains that this verse refers to a generation who went to the pious person and asked him to pray for them but were refused. [7]The verse as explained by Rabbi Ammi reads as follows: If **someone** with a tongue **who is able to pray softly** and effectively **does not pray softly** when entreated to do so, [8]**what benefit does** his ability to pray softly **have?**

וְאִם לָחַשׁ וְלֹא נַעֲנָה [9]Rabbi Ammi now turns to a case in which the pious person agreed to **pray softly** for rain in response to an appeal by his community, **but** his prayers **were not answered,** and rain still did not fall. [10]**What is his remedy?** The answer can be found in the previous verse in Job. [11]The pious person **should go to the** greatest **saint in the generation and let him do much praying for him,** [12]**as it said** (Job 36:32): **"And He has commanded about it because of imploring."** [13]**And** the word **"imploring" has no** other meaning **except "prayer,"** [14]**as it is said** (Jeremiah 7:16): **"And you, do not pray for this nation, and do not lift up a cry or a prayer for them, and do not implore Me."**

וְאִם לָחַשׁ, וְעָלְתָה בְּיָדוֹ [15]Rabbi Ammi now turns to a case in which the pious person agreed to **pray softly** for rain in response to a request by his community, **and** his prayer **was successful.** This pious man achieved

RASHI

משתכין עליו כנחושת – מאדימין פנים, כעין *רודיליי״א, כדאמרינן בבבא מציעא (כו,א): דשתיך טפי – שהעלה חלודה. שנעכרין (מלהוליד) [מלהוריד] טל ומטר. **לוחשי לחישות** – בשביל שאין מתפללים תפלה בלחש. **יגיד עליו רעו** – יתפלל עליו חבירו. וגבי גשמים כתיב, באיוב. **ואין יתרון לבעל הלשון** – כלומר: מה הנאה יש לבעל הלשון שיודע ללחוש ואינו לוחש.

Rav Huna, Rav Ḥisda, and Rav Naḥman. Many teachings are transmitted in his name in the Talmud. He was renowned for his piety, righteousness, and modesty, and lived to an advanced age.

BACKGROUND

לוֹחֲשֵׁי לְחִישׁוֹת **Those who pray softly.** This expression is based on the use of the verb לחש ("to whisper") in the Bible. Those who "whisper whispers" are engaged in prayer, for the central prayer in Judaism is the Amidah, which is recited silently while standing. The emphasis on this silent aspect of prayer is meant to teach us that the essence of prayer is not what may be heard or seen in public, but what is inward and whispered.

LANGUAGE

מִשְׁתַּכִּין **Are rusty.** This verb is mainly used in Aramaic. It usually means "to corrode," although its basic meaning may be "ruin" or "decay." It is probably related to the Syriac שוחתא, which denotes ruin or decay. In Mandaean, the word שותא, a noun meaning "rust," is derived from this root.

LANGUAGE (RASHI)

רודיליי״א* From the Old French *redoilla,* which means "rust."

[1]וּמֵגִיס דַּעְתּוֹ עָלָיו, [2]מֵבִיא אַף לָעוֹלָם, [3]שֶׁנֶּאֱמַר: ״מִקְנֶה אַף עַל עוֹלֶה״.

[4]רָבָא אָמַר: שְׁנֵי תַלְמִידֵי חֲכָמִים שֶׁיּוֹשְׁבִין בְּעִיר אַחַת וְאֵין נוֹחִין זֶה לָזֶה בַּהֲלָכָה, [5]מִתְקַנְּאִין בָּאַף וּמַעֲלִין אוֹתוֹ, שֶׁנֶּאֱמַר: [6]״מִקְנֶה אַף עַל עוֹלֶה״.

[7]אָמַר רֵישׁ לָקִישׁ: מַאי דִּכְתִיב: [8]״אִם יִשֹּׁךְ הַנָּחָשׁ בְּלוֹא לָחַשׁ, וְאֵין יִתְרוֹן לְבַעַל הַלָּשׁוֹן״? [9]לֶעָתִיד לָבוֹא, מִתְקַבְּצוֹת וּבָאוֹת כָּל הַחַיּוֹת אֵצֶל הַנָּחָשׁ, וְאוֹמְרִים לוֹ: [10]״אֲרִי דּוֹרֵס וְאוֹכֵל, זְאֵב טוֹרֵף וְאוֹכֵל; [11]אַתָּה, מָה הֲנָאָה יֵשׁ לְךָ?״ [12]אָמַר לָהֶם: ״וְאֵין יִתְרוֹן לְבַעַל הַלָּשׁוֹן״.

LITERAL TRANSLATION

[1]and he makes his mind become proud, [2]he brings anger to the world, [3]as it is said: "The jealous anger of the storm."

[4]Rava said: [If] two Rabbinic Sages live in one city, and they are not courteous to each other in Halakhah, [5]they arouse anger and cause it to rise up, [6]as it is said: "The jealous anger of the storm."

[7]Resh Lakish said: What is [the meaning of] what is written: [8]"If the snake bites without enchantment, then there is no advantage to the one with a tongue"? [9]In the future, all the animals will gather together and come to the snake and say to him: [10]"A lion mauls and eats, a wolf tears and eats; [11][but] you, what pleasure do you have?" [12]He will say to them: "Then there is no advantage to the one with a tongue."

TRANSLATION AND COMMENTARY

his ability to pray precisely through his isolation and humility, but following his success in bringing rain through his prayers, [1]his fame will now naturally spread **and** there is a danger that this **may make his mind proud** and arrogant. Rabbi Ammi explains that the last part of the verse in Job refers to this case. If the pious person becomes arrogant because of his successful prayers, [2]**he will bring anger to the world,** [3]**as it is said** (Job 36:33): **"The jealous anger of the storm."** Rabbi Ammi gives the verse a figurative interpretation, and explains the words עַל עוֹלֶה, which we have translated as "of the storm," as meaning "upon the one who rises," which is spelled the same way. Thus, as explained by Rabbi Ammi, this verse reads: "Jealous anger is upon the one who rises," and it means that a person who rises in his own estimation brings anger upon himself and, indirectly, upon the world.

רָבָא אָמַר [4]Before giving further examples of Rabbi Ammi's interpretations of verses dealing with prayers for rain, the Gemara now cites two additional interpretations of the verses in Job and Ecclesiastes that we have just considered. The verse in Job was given a figurative explanation by **Rava,** who **said: If two Rabbinic Sages live in one city, and they are not courteous to each other in** discussing and deciding **Halakhah,** [5]**they arouse anger and cause it to rise up,** [6]**as it is said** (Job 36:33): "Its noise will tell about Him, **the jealous anger of the storm."** Rava, too, explains the word רֵעוֹ, which we have translated as "its noise," as "his friend," which is spelled the same way. The words עַל עוֹלֶה, which we have translated as "of the storm," he explains as "will surely rise up," which is spelled the same way. Rava explains the word מִקְנֶה, which we have translated as "jealous," as the closely related verb "arousing." Thus, as explained by Rava, the verse says: If his friend has something to tell about him, he will arouse anger and surely cause it to rise up.

אָמַר רֵישׁ לָקִישׁ [7]The verse in Ecclesiastes was given a different figurative interpretation by **Resh Lakish,** who **said: What is the meaning of what is written** in the verse (Ecclesiastes 10:11): [8]**"If the snake bites without enchantment, then there is no advantage to the one with a tongue"?** [9]Resh Lakish explains that **in the future all the animals will gather together and come to the snake and say to him:** "Why do you bite people? [10]**A lion mauls** only an animal that it wishes to **eat;** similarly, **a wolf tears** to pieces only what it wants to **eat.** [11]**But what pleasure do you have** in biting people and killing them with your venom, because in any case you cannot eat them?" [12]And the snake will **say to them:** "My task is to serve as an example to forked-tongued people, who do harm to others through their words. Gossip and slander are purely malicious **and** bring **no advantage to the one with a tongue.** Thus I, too, strike maliciously, even when it brings me no benefit."

RASHI

מקנה אף על עולה — ״מקנה אף״ — מי שמגיס דעתו ועולה. **ואין נוחין זה לזה כו׳** — והכי משמע: בשביל שצריך להגיד זה לזה ולהיות נוחין בהלכה, ואינן עושין, ״מקנה״ — מתקנאים מתגרים ב״אף״, ומעלים אותו ומביאים אותו עליהן. ויש גורסין: ונוחין זה לזה בהלכה — מתקנאים באף וכו׳, משיגיד עליו רעו שנוחין זה לזה — מתקנאים באף ומעלים אותו מעליהם. **ארי דורס ואוכל** — מיד, ואינו מתירא. **טורף ואוכל** — שמוליך לאחוריו ואוכל שם, שמפחד מן הבריות, ולכולן יש להם הנאה. **ולך מה הנאה יש לך** — שאתה נושך בני אדם והורגן? והוא אומר: מה יתרון לבעל הלשון שמספר לשון הרע, אף על פי שאין לו הנאה. ולפיכך מביאו הקדוש ברוך הוא בדין אצל נחש, כדי שיתביישו, מפני שהסית אדם הראשון, ומתביישין עמו מספרי לשון הרע.

BACKGROUND

וְאֵין נוֹחִין זֶה לָזֶה And they are not courteous to each other. This expression does not refer to personal rivalry between two Sages in a city, but to a harsh and intolerant manner of discussion, in which each controversialist not only insists on the rightness of his own position, but also makes no effort to understand his interlocutor or to explain matters to him. In the Talmudic period, people used to say that relations of this kind were more common in Babylonia, whereas in Eretz Israel the manner of study and discussion was more cordial and pleasant. In any event, intolerant discussion is not likely to deteriorate into personal hatred, but tends to impede clarification of issues and does not usually permit the discovery of truth.

¹אָמַר רַבִּי אַמִי: אֵין תְּפִלָּתוֹ שֶׁל אָדָם נִשְׁמַעַת אֶלָּא אִם כֵּן מֵשִׂים נַפְשׁוֹ בְּכַפּוֹ, ²שֶׁנֶּאֱמַר: ״נִשָּׂא לְבָבֵנוּ אֶל כַּפָּיִם״.
³אִינִי? וְהָא אוֹקִים שְׁמוּאֵל אָמוֹרָא עֲלֵיהּ ⁴וְדָרַשׁ: ״וַיְפַתּוּהוּ בְּפִיהֶם, וּבִלְשׁוֹנָם יְכַזְּבוּ לוֹ, וְלִבָּם לֹא נָכוֹן עִמּוֹ, וְלֹא נֶאֶמְנוּ בִּבְרִיתוֹ״. ⁵וְאַף עַל פִּי כֵן, ״וְהוּא רַחוּם, יְכַפֵּר עָוֹן, וגו׳״.
⁶לָא קַשְׁיָא. כָּאן בְּיָחִיד, ⁷כָּאן בְּצִבּוּר.
⁸אָמַר רַבִּי אַמִי: אֵין גְּשָׁמִים יוֹרְדִין אֶלָּא בִּשְׁבִיל בַּעֲלֵי אֲמָנָה, ⁹שֶׁנֶּאֱמַר: ״אֱמֶת מֵאֶרֶץ תִּצְמָח, וְצֶדֶק מִשָּׁמַיִם נִשְׁקָף״.

LITERAL TRANSLATION

¹Rabbi Ammi said: A man's prayer is not heard unless he puts his soul in his hand, ²as it is said: "Let us lift up our heart with our hands."

³Is that so? But surely Shmuel appointed an interpreter for himself ⁴and he expounded: "But they flattered Him with their mouth, and with their tongue they lied to Him, and their heart was not steadfast with Him, and they were not faithful to His covenant." ⁵But even so, "He is merciful, He forgives sin, etc."

⁶There is no difficulty. Here [it refers] to an individual. ⁷Here [it refers] to a community.

⁸Rabbi Ammi said: Rains fall only because of trustworthy people, ⁹as it is said: "Truth will spring up from the earth, and righteousness will look down from heaven."

TRANSLATION AND COMMENTARY

אָמַר רַבִּי אַמִי ¹The Gemara now cites another interpretation by **Rabbi Ammi, who said: A person's prayer is not heard unless he puts his soul in his hand** when he stretches out his hands in prayer, and his innermost feelings are as sincere as his words, ²**as it is said** (Lamentations 3:41): **"Let us lift up our heart with our hands,** to God in heaven."

אִינִי? ³But, the Gemara objects, **is that so? Surely Shmuel** once discussed this matter in public **and appointed an interpreter for himself** to ensure that everyone understood, ⁴**and he expounded** the following passage (Psalms 78:36-37): **"But they flattered Him with their mouth and with their tongue they lied to Him, and their heart was not steadfast with Him, and they were not faithful to His covenant."** This verse deals specifically with prayer that is not matched by a sincere heart. ⁵**But even so,** the following verse (Psalms 78:38) says: **"But He is merciful, He forgives sin,** and will not destroy, and He has frequently turned away His wrath, and will not awaken all His anger." Thus God forgives insincerity in prayer, and it is sufficient to induce Him to reduce His wrath. How, then, can Rabbi Ammi disagree with this authoritative, public statement of Shmuel?

לָא קַשְׁיָא ⁶The Gemara answers: **There is no difficulty** in reconciling the statement of Rabbi Ammi with that of Shmuel. Rabbi Ammi **was referring to an individual,** ⁷whereas Shmuel **was referring to a community.** The preceding verses in Psalms refer to occasions when the Jewish people as a community declare a public period of repentance and prayer in response to some danger. Inevitably, some of the people taking part do so under social pressure and are not sincere in their prayers, but God still values the public expression of penitence, and forgives at least part of their sins. By contrast, the preceding verses in Lamentations explicitly call on each individual to seek out his own sins and to pray to God for forgiveness, and in this case prayer must be sincere to be heard.

אָמַר רַבִּי אַמִי ⁸The Gemara now cites another statement of Rabbi Ammi about rain. **Rabbi Ammi said: Rains fall only because of trustworthy people,** who are scrupulously honest in their business practices, ⁹**as it is said** (Psalms 85:12): **"Truth will spring up from the earth, and righteousness will look down from heaven."** Rabbi Ammi interprets "truth springing up from the earth" as referring to honesty in earthly matters, and the word צֶדֶק, which we have translated as "righteousness," he interprets as the closely related word "charity," which "will look down from heaven" in the form of rain. Thus the verse connects the idea of earthly truthfulness with heavenly rain, suggesting that the one leads to the other.

RASHI

ולבם לא נכון עמו — עם הקדוש ברוך הוא. **ואף על פי כן** — כתוב בסמוך "והוא רחום יכפר עון" ושומע תפלתם. והיכי אמרת שאין תפלתם נשמעת אלא אם כן משים נפשו בכפו? כלומר, שנפשו מכוונת בכפו. **בצבור** — תפלתם נשמעת, ואף על פי שאין לב כולם שלם, כדכתיב "ויפתוהו בפיהם" בדברים, לשון רבים. **ביחיד** — אינו אלא אם כן לבו מכוון. **בזמן שאמת מארץ תצמח** — שיש אמונה במשא ומתן — אז "צדק משמים נשקף" דהיינו גשמים, שהן צדקה.

BACKGROUND

בַּעֲלֵי אֲמָנָה Trustworthy people. This refers to people whose word may be depended on, who keep their promises, and who do not try to mislead others. There are specific prohibitions in the Torah against criminal deceit and lying. But in many instances people do not keep their promises if this does not entail a specific violation of the law. The Sages spoke approvingly of that small number of people in each generation who, even if they lacked other virtues, were utterly trustworthy.

NOTES

מֵשִׂים נַפְשׁוֹ בְּכַפּוֹ He puts his soul in his hand. The Rishonim explain that a person's prayers are only heard if he places his soul in his hand — in other words, if his innermost thoughts are expressed, so that his prayers express his true feelings (see *Rashi, Shittah*). Some suggest that Rav Ammi is hinting at the notion that a person must steep himself in prayer to the point where he strips himself of all materiality, so that it is only his spirit that communicates with God (see *Nefesh HaHayyim*).

TRANSLATION AND COMMENTARY

וְאָמַר רַבִּי אַמִי [1]On the same theme, **Rabbi Ammi said: Come and see how great is** the power of **trustworthy people,** for God is induced to change the course of history in order to defend their interests. [2]**From where do we learn this? From the** popular legend of the **rat and the pit.** Once upon a time, a young man passed by a pit and heard a voice crying out for help. When he looked into the pit, he saw a young girl in distress. He said to her: "If I save you, will you marry me?" and she said: "Yes." After he rescued her from the pit, they swore to remain faithful to each other, calling on the pit that had brought them together to serve as one witness, and a passing rat to serve as the other. Time went by and the girl remained faithful to her oath, refusing all offers of marriage, but the young man broke his promise, married, and had a son. Shortly afterwards, a rat broke into his house and killed the baby in its crib. The man had another son, who fell into a pit and died. At this point, the man's wife became suspicious, and the story of the girl in distress came out. The wife insisted that her husband give her a divorce and seek out and marry that girl. Rabbi Ammi concludes with another insight into this story. The young man was punished and the girl was defended simply because of the power of trustworthiness. [3]**But if** people **who put their trust in a rat and a pit are so** treated by God, [4]**how much more so will someone who puts his trust** directly **in the Holy One blessed be He** be protected. Accordingly, when people call upon God to serve as their witness in a business transaction, they should know that He will be very exacting indeed if one of the parties abuses the other's trust.

אָמַר רַבִּי יוֹחָנָן [5]The Gemara now cites another interpretation of the verse just cited by Rabbi Ammi in connection with rain. **Rabbi Yoḥanan said: Whoever takes care to behave justly here on earth will be treated justly in Heaven,** [6]**as it is said** (Psalms 85:12): **"Truth will spring up from the earth, and righteousness will look down from heaven."** Rabbi Yoḥanan explains the word צֶדֶק literally as "justice" rather than "charity," as does Rabbi Ammi. According to Rabbi Yoḥanan, this verse reflects the idea that saintly people are often judged more severely by God than are ordinary people.

רַבִּי חִיָּיא בַּר אָבִין [7]**Rabbi Ḥiyya bar Avin said in the name of Rav Huna:** We learn the same idea **from here** (Psalms 90:11): [8]"Who knows the strength of your anger, **and according to the fear of You is Your**

[1]וְאָמַר רַבִּי אַמִי: בֹּא וּרְאֵה כַּמָּה גְּדוֹלִים בַּעֲלֵי אֲמָנָה. [2]מְנַיִין? מֵחוּלְדָּה וּבוֹר. [3]וּמַה הַמַּאֲמִין בְּחוּלְדָּה וּבוֹר כָּךְ, [4]הַמַּאֲמִין בְּהַקָּדוֹשׁ בָּרוּךְ הוּא עַל אַחַת כַּמָּה וְכַמָּה.

[5]אָמַר רַבִּי יוֹחָנָן: כָּל הַמַּצְדִּיק אֶת עַצְמוֹ מִלְּמַטָּה, מַצְדִּיקִין עָלָיו הַדִּין מִלְמַעְלָה, [6]שֶׁנֶּאֱמַר: "אֱמֶת מֵאֶרֶץ תִּצְמָח, וְצֶדֶק מִשָּׁמַיִם נִשְׁקָף".

[7]רַבִּי חִיָּיא בַּר אָבִין אָמַר רַב הוּנָא: מֵהָכָא: [8]"וּכְיִרְאָתְךָ עֶבְרָתֶךָ".

LITERAL TRANSLATION

[1]And Rabbi Ammi said: Come and see how great are trustworthy people. [2]From where [do we learn this]? [3]From [the case of] the rat and the pit. And if someone who puts his trust in a rat and a pit is [treated] so, [4]someone who puts his trust in the Holy One blessed be He how much more so.

[5]Rabbi Yoḥanan said: Whoever makes himself just below, his judgment is made just above, [6]as it is said: "Truth will spring up from the earth, and righteousness will look down from heaven."

[7]Rabbi Ḥiyya bar Avin said in the name of Rav Huna: From here: [8]"And according to the fear of You is Your wrath."

RASHI

מחולדה ובור — שהמיתו שני בני אדם. מצוי הוא באגדה: מעשה בבחור אחד שנתן אמונתו לריבה אחת שישאנה. אמרה: מי מעיד? והיה שם בור אחד וחולדה, אמר הבחור: בור וחולדה עדים בדבר. לימים עבר על אמונתו ונשא אחרת, והוליד שני בנים. אחד נפל לבור ומת, ואחד נשכתו חולדה ומת. אמרה לו אשתו: מה מעשה הוא זה שבנינו מתים במיתה משונה? ואמר לה: כך וכך היה המעשה. **המאמין בהקדוש ברוך הוא** — שמשימו עד בינו לבין חבירו — על אחת כמה וכמה. **המצדיק עצמו** — שמכשיר ומקשט מעשיו. **מצדיקין עליו** — מדקדקין עמו אפילו כחוט השערה, יותר משאילו מקלקל מעשיו כדי למרק עונותיו. **שנאמר אמת מארץ תצמח** — אז "צדק משמים נשקף", "צדקה" אין כתיב כאן, אלא "צדק" — דמשמע דין. **וכיראתך עברתך** — על מי שהוא ירא אותך אתה מחזיק עברתך, כדי למרק עונותיו. ופשט המקרא: "מי יודע עוז אפך" — מי יודע עוז וכח למלוא אותו לנוס מפניך ביום אפך, "וכיראתך עברתך" — כשם שאתה יראוי ומפוחד כך יש להתיירא ולהתפחד מעברתך.

BACKGROUND

כָּל הַמַּצְדִּיק אֶת עַצְמוֹ מִלְּמַטָּה Whoever makes himself just below. The idea presented here in various ways appears in many teachings of the Sages, both in interpretations of other verses and also in explicit statements. As a general rule, greatness and righteousness do not exempt a person from his duties or from the judgment of Heaven. On the contrary, the greater and more pious the person, the more is demanded of him, and the more severe is the punishment for his misdeeds.

SAGES

רַבִּי חִיָּיא בַּר אָבִין Rabbi Ḥiyya bar Avin. The son of Avin Nagara and the brother of Rav Idi bar Avin, Rabbi Ḥiyya bar Avin was a Babylonian Amora of the third and fourth generations. He was the student of Rav Huna in Babylonia and served as רֹאשׁ כַּלָּה — director of study sessions — in his yeshivah. He received the teachings of Rav and Shmuel from Rav Huna. He is found in Halakhic discussions with the Sages of his generation: Rav Yehudah, Rav Naḥman, Rav Ḥisda, Rav Sheshet, Rav Yosef, and others. He immigrated to Eretz Israel and studied in Rabbi Elazar's yeshivah in Tiberias. He debated with Rabbi Zera and Rabbi Assi. In his old age he returned to Babylonia.

רַב הוּנָא Rav Huna. One of the greatest Babylonian Amoraim of the second generation, Rav Huna was most closely associated with his teacher, Rav. Rav Huna was of aristocratic descent, and belonged to the House of the Exilarchs. For many years, however, he lived in great poverty. Later he became wealthy and lived in comfort, distributing his money for the public good.
Rav Huna was the greatest of Rav's students, so much so that Shmuel, Rav's colleague, used to treat him with honor and direct questions to him. After Rav's death Rav Huna became the head of the yeshivah of Sura and occupied that position for about forty years. His eminence in Torah and his loftiness of character helped make the Sura Yeshivah the preeminent center for many centuries. Because of Rav Huna's great knowledge

NOTES

מֵחוּלְדָּה וּבוֹר From the case of the rat and the pit. Rabbi Ammi alludes to a story about a rat and a pit, without elaborating on any of its details. Apparently the story was well known in Talmudic times, and did not require to be retold. The story, which is briefly summarized by *Rashi* and *Tosafot,* is cited by *Arukh* in a much fuller version, which seems to be based on a tradition received from the Geonim.

כָּל הַמַּצְדִּיק אֶת עַצְמוֹ מִלְּמַטָּה Whoever makes himself just below. According to *Rashi* and *Shittah,* a person who

TRANSLATION AND COMMENTARY

wrath." According to its plain meaning, the verse is teaching us that people are unable to bear God's anger and are frightened by it. But Rabbi Ḥiyya bar Avin interprets the last part of this verse as saying that God's anger appears where His fear appears. In other words, God sometimes appears angry toward those who fear Him, and the reason is that he requires a higher standard from them.

רֵישׁ לָקִישׁ אָמַר [1]**Resh Lakish said:** We can learn this idea **from** the plain meaning of the following verse (Isaiah 64:4): [2]**"You have struck down him who rejoiced at doing justice; they will remember You in Your ways; behold You were angry when we sinned; we will be saved by them in the world to come."** This verse tells us that God displays anger specifically toward righteous people, who are held by Him to a higher standard.

אָמַר רַבִּי יְהוֹשֻׁעַ בֶּן לֵוִי [3]The Gemara cites another insight into this latter verse by quoting **Rabbi Yehoshua ben Levi,** who **said: Whoever rejoices in the sufferings that come upon him brings salvation to the world,** [4]**as it is said: "We will be always saved by them in the world to come."** According to Rabbi Yehoshua ben Levi, the verse means that those who continue to rejoice and do justice, even when God strikes them down, bring about the salvation of the world.

אָמַר רֵישׁ לָקִישׁ [5]The Gemara now returns to figurative interpretations of verses dealing with rain. **Resh Lakish said: What is the meaning of what is written** in the following verse (Deuteronomy 11:17): [6]"And the anger of the Lord will be kindled against you, **and He will shut up the heavens,** and there will be no rain"? Rain falling from the heavens is often compared by Scripture to a woman giving birth, and Resh Lakish argues that this verse also employs this metaphor. [7]**When the heavens are prevented from bringing down dew and rain, it is like a woman who is in labor, but does not give birth.** For the Hebrew word עָצַר, which we have translated as "He will shut up," is also used to describe a woman who cannot give birth. [8]The Gemara adds that the idea behind **this** statement of Resh Lakish **is the same as** the idea behind the following statement **that Resh Lakish made in the name of Bar Kappara:** We see many linguistic parallels between rain and childbirth in Scripture. [9]The expression **"shutting up" appears** in Scripture **in connection with rain, and** the same expression **"shutting up" appears** in Scripture **in connection with a woman** giving birth.

[1]רֵישׁ לָקִישׁ אָמַר: מֵהָכָא: [2]״פָּגַעְתָּ אֶת שָׂשׂ וְעֹשֵׂה צֶדֶק; בִּדְרָכֶיךָ יִזְכְּרוּךָ; הֵן אַתָּה קָצַפְתָּ וַנֶּחֱטָא; בָּהֶם עוֹלָם וְנִוָּשֵׁעַ״. [3]אָמַר רַבִּי יְהוֹשֻׁעַ בֶּן לֵוִי: כָּל הַשָּׂמֵחַ בְּיִסּוּרִין שֶׁבָּאִין עָלָיו מֵבִיא יְשׁוּעָה לָעוֹלָם, [4]שֶׁנֶּאֱמַר: ״בָּהֶם עוֹלָם וְנִוָּשֵׁעַ״. [5]אָמַר רֵישׁ לָקִישׁ: מַאי דִּכְתִיב: [6]״וְעָצַר אֶת הַשָּׁמַיִם״? [7]בְּשָׁעָה שֶׁהַשָּׁמַיִם נֶעֱצָרִין מִלְּהוֹרִיד טַל וּמָטָר, דּוֹמֶה לְאִשָּׁה שֶׁמְּחַבֶּלֶת וְאֵינָהּ יוֹלֶדֶת. [8]וְהַיְינוּ דְּאָמַר רֵישׁ לָקִישׁ מִשּׁוּם בַּר קַפָּרָא: [9]נֶאֶמְרָה עֲצִירָה בִּגְשָׁמִים וְנֶאֶמְרָה עֲצִירָה בְּאִשָּׁה.

LITERAL TRANSLATION

[1]Resh Lakish said: From here: [2]"You have struck down him who rejoiced at doing justice; they will remember You in Your ways; behold You were angry when we sinned; we will be saved by them in the world to come."

[3]Rabbi Yehoshua ben Levi said: Whoever rejoices in the sufferings that come upon him brings salvation to the world, [4]as it is said: "We will be always saved by them in the world to come."

[5]Resh Lakish said: What is [the meaning of] what is written: [6]"And he will shut up the heavens"? [7]At a time when the heavens are shut from bringing down dew and rain, it is like a woman who is in labor but does not give birth. [8]And this is the same as what Resh Lakish said in the name of Bar Kappara: [9]"Shutting up" is said about rains, and "shutting up" is said about a woman.

RASHI

פגעת את שש ועושה צדק — כמי ששמח, ו״עושה לדק״, שהן העושים כך — ״בדרכיך״ — יזכירוך, אתה פוגע בו אם חוטא כלום, כמו ״ויפגע בו וימת״. קרא הכי הוא: ״פגעת את שש ועושה לדק״ — והן העושין כך — ״בדרכיך יזכירוך״, באותם דרכים שאתה מייסרן ביסורין יזכירוך לטובה, ואומרים הן: אתה קלפת בשביל שחטאנו, ״בהם עולם ונושע״ — בשבילם נושע לעולם הבא. **שחובלת** — כמו חבלי יולדה, אף השמים עושין כן, וקשה לעולם. ועל חטא הוא.

of Torah, the Halakhah is almost always decided according to his view against all his colleagues and the other members of his generation (except in monetary matters, where Rav Naḥman's views are followed).
Rav Huna had many students, some of whom received their Torah knowledge directly from him; moreover, Rav's younger students continued to study with Rav Huna, his disciple. Rav Huna's son, Rabbah bar Rav Huna, was one of the greatest Sages of the next generation.

NOTES

makes great efforts to act justly and righteously will be treated by God with exacting justice. Such a person will be punished in this world for even the slightest infractions, so that he will be entirely cleansed and ready to receive his full reward in the World to Come. Others explain Rabbi Yoḥanan's statement in the opposite manner: A person who acts in a particularly saintly manner in this world will be treated by God with special compassion and charity (*Rabbenu Elyakim*).

[8B] [1]נֶאֶמְרָה ״עֲצִירָה״ בְּאִשָּׁה, [2]שֶׁנֶּאֱמַר: ״כִּי עָצֹר עָצַר ה׳ בְּעַד כָּל רֶחֶם״. [3]וְנֶאֶמְרָה ״עֲצִירָה״ בִּגְשָׁמִים, [4]דִּכְתִיב: ״וְעָצַר אֶת הַשָּׁמַיִם״.
[5]נֶאֱמַר ״לֵידָה״ בְּאִשָּׁה וְנֶאֱמַר ״לֵידָה״ בִּגְשָׁמִים. [6]נֶאֱמַר ״לֵידָה״ בְּאִשָּׁה, [7]דִּכְתִיב: ״וַתַּהַר וַתֵּלֶד בֵּן״. [8]וְנֶאֱמַר ״לֵידָה״ בִּגְשָׁמִים [9]דִּכְתִיב: ״וְהוֹלִידָהּ, וְהִצְמִיחָהּ״.
[10]נֶאֱמַר ״פְּקִידָה״ בְּאִשָּׁה, וְנֶאֱמַר ״פְּקִידָה״ בִּגְשָׁמִים. [11]נֶאֱמַר ״פְּקִידָה״ בְּאִשָּׁה, [12]דִּכְתִיב: ״וַה׳ פָּקַד אֶת שָׂרָה״. [13]וְנֶאֱמַר ״פְּקִידָה״ בִּגְשָׁמִים, [14]דִּכְתִיב: ״פָּקַדְתָּ הָאָרֶץ וַתְּשֹׁקְקֶהָ; רַבַּת תַּעְשְׁרֶנָּה פֶּלֶג אֱלֹהִים מָלֵא מָיִם״.
[15]מַאי: ״פֶּלֶג אֱלֹהִים מָלֵא מָיִם״?
[16]תָּנָא: ״כְּמִין קוּבָּה יֵשׁ בָּרָקִיעַ, שֶׁמִּמֶּנָּה גְּשָׁמִים יוֹצְאִין.
[17]אָמַר רַבִּי שְׁמוּאֵל בַּר נַחְמָנִי: [18]מַאי דִּכְתִיב: ״אִם לְשֵׁבֶט, אִם לְאַרְצוֹ, אִם לְחֶסֶד, יַמְצִאֵהוּ״?

LITERAL TRANSLATION

[8B] [1]"Shutting up" is said about a woman, [2]as it is said: "For the Lord had surely shut up every womb." [3]And "shutting up" is said about rain, [4]as it is written: "And He will shut up the heavens."

[5]"Giving birth" is said about a woman, and "giving birth" is said about rain. [6]"Giving birth" is said about a woman, [7]as it is written: "And she conceived and gave birth to a son." [8]And "giving birth" is said about rain, [9]as it is written: "And causes it to give birth, and causes it to bud."

[10]"Remembering" is said about a woman, and "remembering" is said about rain. [11]"Remembering" is said about a woman, [12]as it is written: "And the Lord remembered Sarah." [13]And "remembering" is said about rain, [14]as it is written: "You have remembered the earth and You have watered it; You have greatly enriched it, from the river of God which is full of water."

[15]What is [the meaning of]: "The river of God which is full of water"?

[16][A Tanna] taught: "There is a kind of vault in the sky, from which rains come out."

[17]Rabbi Shmuel bar Naḥmani said: [18]What is [the meaning of] what is written: "If for a rod, if for His land, if for kindness, He will cause it to come"?

TRANSLATION AND COMMENTARY

נֶאֶמְרָה ״עֲצִירָה״ בְּאִשָּׁה [8B] [1]The expression **"shutting up" appears** in Scripture **in connection with a woman** giving birth, [2]**as it is said** (Genesis 20:18): **"For the Lord had surely shut up every womb."** [3]**And** the same expression **"shutting up" appears in connection with rain,** [4]**as it is written** (Deuteronomy 11:17): **"And He will shut up the heavens,** and there will be no rain."

נֶאֱמַר ״לֵידָה״ בְּאִשָּׁה [5]There is another linguistic parallel. The expression **"giving birth" appears** in Scripture **in connection with a woman, and** the same expression **"giving birth" appears in connection with rain.** [6]The expression **"giving birth" appears in connection with a woman,** [7]**as it is written** (Genesis 30:23): **"And she conceived and gave birth to a son."** [8]**And** the same expression **"giving birth" appears in connection with rain,** [9]**as it is written** (Isaiah 55:10): **"And causes it to give birth, and causes it to bud."**

נֶאֱמַר ״פְּקִידָה״ בְּאִשָּׁה [10]There is another linguistic parallel. The expression **"remembering" appears** in Scripture **in connection with a woman** giving birth, **and** the same expression **"remembering" appears in connection with rain.** [11]The expression **"remembering" appears in connection with a woman** giving birth, [12]**as it is written** (Genesis 21:1): **"And the Lord remembered Sarah."** [13]**And** the same expression **"remembering"** appears in connection **with rain,** [14]**as it is written** (Psalms 65:10): **"You have remembered the earth and You have watered it; You have greatly enriched it, from the river of God which is full of water."**

מַאי [15]Having mentioned this verse from Psalms, the Gemara asks: **What is** the meaning of the expression in the middle of this verse: **"From the river of God which is full of water"?**

תָּנָא [16]The Gemara answers that **it was taught** in a Baraita: **"There is a kind of vault in the sky, from which rain comes out,** and this is the 'river of God' to which the verse refers."

אָמַר רַבִּי שְׁמוּאֵל בַּר נַחְמָנִי [17]The Gemara concludes this series of figurative interpretations of verses with a statement by **Rabbi Shmuel bar Naḥmani,** who **said: What is the meaning of what is written** in the following verse (Job 37:13): [18]**"If for a rod** [i.e., as a punishment], **if for His land, if for kindness, He will cause it to come"?** This verse belongs to a passage dealing with the manifestation of God's greatness in rain, teaching us that rain can sometimes come as a punishment, it can sometimes come in the normal quantities

RASHI

נאמרה עצירה באשה כו׳ – כלומר, על כולן מבקשים רחמים. **פלג** – בריכה. **כמין קובה** – אהל מלא מים. **אם לשבט** – אם גזר הקדוש ברוך הוא רוב גשמים לרעה – אז יורדים בכח, כשבט שמכה בכח. וחזרו בתשובה – הקדוש ברוך הוא מורידן על הרים וגבעות, מקום שאין שם איש. **אבל אם לחסד** – שיורדין בנחת – ״ימציאהו״, ״לארצו״, לארץ ישראל.

BACKGROUND

נֶאֶמְרָה ״עֲצִירָה״ בְּאִשָּׁה "Shutting up" is said about a woman. Some commentators explain that just as when a woman's womb is blocked, this causes pain to her and to her child, so too does the withholding of rain cause "torments" to Heaven and Earth. Just as giving birth, despite the pain involved, brings relief to the woman, so too does rainfall bring relief to Heaven and Earth. (*Riaf*).

LANGUAGE

קוּבָּה Vault. This word in Mishnaic Hebrew means a small house or a tent. There is a similar word in Arabic قبة . Some authorities believe that both the Hebrew and the Arabic words are borrowed from the Latin word *cuppa,* which has the same meaning.

TRANSLATION AND COMMENTARY

anticipated in God's land, or it can fall in an extraordinarily kindly way, beyond the normal anticipated amounts. But Rabbi Shmuel bar Naḥmani explains this verse in a figurative way as referring only to blessings: [1]**"If for a rod,"** if it has been decreed that the rain will fall with such fury as to be seen as a punishment and cause the people to repent of their misdeeds, then **it falls only on the mountains and on the hills,** where torrential rainfall does little harm, and may even be beneficial. [2]**"If for kindness,"** if the rain falls in a kindly way, **"He will cause it to come for His land"** and the kindly rain **will fall** on Eretz Israel, and especially **on the fields and on the vineyards,** where it is needed most. [3]**"If for a rod,"** if the rain falls with such fury that it would ordinarily be seen as a punishment, **it will fall** only **on the trees,** which benefit from heavy rain. [4]**"If for His land,"** if the rain falls in the normal way that is appropriate for the land, **it will fall on the seeds,** which benefit from moderate rainfall. [5]And **"if for kindness He will cause it to come,"** if there is an extraordinarily good, rainy year, the excess rain will run off into the **pits, ditches and caves** where water is stored for the dry season.

בִּימֵי רַבִּי שְׁמוּאֵל בַּר נַחְמָנִי [6]The Gemara relates that **in the days of Rabbi Shmuel bar Naḥmani there was a famine and a plague** at the same time, and the people gathered together to pray for mercy. [7]Some Sages **said: What shall we do?** [8]**Shall we ask for mercy for both** the famine and the plague? Such a prayer **is impossible.** [9]**Rather, let us ask for mercy concerning the plague,** which is the more severe threat, **and let us bear the famine** patiently. [10]But **Rabbi Shmuel bar Naḥmani** disagreed and **said to them: Let us ask for mercy concerning the famine, for when God gives plenty, He does so in order to help the living,** [11]**as it is written** (Psalms 145:16): **"You open Your hand and satisfy the desire of every living thing."** Therefore, if we are successful in our prayers regarding the famine, God will end the plague as well.

וּמְנָלַן [12]The Gemara asks: **But from where do we know that we may not pray for two things** at the same time?

דִּכְתִיב [13]The Gemara answers that we can infer this from a verse. **For it is written** (Ezra 8:23): **"And we**

[1]״אִם לְשֵׁבֶט״, בֶּהָרִים וּבִגְבָעוֹת. [2]״אִם לְחֶסֶד יַמְצִאֵהוּ לְאַרְצוֹ״, בְּשָׂדוֹת וּבִכְרָמִים. [3]״אִם לְשֵׁבֶט״, לְאִילָנוֹת. [4]״אִם לְאַרְצוֹ״, לִזְרָעִים. [5]״אִם לְחֶסֶד יַמְצִאֵהוּ״, בּוֹרוֹת, שִׁיחִין, וּמְעָרוֹת.

[6]בִּימֵי רַבִּי שְׁמוּאֵל בַּר נַחְמָנִי הֲוָה כַּפְנָא וּמוֹתָנָא. [7]אָמְרִי: הֵיכִי נַעֲבֵיד? [8]נִיבָּעֵי רַחֲמֵי אַתַּרְתֵּי? לָא אֶפְשָׁר. [9]אֶלָּא, לִיבָּעֵי רַחֲמֵי אַמּוֹתָנָא, וְכַפְנָא נִיסְבּוֹל. [10]אֲמַר לְהוּ רַבִּי שְׁמוּאֵל בַּר נַחְמָנִי: נִיבָּעֵי רַחֲמֵי אַכַּפְנָא, דְּכִי יָהֵיב רַחֲמָנָא שׂוֹבְעָא, לְחַיֵּי הוּא דְּיָהֵיב, [11]דִּכְתִיב: ״פּוֹתֵחַ אֶת יָדֶךָ וּמַשְׂבִּיעַ לְכָל חַי רָצוֹן״.

[12]וּמְנָלַן דְּלָא מְצַלֵּינַן אַתַּרְתֵּי? [13]דִּכְתִיב: ״וַנָּצוּמָה וַנְּבַקְשָׁה

LITERAL TRANSLATION

[1]"If for a rod," [it falls] on the mountains and on the hills. [2]"If for kindness He will cause it for His land," [it falls] on the fields and on the vineyards. [3]"If for a rod," it is for the trees. [4]"If for His land," it is for the seeds. [5]"If for kindness He will cause it to come," [it is for] pits, ditches, and caves.

[6]In the days of Rabbi Shmuel bar Naḥmani there was a famine and a plague. [7]They said: What shall we do? [8]Shall we ask for mercy for both [things]? That is impossible. [9]Rather, let us ask for mercy for the plague, and let us bear the famine. [10]Rabbi Shmuel bar Naḥmani said to them: Let us ask for mercy for the famine, for when the Merciful One gives plenty, it is for the living that he gives [it], [11]as it is written: "You open Your hand and satisfy the desire of every living thing."

[12]And from where [do we know] that we do not pray for two [things]? [13]For it is written: "And we fasted and begged

RASHI

אתרתי — לא בעינן רחמי אהדדי, כדלקמן. נבעי רחמי אכפנא — דליתיה שובעא, ומותנא ליבטל ממילא. דכי יהיב רחמנא שובעא לחיי הוא דיהיב — לחיים ולא למתים, דאינו מביא שובעא כדי להמית בני אדם, אלא כדי שיחיו. משביע לכל חי רצון — שובע נותן לבני אדם חיים.

LANGUAGE

בּוֹרוֹת, שִׁיחִין, וּמְעָרוֹת Pits, ditches, and caves. All these terms refer to essentially the same thing — an excavation in the earth for use as a container (generally to hold water). But there are technical differences between these terms (and other terms in the same context): A pit (בּוֹר) is an excavation in the earth with a round opening. A ditch (שִׁיחַ) is long, narrow, and rectangular; while a cave (מְעָרָה) is covered by a roof of sorts.

SAGES

רַבִּי שְׁמוּאֵל בַּר נַחְמָנִי Rabbi Shmuel bar Naḥmani. A Palestinian Amora of the second and third generations, Rabbi Shmuel bar Naḥmani was an important teacher of the Aggadah. He was a disciple of Rabbi Yonatan and transmitted many teachings in his name. He also studied with Rabbi Yehoshua ben Levi. He lived in Lydda in central Palestine.

HALAKHAH

דְּלָא מְצַלֵּינַן אַתַּרְתֵּי That we do not pray for two things. "If a community is suffering from two afflictions, it should petition for mercy for the alleviation of only one of them. Those who pray should say: 'Even though we suffer from many afflictions, it is only with respect to this one affliction that we pray before You.' If the community suffers from famine and plague, it should petition for mercy regarding the famine. For if God answers the people's prayers, He will provide them with food that will restore them to good health." (*Shulḥan Arukh, Oraḥ Ḥayyim* 576:15.)

SAGES

רַבִּי חַגַּי Rabbi Ḥaggai. An Amora of the third and fourth generation, Rabbi Ḥaggai was born in Babylonia, and in his youth he was a student of Rav Huna. He immigrated to Eretz Israel and studied with the senior students of Rabbi Yoḥanan. He is said to have lived a long life, and it was he who brought the coffin of Rav Huna, his teacher, for burial in the cave where the great Amora, Rabbi Ḥiyya, was buried.

Many of the Amoraim of the following generation were his students. His teachings and stories about him are mainly mentioned in the Jerusalem Talmud, for he spent most of his long life in Eretz Israel, but he is also referred to in several places in the Babylonian Talmud.

TRANSLATION AND COMMENTARY

fasted and begged our God for *this*, and He granted it to us." In this verse Ezra relates that he took the Jews returning from Babylonia back to Eretz Israel without any military protection, in order to demonstrate to the non-Jews that he relied on God alone, and he asked the entire congregation to pray to God that no harm befall them on the journey. [1]The Gemara explains that Ezra's use of the word "this" **implies that there was another trouble** for deliverance from which he did not ask the people to fast and pray.

בְּמַעַרְבָא אָמְרִי [2]**In the West,** in Eretz Israel, **they said in the name of Rabbi Ḥaggai that** this idea **comes from** the following verse (Daniel 2:18): **"And to ask for mercy from the God of heaven concerning *this* secret,** so that Daniel and his companions should not perish with the rest of the wise men of Babylonia." The Book of Daniel relates that King Nebuchadnezzar had a frightening dream whose content he forgot. He demanded that his wise men tell him his dream and interpret it for him. When they could not do so, he ordered all the wise men of Babylonia, including Daniel and his three friends, to be killed. But Daniel prayed to God, who revealed the dream and its interpretation to him. [3]The Gemara explains that Daniel's use of the word "this" in this verse **implies that there was another** trouble for deliverance from which he did not pray.

[1]מֵאֱלֹהֵינוּ עַל זֹאת״. [1]מִכְּלָל דְּאִיכָּא אַחֲרִיתֵי.
[2]בְּמַעַרְבָא אָמְרִי מִשְּׁמֵיהּ דְּרַבִּי חַגַּי מֵהָכָא: ״וְרַחֲמִין לְמִבְעֵא מִן קֳדָם אֱלָהּ שְׁמַיָּא עַל רָזָא דְנָה״. [3]מִכְּלָל דְּאִיכָּא אַחֲרִיתֵי.
[4]בִּימֵי רַבִּי זֵירָא, גְּזוּר שְׁמָדָא, [5]וּגְזוּר דְּלָא לְמֵיתַב בְּתַעֲנִיתָא. [6]אֲמַר לְהוּ רַבִּי זֵירָא: נְקַבְּלֵיהּ עִילָּוָון, [7]וּלְכִי בָּטֵיל שְׁמָדָא, לֵיתְבֵיהּ. [8]אָמְרִי לֵיהּ: מְנָא לָךְ הָא? [9]אֲמַר לְהוּ: דִּכְתִיב: [10]״וַיֹּאמֶר אֵלַי: אַל תִּירָא, דָּנִיֵּאל, כִּי מִן הַיּוֹם הָרִאשׁוֹן אֲשֶׁר נָתַתָּ אֶת לִבְּךָ לְהָבִין, וּלְהִתְעַנּוֹת לִפְנֵי אֱלֹהֶיךָ נִשְׁמְעוּ דְבָרֶיךָ״.
[11]אָמַר רַבִּי יִצְחָק: אֲפִילּוּ שָׁנִים

LITERAL TRANSLATION

our God for *this*." [1][This proves] by implication that there was another [trouble].

[2]In the West, they said in the name of Rabbi Ḥaggai [that it comes] from here: "And to ask for mercy from the God of heaven concerning this secret." [3][This proves] by implication that there was another.

[4]In the days of Rabbi Zera, they decreed religious persecution, [5]and they decreed not to sit in a fast. [6]Rabbi Zera said to them: Let us accept it [the fast] upon us, [7]and when the religious persecution is annulled, we will sit [to observe] it. [8]They said to him: From where do you know this? [9]He said to them: For it is written: [10]"And he said to me: Do not fear, Daniel, for from the first day that you set your heart to understand, and to fast before your God, your words were heard."

[11]Rabbi Yitzḥak said: Even [in] years

RASHI

על זאת — על חדא משמע, בעזרא כתיב. **על רזא דנא** — בדניאל כתיב. **דלא ליתבו בתעניתא** — דלא בעו דליתי ברכה לעולם בשבילן. **ניקבל עילוון** — יומי תעניתא, דמשום קבלה מהני לן כתעניתא, וכי בטיל גזרה — עבדין להו. **ומנלן דעבדינן הכי** — כלומר, דמהני אי עבדינן הכי. **אשר נתת לבך להתענות לפני אלהיך נשמעו דבריך** — אלמא: משקיבל עליו נשמעו דבריו.

בִּימֵי רַבִּי זֵירָא [4]In a similar vein, the Gemara relates that **in the days of Rabbi Zera** the Roman government **decreed religious persecution** upon the Jews. [5]In particular, they **decreed** that the Jews were **not** allowed **to fast** to pray for the annulment of the persecution. The usual Jewish response to such persecutions was to pray to God that the evil decree would pass away. But in this case the evil decree was aimed precisely against fasting and prayer, and the people were afraid to fast, lest the Roman government harm them. [6]But **Rabbi Zera said to them: Let us take a fast upon ourselves** without specifying a time for it, [7]**and** later, **when the religious persecution is annulled, we will observe it** by fasting. [8]**They said to him: From where do you know** that **this** is the proper way to proceed? [9]**He said to them:** I know this **from what is written** in the following verse (Daniel 10:12): [10]**"And he said to me: Do not fear, Daniel, for from the first day that you set your heart to understand, and to fast before your God, your words were heard."** Thus we see that the prayers of a person who commits himself to fast are heard even before he actually fasts.

אָמַר רַבִּי יִצְחָק [11]The Gemara now considers some other aspects of rain. **Rabbi Yitzḥak said: Even in years**

HALAKHAH

נְקַבְּלֵיהּ עִילָּוָון **Let us accept the fast upon us.** "If a city is surrounded by a hostile army, or if a single individual is being pursued by enemies, fasting is not permitted, for people under threat must preserve their strength. Rather, they should take it upon themselves to observe a number of fasts after they are no longer in danger," following Rabbi Zera. (*Shulḥan Arukh, Oraḥ Ḥayyim* 571:3.)

כִּשְׁנֵי אֵלִיָּהוּ, [1]וְיָרְדוּ גְּשָׁמִים בְּעַרְבֵי שַׁבָּתוֹת, אֵינָן אֶלָּא סִימַן קְלָלָה.

[2]הַיְינוּ דְּאָמַר רַבָּה בַּר שֵׁילָא: קָשֶׁה יוֹמָא דְּמִיטְרָא כְּיוֹמָא דְּדִינָא.

[3]אֲמַר אַמֵימָר: אִי לָא דִּצְרִיךְ לִבְרִיָּיתָא, [4]בָּעֵינַן רַחֲמֵי וּמְבַטְּלִינַן לֵיהּ.

[5]וְאָמַר רַבִּי יִצְחָק: שֶׁמֶשׁ בְּשַׁבָּת צְדָקָה לַעֲנִיִּים, [6]שֶׁנֶּאֱמַר: "וְזָרְחָה לָכֶם יִרְאֵי שְׁמִי שֶׁמֶשׁ צְדָקָה וּמַרְפֵּא".

[7]וְאָמַר רַבִּי יִצְחָק: גָּדוֹל יוֹם הַגְּשָׁמִים, שֶׁאֲפִילּוּ פְּרוּטָה

LITERAL TRANSLATION

like the years of Elijah, [1]if rains fall on the eves of Sabbaths, it is nothing but a sign of a curse.

[2]This is the same as what Rabbah bar Shela said: A rainy day is as hard as a day of judgment.

[3]Amemar said: Were it not that [rain] is necessary for mankind, [4]we would ask for mercy and annul it.

[5]And Rabbi Yitzḥak said: Sun on Shabbat is charity for the poor, [6]as it is said: "But for you who fear My name a charitable sun will shine with healing [in its wings]."

[7]And Rabbi Yitzḥak said: The day of rains is great, for even

TRANSLATION AND COMMENTARY

like the years of Elijah, when there was a prolonged drought and the people were desperate for rain (see I Kings 17:1), [1]**if rain falls on a Friday, it is nothing but a sign of a curse,** because it disrupts the preparations for Shabbat.

הַיְינוּ [2]The Gemara notes that the idea behind **this** statement **is the same as the idea expressed by Rabbah bar Shela** in the following statement: **A rainy day is as hard as a day of judgment.** Court appearances are inevitably unpleasant and disruptive, just like rainy days.

אֲמַר אַמֵימָר [3]**Amemar said: Were it not** for the fact **that rain is needed by mankind** in order to live, [4]**we would ask** God **for mercy and annul it** altogether, for although rain is indispensable for life, it is inconvenient and disruptive.

וְאָמַר רַבִּי יִצְחָק [5]**And Rabbi Yitzḥak said: Sunny weather on Shabbat is** God's way of giving **charity to the poor,** who benefit from its warmth, [6]**as it is said** (Malachi 3:20): **"But for you who fear My name a charitable sun will shine with healing in its wings,"** and the expression "you who fear my name" is traditionally interpreted as referring to those who observe Shabbat.

וְאָמַר רַבִּי יִצְחָק [7]On the other hand, rain is still a great blessing, as **Rabbi Yitzḥak said: The day of rain is great, for even a coin in the pocket is blessed**

RASHI

כשני אליהו — בימי אחאב, שהיה העולם צריך לגשמים, דכתיב (מלכים א יז) "אם יהיה השנים האלה טל ומטר כי אם לפי דברי". **סימן קללה** — שבני אדם צריכים לחזר בשוק לקנות סעודת שבת. **קשי יומי דמיטרא** — שאין בני אדם יכולין לעשות צרכיהן. **כיומא דדינא** — שני וחמישי, שמתקבצין בני אדם לדון עם חבריהן, כתקנת עזרא. שיש הומות וקולות ואוושות ביום הגשמים כיום הדין. ובערב שבת כל שכן דקשי מיטרא. **והיינו** — דאמר רבי שילא. **ומבטלינהו לירידת גשמים** — שטורחין בני אדם, ואין יכולין לצאת ולבא. **צדקה לעניים** — שמתעדנין בה, ונוח להן יום ברור, ומתחממין בה ביום הצינה. **יראי שמי** — שומרי שבת.

SAGES

רַבָּה בַּר שֵׁילָא **Rabbah bar Shela.** A Babylonian Amora of the third and fourth generations, Rabbah bar Shela was a disciple of Rav Ḥisda, whose teachings he cites. He seems to have lived near Meḥoza, and is usually associated with Rava, who came from Meḥoza. Rabbah bar Shela apparently served as a Rabbinical judge where he lived, and he may have had a small academy of his own there.

אַמֵימָר **Amemar.** One of the greatest Babylonian Amoraim of the fifth and sixth generations, Amemar was born in Neharde'a and was one of its chief Sages. He studied under Rav Zevid and Rav Dimi of Neharde'a, and also with the elders of Pumbedita. He cites the teachings of Rava, Rav Pappa, and others. He was the head of the yeshivah in his city. On several occasions he is found in the company of Mar Zutra and Rav Ashi. Rav Aḥa bar Rava and Rav Gamda were among his most prominent students. He also had a son who was a Sage known as Mar.

NOTES

כְּיוֹמָא דְּדִינָא **As a day of judgment.** According to the standard text of the Talmud, Rabbah bar Shela states that a rainy day is as difficult *as* a day of judgment. *Rashi* explains that people's ordinary activities can be disrupted by rain, just as they can be disrupted by the noise and tumult emanating from the courthouses on Mondays and Thursdays when the courts are in session. All the more so is rain disruptive on Fridays, when preparations for Shabbat must be made.

Maharsha suggests that the text be slightly emended so that it reads: בְּיוֹמָא דְּדִינָא — "*on* a day of judgment." Thus Rabbah bar Shelah is saying that rain causes people difficulty if it falls on a Monday or a Thursday, the days on which the courts are in session, for on rainy days it is difficult for villagers to appear in the courts, which are found only in the larger towns. All the more so is it difficult for people to conclude their Shabbat preparations if it rains on Friday.

שֶׁמֶשׁ בְּשַׁבָּת צְדָקָה לַעֲנִיִּים **Sun on Shabbat is charity for the poor.** Some commentators suggest that it is the poor who are especially in need of sunny weather on Shabbat, for they often do not have warm clothing that is fit for wearing on Shabbat, and they cannot keep themselves warm on Shabbat by engaging in physical labor (*Shittah*). Others explain that the poor suffer from intestinal pains on Shabbat, because they change their dietary habits on that day and eat much more than they do during the rest of the week, and are therefore in particular need of the healing power of sunny weather (*Iyyun Ya'akov* and others).

The proof text cited by Rabbi Yitzḥak poses a certain difficulty, for nowhere in the verse is Shabbat mentioned. *Rashi* explains that "you who fear My name" is an allusion to those who observe Shabbat. Others point out that the verse in Malachi quoted by Rabbi Yitzḥak is based on the following verse in Isaiah (56:6): "Also the sons of the stranger, that join themselves to the Lord to serve Him and to love the name of the Lord, to be His servants, every one that keeps the Sabbath and does not profane it, and take hold of My covenant," which implies that the proper observance of Shabbat is an essential feature of the fear of God (*Riaf*).

TRANSLATION AND COMMENTARY

on it. Business dealings are especially successful on a rainy day, even though there is no direct natural connection between the rain and the business, [1]**as it is said** (Deuteronomy 28:12): "The Lord will open for you His good treasure house, the heavens, **to give the rain of your land in its time and to bless all the work of your hand,** and you will lend to many nations, and you will not need to borrow." Thus we see that the blessing of rain applies to monetary transactions, as well as to agriculture.

וְאָמַר רַבִּי יִצְחָק [2]In his previous statement, Rabbi Yitzḥak referred to the blessing of rain extending to a "coin in the pocket." This is explained by the following statement of the same Sage, who **said: God's special blessing is found only in a thing that is hidden from the eye** — in something unseen and unpredictable — [3]**as it is said** (Deuteronomy 28:8): **"The Lord will command His blessing upon you in your storehouses."** Rabbi Yitzḥak is making a play on the word "storehouses" (אֲסָמֶיךָ), as if the word meant "hidden things," from the root סמה — "to hide." Thus we see that God's blessing falls only on hidden things.

תָּנָא דְּבֵי רַבִּי יִשְׁמָעֵאל [4]The Gemara now quotes a slightly different version of the idea expressed by Rabbi Yitzḥak, in which the Scriptural derivation is based on the literal meaning of the word. A Baraita from **the School of Rabbi Yishmael taught: "Blessing is found only in a thing that is not exposed** to public view, [5]**as it is said** [ibid.]: **'The Lord will command His blessing upon you in your storehouses.'"** The fact that a person keeps his produce in storehouses will be a source of blessing to him, for such produce is not exposed to public view.

תָּנוּ רַבָּנַן [6]On the same theme of blessings in hidden places, the Gemara quotes another statement of the Sages: **Our Rabbis taught** the following Baraita: **"Someone who goes to measure produce in his granary** before separating his tithes **may say** the following prayer: [7]**'May it be Your will, O Lord our God,**

שֶׁבַּכִּיס מִתְבָּרֶכֶת בּוֹ, [1]שֶׁנֶּאֱמַר: "לָתֵת מְטַר אַרְצְךָ בְּעִתּוֹ וּלְבָרֵךְ אֵת כָּל מַעֲשֵׂה יָדֶךָ".
[2]וְאָמַר רַבִּי יִצְחָק: אֵין הַבְּרָכָה מְצוּיָה אֶלָּא בְּדָבָר הַסָּמוּי מִן הָעַיִן, [3]שֶׁנֶּאֱמַר: "יְצַו ה' אִתְּךָ אֶת הַבְּרָכָה בַּאֲסָמֶיךָ".
[4]תָּנָא דְּבֵי רַבִּי יִשְׁמָעֵאל: "אֵין הַבְּרָכָה מְצוּיָה אֶלָּא בְּדָבָר שֶׁאֵין הָעַיִן שׁוֹלֶטֶת בּוֹ, [5]שֶׁנֶּאֱמַר: 'יְצַו ה' אִתְּךָ אֶת הַבְּרָכָה בַּאֲסָמֶיךָ'".
[6]תָּנוּ רַבָּנַן: "הַנִּכְנָס לָמוֹד אֶת גָּרְנוֹ אוֹמֵר: [7]'יְהִי רָצוֹן

LITERAL TRANSLATION

a coin that is in the pocket is blessed on it, [1]as it is said: "To give the rain of your land in its time and to bless all the work of your hand."

[2]And Rabbi Yitzḥak said: Blessing is found only in a thing that is hidden from the eye, [3]as it is said: "The Lord will command the blessing upon you in your storehouses."

[4]The School of Rabbi Yishmael taught: "Blessing is found only in a thing which the eye does not command, [5]as it is said: 'The Lord will command the blessing upon you in your storehouses.'"

[6]Our Rabbis taught: "Someone who goes in to measure [produce in] his granary says: [7]'May it be Your will,

RASHI

פרוטה שבכיס – אפילו מעשה ידים שאינן צריכים לגשמים מתברכין. **ברוך השולח ברכה** – (שיפוע) [ושפע] ומזכיר בה מלכות ואזכרה ככל הברכות כולן. **הרי זו תפילת שוא** – ושוב אין ברכה נכנסת בה. **בדבר הסמוי מן העין** – שאינו יודע הסכום.

NOTES

אֲפִילּוּ פְּרוּטָה שֶׁבַּכִּיס מִתְבָּרֶכֶת בּוֹ **Even a coin that is in the pocket is blessed on it.** *Rashi* notes that rain is not only a blessing for the fields and their produce, but brings plenty to all of a person's business pursuits, even those that are not directly dependent on rain. *Shittah* explains that ample rainfall stimulates the entire economy, even the nonagricultural sector, for when the crops are plentiful, food prices fall and more money is available for other business activities.

בְּדָבָר הַסָּמוּי מִן הָעַיִן **In a thing that is hidden from the eye.** *Sfat Emet* explains that a divine blessing falls under the category of miracles, and miracles are generally performed by God in a discreet manner, for He prefers not to break the natural order publicly. Thus a blessing is to be found only in something that is still hidden from the eye. But once something is exposed to the public gaze it is no longer subject to a divine blessing.

שֶׁאֵין הָעַיִן שׁוֹלֶטֶת בּוֹ **Which the eye does not command.** It is not clear if there is any substantial difference in meaning between Rabbi Yizḥak's version ("hidden from the eye") and the version of the School of Rabbi Yishmael ("which the eye does not command"); *Maharsha* explains that they really mean the same thing. Nevertheless, regarding merchandise that is not exposed to public view, *Rosh* points out that it is considered unwise to do business with large objects such as barrels, since such merchandise attracts too much attention. *Torat Ḥayyim* adds that miracles are normally performed secretly, as it is not considered appropriate to God's honor for uninvolved bystanders to observe their occurrence. (See, for example, II Kings 4:4.)

הַנִּכְנָס לָמוֹד אֶת גָּרְנוֹ **Someone who goes in to measure his produce in his granary.** *Ritva* explains that the blessings prescribed here are recited with the full formula,

HALAKHAH

הַנִּכְנָס לָמוֹד אֶת גָּרְנוֹ **Someone who goes in to measure his produce in his granary.** When a person is about to

TRANSLATION AND COMMENTARY

that You send blessing upon the work of our hands.' [1]**After he has begun to measure, he may say: 'Blessed is He who sends blessing upon this pile.'** [2]But **if he** has already **measured the produce,** it is too late to recite a blessing along these lines; **and** if he does **recite** such a **blessing, it is a vain prayer,** [3]**because blessing is not found in something weighed, or in something measured, or in something counted.** [4]It is **only** found **in something that is hidden from the eye."** According to Jewish law, it is forbidden to say prayers that have no meaning or relevance, for this is a form of taking God's name in vain, which is forbidden by the third of the ten commandments.

קִבּוּץ [5]The Gemara now cites five statements by Rabbi Yoḥanan, and introduces them by the following **mnemonic: Ingathering; armies; charity; tithe; provider."** The five terms in this mnemonic are key expressions employed by Rabbi Yoḥanan in his five statements.

אָמַר רַבִּי יוֹחָנָן [6]In the first statement ("ingathering" in the mnemonic) **Rabbi Yoḥanan said: The day of rain is as great as the day of the ingathering of the exiles,** [7]**as it is said** (Psalms 126:4): **"Turn our captivity, O Lord, like the streams in the desert."** We see from this verse that the ingathering of the exiles is compared to the streams in the desert, [8]**and there is no other meaning of "streams" but** "water," and in particular **"rain,"** [9]**as it is said** (II Samuel 22:16): **"And the streams of the sea appeared."** This latter verse shows us that the word אֲפִיקִים has the connotation of "water," and streams in the desert must therefore refer to the swiftly flowing streams of water created by rainstorms.

וְאָמַר רַבִּי יוֹחָנָן [10]In the second statement ("armies" in the mnemonic) **Rabbi Yoḥanan said: The day of**

מִלְּפָנֶיךָ, ה' אֱלֹהֵינוּ, שֶׁתִּשְׁלַח בְּרָכָה בְּמַעֲשֵׂה יָדֵנוּ'. [1]הִתְחִיל לָמוֹד, אוֹמֵר: 'בָּרוּךְ הַשּׁוֹלֵחַ בְּרָכָה בַּכְּרִי הַזֶּה'. [2]מָדַד וְאַחַר כָּךְ בֵּירַךְ, הֲרֵי זוֹ תְּפִלַּת שָׁוְא, [3]לְפִי שֶׁאֵין הַבְּרָכָה מְצוּיָה, לֹא בְּדָבָר הַשָּׁקוּל וְלֹא בְּדָבָר הַמָּדוּד וְלֹא בְּדָבָר הַמָּנוּי [4]אֶלָּא בְּדָבָר הַסָּמוּי מִן הָעַיִן".

[5]קִבּוּץ; גְּיָיסוֹת; צְדָקָה; מַעֲשֵׂר; פַּרְנָס; סִימָן.

[6]אָמַר רַבִּי יוֹחָנָן: גָּדוֹל יוֹם הַגְּשָׁמִים כְּיוֹם קִבּוּץ גָּלֻיּוֹת, [7]שֶׁנֶּאֱמַר: "שׁוּבָה ה' אֶת שְׁבִיתֵנוּ כַּאֲפִיקִים בַּנֶּגֶב". [8]וְאֵין "אֲפִיקִים" אֶלָּא "מָטָר", [9]שֶׁנֶּאֱמַר: "וַיֵּרָאוּ אֲפִקֵי יָם". [10]וְאָמַר רַבִּי יוֹחָנָן: גָּדוֹל יוֹם הַגְּשָׁמִים, שֶׁאֲפִילּוּ גְּיָיסוֹת

LITERAL TRANSLATION

O Lord our God, that You send blessing upon the work of our hands.'" [1][After] he has begun to measure, he says: 'Blessed is He who sends blessing upon this pile.' [2][If] he measured [the produce] and afterwards said a blessing, this is a vain prayer, [3]because blessing is not found, neither in something that is weighed, nor in something that is measured, nor in something that is counted, [4]but [only] in something that is hidden from the eye."

[5]Mnemonic: Ingathering; armies; charity; tithe; provider.

[6]Rabbi Yoḥanan said: The day of rains is as great as the day of the ingathering of the exiles, [7]as it is said: "Turn our captivity, O Lord, like the streams in the desert." [8]And there is no [other meaning of] "streams" except "rain," [9]as it is said: "And the streams of the sea appeared."

[10]And Rabbi Yoḥanan said: The day of rains is great, for even armies

RASHI

כאפיקים – כאפיקי נחלים. **בנגב** – יבשה, "והנה חרבו" מתרגמינן נגיבו. **אפיקי ים** – מוצאי ים. אלמא: אפיק לשון מים, ו"אפיקים בנגב" נמי לשון גשמים. **גייסות** – חיילות. כשאתה מרווה תלמי הארץ נגשם מיד גדודים נוחין, כדלקמן.

NOTES

"Blessed are You, O Lord our God, King of the Universe, etc." The difficulty with this explanation is that formal blessings are normally recited only in relation to definite occurrences, whereas in this case the farmer is praying for general, unspecified assistance. To resolve this problem, *Ritva* quotes *Ramban,* who explains that this blessing is to be recited only when the farmer is measuring his produce to determine the quantity of tithes to separate, because God promised a blessing to a farmer who tithes his crops (Malachi 3:10).

HALAKHAH

measure the produce in his granary, he should say: 'May it be Your will that You send a blessing on this pile of produce.' Likewise, while actually measuring, he may also recite a blessing: 'Blessed be He who sends a blessing upon this pile of produce.' But if he has completed the measurement, he may no longer recite a blessing. If he does so, it is a vain prayer," following the Gemara. (*Shulḥan Arukh, Oraḥ Ḥayyim* 230:2.)

CONCEPTS

מַעֲשֵׂר Tithe. Certain portions of agricultural produce designated by Torah law for special purposes. According to most opinions, only grain, wine, and olive oil are required by Torah law to be tithed. By Rabbinic decree, however, any food that grows from the ground must be tithed. There are three main types of tithes: מַעֲשֵׂר רִאשׁוֹן — "first tithe"; מַעֲשֵׂר שֵׁנִי — "second tithe"; and מַעְשַׂר עָנִי — "poor man's tithe." These tithes are set aside from foods after they have ripened and been brought into the house. Ownerless food is exempt from tithes, and hence no tithes are taken during the Sabbatical Year, when all food growing from the ground is deemed ownerless. Similarly, food eaten in the course of an אֲכִילַת עֲרַאי — "an incidental meal" (e.g., fruit eaten straight from the tree) — need not be tithed. Most of the laws of tithes appear in tractate *Ma'aserot*.

פּוֹסְקוֹת בּוֹ, [1] שֶׁנֶּאֱמַר: ״תְּלָמֶיהָ רַוֵּה; נַחֵת גְּדוּדֶיהָ״.
[2] וְאָמַר רַבִּי יוֹחָנָן: אֵין הַגְּשָׁמִים נֶעֱצָרִין אֶלָּא בִּשְׁבִיל פּוֹסְקֵי צְדָקָה בָּרַבִּים וְאֵין נוֹתְנִין, [3] שֶׁנֶּאֱמַר: ״נְשִׂיאִים וְרוּחַ, וְגֶשֶׁם אָיִן, אִישׁ מִתְהַלֵּל בְּמַתַּת שָׁקֶר״.
[4] וַאֲמַר רַבִּי יוֹחָנָן: מַאי דִּכְתִיב: [9A] [5] ״עַשֵּׂר תְּעַשֵּׂר״? [6] עַשֵּׂר בִּשְׁבִיל שֶׁתִּתְעַשֵּׁר.

LITERAL TRANSLATION

stop [fighting] on it, [1] as it is said: "You water its ridges abundantly; You settle its furrows."
[2] And Rabbi Yoḥanan said: Rains are withheld only because of those who pledge charity in public but do not give, [3] as it is said: "Clouds and wind, but no rain, is a man who takes pride in a false gift."
[4] And Rabbi Yoḥanan said: What is [the meaning of] what is written: [9A] [5] "You shall surely tithe"? [6] Tithe in order that you may become rich.

RASHI

פוסקי צדקה ברבים — לשם ולפנים, ואורחא דמילתא נקט, שאין אדם עשוי לפסוק צדקה בינו לבין עצמו ואינו נותן. **נשיאים ורוח** — כאין לעולם כאילו גשמים יורדין — ואינן יורדין, בשביל האיש המתהלל במתת שקר. דכשם שהוא עושה לפנים ומחניף את העניים — אף שמים מחניפין את הארץ, שמראין נשיאים ורוח — וגשם אין. אי נמי: ״אין״ קאי אשלשתם, דמכל אלו נעצרין.

TRANSLATION AND COMMENTARY

rain is great, for even armies stop fighting on it, [1] as it is said (Psalms 65:11): **"You water its ridges abundantly; You settle its furrows;** You make it soft with showers; You bless its growth." This verse describes the benefits of the early rain, which falls during the plowing season (see above, 6a). Rabbi Yoḥanan gives this verse a figurative explanation, in which the word גְּדוּדֶיהָ, which we have translated as "its furrows," is explained as "its armies," which is spelled the same way; and the word נחת, which we have translated as "You settle," is explained as "You calm" which is also spelled the same way. Thus the verse, as explained by Rabbi Yoḥanan, teaches us that rain causes armies to refrain from warfare.

וְאָמַר רַבִּי יוֹחָנָן [2] In the third statement ("charity" in the mnemonic) **Rabbi Yoḥanan said: Rain is withheld only because of** the sins of people **who pledge charity in public but do not give** the charity they have pledged, [3] **as it is said** (Proverbs 25:14): **"Clouds and wind, but no rain, is a man who takes pride in a false gift."** For when people fail to fulfill their promises, the clouds and the wind that promise rain fail to provide it.

וְאָמַר רַבִּי יוֹחָנָן [4] In the fourth statement ("tithe" in the mnemonic) **Rabbi Yoḥanan said: What is the meaning of what is written** in the following verse (Deuteronomy 14:22): [9A] [5] **"You shall surely tithe** all the produce of your seed, that comes out in the field year by year"? This verse, which commands us to separate the tithes, uses a double verb form, which we have translated as the emphatic "you shall surely tithe." By making a very slight change in one of the two verbs, [6] Rabbi Yoḥanan interprets the verse as saying: **Tithe in order that you may become rich.**

NOTES

פּוֹסְקֵי צְדָקָה בָּרַבִּים Those who pledge charity in public. *Rashi* explains that Rabbi Yoḥanan specifically refers to those who pledge charity in public, because it is the person who pledges charity in public who sometimes fails to fulfill his pledge, for his promise may only have been made in order to impress others. But it is unusual for someone who pledges charity in private not to fulfill his pledge, for if he did not intend to give the charity he would not have made the pledge in the first place.

Maharsha suggests that it is only those who pledge charity in public and then fail to give the charity they pledged whom Rabbi Yoḥanan holds responsible for the rain being withheld. For it is in response to the disappointment suffered by the poor after someone has made a public pledge of charity and then fails to fulfill that promise that the clouds and the wind cause the world disappointment when the rain they promised fails to fall (see also *Rashi* on Proverbs 25:14).

עַשֵּׂר תְּעַשֵּׂר "You shall surely tithe." Rabbi Yoḥanan's interpretation of the verse is generally understood to be based on a substitution of the Hebrew letter shin (שׁ) for the letter sin (שׂ), so that that the second verb is read as *te'asher* (תְּעַשֵּׁר — "you will become rich"), rather than *te'aser* (תְּעַשֵּׂר — "you will tithe"). Thus the verse promises that a person who carefully tithes his produce will be blessed with wealth. *Rabbenu Ḥananel* (see also *Maharsha*) explains Rabbi Yoḥanan's interpretation of the verse in a different way, and suggests that both verbs refer to tithing: Tithe (עַשֵּׂר) your produce properly in order that you may be blessed with plenty and you may be able to tithe (תְּעַשֵּׂר) your produce many times again.

HALAKHAH

עַשֵּׂר בִּשְׁבִיל שֶׁתִּתְעַשֵּׁר Tithe in order that you may become rich. "The giving of charity brings wealth to the donor. While in general one is forbidden to test God, regarding charity it is permitted. Some authorities say that a person may only test God with respect to the one-tenth of his wealth that he gives away as charity, but not with respect to other forms of charity (*Rema,* in the name of *Bet Yosef*). Others (*Shelah*) say that a person may only test God with respect to the tithe that he sets aside from his produce." (*Shulḥan Arukh, Yoreh De'ah* 247:4.)

TRANSLATION AND COMMENTARY

אַשְׁכַּחֵיהּ [1]The Gemara now relates a story connected with Rabbi Yoḥanan's explanation of this verse in Deuteronomy. Once **Rabbi Yoḥanan came upon the young son of** his foremost disciple and colleague, his brother-in-law **Resh Lakish,** who had died after a dispute with Rabbi Yoḥanan (see *Bava Metzia* 84a). Rabbi Yoḥanan decided to examine the boy's progress in his studies. [2]**He said to** the boy: **"Say your verse to me!** Recite a verse for me that you have just studied." [3]The boy **said to him:** "I have just studied the verse in Deuteronomy: **'You shall surely tithe** all the produce of your seed, that comes out in the field year by year.' " [4]The boy then **said to** Rabbi Yoḥanan: **"What is the meaning of** the double verb form in this verse: **'You shall surely tithe'?"** [5]Rabbi Yoḥanan responded by explaining to the boy the play on words cited above: **"Tithe in order that you may become rich."** [6]The boy **said to** Rabbi Yoḥanan: "This interpretation is very strange. **From where do you know** that someone who tithes is promised wealth? Such a remarkable idea must be based on more than a play on words." [7]Rabbi Yoḥanan **said to** the boy: "You do not need further Scriptural proof. **Go and test** the principle for yourself." [8]The boy **said to** Rabbi Yoḥanan: "How can you say such a thing? **Is it permitted to test the Holy One blessed be He,** by saying to Him, as it were: 'If I fulfill this commandment, I expect to be rewarded in such and such a way'? [9]**But surely it is written** [Deuteronomy 6:16]: **'Do not test the Lord your God,** as you tested Him at Massah' [where the Israelites asked God to prove His power to them by giving them water; Exodus 17:7]!" [10]Rabbi Yoḥanan **said to** the boy in reply: **"This** idea is not my own. My teacher **Rabbi Hoshaya said:** It is forbidden to test God in any way, **except in the** case of tithes, [11]**because it is said** [Malachi 3:10]: **'Bring all the tithes into the storehouse that there may be food in My house, and test Me now by this, said the Lord of Hosts, if I will not open for you the windows of heaven, and pour out for you a blessing until it is more than enough.' "**

[1]אַשְׁכַּחֵיהּ רַבִּי יוֹחָנָן לְיָנוּקָא דְּרֵישׁ לָקִישׁ. [2]אֲמַר לֵיהּ: ״אֵימָא לִי פְּסוּקֵיךְ״. [3]אֲמַר לֵיהּ: ״׳עַשֵּׂר תְּעַשֵּׂר׳״. [4]אֲמַר לֵיהּ: ״וּמַאי ׳עַשֵּׂר תְּעַשֵּׂר׳?״ [5]אֲמַר לֵיהּ: ״עַשֵּׂר בִּשְׁבִיל שֶׁתִּתְעַשֵּׂר״. [6]אֲמַר לֵיהּ: ״מְנָא לָךְ״? [7]אֲמַר לֵיהּ: ״זִיל נַסֵּי״. [8]אֲמַר לֵיהּ: ״וּמִי שָׁרֵי לְנַסּוּיֵיהּ לְהַקָּדוֹשׁ בָּרוּךְ הוּא? [9]וְהָכְתִיב ׳לֹא תְנַסּוּ אֶת ה׳!״ [10]אֲמַר לֵיהּ: ״הָכִי אֲמַר רַבִּי הוֹשַׁעְיָא: חוּץ מִזּוֹ, [11]שֶׁנֶּאֱמַר: ׳הָבִיאוּ אֶת כָּל הַמַּעֲשֵׂר אֶל בֵּית הָאוֹצָר, וִיהִי טֶרֶף בְּבֵיתִי, וּבְחָנוּנִי נָא בָּזֹאת אָמַר ה׳ צְבָאוֹת אִם לֹא אֶפְתַּח לָכֶם אֵת אֲרֻבּוֹת הַשָּׁמַיִם, וַהֲרִיקֹתִי לָכֶם בְּרָכָה עַד בְּלִי דָי׳״.

LITERAL TRANSLATION

[1]Rabbi Yoḥanan came upon the young son of Resh Lakish. [2]He said to him: "Say your verse to me." [3]He said to him: " 'You shall surely tithe.' " [4]He said to him: "But what is [the meaning of] 'you shall surely tithe'?" [5]He said to him: "Tithe in order that you may become rich." [6]He said to him: "From where do you [know this]?" [7]He said to him: "Go [and] test [it]." [8]He said to him: "But is it permitted to test the Holy One blessed be He? [9]But surely it is written: 'You shall not test the Lord'!" [10]He said to him: "This is what Rabbi Hoshaya said: Except for this, [11]for it is said: 'Bring all the tithes into the storehouse, that there may be food in My house, and test Me now by this, said the Lord of Hosts, if I will not open for you the windows of heaven, and pour out for you a blessing until it is more than enough.' "

RASHI

לינוקא דריש לקיש — בן אחותו של רבי יוחנן, ולאחר מיתתו של ריש לקיש, כדמוכח לקמן. **אמר** — ינוקא לרבי יוחנן: מאי ״עשר תעשר״? **אמר ליה ינוקא** — והכתיב ״לא תנסו״.

NOTES

״מְנָא לָךְ?״ ״זִיל נַסֵּי״ "From where do you know this?" "Go and test it." *Gevurat Ari* asks: Why does Resh Lakish's son ask Rabbi Yoḥanan for a source for his statement that a person who tithes his produce is promised wealth? Surely Rabbi Yoḥanan has just told him that his position is based on his interpretation of the expression: "You shall surely tithe"! Moreover, why does Rabbi Yoḥanan respond to the boy that he should go out and tithe and see for himself that he will become wealthy, when he can immediately support his opinion by quoting the verse in Malachi that he later cites in response to the boy's next question?

Gevurat Ari concludes from this that Rabbi Yoḥanan does not interpret the expression — "You shall surely tithe" — merely as a promise that someone who tithes his produce properly is promised wealth, but rather as giving permission for a person to tithe his produce in order to test whether or not God will bless him with wealth. Resh Lakish's son therefore asks him how he knows that the verse should be understood that way and not as a promise. Rabbi Yoḥanan reassures the boy that this is surely the proper interpretation of the verse, and that he may go out and test God to see whether or not He will bless him with wealth if he tithes his produce properly. The boy then raises the difficulty that the verse in Deuteronomy implies that one may not test God, and Rabbi Yoḥanan answers that the verse in Malachi teaches that an exception is made with respect to tithing.

BACKGROUND

יָנוּקָא דְּרֵישׁ לָקִישׁ The young son of Resh Lakish. Resh Lakish married Rabbi Yoḥanan's sister and was his disciple and closest colleague. The differences of opinion and debate between the two Sages were a means of broadening and deepening their understanding. Nevertheless, on one occasion Rabbi Yoḥanan became angry with Resh Lakish and glared at him. The effect of his disapproval was so great that Resh Lakish died.

Resh Lakish had several sons and a daughter, and this יָנוּקָא was most probably the youngest of them. Judging by the subject of study and the style of the remarks recorded here, it seems that he was about seven or eight years old at the time, and his words show the sharpness of his mind as well as his childlike impudence.

This child may have died before reaching manhood, for we do not find that any of Resh Lakish's sons were Sages of the following generation.

SAGES

רַבִּי הוֹשַׁעְיָא Rabbi Hoshaya (or Oshaya). This Sage, usually referred to in the Jerusalem Talmud as Rabbi Hoshaya Rabbah (i.e., "the Great"), to distinguish him from another, later Sage of the same name, lived in Eretz Israel during the transitional period between the Tannaitic and Amoraic eras. Rabbi Hoshaya was the son of a Tanna, Rabbi Ḥama, and the grandson of another Tanna, Rabbi Bisa.

Rabbi Hoshaya lived in Southern Judea during his youth, although he later moved to Tzipori, and from there to Caesarea. His first teacher was Bar Kappara. Later, he became a close disciple of Rabbi Ḥiyya, who was his principal teacher, although he also studied with other students of Rabbi Yehudah HaNasi.

Rabbi Hoshaya was a close friend of the members of the House of the Nasi, and held various important positions. His most noteworthy achievement was the compilation of a collection of Baraitot, which was highly regarded for its accuracy and clarity.

1מַאי: "עַד בְּלִי דָי"?
2אָמַר רָמִי בַּר חָמָא אָמַר רַב: 3עַד שֶׁיִּבְלוּ שִׂפְתוֹתֵיכֶם מִלּוֹמַר: "דַּי".
4אָמַר לֵיהּ: 5"אִי הֲוַת מָטֵי הָתָם לְהַאי פְּסוּקָא, לָא הֲוֵית צְרִיכְנָא לָךְ וּלְהוֹשַׁעְיָא רַבָּךְ".
6וְתוּ אַשְׁכַּחֵיהּ רַבִּי יוֹחָנָן לִינוֹקֵיהּ דְּרֵישׁ לָקִישׁ, דְּיָתֵיב וְאָמַר: 7"'אִוֶּלֶת אָדָם תְּסַלֵּף דַּרְכּוֹ, וְעַל ה' יִזְעַף לִבּוֹ'".
8יָתֵיב רַבִּי יוֹחָנָן וְקָא מַתְמַהּ.
9אֲמַר: "מִי אִיכָּא מִידִי דִּכְתִיבִי בִּכְתוּבֵי דְּלָא רְמִיזִי בְּאוֹרַיְיתָא?" 10אֲמַר לֵיהּ: "אַטּוּ הָא מִי לָא רְמִיזִי? 11וְהָכְתִיב: 'וַיֵּצֵא לִבָּם וַיֶּחֶרְדוּ, אִישׁ אֶל אָחִיו לֵאמֹר: מַה זֹּאת עָשָׂה אֱלֹהִים לָנוּ?'!". 12דַּל עֵינֵיהּ

LITERAL TRANSLATION

[1]What is [the meaning of]: "Until it is more than enough"?

[2]Rami bar Ḥama said in the name of Rav: [3]Until your lips wear out from saying: "Enough."

[4]He said to him: [5]"If I had arrived there at this verse, I would not have needed you and Hoshaya your teacher."

[6]And again Rabbi Yoḥanan came upon the young son of Resh Lakish, who was sitting and saying: [7]"'The foolishness of man perverts his way, and his heart frets against the Lord.'" [8]Rabbi Yoḥanan sat down and wondered. [9]He said: "Is there anything that is written in the Writings that is not hinted at in the Torah?" [10]He said to him: "Is this not hinted at? [11]But surely it is written: 'And their heart failed them and they were afraid, saying one to another: What is this that God has done to us?'!" [12]He raised his eyes

TRANSLATION AND COMMENTARY

מַאי [1]The Gemara digresses briefly from the story of Rabbi Yoḥanan and the young son of Resh Lakish to comment on the verse in Malachi. **What is the meaning of** the words: **"Until it is more than enough"?** The Prophet uses an unusual construction, עַד בְּלִי דָי, which literally means "until without enough."

אָמַר רָמִי בַּר חָמָא [2]The commentators suggest that Malachi means that there will not be enough space for all the plenty. But **Rami bar Ḥama said in the name of Rav** that the meaning of this verse can be brought out even more forcefully through a play on words. The word בְּלִי, which means "without," can also be interpreted as a verb meaning "to wear out." [3]Thus the Prophet is saying that the wealth will be poured out **until your lips wear out from saying: "Enough."**

אָמַר לֵיהּ [4]The Gemara now returns to the story of Rabbi Yoḥanan and the boy. Having heard Rabbi Yoḥanan's explanation, the child responded with childish audacity, **saying to** Rabbi Yoḥanan: "I have not yet studied the Book of Malachi, [5]but **if I had** already **arrived at this verse there, I would not have needed you and Hoshaya your teacher** to inform me that it is permissible to test God's promise that tithing brings wealth."

וְתוּ אַשְׁכַּחֵיהּ רַבִּי יוֹחָנָן [6]Before proceeding to Rabbi Yoḥanan's fifth statement, the Gemara relates that on another occasion **Rabbi Yoḥanan again came upon the young son of Resh Lakish, who was sitting and reciting** the following verse (Proverbs 19:3): [7]**"The foolishness of man perverts his way, and his heart frets against the Lord,"** meaning that when someone gets himself into trouble through his own folly, he tends to blame God for his misfortune. [8]**Rabbi Yoḥanan sat down and wondered.** [9]**He said:** "I have always been troubled by this verse, which seems to be conveying a novel idea not found in the Torah itself. But **is there anything that appears in the Writings that is not hinted at in the Torah** itself? In general, the Torah contains all the basic information we need. The Prophets and the authors of the Writings (Psalms, Proverbs, etc.) did not originate truly novel ideas. Where, then, does the principle contained in this verse appear in the Torah? [10]The boy **said to** Rabbi Yoḥanan: "**Is this** idea **not hinted at** in the Torah? [11]**Surely** the same idea **is written** in connection with the story of Joseph and his brothers [Genesis 42:28]." Joseph decided to frighten his brothers by having their money returned to them after they bought grain, thus exposing them to charges of theft. The verse relates that one of the brothers opened his sack on the journey back from Egypt to Canaan. "Surely," the boy continued, "the verse says: 'And he said to his brothers: "My money has been returned, and here it is in my sack." **And their heart failed them and they were afraid, saying one to another: What is this that God has done to us?'!"** The brothers immediately blamed God for their misfortune, even though in fact they had brought it on themselves by mistreating Joseph. [12]The Gemara relates that Rabbi Yoḥanan **raised his eyes**

RASHI

שיבלו — כלומר: שייגעו = *דולוראנ"ט בלעז. **אי הוה מטינא להתם** — להאי קרא ד"הביאו את כל המעשר" הוה ידעית ליה ממילא. **לרבי הושעיא רבך** — דאמרית לי משמיה. **אולת אדם תסלף דרכו ועל ה' יזעף לבו** — כשאדם חוטא מסלף דרכו, שבאין עליו פגעים — "ועל השם יזעף לבו", שכועס ואומר: מפני מה אירע לי פגע זה? **ולא רמזה** — משה באורייתא, שהחומש הוא יסוד נביאים וכתובים, וכולן יש סמך למצוא מן התורה. **דלי עיניה** — רבי יוחנן, שהיו עפעפיו מכסין את עיניו, ומגביהין במזלגי דכספא, בבבא קמא בפרק אחרון (קיז,א). שהיה רוצה לראותו, מפני שהוא חריף.

The leading Amoraim of the next generation (among them Rabbi Yoḥanan, Resh Lakish, and some of their students) studied with Rabbi Hoshaya and cited his teachings. Rabbi Hoshaya was skilled at disputing with non-Jewish scholars and explaining Jewish law to them. He was particularly noted for his fine character, and for the great respect in which he held his fellow men. He was apparently a pauper for most of his life, in spite of the important positions he held. He lived to a great age, and had a son named Rabbi Marinos, who was also a Sage.

SAGES

רָמִי בַּר חָמָא **Rami bar Ḥama.** Rami (Rabbi Ammi) bar Ḥama was one of the most important Babylonian Amoraim of the fourth generation. As a boy he was the outstanding student of Rav Ḥisda, whose daughter he subsequently married. Rami bar Ḥama learned Torah from Rav Naḥman and Rav Sheshet, and also discussed Halakhic issues with them. He was famous for his brilliant intellect, but some of his contemporaries observed that because of his great intelligence and creativity, he did not always submit problems to precise analysis. Rami bar Ḥama had close ties with his younger colleague, Rava, who survived him and married his widow. Rami bar Ḥama's daughter was the mother of the Amora Amemar.

LANGUAGE (RASHI)

דולוראנ"ט* From the Old French *dolorent*, which means "very tired," or "exhausted."

TRANSLATION AND COMMENTARY

and looked at the boy. [1]The boy's **mother** saw this and quickly **came and took him away.** [2]**She said to him: "Come away from** Rabbi Yoḥanan, **so that he does not do to you as he did to your father,** Resh Lakish." For Resh Lakish had died after an argument concerning Torah with Rabbi Yoḥanan which had ended with an offended look from Rabbi Yoḥanan. Resh Lakish's widow was afraid that Rabbi Yoḥanan was about to be offended by her child's precocity, and that this might lead to the child's death.

אָמַר רַבִּי יוֹחָנָן [3]The Gemara now turns to the fifth in the series of statements by Rabbi Yoḥanan ("provider" in the mnemonic). **Rabbi Yoḥanan said:** God sometimes causes **rain to fall for the sake of an individual** righteous person who needs it. [4]**Sustenance,** on the other hand, **is granted** only **for the sake of many** worthy people who need it, but not for the sake of an individual. In this context, "sustenance" refers to blessings beyond those needed for bare subsistence. [5]Rabbi Yoḥanan explains: We see that God sometimes causes **rain to fall for the sake of an individual,** [6]**as it is written** (Deuteronomy 28:12): **"The Lord will open for you** [second person singular] **His good storehouse,** the heavens, **to give the rain of your** [second person singular] **land."** We see from the use of the second person singular in this verse that God promises rain to each individual if he merits it. [7]Sustenance, on the other hand, **is granted** only **for the sake of many** worthy people who need it, [8]**as it is written** concerning the manna that God provided for the Israelites in the wilderness (Exodus 16:4): **"Behold I will rain down bread for you** [second person plural] from the heavens." In this verse God uses the second person plural. From this we see that the manna, which provided much more than basic subsistence, was not granted by God on an individual basis, but only to the Children of Israel as a whole.

מֵיתִיבִי [9]The Gemara now **raises an objection** against Rabbi Yoḥanan's statement by citing a Baraita which implies that sustenance, too, is provided for the sake of an individual, if he is extremely meritorious: [10]**"Rabbi Yose the son of Rabbi Yehudah says: Three good leaders rose up for Israel, and these are they:**

וַחֲזָא בֵּיהּ. [1]אָתְיָא אִימֵּיהּ אַפִּיקְתֵּיהּ. [2]אֲמָרָה לֵיהּ: "תָּא מִקַּמֵּיהּ, דְּלָא לִיעֲבַד לָךְ כְּדַעֲבַד לַאֲבוּךְ".

[3]אָמַר רַבִּי יוֹחָנָן: מָטָר בִּשְׁבִיל יָחִיד. [4]פַּרְנָסָה בִּשְׁבִיל רַבִּים. [5]מָטָר בִּשְׁבִיל יָחִיד, [6]דִּכְתִיב: "יִפְתַּח ה׳ לְךָ אֶת אוֹצָרוֹ הַטּוֹב... לָתֵת מְטַר אַרְצְךָ". [7]פַּרְנָסָה בִּשְׁבִיל רַבִּים, [8]דִּכְתִיב: "הִנְנִי מַמְטִיר לָכֶם לֶחֶם".

[9]מֵיתִיבִי: [10]"רַבִּי יוֹסֵי בְּרַבִּי יְהוּדָה אוֹמֵר: שְׁלֹשָׁה פַּרְנָסִים טוֹבִים עָמְדוּ לְיִשְׂרָאֵל, אֵלּוּ הֵן:

LITERAL TRANSLATION

and looked at him. [1]His mother came [and] took him away. [2]She said to him: "Come away from him, so that he does not do to you as he did to your father."

[3]Rabbi Yoḥanan said: Rain [falls] for the sake of an individual. [4]Sustenance [is granted] for the sake of the many. [5]Rain [falls] for the sake of an individual, [6]as it is written: "The Lord will open for you [singular] His good storehouse...to give the rain of your [singular] land." [7]Sustenance [is granted] for the sake of the many, [8]as it is written: "Behold I will rain down bread for you [plural]."

[9]An objection was raised: [10]"Rabbi Yose the son of Rabbi Yehudah says: Three good leaders rose up for Israel, [and] these are they:

SAGES

רַבִּי יוֹסֵי בְּרַבִּי יְהוּדָה Rabbi Yose the son of Rabbi Yehudah. A Tanna of the last generation, Rabbi Yose was the son of the Tanna Rabbi Yehudah (ben Il'ai). He was apparently a close disciple of his father, though he occasionally disagreed with him about the Halakhah, and he was a colleague of Rabbi Yehudah HaNasi. He also discussed the Halakhah with other Sages of his generation. In his work as a Halakhic authority he was apparently closely associated with Rabbi Yehudah HaNasi, and his teachings are mentioned a number of times in the Mishnah, and very often in the Tosefta and elsewhere. He was also very prolific in the area of Aggadah, and some well-known sayings are transmitted in his name.

RASHI

דלא ליעביד לך כדעבד לאבוך – שלא יתן עיניו בך כמו שנתן באביך והמיתו, בבבא מציעא (פד,א). **מטר בשביל יחיד** – שאם אין צריך מטר אלא לאדם אחד, כגון שזרע אחר זמן זריעת בני אדם, או שדר בעיר שכולה נכרים וצריך למטר – בא בזכותו. ופרנסה, שפע טובה ומחיה לכל העולם, אינו בא לעולם בזכות אחד אלא בשביל רבים. שאם רבים צריכין שובע, שתשלח ברכה בתבואה – הקדוש ברוך הוא עושה, אם זכו. אבל יחיד הצריך שיתברכו תבואותיו – אין הקדוש ברוך הוא משנה בעבורו דין השנה, אלא כפי ברכותיה. ואף על פי שמוריד בשביל יחיד מטר זה להשביח תבואותיו, שלא יהו גרועות משל אחרים – אבל לעשות שדהו כשדה שובע – לא. **מטר ארצך** – של אחד משמע. **ממטיר לכם** – לשון רבים.

NOTES

פַּרְנָסָה בִּשְׁבִיל רַבִּים Sustenance is granted for the sake of the many. According to *Rashi,* when Rabbi Yoḥanan says that rain falls even for an individual, he is referring to rain that that individual requires so that his crops will not fail or produce yields inferior to those of his neighbors. And when he says that sustenance is provided only when it is merited by the community, he is referring to a state of prosperity that is not granted solely for the sake of an individual. *Maharsha* explains that rain, which naturally leads to prosperity, falls even for the sake of a single worthy individual, but sustenance provided by supernatural means, such as manna from Heaven, is provided only when the entire community is considered worthy.

משֶׁה, וְאַהֲרֹן, וּמִרְיָם. [1]וְשָׁלשׁ מַתָּנוֹת טוֹבוֹת נִיתְּנוּ עַל יָדָם, וְאֵלּוּ הֵן: בְּאֵר, וְעָנָן, וּמָן. [2]בְּאֵר בִּזְכוּת מִרְיָם. [3]עַמּוּד עָנָן בִּזְכוּת אַהֲרֹן. [4]מָן בִּזְכוּת משֶׁה. [5]מֵתָה מִרְיָם, נִסְתַּלֵּק הַבְּאֵר. [6]שֶׁנֶּאֱמַר: ׳וַתָּמָת שָׁם מִרְיָם׳, [7]וּכְתִיב בַּתְרֵיהּ: ׳וְלֹא הָיָה מַיִם לָעֵדָה׳. [8]וְחָזְרָה בִּזְכוּת שְׁנֵיהֶן. [9]מֵת אַהֲרֹן, נִסְתַּלְּקוּ עַנְנֵי כָבוֹד, [10]שֶׁנֶּאֱמַר: ׳וַיִּשְׁמַע הַכְּנַעֲנִי, מֶלֶךְ עֲרָד׳. [11]מַה שְּׁמוּעָה שָׁמַע? שָׁמַע שֶׁמֵּת אַהֲרֹן וְנִסְתַּלְּקוּ עַנְנֵי כָבוֹד, [12]וּכְסָבוּר נִיתְּנָה לוֹ רְשׁוּת לְהִלָּחֵם בְּיִשְׂרָאֵל. [13]וְהַיְינוּ דִּכְתִיב [14]׳וַיִּרְאוּ כָּל הָעֵדָה כִּי גָוַע אַהֲרֹן׳ ״.

LITERAL TRANSLATION

Moses, and Aaron, and Miriam. [1]And three good gifts were given at their hand, and these are they: The well, and the cloud, and the manna. [2]The well was because of the merit of Miriam. [3]The pillar of cloud was because of the merit of Aaron. [4]The manna was because of the merit of Moses. [5][When] Miriam died, the well disappeared, [6]as it is said: 'And Miriam died there,' [7]and it is written after it: 'And there was no water for the congregation.' [8]But it returned because of the merit of both of them. [9][When] Aaron died, the clouds of glory disappeared, [10]as it is said: 'And the Canaanite, the king of Arad, heard.' [11]What report did he hear? He heard that Aaron had died and the clouds of glory had disappeared, [12]and he thought [that] permission had been given to him to go to war against Israel. [13]And this is [the meaning of] what is written: [14]'And all the congregation saw that Aaron was dead.'"

TRANSLATION AND COMMENTARY

Moses, Aaron, and Miriam. [1]**And three good gifts were given at their hand** when the Israelites were wandering in the wilderness: **The well,** from which they drank; **the** pillar of **cloud,** which guided them and protected them from harm; **and the manna,** which they ate. [2]**The well was** given to the Israelites by God **because of the merit of Miriam.** [3]**The pillar of cloud was** given **because of the merit of Aaron.** [4]**The manna was** given **because of the merit of Moses.** [5]We know that the well was given because of Miriam's merit, for **when Miriam died, the well disappeared,** [6]**as it is said** [Numbers 20:1]: **'And Miriam died there,'** [7]**and** immediately **afterwards** in the next verse **it is written: 'And there was no water for the congregation.'** At the beginning of their wanderings, the Israelites repeatedly complained about the lack of water, until a well miraculously opened up for them [Exodus 17:1-7]. From that time until the death of Miriam nearly forty years later there were no further complaints about lack of water. Thus we see that the well that had sustained them all that time was given to them because of Miriam's merit. [8]**But** even though the well disappeared when Miriam died, **it returned because of the merit of both** Moses and Aaron. As soon as the well disappeared and the people complained about the lack of water, God commanded Moses and Aaron to go together to a rock and command it to deliver up water [Numbers 20:8]. [9]We know that the pillar of cloud was given because of Aaron's merit, for **when Aaron died, the clouds of glory disappeared,** [10]**as it is said** [Numbers 21:1]: **'And the Canaanite, the king of Arad,** who dwelt in the south, **heard** that Israel had come... he fought against Israel.' The verse implies that the king of Arad had received a report that led to this attack. [11]**What report did he hear? He heard that Aaron had died,** the topic of the verses immediately preceding [Numbers 20:22-29], **and** that this had led to **the disappearance of the clouds of glory** that had hitherto protected the Israelites from attack. [12]Accordingly, **he thought that he had been given permission to go to war against Israel,** and this led to his attack. [13]**And this is the meaning of what is written** in the verse immediately preceding the one that mentions the attack by the king of Arad [Numbers 20:29]: [14]**'And all the congregation saw that Aaron was dead,** and all the house of Israel mourned for Aaron for thirty days.'"

RASHI

בארה של מרים — סלע, וזבין ממנו מים, והיה מתגלגל והולך עם ישראל. והוא הסלע שבו הכה משה, שלא היה רוצה להזיל מימיו בשבילו, לפי שמתה מרים. **ונסתלקו ענני כבוד** — ענני רקיע וענני עשן, ושאר עננים אינן של כבוד. **חזרה בזכות שניהן** — שכן כתיב "ודברתם שניכם אל הסלע ונתן מימיו".

NOTES

וְחָזְרָה בִּזְכוּת שְׁנֵיהֶן But it returned because of the merit of both of them. Some commentators ask: If the miraculous well from which the Israelites drew their water was returned to them after Miriam's death because of the merit of Moses and Aaron, then their merit should certainly have sufficed for the well not to disappear when Miriam died! It has been suggested that, although the well returned because of the merit of Moses and Aaron, it did not sustain the people after Miriam's death in the same manner as it sustained them during Miriam's lifetime (*Ahavat Eitan*). *Maharsha* suggests that the well disappeared when Miriam died in order to show the Israelites that during her lifetime the well was provided primarily because of her merit.

TRANSLATION AND COMMENTARY

אָמַר רַבִּי אַבָּהוּ [1]The Gemara interprets the Baraita in order to explain that the verse is specifically referring to the disappearance of the clouds of glory, for **Rabbi Abbahu said: Do not read: "And they saw"** (וַיִּרְאוּ), [2]**but rather: "And they were seen"** (וַיֵּרָאוּ). The congregation were revealed to the eyes of potential enemies because Aaron had died, because Aaron's death had brought about the dispersal of the clouds of glory which had enveloped and protected them. The Gemara adds that Rabbi Abbahu's interpretation implies that the word "כִּי", which we originally translated as "that," must be translated as "because." The Israelites did not see *that* Aaron was dead; they were seen *because* Aaron was dead. This change in translation is legitimate, since כִּי has many different meanings, [3]**in accordance with the** following **explanation by Resh Lakish.** [4]**For Resh Lakish said: The word "*ki*"** (כִּי) **serves four meanings:** [5]**"If," "perhaps," "but," and "because."** Thus in the present context כִּי can appropriately be translated as "because," and the sense of the passage is that Aaron's death led to the disappearance of the clouds of glory and to the exposure of the Israelites to attack.

חָזְרוּ שְׁנֵיהֶם [6]We now return to the Baraita, which has just related that the well disappeared upon the death of Miriam, and the clouds of glory disappeared upon the death of Aaron. The Baraita continues: "Nevertheless, **they both returned, because of the merit of Moses** alone. [7]**But when Moses died,** the well, the clouds, and the manna **all disappeared** forever, [8]**as it is said** [Zechariah 11:8]: **'And I destroyed the three shepherds in one month.'** This verse refers to Moses, Aaron, and Miriam, the three shepherds of the Israelites in the wilderness. [9]**But did they** really **die in one month?** [10]**Surely Miriam died in Nisan**, the first month [as the Torah says explicitly in Numbers 20:1], **and Aaron** died **in Av**, the fifth month [as the Torah says explicitly in Numbers 33:38], **and Moses** died **in Adar**, the twelfth month [as can be calculated by comparing Deuteronomy 34:8, Joshua 1:11, and Joshua 4:19]! [11]**Rather,** the verse in Zechariah **teaches us that** when **the three good gifts that were given at their hand were** permanently **annulled, they all disappeared in one month,** the month following the death of Moses [see Deuteronomy 34:8]." [12]**Thus we see from this** Baraita **that we can find** a case in which **sustenance was granted for the sake of an individual,** for the manna was granted because of the merit of Moses alone! How, then, can Rabbi Yoḥanan say that sustenance is never granted for the sake of an individual?

[1]אָמַר רַבִּי אַבָּהוּ: אַל תִּקְרִי: "וַיִּרְאוּ", [2]אֶלָּא: "וַיֵּרָאוּ", [3]כִּדְדָרֵישׁ רֵישׁ לָקִישׁ. [4]דְּאָמַר רֵישׁ לָקִישׁ: "כִּי" מְשַׁמֵּשׁ בְּאַרְבַּע לְשׁוֹנוֹת: [5]"אִי", "דִּלְמָא", "אֶלָּא", "דְּהָא". [6]חָזְרוּ שְׁנֵיהֶם בִּזְכוּת מֹשֶׁה. [7]מֵת מֹשֶׁה, נִסְתַּלְּקוּ כּוּלָּן, [8]שֶׁנֶּאֱמַר: 'וָאַכְחִד אֶת שְׁלֹשֶׁת הָרֹעִים בְּיֶרַח אֶחָד'. [9]וְכִי בְּיֶרַח אֶחָד מֵתוּ? [10]וַהֲלֹא מִרְיָם מֵתָה בְּנִיסָן, וְאַהֲרֹן בְּאָב, וּמֹשֶׁה בַּאֲדָר? [11]אֶלָּא, מְלַמֵּד שֶׁנִּתְבַּטְּלוּ שָׁלֹשׁ מַתָּנוֹת טוֹבוֹת שֶׁנִּתְּנוּ עַל יָדָן, וְנִסְתַּלְּקוּ כּוּלָּן בְּיֶרַח אֶחָד". [12]אַלְמָא אַשְׁכַּחַן פַּרְנָסָה בִּשְׁבִיל יָחִיד!

LITERAL TRANSLATION

[1]Rabbi Abbahu said: Do not read: "And they saw," [2]but rather: "And they were seen," [3]as Resh Lakish expounded. [4]For Resh Lakish said: [The word] *"ki"* (כִּי) serves four meanings: [5]"If," "perhaps," "but," [and] "because."

[6]"They both returned because of the merit of Moses. [7][When] Moses died, they all disappeared, [8]as it is said: 'And I destroyed the three shepherds in one month.' [9]But did they die in one month? [10]But did not Miriam die in Nisan, and Aaron in Av, and Moses in Adar? [11]Rather, it teaches [us] that the three good gifts that were given at their hand were annulled, and they all disappeared in one month." [12]From here we find that sustenance [is granted] for the sake of an individual!

RASHI

כי משמש ארבע לשונות אי דלמא אלא דהא – כל מקום שצריך לדרוש 'כי' בין לענין דרשה בין למשמעות המקרא – תוכל לשנותו באחד מהני ארבע לשונות, דלשון 'כי' משמע בכולם. וכן, 'וכד' 'וברם', 'וארי' בכלל הני ארבע הן. והאי ד"כי גוע אהרן" משתמש בלשון דהא, ושמעינן מינה טעמא דקרא: דמה טעם נתראו – דהא מית, שהרי מת אהרן. וריש לקיש לא אתי למימר דלא מתרגמינן שום "כי" בעולם אלא מהני לשונות, אלא אפילו מתרגם דלמא, ארי – דרשינן משמעותיה כמשמעות "דהא", ומאן דמתרגם "וחזיאו כל כנישתא דהא מית" – טועה הוא, דאם כן "ואתחזיאו" מיבעי ליה. "וַיִּרְאוּ כל העדה" במשקל "וַיֵּרָאוּ ראשי הבדים" "וירפו המים" "ויעלו מעל משכן קרח". **חזרו שניהם בזכות משה** – מדכתיב "ואכחיד את שלשת הרועים" פשיטא לן דבדידהו משתעי, שלא מצינו פרנסים לישראל שלשה כאחד אלא הם. **מתה בניסן** – שנאמר (במדבר כ) "ויבואו בני ישראל כל העדה מדבר צין בחדש הראשון וישב העם בקדש ותמת שם מרים ותקבר שם", [בפרשת] פרה אדומה. **אהרן מת** – באחד לחדש.

NOTES

"כִּי" מְשַׁמֵּשׁ בְּאַרְבַּע לְשׁוֹנוֹת The word "כִּי" serves four meanings. In his Aramaic translation of the Torah, Onkelos consistently translates the Hebrew word כִּי with the Aramaic word אֲרֵי. But it can be argued that the Aramaic word אֲרֵי has

TRANSLATION AND COMMENTARY

שָׁאנֵי מֹשֶׁה [1]The Gemara answers: **Moses is different,** for Moses was not in need of sustenance for himself personally. Rather, he asked God to provide it for the Children of Israel. [2]And **since he asked for it for the many** people who needed it, **he was regarded** as if he were **many** people and his merit benefited them all.

רַב הוּנָא בַּר מָנוֹחַ [3]Having mentioned the verse in Zechariah, the Gemara now relates a story connected to it. **Rav Huna bar Manoaḥ and Rav Shmuel bar Idi and Rav Ḥiyya from Vastanya** went **regularly to Rava** to study from him. [4]**When Rava died, they went to Rav Pappa** instead. But they did not have the same confidence in Rav Pappa as they had had in Rava, [5]and **whenever** Rav Pappa **would give them a Talmudic discourse which did not make sense to them,** [6]**they would gesture to each other,** indicating that Rav Pappa was not of the stature of Rava. [7]Rav Pappa **was** greatly **hurt** by this behavior.

אַקְרוּיֵהּ בְּחֶלְמֵיהּ [9B] [8]One night, he had a **dream** in which the verse from Zechariah (11:8) **was read to him: "And I destroyed the three shepherds."** Rav Pappa interpreted this dream to mean that God was planning to punish the three Sages for hurting Rav Pappa. [9]**The next day, when** the three of them **were parting from** Rav Pappa, [10]**he said to them: "May the Rabbis go in peace,"** using a phrase said at funerals, because Rav Pappa did not expect to see them again.

רַב שִׁימִי בַּר אַשִׁי [11]The Gemara now presents another story about Rav Pappa. **Rav Shimi bar Ashi came regularly before Rav Pappa** to study from him. [12]**He would raise many difficulties for Rav Pappa,** obstinately asking questions that Rav Pappa did not know how to answer. [13]**One day,** Rav Shimi **saw** Rav Pappa **fall on his face** in prayer. [14]**He heard him say: "May the Merciful One save me from the embarrassment** I am suffering

LITERAL TRANSLATION

[1]Moses is different. [2]Since he asked [for it] for the many, he was regarded like the many.

[3]Rav Huna bar Manoaḥ and Rav Shmuel bar Idi and Rav Ḥiyya from Vastanya were [found] regularly before Rava. [4]When Rava died, they came before Rav Pappa. [5]Whenever he would say a Halakhah to them and it did not make sense to them, [6]they would gesture to each other. [7]He was upset (lit., "his mind was weak").

[9B] [8]They read to him in his dream: "And I destroyed the three shepherds." [9]The next day, when they were parting from him, [10]he said to them: "May the Rabbis go in peace."

[11]Rav Shimi bar Ashi was [found] regularly before Rav Pappa. [12]He would raise many difficulties for him. [13]One day, he saw him fall on his face. [14]He heard him say: "May the Merciful One save

[1]שָׁאנֵי מֹשֶׁה. [2]כֵּיוָן דִּלְרַבִּים הוּא בָּעֵי, כְּרַבִּים דָּמֵי.

[3]רַב הוּנָא בַּר מָנוֹחַ וְרַב שְׁמוּאֵל בַּר אִידִי וְרַב חִיָּיא מִוּוֹסְתָּנְיָא הָווּ שְׁכִיחִי קַמֵּיהּ דְּרָבָא. [4]כִּי נָח נַפְשֵׁיהּ דְּרָבָא אָתוּ לְקַמֵּיהּ דְּרַב פַּפָּא. [5]כָּל אֵימַת דַּהֲוָה אָמַר לְהוּ שְׁמַעְתָּא וְלָא הֲוָה מִסְתַּבְּרָא לְהוּ, [6]הָווּ מְרַמְּזִי אַהֲדָדֵי. [7]חֲלַשׁ דַּעְתֵּיהּ.

[9B] [8]אַקְרוּיֵהּ בְּחֶלְמֵיהּ: "וָאַכְחִד אֶת שְׁלֹשֶׁת הָרֹעִים". [9]לְמָחָר, כִּי הָווּ מִיפְּטְרוּ מִינֵּיהּ, [10]אֲמַר לְהוּ: "לֵיזְלוּ רַבָּנַן בִּשְׁלָמָא".

[11]רַב שִׁימִי בַּר אַשִׁי הֲוָה שְׁכִיחַ קַמֵּיהּ דְּרַב פַּפָּא. [12]הֲוָה מַקְשֵׁי לֵיהּ טוּבָא. [13]יוֹמָא חַד, חַזְיֵיהּ דִּנְפַל עַל אַפֵּיהּ. [14]שְׁמָעֵיהּ דְּאָמַר: "רַחֲמָנָא לִיצְלַן

RASHI

מווסתניא — מאותו מקום. **אחוו להדדי** — מראין ומביטין זה לזה, דלא סלקא להו שמעתא כרבא. **אקרויה** — היו מקרין אותו מקרא זה בחלום: "ואכחיד את שלשת הרועים בירח אחד" שרוצין לעונשן בשמים, משום דמכספי ליה.

SAGES

רַב הוּנָא בַּר מָנוֹחַ **Rav Huna bar Manoaḥ.** A fifth-generation Babylonian Amora, Rav Huna bar Manoaḥ was a disciple of Rav Aḥa the son of Rav Ika, whose teachings he frequently cites. Rav Huna bar Manoaḥ also studied with Rava. After Rava's death, Rav Huna bar Manoaḥ studied in Rav Pappa's yeshivah, and became a student-colleague of his.

רַב שְׁמוּאֵל בַּר אִידִי **Rav Shmuel bar Idi.** This fifth-generation Babylonian Amora was a student of Rava and, after Rava's death, of Rav Pappa. Few of his teachings are recorded in the Talmud.

רַב חִיָּיא מִוּוֹסְתָּנְיָא **Rav Ḥiyya from Vastanya.** This fifth-generation Babylonian Amora was a student of Rava, as is related here. Little is known about him, and he is very rarely mentioned in the Talmud.

רַב שִׁימִי בַּר אַשִׁי **Rav Shimi bar Ashi.** A Babylonian Amora of the fifth generation, Rav Shimi bar Ashi was a close disciple of Abaye, and also studied with Rava. After his teachers died he attended Rav Pappa's yeshivah, and the members of his generation regarded him as a great man and honored him. His teachings are transmitted by a number of Sages of the following generation, although he apparently did not have a yeshivah of his own. In several places in the Talmud he is shown to have been extremely sharp-witted, so that his contemporaries feared his questions. He may have been a physician by profession, but we do not have detailed information about his life.

BACKGROUND

אָתוּ לְקַמֵּיהּ דְּרַב פַּפָּא **They came before Rav Pappa.** Rav Pappa was a student of the greatest scholars of the preceding generation, but he was in particular a close disciple of Rava. After Rava's death Rava's yeshivah in Meḥoza was divided. Rav Pappa became head of the part of the yeshivah that was transferred to the city of Neresh, and over time he trained many students.

Rav Huna bar Manoaḥ and his friends had also been

NOTES

the same wide spectrum of meanings as does the Hebrew word כִּי (*Arukh, Rashi*). Thus Onkelos intentionally maintains the ambiguity in meaning that he found in the Hebrew original.

It has been noted that in fact the word כִּי has other meanings in addition to the four suggested by Resh Lakish. For example, the word כִּי often has the meaning of כַּאֲשֶׁר — "when." Thus Resh Lakish is not to be understood as having provided a full list of the possible meanings of the word. All that he means to say is that we should not make the mistake of thinking that the word כִּי has one uniform meaning.

לֵיזְלוּ רַבָּנַן בִּשְׁלָמָא **May the Rabbis go in peace.** The story reported here can be understood in the light of a teaching in tractate *Berakhot* (64a), that someone who bids farewell should say: "Go *for* peace [לֵךְ לְשָׁלוֹם]," whereas to the dead one says: "Go *in* peace [לֵךְ בְּשָׁלוֹם]." Thus, when Rav Pappa said to the younger Sages: "לֵיזְלוּ בִּשְׁלָמָא," he was using the formula for taking leave of the dead. He thought that this was appropriate, because he interpreted his dream as a divine revelation that the three Sages would soon meet their deaths. A variant reading is found in some texts of the Talmud and in other sources, according to which Rav Pappa said: "לֵיזְלוּ לִשְׁלָמָא," using the formula reserved for the living. According to this reading, we must understand that the verse in Zechariah was read to Rav Pappa as a question: "Am I to destroy the three shepherds?" Therefore, Rav Pappa told his younger colleagues to go *for* peace, for he did not want them to be punished on his account (*Shittah*), or he wished to hint to them that it would be better for them to go and study somewhere else (*Sfat Emet*).

TRANSLATION AND COMMENTARY

because **of Shimi."** Rav Shimi bar Ashi realized that his behavior had greatly hurt Rav Pappa. [1]**He took upon himself** a vow of **silence** when studying before Rav Pappa, [2]**and did not raise any further difficulties** for Rav Pappa from that time onward.

וְאַף רֵישׁ לָקִישׁ [3]The Gemara now returns to the subject of God blessing the world for the sake of meritorious people. We have seen that Rabbi Yoḥanan believed that God sometimes causes rain to fall for the sake of a single righteous individual, although He does not bestow sustenance in such a case. **And Resh Lakish, too, maintained that** God sometimes causes **rain to fall for the sake of an individual** righteous person, [4]**for Resh Lakish asked rhetorically: From where do we know that** God sometimes causes **rain to fall for the sake of an individual** righteous person in this way? Resh Lakish answers that we know this from a verse, [5]**for it is written** (Zechariah 10:1): **"Ask of the Lord rain at the time of the latter rain; the Lord makes thunderclouds, and He will give them showers of rain; for each man grass in the field."** [6]Resh Lakish explains: **Could it be that** the verse means that when all the Jewish people behave righteously, the rain will fall **for everyone?** [7]**The verse teaches us** that this is not so by saying that the rain will be given **"for each man"** individually. [8]**And** this point was developed further in a Baraita, where **it was taught:** "Granted that the verse teaches us that the rain will be given **for each man** individually, **could it** nevertheless **be that** the verse means that the rain will fall **on all his fields** indiscriminately, both on the ones that need rain and on those that do not? [9]The verse **teaches us** that this is not so by saying that the rain will fall **'in the field,'** employing the singular form of the noun. Thus we see that God will cause the rain to fall only on those fields of the righteous person where it is needed, and not on his other fields. [10]Moreover, granted that the verse teaches us that the rain will fall on each **field** individually, **could it** nevertheless **be that** the verse means that the rain will fall **on the entire field** indiscriminately, both on the part that needs rain and on the part that does not? [11]**The verse teaches us** that this is not so by saying that the rain will fall on the **'grass'** of the field, employing a word (עֵשֶׂב) that suggests an individual plant." Thus we see that God will cause the rain to fall only on those plants of the righteous person that need it, and not on the other plants in his field.

כִּי הָא [12]The Gemara notes that Resh Lakish's explanation of this verse **is reminiscent of the following story**

מִכִּיסוּפָא דְשִׁימִי״. [1]קַבֵּיל עֲלֵיהּ שְׁתִיקוּתָא, [2]וְתוּ לָא אַקְשֵׁי לֵיהּ. [3]וְאַף רֵישׁ לָקִישׁ סָבַר מָטָר בִּשְׁבִיל יָחִיד. [4]דְּאָמַר רֵישׁ לָקִישׁ: מִנַּיִן לְמָטָר בִּשְׁבִיל יָחִיד? [5]דִּכְתִיב: ״שַׁאֲלוּ מֵה׳ מָטָר בְּעֵת מַלְקוֹשׁ; ה׳ עֹשֶׂה חֲזִיזִים, וּמְטַר גֶּשֶׁם יִתֵּן לָהֶם; לְאִישׁ עֵשֶׂב בַּשָּׂדֶה״. [6]יָכוֹל לַכֹּל? [7]תַּלְמוּד לוֹמַר: ״לְאִישׁ״. [8]וְתַנְיָא: ״אִי ׳לְאִישׁ׳ יָכוֹל לְכָל שְׂדוֹתָיו? [9]תַּלְמוּד לוֹמַר: ׳שָׂדֶה׳. [10]אִי שָׂדֶה, יָכוֹל לְכָל הַשָּׂדֶה? [11]תַּלְמוּד לוֹמַר: ׳עֵשֶׂב׳. [12]כִּי הָא דְּרַב דָּנִיֵּאל בַּר קְטִינָא.

LITERAL TRANSLATION

me from the embarrassment of Shimi." [1]He accepted silence upon himself, [2]and did not raise any further difficulties for him.

[3]And Resh Lakish too maintained [that] rain [falls] for the sake of an individual. [4]For Resh Lakish said: From where [do we know] that rain [falls] for the sake of an individual? [5]For it is written: "Ask of the Lord rain at the time of the latter rain; the Lord makes thunderclouds, and He will give them showers of rain; for each man grass in the field." [6]Could it be [that] it is for everyone? [7]The verse states: "For each man." [8]And it was taught: "If it is 'for each man,' could it be [that] it is for all his fields? [9]The verse states: 'Field.' [10]If it is a field, could it be [that] it is for the entire field? [11]The verse states: 'Grass.'"

[12]It is like the following [story] about Rav Daniel bar Ketina.

RASHI

קבל עליו — רב שימי שתיקותא מלהקשות עוד. **יכול לכל** — כלומר, יכול אין נותן מטר אלא אם כן הכל צריכין לו. **תלמוד לומר לאיש** — אפילו בשביל אחד. **אי לאיש יכול לכל שדותיו** — כלומר, אינו יורד עד שהוא צריך לכל שדותיו. **תלמוד לומר שדה** — אפילו אינו צריך אלא בשדה אחד. **אי בשדה יכול עד שיצטרך לכל השדה תלמוד לומר עשב** — אפילו אינו צריך אלא לעשב אחד, (עשב) בשביל ירק אחד יורד עליו מטר.

students of Rava, and after his death they went to sit before the new head of the yeshivah. But since he had previously been their colleague, they did not treat him with the proper respect.

BACKGROUND

רַחֲמָנָא לִיצְּלַן מִכִּיסוּפָא דְשִׁימִי May the Merciful One save me from the embarrassment of Shimi. The normal manner of study in the Academy was for the Rabbi to give a lesson in Halakhah or an interpretation of the Mishnah. The students would respond with questions and explanations according to their understanding of the matter. Rav Shimi bar Ashi was particularly sharp-witted in posing questions which Rav Pappa often found impossible to answer, and thus he would be disconcerted. The Sages taught that one should not ask difficult questions in front of a large audience so as not to confuse the audience or embarrass the Rabbi who is teaching. Presumably, Rav Shimi bar Ashi acted in this fashion, for after he realized that Rav Pappa had been disconcerted by his questions, Rav Shimi stopped asking them in public.

SAGES

רַב דָּנִיֵּאל בַּר קְטִינָא Rav Daniel bar Rav Ketina. A third-generation Babylonian Amora, Rav Daniel studied with his father who was a distinguished Torah scholar in his own right. Rav Daniel frequently cites the teachings of Rav, Rav Huna, and Rav Assi. The Gemara relates that Rav Daniel bar Ketina was exceptionally pious, and that his prayers were always answered.

NOTES

עֹשֶׂה חֲזִיזִים Makes thunderclouds. The statement of Rabbi Yose the son of Rabbi Ḥanina is based on the fact that the word חֲזִיזִים — "thunderclouds" — is plural, whereas all the other words in the verse that refers to rain — מַלְקוֹשׁ, גֶּשֶׁם, מָטָר — are in the singular form. Thus Rabbi Yose the son of Rabbi Ḥanina explains the verse as meaning that a separate thundercloud is formed for each and every righteous person.

BACKGROUND

פורחות Flying clouds. This description suggests the cumulus clouds of modern meteorology. They usually comprise a thick layer of clouds under which are small, thin, clouds. Clouds like these are typical rain clouds. Nevertheless, actual rainfall depends not only on the presence of the right kind of clouds, but also on wind conditions and ground temperature. For that reason, rain clouds over Eretz Israel do not always result in rainfall there, for the climate is very different from that of Babylonia.

TRANSLATION AND COMMENTARY

about Rav Daniel bar Katina, [1]**who had a garden.** [1]**Every day, he would go and inspect it.** [2]**He would say: "This bed needs water, and that bed does not need water."** [3]**And rain would come and water every part that needed water.**

מאי [4]Having mentioned the verse in Zechariah (10:1), the Gemara asks: **What is the meaning of** the expression **"the Lord makes thunderclouds"?** Why is the plural form of the noun used?

אָמַר רַבִּי יוֹסֵי בְּרַבִּי חֲנִינָא [5]**Rabbi Yose the son of Rabbi Ḥanina said** in reply: [6]The verse **teaches us that for every righteous person the Holy One blessed be He makes a separate** and distinct **thundercloud.**

מַאי "חֲזִיזִים" [7]The Gemara now asks: **What is the** precise **meaning of** the word **"thunderclouds"** (in Hebrew, חֲזִיזִים)?

אָמַר רַב יְהוּדָה [8]**Rav Yehudah said: Flying clouds.**

אָמַר רַבִּי יוֹחָנָן [9]**Rabbi Yoḥanan said: Flying clouds are** a sure **sign of rain.**

מַאי פּוֹרְחוֹת [10]The Gemara asks: **What are "flying clouds"?**

אָמַר רַב פַּפָּא [11]**Rav Pappa said: A thin cloud under a thick cloud.** Clouds of this kind seem to move more quickly than the more dense clouds above them, and that is why they are given the name "flying clouds."

אָמַר רַב יְהוּדָה [12]The Gemara now cites other indications of imminent rain. **Rav Yehudah said: Drizzle before rain means that rain is coming.** [13]But if drizzle occurs **after rain, it means that the rain is stopping.** [14]Rav Yehudah uses an analogy: **Drizzle before rain means** that **rain is coming, and your sign** for appreciating this **is a sieve.** Just as light flour drops from a sieve before coarse flour, a light drizzle indicates that heavier rain is about to fall. [15]**Drizzle after rain means that the rain is stopping, and your sign is goat dung.** Goats drop large pieces of dung at first, and finish defecating with small pieces, so that the appearance of these small pieces is a clear indication that the goat is about to finish. By analogy, the appearance of small drops of rain is a clear sign that the rainstorm is at an end.

[1]הֲוָה לֵיהּ הַהִיא גִּינְּתָא. [2]כָּל יוֹמָא, הֲוָה אָזֵיל וְסָיֵיר לַהּ. [3]אָמַר: "הָא מִישְׁרָא בָּעֲיָא מַיָּא, וְהָא מִישְׁרָא לָא בָּעֲיָא מַיָּא". [3]וַאֲתָא מִיטְרָא וְקָמַשְׁקֵי כָּל הֵיכָא דְּמִיבָּעֵי לֵיהּ מַיָּא.
[4]מַאי "ה' עֹשֶׂה חֲזִיזִים"?
[5]אָמַר רַבִּי יוֹסֵי בְּרַבִּי חֲנִינָא: [6]מְלַמֵּד שֶׁכָּל צַדִּיק הַקָּדוֹשׁ בָּרוּךְ הוּא עוֹשֶׂה לוֹ חָזִיז בִּפְנֵי עַצְמוֹ.
[7]מַאי "חֲזִיזִים"?
[8]אָמַר רַב יְהוּדָה: פּוֹרְחוֹת.
[9]אָמַר רַבִּי יוֹחָנָן: סִימָן לְמָטָר פּוֹרְחוֹת.
[10]מַאי "פּוֹרְחוֹת"?
[11]אָמַר רַב פַּפָּא: עֵיבָא קְלִישָׁא תּוּתֵי עֵיבָא סְמִיכְתָּא.
[12]אָמַר רַב יְהוּדָה: נְהִילָא מִקַּמֵּי מִיטְרָא אָתֵי מִיטְרָא. [13]בָּתַר מִיטְרָא פָּסֵיק מִיטְרָא. [14]מִקַּמֵּי מִיטְרָא אָתֵי מִיטְרָא, וְסִימָנֵיךְ מְהוֹלְתָּא. [15]דְּבָתַר מִיטְרָא פָּסֵיק מִיטְרָא, וְסִימָנֵיךְ חַרְיָא דְעִיזֵּי.

LITERAL TRANSLATION

[1]He had a garden. [2]Every day, he would go and inspect it. [3]He would say: "This bed needs water, and that bed does not need water." [3]And rain would come and water everywhere that needed water.

[4]What is [the meaning of] "the Lord makes thunderclouds"?

[5]Rabbi Yose the son of Rabbi Ḥanina said: [6]It teaches [us] that, for every righteous person, the Holy One blessed be He makes a separate thundercloud.

[7]What is [the meaning of] "thunderclouds"?

[8]Rav Yehudah said: Flying clouds.

[9]Rabbi Yoḥanan said: Flying clouds are a sign of rain.

[10]What are "flying clouds"?

[11]Rav Pappa said: A thin cloud under a thick cloud.

[12]Rav Yehudah said: Drizzle before rain [means that] rain is coming. [13]After rain [it means that] rain is stopping. [14]Drizzle before rain [means that] rain is coming, and your sign is a sieve. [15]After rain [it means that] the rain is stopping, and your sign is goat dung.

RASHI

וסייר — מְעַיין. **מישרא** — ערוגה. **עושה לו חזיז** — לכל צדיק הבא בעולם הזה, להריק לו גשמים על שדותיו, ברישא בעי: מאי "חזיזים" לשון רבים, והדר בעי: ומאי נינהו חזיזים, מאי נינהו דקרי חזיזי? הכי גרסינן: עיבא קלישתא דתותי עיבא סמיכתא — דתותי עיבא — כלפי הארץ. **הילא** — כמו קיטמא נהילא (חולין נא,ב) שהיא דקה, גשמים דקים כקמחא נהילא, שהיא דקה, הבאין תחילה למטר, ואחר כך בא מטר. **אתי מיטרא** — גשמים יורדין לרוב, ואין פוסקין מהר, אבל בא מטר תחילה ומתחילין דקין לבא — פוסקין מיד. **מהולתא** — שמתחילה יוצא קמח דק, ולבסוף סובין גסין. **חריא דעיזי** = ריעי של עזים, בתחילה יוצאה גסה, ולבסוף דקה, ופוסק.

NOTES

חַרְיָא דְעִיזֵּי Goat dung. *Arukh* cites a variant reading: דַּדְיָא דְעִיזֵּי — "goat teats." When one begins to milk a goat, the milk gushes out; but as the milking draws to a close, the milk comes out in small drops. Just as the appearance of these small drops of milk signifies that there is little milk left, so too is the light drizzle at the end of a rainstorm a sure sign that the rain is coming to an end.

TRANSLATION AND COMMENTARY

עוּלָּא [1]The previous statements about flying clouds being a sure sign of rain were made by Rabbi Yoḥanan and Resh Lakish, who lived in Eretz Israel. The Gemara now relates that when **Ulla arrived in Babylonia** from Eretz Israel, **he saw flying clouds.** [2]**He said to** the people around him: **"Put away your things in the house, because now rain is coming."** [3]But **in the end rain did not fall.** Seeing that the weather patterns in Babylonia were not the same as those in Eretz Israel, [4]Ulla **said: "Just as the Babylonians are deceptive** people, **so too is their rain deceptive."**

עוּלָּא [5]The Gemara now relates another incident that occurred when **Ulla arrived in Babylonia.** [6]**He saw a basket full of dates** being offered for sale **for a zuz**, whereas in Eretz Israel they would have been far more expensive. [7]He drew a moral from this incident, **saying: "A full basket of** date **honey** can be bought **for a zuz** in this country. [8]**Yet the Babylonians do not occupy themselves with Torah,** which they could readily do since their material needs are so easily taken care of." Ulla then bought a basket of dates and ate them. [9]**During the night, they caused him** stomach **pain** and diarrhea. As a result of this incident he changed his opinion, [10]**saying:** "Now I am impressed with Babylonia. **A full basket of** things that hurt like **knives** can be bought **for a zuz**! [11]Yet the **Babylonians** still succeed in **occupying themselves with Torah,** despite the fact that they suffer pain from the food they eat."

תַּנְיָא [12]The Gemara now discusses the source of rain. **It was taught** in a Baraita that there was a Tannaitic dispute on this subject: **"Rabbi Eliezer said:** [13]**The entire world derives its rain from the waters of the ocean, as it is said** [Genesis 2:6]: **'And a mist rose from the earth and watered the whole face of the ground.'** Thus we see that the source of rain is in mist that rises from the earth and becomes rainclouds, and not in some source of water in the heavens. [14]**Rabbi Yehoshua said to him:** Your viewpoint is logically flawed, because rainwater is fresh **but the waters of the ocean are salty.** [15]Rabbi Eliezer **said to** Rabbi Yehoshua in reply: The ocean mist begins by being salty, but the rain water **is sweetened in the clouds.** [16]**Rabbi**

[1]עוּלָּא אִיקְלַע לְבָבֶל. חֲזָא פּוֹרְחוֹת. [2]אֲמַר לְהוּ: "פַּנּוּ מָאנֵי, דְּהָשְׁתָּא אָתֵי מִיטְרָא". [3]לְסוֹף לָא אָתֵי מִיטְרָא. [4]אֲמַר: "כִּי הֵיכִי דִּמְשַׁקְּרִי בַּבְלָאֵי, הָכִי מְשַׁקְּרִי מִיטְרַיְיהוּ".

[5]עוּלָּא אִיקְלַע לְבָבֶל. [6]חָזֵי מְלָא צַנָּא דְּתַמְרֵי בְּזוּזָא. [7]אֲמַר: "מְלָא צַנָּא דְּדוּבְשָׁא בְּזוּזָא, [8]וּבַבְלָאֵי לָא עָסְקֵי בְּאוֹרַיְיתָא!" [9]בְּלֵילְיָא צַעֲרוּהוּ. [10]אֲמַר: "מְלָא צַנָּא דְּסַכִּינָא בְּזוּזָא, [11]וּבַבְלָאֵי עָסְקֵי בְּאוֹרַיְיתָא!"

[12]תַּנְיָא: "רַבִּי אֱלִיעֶזֶר אוֹמֵר: [13]כָּל הָעוֹלָם כּוּלּוֹ מִמֵּימֵי אוֹקְיָינוֹס הוּא שׁוֹתֶה, שֶׁנֶּאֱמַר: 'וְאֵד יַעֲלֶה מִן הָאָרֶץ וְהִשְׁקָה אֶת כָּל פְּנֵי הָאֲדָמָה'. [14]אָמַר לוֹ רַבִּי יְהוֹשֻׁעַ: וַהֲלֹא מֵימֵי אוֹקְיָינוֹס מְלוּחִין הֵן? [15]אָמַר לוֹ: מְמַתְּקִין בֶּעָבִים. [16]רַבִּי

LITERAL TRANSLATION

[1]Ulla happened to come to Babylonia. He saw flying clouds. [2]He said to them: "Put away the things, for now rain is coming." [3]In the end, rain did not come. [4]He said: "Just as the Babylonians lie, so do their rains lie."

[5]Ulla happened to come to Babylonia. [6]He saw a basket full of dates for a zuz. [7]He said: "A full basket of honey for a zuz, [8]and [yet] the Babylonians do not occupy themselves with Torah!" [9]In the night, they caused him pain. [10]He said: "A full basket of knives for a zuz, [11]and [yet] the Babylonians occupy themselves with Torah!"

[12]It was taught: "Rabbi Eliezer says: [13]The entire world drinks from the waters of the ocean, as it is said: 'And a mist rose from the earth and watered the whole face of the ground.' [14]Rabbi Yehoshua said to him: But are not the waters of the ocean! [15]He said to him: They are sweetened in the clouds. [16]Rabbi

RASHI

דתמרי — דבש עושין מהן. **ובבלאי לא עסקי** — כלומר, יכולין הן לעסוק תמיד, שיש להן מזונות בזול ובלא טורח. **מצערים** — בשלשול, דאמרו (גיטין ע,א): תמרי משחנן ומשלשלן. **מלא צנא דסכיני בזוזא** — שמתוך שלוקחין אותו בזול אוכלין מהן הרבה, ומצערים אותן. **ממימי אוקיינוס** — כלומר: ממים של מטה, ולא ממים של מעלה, שנאמר "ואד יעלה מן הארץ" שעתה בארץ ועלה. **מלוחין הן** — ואין תבואה גדילה מהן.

BACKGROUND

כִּי הֵיכִי דִּמְשַׁקְּרִי בַּבְלָאֵי Just as the Babylonians lie. People from Eretz Israel had a poor opinion of Babylonians, regarding them as uncultivated, unmannered, and unethical. That is why Ulla used this expression.

מְלָא צַנָּא דְּדוּבְשָׁא בְּזוּזָא A full basket of honey for a zuz. Although date palms are found in Eretz Israel, the climate of Babylonia and the combination of hot weather with an aquifer close to the surface make it a center for growing dates to this day. They grow in large quantities and are therefore quite cheap.

Dates have great nutritive value because of their high concentration of sugar, and the Sages praised their beneficial effect on those who eat them. At first Ulla, who was from Eretz Israel, thought that one could live only on dates, and for that reason he reprimanded the people of Babylonia, who did not study Torah enough, even though they could supposedly live a comfortable life with little work. After eating a large number of dates, however, which caused him stomach cramps and diarrhea, Ulla realized that dates could only be an addition to other foods, and that Babylonians still had to work hard to survive.

LANGUAGE

אוֹקְיָינוֹס The ocean. The source of this word is the Greek Ὠκεανός, *Oceanos,* which means, among other things, the outer ocean surrounding the world, as opposed to the Mediterranean Sea.

NOTES

רַבִּי אֱלִיעֶזֶר וְרַבִּי יְהוֹשֻׁעַ Rabbi Eliezer and Rabbi Yehoshua. According to the straightforward understanding of the dispute between Rabbi Eliezer and Rabbi Yehoshua, the two Tannaim are debating a scientific question regarding the source of rainwater — whether rain is recycled water from the ocean, or whether it is derived from some heavenly source (see *Maharsha*).

Some commentators suggest that this discussion is an allusion to a dispute regarding the mutual influences of the heavenly and the mundane worlds. Is the source of all bounty to be found in the heavens, human endeavor serving merely as a receptacle for that bounty, or is divine bounty dependent on human activity? (See *Otzar HaKavod* and others.)

יְהוֹשֻׁעַ אוֹמֵר: [1]כָּל הָעוֹלָם כּוּלּוֹ מִמַּיִם הָעֶלְיוֹנִים הוּא שׁוֹתֶה, [2]שֶׁנֶּאֱמַר: ׳לִמְטַר הַשָּׁמַיִם תִּשְׁתֶּה מָּיִם׳. [3]אֶלָּא מָה אֲנִי מְקַיֵּים ׳וְאֵד יַעֲלֶה מִן הָאָרֶץ׳? [4]מְלַמֵּד שֶׁהָעֲנָנִים מִתְגַּבְּרִים וְעוֹלִים לָרָקִיעַ, [5]וּפוֹתְחִין פִּיהֶן כְּנוֹד וּמְקַבְּלִין מֵי מָטָר, [6]שֶׁנֶּאֱמַר: ׳יָזֹקּוּ מָטָר לְאֵדוֹ׳. [7]וּמְנוּקָּבוֹת הֵן כִּכְבָרָה, וּבָאוֹת וּמְחַשְּׁרוֹת מַיִם עַל גַּבֵּי קַרְקַע, [8]שֶׁנֶּאֱמַר: ׳חַשְׁרַת מַיִם, עָבֵי שְׁחָקִים׳. [9]וְאֵין בֵּין טִיפָּה לְטִיפָּה אֶלָּא כִּמְלֹא נִימָא, [10]לְלַמֶּדְךָ שֶׁגָּדוֹל יוֹם הַגְּשָׁמִים כְּיוֹם שֶׁנִּבְרְאוּ בּוֹ שָׁמַיִם וָאָרֶץ, [11]שֶׁנֶּאֱמַר: עֹשֶׂה גְדֹלוֹת וְאֵין חֵקֶר׳. [12]וּכְתִיב: ׳הַנֹּתֵן מָטָר עַל פְּנֵי אָרֶץ׳. [13]וּכְתִיב לְהַלָּן: ׳הֲלוֹא יָדַעְתָּ? אִם לֹא שָׁמַעְתָּ? [14]אֱלֹהֵי עוֹלָם, ה׳,... אֵין חֵקֶר לִתְבוּנָתוֹ׳. [15]וּכְתִיב: ׳מֵכִין הָרִים בְּכֹחוֹ, וְגוֹ׳׳״.

[16]כְּמַאן אָזְלָא הָא דִּכְתִיב:

LITERAL TRANSLATION

Yehoshua says: [1]The entire world drinks from the upper waters, [2]as it is said: 'From the rain of the heavens you will drink water.' [3]Then what do I learn from 'and a mist rose from the earth'? [4]It teaches that the clouds grow stronger and rise to the firmament, [5]and open their mouths like a leather bottle and receive the rainwaters, [6]as it is said: 'They pour down rain into His mist.' [7]And they are perforated like a sieve, and they come and sprinkle water onto the ground, [8]as it is said: 'Sprinkling water, the clouds of the skies.' [9]And between drop and drop there is nothing but a hairsbreadth, [10]to teach you that the day of rains is as great as the day on which Heaven and Earth were created, [11]as it is said: 'He does great things and there is no comprehension.' [12]And it is written: 'Who gives rain on the face of the earth.' [13]And it is written elsewhere: 'Did you not know? Have you not heard? [14]The God of the world, the Lord... there is no comprehension of His wisdom.' [15]And it is written: 'He sets firm the mountains with His strength, etc.'"

[16]According to whom does the following [statement] that is

TRANSLATION AND COMMENTARY

Yehoshua says: [1]**The entire world derives its rain from waters in the upper** regions, above the firmament of the sky, [2]**as it is said** [Deuteronomy 11:11]: **'From the rain of the heavens you will drink water.'** Thus we see that water does not rise from the earth and fall again as rain, but is derived from a source in the heavens. Rabbi Yehoshua now asks a rhetorical question: [3]**Then what do I learn from** the verse cited by Rabbi Eliezer: **'And a mist rose from the earth'?** [4]**It teaches** us **that the clouds grow stronger and rise** from their original position over the surface of the earth. [5]They rise **to the firmament** of the sky **and open their mouths like a leather water bottle, and receive the rainwaters** from their source in the heavens, [6]**as it is said** [Job 36:27]: **'They pour down rain into His mist.'** [7]Rabbi Yehoshua continues to explain that the clouds **are perforated like a sieve, and** when they are filled with water from heaven, **they come and sprinkle the water onto the ground,** [8]**as it is said** [II Samuel 22:12]: **'Sprinkling water, the clouds of the skies.'** [9]Rabbi Yehoshua notes that the clouds are so finely perforated that **the gap between drop and drop is no more than a hairsbreadth.** [10]This can serve **to teach you that the day** when **rain** falls **is as great as the day on which Heaven and Earth were created,** [11]**as it is said** [Job 5:9]: **'He does great things and there is no comprehension,** and wonders without number.' [12]**And it is** further **written** in the next verse: 'Who **gives rain on the face of the earth.'** Thus we see that the 'great things' and the 'wonders' refer to rain. Rainfall is compared to creation by means of a hermeneutical rule called a *gezerah shavah*, whereby verses in separate contexts can be compared when the same word appears in both of them. In this case, the word 'comprehension' appears in the verse in Job and also in a verse dealing with the creation of the world. [13]For **it is written elsewhere** [Isaiah 40:28]: **'Did you not know? Have you not heard?** [14]**The God of the world, the Lord,** the Creator of the ends of the earth, does not faint and is not weary; **there is no comprehension of His wisdom.'** Thus we see that the word 'comprehension' appears both in connection with the creation of the world and in connection with rain, and this teaches us that the creation and rain are comparable. [15]**And** we know that the creation of the world is the ultimate reflection of God's power, as **it is written** [Psalms 65:7]: **'He sets firm mountains with His strength.'** Thus we may infer that rain is as much a reflection of God's power as is the creation of the world."

כְּמַאן אָזְלָא הָא דִּכְתִיב [16]In the light of these two Tannaitic opinions as to the source of rain, the Gemara asks: **Which** view **does the following** Amoraic **statement reflect? For it is written** (Psalms 104:13):

RASHI

יזקו מטר לאדו — רקיעין מוליאין מים לעבים. **יזקו** — כמו ״ינוקו״, ״לק לעס ויאכלו״ (מלכים ב ז). **חשרת מים עבי שחקים** — העבים מחסרין, כלומר: מסירין המים לארץ. **ללמדך** — אקרא דלקמן קאי, ואומר מכין הרים — לא גרסינן הכא.

LANGUAGE

וּמְחַשְּׁרוֹת And sprinkle. This verb describes the way flour falls from a sieve or the way rain falls — in drops or small particles. It may be related to the Arabic حشر, meaning "dense," or "thick."

BACKGROUND

וְאֵין בֵּין טִיפָּה לְטִיפָּה And between drop and drop there is nothing. The details of the process of rain production are an important area of scientific study today. The systems that produce rain (the presence of water vapor in sufficient concentration, the temperature at which tiny ice crystals are formed, the creation of drops and their structure) are complicated, and have led to the creation of a "physics of chaos," dealing with the combination of the many factors, large and small, that produce a single event.

The creation of drops, the inner cohesion of the water molecules that form each drop, the fact that these drops receive a characteristic shape and do not fall in a continuous flow — all these are extremely complex matters.

Therefore the Gemara speaks of the miracle of the creation of rain. Although this is a common event, it is also difficult to understand, like well-known miracles. The creation of rainfall is in its own way as elaborate and complicated as the creation of the entire universe.

[1]״מַשְׁקֶה הָרִים מֵעֲלִיּוֹתָיו״? [2]וְאָמַר רַבִּי יוֹחָנָן: מֵעֲלִיּוֹתָיו שֶׁל הַקָּדוֹשׁ בָּרוּךְ הוּא. [3]כְּמַאן? [4]כְּרַבִּי יְהוֹשֻׁעַ. [5]וְרַבִּי אֱלִיעֶזֶר? [6]כֵּיוָן דְּסָלְקֵי לְהָתָם ״מַשְׁקֶה מֵעֲלִיּוֹתָיו״ קָרֵי לְהוּ. [7]דְּאִי לָא תֵּימָא הָכִי, [8]״אָבָק וְעָפָר מִן הַשָּׁמַיִם״ הֵיכִי מַשְׁכַּחַת לָהּ? [9]אֶלָּא, כֵּיוָן דְּמִדְלֵי לְהָתָם, [10]״מִן הַשָּׁמַיִם״ קָרֵי לֵיהּ. [11]הָכִי נַמִי, דְּסָלְקֵי לְהָתָם, [12]״מֵעֲלִיּוֹתָיו״ קָרֵי לֵיהּ.

[13]כְּמַאן אָזְלָא הָא דְּאָמַר רַבִּי חֲנִינָא: [14]״כֹּנֵס כַּנֵּד מֵי הַיָּם; נֹתֵן בְּאוֹצָרוֹת תְּהוֹמוֹת״. [15]מִי גָּרַם לָאוֹצָרוֹת שֶׁיִּתְמַלְּאוּ בָּר? תְּהוֹמוֹת.

[16]כְּרַבִּי אֱלִיעֶזֶר.

[17]וְרַבִּי יְהוֹשֻׁעַ?

[18]הַהוּא [10A] בִּבְרִיָּיתוֹ שֶׁל עוֹלָם.

LITERAL TRANSLATION

written go: [1]He waters the mountains from His upper chambers? [2]And Rabbi Yoḥanan said: From the upper chambers of the Holy One blessed be He. [3]According to whom?

[4]According to Rabbi Yehoshua.

[5]And Rabbi Eliezer?

[6]Since they go up to there, they are called: He waters from His upper chambers. [7]For if you do not say so, [8]how can "powder and dust from the heavens be found? [9]Rather, since it goes up to there, [10]it is called: From the heavens. [11]Here too, [since] they go up to there, they are called: [12]From His upper chambers.

[13]According to whom does the following [statement] that Rabbi Ḥanina said go: [14]He gathers together like a heap the waters of the sea; He puts the depths in storehouses. [15]Who caused the storehouses to be filled with grain? The depths.

[16]According to Rabbi Eliezer.

[17]And Rabbi Yehoshua?

[18]That [verse] [10A] is about the creation of the world.

TRANSLATION AND COMMENTARY

[1]**He waters the mountains from His upper chambers.** [2]**And Rabbi Yoḥanan said** that this verse means that the rain comes **"from the upper chambers of the Holy One blessed be He,"** meaning the upper chambers of the sky. [3]**According to which** of the two Tannaim is Rabbi Yoḥanan's statement?

כְּרַבִּי יְהוֹשֻׁעַ [4]The Gemara answers: Rabbi Yoḥanan's statement clearly **reflects** the viewpoint of **Rabbi Yehoshua** that the source of rain is above the sky.

וְרַבִּי אֱלִיעֶזֶר [5]The Gemara asks: **And Rabbi Eliezer?** How does he explain this verse?

כֵּיוָן [6]The Gemara answers that, according to Rabbi Eliezer, **since** clouds **rise** from the ocean **to** the sky and only then bring rain down to the earth, the process **is called watering from** God's **upper chambers.** [7]**For if you do not say** that this interpretation is correct, [8]**how can you explain** the following verse (Deuteronomy 28:24): The Lord will make the rain of your land **powder and dust; from the heavens** it will fall on you until you are destroyed. The verse is saying that dust and dirt will fall from the heavens. But where can we find dust and dirt that originate in the heavens? [9]**Rather,** the dust and the dirt originate on the ground and then rise to the sky before falling again, and **since** the dust and the dirt **rise to** the sky before falling, [10]the process **is called:** Falling **from the heavens.** [11]We may apply this interpretation **here, too,** and say that **since** clouds **rise** from the ocean **to** the sky and then cause rain to fall on the earth, [12]the process **is called** "watering **from** God's **upper chambers."**

כְּמַאן אָזְלָא [13]Similarly, the Gemara asks: Which of the two Tannaitic views **does the following statement of Rabbi Ḥanina reflect?** Rabbi Ḥanina commented on the following verse (Psalms 33:7): [14]**"He gathers together like a heap the waters of the sea; He puts the depths in storehouses."** Rabbi Ḥanina said: The word "storehouses" in this verse refers to granaries. But the depths themselves are not put in granaries. [15]Rather, this verse teaches us that **it is the depths that cause the storehouses to be filled with grain,** by returning their water to the land in the form of rain.

כְּרַבִּי אֱלִיעֶזֶר [16]The Gemara answers: Rabbi Ḥanina's statement clearly **reflects** the viewpoint of **Rabbi Eliezer** that the source of rain is the depths of the ocean.

וְרַבִּי יְהוֹשֻׁעַ [17]The Gemara asks: **And** how does **Rabbi Yehoshua** explain this verse?

הַהוּא [18]The Gemara answers that, according to Rabbi Yehoshua, **that** particular **verse** in Psalms is not referring to rainfall at all. [10A] It **is** talking **about the creation of the world.** The "storehouses" are

RASHI

ואמר רבי יוחנן מעליותיו של מעלה — כלומר ממים העליונים, ורבי יוחנן מים העליונים אתא לאשמועינן, דאי לאו רבי יוחנן — הוי אמינא דהכי קאמר: מעליות שהקדוש ברוך הוא עומד בהם הוא משקה אותן למטה, ולעולם המים מאוקיינוס. **כרבי יהושע** — דאמר ממים העליונים. **ורבי אליעזר** — אמר לעולם מעליותיו של הקדוש ברוך הוא, כרבי יוחנן וכו׳. **תהומות** — מים של מטה, כדכתיב ״תהומות יכסיומו״ (שמות טו). **בבריותו של עולם** — כתיב, שהיה כל העולם שטוף במים, והקדוש ברוך הוא כונסן במקום אחד כמכנים מים בנאד, שנתנם באוצרות, דכתיב ״נותן באוצרות תהומות״ שם חול גבולו ואוצר לים.

TRANSLATION AND COMMENTARY

metaphorical storehouses, in which the depths of the ocean are themselves retained to prevent them from flooding the earth. Thus the verse is saying that when God separated the waters from the dry land, He gathered all the waters of the seas into one place, as though behind a wall, and kept them there, as though the depths of the seas were placed in a storehouse.

תָּנוּ רַבָּנַן [1]Before continuing its analysis of the dispute between Rabbi Eliezer and Rabbi Yehoshua, the Gemara interjects with a Baraita describing the superiority of Eretz Israel to the rest of the world. **Our Rabbis taught** the following Baraita: **"Eretz Israel was created first and the entire** rest of the **world was created later,** [2]**as it is said** in a verse discussing the creation (Proverbs 8:26): **'He had not yet made the land and the outlying areas.'"** This Baraita understands the term "land" to refer to Eretz Israel, and the term חוּצוֹת, which we have translated as "outlying areas," to refer to the parts of the world outside Eretz Israel. Thus the verse describes God as first creating Eretz Israel and then the outlying areas outside it. A similar distinction can be found in a verse in Job dealing with rain: [3]**"Eretz Israel is watered by the Holy One blessed be He Himself,** whereas **the entire** rest of the **world is watered through an agent,** [4]**as it is said** [Job 5:10]: **'Who gives rain on the face of the land, and sends water on the face of the outlying areas.'"** The verse in Job describes God as bestowing rain directly on the land (i.e., on Eretz Israel), whereas He merely sends it by intermediary to the areas outside Eretz Israel. [5]Along the same lines the Baraita declares: **"Eretz Israel drinks** true **rainwater,** whereas the water **the entire world drinks** is merely **the residue** left over in the clouds, [6]**as it is said** [ibid.]: **'Who gives rain on the face of the land,** and sends water on the face of the outlying areas.'" The verse in Job describes God as bestowing *rain* on the land (Eretz Israel), and sending mere *water* to the outlying areas. [7]In the same vein the Baraita declares: **"Eretz Israel drinks first** (in that God decides first how much rain to give to Israel), **and** the decision about the rain falling on **the entire** rest of the **world** comes **later,** [8]**as it is said** in the same verse in Job: **'Who gives rain on the face of the land,** and sends water on the face of the outlying areas.'" God brings rain to the world in two stages: First to Eretz Israel, and then to the areas outside Eretz Israel. The Baraita concludes: [9]"The selection of Eretz Israel **is analogous to a person who kneads cheese** after it has curdled. [10]**He takes the food** [the curds], **and leaves the refuse** [the whey]. This is the relationship between Eretz Israel and the rest of the world in the eyes of God."

אָמַר מָר [11]The Gemara now returns to the dispute between Rabbi Eliezer and Rabbi Yehoshua. **It was stated above** that Rabbi Yehoshua had objected to Rabbi Eliezer that the source of rain could not be the mists rising from the oceans, since the oceans are salty, whereas rainwater is sweet. And Rabbi Eliezer had said to Rabbi Yehoshua in reply: [12]"The ocean mist begins by being salty, but the rain water **is sweetened**

[1]תָּנוּ רַבָּנַן: "אֶרֶץ יִשְׂרָאֵל נִבְרֵאת תְּחִילָּה וְכָל הָעוֹלָם כּוּלּוֹ נִבְרָא לְבַסּוֹף, [2]שֶׁנֶּאֱמַר: 'עַד לֹא עָשָׂה אֶרֶץ וְחוּצוֹת'. [3]אֶרֶץ יִשְׂרָאֵל מַשְׁקָה אוֹתָהּ הַקָּדוֹשׁ בָּרוּךְ הוּא בְּעַצְמוֹ, וְכָל הָעוֹלָם כּוּלּוֹ עַל יְדֵי שָׁלִיחַ, [4]שֶׁנֶּאֱמַר: הַנֹּתֵן מָטָר עַל פְּנֵי אָרֶץ, וְשֹׁלֵחַ מַיִם עַל פְּנֵי חוּצוֹת'. [5]אֶרֶץ יִשְׂרָאֵל שׁוֹתָה מֵי גְשָׁמִים, וְכָל הָעוֹלָם כּוּלּוֹ מִתַּמְצִית, [6]שֶׁנֶּאֱמַר: 'הַנֹּתֵן מָטָר עַל פְּנֵי אָרֶץ, וגו'. [7]אֶרֶץ יִשְׂרָאֵל שׁוֹתָה תְּחִילָּה, וְכָל הָעוֹלָם כּוּלּוֹ לְבַסּוֹף, [8]שֶׁנֶּאֱמַר: הַנֹּתֵן מָטָר עַל פְּנֵי אָרֶץ, וגו'. [9]מָשָׁל לְאָדָם שֶׁמְּגַבֵּל אֶת הַגְּבִינָה. [10]נוֹטֵל אֶת הָאוֹכֶל וּמַנִּיחַ אֶת הַפְּסוֹלֶת".

[11]אָמַר מָר: [12]מִמַּתְּקִין הֵן

LITERAL TRANSLATION

[1]Our Rabbis taught: "Eretz Israel was created first and the entire world was created last, [2]as it is said: 'He had not yet made the land and the outlying areas.' [3]Eretz Israel is watered by the Holy One blessed be He Himself, and the entire world [is watered] through an agent, [4]as it is said: 'Who gives rain on the face of the land, and sends water on the face of the outlying areas.' [5]Eretz Israel drinks rainwater, and the entire world [drinks] from the residue, [6]as it is said: 'Who gives rain on the face of the land, etc.' [7]Eretz Israel drinks first, and the entire world [drinks] last, [8]as it is said: 'Who gives rain on the face of the land, etc.' [9]It is like a man who kneads cheese. [10]He takes the food and leaves the refuse."

[11]The master said: [12]"They are made sweet in the

RASHI

משיורי תמצית — מה שנשאר בעבים אחר שתייתה. **על פני ארץ** — ארץ ישראל. **בתחילה שותה** — שם יורדין הגשמים תחילה, כך שמעתי.

NOTES

אֶרֶץ יִשְׂרָאֵל וְכָל הָעוֹלָם **Eretz Israel and the entire world.** *Rashba* writes that the comparisons and distinctions drawn here between Eretz Israel and the rest of the world are expressions of the idea that the world was created for the

TRANSLATION AND COMMENTARY

in the clouds." [1]The Gemara asks: **From where does** Rabbi Eliezer **know** that the clouds have the power to remove the salt from seawater?

דְּאָמַר רַב יִצְחָק בַּר יוֹסֵף [2]The Gemara explains that Rabbi Eliezer infers this idea from a Biblical verse. **For Rav Yitzḥak bar Yosef said in the name of Rabbi Yoḥanan:** [3]**It is written** (Psalms 18:12): **"The darkness of water, the clouds of the sky,"** [4]**and it is written** (II Samuel 22:12): **"Sprinkling water, the clouds of the sky."** Psalm 18 and chapter 22 of II Samuel are two versions of the same song, written by King David "on the day when God delivered him from all his enemies." The two versions vary in only a few words, and were traditionally understood to complement each other. Here the two versions vary in only one word — "darkness" (חֶשְׁכַת) as against "sprinkling" (חַשְׁרַת). Moreover, these two words differ in only one letter — kaph (כ) as against resh (ר). Rabbi Yitzḥak bar Yosef explains that the two variant versions are intended to hint at yet a third possibility: [5]**Take the letter kaph** from the version in Psalms ("darkness") **and place it next to the letter resh** in the version in II Samuel ("sprinkling"), thereby creating a new word containing both letters: חַכְשָׁרַת. This word means nothing in Hebrew, but if the first letter heth (ח) is replaced by the letter he (ה) it becomes the word הַכְשָׁרַת, which means "rendering fit." [6]Thus we may **read** the verse **as** saying: **"The rendering fit** of water is [done by] the clouds of the sky," which teaches us that the clouds remove salt from the water of the ocean and make it fit to drink.

וְרַבִּי יְהוֹשֻׁעַ [7]The Gemara asks: **And Rabbi Yehoshua?** Clearly he does not agree with the above explanation of this verse, because he maintains that the clouds do not sweeten the water. [8]**How,** then, **does he interpret** the difference between **these** two **verses?**

סָבַר לָהּ [9]The Gemara answers: Rabbi Yehoshua's **opinion about** these verses **is as follows:** [10]**When Rav Dimi came** from Eretz Israel to Babylonia, **he said: They say in Eretz Israel:** [11]**When clouds are bright, they have little water; when clouds are dark, they have much water,** and the two versions of David's song refer to these two types of rainfall. The verse in Psalms refers to the heavy rainfall that comes from "the darkness in the clouds," whereas the verse in Samuel refers to the fine rain that comes from "the sprinkling of the clouds."

כְּמַאן אָזְלָא הָא דְּתַנְיָא [12]The Gemara now examines one further statement in the light of the two Tannaitic opinions as to the source of rain. The Gemara asks: **Which** of the two Tannaitic views, that of Rabbi Eliezer or that of Rabbi Yehoshua, **does the following Baraita reflect?** [13]**For it was taught:** "The Torah [Genesis 1:6] states that God created the firmament to divide the lower waters on earth from the upper waters above the sky. **The upper waters** do not rest on the sky, but **are suspended** above the sky **by the Word of God,**

בֶּעָבִים". [1]מְנָלֵיהּ?
[2]דְּאָמַר רַב יִצְחָק בַּר יוֹסֵף אָמַר רַבִּי יוֹחָנָן: [3]כְּתִיב: "חֶשְׁכַת מַיִם, עָבֵי שְׁחָקִים", [4]וּכְתִיב: "חַשְׁרַת מַיִם, עָבֵי שְׁחָקִים." [5]שְׁקוֹל כַּף וּשְׁדֵי אֲרֵישׁ, [6]וּקְרֵי בֵּיהּ "חַכְשָׁרַת".
[7]וְרַבִּי יְהוֹשֻׁעַ, [8]בְּהָנֵי קְרָאֵי מַאי דָּרֵישׁ בְּהוּ?
[9]סָבַר לָהּ כִּי הָא: [10]דְּכִי אֲתָא רַב דִּימִי, אֲמַר: אָמְרִי בְּמַעְרְבָא: [11]נְהוֹר עֲנָנֵי, זְעִירִין מוֹהִי; חֲשׁוֹךְ עֲנָנֵי, סָגְיָין מוֹהִי.
[12]כְּמַאן אָזְלָא הָא דְּתַנְיָא: [13]"מַיִם הָעֶלְיוֹנִים בְּמַאֲמָר הֵם

LITERAL TRANSLATION

clouds." [1]From where does he [know this]? [2]For Rav Yitzḥak bar Yosef said in the name of Rabbi Yoḥanan: [3]It is written: "The darkness of water, the clouds of the sky," [4]and it is written: "Sprinkling water the clouds of the sky." [5]Take the [letter] kaph and place it next to (lit., "throw it on") the [letter] resh, [6]and read it as "rendering fit." [7]And Rabbi Yehoshua, [8]how does he interpret these verses? [9]He thinks about it like the following: [10]For when Rav Dimi came, he said: They say in Eretz Israel (lit., "the West"): [11][When] clouds are bright, [they have] little water; [when] clouds are dark [they have] much water. [12]According to whom goes the following [thing] that was taught: [13]"The upper waters are suspended by the Word [of

RASHI

חשרת מים וחשכת מים — שני מקראות הן, חד בתהלים וחד בשמואל, ב"וידבר דוד". **הכי גרסינן: שקול כף ושדי אריש** — כלומר: קח כף שבמלת "חשכת", וצרפו עם מלת "חשרת", וקרי ביה חכשרת — שממתקין ומכשירין בעבים. **חשוך ענני סגיאין מימוהי** — והיינו דכתיב "חשכת מים". **נהור ענני** — כשהענן קלים זעירין מימוהי, ומכלל חשוך סגיאין, אתה למד: אבל נהור עירין, ו"חשרת" — לשון השרה, כמו "אין שורין דיו" (שבת יז,ב) כו' כדדריש ליה רבי יהושע לעיל, אבל "חשכת" מיבעי ליה להכי ולהכי. **במאמר הן תלוין** — אינן נחות על שום דבר, אלא מכונסות ועומדות כמין בריכה, ותלויות במאמרו של הקדוש ברוך הוא.

NOTES

sake of Eretz Israel, that the most significant events occurring in the world take place in Eretz Israel, that the rest of the world plays a role secondary to that of Eretz Israel, and that the rest of the world benefits from the divine bounty that is intended primarily for Eretz Israel.

LANGUAGE

חַכְשָׁרַת Rendering fit. The statement in the name of Rabbi Yoḥanan takes the initial letter heth (ח) as being equivalent to the letter he (ה) and interprets the word as meaning "preparation." No comment is made about this change in letters because they are similar both in form and in pronunciation, and in Talmudic times there were already a great many people who found it difficult to distinguish between the two. The Sages say explicitly that it is permitted to draw Midrashic meaning from Biblical verses by substituting one of these letters for the other (see Jerusalem Talmud, *Shabbat* 7:2).

SAGES

רַב יִצְחָק בַּר יוֹסֵף Rav Yitzḥak bar Yosef. An Amora of the fourth generation, Rav Yitzḥak bar Yosef was born in Babylonia, but studied in Eretz Israel. He was one of the נְחוּתֵי, the emissaries from Eretz Israel who would travel to Babylonia to report the teachings of Eretz Israel. Rav Yitzḥak bar Yosef studied with Rabbi Yoḥanan's students and may have had the privilege of studying with Rabbi Yoḥanan himself. He is mentioned in the Babylonian Talmud as transmitting many of Rabbi Yoḥanan's teachings and also those of other important Palestinian Sages. At the same time, he was not as highly regarded as his colleagues, Rav Dimi and Ravin, because it was suspected that he was not accurate in transmitting the teachings. Almost nothing is known of his biography, except that he had a nickname, יִצְחָק סוּמְקָא (Red Isaac), suggesting that he had a ruddy complexion or red hair.

רַב דִּימִי Rav Dimi. An Amora of the third and fourth generations, Rav Dimi lived both in Babylonia and in Eretz Israel. He seems to have been a Babylonian who moved to Eretz Israel in his youth. He returned to Babylonia several times, taking with him the teachings of Eretz Israel. Rav Dimi was responsible for the transmission of these teachings, and in the Jerusalem Talmud he is called Rav Avdimi (or Avduma) Naḥota. He was one of the

Sages who were given the title רַבָּנַן נְחוּתֵי — "the emigrant Rabbis" — because they carried the teachings of Eretz Israel to Babylonia, mainly the teachings of Rabbi Yoḥanan, Resh Lakish, and Rabbi Elazar. Others who shared in this task were Rabbah bar Bar Ḥanah and Ulla, and later Ravin, Rav Shmuel bar Yehudah, and others. The Talmud reports dozens of Halakhic decisions that Rav Dimi took from one Torah center to the other, and he debated with the greatest Sages of his generation about them. At the end of his life he seems to have returned to Babylonia, where he died.

BACKGROUND

נְהוֹר עֲנָנֵי When clouds are bright. A cloud's darkness is a sign of its density, which in itself is a condition for rain to fall. A cloud's darkness also shows the presence of water droplets and particles of ice in the cloud. Bright clouds generally bring little or no rain.

LANGUAGE

תַּרְקַב Tarkav. The origin of this word is not clear. Some authorities maintain that it derives from the Greek τρίκαβος, *trikabos,* meaning three *kabbin* (units of capacity). But this etymology is difficult to accept, because generally the Greek letter tau (τ) becomes teth (ט) in Hebrew. Others claim that it is an abbreviation of תְּרֵי and קַב, meaning two *kabbin* and another one. Others maintain that it was originally a unit of two *kabbin,* but the size of the units was changed. In any event, the Talmud always uses תַּרְקַב to describe a measure that is three *kabbin,* the equivalent of half a *se'ah.*

TRANSLATION AND COMMENTARY

and **the rainwater is** produced by them without diminishing their quantity, as a tree produces **fruit,** [1]**as it is said** [Psalms 104:13]: 'He waters the mountains from His upper chambers; **from the fruit of your works the earth is satiated.'"** [2]**Which of** the two Tannaitic views, that of Rabbi Eliezer or that of Rabbi Yehoshua, is reflected in this Baraita?

כְּרַבִּי יְהוֹשֻׁעַ [3]The Gemara answers: The Baraita is **in accordance with** the viewpoint of **Rabbi Yehoshua** that rain **has its source in** the upper waters above the sky.

וְרַבִּי אֱלִיעֶזֶר [4]The Gemara asks: **And** how does **Rabbi Eliezer** explain the verse in Psalms?

הַהוּא [5]The Gemara answers that Rabbi Eliezer would argue that the word "works" in **that** particular **verse** in Psalms does not refer to the immediate source of rainfall, but **is describing the handicraft of the Holy One blessed be He.** All of creation, including the oceans and the rain, was created by God and set in motion by Him.

אָמַר רַבִּי יְהוֹשֻׁעַ בֶּן לֵוִי [6]Having concluded its discussion of the dispute between Rabbi Eliezer and Rabbi Yehoshua, the Gemara now continues on the subject of rain. **Rabbi Yehoshua ben Levi said:** [7]The water **the entire world drinks** is merely **the residue** left over **from** the water in **the Garden of Eden,** [8]**as it is said** (Genesis 2:10): **"And a river went out from Eden,** to water the garden, and from there it divided and became four heads." Thus we see that the main purpose of the river was to water the garden, and only afterwards did it go into the outside world in the form of four major rivers. [9]We can understand better what this means from what **was taught** in the following Baraita: **"From the residue of a** ***bet kor*** [a very large field, approximately five acres in area] **a** ***tarkav*** [a field one-sixtieth the size of a *bet kor*] **can drink."** It is normal for a certain amount of water to run off when a field is irrigated, and if this water is collected, it is sufficient to water a field one-sixtieth the size of the original field. Thus we may conclude that the world receives only one-sixtieth of the water that was used to water the Garden of Eden.

תָּנוּ רַבָּנַן [10]Having mentioned that the Garden of Eden receives sixty times as much rain as the whole of the rest of the world, the Gemara now cites another Baraita that states that the Garden is in fact sixty times the size of the rest of the world. **Our Rabbis taught: "The area of the land of Egypt is four hundred parasangs by four hundred parasangs** [a parasang is a measurement of length, about four kilometers]. [11]**And** Egypt **is one-sixtieth** the size **of Kush** [generally used to refer to Ethiopia]. [12]**And Kush is one-sixtieth of** the size of **the world.** [13]**And the world is one-sixtieth of** the size of **the Garden** of Eden [as we saw from the previous passage, which stated that the world drinks from the residue of the Garden]. [14]**And the Garden** of Eden **is one-sixtieth of** the size of **Eden** itself, of which the Garden is merely a part. [15]**And Eden is**

תְּלוּיִם, וּפֵירוֹתֵיהֶן מֵי גְשָׁמִים, [1]שֶׁנֶּאֱמַר: ׳מִפְּרִי מַעֲשֶׂיךָ תִּשְׂבַּע הָאָרֶץ׳.״ [2]כְּמַאן? [3]כְּרַבִּי יְהוֹשֻׁעַ. [4]וְרַבִּי אֱלִיעֶזֶר? [5]הַהוּא בְּמַעֲשֵׂה יָדָיו שֶׁל הַקָּדוֹשׁ בָּרוּךְ הוּא הוּא דִּכְתִיב. [6]אָמַר רַבִּי יְהוֹשֻׁעַ בֶּן לֵוִי: [7]כָּל הָעוֹלָם כּוּלּוֹ מִתַּמְצִית גַּן עֵדֶן הוּא שׁוֹתֶה, [8]שֶׁנֶּאֱמַר: ״וְנָהָר יֹצֵא מֵעֵדֶן, וגו׳״. [9]תָּנָא: ״מִתַּמְצִית בֵּית כּוֹר שׁוֹתֶה תַּרְקַב.

[10]תָּנוּ רַבָּנַן: ״אֶרֶץ מִצְרַיִם הָוְיָא אַרְבַּע מֵאוֹת פַּרְסָה עַל אַרְבַּע מֵאוֹת פַּרְסָה. [11]וְהוּא אֶחָד מִשִּׁשִּׁים בְּכוּשׁ. [12]וְכוּשׁ אֶחָד מִשִּׁשִּׁים בָּעוֹלָם. [13]וְעוֹלָם אֶחָד מִשִּׁשִּׁים בַּגַּן. [14]וְגַן אֶחָד מִשִּׁשִּׁים לְעֵדֶן. [15]וְעֵדֶן אֶחָד

LITERAL TRANSLATION

God], and their fruits are rainwater, [1]as it is said: 'From the fruit of your works the earth is satiated.'"

[2]According to whom?

[3]According to Rabbi Yehoshua.

[4]And Rabbi Eliezer?

[5]That [verse] is written about the handiwork of the Holy One blessed be He.

[6]Rabbi Yehoshua ben Levi said: [7]The entire world drinks from the residue of the Garden of Eden, [8]as it is said: "And a river went out from Eden, etc." [9][A Tanna] taught: "From the residue of a *bet kor* a *tarkav* can drink."

[10]Our Rabbis taught: "The land of Egypt is four hundred parasangs by four hundred parasangs. [11]And it is one-sixtieth of Kush. [12]And Kush is one-sixtieth of the world. [13]And the world is one-sixtieth of the Garden. [14]And the Garden is one-sixtieth of Eden. [15]And Eden is one-sixtieth

RASHI

ופירותיהן מי גשמים — משום לישנא דקרא נקט הכי, משום דכתיב "מפרי מעשיך תשבע הארץ", ופירותיהם, כלומר מזיעת המים, שאין נחסרין כלום, כדכתיב (תהלים סה) "פלג אלהים מלא מים", כל שעה, והקרן קיימת, ופירותיהן מי גשמים, וכן מפורש בבראשית רבה. ונהר יוצא מעדן — סימן לדבר שגן עדן שותה מן הגשמים תחילה, דכתיב "ונהר יוצא מעדן להשקות את הגן" וגו׳. **תנא מתמצית בית כור** — כלי שמשקין במימיו בית כור יכולין להשקות בתמציתו שיעור זריעת תרקב, שהוא אחד מששים בבית כור. והכי נמי, עולם אחד מששים בגן עדן, ודי לו בתמצית העננים המשקין את הגן, גן לפני כל העולם כולו כעדן לגן.

TRANSLATION AND COMMENTARY

one-sixtieth of the size of **Gehenna,** the netherworld where the wicked are punished. [1]**It thus** turns **out that the entire world is** merely **a pot cover for** the steaming cauldron of **Gehenna,** as the size of Gehenna is vastly greater than that of the world. [2]**And some say that Gehenna** is so large it **cannot be measured.** [3]**And some say** that **Eden,** too, is so large it **cannot be measured."**

אָמַר רַבִּי אוֹשַׁעְיָא [4]Having discussed rainfall in Eretz Israel and in the Garden of Eden, the Gemara now turns to Babylonia. **Rabbi Oshaya said: What is the meaning of what is written** in the following verse (Jeremiah 51:13): [5]**"You who dwell on many waters, abundant in storehouses**, your end is come, the measure of your greed"? In this chapter Jeremiah prophesies the destruction of Babylon, and in this verse he addresses himself to the wealth of Babylon at the height of its power, noting its water resources and storehouses. Rabbi Oshaya explains that the two points are connected. [6]**What caused Babylonia to have storehouses full of grain?** [7]**You have to say that it is because it dwells on many waters,** the two mighty rivers, the Tigris and the Euphrates.

אָמַר רַב [8]**Rav said: Babylonia is wealthy because it can harvest** its crops even **without** any **rain** at all, as its fields are watered by the two great rivers. Hence Babylonia has no real need for rain. [9]**Abaye said: We have a tradition that it is better** for a country **to be swampy,** like Babylonia, **and not dry,** like other countries.

MISHNAH בִּשְׁלֹשָׁה בְּמַרְחֶשְׁוָן The previous Mishnayot discussed the date from which we begin inserting the words "You cause the wind to blow and the rain to fall" in the second blessing of the Amidah, and the date from which we cease making further mention of rain in our prayers with the onset of the dry season. The present Mishnah discusses the date from which we begin praying explicitly for rain by inserting the words "and give dew and rain for a blessing on the face of the earth" in the ninth blessing of the Amidah. We have seen earlier that this insertion may not be made until Sukkot is over and the time for rain has fully arrived. This Mishnah notes that there is a Tannaitic dispute about the precise date when we begin praying for rain. [10]The first Tanna says: **On the third** day **of** the month of **Marḥeshvan,** eleven days after the last day of Sukkot, **we** begin to **pray for rain,** for we have already seen (above, 6a) that the earliest date in the autumn when rainfall is considered normal is the third of Marḥeshvan. [11]**Rabban Gamliel says:** We begin reciting this prayer only **on the seventh of** Marḥeshvan, **fifteen days after the Sukkot Festival.**

מִשִּׁשִּׁים לְגֵיהִנָּם. [1]נִמְצָא כָּל הָעוֹלָם כּוּלּוֹ כְּכִיסּוּי קְדֵרָה לְגֵיהִנָּם. [2]וְיֵשׁ אוֹמְרִים: גֵּיהִנָּם אֵין לָהּ שִׁיעוּר. [3]וְיֵשׁ אוֹמְרִים: עֵדֶן אֵין לָהּ שִׁיעוּר".

[4]אָמַר רַבִּי אוֹשַׁעְיָא: מַאי דִּכְתִיב: [5]"שָׁכַנְתְּ עַל מַיִם רַבִּים, רַבַּת אוֹצָרֹת"? [6]מִי גָּרַם לְבָבֶל שֶׁיְּהוּ אוֹצְרוֹתֶיהָ מְלֵאוֹת בָּר? [7]הֱוֵי אוֹמֵר מִפְּנֵי שֶׁשּׁוֹכֶנֶת עַל מַיִם רַבִּים.

[8]אָמַר רַב: עֲתִירָה בָּבֶל דְּחָצְדָא בְּלָא מִיטְרָא. [9]אֲמַר אַבַּיֵי: נְקִיטִינַן טוּבְעָנֵי וְלָא יוּבְשָׁנֵי.

מ ש נ ה [10]בִּשְׁלֹשָׁה בְּמַרְחֶשְׁוָן שׁוֹאֲלִין אֶת הַגְּשָׁמִים. [11]רַבָּן גַּמְלִיאֵל אוֹמֵר: בְּשִׁבְעָה בּוֹ, חֲמִשָּׁה עָשָׂר יוֹם

LITERAL TRANSLATION

of Gehenna. [1]It turns out [that] the entire world is like a pot cover for Gehenna. [2]And some say: Gehenna has no measure. [3]And some say: Eden has no measure."

[4]Rabbi Oshaya said: What is [the meaning of] what is written: [5]"You who dwell on many waters, abundant in storehouses"? [6]What caused Babylonia that its storehouses should be full of grain? [7]You have to say [that it is] because it dwells on many waters.

[8]Rav said: Babylonia is wealthy because it harvests without rain. [9]Abaye said: We hold [that it is better to be] flooded and not dry.

MISHNAH [10]On the third of Marḥeshvan we pray (lit., "ask") for rains. [11]Rabban Gamliel says: On the seventh of it, fifteen days

RASHI

נמצא כל העולם ככיסוי קדרה — הקטן כנגד הקדרה. **"שוכנת על מים רבים** רבת אוצרות בא קצך אמת בצעך". **שרבו אוצרותיה** — שקנו עושר. **מים רבים** — שמשקין שדותיהן, דבבל עמוקים מכל הארצות, וגשמים מטפטפין ויורדין שם. **עתירה בבל** — עשירה היא בבל, שקוצרין בה תבואה בלא מטר, שאין צריכים לגשמים. **נקיטינן** — דהכי חצדא בבל בלא מיטרא. **דטובעני** — היא מקום מצולה ורקק. **ולא יובשני** — שאינה יבשה.

משנה בשלשה במרחשון שואלין את הגשמים וכו' רבן גמליאל אומר בשבעה בו בחמשה עשר יום

BACKGROUND

מִצְרַיִם וְכוּשׁ, גַּן עֵדֶן וְגֵיהִנָּם Egypt and Kush, the Garden of Eden and Gehenna. On this subject, as in several other Aggadic matters found both in this tractate and elsewhere in the Talmud, there is a tacit transition from an empirical discussion to abstract, metaphysical subjects. Continuing from the discussion of the size of various regions in the world, the discussion passes to the entire world, and from there to the Garden of Eden and to Gehenna.

אֶחָד מִשִּׁשִּׁים בַּגַּן One-sixtieth of the Garden. Usually the expression "one-sixtieth" does not refer to an exact numerical quantity, but to the Halakhic concept of בָּטֵל בְּשִׁשִּׁים, meaning a negligible quantity, for anything that makes up only one-sixtieth of a whole is regarded as non-existent from the point of view of the Halakhah. Therefore the remark that the world is one-sixtieth of the Garden of Eden must be understood in the same way: the whole world is insignificant in comparison to the Garden of Eden, the spiritual reality that comes after it. The relative difference between the Garden of Eden and Gehenna is also an indication of the number of people worthy of receiving a reward versus those who sin and are worthy of Gehenna. Hence the conclusion that the entire world is merely the pot cover for Gehenna comprises a severe warning regarding the spiritual danger lying in wait for a person in his lifetime: Every sin and transgression can incur a severe spiritual punishment, and the temptation and the punishment are more comprehensive and larger than empirical existence itself.

עֲתִירָה בָּבֶל Babylonia is wealthy. The soil of Babylonia is extremely fertile, because it is composed of silt from the rivers. Rainfall in Babylonia is very slight, only 100-200 cm. annually, but the strong flow of the rivers and the canals that have been constructed between them supply water in abundance, so that Babylonia can produce crops without rain.

NOTES

עֲתִירָה בָּבֶל Babylonia is wealthy. According to a variant reading, Rav is stating that, in the future (עֲתִידָה), Babylonia will be desolate, as her sources of water will dry up, and the rain falling there will be insufficient to meet her needs (see *Arukh*).

TRANSLATION AND COMMENTARY

[1]Rabban Gamliel explains that we wait these extra four days **so that the last pilgrim from** Eretz **Israel** who traveled to Jerusalem for the Sukkot Festival **can reach** his home on the banks of **the Euphrates River** without being inconvenienced by the rain.

GEMARA אָמַר רַבִּי אֶלְעָזָר [2]**Rabbi Elazar said:** The Halakhah **is in accordance with Rabban Gamliel,** and we do not begin to pray for rain until fifteen days after Sukkot.

תַּנְיָא [3]**It was taught** in a Baraita: **"Hananyah said:** The difference of opinion in the Mishnah applies only to Eretz Israel, where the winter rains normally start at the beginning of the month of Marḥeshvan. [4]**But in the Diaspora** [Babylonia], where the rainy season begins somewhat later, **we do not begin** to pray for rain **until sixty days into the autumn season,** the period of three months from the autumnal equinox until the winter solstice."

אָמַר רַב הוּנָא בַּר חִיָּיא [5]**Rav Huna bar Ḥiyya said in the name of Shmuel: The Halakhah is in accordance with Ḥananyah,** and in Babylonia we do not begin to pray for rain until sixty days have passed, counting from the autumnal equinox.

אַחַר הַחַג, [1]כְּדֵי שֶׁיַּגִּיעַ אַחֲרוֹן שֶׁבְּיִשְׂרָאֵל לִנְהַר פְּרָת.

גמרא [2]אָמַר רַבִּי אֶלְעָזָר: הֲלָכָה כְּרַבָּן גַּמְלִיאֵל.

[3]תַּנְיָא: "חֲנַנְיָה אוֹמֵר: [4]וּבַגּוֹלָה עַד שִׁשִּׁים בַּתְּקוּפָה". [5]אָמַר רַב הוּנָא בַּר חִיָּיא אָמַר שְׁמוּאֵל: הֲלָכָה כַּחֲנַנְיָה.

LITERAL TRANSLATION

after the [Sukkot] Festival, [1]in order that the last [pilgrim] in Israel may reach the Euphrates River.

GEMARA [2]Rabbi Elazar said: The Halakhah is in accordance with Rabban Gamliel.

[3]It was taught: "Ḥananyah says: [4]And in the Diaspora [we do not begin] until sixty [days] in the [autumn] season." [5]Rav Huna bar Ḥiyya said in the name of Shmuel: The Halakhah is in accordance with Ḥananyah.

RASHI

אחר החג – כלומר, בשבעה במרחשון הוא חמשה עשר אחר החג. **כדי שיגיע האחרון** – כלומר, קודם ביאת מים לנהר פרת, שהוא רחוק יותר.

גמרא ובגולה ששים – ובגולה אין שואלין עד ששים בתקופה, לפי שהוא מקום נמוך, ואין צריכים מטר כל כך.

BACKGROUND

שֶׁיַּגִּיעַ...לִנְהַר פְּרָת **May reach the Euphrates River.** There were several routes from Eretz Israel to Babylonia. The main route passed through Damascus, and from there north to the Euphrates at Thapsacus, and then southeast to Babylonia. This route, which passed through inhabited regions, was long, the diversion via Thapsacus making the distance 500 kilometers, but it was suitable for large caravans, sometimes including women and children, which traveled thirty to forty kilometers per day and took about fifteen days. By taking shorter routes through the desert and traveling very quickly, it was possible to arrive in approximately seven days.

SAGES

חֲנַנְיָה **Ḥananyah.** He was a nephew of Rabbi Yehoshua and belonged to the fourth generation of Tannaim. His principal teacher was his uncle, Rabbi Yehoshua, but he also learned Torah from other important Sages of that generation.

He seems to have gone to live in Babylonia before the Bar Kokhba revolt. After the war and the persecutions that followed it, he remained among the remnants of the important Sages of that generation. This led him to attempt to regulate the Hebrew calendar in Babylonia, since, following the decrees of Hadrian, it was difficult to do so in Eretz Israel. This effort, which was tantamount to a challenge to the supreme authority of Eretz Israel, led to a sharp response from the Palestinian Sages, who ultimately succeeded in changing Ḥananyah's mind. However, it did not succeed in entirely undoing the results of his action. The Sages viewed this action as so grave that they spoke of a curse upon his descendants because of "the sin of Ḥananyah."

He lived a long life and died in Babylonia. The great Amora, Shmuel, may have been one of his descendants.

NOTES

וּבַגּוֹלָה **And in the Diaspora.** When this term is used in the Bible with reference to a specific place, it means the Babylonian exile (see Ezekiel 1:1 and many other passages there). Not only was Babylonia the place to which the majority of the Israelites were exiled at the time, but it also became a national spiritual center in its own right. The connections and relations between the Eretz Israel and the Diaspora refer mainly to the large and important Jewish community in Babylonia.

Sometimes the term has an even more restricted meaning and refers to the city of Pumbedita and its surroundings, which apparently were the places where the Jews first settled when they went into exile in Babylonia.

עַד שִׁשִּׁים בַּתְּקוּפָה **Until sixty days in the autumn season.** The Rishonim disagree about what Ḥananyah meant when he said that in the Diaspora we do not insert the prayer for rain until sixty days after the autumnal equinox. Was he referring only to Babylonia, the principal Diaspora community in the Talmudic period, where (as was stated above) the land is watered by rivers, and rain is not needed until later in the winter, or was he referring to all the Jewish communities outside Eretz Israel? Many commentators argue that it makes no sense to require those living in areas where rain is needed immediately after Sukkot or shortly thereafter to wait until sixty days after the autumnal equinox before inserting the prayer for rain into the Amidah (see *Rosh, Ritva*).

In some places it was customary to insert the prayer for rain immediately after Sukkot (in accordance with the viewpoint of Rabbi Yoḥanan; above, 4b), or on the seventh of Marḥeshvan (in accordance with the viewpoint of Rabban Gamliel in our Mishnah). But the custom that prevailed in most Diaspora communities was that the prayer for rain was not said until sixty days after the equinox. *Ritva* and others explain that the Rabbis decreed two dates on which to begin praying for rain, one for Eretz Israel and one for Babylonia. All other places must follow either Eretz Israel or Babylonia, for a third date was not decreed. The Geonim ruled that all communities should wait until sixty days after the equinox before inserting the prayer for rain

HALAKHAH

וּבַגּוֹלָה עַד שִׁשִּׁים בַּתְּקוּפָה **And in the Diaspora we do not begin until sixty days in the autumn season.** "Those who live outside Eretz Israel begin to insert the prayer for rain in the ninth blessing of the Amidah prayer on the night of the sixtieth day after the autumnal equinox. The equinox for this purpose is determined according to the calculations of the Amora Shmuel, following the tradition received by the Geonim. In an ordinary year the prayer for rain is first inserted on December 5, and in a leap year it is first inserted on December 6.

"The Aḥaronim disagree about the law applying to a resident of Eretz Israel who travels abroad during this period of the year. Some authorities maintain that he inserts the prayer for rain from the seventh of Marḥeshvan, according to the custom in Eretz Israel (*Ya'akov Castro*). Others maintain that he follows the practice observed in the Diaspora and does not pray for rain until sixty days from the equinox (*Mishnah Berurah*). Some argue that the law applying to such a person depends on when he intends to return to Eretz Israel (*Pri Ḥadash*). In practice, different communities follow different customs on the matter." (*Shulḥan Arukh, Oraḥ Ḥayyim* 117:1.)

[1]אִינִי? [2]וְהָא בָּעוּ מִינֵּיהּ מִשְּׁמוּאֵל: מֵאֵימַת מַדְכָּרִינַן: [3]״וְתֵן טַל וּמָטָר״? [4]אֲמַר לְהוּ: מִכִּי מְעַיְּילִי צִיבֵי לְבֵי טָבוּת רִישְׁבָּא.

[5]דִּילְמָא אִידִי וְאִידִי חַד שִׁיעוּרָא הוּא.

[6]אִיבַּעְיָא לְהוּ: [7]יוֹם שִׁשִּׁים כִּלְפְנֵי שִׁשִּׁים אוֹ כִּלְאַחַר שִׁשִּׁים?

[8]תָּא שְׁמַע: רַב אָמַר: יוֹם שִׁשִּׁים כִּלְאַחַר שִׁשִּׁים. [9]וּשְׁמוּאֵל אָמַר: יוֹם שִׁשִּׁים כִּלְפְנֵי שִׁשִּׁים.

[10]אֲמַר רַב נַחְמָן בַּר יִצְחָק: [11]וְסִימָנָךְ: עִלָּאֵי בָּעוּ מַיָּא, [12]תַּתָּאֵי לָא בָּעוּ מַיָּא.

LITERAL TRANSLATION

[1]Is that so? [2]But surely they asked Shmuel: From when do we mention: [3]"And give dew and rain"? [4]He said to them: From when they bring wood into the house of Tavut the bird hunter.

[5]Perhaps this and that are one measure.

[6]It was asked of them: [7]Is the sixtieth day like before sixty or like after sixty?

[8]Come and hear: Rav said: The sixtieth day is like after sixty. [9]And Shmuel said: The sixtieth day is like before sixty.

[10]Rav Naḥman bar Yitzḥak said: [11]And your sign is: [12]Those above need water, those below do not need water.

TRANSLATION AND COMMENTARY

אִינִי [1]But, the Gemara objects, **is this so?** Did Shmuel really rule that we begin reciting this prayer on this date? [2]**Surely Shmuel's** students **asked him: From when do we** in Babylonia begin to **mention** [3]**"and give dew and rain"** in the ninth blessing of the Amidah? [4]And **he said to them** in reply: **From** the day **when they bring wood into the house of Tavut, the bird hunter,** who owned a big building where the local people stored their firewood during the winter to prevent it from getting wet. This date does not appear to be connected with a specific time after the autumnal equinox.

דִּילְמָא [5]The Gemara answers: **Perhaps both are one** and the same **measure** of time. The wood was in fact brought into Tavut's house sixty days after the equinox. But it was easier for the students to note the time when the wood was brought in than to calculate the equinox.

אִיבַּעְיָא לְהוּ [6]**The** following **question was raised** in the Academy: Ḥananyah ruled that the prayer for rain begins to be inserted sixty days after the autumnal equinox. [7]But **is the sixtieth day** counting from the equinox (fifty-nine days after the equinox) treated **like** the days **before the sixtieth** day **or like** the days **after the sixtieth** day? In other words, do we begin to recite the prayer on the sixtieth day or on the next day?

תָּא שְׁמַע [8]**Come and hear** that the answer to this problem is the subject of disagreement between Amoraim: **Rav said: The sixtieth day is** treated **like** the days **after the sixtieth** day, and we begin reciting the prayer for rain on the sixtieth day itself. [9]**Shmuel said: The sixtieth day is** treated **like** the days **before the sixtieth** day, and we refrain from reciting this prayer until the sixty-first day.

אֲמַר רַב נַחְמָן בַּר יִצְחָק [10]**Rav Naḥman bar Yitzḥak said:** Rav, who says that the sixtieth day is like the days *after* the sixtieth day, means that we begin to recite the prayer *earlier*, whereas Shmuel, who says that the sixtieth day is like the days *before* the sixtieth day, means that we begin to recite the prayer *later*. [11]If you wish to remember which Amora issued which opinion, **you can use** the following **mnemonic:** [12]People who live **above,** in mountainous regions, **need water** more, whereas people who live **below,** in the valleys, **do not need water** as much. Rav, who came from the mountains of Eretz Israel and only moved to Babylonia

RASHI

מכי מעיילי ציבי לבי טבות רישבא – משעה שמכניסין עצים לאוצר לצורך ימות הגשמים, היו נוהגין, לפי שהיו יודעין שזמן גשמים הוא משם ואילך, ולא היו יכולין לחטוב עצים ביער. **רישבא** = צייד עופות, כמו ״אין פורשין רשבים ליונים״ (בבא קמא עט,ב), טבות – שם אדם. **כלפני ששים** – ולא מדכרינן. **כלאחר ששים** – ומדכרינן. **עילאי בעו מים** – העומדים בהרים צריכין יותר מים, מפני שהגשמים מתגלגלים ויורדין למטה. **תתאי לא בעו מים** – שמתכנסין כל מימי ההרים לבקעה, הכי נמי, רב שהיה מארץ ישראל כדאמרינן בעלמא (גיטין ו,א): מכי אתא רב לבבל, וארץ ישראל גבוהה מכל הארצות, משום הכי אמר כלאחר ששים. ובבבל, בגולה מתוך שאינן צריכין לגשמים – אין שואלין עד ששים לתקופת תשרי, וכן אנו נוהגים, שכל מנהגינו אחר בני בבל.

NOTES

into the Amidah, because in all matters the Diaspora communities follow the practices of Babylonia. Moreover, it is preferable for there to be a uniform date throughout the Diaspora on which to begin praying for rain, and in any event the prayer cannot be inserted immediately after Sukkot as in Eretz Israel, since in most Diaspora communities there is still grain in the fields which must be gathered in before the rains come.

רִישְׁבָּא The bird hunter. רִישְׁבָּא is the Rabbinic Hebrew word for a net used to catch animals, mainly birds, and in Syriac it is *"nishba."* The name "Tavut Rishba" thus refers to someone with nets, a hunter. However, it is reported in the name of the Geonim that רִישְׁבָּא is an abbreviation of רֵישׁ בֵּי אַבָּא ("the head of a family"), so that this Tavut may have been an important personage, the head of a large family.

עִלָּאֵי...תַּתָּאֵי Those above...those below. *Rabbenu Ḥananel* (following the Geonim) has a reading opposite to

TRANSLATION AND COMMENTARY

as an adult, ruled that we should begin to recite the prayer for rain earlier, whereas Shmuel, who was a native of the Babylonian lowlands, ruled that we should begin to recite the prayer later.

אֲמַר רַב פַּפָּא [1]**Rav Pappa said: The Halakhah is** in accordance with Rav in this matter, [2]and **the sixtieth day is** treated **like** the days **after the sixtieth** day. Hence, we begin to recite the prayer on the sixtieth day starting with the equinox — i.e., fifty-nine days after the equinox. According to the Gregorian calendar, this coincides with December 5 in the present century.

MISHNAH הִגִּיעַ From here to the end of the second chapter of the tractate, the subject moves from the topic of regular prayers for rain to the topic of the special prayers that are recited when there is a drought. The previous Mishnah ruled that we begin to pray for rain from the third, or the seventh, of Marḥeshvan. We have seen (above, 6a) that these dates correspond to when rainfall is normally expected in early and average years, and that the latest date that can still be considered normal is the seventeenth of Marḥeshvan. [3]So, **if rain had** still **not fallen by the seventeenth of Marḥeshvan,** it was considered to be a sign of drought. Special prayers were not yet introduced, however, because the rain was only slightly late. [4]But pious **individuals** would **begin to fast** a series of **three fasts**. [5]Those fasting could **eat and drink from** the time **when it became dark** until morning, and would begin fasting only after dawn. Similarly, those fasting were only required to abstain from food and drink. [6]They **were permitted** to do any kind of **work,** to **bathe,** to **anoint** themselves with oil, to **wear shoes, and** to engage in **marital relations.** These other activities are forbidden on strict fasts like Yom Kippur and the Ninth of Av, and they are also forbidden on the fasts that are decreed if the drought continues for a long time (below, 12b), but at this early stage in the drought there is no need to observe these additional stringencies.

הִגִּיעַ [7]The first three fasts by individuals are held during the final part of Marḥeshvan. **If the beginning of the month of Kislev arrives, and rain has** still **not fallen,** this is the sign that drought has begun and special prayers are introduced. [8]Accordingly, **the court decrees three** daytime **fasts** to be observed **by the** entire **community,** to be held on the first Monday after the first of Kislev, on the following Thursday,

[1]אֲמַר רַב פַּפָּא: הִלְכְתָא: [2]יוֹם שִׁשִּׁים כִּלְאַחַר שִׁשִּׁים.

מִשְׁנָה [3]הִגִּיעַ שִׁבְעָה עָשָׂר בְּמַרְחֶשְׁוָן, וְלֹא יָרְדוּ גְּשָׁמִים, [4]הִתְחִילוּ הַיְּחִידִים מִתְעַנִּין שָׁלֹשׁ תַּעֲנִיּוֹת. [5]אוֹכְלִין וְשׁוֹתִין מִשֶּׁחָשֵׁיכָה, [6]וּמוּתָּרִין בִּמְלָאכָה, וּבִרְחִיצָה, וּבְסִיכָה, וּבִנְעִילַת הַסַּנְדָּל, וּבְתַשְׁמִישׁ הַמִּטָּה.

[7]הִגִּיעַ רֹאשׁ חֹדֶשׁ כִּסְלֵיו, וְלֹא יָרְדוּ גְּשָׁמִים, [8]בֵּית דִּין גּוֹזְרִין שָׁלֹשׁ תַּעֲנִיּוֹת עַל הַצִּבּוּר.

LITERAL TRANSLATION

[1]Rav Pappa said: The Halakhah is: [2]The sixtieth day is like after sixty.

MISHNAH [3][If] the seventeenth of Marḥeshvan arrived, and rain had not fallen, [4]individuals began to fast three fasts. [5]They eat and drink from when it is dark, [6]and they are permitted work, and bathing, and anointing, and wearing shoes, and marital relations.

[7][If] the New Moon of Kislev has arrived, and rain has not fallen, [8]the court decrees three fasts on the community.

RASHI

משנה הגיע שבעה עשר וכו' — אוכלין ושותין משחשיכה, שאין אוכלין מבעוד יום כיום הכפורים ותשעה באב.

NOTES

that found in the standard texts of the Talmud: Rav said that the sixtieth day is treated like the days before the sixtieth day, and Shmuel said that the sixtieth day is treated like the days after the sixtieth day. According to this reading, Shmuel is considered the one who lives "above" and therefore needs the rain, because he lived in Neharde'a which was situated higher up the Euphrates River. And Rav is considered the one who lives "below" and does not need the rain, because when he emigrated to Babylonia, he established his academy in Sura, a place lower down the Euphrates than Neharde'a. (See also *Rabbi Ya'akov Emden,* who suggests a somewhat similar explanation for the reading found in the standard texts of the Talmud.)

HALAKHAH

הִגִּיעַ שִׁבְעָה עָשָׂר בְּמַרְחֶשְׁוָן **If the seventeenth of Marḥeshvan arrived.** "If the seventeenth of Marḥeshvan has arrived, and rain has still not fallen, Rabbinic scholars ('individuals') begin a series of three fasts — on Monday, the following Thursday, and the next Monday. These fasts are treated as individual fasts." (*Shulḥan Arukh, Oraḥ Ḥayyim* 575:1.)

הִגִּיעַ רֹאשׁ חֹדֶשׁ כִּסְלֵיו **If the New Moon of Kislev has arrived.** "If the beginning of the month of Kislev has arrived, and it has still not rained, the court decrees a series of three fasts on the entire community — on Monday, the following Thursday, and the next Monday. On these fasts, the prayer services are conducted as on all other communal fasts." (Ibid., 575:2.)

TRANSLATION AND COMMENTARY

and on the following Monday. [1]Those fasting can **eat and drink from** the time **when it** becomes **dark** until morning, and begin fasting only after dawn. Similarly, they are required to abstain from food and drink alone, [2]but **are permitted** to do any kind of **work,** to **bathe,** to **anoint** themselves with oil, to **wear shoes, and** to engage in **marital relations,** since the rain is still only moderately late and the drought is not yet severe.

GEMARA מַאן יְחִידִים [3]The Gemara asks: **Who are the "individuals"** mentioned in the first clause of the Mishnah?

אָמַר רַב הוּנָא [4]**Rav Huna said** in reply: **The Rabbis.** Torah scholars are expected to undertake these fasts, but ordinary people are not.

וְאָמַר רַב הוּנָא [5]**And Rav Huna said** further: When the **individuals fast,** they do so on **three fast** days. [6]They start on a **Monday, and** they continue on the following **Thursday, and** on the following **Monday.**

מַאי קָמַשְׁמַע לָן [7]The Gemara asks: **What is** Rav Huna **teaching us** by this ruling? Ostensibly, he is teaching us that the fasts are held on Monday, Thursday, and Monday, in that order. [8]But **we have already learned this** in a Mishnah (below, 15b), which rules: **"We do not decree a fast on the community beginning on a Thursday, so as not to cause an increase in prices.** Thursday is the most important market day, when people buy supplies for Shabbat, and on the first day of a series of fasts there is a tendency for demand to increase, because people need food for breaking the fast. Thus, if the first fast were to take place on a Thursday, the market would not have time to adjust itself, and prices would rise excessively. [9]**Rather, the first three fasts are on Monday and Thursday and Monday."** Since the sequence of the fasts has already been established by the Mishnah, what was Rav Huna teaching us that we did not already know?

[1]אוֹכְלִין וְשׁוֹתִין מִשֶּׁחָשֵׁיכָה, [2]וּמוּתָּרִין בִּמְלָאכָה, וּבִרְחִיצָה, וּבְסִיכָה, וּבִנְעִילַת הַסַּנְדָּל, וּבְתַשְׁמִישׁ הַמִּטָּה.

גמרא [3]מַאן "יְחִידִים"? [4]אֲמַר רַב הוּנָא: רַבָּנַן. [5]וְאָמַר רַב הוּנָא: יְחִידִים מִתְעַנִּין שָׁלֹשׁ תַּעֲנִיּוֹת, [6]שֵׁנִי וַחֲמִישִׁי וְשֵׁנִי.

[7]מַאי קָמַשְׁמַע לָן? [8]תָּנֵינָא: "אֵין גּוֹזְרִין תַּעֲנִית עַל הַצִּבּוּר בַּתְּחִילָּה בַּחֲמִישִׁי, שֶׁלֹּא לְהַפְקִיעַ אֶת הַשְּׁעָרִים. [9]אֶלָּא שָׁלֹשׁ תַּעֲנִיּוֹת הָרִאשׁוֹנוֹת שֵׁנִי וַחֲמִישִׁי וְשֵׁנִי".

LITERAL TRANSLATION

[1]They eat and drink from when it is dark, [2]and they are permitted work, and bathing, and anointing, and wearing shoes, and marital relations.

GEMARA [3]Who are the "individuals"?

[4]Rav Huna said: The Rabbis.

[5]And Rav Huna said: Individuals fast three fasts, [6]Monday and Thursday and Monday.

[7]What is he teaching us? [8]We have [already] learned [this]: "We do not decree a fast on the community beginning on Thursday, in order not to raise prices. [9]Rather, the first three fasts are [on] Monday and Thursday and Monday."

RASHI

גמרא מאי קא משמע לן – האי דקאמר "שני וחמישי ושני". **תנינא** – בפירקין דלקמן (טו,ג): אין גוזרין תענית כו' שלא להפקיע את השערים, שאם היו מתחילין להתענות בחמישי היו קונין למוצאי התענית שתי סעודות גדולות, אחד לתענית ואחד לשבת, וכסבור המוכר שרעב בא לעולם ואתי לאפקועי שערים. **אפקועי** – מבטל שיעור מדה הראשונה, וממעטה.

TERMINOLOGY

תָּנֵינָא **We have already learned this.** A term used to introduce an objection based on a statement in a Mishnah or a Baraita which makes a prior statement or question seem superfluous, since it is already covered in a Mishnah or a Baraita.

NOTES

שֶׁלֹּא לְהַפְקִיעַ אֶת הַשְּׁעָרִים **In order not to raise prices.** According to the straightforward explanation of this Mishnah, the court may not decree a fast for the first time on a Thursday, because Thursday is already a busy market day when people buy supplies for Shabbat. Were the first of a series of fasts to be declared on a Thursday, the demand for food would increase further, because people go to the market to provide themselves with food to break the fast. Thus there is concern that the merchants may take advantage of the sudden rise in demand and increase their prices. *Rabbenu Gershom* adds that if the first of a series of fasts were to be declared on a Thursday, the villagers who come into town on that day to supply the townspeople with their produce might not hear about the fast in time to bring in more produce than usual. Thus food prices will rise on account of the increase in demand. *Eshkol* suggests that the first of a series of fasts may not be declared on a Thursday, lest the suppliers not come into town at all on that day on account of the fast and thereby cause a sudden rise in the price of food.

HALAKHAH

אֵין גּוֹזְרִין תַּעֲנִית עַל הַצִּבּוּר בַּתְּחִילָּה בַּחֲמִישִׁי **We do not decree a fast on the community beginning on Thursday.** "The court does not decree the first of a series of fasts on a Thursday, so as not to cause a rise in food prices. This ruling applies even in places where there is no concern that food prices will rise as a result of the declaration of a fast. According to some authorities, in places where there is no concern about a sudden rise in food prices, the first of a series of fasts may indeed be decreed on a Thursday (*Magen Avraham*). The common practice follows the second opinion." (*Shulḥan Arukh, Oraḥ Ḥayyim* 572:2.)

TERMINOLOGY

תַּנְיָא נַמִי הָכִי It was also taught thus. A term used to introduce a Baraita which supports the previous statement by the Gemara or by an individual Amora.

CONCEPTS

מְגִילַּת תַּעֲנִית ***Megillat Ta'anit.*** This is an ancient list, mainly compiled during Second Temple times, enumerating days commemorating joyful occasions on which it was forbidden to fast or to make public eulogies. Most of the events on the list derive from Hasmonean times, and recall victories and other joyous events that took place then. The main list is written in Aramaic and is accompanied by a broader explanation of each event in Hebrew. This list was the first part of the Oral Law to be written down over the generations.

BACKGROUND

תַּלְמִיד **A student.** Torah scholars enjoyed a high status, which conferred benefits upon them both in the social realm (places of honor at public gatherings, and the like), and in the economic sphere, where they received preferential treatment in business dealings and exemptions from certain taxes. In some places, especially Babylonia, Torah scholars wore special clothes, to make their status more conspicuous. Our passage warns that not every man can confer this status upon himself, unless his way of life and his knowledge make him worthy of it.

TRANSLATION AND COMMENTARY

מַהוּ דְּתֵימָא [1]The Gemara answers: If it were not for Rav Huna, **you might have said** that the Mishnah's ruling **applies to** the three fasts imposed on **the community that are** described in the latter part of our Mishnah, [2]**but not to** the three fasts undertaken by **individuals** that are described in the first part of our Mishnah. For the small number of Torah scholars who fast on these days have little effect on prices. Hence we might have thought that they should begin fasting on a Thursday, if the seventeenth of Marḥeshvan falls on a Tuesday or a Wednesday. [3]**Accordingly,** Rav Huna **informs us that this is not so.** Even though the reason for the rule given below by the Mishnah does not apply to these fasts, the rule itself does apply, and the fasts begin on a Monday.

תַּנְיָא נַמִי הָכִי [4]The Gemara notes that Rav Huna's ruling has Tannaitic support, as the same principle **was also taught** in the following Baraita: **"When the individuals began to fast, they would fast on Monday and Thursday and Monday,"** in that order, just as Rav Huna ruled. [5]The Baraita notes further that they would **interrupt** the series of fasts if **the first day of a month** happened to fall on one of the fast days, since Rosh Ḥodesh, the first day of a month, is a minor holiday, on which it is forbidden to fast. [10B] [6]Likewise, they would interrupt the series of fasts if a **festival that was written in *Megillat Ta'anit*** happened to fall on one of the fast days, since it is also forbidden to fast on these days." *Megillat Ta'anit* (literally, "The Scroll of Fasts") was a list of minor festivals that were celebrated during the Second Temple period (see below, 17b-18b). On all these occasions, it was forbidden to fast, and in some cases additional celebrations were ordained. Most of these festivals ceased to be observed after the destruction of the Temple (*Rosh HaShanah* 19b).

תָּנוּ רַבָּנַן [7]The Gemara now returns to Rav Huna's first ruling — that when the Mishnah refers to "individuals" fasting, it is in fact referring to Torah scholars. The Gemara cites a Baraita which elaborates on this point. **Our Rabbis taught:** "When the rains fail, and individuals begin to fast, **a man** who is a Torah scholar **should not** be excessively modest and **say: 'I am a** mere **student,** not a true scholar. [8]Therefore **I am not worthy to** consider myself a true scholar by fasting with the **individuals.'** [9]**Rather, all Torah scholars** who meet the following criterion **are** considered to be **individuals** for this purpose, and it does not depend on self-evaluation." [10]The Baraita explains the criterion: **"Which Torah scholars are** considered **individuals**

[1]מַהוּ דְּתֵימָא: הָנֵי מִילֵּי צִבּוּר, [2]אֲבָל יָחִיד לָא. [3]קָמַשְׁמַע לָן. [4]תַּנְיָא נַמִי הָכִי: כְּשֶׁהִתְחִילוּ הַיְּחִידִים לְהִתְעַנּוֹת, מִתְעַנִּין שֵׁנִי וַחֲמִישִׁי וְשֵׁנִי, [5]וּמַפְסִיקִין בְּרָאשֵׁי חֳדָשִׁים [10B] [6]וּבְיָמִים טוֹבִים הַכְּתוּבִין בִּמְגִילַּת תַּעֲנִית".

[7]תָּנוּ רַבָּנַן: "אַל יֹאמַר אָדָם: 'תַּלְמִיד אֲנִי; [8]אֵינִי רָאוּי לִהְיוֹת יָחִיד'. [9]אֶלָּא, כָּל תַּלְמִידֵי חֲכָמִים יְחִידִים. [10]אֵי זֶהוּ יָחִיד

LITERAL TRANSLATION

[1]You might have said: This applies to (lit., "these words") a community, [2]but not to an individual. [3][Therefore] he tells us [that this is not so]. [4]It was also taught thus: "When the individuals began to fast, they would fast [on] Monday and Thursday and Monday, [5]and stop on New Moons [10B] [6]and on festivals that are written in *Megillat Ta'anit.*"

[7]Our Rabbis taught: "A man should not say: 'I am a student; [8]I am not worthy to be an individual.' [9]Rather, all Torah scholars are individuals. [10]Who is an individual

RASHI

אבל יחידים לא – שלש תעניות שהיחידין עושין קודם לצבור – אינן זקוקין להתחיל בשני, דליכא אפקיעת שערים משום יחידים לחודייהו, והללו שלש תעניות דיחידים אינן בכלל שלש עשרה תעניות דצבור, תדע דקא חשיב במתניתין שלש ושלש ושבע. **ומפסיקין בראשי חדשים** – שאם חל ראש חדש בשני ובחמישי לאחר שהתחילו להתענות – פוסקין תעניתם. **וכן בימים טובים** – הכתובים במגילת תענית. **תלמיד אני** – ואיני חשוב כל כך כיחידים, כלומר: איני ראוי להתחיל תענית עם היחידים.

NOTES

אֵי זֶהוּ יָחִיד **Who is an individual?** According to the Jerusalem Talmud, when our Mishnah refers to "individuals," it is referring to those Torah scholars who have already been appointed to positions of leadership in the

HALAKHAH

וּמַפְסִיקִין בְּרָאשֵׁי חֳדָשִׁים **And stop on New Moons.** "Individuals who have undertaken a series of fasts (including Rabbinic scholars who are fasting as individuals on account of a drought) may interrupt the series if one of the fast days falls on Rosh Ḥodesh, on Hanukkah, or on Purim." (*Shulḥan Arukh, Oraḥ Ḥayyim* 575:7.)

יְחִידִים **Individuals.** "If the seventeenth day of Marḥeshvan has arrived and it has still not rained, Rabbinic scholars fast on Monday, on the following Thursday, and on the next Monday. (The Aḥaronim disagree regarding a case where the seventeenth of Marḥeshvan falls on a Monday as to whether the series of fasts observed by Rabbinic scholars begins on that day or only on the following Monday; see *Mishnah Berurah.*) Whoever can be categorized as a 'scholar' is fit to observe these three fasts." (Ibid., 575:1.)

וְאֵיזֶהוּ תַּלְמִיד? [1]יָחִיד כָּל שֶׁרָאוּי לְמַנּוֹתוֹ פַּרְנָס עַל הַצִּבּוּר. [2]תַּלְמִיד כָּל שֶׁשּׁוֹאֲלִין אוֹתוֹ דְּבַר הֲלָכָה בְּתַלְמוּדוֹ וְאוֹמֵר, [3]וַאֲפִילּוּ בְּמַסֶּכֶת דְּכַלָּה״.

[4]תָּנוּ רַבָּנַן: ״לֹא כָּל הָרוֹצֶה לַעֲשׂוֹת עַצְמוֹ יָחִיד עוֹשֶׂה; [5]תַּלְמִיד, עוֹשֶׂה. [6]דִּבְרֵי רַבִּי מֵאִיר. [7]רַבִּי יוֹסֵי אוֹמֵר: עוֹשֶׂה, וְזָכוּר לְטוֹב. [8]לְפִי שֶׁאֵין שֶׁבַח הוּא לוֹ, אֶלָּא צַעַר הוּא לוֹ״.

LITERAL TRANSLATION

and who is a student? [1]An individual is anyone who is worthy to be appointed leader of the community. [2]A student is anyone who is asked a matter of Halakhah in his studies and answers (lit., 'says') [3]even in tractate *Kallah*."

[4]Our Rabbis taught: "Not everyone who wishes to make himself an individual may do so; [5][to make himself] a student, he may do so. [6][These are] the words of Rabbi Meir. [7]Rabbi Yose says: He may do so, and he is remembered for good, [8]because it is not [a source of] praise for him, but rather it is [a source of] pain for him."

TRANSLATION AND COMMENTARY

and which Torah scholars **are** considered **students?** [1]**An individual is any** Torah scholar **who is worthy to be appointed leader of the community and** to assume the public offices reserved for Torah scholars." Elsewhere (*Shabbat* 114a), the Gemara explains that only a Torah scholar who can answer a question on any part of the Talmud belongs in this category. [2]The Baraita continues: **"A student is any** Torah scholar **who** is not yet worthy of public office, but **is able to answer if asked a matter of Halakhah in** those parts of the Talmud that **he has studied,** [3]**even if** he has studied only **tractate *Kallah*,"** one of the so-called "minor tractates", whose material is mostly about social behavior and is tangential to the mainstream of Talmud study. A person in this category need not fast with the individuals, although he is entitled to some of the status due to students of Torah.

תָּנוּ רַבָּנַן [4]The previous Baraita considered the case of an individual who humbly claims to be merely a student. The Gemara now cites another Baraita, which deals with the converse case — a student who wishes to fast together with the individuals. **Our Rabbis taught: "Not everyone who wishes to make himself an individual may do so.** [5]Likewise, not everyone who wishes to call himself **a student may do so.** If a novice is in fact not yet even a student — in accordance with the definition in the previous Baraita — he has no right to pretend to a distinction that he does not have. [6]**This is the opinion of Rabbi Meir.** [7]But **Rabbi Yose says:** A student who wishes to fast together with the individuals **may do so, and he is** even **remembered for good** for his piety, [8]**because** his fasting **is not a source of praise for him, but rather a source of pain."** Hence it is not considered inconsistent with the humility demanded of Torah scholars.

RASHI

לא כל הרוצה לעשות עצמו יחיד — לענין תענית. **עושה** — דנראה מגסי הרוח, ותנן (אבות פרק ג משנה י): כל שרוח הבריות נוחה הימנו כו'. הכי גרסינן: **התלמידים עושין עצמן** — כדאמרינן לעיל, שכל התלמידים ראוין לכך, ואין בהם משום גסות הרוח. **רבי יוסי אומר כל אדם** — ואפילו שאינו תלמיד, עושה עצמו יחיד להתענות וזכור לטוב, דצער הוא לו ולא גסות. לישנא אחרינא גרסינן: לא כל הרוצה לעשות עצמו יחיד עושה, תלמיד עושה, כלומר: ולא כל הרוצה נמי לעשות עצמו תלמיד, להתנהג עצמו במדת תלמיד בחלוקו ובמטתו, ולהתנאות בסודר של תלמידי חכמים ושאר דברים עושה, דכל הרוצה ליטול לו את השם לא יטול. ורבי יוסי ארישא. ומסתבר כי האי לישנא. מדקא מהדר רבן שמעון בן גמליאל: דבר של שבח — אינו עושה, מכלל דאיירי בשבח.

BACKGROUND

וְזָכוּר לְטוֹב And he is remembered for good. If a person takes stringencies upon himself that are not required of everyone, this should not be seen as pride. On the contrary, such a person is regarded as volunteering to do more than he is obliged to do. Indeed, the Sages debated throughout the generations as to the stringencies an ordinary person is permitted to take upon himself and the honors he is permitted to assume if these do not conform to his general status, his knowledge of Torah, or his scrupulousness in observing the commandments.

NOTES

community and who have been found trustworthy. Such people are fit to fast and to offer prayers on behalf of the entire community in times of trouble.

וַאֲפִילּוּ בְּמַסֶּכֶת דְּכַלָּה Even if it is in tractate *Kallah*. The Rishonim disagree about the meaning of this phrase. Some (*Rabbenu Ḥananel, Ri* cited by *Tosafot, Shabbat* 114a) explain that the Baraita is referring to the tractate studied at the assemblies held twice a year at the Talmudic academies during the months of Adar and Elul. During each *Kallah* month, one specific tractate was studied, and public lessons were delivered on the topics it contained, so that the material was familiar even to ordinary people who did not devote all their time to Torah study. Thus the Baraita is teaching us that a man is regarded as a student of Torah even if he can answer questions only on the tractate studied in a *Kallah* month.

Others (*Rashi* and *Tosafot, Shabbat* 114a, *Ritva, Rabbenu Yehonatan,* and others) maintain that the Baraita is referring to the minor tractate known as tractate *Kallah*, so named because it opens with a discussion regarding a certain regulation applying to a bride (כַּלָּה — *kallah*). This tractate is not a part of the Talmud, but is a collection of Baraitot.

HALAKHAH

וְאֵיזֶהוּ תַּלְמִיד And who is a student? "If a person is able to answer a question posed to him regarding those parts of the Talmud that he has studied, or even a question regarding the laws pertaining to the Festivals — matters that are reviewed in public discourses before each Festival — he is regarded as a 'student,' both with respect to fast days and with respect to a betrothal which was entered into on condition that the groom was a 'student.'" (*Shulḥan Arukh, Even HaEzer* 38:27.)

LITERAL TRANSLATION

[1] Another [Baraita] was taught: "Not everyone who wishes to make himself an individual may do so; [2] [to make himself] a student, he may do so. [3] [These are] the words of Rabbi Shimon ben Elazar. [4] Rabban Shimon ben Gamliel says: In what [case] are these things said? [5] About a matter [that is a source] of praise, [6] but about a matter [that is a source] of pain he may do so, and he is remembered for good, [7] because it is not [a source of] praise for him, but rather it is [a source of] pain for him."

[8] Our Rabbis taught: "Someone who was fasting over a trouble and it passed, [9] [or] over a sick person and he recovered, should fast and complete. [10] Someone who is going from a place where they are not fasting to a place where they are fasting should fast with them.

[1] תַּנְיָא אִידָךְ: ״לֹא כָּל הָרוֹצֶה לַעֲשׂוֹת עַצְמוֹ יָחִיד עוֹשֶׂה; [2] תַּלְמִיד, עוֹשֶׂה. [3] דִּבְרֵי רַבִּי שִׁמְעוֹן בֶּן אֶלְעָזָר. [4] רַבָּן שִׁמְעוֹן בֶּן גַּמְלִיאֵל אוֹמֵר: בַּמֶּה דְּבָרִים אֲמוּרִים? [5] בְּדָבָר שֶׁל שֶׁבַח, [6] אֲבָל בְּדָבָר שֶׁל צַעַר עוֹשֶׂה, וְזָכוּר לְטוֹב, [7] שֶׁאֵין שֶׁבַח הוּא לוֹ, אֶלָּא צַעַר הוּא לוֹ״.

[8] תָּנוּ רַבָּנַן: ״מִי שֶׁהָיָה מִתְעַנֶּה עַל הַצָּרָה וְעָבְרָה, [9] עַל הַחוֹלֶה וְנִתְרַפֵּא, הֲרֵי זֶה מִתְעַנֶּה וּמַשְׁלִים. [10] הַהוֹלֵךְ מִמָּקוֹם שֶׁאֵין מִתְעַנִּין לְמָקוֹם שֶׁמִּתְעַנִּין הֲרֵי זֶה מִתְעַנֶּה עִמָּהֶן.

TRANSLATION AND COMMENTARY

תַּנְיָא אִידָךְ [1] The Gemara notes that a slightly different version of the previous Baraita's ruling **was taught in another Baraita: "Not everyone who wishes to make himself an individual may do so.** [2] Likewise, not everyone who wishes to call himself **a student may do so.** [3] **This is the opinion of Rabbi Shimon ben Elazar.** [4] **Rabban Shimon ben Gamliel says: In what case are these things said?** When is it true that a student must not assume the status of a full scholar, and a novice must not assume the status of a student? [5] It is true only **of a matter that is a source of praise,** such as public office and the like. [6] **But when a matter is a source of pain,** such as fasting, a student who wishes to fast together with the individuals **may do so, and he is** even **remembered for good** for his piety, [7] **because** his fasting **is not a source of praise for him, but rather a source of pain."**

תָּנוּ רַבָּנַן [8] The Gemara now cites another Baraita on the topic of private fasts. The Mishnah (below, 19a) rules that if a public fast has been decreed because of drought, and rain falls during the morning of the fast day, the community need not complete the fast. But the rule regarding private fasts is different, as **our Rabbis taught** in the following Baraita: "If **someone is fasting** on a private basis **because of a serious personal problem, and** before the day has come to an end, the problem that caused him to fast has in fact **passed,** he must still continue the fast until the evening. [9] Likewise, if a person is fasting **over a sick person,** praying for his recovery, **and** the sick person **recovers** before the fast has come to an end, the person must **complete his fast."** [10] The Baraita continues: "If **someone travels from a place where they are not fasting to a place where they are fasting** because of some local calamity, the traveler must **fast with** the local people, even if he is not personally affected by their problems and plans to return

RASHI

על החולה ונתרפא — הוא הדין אם מת החולה, בעי לקיומי נדרו. **על הצרה ועברה** — מתענה ומשלים, ואם לאו — נראה כמַתְנֶה עם קונו: אם תעבור [לא] אתענה, ואם לאו — אתענה.

SAGES

רַבִּי שִׁמְעוֹן בֶּן אֶלְעָזָר **Rabbi Shimon ben Elazar.** One of the Sages of the Mishnah during the last generation of Tannaim. We know practically nothing about his life or family, and, because he belonged to the generation in which the Mishnah was edited, not many of his teachings appear in the Mishnah itself (although they are found in Baraitot and in the Talmud). Rabbi Shimon ben Elazar was a friend of Rabbi Yehudah HaNasi, and controversies between them are mentioned several times. He received most of his knowledge of the Torah from his teacher, Rabbi Meir, to whom he was devoted, and he customarily reports teachings in Rabbi Meir's name. Rabbi Shimon ben Elazar lived in or near Tiberias, and although he apparently did not have an academy of his own, many teachings are cited in his name, both in the Halakhah and in the Aggadah.

רַבָּן שִׁמְעוֹן בֶּן גַּמְלִיאֵל **Rabban Shimon ben Gamliel.** There were two Sages of this name. The first lived at the end of the Second Temple period and was executed by the Romans as a leader of the great Jewish revolt. The second, his grandson, was Rabban Shimon, the son of Rabban Gamliel of Yavneh. Here and in general, the Sage cited in the Talmud is the second of the two, the father and teacher of Rabbi Yehudah HaNasi. Rabban Shimon ben Gamliel the second apparently became president (Nasi) of the Sanhedrin after the Bar Kokhba revolt, when the situation of the Jews in Eretz Israel was extremely difficult and a great deal of political talent was needed to restore Jewish life in the country. Indeed, his father Rabban Gamliel traveled to Rome several times to intervene with the Emperor for this purpose. Rabban Shimon ben Gamliel was apparently the youngest of the great Sages of his generation: Rabbi Yehudah, Rabbi Yose, Rabbi Meir, and Rabbi Shimon bar Yoḥai were all disciples of Rabbi Akiva. Rabban Shimon ben Gamliel regarded himself as inferior to them in status, and he esteemed their greatness. On

NOTES

The material covered in the tractate is regarded as being intellectually undemanding. Thus the Baraita is informing us that if a person can intelligently discuss those parts of the Talmud that he has studied, even if he has only studied tractate *Kallah*, he is regarded as a Talmudic student. Elsewhere (*Shabbat* 114a), the Gemara states that a Talmudic scholar is deemed worthy of public office if he can answer Halakhic questions on any part of the Talmud, even tractate *Kallah*. The Rishonim explain that, although this tractate was considered relatively easy, it was not studied regularly in the academies, so mastery of it was regarded as a sign of great erudition.

הַהוֹלֵךְ מִמָּקוֹם שֶׁאֵין מִתְעַנִּין לְמָקוֹם שֶׁמִּתְעַנִּין **Someone who is going from a place where they are not fasting to a place where they are fasting.** As a rule, a person who intends to return home at the end of his journey is not

HALAKHAH

מִי שֶׁהָיָה מִתְעַנֶּה עַל הַצָּרָה וְעָבְרָה **Someone who was fasting over a trouble and it passed.** "If an individual was fasting in order to avert a certain calamity, and the calamity passed, or if he was fasting on behalf of a sick person, and the patient recovered or died, he must complete the fast (or the series of fasts) that he took upon himself (unless he stipulated at the outset that he would not complete his fast or fasts if the calamity was averted, or the patient recovered or died; *Darkhei Moshe, Yoreh De'ah* 220)." (*Shulḥan Arukh, Oraḥ Ḥayyim* 569:1.)

הַהוֹלֵךְ מִמָּקוֹם שֶׁאֵין מִתְעַנִּין לְמָקוֹם שֶׁמִּתְעַנִּין **Someone who is going from a place where they are not fasting to a place where they are fasting.** "If someone goes from a place where they are not fasting to a place where they are

the other hand, he sought to strengthen the position of the office of Nasi. This led to an effort to remove him from office, though he remained Nasi in that generation, and those who sought to depose him were severely reprimanded. Although not many Halakhot are taught in his name, the Amoraim ruled that in almost every place where he presents a ruling, even against an anonymous Mishnah, the Halakhah is in accordance with him. Since he was the head of a yeshivah, he did not have individual disciples, except for his eminent son, Rabbi Yehudah HaNasi.

[1]מִמָּקוֹם שֶׁמִּתְעַנִּין לְמָקוֹם שֶׁאֵין מִתְעַנִּין הֲרֵי זֶה מִתְעַנֶּה וּמַשְׁלִים. [2]שָׁכַח וְאָכַל וְשָׁתָה, אַל יִתְרָאֶה בִּפְנֵי הַצִּבּוּר, [3]וְאַל יַנְהִיג עִידּוּנִין בְּעַצְמוֹ, [4]שֶׁנֶּאֱמַר: ׳וַיֹּאמֶר יַעֲקֹב לְבָנָיו: לָמָּה תִּתְרָאוּ?׳ [5]אָמַר לָהֶם יַעֲקֹב לְבָנָיו: אַל תַּרְאוּ עַצְמְכֶם כְּשֶׁאַתֶּם שְׂבֵעִין, לֹא בִּפְנֵי עֵשָׂו, וְלֹא בִּפְנֵי יִשְׁמָעֵאל, [6]כְּדֵי שֶׁלֹּא יִתְקַנְּאוּ בָּכֶם״.

LITERAL TRANSLATION

[1]From a place where they are fasting to a place where they are not fasting, he should fast and complete. [2][If] he forgot, and ate and drank, he should not appear before the community, [3]and he should not indulge in luxuries (lit., 'follow the custom of luxuries with himself'), [4]as it is said: 'And Jacob said to his sons: Why do you show yourselves?' [5]Jacob said to his sons: Do not show yourselves when you are satiated, not before Esau, and not before Ishmael, [6]in order that they should not be jealous of you."

RASHI

למקום שאין מתענין הרי זה מתענה ומשלים — כל התעניות שקבלו עליהן בני עירו, דנותנין עליו חומרי המקום שיצא משם. **אכל ושתה** — דיעבד. **אל יתראה בפניהן** — שנראה כחתן בין אבלים, ויתקנאו בו. **ואל ינהיג עדונים בעצמו** — שלא יאמר: הואיל ואכלתי כל שהוא — אוכל הרבה. **אל תראו עצמכם** — שיש לכם חטים הרבה, ולא הלכו אלא בשביל דבר זה, שלא להתראות בפני בני עשו, שהיו לעורים ורעבים.

TRANSLATION AND COMMENTARY

home the next day. [1]Conversely, if he travels on the fast day itself **from a place where they are fasting to a place where they are not fasting,** in such a case the traveler must **complete his fast** like the people of his home town, even though the people around him are not fasting." [2]The Baraita continues: **"If** a traveler from a city that is not fasting visits a city that is fasting, and **forgets** himself **and eats and drinks, he should not show himself before the** members of the **community** who are fasting. [3]Likewise, **he should not indulge in luxuries,** arguing that since he has already broken his fast, it does not matter what he eats. Rather, he must stop eating as soon as he realizes that he has violated the local fast." The Baraita now cites Scriptural support for its first contention: [4]**"As it is said** [Genesis 42:1]: 'And Jacob saw that there was grain in Egypt, **and Jacob said to his sons: Why do you show yourselves?'"** According to the plain meaning of the verse, Jacob and his sons were suffering from the famine that had befallen Canaan, and when Jacob heard that there was grain in Egypt, he asked his sons to travel there to buy it. But it is not clear what Jacob meant by "showing yourselves." The traditional explanation of this verse is that Jacob had sufficient food for himself and for his family but did not want the people living near him, who were indeed suffering from famine, to know this. Accordingly, he gave the impression that he was in need himself. [5]"Thus," the Baraita explains, **"Jacob was saying to his sons: Do not show yourselves when you have satisfied your hunger, neither before** the children of **Esau, nor before** the children of **Ishmael,** [6]**in order that they should not be jealous of you."** But when it became difficult to maintain this pretense, Jacob sent his sons to Egypt to provide a convincing explanation for their ability to withstand the famine.

NOTES

required to adopt the stringencies of the places he is visiting (see *Pesaḥim* 51a). Here, however, the Baraita requires the traveler to observe the fast with the rest of the community he is visiting. *Rabbenu Yehonatan* writes that he must observe the fast even if he plans to return home, because a person may not separate himself from the distress experienced by the community in which he finds himself, even if his stay in that community is only temporary.

מִתְעַנֶּה וּמַשְׁלִים He should fast and complete. Elsewhere (below, 19a), the Mishnah states that if a fast is being observed on account of drought, and it begins to rain

HALAKHAH

fasting, he must fast with them (even if he has already eaten earlier in the day; *Eliya Rabbah*), even if he plans to return to the place he came from, where they are not fasting. Nevertheless, since he did not take the fast upon himself, once he leaves the city boundary he is permitted to eat. *Rema* adds that if he arrived in that place on the day before the fast, he is required to take the fast upon himself together with the rest of the community, and then he is required to complete his fast with them even if he leaves the city." (*Shulḥan Arukh, Oraḥ Ḥayyim* 574:2.)

מִמָּקוֹם שֶׁמִּתְעַנִּין לְמָקוֹם שֶׁאֵין מִתְעַנִּין From a place where they are fasting to a place where they are not fasting. "If someone goes from a place where they are fasting to a place where they are not fasting, and he plans to return to the place where they are fasting, he is required to observe all the fasts that his fellow townspeople have undertaken (even if he did not take those fasts upon himself; *Taz*). If he was not in his own town at the time that the fast was accepted, he is not required to observe the fast (*Arukh HaShulḥan*). But if the fast was decreed not on account of an impending calamity but to commemorate some past calamity, he is required to observe the fast, even if he was not there when the fast was accepted, because he must accept the stringencies of his community as long as he plans to return there (*Eliya Rabbah, Pri Megadim*)." (Ibid., 574:1.)

שָׁכַח וְאָכַל וְשָׁתָה If he forgot and ate and drank. "If someone is required to fast because he has arrived in a place where the community is observing a fast, and he forgets and eats and drinks, he should not appear in public

SAGES

רַבִּי אִלְעַאי בַּר בֶּרֶכְיָה Rabbi Il'ai bar Berekhyah. A Palestinian Amora of the third generation. A few Aggadic teachings are reported in his name in the Babylonian Talmud. Nothing is known of the details of his personal life.

BACKGROUND

רְאוּיִין לִישָּׂרֵף Are fit to be burned. People, especially Torah scholars, who waste their time and do not study Torah are guilty of the sin of בִּיטּוּל תּוֹרָה, nullification of Torah, for whenever one has free time one is required to study. Therefore anyone who is traveling and has no other business must study Torah to the degree that time and circumstances permit it.

LITERAL TRANSLATION

[1]"Do not become distressed on the road." [2]Rabbi Elazar said: Joseph said to his brothers: [3]Do not become involved in a matter of Halakhah, lest you make the road distressing for you.

[4]Is this so? [5]But surely Rabbi Il'ai bar Berekhyah said: Two Torah scholars who are walking along the road, and there are no words of Torah between them, are fit to be burned, [6]as it is said: "And it came to pass as they were walking, walking and talking, that behold a chariot of fire and horses of fire appeared and separated the two of them." [7]The reason is because there was speech, [8]but if there had been no speech, they would have been fit to be burned!

[1]"אַל תִּרְגְּזוּ בַּדָּרֶךְ". [2]אָמַר רַבִּי אֶלְעָזָר: אָמַר לָהֶם יוֹסֵף לְאֶחָיו: [3]אַל תִּתְעַסְּקוּ בִּדְבַר הֲלָכָה, שֶׁמָּא תִּרְגְּזוּ עֲלֵיכֶם הַדֶּרֶךְ.

[4]אִינִי? [5]וְהָאָמַר רַבִּי אִלְעַאי בַּר בֶּרֶכְיָה: שְׁנֵי תַלְמִידֵי חֲכָמִים שֶׁמְּהַלְּכִים בַּדֶּרֶךְ, וְאֵין בֵּינֵיהֶן דִּבְרֵי תוֹרָה, רְאוּיִין לִישָּׂרֵף, [6]שֶׁנֶּאֱמַר: "וַיְהִי הֵמָּה הֹלְכִים, הָלוֹךְ וְדַבֵּר, וְהִנֵּה רֶכֶב אֵשׁ וְסוּסֵי אֵשׁ וַיַּפְרִדוּ בֵּין שְׁנֵיהֶם". [7]טַעֲמָא דְּאִיכָּא דִּיבּוּר, [8]הָא לֵיכָּא דִּיבּוּר, רְאוּיִין לִישָּׂרֵף!

TRANSLATION AND COMMENTARY

אַל תִּרְגְּזוּ בַּדָּרֶךְ [1]Having cited this Baraita, the Gemara now presents another piece of advice related to the story of Joseph and his brothers. After Joseph has revealed himself to his brothers, the Torah continues (Genesis 45:24): "And he sent his brothers away and they went, and he said to them: **Do not become distressed on the road.**" What did Joseph mean by this piece of advice? [2]**Rabbi Elazar said: Joseph was saying to his brothers:** Concentrate on your journey. [3]**Do not become involved in** discussing a difficult **matter of Halakhah, lest you make the road distressing for you** and you lose your way. Thus this verse is apparently teaching us that it is not wise to study Torah while traveling.

אִינִי [4]The Gemara objects: **Is this really so?** [5]Is it really unwise to study Torah while traveling? **But surely Rabbi Il'ai bar Berekhyah said: If two Torah scholars are walking along the road and there are no words of Torah between them, they are fit to be burned** to death! Thus we see that the study of Torah while traveling is in fact required! Rabbi Il'ai bar Berekhyah brings Scriptural support for his contention, [6]**for it is said** (II Kings 2:11): **"And it came to pass as they were walking, walking and talking, that behold a chariot of fire and horses of fire appeared and separated the two of them,** and Elijah went up to heaven in a storm." This verse describes the parting of the Prophet Elijah from his disciple Elisha. Elisha had been told that if he was privileged to see Elijah's departure from the earth, he could be confident that Elijah's spirit would rest upon him. Accordingly, he remained close to Elijah until a fiery chariot took Elijah to Heaven. Rabbi Il'ai bar Berekhyah notes that the chariot was of fire, and the verse describes Elijah and Elisha as constantly in conversation as they traveled from place to place, and their conversation must presumably have been about Torah matters. [7]Accordingly, **the reason** why the chariot took Elijah up to Heaven and left Elisha untouched **was because** they **were speaking** words of Torah; [8]**but had they not been speaking** words of Torah, **they would have been fit to be burned** to death. Rabbi Il'ai bar Berekhyah

RASHI

תרגזו עליכם הדרך — תתעו. **לישרף באש** — דכתיב "והנה סוסי אש" וכתיב בההוא עניינא "הלוך ודבר", והכי כתביה, לאשמועינן דאי לאו שהיו הולכין בעומקה של הלכה — לא [היו ניצולין].

NOTES

before noon, there is no need to complete the fast. *Ra'avad* (in his note to *Rambam, Hilkhot Ta'aniyyot* 1:15-16) distinguishes between a fast observed on account of a drought and all other fasts. If it rains on the day that a fast is being observed on account of a drought, there is no longer any reason to continue the fast, because the community is no longer faced with danger. But if a fast is being observed in order to avert some other calamity, the fast must be completed even if the calamity has passed, for it may not have passed completely. Most other Rishonim (*Rambam, Ramban,* and others) distinguish between an individual fast and a public fast. Our Baraita deals with an individual fast, which must be completed even if the calamity on account of which the fast was undertaken has already passed. The Mishnah below deals with a public fast, which does not have to be completed if the calamity has already passed, so as not to cause the community unnecessary hardship. A public fast is always regarded as having been decreed with the stipulation that it will not have to be completed if the calamity on account of which it was decreed has passed.

שֶׁמָּא תִּרְגְּזוּ עֲלֵיכֶם הַדֶּרֶךְ Lest you make the road distressing for you. Our commentary follows *Rashi,* who explains

HALAKHAH

before the community that is fasting, nor should he indulge in luxuries, arguing that since he has already broken his fast he may continue to eat. Rather, he must stop eating as soon as he remembers that he is supposed to be fasting. *Rema* adds that he may not indulge in luxuries even if he is not in the presence of the community that is fasting." (*Shulḥan Arukh, Oraḥ Ḥayyim* 574:3.)

TRANSLATION AND COMMENTARY

infers from this incident that it is obligatory to speak words of Torah while traveling, thus contradicting Rabbi Elazar's ruling that it is forbidden to study Torah when traveling.

לָא קַשְׁיָא [1]The Gemara answers: **There is no difficulty** in resolving the contradiction between the two rulings. Rabbi Il'ai bar Berekhyah was referring **to learning by rote,** [2]whereas Rabbi Elazar **was referring to learning in depth.** While traveling, it is obligatory to study and review material that has already been learned, but it is forbidden to become involved in deep Torah discussions that can distract one's attention from the road.

בְּמַתְנִיתָא תָּנָא [3]The Gemara notes that a different explanation of Joseph's advice to his brothers **was taught in a Baraita.** According to this Baraita, when Joseph said to his brothers: "Do not become distressed on the road," he meant that they should not be careless. [4]The Baraita explains: "Joseph said to them: **Do not stride with large strides,** but walk at a normal pace, **and bring the sun into the city** by finding a place to spend the night before the sun sets." [5]The Gemara explains why these safety precautions are important: **"Do not stride with large strides," because a Master has said** (*Berakhot* 43b) [6]that the stress involved in taking **large strides takes away one five-hundredth of the light of a man's eyes.** [7]**"And bring the sun into the city," in accordance with what Rav Yehudah said in the name of Rav.** [8]**For Rav Yehudah said in the name of Rav: A man should always leave** a city when the light — of which God has said (Genesis 1:4) **"that it was good"** — has already appeared in the morning, [9]**and** he should always **come in** to a city to spend the night while the light — of which God has said **"that it was good"** — is still there in the late afternoon. For the good light is a help to travelers, and it is unsafe to travel in the dark. Rav Yehudah brings Scriptural support for his statement, [10]**as it is said** (Genesis 44:3): **"The morning was light, and the men were sent away,** they and their asses." Thus we see that Joseph did not send his brothers away until it was light outside.

אָמַר רַב יְהוּדָה [11]The Gemara now cites another piece of advice for travelers. **Rav Yehudah said in the name of Rabbi Ḥiyya:** [12]**Someone who is traveling along the road should not eat more than** he would eat **in time of famine** (see below, 11a).

LITERAL TRANSLATION

[1]There is no difficulty. This [refers] to learning by rote; [2]that [refers] to learning in depth.

[3][A Tanna] taught in a Baraita: [4]"Do not stride with large strides, and bring the sun into the city." [5]"Do not stride with large strides," for the Master said: [6]Large strides take away one five-hundredth of the light of a man's eyes. [7]"And bring the sun into the city," in accordance with what Rav Yehudah said in the name of Rav. [8]For Rav Yehudah said in the name of Rav: A man should always go out with "that it was good" [9]and come in with "that it was good," [10]as it is said: "The morning was light, and the men were sent away."

[11]Rav Yehudah said in the name of Rabbi Ḥiyya: [12]Someone who is traveling along the road should not eat more than [in] years of famine.

[1]לָא קַשְׁיָא. הָא לְמִיגְרַס; [2]הָא לְעִיּוּנֵי.

[3]בְּמַתְנִיתָא תָּנָא: [4]"אַל תַּפְסִיעוּ פְּסִיעָה גַּסָּה, וְהַכְנִיסוּ חַמָּה לָעִיר". [5]"אַל תַּפְסִיעוּ פְּסִיעָה גַּסָּה," דְּאָמַר מָר: [6]פְּסִיעָה גַּסָּה נוֹטֶלֶת אֶחָד מֵחֲמֵשׁ מֵאוֹת מִמְּאוֹר עֵינָיו שֶׁל אָדָם. [7]"וְהַכְנִיסוּ חַמָּה לָעִיר," כִּדְרַב יְהוּדָה אָמַר רַב. [8]דְּאָמַר רַב יְהוּדָה אָמַר רַב: לְעוֹלָם יֵצֵא אָדָם בְּ"כִי טוֹב" [9]וְיִכָּנֵס בְּ"כִי טוֹב", [10]שֶׁנֶּאֱמַר: "הַבֹּקֶר אוֹר, וְהָאֲנָשִׁים שֻׁלְּחוּ".

[11]אָמַר רַב יְהוּדָה אָמַר רַבִּי חִיָּיא: [12]הַמְהַלֵּךְ בַּדֶּרֶךְ אַל יֹאכַל יוֹתֵר מִשְּׁנֵי רְעָבוֹן.

RASHI

במתניתא תנא — מאי "אל תרגזו בדרך" — אל תזיקו עצמכם בפסיעה גסה. **והכניסו חמה לעיר** — כשאתם לנין ושוכבין בדרך בעיירות, הכניסו לעיר בעוד שהחמה זורחת. **יצא אדם בכי טוב** — שימתין עד שיאור, כמו "וירא אלהים את האור כי טוב" (בראשית א). **ויכנס בכי טוב** — בערב בעוד שהחמה זורחת, שאין ליסטין מצויין, אי נמי: שלא יפול בבורות ובקעים שבעיר, שלא יעלילו עליו עלילות: מרגל אתה או גנב. **הבוקר אור והאנשים שולחו המה וחמוריהם** — מיכן שיצאו בכי טוב, והוא הדין ליכנס בכי טוב. יש ספרים דלא כתיב בהו האי קרא, אלא מילתא דרב יהודה סברא הוא, ולא בעינן קרא. **לא יאכל יותר ממה שאוכל בשני רעבון** — דאמר לקמן (יא,א): שצריך להרעיב עצמו בשני רעבון.

NOTES

that Torah scholars who are on a journey should not become involved in a discussion of a difficult matter of Halakhah, lest they lose their way. Similarly, *Meiri* writes that they should not engage in a Halakhic discussion, lest

HALAKHAH

הַמְהַלֵּךְ בַּדֶּרֶךְ אַל יֹאכַל יוֹתֵר מִשְּׁנֵי רְעָבוֹן Someone who is traveling along the road should not eat more than in years of famine. "A person who is on a journey should not eat more than he would eat in years of famine, lest he suffer intestinal problems." (*Magen Avraham, Shulḥan Arukh, Oraḥ Ḥayyim* 110, note 10.)

BACKGROUND

נוֹטֶלֶת אֶחָד מֵחֲמֵשׁ מֵאוֹת מִמְּאוֹר עֵינָיו שֶׁל אָדָם Take away one five-hundreth of the light of a man's eyes. People whose ocular nerves are weak are liable to endanger their vision by excessive physical effort. A significant muscular effort is liable to interfere with the muscles that control the movement of the eyes. Although such damage occurs only to a relatively small number of people, the Sages recommended that one avoid such physical exertion so as not to endanger one's vision.

לְעוֹלָם יֵצֵא אָדָם בְּ"כִי טוֹב" A man should always go out with "that it was good." This recommendation applies especially to people traveling on unfamiliar roads. In darkness a person is liable to encounter obstacles in his path, and often goes astray on a road that he does not know well. It should be added that at night there is increased danger from wild animals and robbers. Therefore someone who travels by daylight is more likely to reach his destination safely, even if this forces him to make frequent overnight stops.

SAGES

רַבִּי חִיָּיא Rabbi Ḥiyya. Originating from the town of Kafri in Babylonia, Rabbi Ḥiyya was one of the last of the Tannaim, and a student and colleague of Rabbi Yehudah HaNasi.

Rabbi Ḥiyya came from a distinguished family that was descended from King David and produced many Sages. While he still lived in Babylonia he was already considered a great Torah scholar, and when he left Babylonia with the members of his family to settle in Eretz Israel, there were those who said, in exaggeration, that the Torah would have been forgotten in Eretz Israel had he not arrived from Babylonia to reestablish it. Upon his arrival in Eretz Israel, he became the student and colleague of Rabbi Yehudah HaNasi. He also became a close friend of Rabbi Yehudah HaNasi and in particular of his son, Rabbi Shimon, who was Rabbi Ḥiyya's business partner. Rabbi Ḥiyya was one of the greatest Sages of his

TRANSLATION AND COMMENTARY

מַאי טַעֲמָא [1]The Gemara asks: **What is the reason?**

הָכָא תַּרְגִּימוּ [2]The Gemara answers: **Here** in Babylonia **they explained** that **it is because of one's bowels.** If a person eats normally and then, in order to reach his destination, he exerts himself more than he is accustomed, he is liable to suffer from diarrhea. [3]**In Eretz Israel they explained** that it **is because** he can carry only a small amount **of food**, and if he eats too much, he will find it difficult to replenish his supplies during the journey.

מַאי בֵּינַיְיהוּ [4]The Gemara asks: **What is the difference between** these two explanations?

אִיכָּא בֵּינַיְיהוּ [5]The Gemara answers: **There is a** case where one can see the **difference between them:** [11A] [6]For example, **where he was traveling in a boat.** A person on a sea voyage does not need to exert himself and should not have any digestive problems. Hence, according to the explanation given in Babylonia, he should be permitted to eat normally. But according to the explanation given in Eretz Israel, he should still refrain, in case he uses up his supplies and later finds it difficult to buy provisions during the voyage. [7]**Alternatively,** there is another case where only one of these reasons applies: For example, **where he was traveling from one lodging to another.** Such a person need not carry much food with him, because he can always buy it on his journey. Hence, according to the explanation given in Eretz Israel, he should be permitted to eat normally. But according to the explanation given in Babylonia, he should still refrain, in case he suffers digestive problems because of the exertion of the journey.

דְּיָתֵיב בְּאַרְבָּא [8]The Gemara relates that when **Rav Pappa** traveled, he **would eat a loaf of bread every single parasang** (about four kilometers) of his journey. [9]The Gemara explains that Rav Pappa **was of the opinion** that the sole reason for the injunction to eat sparingly on a journey was the one given in Babylonia — to avoid diarrhea. Accordingly, Rav Pappa felt that this prohibition did not apply to a heavy eater like himself, because travel did not interfere with his digestion.

אָמַר רַב יְהוּדָה [10]**Rav Yehudah said in the name of Rav: Anyone who** has enough food for himself but **makes**

[1]מַאי טַעֲמָא?
[2]הָכָא תַּרְגִּימוּ: מִשּׁוּם מַעֲיָינָא.
[3]בְּמַעַרְבָא אָמְרִי: מִשּׁוּם מְזוֹנֵי.
[4]מַאי בֵּינַיְיהוּ?
[5]אִיכָּא בֵּינַיְיהוּ [11A] [6]דְּיָתֵיב בְּאַרְבָּא. [7]אִי נַמִי: דְּקָאָזֵיל מֵאַוְונָא לְאַוְונָא.
[8]רַב פַּפָּא כָּל פַּרְסָה וּפַרְסָה אָכֵיל חֲדָא רִיפְתָּא. [9]קָסָבַר: מִשּׁוּם מַעֲיָינָא.
[10]אָמַר רַב יְהוּדָה אָמַר רַב: כָּל הַמַּרְעִיב עַצְמוֹ בִּשְׁנֵי רְעָבוֹן

LITERAL TRANSLATION

[1]What is the reason?
[2]Here they explained: Because of the bowels. [3]In Eretz Israel (lit., "in the West") they explained: Because of food.
[4]What is [the difference] between them?
[5]There is [a difference] between them [11A] [6]where he is sitting in a boat. [7]Or alternatively: Where he is going from station to station.
[8]Rav Pappa would eat one [loaf of] bread every single parasang. [9]He maintained: It is because of the bowels.
[10]Rav Yehudah said in the name of Rav: Anyone who starves himself in years of famine

RASHI

(הכא — [תלמוד] זה בבלי הוא, וכי משתעי בבבל קאמר הכא, וכל "הא לן והא להו" בבבל קאמר). **משום מעיינא** — שלא יתחלחלו מעיו של אדם ברוב אכילתו מפני טורח הדרך, יש אומרים: יהיו מעיו של אדם שופכין זה לזה כעין מעיין. **משום מזוני** — שמא אין לו לאחר כך. **דיתיב בארבא** = שהולך בספינה, משום מזוני — איכא, משום מעיינא — ליכא. **מאוונא לאוונא** — מקום מלון התגרים מכפר לכפר, דמשתכחי מזוני, וליכא למיחש למזוני, ולמעיינא איכא למיחש. **כל פרסה ופרסה אכל ריפתא** — קסבר רב פפא: הא דאמור רבנן לא ליכול טפי — משום מעיינא, ואיהו לא מיסתפי ממעיינא, דבעל בטן הוה, ענין אחר: כריסו רחבה, כדאיתא בבבא מציעא (פד,א) דקא חשיב אבריה דרב פפא, וכאיש גבורתו, ולפיכך יכול לאכול הרבה ואינו מזיק לו.

generation. Not only was he a great Torah scholar, but he was also very pious, as is related in many places in the Talmud. His great achievement was the editing of collections of Baraitot, as a kind of supplement to the Mishnah edited by Rabbi Yehudah HaNasi. These collections, which he seems to have edited in collaboration with his colleague and student, Rabbi Oshaya, were considered extremely reliable, so much so that it was said that any Baraitot not reported by them were not worthy of being cited in the House of Study. It seems that, upon his arrival in Eretz Israel, he received some financial support from the House of the Nasi, but he mainly earned his living from international trade on a large scale, especially in silk. He had twin daughters, Pazi and Tavi, from whom important families of Sages were descended. He also had twin sons, Yehudah (Rabbi Yannai's son-in-law) and Ḥizkiyah, who were important scholars during the transitional generation between the Tannaim and the Amoraim. They apparently took their father's place at the head of his yeshivah in Tiberias, where he lived. All of Rabbi Yehudah HaNasi's students were Rabbi Ḥiyya's colleagues, and he was also on close terms with the Tanna Rabbi Shimon ben Ḥalafta. Rabbi Yehudah HaNasi's younger students (Rabbi Ḥanina, Rabbi Oshaya, Rabbi Yannai, and others) all studied under Rabbi Ḥiyya as well, and to some degree were considered his disciples. Rabbi Ḥiyya's nephews, Rabbah bar Ḥana, and, above all, the great Amora Rav, were his outstanding disciples. He also appears as one of the central figures in the *Zohar*. Rabbi Ḥiyya was buried in Tiberias, and his two sons were later buried at his side.

LANGUAGE

אַוְונָא Lodging place. In Syriac this word means "station" or "inn." Some, however, derive it from the Greek εὐνή, *eune*, meaning "bed."

BACKGROUND

כָּל פַּרְסָה וּפַרְסָה Every single parasang. Stomach disorders that often affect

NOTES

they do not notice an obstacle found on the road and they get hurt. *Rabbenu Gershom* explains the issue differently. Torah scholars who are on a journey should not become involved in a heated discussion regarding a Halakhic matter, lest onlookers think that the scholars are quarreling and come to think badly of them.

מַעֲיָינָא The bowels. Our commentary follows *Rabbenu Ḥananel*, who explains that this is a reference to diarrhea. If a traveler eats in his customary way, he is likely to suffer from diarrhea and be unable to continue his journey. *Rabbenu Gershom* notes that if a person who wishes to set out on a journey eats too much, his full stomach will weigh him down and make it difficult for him to travel as planned.

כָּל פַּרְסָה וּפַרְסָה Every single parasang. Some commentators suggest that Rav Pappa understood that the advice to a traveler to eat sparingly was in order to avoid problems of

HALAKHAH

כָּל הַמַּרְעִיב עַצְמוֹ בִּשְׁנֵי רְעָבוֹן Anyone who starves himself in years of famine. "In years of famine, a person should reduce the amount of food that he eats and allow himself to go hungry, following Rav Yehudah. In years of famine, a man is forbidden to engage in sexual relations with his wife, except on the night she undergoes ritual immersion.

TRANSLATION AND COMMENTARY

himself go hungry in years of famine out of sympathy for his fellowmen, [1]**will be saved from an unnatural death** — a term referring to an untimely or undignified or painful death — and will die in his time in his bed, [2]**as it is said** (Job 5:20): **"In famine, He redeemed you from death,** and in war from the hand of the sword." In the context, Job is being told that God will save him from death when the rest of the world is dying from hunger. But why does the verse say that in time of famine God redeems him "from death" in general? [3]**It should have** specifically **said** that He redeems him **"from famine,"** just as it specifically says that in time of war He redeems him from the sword! [4]**Rather,** argues Rav Yehudah, **this is what** the verse in Job **is saying:** [5]Job is being told that **as a reward for making himself go hungry in years of famine,** God has promised that Job **will be saved,** not only from the famine itself, but also **from** all other forms of **unnatural death.**

אָמַר רֵישׁ לָקִישׁ [6]Similarly, **Resh Lakish said: It is forbidden for a person to have marital relations in years of famine,** out of sympathy for the plight of his fellowmen, even if the person himself has adequate food, [7]**as it is said** (Genesis 41:50): **"And to Joseph were born two sons before the year of famine came,** whom Asenath the daughter of Potipherah the priest of On bore him." We see from this verse that from the time when the famine began, Joseph had no further children. Joseph was viceroy of Egypt and in no personal danger of starvation, yet he refrained from marital relations out of sympathy for the plight of his fellowmen.

תָּנָא [8]The Gemara notes that in spite of Resh Lakish's ruling **a Tanna taught** in a Baraita that **"those** couples who are as yet **without children may have marital relations in years of famine,"** because Resh Lakish's ruling applies only to people like Joseph, who had already begotten children during the years preceding the famine in Egypt.

[1]נִיצַּל מִמִּיתָה מְשׁוּנָּה, [2]שֶׁנֶּאֱמַר "בְּרָעָב פָּדְךָ מִמָּוֶת". [3]"מֵרָעָב" מִיבָּעֵי לֵיהּ! [4]אֶלָּא, הָכִי קָאָמַר: [5]בִּשְׂכַר שֶׁמַּרְעִיב עַצְמוֹ בִּשְׁנֵי רְעָבוֹן, נִיצּוֹל מִמִּיתָה מְשׁוּנָּה. [6]אָמַר רֵישׁ לָקִישׁ: אָסוּר לְאָדָם לְשַׁמֵּשׁ מִטָּתוֹ בִּשְׁנֵי רְעָבוֹן, [7]שֶׁנֶּאֱמַר: "וּלְיוֹסֵף יֻלַּד שְׁנֵי בָנִים בְּטֶרֶם תָּבוֹא שְׁנַת הָרָעָב". [8]תָּנָא: "חֲסוּכֵי בָנִים מְשַׁמְּשִׁין מִטּוֹתֵיהֶן בִּשְׁנֵי רְעָבוֹן".

LITERAL TRANSLATION

[1]is saved from an unnatural death, [2]as it is said: "In famine, He redeemed you from death." [3]It should have [said]: "From famine"! [4]Rather, this is what it says: [5]As a reward for starving himself in years of famine, he is saved from an unnatural death.

[6]Resh Lakish said: It is forbidden for a man to have marital relations in years of famine, [7]as it is said: "And to Joseph were born two sons before the year of famine came."

[8][A Tanna] taught: "Those without children may have marital relations in years of famine."

RASHI

מיתה משונה — מת בחרב וברעב, וכל מיתה שאינה בידי מלאך המות כדרך כל אדם על מטתו. **בשכר שמצער עצמו** — כשישראל בצער. **אסור לשמש מטתו בשני רעבון** — דצריך אדם לנהוג צער בעצמו. **חסוכי בנים** — חסירי בנים, דגרסינן במנחות (כט,א) לגבי מנורה: ומי חסיכי כולי האי, שלא קיימו פריה ורביה.

travelers can be caused by changes in diet and water, which expose a person to germs to which the body is not accustomed, and they typically cause diarrhea. On the other hand, a traveler often places an excessive burden on his digestive system by eating heavy meals quickly in the morning and in the evening. Rav Pappa believed that the main problem was the sudden burden on the digestive system following too copious a meal, and therefore he divided his food into small meals eaten every hour. This would certainly help alleviate various digestive problems such as a stomach ulcer.

NOTES

digestion that might result from eating a heavy meal. Thus he divided his rations into small quantities, and ate a large number of small meals, rather than a single heavy meal (*Sfat Emet*).

חֲסוּכֵי בָנִים Those without children. Most Rishonim explain this expression as referring to couples without children, who are permitted to engage in marital relations even during years of famine. The Rishonim and the Aḥaronim disagree about the precise meaning of the phrase — whether it refers only to those who have no children at all (*Ri of Lunel, Meiri, Taz*), or whether it refers even to those who have a son or a daughter, but not both, and so have not fulfilled their religious obligation to procreate (*Rashi, Ran, Talmid HaRamban*).

According to the Jerusalem Talmud, even those couples who are without children (the Jerusalem Talmud uses the expression תְּאֵבֵי בָנִים — "those who are desirous of children") may engage in marital relations during years of famine only on the night that the woman undergoes ritual immersion, the night that conception is most likely.

Ritva suggests an entirely different explanation of this passage, which he bases on a variant reading found in the Talmudic texts available to many of the Rishonim: חֲשׁוּכֵי בָנִים — "those whose children are dark." Those couples whose children do not turn out well ("are dark") are those who engaged in marital relations during years of famine.

HALAKHAH

But couples who are as yet without children may engage in sexual relations even during years of famine. Many authorities (see *Sha'arei Teshuvah*) rule leniently on this matter, following the opinion that refraining from sexual relations during years of famine is an act of piety, not a strict requirement. *Rema* notes that these regulations are not limited to years of famine, but apply whenever the community is faced with an impending calamity." (*Shulḥan Arukh, Oraḥ Ḥayyim* 574:4.)

[1]תָּנוּ רַבָּנַן: ״בִּזְמַן שֶׁיִּשְׂרָאֵל שְׁרוּיִין בְּצַעַר, [2]וּפֵירַשׁ אֶחָד מֵהֶן, בָּאִין שְׁנֵי מַלְאֲכֵי הַשָּׁרֵת שֶׁמְּלַוִּין לוֹ לְאָדָם וּמַנִּיחִין לוֹ יְדֵיהֶן עַל רֹאשׁוֹ וְאוֹמְרִים: [3]׳פְּלוֹנִי זֶה, שֶׁפֵּירַשׁ מִן הַצִּבּוּר, אַל יִרְאֶה בְּנֶחָמַת צִבּוּר׳״. [4]תַּנְיָא אִידָךְ: ״בִּזְמַן שֶׁהַצִּבּוּר שָׁרוּי בְּצַעַר, [5]אַל יֹאמַר אָדָם: ׳אֵלֵךְ לְבֵיתִי וְאוֹכַל וְאֶשְׁתֶּה, וְשָׁלוֹם עָלַיִךְ, נַפְשִׁי׳. [6]וְאִם עוֹשֶׂה כֵּן, עָלָיו הַכָּתוּב אוֹמֵר: [7]׳וְהִנֵּה שָׂשׂוֹן וְשִׂמְחָה, הָרֹג בָּקָר וְשָׁחֹט צֹאן, אָכֹל בָּשָׂר וְשָׁתוֹת יָיִן. אָכוֹל וְשָׁתוֹ, כִּי מָחָר נָמוּת׳. [8]מַה כְּתִיב בַּתְרֵיהּ? [9]״וְנִגְלָה בְאָזְנָי ה׳ צְבָאוֹת: אִם יְכֻפַּר הֶעָוֹן הַזֶּה לָכֶם עַד תְּמֻתוּן׳. [10]עַד כָּאן

LITERAL TRANSLATION

[1]Our Rabbis taught: "At a time when Israel is immersed in distress, [2]and one of them has separated himself, the two ministering angels who accompany a man come and place their hands on his head and say: [3]'This man, So-and-so, who has separated himself from the community, let him not see the consolation of the community.'" [4]Another [Baraita] was taught: "At a time when Israel is immersed in distress, [5]a person should not say: 'I will go to my home and I will eat and drink, and peace be upon you, my soul.' [6]And if he does so, of him the verse says: [7]'And behold joy and gladness, killing cattle and slaughtering sheep, eating meat and drinking wine. Eat and drink, for tomorrow we die.' [8]What is written after it? [9]'And it was revealed in my ears by the Lord of Hosts: Surely this iniquity will not be atoned for you until you die.' [10]Up to here

TRANSLATION AND COMMENTARY

תָּנוּ רַבָּנַן [1]The Gemara now cites a Baraita on the same theme. **Our Rabbis taught** the following Baraita: **"At a time when** the community of **Israel** as a whole **is immersed in distress,** everyone is required to share in the burden of the community. [2]If **one of** the members of the community **separates himself** from the community in its hour of need in order to save himself from its problems, **the two ministering angels who accompany a person come and place their hands on his head and say:** [3]**'This man, So-and-so, who has separated himself from the community, let him not see the consolation of the community.'"** The Gemara (*Shabbat* 119b) informs us that two angels accompany every person, one good angel and one bad. This Baraita informs us that these two angels also appear when the person's community is in trouble, and based on the person's behavior they determine whether or not he will be judged worthy of joining the community on its day of joy.

תַּנְיָא אִידָךְ [4]A similar idea **was taught in another Baraita: "At a time when** the community of **Israel** as a whole **is immersed in distress,** everyone is required to share in the burden of the community. [5]**A person should not say** to himself: **'I will go to my home and I will eat and drink, and peace be upon you, my soul.'** [6]**And if he does** withdraw from the community in this way, **of him the verse says** [Isaiah 22:13]: [7]**'And behold joy and gladness, killing cattle and slaughtering sheep, eating meat and drinking wine. Eat and drink, for tomorrow we die.'"** In this prophecy, Isaiah describes the terrible danger confronting the Kingdom of Judah. Many of the people of Jerusalem had apparently despaired of victory. However, instead of turning to God in fasting and prayer and repentance, they decided to enjoy what was left of their lives in mirth and revelry, in an open affront to God who desired only their repentance. The Baraita sees this behavior as an affront to their fellowmen as well, because these people were ignoring the plight of the rest of the population and abandoning themselves to their revels. The Baraita notes that this behavior was explicitly condemned by the Prophet in the strongest language: [8]"For **what is written** in the next verse **after** this [verse 14]? [9]**'And it was revealed in my ears by the Lord of Hosts: Surely this iniquity will not be atoned for you until you die,** said the Lord God of Hosts.'" Thus we see that people who withdraw from the community in its hour of need commit so grievous a sin that it can be atoned for only through death. The Baraita continues: [10]"**Up to this point,** the Prophet Isaiah is writing about **the measure** meted out

RASHI

שני מלאכי שרת מלוין לו לאדם – אחד מימינו ואחד משמאלו, דכתיב (תהלים צא) "כי מלאכיו יצוה לך". **הנה ששון ושמחה** – "הרוג בקר ושחוט צאן אכול בשר ושתות יין כי מחר נמות ונגלה באזני ה׳ צבאות אם יכופר העון הזה לכם עד תמותון."

HALAKHAH

וּפֵירַשׁ אֶחָד מֵהֶן **And one of them has separated himself.** "Whoever separates himself from the community when it is in distress (and when it is in his power to help the community in some way; *Magen Avraham*) will not merit to see the consolation of the community when it eventually comes. But whoever joins in the community's distress will merit to see its consolation." (*Shulḥan Arukh, Oraḥ Ḥayyim* 574:5.)

מִידַּת בֵּינוֹנִים, [1]אֲבָל בְּמִדַּת רְשָׁעִים מַה כְּתִיב? [2]׳אֵתָיוּ, אֶקְחָה יַיִן, וְנִסְבְּאָה שֵׁכָר, וְהָיָה כָּזֶה יוֹם מָחָר׳. [3]מַה כְּתִיב בַּתְרֵיהּ? ׳הַצַּדִּיק אָבָד וְאֵין אִישׁ שָׂם עַל לֵב...כִּי מִפְּנֵי הָרָעָה נֶאֱסַף הַצַּדִּיק׳. [4]אֶלָּא, יְצַעֵר אָדָם עִם הַצִּבּוּר. [5]שֶׁכֵּן מָצִינוּ בְּמֹשֶׁה רַבֵּינוּ, שֶׁצִּיעֵר עַצְמוֹ עִם הַצִּבּוּר, [5]שֶׁנֶּאֱמַר: ׳וִידֵי מֹשֶׁה כְּבֵדִים וַיִּקְחוּ אֶבֶן וַיָּשִׂימוּ תַחְתָּיו וַיֵּשֶׁב עָלֶיהָ׳, [6]וְכִי לֹא הָיָה לוֹ לְמֹשֶׁה כַּר אֶחָד אוֹ כֶּסֶת אַחַת לֵישֵׁב עָלֶיהָ? [7]אֶלָּא, כָּךְ אָמַר מֹשֶׁה: הוֹאִיל וְיִשְׂרָאֵל שְׁרוּיִין בְּצַעַר,

LITERAL TRANSLATION

is the measure of average people, [1]but what is written about the measure of the wicked? [2]'Come, I will take wine, and we will become drunk with strong drink, and tomorrow will be like this.' [3]What is written after it? 'The righteous has perished and no man has taken to heart...that because of the evil the righteous has been gathered in.' [4]Rather, a man should be distressed together with the community, for thus have we found regarding Moses our teacher, that he distressed himself together with the community, [5]as it is said: 'And Moses' hands were heavy, and they took a stone and put it under him, and he sat upon it.' [6]But did Moses not have one pillow or one cushion to sit upon? [7]Rather, this is what Moses said: Since Israel is immersed in distress,

TRANSLATION AND COMMENTARY

to **ordinary people** (not good, but not absolutely wicked), who are guilty of withdrawing from the community in its hour of need, but who at least recognize that they will die on the morrow. [1]**But what is written about the measure** meted out to **the** truly **wicked** who try to turn the troubles of the community to their own material advantage?" The Baraita answers: "It is to this person that Isaiah addresses himself in the following verse [Isaiah 56:12]: [2]**'Come, I will take wine, and we will become drunk with strong drink, and tomorrow will be like this,** only very much more so.'" In this prophecy, Isaiah condemns the corrupt leaders of the people. They are described as shepherds who abandon their sheep to the mercies of wild animals, while they themselves pursue corrupt profit, imagining that this behavior can continue indefinitely. The Baraita sees in this behavior an even greater affront than in the previous "ordinary" case and notes that such wicked behavior cannot be atoned through the sinner's death, as in the previous case: [3]"For **what is written** in the next verse **after** this [57:1]? **'The righteous has perished, and no man has taken to heart...that because of the evil the righteous has been gathered in.'"** Thus we see that such behavior causes God to remove the righteous from the community so that it deteriorates to the point of catastrophe. [4]**"Rather,"** the Baraita continues, **"a man should be distressed together with the community,** even if he is not personally affected by its troubles." The Baraita cites Scriptural support for this advice: [5]**"As it is said** in a passage dealing with the war of the Israelites against Amalek [Exodus 17:12]. The Torah relates that Joshua led an army into battle against Amalek, while Moses, Aaron, and Hur went up to the mountain to pray for God's assistance. So long as Moses' hands were raised in prayer, the Israelites were victorious, but when he felt weak and lowered them, the Amalekites recovered. **'And Moses' hands were heavy, and they took a stone and put it under him, and he sat upon it,** and Aaron and Hur supported his hands, the one from this side and the one from that side, and his hands were steady until the going down of sun.'" [6]The Baraita asks: "Why did Aaron and Hur seat Moses on a stone? **Did Moses not have one pillow or one cushion to sit upon? [7]Rather, this is what Moses said: Since Israel is immersed in distress,**

RASHI

זו מידת בינונים – שיצאין מן המיתה, כדכתיב בהו "כי מחר נמות". **אתיו אקחה יין ונסבאה שכר והיה כזה יום מחר** – גדול יותר מאד. **הצדיק אבד ואין איש שם על לב** – מפני מה הוא מת – "מפני הרעה נאסף הצדיק", מפני שלא יצטער הוא ברעה, ואחר שהיא גזרה מלפניו, כי מפני הרעה נאסף הצדיק, לשון אחר: מפני רעות של אלו הוא נאסף, שאין הקדוש ברוך הוא רוצה שיבקש עליהם רחמים.

NOTES

בֵּינוֹנִים...רְשָׁעִים Average people...the wicked. The commentators offer various explanations as to the difference between those who are considered "average," i.e., neither righteous nor wicked, and those who are considered "wicked." Our commentary follows *Rashi,* who explains that although the members of the middle group refuse to show sympathy toward those who are already in distress, they do recognize that they themselves are in danger, whereas the really wicked believe that they are immune to the dangers threatening the community.

Rabbenu Elyakim suggests that although the members of the middle group withdraw from the community in their time of need, they do so only in private, whereas the wicked publicly declare that they are unaffected by the distress suffered by the rest of the community.

Other commentators argue that although the members of the middle group are indifferent to the troubles suffered by the rest of the community, they are ready to repent when they themselves are struck by the same afflictions. But the wicked fail to repent even when the suffering reaches their own doors (*Ritva* and others).

BACKGROUND

מִדַּת בֵּינוֹנִים וּרְשָׁעִים The measure of average people ...the measure of the wicked. The average people mentioned here are those who do not yet suffer from the problem afflicting the community, and who ignore other people's problems and continue their ordinary way of life. But the wicked are those who become dissolute in times of public distress, and try to enjoy every possible pleasure while they are still alive.

SAGES

דְּבֵי רַבִּי שֵׁילָא In the School of Rabbi Shela. Rabbi Shela was a Babylonian Sage of the transitional generation between the Tannaim and the Amoraim. His school played an important role in Babylonia, and before the advent of Rav it was the only important yeshivah there.

The important Amoraim, Rav and Shmuel, treated Rabbi Shela with respect, and when they established Torah centers they did so in other cities, so as not to detract from his honor.

Rabbi Shela's yeshivah seems to have remained active for a considerable time after his death, and therefore we have teachings delivered in the name of the School of Rabbi Shela.

רַבִּי חִידְקָא Rabbi Ḥidka. He seems to have belonged to the fifth generation of Tannaim. He was probably one of the first and oldest students of Rabbi Akiba. Only a few of his teachings are extant, presented in Baraitot but not in the Mishnah. His most famous Halakhah is that a person must eat four meals on Shabbat.

BACKGROUND

שְׁנֵי מַלְאֲכֵי הַשָּׁרֵת The two ministering angels. This idea is based on Psalm 91:11, "For He shall give His angels charge over you, to keep you in all your ways," from which we learn that everyone has at least two angels to watch over him at all times. The Rabbis add that these angels do not merely guard a person but also bear witness to his deeds, and to a certain degree they judge him at every turning point in his life.

TRANSLATION AND COMMENTARY

fighting a difficult and dangerous battle, [1]**I too will be with them in distress.** [2]And we may conclude from this example that **anyone who distresses himself together with the community,** taking part in their suffering in whatever way he can, **will merit seeing the consolation of the community** when it eventually comes." Having stressed the importance of participating in the sufferings of the community, even in private, [3]the Baraita continues: **"And lest a man say: 'Who will testify against me?** How will anyone know what I did in the privacy of my own home?' [4]**A man** should know that it is impossible to hide his behavior, because **the stones of his house and the beams of his house will testify against him,** [5]**as it is said** [Habakkuk 2:11]: **'For a stone will cry out from the wall, and the beam from the wood will answer it.'"** [6]The Baraita notes: **"In the School of Rabbi Shela,** a different answer was given to the question, 'Who will testify if I sin in private?' **They said:** [7]**The two ministering angels who accompany a man will testify against him** on the day of judgment, [8]**as it is said** [Psalms 91:11]: **'For He will command His angels about you,** to guard you in all your ways.'" Rabbi Shela interprets this verse as referring specifically to the two angels, one good and one bad, who accompany every person. Thus we see that these two angels observe a person's ways and take note of everything he does. [9]The Baraita continues: "Another answer to the rhetorical question was given by **Rabbi Ḥidka, who said: A man's soul testifies against him** on the day of judgment, [10]**as it is said** [Micah 7:5]: 'Do not trust in a friend; do not place your confidence in an official. **From that which lies in your bosom guard the openings of your mouth.'"** In context, the expression '"that which lies in your bosom" refers to a man's wife, and the Prophet is teaching us that it is impossible to rely on any human being, but only on God. But Rabbi Ḥidka interprets this expression as referring to a man's soul, which will not keep his deeds secret on the day of judgment. [11]The Baraita continues: **"Some say** that yet another answer can be given to the rhetorical question: **A man's limbs will testify against him** on the day of judgment, [12]**as it is said** [Isaiah 43:12]: "I have declared and I have saved, and I have made heard and there is no stranger among you, and **you are my witnesses, says the Lord,** that I am God.'" The Prophet is stating that Israel has itself seen the justice of divine providence in its history, and can itself testify to this without needing to invoke strangers. The Baraita expands this idea to refer to each individual, who can testify that God has judged him fairly in accordance with his behavior. And because of the plural language used in the verse, the Baraita describes each part of a person's body as taking part in this testimony. [13]Having mentioned the idea that both a man's body and his soul will testify about his behavior on the day of judgment, the Baraita employs a similar metaphor to explain a verse in Deuteronomy (32:4): "The verse reads: 'The work of the Rock is perfect, for all His ways are by judgment; **a God of faithfulness,**

[1]אַף אֲנִי אֶהְיֶה עִמָּהֶם בְּצַעַר. [2]וְכָל הַמְצַעֵר עַצְמוֹ עִם הַצִּבּוּר זוֹכֶה וְרוֹאֶה בְּנֶחָמַת צִבּוּר. [3]וְשֶׁמָּא יֹאמַר אָדָם: ׳מִי מֵעִיד בִּי?׳ [4]אַבְנֵי בֵיתוֹ שֶׁל אָדָם וְקוֹרוֹת בֵּיתוֹ שֶׁל אָדָם מְעִידִים בּוֹ, [5]שֶׁנֶּאֱמַר: ׳כִּי אֶבֶן מִקִּיר תִּזְעָק, וְכָפִיס מֵעֵץ יַעֲנֶנָּה׳. [6]דְּבֵי רַבִּי שֵׁילָא אָמְרִי: [7]שְׁנֵי מַלְאֲכֵי הַשָּׁרֵת הַמְלַוִּין לוֹ לְאָדָם הֵן מְעִידִין עָלָיו, [8]שֶׁנֶּאֱמַר: ׳כִּי מַלְאָכָיו יְצַוֶּה לָּךְ׳. [9]רַבִּי חִידְקָא אוֹמֵר: נִשְׁמָתוֹ שֶׁל אָדָם הִיא מְעִידָה עָלָיו, [10]שֶׁנֶּאֱמַר: ׳מִשֹּׁכֶבֶת חֵיקֶךָ שְׁמֹר פִּתְחֵי פִיךָ׳. [11]וְיֵשׁ אוֹמְרִים: אֵבָרָיו שֶׁל אָדָם מְעִידִים בּוֹ, [12]שֶׁנֶּאֱמַר: ׳אַתֶּם עֵדַי, נְאֻם ה׳. [13]׳אֵל אֱמוּנָה,

LITERAL TRANSLATION

[1]I too will be with them in distress. [2]And anyone who distresses himself together with the community merits to see the consolation of the community. [3]And lest a man say: 'Who will testify against me?' [4]The stones of a man's house and the beams of a man's house will testify against him, [5]as it is said: "For the stone will cry out from the wall, and the beam from the wood will answer it.' [6]In the School of Rabbi Shela, they said: [7]The two ministering angels who accompany a man will testify against him, [8]as it is said: 'For He will command His angels about you.' [9]Rabbi Ḥidka said: A man's soul testifies against him, [10]as it is said: 'From that which lies in your bosom guard the openings of your mouth.' [11]And some say: A man's limbs testify against him, [12]as it is said: 'You are my witnesses, says the Lord.' [13]'A God of faithfulness,

RASHI

כפיס — חצי לבינה, ורגילין לתתה בין שתי נדבכי העצים. הכי גרסינן: **אבריו של אדם הן מעידין בו שנאמר ואתם עדי** — לשון רבים, "נאם ה'".

NOTES

מִי מֵעִיד בִּי Who will testify against me? *Rashba* explains that the "testimony" mentioned here should be understood in the sense of "revealing the truth." The beams of a person's house, the angels who accompany him, his soul, and his very body will reveal a person's true behavior during those times when the community is suffering

וְאֵין עָוֶל׳. [1]׳אֵל אֱמוּנָה׳: כְּשֵׁם שֶׁנִּפְרָעִין מִן הָרְשָׁעִים לָעוֹלָם הַבָּא אֲפִילּוּ עַל עֲבֵירָה קַלָּה שֶׁעוֹשִׂין. [2]כָּךְ נִפְרָעִין מִן הַצַּדִּיקִים בָּעוֹלָם הַזֶּה עַל עֲבֵירָה קַלָּה שֶׁעוֹשִׂין. [3]׳וְאֵין עָוֶל׳: כְּשֵׁם שֶׁמְּשַׁלְּמִין שָׂכָר לַצַּדִּיקִים לָעוֹלָם הַבָּא אֲפִילּוּ עַל מִצְוָה קַלָּה שֶׁעוֹשִׂין, [4]כָּךְ מְשַׁלְּמִין שָׂכָר לָרְשָׁעִים בָּעוֹלָם הַזֶּה אֲפִילּוּ עַל מִצְוָה קַלָּה שֶׁעוֹשִׂין. [5]׳צַדִּיק וְיָשָׁר הוּא׳: [6]אָמְרוּ: בִּשְׁעַת פְּטִירָתוֹ שֶׁל אָדָם לְבֵית עוֹלָמוֹ, כָּל מַעֲשָׂיו נִפְרָטִין לְפָנָיו, [7]וְאוֹמְרִים לוֹ: ׳כָּךְ וְכָךְ עָשִׂיתָ בְּמָקוֹם פְּלוֹנִי

LITERAL TRANSLATION

and without iniquity.' [1]'A God of faithfulness': Just as punishment is exacted from the wicked in the world to come even for a light transgression that they do, [2]so too is punishment exacted from the righteous in this world for a light transgression that they do. [3]'And without iniquity': Just as reward is paid to the righteous in the world to come even for a light commandment that they do, [4]so too is reward paid to the wicked in this world even for a light commandment that they do. [5]'He is just and righteous': [6]They said: At the hour of a man's departure to his eternal home, all his deeds are enumerated before him, [7]and they say to him: 'You did such and such in such and such a place

RASHI

מאי דכתיב אל אמונה ואין עול כשם שמשלם כו׳ — כך משלם לרשעים בעולם הזה, כדי לטורדן מן העולם הבא, וכדכתיב (דברים ז) "ומשלם לשונאיו אל פניו להאבידו". **ואין עול** — שאין עושה דין בלא דין אמת וצדק. **צדיק וישר** — מצדיק הדין על הצדיקים לפרוע מהם, ועושה טובה וישרות עם הרשעים לפרוע כל זכותם בעולם הזה, כדי לטורדן.

TRANSLATION AND COMMENTARY

and without iniquity, He is just and righteous.'" This verse teaches us that God's judgment is perfect, although it is sometimes difficult to understand. Each of the sections of the second half of this verse will now be explained in turn: [1]"The first section — **'A God of faithfulness'** — teaches us that God can be trusted not to punish where it is not warranted. All sins are punished, but righteous people are punished in this world, whereas wicked people are punished in the World to Come. And **just as punishment is exacted from the wicked in the World to Come even for a light transgression that they commit, [2]so too is punishment exacted from the righteous in this world for a light transgression that they commit.** God is very scrupulous in holding righteous people to high standards in this world, just as he can be trusted to be scrupulous with the wicked in the World to Come. [3]The second section — **'and without iniquity'** — teaches us the converse: God never fails to reward good behavior, but wicked people are rewarded in this world, whereas righteous people are rewarded in the world to come. [4]And **just as reward is paid to the righteous in the World to Come even for a light commandment that they fulfill, so too is reward paid to the wicked in this world even for a light commandment that they fulfill.** God is very scrupulous in rewarding wicked people for their few good deeds in this world, in order not to deprive them of what is their due, just as He is scrupulous with the righteous in the World to Come. [5]The third section — **'He is just and righteous'** — teaches us that God causes justice not only to be done, but to be seen to be done. [6]The Rabbis **said: At the hour of a man's departure to his eternal home, all his deeds are enumerated before him, [7]and they say to him: 'You did such and such in such and such a place**

NOTES

distress. The "beams" of a person's house are the person's neighbors who are aware of what he does in the privacy of his own home and reveal what they know to the rest of the community. The angels reveal the person's true character to the public when they withdraw from him the protection that had until that point shielded him from calamity. A person's soul sheds light on his conduct when it receives its fitting punishment in the World to Come. And a person's own body reveals his true character when his organs are afflicted in this world.

וְאֵין עָוֶל And without iniquity. The Rishonim cite different readings and interpretations of our passage. According to the standard Talmud text, the first part of the verse, "a God of faithfulness," teaches that punishment is exacted from the righteous in this world for even the slightest transgression they do, and the second part of the verse, "and without iniquity," teaches that reward is paid to the wicked in this world for even the slightest good deed they perform. *Rashi,* in his commentary on Deuteronomy 32:4, explains that both parts of the verse promise that a person's good deeds will ultimately be rewarded. "A God of faithfulness" teaches that God will reward the righteous in the World to Come, and "without iniquity" teaches that He will reward the wicked in this world.

Maharsha prefers the reading found in *Yalkut Shimoni,* according to which the first part of the verse refers to all aspects of God's justice — the reward paid to the righteous and to the wicked, as well as the punishment meted out to the righteous and to the wicked. The second part of the verse teaches what appears next in the Baraita — that when a person dies, all his deeds appear before him and remind him of all that he did in the course of his lifetime. The third part of the verse, "He is just and righteous," teaches that when the deceased receives his punishment, he justifies the judgment and explicitly confesses his sins.

בְּיוֹם פְּלוֹנִי׳, [1]וְהוּא אוֹמֵר: ׳הֵן׳ וְאוֹמְרִים לוֹ: ׳חֲתוֹם׳, וְחוֹתֵם, [2]שֶׁנֶּאֱמַר: ׳בְּיַד כָּל אָדָם יַחְתּוֹם׳. [3]וְלֹא עוֹד, אֶלָּא שֶׁמַּצְדִּיק עָלָיו אֶת הַדִּין, [4]וְאוֹמֵר לָהֶם: ׳יָפֶה דַּנְתּוּנִי׳, [5]לְקַיֵּים מַה שֶּׁנֶּאֱמַר: [6]׳לְמַעַן תִּצְדַּק בְּדָבְרֶךָ׳״.

[7]אָמַר שְׁמוּאֵל: כָּל הַיּוֹשֵׁב בְּתַעֲנִית נִקְרָא חוֹטֵא.

[8]סָבַר כִּי הַאי תַּנָּא, דְּתַנְיָא: [9]״רַבִּי אֶלְעָזָר הַקַּפָּר בְּרַבִּי אוֹמֵר: מַה תַּלְמוּד לוֹמַר: [10]׳וְכִפֶּר עָלָיו מֵאֲשֶׁר חָטָא עַל הַנָּפֶשׁ׳? [11]וְכִי בְּאֵיזֶה נֶפֶשׁ חָטָא זֶה? [12]אֶלָּא, שֶׁצִּיעֵר עַצְמוֹ מִן

LITERAL TRANSLATION

on such and such a day,' [1]and he says: 'Yes.' And they say to him: 'Sign,' and he signs, [2]as it is said: 'He makes the hand of every man sign.' [3]And not only this, but he justifies the judgment on himself, [4]and he says to them: 'You have judged me well,' [5]in order to fulfill what is said: [6]'In order that You may be justified in Your speaking.'"

[7]Shmuel said: Whoever fasts (lit., "sits in a fast") is called a sinner.

[8]He agrees with the following Tanna, for it was taught: [9]"Rabbi Elazar HaKappar the Great says: What is [the Torah] teaching us by saying: [10]'And he will atone for him for what he sinned concerning the soul'? [11]But concerning which soul did this [man] sin? [12]Rather, it is because he distressed himself [by abstaining]

TRANSLATION AND COMMENTARY

on such and such a day,' [1]**and he says: 'Yes.' And they say to him: 'Sign,' and he signs,** [2]**as it is said** [Job 37:7]: **'He makes the hand of every man sign.'** [3]**And not only this, but** the dead man **justifies the judgment on himself,** [4]**and says** to his deeds that have been enumerated before him: **'You have judged me well,'** [5]**in order to fulfill what is said** [Psalms 51:6]: [6]'Against You alone have I sinned, and what is evil in Your eyes have I done, **in order that You may be justified in Your speaking.'"** The Psalmist states that ultimately the sinner will confess his sins explicitly, in order that God's judgment may be seen to have been correct.

אָמַר שְׁמוּאֵל [7]The Gemara now returns to the subject of the private fasts of "individuals." We have seen that such fasts are called for when the seasonal rain is even slightly delayed, and even students who are not yet "individuals" are permitted to fast, according to some opinions. The Gemara now considers the case of someone who chooses to fast as an act of piety entirely on his own initiative. **Shmuel said: Whoever fasts** in this way **is called a sinner.**

סָבַר כִּי הַאי תַּנָּא [8]The Gemara cites a source for Shmuel's ruling: **He agrees with the following Tanna, for it was taught** in a Baraita: [9]**"Rabbi Elazar HaKappar the Great says: What is the Torah teaching us by saying** [Numbers 6:11]: [10]'And the priest will offer one for a sin-offering and one for a burnt-offering, **and he will atone for him for what he sinned concerning the soul.'** The verse is referring to a Nazirite, a person who took a vow of self-abnegation for a specified period of time, as an act of piety and entirely on his own initiative. The Nazirite is forbidden to drink wine or to come into physical contact with the dead, or to cut his hair. The Torah teaches us that if he accidentally comes into contact with a dead body, he must bring a sacrifice and begin his period of self-abnegation again. The Torah uses an unusual choice of words for this sacrifice, describing the Nazirite as 'sinning concerning the soul.' [11]**But concerning which soul did this** Nazirite **sin?** [12]**Rather,** the verse describes the Nazirite as sinning concerning his own soul, **because he distressed himself by abstaining from wine** unnecessarily; and this was a sin against his own soul, because

RASHI

ביד כל אדם יחתום — כותב מעשה כל אדם, ומחתים יד על כל מעשיו. **למען תצדק בדברך** — שהוא מצדיק עליו בדבריך, שאתה מראה לו.

NOTES

כָּל הַיּוֹשֵׁב בְּתַעֲנִית נִקְרָא חוֹטֵא Whoever fasts is called a sinner. The Rishonim and the Aḥaronim discuss at length the broader question of the place of fasting and asceticism in Judaism. *Tosafot* attempts to reconcile the seemingly contradictory Talmudic sources and argues that while a person who observes a fast is called a sinner, the righteous deed he performs when he fasts outweighs the sin he commits when he causes his body distress.

Meiri distinguishes between a fast observed as an act of penance and one observed as a means of attaining holiness. In the former case, the person fasting is called a sinner — not because of the fast, but because of the transgressions that made the fast necessary. When he observes the fast, he acts correctly, but the fast does not turn him into a holy or pious man. But in the latter case, the person fasting is regarded as a holy and pious man, for his purpose in fasting is to reach a state of holiness and closeness to God.

Riaf argues that a person who observes a fast is called a sinner only if he observes the fast and fails to repent his sins. In addition to the sins he committed in the past, he is now guilty of the additional sin of causing his body distress. But if he observes a fast and arrives at sincere repentance, he is certainly regarded as a holy man, for by means of the fast he cleansed himself of his sins.

BACKGROUND

כָּל הַיּוֹשֵׁב בְּתַעֲנִית נִקְרָא חוֹטֵא Whoever fasts is called a sinner. The Gemara shows here that there were differences in attitude toward asceticism. One approach, expressed clearly by Shmuel and Rabbi Elazar HaKappar, is that self-mortification is a sin toward oneself and an unworthy way of seeking to exalt the soul. But the other approach, which is expressed in the words of various Sages below, is ascetic, seeing mortification of the body, at least when this does not cause physical or psychological damage, as an important means of aiding the spirit to overcome the flesh, and as a means of spiritual progress.

SAGES

רַבִּי אֶלְעָזָר הַקַּפָּר Rabbi Elazar HaKappar. He was a Sage of the last generation of Tannaim. Some of his Halakhic teachings are found in Baraitot and in Halakhic Midrashim. We possess no details about his life except that he had a son named Rabbi Elazar. It seems that for some time he lived and worked in the city of Lydda, and Rabbi Yehoshua ben Levi was his disciple. The meaning of the epithet הַקַּפָּר is not clear. It may be a place name, or it may refer to a profession (perhaps someone who dealt in wool). There has also been much speculation regarding the connection between Rabbi Elazer HaKappar and the Sage Bar Kappara..

LANGUAGE

בְּרַבִּי The Great. When the epithet בְּרִיבִּי or בְּרַבִּי appears after the name of a Sage, this does not mean that he was the son of a Rabbi, unless a specific Rabbi is named, as in רַבִּי יוֹסֵי בְּרַבִּי יְהוּדָה meaning "Rabbi Yose the son of Rabbi Yehudah." The term בְּרַבִּי is simply an honorific, meaning son of great men, the son of the Rabbis and great scholars of the generation. However, since it is an honorific expression, it does not mean that the person to whom it is applied is actually the son of great Sages, but rather that he himself is an important Sage of his generation.

הַיַּיִן. [1]וַהֲלֹא דְּבָרִים קַל וָחוֹמֶר? [2]וּמַה זֶּה, שֶׁלֹּא צִיעֵר עַצְמוֹ אֶלָּא מִן הַיַּיִן, נִקְרָא חוֹטֵא, [3]הַמְצַעֵר עַצְמוֹ מִכָּל דָּבָר וְדָבָר, [4]עַל אַחַת כַּמָּה וְכַמָּה!

[5]רַבִּי אֶלְעָזָר אוֹמֵר: נִקְרָא קָדוֹשׁ, [6]שֶׁנֶּאֱמַר: "קָדוֹשׁ יִהְיֶה, גַּדֵּל פֶּרַע שְׂעַר רֹאשׁוֹ". [7]וּמַה זֶּה, שֶׁלֹּא צִיעֵר עַצְמוֹ אֶלָּא מִדָּבָר אֶחָד, נִקְרָא קָדוֹשׁ, [8]הַמְצַעֵר עַצְמוֹ מִכָּל דָּבָר, [9]עַל אַחַת כַּמָּה וְכַמָּה!

[10]וְלִשְׁמוּאֵל, [11]הָא אִיקְּרֵי קָדוֹשׁ!

[12]הַהוּא אַגִּידּוּל פֶּרַע קָאֵי.

[13]וּלְרַבִּי אֶלְעָזָר, [14]הָא נִקְרָא חוֹטֵא!

[15]הַהוּא דְּסָאֵיב נַפְשֵׁיהּ.

LITERAL TRANSLATION

from wine. [1]And are not the matters a *kal vahomer?* [2]If this [man], who distressed himself [by abstaining] only from wine, is called a sinner, [3]someone who distresses himself [by abstaining] from every single thing, [4]how much more so!"

[5]Rabbi Elazar says: He is called holy, [6]as it is said: "He will be holy, and will let the locks of the hair of his head grow." [7]If this [man], who distressed himself [by abstaining] only from wine, is called holy, [8]someone who distresses himself [by abstaining] from every single thing, [9]how much more so!

[10]But according to Shmuel, [11]surely he is called holy!

[12]That is referring to the growth of the locks.

[13]But according to Rabbi Elazar, [14]surely he is called a sinner!

[15]That is because he rendered himself ritually impure.

TRANSLATION AND COMMENTARY

he deprived himself of pleasures that the Torah permits. [1]**And is not this matter** the basis for **a *kal vahomer*** (*a fortiori*) inference? [2]**If this** Nazirite, **who distressed himself by abstaining only from wine, is called a sinner,** [3]**someone who distresses himself by abstaining from** eating **every single thing,** by choosing to fast on his own initiative, [4]**how much more so** should he be called a sinner!"

רַבִּי אֶלְעָזָר אוֹמֵר [5]The Gemara notes that Shmuel's ruling is not universally accepted, for **Rabbi Elazar says:** A Nazirite who chooses voluntarily to abstain from wine in this way, far from being considered a sinner, **is called holy,** [6]**as it is said** (Numbers 6:5): "All the days of his Nazirite vow, a razor shall not pass over his head; until the days that he vowed to God are fulfilled, **he will be holy, and will let the locks of the hair of his head grow."** Thus we see that during the period of his vow the Nazirite is called "holy." And Rabbi Elazar, too, employs a *kal vahomer* argument: [7]**If this** Nazirite, **who distressed himself** by abstaining **only from wine, is called holy,** [8]**someone who distresses himself by abstaining from** eating **every single thing,** by choosing to fast on his own initiative, [9]**how much more so** should he be considered holy!

וְלִשְׁמוּאֵל [10]Having cited the dispute between Shmuel and Rabbi Elazar, the Gemara now questions how each one accounts for the other's Scriptural support and asks: **But according to Shmuel,** how can we explain Rabbi Elazar's verse? [11]**Surely** that verse states explicitly that the Nazirite **is called holy!**

הַהוּא אַגִּידּוּל פֶּרַע קָאֵי [12]The Gemara answers: Shmuel can argue that the word "holy" in **that** verse **is referring to the growth of the locks** of his hair. The hair of the Nazirite is considered "holy" in the technical, legal sense that it must be allowed to grow freely until it is cut in the Temple. But no general spiritual holiness is implied.

וּלְרַבִּי אֶלְעָזָר [13]The Gemara now considers the converse case and asks: **But according to Rabbi Elazar,** how can we explain Shmuel's verse? [14]**Surely** that verse states explicitly that the Nazirite **is called a sinner!**

הַהוּא דְּסָאֵיב נַפְשֵׁיהּ [15]The Gemara answers: Rabbi Elazar can argue that the Nazirite is accused in **that** verse of "sinning concerning the soul," **because he rendered himself ritually impure** by coming into contact with a dead body. The Nazirite is guilty of the sin of contact with a dead body, but no spiritual condemnation is implied, and the Nazirite, who is considered to be holy, is certainly not a sinner.

RASHI

לשמואל קדוש יהיה אגדל פרע קאי — שׂשערו אסור בהנאה, אבל הוא עצמו לא נקרא קדוש, ולרבי אלעזר חוטא, דסאיב כתרגומו "מאשר חטא על הנפש", פשט המקרא — על שנטמא במת. וכי **באיזה נפש חטא זה** — מי הרג שנקרא חוטא? שאין מלוה לצער עצמו, כדאמרינן: לדיקי [אי] אכלי האי עלמא (והאיך) מי סני להו, במסכת הוריות (פרק שלישי י,ב). **נקרא קדוש** — רישיה דקרא קא דריש, בשביל שמתוך כך מתמרקין עונותיו שמתענה.

NOTES

הַהוּא אַגִּידּוּל פֶּרַע **That is referring to the growth of the locks.** The commentators disagree about the meaning of this phrase — whether it means to imply that the Nazirite's hair itself is regarded as holy, or whether it means to say that the Nazirite's letting his hair grow is the holy act associated with being a Nazirite, and not his abstention from wine. A number of Rishonim (see *Rabbenu Hananel* and *Rabbenu Gershom*) had the reading הַהוּא דִּמְדַכֵּי נַפְשֵׁיהּ — "that is referring to where he purifies his soul." A Nazirite is regarded as holy, not because he refrains from drinking wine, but because he purifies his soul by avoiding contact with the dead.

¹וּמִי אָמַר רַבִּי אֶלְעָזָר הָכִי? ²וְהָאָמַר רַבִּי אֶלְעָזָר: לְעוֹלָם יָמוּד אָדָם עַצְמוֹ [11B] כְּאִילּוּ קָדוֹשׁ שָׁרוּי בְּתוֹךְ מֵעָיו, ³שֶׁנֶּאֱמַר "בְּקִרְבְּךָ קָדוֹשׁ וְלֹא אָבוֹא בְּעִיר"!

⁴לָא קַשְׁיָא. ⁵הָא דְּמָצֵי לְצַעוּרֵי נַפְשֵׁיהּ; ⁶הָא דְּלָא מָצֵי לְצַעוּרֵי נַפְשֵׁיהּ.

⁷רֵישׁ לָקִישׁ אָמַר: נִקְרָא חָסִיד,

LITERAL TRANSLATION

[1]But did Rabbi Elazar say this? [2]But surely Rabbi Elazar said: A person should always regard himself [11B] as if a holy thing is within in his bowels, [3]as it is said: "In your midst is the Holy One, and I will not come into the city"!

[4]There is no difficulty. [5]This is where he is able to distress himself; [6]that is where he is not able to distress himself.

[7]Resh Lakish said: He is called pious,

TRANSLATION AND COMMENTARY

וּמִי אָמַר רַבִּי אֶלְעָזָר הָכִי [1]**But,** the Gemara objects, **did Rabbi Elazar** really **say** that self-deprivation is a virtue? [2]**Surely Rabbi Elazar** once made a statement that agreed with Shmuel, **saying: A person should always consider himself** [11B] **as if a holy thing were immersed in his bowels** in other words, he should treat his body as though it were holy, and should not mortify his flesh by fasting, [3]**as it is said** (Hosea 11:9): "I will not execute the fierceness of my anger. I will not return to destroy Ephraim, for I am God and not a man. **In your midst is the Holy One, and I will not come into the city"!** This verse was discussed in detail above (5a). Rabbi Elazar is not attempting to give the verse another interpretation. He is focusing on the words in the middle of the verse ("In your midst is the Holy One") regardless of this context, and is making a play on words. The word בְּקִרְבְּךָ, which we have translated as "in your midst," can also mean "in your bowels," and the word קָדוֹשׁ, which we have translated as "the Holy One," can also be translated as "a holy thing." Thus these words can be read as saying that what is in a person's bowels is holy. We see from this statement that Rabbi Elazar agrees with Shmuel that mortification of the flesh and voluntary fasting are forbidden. How, then, can Rabbi Elazar say that someone who voluntarily undertakes to fast is considered holy?

לָא קַשְׁיָא [4]The Gemara answers: **There is no difficulty** in resolving the seeming contradiction between Rabbi Elazar's two rulings. The first ruling — that he who fasts is holy: [5]**This is** referring to a person **who is able to distress himself** without causing himself any bodily harm. The second ruling — that a person's body is holy and should not be mistreated: [6]**That is** referring to a person **who is not able to distress himself** without causing himself bodily harm. Rabbi Elazar does not agree with Shmuel that fasting is intrinsically wrong. Rather, it is an act of holiness to abstain from the pleasures of this world, if one's health is not damaged by such action. But Rabbi Elazar would agree that it is strictly forbidden to damage one's body by mortifying one's flesh in an act of misplaced piety.

רֵישׁ לָקִישׁ אָמַר [7]The Gemara now cites a single statement expressing the Gemara's distinction between the two rulings of Rabbi Elazar. **Resh Lakish said:** A person who is physically able to fast and does so **is called**

RASHI

כאילו קדוש שרוי בתוך מעיו — כאילו כל מעיו קדוש, ואסור להכחישן, דהכי משמע: "בקרבך קדוש", כלומר: דאסור להתענות — "בקרבך קדוש" רישיה דקרא קדריש, בשביל שקדוש שרוי בקרבך — "לא אבוא בעיר" של מעלה, עד שאבנה ירושלים של מטה, ורמיזא בעלמא הוא. **הא דמצי מצער נפשיה** — שיכול לסבול התענית — משבחו הקדוש ברוך הוא, אבל מי שאינו יכול להתענות נקרא חוטא. **נקרא חסיד** — המתענה, דכתיב "גומל נפשו איש חסד" — מפריש עצמו ממאכל ומשתה, כמו "ביום הגמל את יצחק" (בראשית כא) — *שברי"ר בלעז. מפי מורי. אי נמי: גומל — לשון תגמול, שמשלים נפשו לקונו.

LANGUAGE (RASHI)

שברי"ר* From the Old French *sevrer,* meaning "to wean."

NOTES

בְּקִרְבְּךָ קָדוֹשׁ In your midst is the Holy One. Our commentary follows *Rashi,* who explains that Rabbi Elazar is saying that a person should always assess himself as if there were something holy immersed in his bowels. According to this interpretation, the verse is to be understood as follows: Since what is holy inside you (בְּקִרְבְּךָ קָדוֹשׁ) is suffering distress because you are fasting, I will not come into the city.

Tosafot interprets Rabbi Elazar as saying that a person should always assess himself as if the Holy One were immersed in his bowels, as the verse itself says: "The Holy one is inside you [בְּקִרְבְּךָ קָדוֹשׁ]." According to this explanation, there is no need to make reference to the rest of the verse, and indeed the words וְלֹא אָבוֹא בְּעִיר are missing in certain manuscripts.

HALAKHAH

דְּמָצֵי לְצַעוּרֵי נַפְשֵׁיהּ Where he is able to distress himself. "A person who observes a fast when he is able to do so without causing himself bodily harm is regarded as holy. But a person who observes a fast when he is weak or ill is regarded as a sinner, following Rabbi Elazar according to the Gemara's conclusion. The ruling regarding a fast when he is weak or ill applies only in the case of a person who observes the fast as an act of piety. But a person who knows that he has committed a transgression is required to fast, even if he is weak or ill (*Taz*). Rabbinic authorities associated with the *Musar* [moralist] movement have suggested a variety of alternatives to fasting for those who seek atonement for their sins. These alternatives include refraining from eating certain foods, refraining from speech, and going into isolation (see *Shelah, Magen Avraham,* and others)." (*Shulḥan Arukh, Oraḥ Ḥayyim* 571:1.)

TRANSLATION AND COMMENTARY

pious, [1]**as it is said** (Proverbs 11:17): **"He who does good to his soul is a pious man, but he who damages his flesh** is cruel." This verse teaches us that a truly pious person must be as kind to himself as he is to others, whereas a person who abuses his body is being cruel. Resh Lakish's interpretation is based on the verb גֹּמֵל, which we have translated as "does good." This verb can also mean "weaning" — abstaining from unnecessary pleasures, which is how Resh Lakish reads it for the purpose of his homiletic interpretations. Thus the first part of this verse teaches us that a person who weans his soul away from the pleasures of this world by fasting is considered pious. But he must not damage his health, as we see from the end of this verse: "But he who damages his flesh is cruel."

אָמַר רַב שֵׁשֶׁת [2]The Gemara now cites several further statements forbidding voluntary fasting to certain people. **Rav Sheshet said:** If **a student** of Torah **fasts,** [3]it has the same spiritual value as though **a dog ate his meal.**

אָמַר רַב יִרְמְיָה בַּר אַבָּא [4]**Rav Yirmeyah bar Abba said: There are no** fully stringent **public fasts** imposed by the Rabbis **in Babylonia except the Ninth of Av alone.** As we have seen in our Mishnah, the first fasts that are decreed when rain is slightly late in autumn are relatively mild. The next Mishnah (below, 12b) teaches us that the later fasts, which are imposed if the rain is very late, are much more stringent. They last for a full twenty-four hours, and include refraining from pleasures in addition to not eating and drinking. These same restrictions apply to the fast of Yom Kippur, which is the only fast required by Torah law, but they do not apply to any public fasts imposed by the Rabbis on specific dates in the calendar, except for the fast of the Ninth of Av, Tisha B'Av, when we mourn the destruction of the Temple. In Babylonia, even if a public fast was decreed, these stringencies did not apply.

אָמַר רַב יִרְמְיָה בַּר אַבָּא [5]The Gemara now cites another statement by **Rav Yirmeyah bar Abba** on this topic, which he **said in the name of Resh Lakish:** [6]**A Torah scholar is not permitted to** undertake a voluntary **fast,** even if he is physically capable of doing so without causing himself any bodily harm,

[1]שֶׁנֶּאֱמַר: ״גֹּמֵל נַפְשׁוֹ אִישׁ חָסֶד, וְעֹכֵר שְׁאֵרוֹ, וגו׳״. [2]אָמַר רַב שֵׁשֶׁת: הַאי בַּר בֵּי רַב דְּיָתֵיב בְּתַעֲנִיתָא, [3]לֵיכוּל כַּלְבָּא לְשֵׁירוּתֵיהּ. [4]אָמַר רַב יִרְמְיָה בַּר אַבָּא: אֵין תַּעֲנִית צִיבּוּר בְּבָבֶל אֶלָּא תִּשְׁעָה בְּאָב בִּלְבַד. [5]אָמַר רַב יִרְמְיָה בַּר אַבָּא אָמַר רֵישׁ לָקִישׁ: [6]אֵין תַּלְמִיד חָכָם רַשַּׁאי לֵישֵׁב בְּתַעֲנִית,

LITERAL TRANSLATION

[1]as it is said: "He who does good to his soul is a pious man, but he who damages his flesh, etc." [2]Rav Sheshet said: A student (lit., "the son of the house of a teacher") who fasts, [3]let a dog eat his meal.

[4]Rav Yirmeyah bar Abba said: There is no public fast in Babylonia except the Ninth of Av alone.

[5]Rav Yirmeyah bar Abba said in the name of Resh Lakish: [6]A Torah scholar is not permitted to fast,

RASHI

ועוכר שארו — המתענה ומכחיש בשרו נקרא אכזר. **שממעט במלאכת שמים** — חלש הוא, ואינו יכול ללמוד. **שירותיה** = סעודתו, כלבא ליכול סעודתו, ולכך המתענה אינו מועיל לו, אלא כמי שמתענה מפני שאין לו מה יאכל. **אין תענית צבור בבבל** — לענין איסורי חומרי תענית אמר רבי ירמיה למילתיה, שהיו נוהגין בו כעין אבילות, שהיו אוכלין מבעוד יום ואסורין בנעילת הסנדל, אלא תשעה באב בלבד.

NOTES

גֹּמֵל נַפְשׁוֹ **He who does good to his soul.** In our commentary we have followed *Rashi* and others who explain that Resh Lakish, like Shmuel and Rabbi Elazar, is referring to a person who voluntarily observes a fast. Such a person, argues Resh Lakish, is pious, as the verse teaches: He who weans his soul (גּוֹמֵל נַפְשׁוֹ) by abstaining from food is a pious person.

Tosafot interprets Resh Lakish as referring to a person who *refrains from* fasting. Such a person, argues Resh Lakish, is pious, as the verse says: He who acts kindly to his soul [גּוֹמֵל נַפְשׁוֹ] by feeding it is a pious person.

לֵיכוּל כַּלְבָּא לְשֵׁירוּתֵיהּ **Let a dog eat his meal.** *Rashi* explains that a Talmudic scholar who observes a fast gains nothing, since he is viewed as someone who is refraining from eating because a dog has eaten his meal. Some texts read אֲכוּל כַּלְבָּא שֵׁירוּתֵיהּ, interpreting Rav Sheshet's remark as a curse: As for a Talmudic scholar who observes a fast, may a dog eat his meal (*Shittah*).

אֵין תַּעֲנִית צִיבּוּר בְּבָבֶל **There is no public fast in Babylonia.** Several explanations have been offered for this regulation

HALAKHAH

אֵין תַּעֲנִית צִיבּוּר בְּבָבֶל **There is no public fast in Babylonia.** "The only severe public fast that is observed in Babylonia or the rest of the Diaspora — a fast that begins on the previous evening at sundown and on which work is forbidden — is the fast of the Ninth of Av. Therefore, if an individual takes it upon himself to fast, there is no concern that he has undertaken to observe a public fast. But it is preferable that he state explicitly at the time that he accepts the fast that it is an individual fast. Furthermore, all fasts that are decreed upon the community in Babylonia and the rest of the Diaspora are treated as individual fasts." (*Shulhan Arukh, Orah Hayyim* 568:6; 575:10.)

אֵין תַּלְמִיד חָכָם רַשַּׁאי לֵישֵׁב בְּתַעֲנִית **A Torah scholar is not permitted to fast.** "A Torah scholar is not permitted

SAGES

רַב שֵׁשֶׁת **Rav Sheshet.** He was a famous Babylonian Amora of the second and third generations, a colleague of Rav Naḥman and of Rav Ḥisda. He was outstanding in his knowledge of Mishnayot and Baraitot, which he had acquired through his exceptional diligence. In his controversies with Rav Naḥman, the Geonim decided the Halakhah according to him in all matters of ritual law. He was blind. Many of the Amoraim of the third and fourth generations, including Rava, were his students.

רַב יִרְמְיָה בַּר אַבָּא **Rav Yirmeyah bar Abba.** A Babylonian Amora of the first and second generations, Rav Yirmeyah bar Abba was one of the first Sages who went to study under Rav when the latter arrived in Babylonia. Rav Yirmeyah bar Abba reports a large number of rulings in Rav's name, and many Sages from both Babylonia and Eretz Israel studied with him. His son, Rav Huna, was a Sage, as was his son-in-law, Rav Huna bar Ḥiyya, and his daughter's son, Levi ben Rav Huna bar Ḥiyya.

BACKGROUND

תַּעֲנִית צִיבּוּר **A public fast.** The ceremonial and Halakhic details accompanying a public fast are described in the third chapter of our tractate. These ceremonies were performed only while the Temple was still standing, as is explained there. However, according to Rav Yirmeyah bar Abba, the Halakhic stringencies that apply to a full public fast (fasting at night, the prohibition against work, and other hardships beyond the prohibition against eating and drinking) should also be practiced only in Eretz Israel. For elsewhere the community is not viewed as a full national entity, but as a group of individuals who practice the customs of individual fasts. The only exception to this rule is Tisha B'Av, which, because of the many calamities that occurred on that date, was observed throughout the Jewish Diaspora with great stringency, both with respect to the length of the fast and the prohibition against other pleasures, as well as the observance of mourning practices.

[1]מִפְּנֵי שֶׁמְּמַעֵט בִּמְלֶאכֶת שָׁמַיִם.

[2]״אוֹכְלִין וְשׁוֹתִין מִשֶּׁחָשֵׁיכָה, כו׳״. [3]אָמַר רַבִּי זְעֵירָא אָמַר רַב הוּנָא: יָחִיד שֶׁקִּיבֵּל עָלָיו תַּעֲנִית, [4]אֲפִילּוּ אָכַל וְשָׁתָה כָּל הַלַּיְלָה, [5]לְמָחָר הוּא מִתְפַּלֵּל

LITERAL TRANSLATION

[1]because he lessens the work of Heaven.

[2]"They eat and drink from when it is dark, etc." [3]Rabbi Zera said in the name of Rav Huna: An individual who accepted upon himself a fast, [4]even if he ate and drank all the night, [5]the next day he prays

RASHI

יחיד שקיבל עליו תענית — מאתמול: הרי אני יושב בתענית למחר, אפילו אכל ושתה כל הלילה עד עמוד השחר — למחר מתפלל תפלת תענית "עננו".

TRANSLATION AND COMMENTARY

[1]**because he** thereby **lessens the work of Heaven,** since he will inevitably be less able to concentrate on his studies while he is fasting.

אוֹכְלִין וְשׁוֹתִין [2]The Gemara now returns to its analysis of our Mishnah, which stated that those who undertook to fast after the seventeenth of Marḥeshvan "**would eat and drink from** the time **when it became dark** until morning, and would begin fasting only after dawn." [3]On this clause **Rabbi Zera said in the name of Rav Huna:** Regarding a pious **individual who undertook to fast** by making a declaration before sunset that he would fast the following day, [4]**even if he eats and drinks throughout the whole night** before the morning he is due to begin his fast, [5]nevertheless **the following morning he includes** in the Amidah **the** special *anenu* **prayer** recited **on**

NOTES

that there are no severe public fasts in Babylonia, except for the Ninth of Av. *Tosafot* and others suggest that the stringencies associated with public fasts — starting the fast at sundown, the prohibitions against working, bathing, anointing oneself, and wearing leather shoes — were not observed in Babylonia, because in Babylonia there was seldom any shortage of rain for which to decree a severe fast, agriculture there being dependent on water from rivers. *Ramban* objects to this explanation, arguing that if this is the reason, severe public fasts should be decreed in the rest of the Diaspora, wherever periods of drought are common. Moreover, even in Babylonia, severe public fasts should be decreed if calamities other than drought threaten the community.

Ra'avad suggests that there were no severe public fasts in Babylonia because the Jews in Babylonia were especially poor, and it would have been difficult for them to refrain from working on public fast days. In addition, the Babylonian Jews were not as physically fit as the Jews of Eretz Israel, and prohibitions against bathing, anointing themselves, and wearing leather shoes would have been particularly burdensome to them. *Ramban* raises the same objection to this explanation, namely that if this is the reason, the regulation should be limited to Babylonia, where the people were poor and frail. But in other places it should be possible to decree severe fasts. However, it is generally accepted that severe public fasts are not decreed anywhere outside Eretz Israel. *Ramban* himself and others suggest that there are no severe public fasts in Babylonia or anywhere else in the Diaspora, because there are no courts outside Eretz Israel with the authority to decree such fasts.

יָחִיד שֶׁקִּיבֵּל עָלָיו תַּעֲנִית An individual who accepted upon himself a fast. Our translation and commentary follow the reading of *Rashi,* according to which the Gemara is referring here to a person who has committed himself to fast for a single day. Rav Huna teaches that, even though he eats and drinks all night before the fast, the next day he inserts the *anenu* prayer in the Amidah. But if he continues his fast the following night, he does not recite the *anenu* prayer on the next day, because he did not impose that day upon himself as a fast day.

Rif, Rambam, and many others have a different reading, according to which the Gemara is referring to a person who committed himself to fast on two successive days. Rav Huna teaches us that even though that person eats and drinks during the intervening night, he still recites the *anenu* prayer on the second day of his fast, for at the outset he committed himself to two consecutive fast days. But if he committed himself to only one day of fasting but continued to fast for a second day, he does not recite the *anenu* prayer on the second day. Some commentators explain that this disagreement has ramifications with respect to the question of whether or not the *anenu* prayer is inserted in the evening Amidah, a matter which is in dispute between the Rishonim.

HALAKHAH

to fast, because fasting decreases his ability to engage in worthy activities. But if the entire community is fasting, he must fast with them, because he must not separate himself from the community. If a person's primary occupation is the study of Torah, he is regarded as a Torah scholar for this purpose (*Magen Avraham*). Primary-school teachers are treated as Torah scholars for this purpose, as is explained in the Jerusalem Talmud." (*Shulḥan Arukh, Oraḥ Ḥayyim* 571:2.)

יָחִיד שֶׁקִּיבֵּל עָלָיו תַּעֲנִית, אֲפִילּוּ אָכַל וְשָׁתָה כָּל הַלַּיְלָה An individual who accepted upon himself a fast, even if he ate and drank all the night. "If a person accepts a fast during the afternoon service, he is permitted to eat during the entire night. And similarly, if he commits himself to fast for several days in a row, he is permitted to eat and drink on each of the intervening nights. *Rema* adds that on each of the days that the person has committed himself to fast he inserts the *anenu* prayer into the afternoon Amidah prayer." (Ibid., 562:7.)

BACKGROUND

מִפְּנֵי שֶׁמְּמַעֵט בִּמְלֶאכֶת שָׁמַיִם Because he lessens the work of Heaven. According to the Halakhah, a hired worker is not permitted to fast, because by weakening his body he renders himself capable of less work than he was hired to do. Similarly, Torah scholars and schoolteachers are viewed as working for the Holy One, blessed be He, so they too are not permitted to fast, because by so doing they perform their holy work in an unsatisfactory manner.

יָחִיד שֶׁקִּיבֵּל עָלָיו תַּעֲנִית An individual who accepted upon himself a fast. The Gemara explains that a fast is not considered Halakhically significant unless a person has committed himself to it in advance. One reason for this is the view that it is more meritorious to do something when commanded to do so than when not commanded. Thus, when someone commits himself to fast, he knows that he has an obligation and that abstaining from food and drink is not merely a voluntary act that can be revoked at any moment.

TRANSLATION AND COMMENTARY

fast days. His eating and drinking during the night in no way affect his previous commitment to fast the following morning. [1]But if a man completes at nightfall a fast that he formally undertook the previous day, but **keeps** fasting **throughout the night** after his fast was completed, [2]**he does not include** in the Amidah the following morning **the** special *anenu* **prayer** recited **on fast days,** even though he has not yet broken the fast he began to observe the day before. As will be explained below (13b), a special prayer which opens with the word *anenu* (עֲנֵנוּ — "answer us") is inserted in the Amidah prayer on fast days. Rav Huna teaches us that the recitation of *anenu* by an individual who is fasting does not depend on how long he has been fasting when he says the prayer, but rather on his commitment to the fast on the afternoon of the day before. Thus, in our case, the person fasting inserts the *anenu* prayer in the Amidah before he has begun to feel the effects of the fast, because he formally committed himself the previous afternoon. But he does not recite the *anenu* prayer on the morning of the second day, even if he is in fact still fasting, because he made no formal commitment to continue his fast beyond nightfall of the previous day.

אֲמַר רַב יוֹסֵף [3]The Gemara now seeks to understand the second part of Rav Huna's ruling. **Rav Yosef said: What does Rav Huna maintain** when he says that a person who has observed an individual fast for one day, and has then continued his fast overnight, does not insert the *anenu* prayer in the Amidah the following morning? [4]**Does he maintain that there is no** such thing as a **fast** that is observed **for** only a few **hours?** His position would then be that a person is not regarded as observing a fast unless he plans to refrain from eating for an entire day. His not eating throughout the night does not constitute a fast, hence he does not recite the *anenu* prayer in the Amidah. [5]**Or** does Rav Huna **perhaps** maintain that **there is** such a thing as **a fast** that is observed **for** only a few **hours** of the day, [6]**but someone who fasts for** only a few **hours does not insert the** *anenu* **prayer** recited **on fast days** into the Amidah, because such a fast is not treated as stringently as a fast observed for an entire day?

אֲמַר לֵיהּ אַבַּיֵי [7]**Abaye said to** Rav Yosef in reply: **In fact, Rav Huna maintains that** generally speaking **there is** such a thing as **a fast** that is observed **for** only a number of **hours,** [8]**and** he also maintains that **someone who fasts for** only a number of **hours does insert the** *anenu* **prayer** recited **on fast days** into the

תְּפִילַּת תַּעֲנִית. [1]לָן בְּתַעֲנִיתוֹ, [2]אֵינוֹ מִתְפַּלֵּל שֶׁל תַּעֲנִית. [3]אֲמַר רַב יוֹסֵף: מַאי קָסָבַר רַב הוּנָא? [4]סְבִירָא לֵיהּ אֵין מִתְעַנִּין לְשָׁעוֹת? [5]אוֹ דִּלְמָא, מִתְעַנִּין לְשָׁעוֹת, [6]וְהַמִּתְעַנֶּה לְשָׁעוֹת אֵינוֹ מִתְפַּלֵּל תְּפִלַּת תַּעֲנִית? [7]אֲמַר לֵיהּ אַבַּיֵי: לְעוֹלָם קָסָבַר רַב הוּנָא מִתְעַנִּין לְשָׁעוֹת, [8]וְהַמִּתְעַנֶּה לְשָׁעוֹת מִתְפַּלֵּל

LITERAL TRANSLATION

the prayer of a fast. [1][If] he stayed overnight in his fast, [2]he does not pray [the prayer] of a fast.

[3]Rav Yosef said: What does Rav Huna maintain? [4]Does he maintain [that] we do not fast for hours? [5]Or perhaps, we do fast for hours, [6]but he who fasts for hours does not pray the prayer of a fast?

[7]Abaye said to him: In fact Rav Huna maintains [that] we fast for hours, [8]and he who fasts for hours prays

RASHI

לן בתעניתו — באותו תענית שקיבל עליו, שלא אכל במוצאי תעניתו, ולן כל אותו הלילה בשם תענית עד הבקר. **למחר אין מתפלל תפלת תענית** — אינו יכול להתפלל "עננו" קודם שיאכל, כדי לצאת ידי חובת תענית של לילה, אף על פי שהוא יום אחד כדכתיב (בראשית א) "ויהי ערב ויהי בוקר יום אחד", ולקמן מפרש ואזיל מאי קסבר רב הונא, מאי טעמא אין מתפלל למחר "עננו". **והכי גרסינן: מאי קסבר רב הונא מיסבר קסבר אין מתענין לשעות או דלמא קסבר מתענין לשעות והמתענה לשעות אינו מתפלל תפלת תענית אמר אביי לעולם קסבר מתענין לשעות ומתפלל תפלת תענית כו'** — פירוש: מאי קסבר רב

BACKGROUND

מִתְעַנִּין לְשָׁעוֹת **We fast for hours.** The problem troubling the Sages regarding a fast for a limited number of hours is whether such a vow (which is certainly valid, like any other vow a person may make) belongs to the category of fasting or the category of private self-mortification. The question is really whether a fast must last at least a day, or whether refraining from eating and drinking for a shorter time comes under the same category. This Halakhic issue is also connected to the recital of the special *anenu* prayer recited in the Amidah on a fast day. If someone is fasting for no more than a few hours, must he recite that prayer?

NOTES

סְבִירָא לֵיהּ אֵין מִתְעַנִּין לְשָׁעוֹת **Does he maintain that we do not fast for hours?** The Gemara raises the question here as to whether a fast may be observed for only a portion of a day, and it concludes that there is indeed such a thing as a fast that is observed for only a few hours. *Rashi* explains the question as follows: If a person undertakes to fast for a few hours, is he required to refrain from eating during that period or not? *Ritva* raises an objection: If a person undertakes to fast for a few hours, why should he not be required to fast during that period? Surely the undertaking of a fast is regarded as a vow, and the vow must be fulfilled even if the person only committed himself to fast for a short period of time.

Ritva explains that while the undertaking of a fast is regarded as a vow, it is not treated as a vow by which a person can forbid to himself something that is ordinarily permitted to him, for in that case it would be obvious that a person can indeed forbid food to himself even for no more than a minute. Rather, the undertaking of a fast is regarded as a vow to perform a meritorious deed, because fasting leads to submission to God and to true penance. Thus the Gemara asks: If a person commits himself to fast for a few hours, has he vowed to perform a meritorious deed? If so, the vow is binding. But perhaps a fast that is observed for less than a full day is an insignificant matter and not a meritorious deed, in which case the vow is not binding and he may eat even during those hours that he had committed himself to fast.

LITERAL TRANSLATION

the prayer of a fast. [1]But it is different here, [2]for there are the hours of the night that he did not accept upon himself from the outset.

[3]Mar Ukva happened to come to Ginzak. [4]They asked him: [5]"Do we fast for hours, [6]or do we not fast for hours?" [7][The answer] was not in his hand. [8]"Are the jars of non-Jews forbidden or permitted?" [9][The answer] was not in his hand. [10]"In what [garment] did Moses serve [during] all the seven

תְּפִלַּת תַּעֲנִית. [1]וְשָׁאנֵי הָכָא, [2]דְּאִיכָּא שָׁעוֹת דְּלֵילְיָא דְּלָא קַבֵּיל עֲלֵיהּ מֵעִיקָּרָא.
[3]מָר עוּקְבָא אִיקְלַע לְגִינְזַק. [4]בְּעוּ מִינֵּיהּ: [5]"מִתְעַנִּין לְשָׁעוֹת, [6]אוֹ אֵין מִתְעַנִּין לְשָׁעוֹת"? [7]לָא הֲוָה בִּידֵיהּ. [8]"קַנְקַנִּין שֶׁל נָכְרִים אֲסוּרִין אוֹ מוּתָּרִין"? [9]לָא הֲוָה בִּידֵיהּ. [10]"בַּמֶּה שִׁימֵּשׁ מֹשֶׁה כָּל שִׁבְעַת

TRANSLATION AND COMMENTARY

Amidah. [1]**But it is different here,** because a person who wishes to observe an individual fast, even if only for a few hours, must make a commitment to impose that fast upon himself before he actually observes it, and in the absence of such an acceptance of the fast, his refraining from eating is not regarded as a fast. Here we are dealing with the case of a person who committed himself to fast for one day, and then continued his fast the next night. [2]**Those hours of the** second **night** during which he refrained from eating **he did not accept from the outset,** so they are not regarded as a fast, and he does not insert the *anenu* prayer in the Amidah the following day.

מָר עוּקְבָא [3]The Gemara relates that **Mar Ukva happened to come to** the city of **Ginzak,** [4]**where he was asked** a series of questions. [5]He was first questioned about the matter discussed above: "**Is there** such a thing as **a fast** that is observed **for** only a few **hours,** [6]**or is there no** such thing as a **fast** that is observed **for** only a few **hours?"** [7]Mar Ukva **was unable to answer** the question. [8]He was then asked a second question: "Are **the** earthenware **jars of non-Jews,** in which they store their wine, permanently **forbidden** for use **or** are they **permitted** after the passage of a certain amount of time?" [9]Mar Ukva **was** also **unable to answer** this question. [10]A third question was then presented to him: "**What garment did Moses** wear when he **served** in the Tabernacle **during the seven days**

RASHI

הונא אין מתענין לשעות, כלומר, האי דקאמר: למחר אין מתפלל תפלת תענית — לכך אינו מתפלל, דקבלת תענית זה אינו קבלה, ואינו תענית כלל, ואם רוצה לאכול ולסעוד בתוך התענית — הרשות בידו, דאין מקבלין תענית לשעות, כגון זה שלא קיבל תענית של לילה זה מאתמול, כדקתני: לן בתעניתו, דמשמע: מאליו, כשהחשיך ובא לסעוד עמד ולא אכל, כלומר, שהיה בדעתו לאכול עד שעבר מקצת הלילה שעה אחת או שתי שעות, ואחר כך נמלך ולן בתעניתו. או דלמא האי דקאמר רב הונא: למחר אין מתפלל תפלת תענית — לאו משום דאין מתענין לשעות, דשם תענית עליו, ואם רוצה לחזור בו ולטעום אחר שהתחיל בתענית — אינו יכול, אלא להכי אינו מתפלל תפלת תענית, דסבר: אין תענית של שעות חשוב וחמור כל כך שיהא צריך להתפלל עליו "עננו". **לעולם קסבר** — בעלמא דמתענין לשעות, והמתענה לשעות מתפלל תפלת תענית, והכא מאי טעמא אין מתפלל תפלת תענית דשאני הכא היכא דהתענה אתמול ובלילה לן בתעניתו דלא קיבלה עילויה, שלא קיבל עליו תענית זה בפני עצמו מאתמול כדרך שאר מתענין לשעות, ואינו חשוב להתפלל עליו "עננו". **מר עוקבא איקלע לגינזק** — גרסינן, דאילו רבי עקיבא לא היה מסתפק לו הנך בעיי, ועוד, דבלשון ברייתא הוה משתעי ביה: מעשה ברבי עקיבא כו׳, ולא בגמרא. **קנקנים של חרס** — שמכניסין בהן יין לקיום — אסור להשתמש בהן. **במה שימש משה** — דאילו באהרן כתיב בגדי כהונה, דכתיב (שמות כט) "והלבשתם", שבשעה שהיה משה עובד, אהרן היה לבוש בגדי כהונה, ועבודה דמשה גזירת הכתוב הוא, ובגדי כהונה לא מצינו בו, ומסתמא אין הדבר כשר שהיה עובד בבגדיו של חול, שיוצא בהן לשוק. **לאחר שנים עשר חדש** — הולך טעם יין נסך, ומותרים בלא עירוי מים, אבל תוך שנים עשר חדש — צריך עירוי שלשה ימים מעת לעת.

SAGES

מָר עוּקְבָא **Mar Ukva.** He was the Exilarch during the first and second generations of Amoraim in Babylonia. He was famous not only for occupying this elevated position but also for his learning and piety. Mar Ukva was very close to the circles of the Amora Shmuel, who respected him greatly. Mar Ukva was also famous for his generosity in donating charity and for his great modesty. According to various traditions, Mar Ukva was called "Nathan Dezuzita," and he was a famous penitent in his generation. He seems to have had two sons who were also Sages.

BACKGROUND

גִּינְזַק **Ginzak.** The Sages identified Ginzak as the city Gozan mentioned in I Chronicles 5:26. The location of this city is not clear. Some scholars believe it is Ganzaka, located to the southeast of Lake Urmia [in present-day Iran]. Other scholars believe that it is south of the Caspian Sea. Still others say that it is in the vicinity of the city of Neharawan. In any case, it seems that this Jewish center was isolated from the Babylonian Jewish community, but was significant enough for a number of Sages and important leaders to visit it.

לָא הֲוָה בִּידֵיהּ **The answer was not in his hand.** Sometimes a Sage is asked a question in private or in public, and he has no answer. This may be because the answer is complex or the subject of controversy, and sometimes because it depends on tradition not widely known. The story here is given prominence because an important Sage and a great man like Mar Ukva was not ashamed to admit that he did not know the answers to these questions, and that he had to go to the yeshivah to clarify them.

CONCEPTS

קַנְקַנִּין שֶׁל נָכְרִים **The jars of non-Jews.** In the Torah (Numbers 31:22-23) it is stated that utensils which non-Jews have used for food forbidden to Jews must be specially cleaned before

NOTES

בַּמֶּה שִׁימֵּשׁ מֹשֶׁה? **In what garment did Moses serve?** Our commentary follows *Rashi* here and in *Avodah Zarah* (34a), who explains that Moses could not have worn the priestly garments when he served during the seven days of inauguration, because those garments were designated for Aaron and his sons, and Moses was not a priest. *Tosafot* (*Avodah Zarah* 34a) objects that Moses could indeed have worn the priestly garments, for the Gemara states elsewhere (*Zevaḥim* 101b) that during the forty years that the Israelites were in the wilderness Moses had the status of a High Priest. According to *Tosafot,* our Gemara is asking only about what Moses wore during the seven days of inauguration, for at that time the priestly garments had not yet been consecrated. *Rabbi Ya'akov of Orleans* suggests that even if the priestly garments had already been consecrated, Moses could not have worn them during the seven days of inauguration, for at that time the Tabernacle was regarded as a בָּמָה, an improvised altar, and the priestly garments are not worn when sacrifices are offered on an improvised altar. *Riaf* maintains that it was clear to the Gemara that Moses wore priestly garments during the seven days of inauguration. The question raised was whether he wore the eight garments worn by a High Priest or the four garments worn by an ordinary priest.

HALAKHAH

קַנְקַנִּין שֶׁל נָכְרִים **The jars of non-Jews.** "Any utensil that has been used for the storage of non-kosher wine is permitted to be used after twelve months have passed, for by that time there are certainly no traces of the wine in the utensil." (*Shulḥan Arukh, Yoreh De'ah* 135:16.)

TRANSLATION AND COMMENTARY

of inauguration?" After the Tabernacle was inaugurated, Aaron and his sons were in charge of the sacrificial service. While they served, they wore the special priestly garments without which their sacrifices would have been disqualified. But during the seven days of inauguration, it was Moses who by special divine decree conducted the whole service. It stands to reason that he did not wear his ordinary clothing while performing the sacrificial service in the Tabernacle, but there is no indication in the Torah that he wore the priestly garments. What, then, did Moses wear when he served in the Tabernacle? [1]Mar Ukva **was** also **unable to answer** this third question. [2]**He went and posed these questions in the Academy,** [3]and his colleagues there **said to him:** [4]**The law** regarding the first matter **is** that **there is** such a thing as **a fast** that is observed **for** only a few **hours,** [5]**and** someone who fasts for only a few hours **inserts into the** Amidah **prayer the** special *anenu* **prayer** recited **on fast days.** [6]**And the law** regarding the second issue **is** that **the** wine **jars of non-Jews are permitted** for use **after twelve months** have passed since they were last used by a non-Jew for storing wine. [7]And as for the third question — **what** garment **did Moses** wear when he **served** in the Tabernacle **during the seven days of inauguration?** — the answer is as follows: He wore neither his regular clothing nor the priestly garments, [8]but rather **a white** linen **shirt** especially designated for this purpose. [9]**Rav Kahana taught** a Baraita which stated: "During the seven days of inauguration, Moses served **in a white shirt that did not have a** folded **hem."**

אָמַר רַב חִסְדָּא [10]**Rav Hisda said:** [12A] [11]Even though **it has been said that there is** such a thing as **a fast** that is observed **for** only a few **hours** and not the whole day, this does not mean that a person may eat

יְמֵי הַמִּלּוּאִים״? [1]לָא הֲוָה בִּידֵיהּ. [2]אֲזַל וּשְׁאֵיל בֵּי מִדְרָשָׁא. [3]אֲמַרוּ לֵיהּ: [4]הִלְכְתָא: מִתְעַנִּין לְשָׁעוֹת, [5]וּמִתְפַּלְּלִין תְּפִלַּת תַּעֲנִית. [6]וְהִלְכְתָא: קַנְקַנִּין שֶׁל נָכְרִים לְאַחַר שְׁנֵים עָשָׂר חֹדֶשׁ מוּתָּרִין. [7]בַּמֶּה שִׁימֵּשׁ מֹשֶׁה כָּל שִׁבְעַת יְמֵי הַמִּלּוּאִים? [8]בְּחָלוּק לָבָן. [9]רַב כָּהֲנָא מַתְנֵי: ״בְּחָלוּק לָבָן שֶׁאֵין לוֹ אִימְרָא״.
[10]אֲמַר רַב חִסְדָּא: [12A] [11]הָא דְּאָמְרַתְּ מִתְעַנִּין לְשָׁעוֹת —

LITERAL TRANSLATION

days of inauguration?" [1][The answer] was not in his hand. [2]He went and asked in the Academy. [3]They said to him: [4]The law is: We fast for hours, [5]and we pray the prayer of a fast. [6]And the law is: The jars of non-Jews are permitted after twelve months. [7]In what [garment] did Moses serve [during] all the seven days of inauguration? [8]In a white shirt. [9]Rav Kahana taught: "In a white shirt that does not have a hem."

[10]Rav Hisda said: [12A] [11]What you said [that] we fast for hours —

RASHI

בחלוק לבן — של פשתן, עשוי לשם כך. **רב כהנא מתני** — כי האי לישנא. **בחלוק לבן שאין בו אימרא** — "שפה" מתרגמינן אימרא (שמות כח) כלומר, תחוב היה מחוט אחד כל החלוק, ולא כבגדים שלנו שבתי הידים מדובקין בבגד הגוף בתפירה, כדי שלא יחשדוהו שמא בתוכה שפה הוציא מעות הקודש, משום שנאמר (במדבר לב) "והייתם נקיים מה׳ ומישראל".

Jews are permitted to use them. The purpose of this cleaning is not only to remove remnants of food left in the utensils, but also to remove the taste and smell that the utensils have absorbed. The Torah explains how utensils of various kinds should be cleaned in order to make them fit for use. To this day the same process is used. The utensils are either scalded by boiling water in them or are heated in fire. But eathenware utensils cannot be boiled or heated in fire. Therefore it is asked whether there is any way of rendering them fit for use. The answer is that if they have not been used for twelve months, we assume that the remnants of food in them have undergone chemical changes sufficient to remove all the original smell and taste, and they have become permitted for use.

NOTES

בְּחָלוּק לָבָן שֶׁאֵין לוֹ אִימְרָא In a white shirt that does not have a hem. Most Rishonim explain the word אִימְרָא as meaning the border of a hem at the bottom of a garment. The white shirt that Moses wore during the seven days of inauguration did not have a border, neither a folded hem nor an additional piece of material sewn to the bottom of the garment. *Rashi* explains here that the shirt was made without a border, so that people should not suspect Moses of illicitly removing some of the money consecrated for the Tabernacle in the border of his garment. Elsewhere (*Avodah Zarah* 34a), *Rashi* himself rejects this explanation, arguing that by the time the Tabernacle was inaugurated the money donated for its construction had already been spent.

Tosafot (*Avodah Zarah* 34a) suggests that Moses' shirt was made without a border, so that it should be clear to all that it was new and had never been worn before. Alternatively, it was made without a border in order to prevent people from thinking that some defect had been found in Moses when they saw that he was being replaced by Aaron at the end of the seven days of inauguration. Since the shirt that Moses wore was made without a border, it would be apparent to all that it had been intended from the outset to be worn for only a short while. *Tosafot* also gives another explanation of the word אִימְרָא — as meaning עַמְרָא, "wool." The priestly garments were made of wool and linen, a combination that is ordinarily forbidden on account of the prohibition against wearing garments of *sha'atnez*. According to this explanation, Rav Kahana is informing us that since the shirt that Moses wore was not a priestly garment, it was made of linen without any admixture of wool.

HALAKHAH

מִתְעַנִּין לְשָׁעוֹת We fast for hours. "A person may observe a fast for a few hours, provided that he does not eat the entire day. How so? If a person is involved in his affairs and does not eat for the first part of the day, and then decides that he wants to observe a fast during the remainder of the day, he may do so and may insert the *anenu* prayer into the Amidah. However, according to some authorities, even a fast that is observed for only a few hours must already have been accepted the previous afternoon. If a person takes it upon himself to fast for the

¹וְהוּא שֶׁלֹּא טָעַם כְּלוּם עַד הָעֶרֶב.
²אֲמַר לֵיהּ אַבַּיֵי: הָא תַּעֲנִית מַעַלְיְיתָא הִיא!
³לָא, צְרִיכָא דְּאִימְלַךְ אִימְלוּכֵי.
⁴וְאָמַר רַב חִסְדָּא: כָּל תַּעֲנִית שֶׁלֹּא שָׁקְעָה עָלָיו חַמָּה לָא שְׁמֵיהּ תַּעֲנִית.

LITERAL TRANSLATION

[1] that is provided that he did not taste anything until the evening.

[2] Abaye said to him: Surely that is a proper fast!

[3] No, it is necessary where he changed his mind.

[4] And Rav Ḥisda said: Any fast on which the sun did not set is not regarded as a fast.

TRANSLATION AND COMMENTARY

food in the morning and then fast for a few hours, and still be regarded as having observed a fast. The innovation of a fast observed for only a few hours is that it can be undertaken without a prior commitment to fast for a whole day, yet it is regarded as a fast [1] **if** in fact the person fasting **did not taste any** food from the beginning of the day **until the evening.**

אֲמַר לֵיהּ אַבַּיֵי [2] **Abaye said to** Rav Ḥisda: But if a person fasts the entire day, even if he only undertook to fast for a few hours, he should **surely** be regarded as having observed **a proper** full-day **fast!** Why, then, was it necessary to teach the law that a fast observed for a few hours is regarded as a fast?

לָא, צְרִיכָא [3] The Gemara answers: **No, it was necessary** to cover the following eventuality: **If** at the beginning of the day someone had no intention of fasting, but for some reason he happened not to eat anything all morning, and then **he decided** to continue fasting for another few hours until the end of the day, we might have thought that this does not count as a fast. Hence the law was taught that since he did not eat anything in the morning, and the rest of the day he deliberately afflicted himself with a fast, the additional hours he observed as a fast do indeed constitute a fast.

וְאָמַר רַב חִסְדָּא [4] **Rav Ḥisda stated** another law on the subject of a fast observed for a period of hours: **Any fast that does not last until sunset is not regarded as a fast.** Just as a person cannot eat in the morning, and then observe a fast for a few hours later on, so too he cannot observe a fast in the morning and then eat in the afternoon. As we said above, a person is regarded as having observed a fast only if he ate nothing all day.

RASHI

הא דאמרת מתענין לשעות והוא שלא טעם כלום כל אותו היום — כלומר, לא אמרו במתענה שאכל בו ביום, כגון שהתחיל להתענות עד חצי היום ואחר כך אכל — דאין זה עינוי. ואם אכל קודם חצות — אין בכך כלום, דאינו תענית של כלום, אלא כשהשלים כל היום, אף על פי שלא קיבלו עליו מאתמול. ופריך: אי דקבל עליו להתענות עד חצי יום, והדר מתענה כל היום — האי תעניתא מעלייתא הוא, ופשיטא דתענית גמור הוא, ואפילו תפלת תענית נמי מתפלל עליו. ולא איצטריך לאוקומי הלכה בהכי, דזהו תענית גמור. והאי מקשה סבר: דהאי הלכה מתענין לשעות — כמשמעו, דיכול להתענות עד חצי היום — ״מתענה״ קרינא ביה. **לא צריכנא דממליך אימלוכי** — כלומר, לא היה בדעתו כלל להתענות, אלא אתא ליה טרדא ולא אכל עד חצי היום, וכי מטא חצי יום ממליך אמר: הואיל והתעניתי עד חצי היום — אתענה כל היום. **שלא שקעה עליו חמה** — שלא התענה עד אותה שעה.

NOTES

וְאָמַר רַב חִסְדָּא: כָּל תַּעֲנִית And Rav Ḥisda said: Any fast. The Rishonim point out a difficulty regarding the two statements of Rav Ḥisda: His first statement, that someone who fasts for hours may not taste anything until evening, seems to be identical with his second statement, that a fast that does not continue until sunset is not regarded as a fast. This difficulty disappears if we follow the reading of *Rabbenu Ḥananel* and others: ורב חסדא לטעמיה, "And Rav Ḥisda follows his own opinion," for according to that reading the Gemara itself is stating that the two rulings are teaching the same thing.

Ritva and others explain that Rav Ḥisda's first statement teaches us that a person cannot eat in the morning and then observe a fast for hours during the second part of the day. His second statement teaches us that a person cannot observe a fast in the morning and then eat in the afternoon.

Ra'avad suggests that Rav Ḥisda's first statement refers to the *anenu* prayer. A person observing a fast for hours is regarded as observing a fast with respect to the reciting of *anenu* only if he does not taste any food from the beginning of the day until evening. Rav Ḥisda's second statement

HALAKHAH

first part of a day, and then eats, or if he has eaten during the first part of the day and then takes it upon himself to fast for the rest of the day, he is not regarded as observing a fast requiring recital of the *anenu* prayer, but he is required to observe the fast as he had taken it upon himself." (*Shulḥan Arukh, Oraḥ Ḥayyim* 562:10-11.)

כָּל תַּעֲנִית שֶׁלֹּא שָׁקְעָה עָלָיו חַמָּה Any fast on which the sun did not set. "A fast that is not observed until nightfall, after three medium-sized stars have appeared, is not regarded as a fast. Thus, if a person who is fasting intends to break his fast before that time, he may not recite the *anenu* prayer. *Rema* notes that, according to some authorities, the *anenu* prayer may be inserted even if the fast does not continue until nightfall. *Rema* rules that an individual may insert the *anenu* prayer into the sixteenth blessing of the Amidah ['He who hearkens unto prayer'], even if he does not intend to continue his fast until nightfall, but the prayer leader may not recite the *anenu* prayer unless a fast accepted by the community is to be continued until nightfall." (Ibid., 562:1.)

TRANSLATION AND COMMENTARY

מֵיתִיבִי [1]**An objection was raised** against Rav Ḥisda's ruling from a Mishnah found later in our tractate (below, 15b), which states: "On the first three fasts that the court imposes on the community during periods of drought, [2]**the members of the *mishmar*** — the "watch" of priests whose week it is to serve in the Temple — observe the **fast,** [3]**but they do not complete their fast** by abstaining from food until nightfall, because they must preserve their strength to perform the Temple service." Thus we see that a fast observed in the morning is regarded as a fast, even though the fast does not last until the end of the day, and this contradicts the ruling of Rav Ḥisda!

הָתָם [4]The Gemara responds: A fast that is not continued until sunset is indeed not regarded as a fast, as was argued by Rav Ḥisda. But **there,** in the Mishnah quoted, the members of the *mishmar* refrain from eating during the first part of the day not because they are required to fast, but **merely in order to cause themselves distress** and thus share in the suffering of the rest of the community who are required to fast the entire day.

תָּא שְׁמַע [5]The Gemara now raises another objection against Rav Ḥisda's ruling: **Come and hear** the story related in the following Baraita: **"Rabbi Elazar the son of Rabbi Tzadok said:** [6]**I am** one **of the descendants of Sena'ah,** the ancestor **of** a distinguished family belonging to **the tribe of Benjamin."** When the Jews first returned to Eretz Israel after the destruction of the First Temple and the exile in Babylonia, and the Second Temple was built, there was a serious shortage of wood, which was absolutely necessary for the daily service in the Temple. A number of families volunteered to donate the wood that was needed. It was then enacted that those families would thenceforth be entitled to donate wood to the Temple on specified dates each year, even if the Temple woodsheds were full and there was no need for individual donations, and that their donations would be used to feed the fire burning on the altar. One of the families that enjoyed this privilege was that of the descendants of Sena'ah. They would bring wood to the Temple on the tenth of Av, and celebrate that day as a family festival. [7]"Now," continued Rabbi Elazar the son of Rabbi Tzadok, "it **once** happened that **the Ninth of Av,** the day of mourning for the destruction of the Temple, **fell on Shabbat,** [8]**and** the fast that was to be observed on that day **was postponed until after**

[1]מֵיתִיבִי: [2]״אַנְשֵׁי מִשְׁמָר מִתְעַנִּין, [3]וְלֹא מַשְׁלִימִין״. [4]הָתָם לְצַעוּרֵי נַפְשֵׁיהּ בְּעָלְמָא הוּא.

[5]תָּא שְׁמַע: ״דְּאָמַר רַבִּי אֶלְעָזָר בְּרַבִּי צָדוֹק: [6]אֲנִי מִבְּנֵי בָנָיו שֶׁל סְנָאָה בֶּן בִּנְיָמִין. [7]וּפַעַם אַחַת חָל תִּשְׁעָה בְּאָב לִהְיוֹת בְּשַׁבָּת, [8]וּדְחִינוּהוּ לְאַחַר

LITERAL TRANSLATION

[1]They raised an objection: [2]"The members of the *mishmar* fast, [3]but they do not complete [their fast]." [4]There it was merely to distress himself.

[5]Come [and] hear: "Rabbi Elazar the son of Rabbi Tzadok said: [6]I am of the descendants of Sena'ah of the tribe of (lit., 'the son of') Benjamin. [7]And once the Ninth of Av fell on Shabbat, [8]and we postponed it until after

RASHI

אנשי משמר — כהנים ולוים העובדין מתענין, כדלקמן בפרק ״סדר תעניות״. **ולא משלימין** — לפי שהן עסוקין בעבודה, ואין יכולים להשלים, אלמא, אף על גב דאינו משלים — ״מתענה״ קרי ליה. **לצעורי נפשייהו** — עם הצבור, אבל אינו תענית לא להתפלל תפלת ״עננו״ ולא לקובעו עליו חובה כלל, וכל שעה שהוא רוצה לאכול — אוכל. **מבני סנאה בן בנימין** — משבט בנימין.

NOTES

refers to whether or not the fast is regarded as a fast to the extent that it fulfills a vow to observe a fast. If a person vowed to observe a fast and then observed a fast for a number of hours but did not continue until sunset, his vow to observe a fast remains unfulfilled.

Rambam (*Hilkhot Ta'aniyyot* 1:13) rules that if for some reason a person does not eat in the morning and then decides to observe a fast for the rest of the day, he is regarded as observing a fast for a number of hours and he recites the *anenu* prayer. Even if he ate in the morning and then decided to fast for the rest of the day, he is regarded as observing a fast for hours. The Rishonim and the Aḥaronim discuss this ruling and the relationship between it and the statements of Rav Ḥisda. *Maggid Mishneh* and others suggest that *Rambam* understood Rav Ḥisda's first statement, that the person fasting may not eat anything until evening, as referring to the rest of the day after he begins his fast. But if he eats in the morning, before beginning his fast, the fast that he observes in the latter part of the day is still regarded as a fast.

אַנְשֵׁי מִשְׁמָר מִתְעַנִּין וְלֹא מַשְׁלִימִין The members of the *mishmar* fast, but they do not complete their fast. *Rashi* (below, 15b) explains that the members of the *mishmar* whose week it is to serve in the Temple observe each fast imposed on the community during periods of draught, but do not continue their fast until nightfall, because they must preserve their strength, lest the work that has to be done in the Temple be too much for the members of the *bet av* (בֵּית אָב — "family") whose day it is to serve, and the other members of the *mishmar* have to be called in to help them. Others suggest that they do not complete the fast because they must sometimes help eat the sacrifices offered that day, preventing them from being left over after the time permitted for them to be eaten (*Rabbenu Elyakim*).

CONCEPTS

מִשְׁמָר ***Mishmar,* watch.** The priests who served in the Temple were divided into twenty-four groups, called "watches." Each watch served for one week at a time. Thus each watch performed the Temple service for approximately two weeks every year. During the Pilgrim Festivals, all the watches went to the Temple and performed the Temple service together. Each watch received the מַתְּנוֹת כְּהֻנָּה — priestly gifts — which were contributed to the Temple during their week of Temple service. The watches were divided into בָּתֵּי אָב — "families." Corresponding to each watch there was a מַעֲמָד — "post" or "division" — a group of non-priests who accompanied the members of the watch to Jerusalem. The priests were originally divided into watches in the time of King David. During the Second Temple period, when many of the Jews who had been exiled to Babylonia after the destruction of the First Temple returned to Eretz Israel, some of the watches remained in Babylonia. Those priests who did return to Eretz Israel had to be divided once again into twenty-four watches.

BACKGROUND

מִבְּנֵי סְנָאָה בֶּן בִּנְיָמִין **Of the descendants of Sena'ah of the tribe of Benjamin.** This statement informs us that the festive days observed by families who brought the wood for the Temple were observed by all the members of the family, for Rabbi Elazar the son of Rabbi Tzadok was a priest and apparently belonged to the Sena'ah family on his mother's side.

SAGES

רַבִּי אֶלְעָזָר בְּרַבִּי צָדוֹק **Rabbi Elazar the son of Rabbi Tzadok.** He lived at the time of the destruction of the Temple, and was the son of a Sage of the previous generation who was famous for his piety and many fasts and one of the important priests in the Temple. The family of Rabbi Tzadok were extremely important to the Sages, and Rabban Yoḥanan Ben Zakkai tried to save them from the

הַשַּׁבָּת, [1]וְהִתְעַנֵּינוּ בּוֹ, וְלֹא הִשְׁלַמְנוּהוּ, [2]מִפְּנֵי שֶׁיּוֹם טוֹב שֶׁלָּנוּ הוּא".
[3]הָתָם נַמִי לְצַעוּרֵי נַפְשֵׁיהּ בְּעָלְמָא הוּא.
[4]תָּא שְׁמַע, דְּאָמַר רַבִּי יוֹחָנָן: [5]אֱהֵא בְּתַעֲנִית עַד שֶׁאָבוֹא לְבֵיתִי.
[6]הָתָם לְשַׁמּוּטֵיהּ נַפְשֵׁיהּ מִבֵּי נְשִׂיאָה הוּא דַּעֲבַד.
[7]אָמַר שְׁמוּאֵל: כָּל תַּעֲנִית שֶׁלֹּא קִיבֵּל עָלָיו מִבְּעוֹד יוֹם

LITERAL TRANSLATION

Shabbat, [1]and we fasted on it, but we did not complete it, [2]because it is a festival for us."
[3]There too it was merely to distress himself.
[4]Come [and] hear, for Rabbi Yoḥanan said: [5]I shall be in a fast until I come to my house.
[6]There he did [it] to extricate himself from the House of the Nasi.
[7]Shmuel said: Any fast that he did not accept upon himself while it was still day

TRANSLATION AND COMMENTARY

Shabbat and was observed on Sunday, the tenth of Av. [1]**We,** the descendants of Sena'ah, **fasted on that** day, **but we did not complete the fast** by fasting until nightfall, [2]**because it is a festival for our** family." We see from this story that a fast observed in the morning is regarded as a fast, even if it is not observed until the end of the day. Thus the Baraita contradicts Rav Ḥisda, who said that a fast that is not observed until the end of the day is not a fast!

הָתָם [3]The Gemara answers this objection in the same way that it answered the objection raised above: **There too**, in the Baraita just quoted, the family of Sena'ah were exempt from fasting because the day was considered a family festival. They **merely** refrained from eating **in order to cause themselves distress** and thus share in the mourning for the Temple being observed by the rest of the community. Ordinarily, however, a fast that is not completed is not regarded as a fast, as was argued by Rav Ḥisda.

תָּא שְׁמַע [4]The Gemara now tries again to disprove the ruling of Rav Ḥisda: **Come and hear** what **Rabbi Yoḥanan** used to **say:** [5]**I shall observe a fast until I come to my house.** Rabbi Yoḥanan's statement implies that he took it upon himself to fast only until he arrived at his house, but once he reached home he would eat, even if he returned home in the middle of the day. Thus, we see that a fast that is observed during the first part of the day is indeed regarded as a fast, even if it does not continue until the end of the day, and this contradicts the ruling of Rav Ḥisda!

הָתָם [6]The Gemara explains: **There** Rabbi Yoḥanan did not really undertake to fast. **He said** what he said only in order **to excuse himself from** remaining at **the House of the Nasi.** There were times when Rabbi Yoḥanan was invited to dine with the Nasi but did not wish to accept the invitation. To avoid offending the Nasi, he would claim that he had undertaken to observe a fast until he arrived at his house. Since he had not undertaken to fast all day, he was permitted to eat when he arrived home.

אָמַר שְׁמוּאֵל [7]**Shmuel said: Any fast that a person did not take upon himself** on the day before his fast

RASHI

שיום טוב שלנו היה — כדלקמן בשלשה פרקים (כו,א): זמן עצי כהנים והעם כו', עד בחמשה באב בני פרעוש בן יהודה, בעשרה בו בני סנאה בן בנימין. שעל ידי מעשה קבעו להן חכמים להתנדב עצים ולהביא למערכה, וכשמגיע זמנו מביאין אותן ומדליקין אותן על גבי המזבח, אף על פי שהיו שם שאר עצים הרבה. מה שאין כן בשאר מתנדבי עצים, דאין מבערין אותן בזמן שיש עצים אחרים. במסכת מנחות (קו,ב) אמרינן: המתנדב עצים לא יפחות משני גזירין, ועצים טעונין קמיצה, טעונים הגשה כו'. **דאמר רבי יוחנן** — פעמים שהיה אומר: אהא בתענית עד שאבוא לביתי, ואי מטי לביתיה בשתים או בשלש שעות ביום — הוה אכיל, וקרי ליה "מתענה". **לשמוטיה נפשיה מבי נשיאה** — דלא ליטרחוהו למיכל בהדייהו, שהיה מבקש

destruction. Rabbi Elazar the son of Rabbi Tzadok was one of the friends of the Nasi, Rabban Gamliel of Yavneh, and was active in the great assembly of Sages that met in Yavneh. His teachings and personal memories are found in many places in the Mishnah among the important testimonies of the Sages. He was apparently a merchant by profession, and his righteous behavior and piety are regarded in the Talmud as exemplary. He appears to have lived a long life and was active for many years. There were two Sages of this name, and the second of them was one of the last of the Tannaim, a member of the generation of Rabbi Yehudah HaNasi.

BACKGROUND

וּדְחִינוּהוּ לְאַחַר הַשַּׁבָּת **And we postponed it until after Shabbat.** In this case there was a double reason not to complete the fast of the Ninth of Av. Since it was a postponed fast, it did not have the obligatory force of a fast observed at the right time. Furthermore, it was a festive day for the family. It should also be noted that since this incident occurred while the Second Temple was still standing, the fast of the Ninth of Av did not yet include the additional severity of mourning for its destruction.

כָּל תַּעֲנִית שֶׁלֹּא קִיבֵּל עָלָיו **Any fast that he did not accept upon himself.** Most Rishonim explain that if a person wishes to observe an individual fast, he is required to take that fast upon himself by making a verbal statement: Tomorrow I shall observe a fast. *Rabbenu Tam* (cited by *Rosh;* see also *Tosafot, Avodah Zarah* 34a) argues that while it is preferable to make a verbal statement out loud, nevertheless if a person decides in his heart that he will fast the next day, that too is considered a binding acceptance of a fast.

NOTES

לְשַׁמּוּטֵיהּ נַפְשֵׁיהּ מִבֵּי נְשִׂיאָה **To extricate himself from the House of the Nasi.** The Jerusalem Talmud (*Nedarim* 8:1) infers from a similar statement made by Rabbi Yoḥanan that a person may take it upon himself to fast for a period of hours or until a certain event occurs. Thus the Jerusalem Talmud seems to understand that Rabbi Yoḥanan did indeed accept a fast for hours, and that a person who commits himself to fast in the morning and then eats in the afternoon is regarded as having observed a fast, against the view of Rav Ḥisda cited in our Gemara. Some Rishonim attempt to reconcile the positions of the two Talmuds (see *Ritva* and *Meiri*).

כָּל תַּעֲנִית שֶׁלֹּא קִיבֵּל עָלָיו **Any fast that he did not accept upon himself.** *Rif* observes that the rule that a person must

HALAKHAH

מִפְּנֵי שֶׁיּוֹם טוֹב שֶׁלָּנוּ הוּא **Because it is a festival.** "During the Temple period, there were fixed dates on which certain families were entitled to donate the wood to be used for the fire on the altar. These dates were treated by the families as festivals on which eulogizing the dead, fasting, and working were forbidden." (*Rambam, Sefer Avodah, Hilkhot Klei HaMikdash* 6:9.) "If the Ninth of Av falls on Shabbat, so that it is deferred and observed on the Sunday, the father of an infant requiring circumcision on the Sunday may recite his afternoon prayers early in the afternoon, and may then bathe and eat, for the day is regarded as a festival for him." (*Shulḥan Arukh, Oraḥ Ḥayyim* 559:9.)

כָּל תַּעֲנִית שֶׁלֹּא קִיבֵּל עָלָיו מִבְּעוֹד יוֹם **Any fast that he did**

לָאו שְׁמֵיהּ תַּעֲנִית.
[1]וְאִי יָתֵיב, מַאי?
[2]אֲמַר רַבָּה בַּר שֵׁילָא: דָּמֵי לְמַפּוּחָא דְּמַלְיָא זִיקָא.
[3]אֵימַת מְקַבֵּיל לֵיהּ?
[4]רַב אָמַר: בְּמִנְחָה. [5]וּשְׁמוּאֵל אָמַר: בִּתְפִלַּת הַמִּנְחָה.
[6]אֲמַר רַב יוֹסֵף: כְּוָותֵיהּ דִּשְׁמוּאֵל מִסְתַּבְּרָא, [7]דִּכְתִיב

LITERAL TRANSLATION

is not regarded as a fast.

[1]And if he sat [in a fast], what [is the law]?

[2]Rabbah bar Shela said: He is like a bellows that is full of air.

[3]When does he accept [a fast] upon himself?

[4]Rav said: During the afternoon. [5]And Shmuel said: During the afternoon prayer.

[6]Rav Yosef said: It stands to reason according to Shmuel, [7]for it is written

TRANSLATION AND COMMENTARY

while it was still day is not regarded as a fast. If a person wishes to observe an individual fast, he must say: "Tomorrow I will observe a fast."

וְאִי יָתֵיב [1]The Gemara asks: **And if a person observed a fast** without having accepted the fast upon himself on the previous day, **what is the law?**

אֲמַר רַבָּה בַּר שֵׁילָא [2]**Rabbah bar Shela said** in reply: **He is** regarded **like a bellows that** the smith **fills with air.** His self-deprivation does not have the religious significance of a fast.

אֵימַת מְקַבֵּיל לֵיהּ [3]The Gemara asks: A person who wishes to observe an individual fast is required to accept that fast upon himself on the day prior to his proposed fast. **When** precisely **should a person accept the commitment to fast?**

רַב אָמַר [4]**Rav said:** The fast should be accepted **during the afternoon** on the day prior to the proposed fast, and one must say: "Tomorrow I will observe a fast." [5]**And Shmuel said:** The fast must be accepted **during the afternoon prayer** service, either during or after the Amidah prayer.

אֲמַר רַב יוֹסֵף [6]**Rav Yosef said: It stands to reason** that the Halakhah is **in accordance with Shmuel** that the fast must be accepted during the afternoon prayer, [7]**for** at the end of ***Megillat Ta'anit*** — a list of thirty-six minor festivals on which the Rabbis forbade fasting, on account of happy events that occurred to the Jewish

RASHI

הימנו שיאכל עמו, היה אומר כן, שלא יטריחנו לאכול עמו ומיהו לא הוי תענית, שאם היה רוצה — היה אוכל מיד, ואין בנדרו כלום. **ואי יתיב מאי** — מי סליק לתענית אי לא. **למפוחא** — הוא המפוח שנופחין בו הנפחין את האור, המתמלא ברוח, אף זה נתמלא רוח — שלא אכל בחנם. **במנחה** — בזמן המנחה, ואפילו בשוק אומר: הריני מחר בתענית. **בתפלת המנחה** — בסופה, תוספת ריצוי ותחנונים, עד שאומר: הריני מחר בתענית. ודוקא נקט מנחה, משום דסמוך לתחלת יום תעניתו, לאפוקי תפלת יוצר. ודיקא נמי, מדפסיק שמואל ופליג אדרב דאמר בזמן המנחה, שיעורא יתירא.

NOTES

commit himself to fast on the afternoon prior to the proposed fast is derived from the verse (Joel 1:14): "Sanctify a fast," which teaches that a fast day must be fixed and sanctified before it actually begins.

בְּמִנְחָה **During the afternoon.** Most Rishonim explain that, even according to Rav, a person who wishes to observe an individual fast is required to take that fast upon himself during the afternoon of the day before. *Rav Hai Gaon* states that the fast must be accepted during the second half of the day (from the time of *minḥah gedolah* [מִנְחָה גְּדוֹלָה], half an hour after midday), whereas *Rabbenu Gershom* says that the fast must be accepted during the final quarter of the day (from the time of *minḥah ketanah* [מִנְחָה קְטַנָּה], nine-and-a-half hours after the beginning of the day). According to some Rishonim (*Ritva, Ran*), Rav says that the fast must be accepted during the afternoon only to distance himself from the viewpoint of Shmuel that this must be done during the afternoon prayer. In fact, however, a person who wishes to observe an individual fast may take it upon himself well in advance. These Rishonim explain the dispute between Rav and Shmuel as follows: According to Rav, the undertaking of a fast is viewed as a vow to perform a meritorious deed. Such a vow is binding even if it is taken well in advance. Shmuel argues that a person who undertakes to observe a fast does not appear to be taking a vow to perform a meritorious deed, for on the surface he is taking a vow to cause himself distress. Thus he must accept the fast in the manner in which a person accepts Shabbat or a Festival, in the prayer that he recites shortly before the onset of the fast.

בִּתְפִלַּת הַמִּנְחָה **During the afternoon prayer.** The Rishonim disagree about the wording of the commitment to fast, and

HALAKHAH

not accept upon himself while it was still day. "If a person did not take the obligation of observing an individual fast upon himself on the afternoon of the day before the proposed fast, the fast is not regarded as a fast, neither with respect to the reciting of the *anenu* prayer, nor with respect to the fulfillment of a vow. *Rema* notes that some authorities maintain that an individual should recite the *anenu* prayer even if he did not take the fast upon himself the previous day. All agree that a person who has a disturbing dream during the night may fast the next day in order to redress the dream's bad effects, even though he did not take the fast upon himself the day before." (*Shulḥan Arukh, Oraḥ Ḥayyim* 562:5.)

בִּתְפִלַּת הַמִּנְחָה **During the afternoon prayer.** "If an individual wishes to observe a fast, he must commit himself to it on the day before during the afternoon service, either

SAGES

רַבָּה בַּר שֵׁילָא **Rabbah bar Shela.** A Babylonian Amora of the third and fourth generations, Rabbah bar Shela was a disciple of Rav Ḥisda, whose teachings he cites. He seems to have lived near Meḥoza and is usually associated with Rava, who came from Meḥoza. Rabbah bar Shela apparently served as a Rabbinic judge where he lived, and he may have had a small academy of his own there.

SAGES

רַבִּי שִׁמְעוֹן בְּרַבִּי Rabbi Shimon, the son of Rabbi Yehudah HaNasi. Rabbi Yehudah HaNasi's youngest son, Rabbi Shimon, was also his closest disciple. Exchanges between father and son are mentioned several times in the Talmud. This son of Rabbi Yehudah HaNasi became one of the most important Sages of his generation, and Rabbi Yehudah HaNasi's other disciples — even those who were older than Rabbi Shimon — were his students. He was a particularly close friend of Rabbi Ḥiyya, who was his partner in the silk trade. Rabbi Shimon discussed Halakhic issues with the other Sages of his generation, and his name is mentioned once in the Mishnah. Because he was Rabbi Yehudah HaNasi's youngest son, he did not assume his position as Nasi, president of the Sanhedrin, but his father did appoint him to take over the important position of Ḥakham in his yeshivah after his death. This was the third most important position in the Sanhedrin.

בְּמְגִילַּת תַּעֲנִית: [1]"לָהֵן, כָּל אִינִישׁ דְּיֵיתֵי עֲלוֹהִי מִקַּדְמַת דְּנָא יֵיסַר". [2]מַאי לָאו יֵיסַר עַצְמוֹ בִּצְלוֹ? [3]לָא. [4]יֵאָסֵר עַצְמוֹ. [5]פְּלִיגִי בָּהּ רַבִּי חִיָּיא וְרַבִּי שִׁמְעוֹן בְּרַבִּי: [6]חַד אָמַר: "יֵיסַר", [7]וְחַד אָמַר: "יֵאָסֵר".

LITERAL TRANSLATION

in *Megillat Ta'anit*: [1]"Therefore, any person upon whom [a fast] will come from beforehand shall bind himself." [2]Is it not [that] he shall bind himself during prayer?

[3]No. [4]He shall himself be forbidden.

[5]Rabbi Ḥiyya and Rabbi Shimon the son of Rabbi disagreed about this: [6]One said: "He shall bind himself." [7]And one said: "He shall be forbidden."

TRANSLATION AND COMMENTARY

people during the Second Temple period — **it is written:** [1]**"Therefore, if a person has taken a fast upon himself from beforehand,** if, for example, he has committed himself to fast well in advance of the day on which he intends to fast, and it then turns out that the proposed fast falls on a day recorded in *Megillat Ta'anit* as one on which fasting is forbidden, **he shall bind himself** ([יֵיסַר]) to the fast, and if he fails to do so, he is not required to observe the fast." Rav Yosef proposes the following interpretation of the difficult expression, "he shall bind himself": [2]**Does it not mean he shall bind himself** to the fast by taking the fast upon himself **during** the afternoon **prayer** on the day before his proposed fast, as argued by Shmuel?

לָא [3]The Gemara answers: We **cannot** adduce support for Shmuel's position from *Megillat Ta'anit,* because the text of the scroll should be emended to read: [4]**He shall be forbidden** (יֵאָסֵר). If a person has undertaken to fast on a day recorded in *Megillat Ta'anit* as one on which fasting is prohibited, he is forbidden to eat on that day, irrespective of whether he imposed the fast upon himself during the afternoon prayer on the day prior to his proposed fast.

פְּלִיגִי בָּהּ רַבִּי חִיָּיא [5]The Gemara notes that **Rabbi Ḥiyya and Rabbi Shimon the son of Rabbi** Yehudah HaNasi **disagreed about this** very matter: [6]**One** Sage **said:** The text of the scroll reads יֵיסַר, **"he shall bind himself,"** implying that if a person binds himself to the fast by taking it upon himself during the afternoon service on the day before his proposed fast, he must observe the fast, and if not, the fast is not binding. [7]**And** the other Sage **said:** The text of the scroll reads יֵאָסֵר and teaches that a person **is forbidden** to eat on a fast that he has undertaken, even if he did not take the fast upon himself during the afternoon prayer on the day before.

RASHI

כדכתיב במגילת תענית — לסוף ימים טובים הכתובים במגילת תענית כתיב בה: מקדמת דנא ייסר לעיל מינה תני אילין יומיא די לא להתענאה בהון, להן כל איניש דייתי עלוהי תענית מן קדמת דנא, לפני אלו ימים טובים. כגון שקיבל עליו עשרה תעניות או עשרים, ונכנסו אלו הימים בהם. **ייסר בצלו** — בתפלה. ואי לא קבליה עליה בתפלת המנחה — לא דחי להנך ימים טובים. אלמא: דעיקר תענית בעי לקבולי בתפלת המנחה עילויה, ואי לא קבליה עילויה בתפלת המנחה — לא עשה כלום. **ייסר** — לשון "ואסרה אסר" (במדבר ל). **בצלו** — צלותא, איכא דאמרי: לשון נדר, שקבל עליו להתענות, כמו "הרימותי ידי אל ה'" (בראשית יד) דמתרגמינן: ארימיה ידי בצלו, ואין רבי מודה. האי דקתני "דכתיב" — משום דמגילת תענית היתה נכתבת לבד, לזכרון נסים. **וחד אמר יאסר** — דלא הוי תני "ייסר בצלו", דמשמע דוקא כדאמרינן אי מקבל בתפלת המנחה — אין, ואי לא — לא. אלא "יאסר", דמשמע: יהא אסור לאכול אי אתי עליה תעניות מן קדמת דנא. בין בתפלה בין שלא בתפלה.

NOTES

about the precise point in the afternoon prayer that it should be made. According to *Rambam* (see *Maggid Mishneh* to *Hilkhot Ta'aniyyot* 1:10; see also *Teshuvot HaRambam*, ed. Blau, no. 160), a person who wishes to observe an individual fast must recite the *anenu* prayer in the sixteenth blessing of the afternoon Amidah on the day before. Many authorities reject this view, arguing that the Talmudic sources imply that the *anenu* prayer is recited only on the fast day itself. (*Rambam* himself apparently revised his view, for this position does not appear in the standard version of his code.)

Most Rishonim maintain that the fast must be accepted by using the formula: "Tomorrow I shall observe a fast." According to some, this formula is inserted into the sixteenth blessing of the afternoon Amidah. According to others, it is inserted at the end of the Amidah, immediately before the concluding line, "May the words of my mouth and the meditation of my heart be acceptable before You," or immediately after that line before the person takes his three steps backward, indicating that his Amidah prayer is finished.

מַאי לָאו יֵיסַר עַצְמוֹ בִּצְלוֹ Is it not that he shall bind himself during prayer? *Ritva* asks: Why does the reading יֵיסַר, he shall bind himself, support Shmuel? Surely Rav agrees that

HALAKHAH

in the sixteenth blessing of the Amidah or at the conclusion of the Amidah, following Shmuel. He should state explicitly (or mentally verbalize): 'Tomorrow I will observe an individual fast.' *Rema* rules that it is preferable to accept the fast after completing the Amidah, so as not to interrupt one's prayer. If a person did not take the fast upon himself during the afternoon service, he may do so later in the afternoon as long as it is still day (*Baḥ, Magen Avraham*)." (*Shulḥan Arukh, Oraḥ Ḥayyim* 562:6.)

TRANSLATION AND COMMENTARY

מַאן דְּאָמַר יֵיסַר [1]The Gemara continues: According to **the** Sage **who said** that the scroll reads: "**He shall bind himself,**" the scroll **teaches us what we said** above, that if a person commits himself to fast well in advance of the date of his proposed fast, he must formally confirm that fast in the afternoon prayer on the day immediately preceding his fast. [2]**But according to the** Sage **who said** that the scroll reads: **"He shall be forbidden,"** [3]**what is** *Megillat Ta'anit* **teaching us?** Surely, if a person has accepted a fast upon himself, he is forbidden to eat on the day of his fast!

דְּתַנְיָא בִּמְגִילַּת תַּעֲנִית [4]The Gemara answers: The explanation **was taught in** ***Megillat Ta'anit***: [5]**"If a person has taken a fast upon himself from beforehand, he shall be forbidden** to eat on that day. [6]**How so? If an individual accepts upon himself** to fast on every **Monday and Thursday throughout the year,** [7]**and** it turns out that one of **the festivals recorded in *Megillat Ta'anit*** as days on which fasting is forbidden **falls on** a Monday or a Thursday, the following distinction applies: [8]**If the vow** by which he accepted those fasts upon himself **preceded our decree** forbidding fasting on these days, **his vow cancels our decree,** and he is forbidden to eat even on those days that fall on the festivals recorded in the scroll. [9]**But if our decree** forbidding fasting on those days **preceded the vow** by which he took it upon himself to fast, **our decree cancels his vow,** and he is forbidden to fast

[1]מַאן דְּאָמַר "יֵיסַר", כִּדְאָמְרִינַן. [2]לְמַאן דְּאָמַר: "יֵאָסֵר", [3]מַאי הִיא? [4]דְּתַנְיָא בִּמְגִילַּת תַּעֲנִית: [5]"כָּל אִינִישׁ דְּיֵיתֵי עֲלוֹהִי מִקַּדְמַת דְּנָא יֵאָסֵר. [6]כֵּיצַד? יָחִיד שֶׁקִּיבֵּל עָלָיו שֵׁנִי וַחֲמִישִׁי וְשֵׁנִי שֶׁל כָּל הַשָּׁנָה כּוּלָּהּ, [7]וְאֵירְעוּ בָּם יָמִים טוֹבִים הַכְּתוּבִין בִּמְגִילַּת תַּעֲנִית, [8]אִם נִדְרוֹ קוֹדֶם לִגְזֵרָתֵנוּ, יְבַטֵּיל נִדְרוֹ אֶת גְּזֵרָתֵנוּ; [9]וְאִם גְּזֵרָתֵנוּ קוֹדֶמֶת לְנִדְרוֹ, תְּבַטֵּל גְּזֵרָתֵנוּ אֶת נִדְרוֹ".

LITERAL TRANSLATION

[1]The one who said: "He shall bind himself," [means] as we said. [2][But] according to the one who said: "He shall be forbidden," [3]what [does] it [mean]?

[4]For it was taught in *Megillat Ta'anit*: [5]"Any person upon whom [a fast] will come from beforehand shall be forbidden. [6]How so? [If] an individual accepted upon himself Monday, Thursday, and Monday of the entire year, [7]and the festivals written in *Megillat Ta'anit* fell on them, [8]if his vow was before our decree, his vow will annul our decree; [9]but if our decree preceded his vow, our decree will annul his vow."

RASHI

מאי היא – מאי קסבר? ומשני: **כדתניא:** יחיד שקבל עליו תענית שני וחמישי של כל השנה כולה, כלומר, כדמפרש בהדיא: אם נדרו קודם לגזרתנו כו׳ ולא שנא בין בתפלה בין שלא בתפלה. **קודם גזרתנו** – קודם שגזרו חכמים ימים טובים הללו. אבל משגזרו, אף על פי שהתחיל תעניותיו קודם הזמנים הללו – לא דמו.

NOTES

a person who wishes to observe a fast must obligate himself before the fast! Thus Rav can explain this passage as saying that the person must commit himself on the afternoon before his proposed fast.

Ritva answers: Rav maintains that a person is not required to accept his proposed fast in the afternoon prayer, because he regards the acceptance of a fast as a vow to perform a meritorious deed. Thus it also follows that it is not necessary for him to accept the fast on the previous day. In fact, he can accept the fast well in advance. Hence, if a person accepted a fast in advance, there would be no need for him to bind himself to the fast once again on the day before it. Therefore, argues the Gemara, this passage of *Megillat Ta'anit* cannot be in accordance with the view of Rav. The Gemara answers that the text of the scroll must be amended to read: "He shall be forbidden." The scroll teaches us that if a person has accepted a fast beforehand, he is forbidden to eat on that day, even if it turns out to be a day on which fasting is prohibited.

אִם נִדְרוֹ קוֹדֶם לִגְזֵרָתֵנוּ **If his vow was before our decree.** The Rishonim offer several interpretations of this passage. *Rashi* and many other Rishonim explain that the Baraita is referring to the time that the Rabbis first instituted the semi-festivals recorded in *Megillat Ta'anit.* If the vow preceded the decree, it is valid, but if the decree preceded the vow, it is canceled.

Ra'avad (notes on *Rif,* end of *Pesaḥim*) understands the passage differently: If a person has committed himself to a series of fasts, and he has already observed one or more

HALAKHAH

יָחִיד שֶׁקִּיבֵּל עָלָיו שֵׁנִי וַחֲמִישִׁי וְשֵׁנִי **If an individual accepted upon himself Monday, Thursday, and Monday.** "If an individual has committed himself to a series of fasts, and one of the days on which he is supposed to fast turns out to be a Shabbat, or a Festival, or Rosh Ḥodesh, or Ḥanukkah, or Purim, the following distinction applies: If he accepted the fasts using the ordinary formulation for accepting fasts, he is not required to fast on those days, but if he accepted the fasts by taking a vow, the vow is binding and requires annulment (*Ramban* and others). *Rambam* maintains that if he accepted the fasts by taking a vow, and one of the days on which he is supposed to fast turns out to be a day on which fasting is forbidden by Torah law, the vow is binding and requires annulment. But if it turns out to be Ḥanukkah or Purim, days on which fasting is forbidden by Rabbinic decree, the vow is not binding. *Rema* notes that the custom follows the first view." (*Shulḥan Arukh, Oraḥ Ḥayyim* 570:1.)

TRANSLATION AND COMMENTARY

on those days."

תָּנוּ רַבָּנַן [1]**Our Rabbis taught** a Baraita, which stated: "On all those fasts undertaken by individuals or on the less stringent public fasts that are observed only during the daytime and not from the previous evening, **until when may a person eat and drink?** [2]**Until the rise of the dawn** when the light of day can first be detected, which in Eretz Israel occurs approximately one-and-a-quarter hours before sunrise. [3]**This is the opinion of Rabbi** Yehudah HaNasi. [4]**Rabbi Elazar the son of Rabbi Shimon** disagrees and **says:** He may eat only **until** the first **cockcrow,** which occurs even before the break of dawn."

אָמַר אַבַּיֵי [5]**Abaye said: This** ruling, that on the less stringent fasts a person may eat all night, **applies only if he has not** yet **finished his** evening **meal,** which he may prolong until morning — whether until dawn, according to Rabbi Yehudah HaNasi, or until cockcrow, according to Rabbi Elazar the son of Rabbi Shimon. [6]**But if he has** already **finished his** evening **meal,** then all agree that **he may not eat** anything else, for once a person has finished his supper, he has in mind to eat nothing more until morning.

אֵיתִיבֵיהּ רָבָא [7]**Rava raised an objection against** the distinction proposed by Abaye from the following Baraita, which stated: [8]**"If** a person intending to fast the next day **has finished** his evening meal, **and has** then **stood up** from the table, **he may** still **eat** later that night." Thus we see that the fast does not come into effect as soon as he finishes his evening meal, and this contradicts the ruling of Abaye!

הָתָם [9]The Gemara answers: **There** the Baraita **is** referring to a case **where** the person intending to fast the next day **has not** yet **removed the table** at which he ate. During the Mishnaic period, people took their meals on small, individual tables. As long as these tables have not yet been removed, then, even if all the food has been eaten, the meal is not over. Thus a person may continue to eat as long as the table has not yet been removed, for until the table has been removed, he has not yet decided to stop eating.

[1]תָּנוּ רַבָּנַן: "עַד מָתַי אוֹכֵל וְשׁוֹתֶה"? [2]עַד שֶׁיַּעֲלֶה עַמּוּד הַשַּׁחַר. [3]דִּבְרֵי רַבִּי. [4]רַבִּי אֶלְעָזָר בְּרַבִּי שִׁמְעוֹן אוֹמֵר: עַד קְרוֹת הַגֶּבֶר".

[5]אָמַר אַבַּיֵי: לֹא שָׁנוּ אֶלָּא שֶׁלֹּא גָּמַר סְעוּדָתוֹ. [6]אֲבָל גָּמַר סְעוּדָתוֹ אֵינוֹ אוֹכֵל.

[7]אֵיתִיבֵיהּ רָבָא: [8]"גָּמַר וְעָמַד, הֲרֵי זֶה אוֹכֵל".

[9]הָתָם כְּשֶׁלֹּא סִילֵּק.

LITERAL TRANSLATION

[1]Our Rabbis taught: "Until when may he eat and drink? [2]Until the dawn arises. [3][These are] the words of Rabbi. [4]Rabbi Elazar the son of Rabbi Shimon says: Until cockcrow."

[5]Abaye said: They only taught [this] if he did not finish his meal. [6]But [if] he finished his meal, he may not eat.

[7]Rava raised an objection against him: [8]"[If] he finished and stood [up], he may eat."

[9]There it is where he did not remove [the table].

RASHI

עד מתי אוכל ושותה — בלילה, כשמתענה למחר, בכל תעניות שהוא אוכל משתחשך, ואפילו בתענית יחיד קא מיירי. **עד קרות הגבר** — אפילו פעם ראשונה קאמר, מדקאמר גבי "יוצא יחידי בלילה" בסדר יומא (כא, א): עד שישלש. **שלא גמר סעודתו** — אבל גמר דברי הכל אינו אוכל. **אכל ועמד** — אף על פי שבירך ועמד משולחנו — חוזר ואוכל, ואין בכך כלום. **שלא סילק** — את הטבלא, דלאו עקירה היא, ולא אסח דעתיה מאכילה, וכסעודה אריכתא דמיא.

NOTES

of them, and the next fast falls on a day recorded in *Megillat Ta'anit,* his vow cancels the Rabbis' decree and he observes the fast. But if he has not yet observed any of his fasts, and the first of the series falls on a day recorded in the scroll, the Rabbis' decree cancels his vow, and fasting is forbidden.

Rabbenu Gershom explains that if a person took a vow committing himself to a series of fasts before the Rabbinical Court declared the beginning of the new month, so that when he took the vow he could not have known that his fasts would fall on days recorded in *Megillat Ta'anit,* his vow cancels the Rabbis' decree. But if the person took his vow after the court had already declared the beginning of the new month, so that he already knew that his fasts would fall on days recorded in *Megillat Ta'anit,* the Rabbis' decree cancels his vow.

HALAKHAH

עַד מָתַי אוֹכֵל וְשׁוֹתֶה **Until when may he eat and drink.** "On any fast that is observed only during the daytime hours, whether it be an individual fast or a communal fast, a person may eat and drink all night until dawn, following Rabbi Yehudah HaNasi. If he falls soundly asleep, he may not eat when he wakes up, unless he has stipulated that he will eat then. But if he only dozes off, he is permitted to eat until morning. According to some authorities, he may drink until morning, even if he fell into a sound sleep without stipulating that he would drink when he woke up, for he surely had in mind that he should be permitted to drink when he woke up (*Rema,* following *Mordekhai* and *Tur*). Some authorities maintain that it is nonetheless preferable to stipulate about drinking as well (*Magen Avraham*). Others argue (*Arukh HaShulhan*) that today, when all are accustomed to drink when waking up, such a stipulation is not necessary." (*Shulhan Arukh, Orah Hayyim* 564:1.)

SAGES

רַבִּי אֶלְעָזָר בְּרַבִּי שִׁמְעוֹן **Rabbi Elazar the son of Rabbi Shimon.** A contemporary of Rabbi Yehudah HaNasi, Rabbi Elazar the son of Rabbi Shimon was a distinguished scholar, like his father, Rabbi Shimon bar Yohai. Rabbi Elazar's remarkable personality was the subject of numerous anecdotes. When Rabbi Shimon bar Yohai, who was strongly opposed to Roman rule, was betrayed to the Roman authorities by informers, Rabbi Elazar fled with his father and lived with him in a cave for thirteen years. There the two subsisted on the barest essentials and spent their time studying Torah. During this period, Rabbi Elazar learned almost everything he knew from his father, who was his principal teacher (although Rabbi Elazar occasionally disagreed with his father's Halakhic decisions). Rabbi Elazar also studied with other scholars of his father's generation, e.g., Rabbi Yehudah, Rabbi Elazar (ben Shammua), and Rabbi Meir.

Later, Rabbi Elazar was forced to accept the unpopular position of a law-enforcement officer, and his acceptance of the post aroused opposition among the Sages. His spiritual independence led to friction between him and various other Rabbis, and to cooler relations with Rabbi Yehudah HaNasi, who was his boyhood friend.

Nevertheless, all acknowledged his personal piety, asceticism, and greatness in Torah knowledge. His father, Rabbi Shimon, considered him one of the most pious people of all time, and he was apparently considered exceptionally pious by the common people as well. Rabbi Elazar is also one of the most prominent figures in the Zohar. When he died, he was eulogized for his great achievements as a student of the Torah, both written and oral, as a preacher, and as a composer of liturgical poetry. The Gemara tells us that he was buried next to his father's grave in Meron.

Rabbi Elazar's teachings are quoted explicitly in several places in the Mishnah, while many other rulings of his

[1]אִיכָּא דְּאָמְרִי אָמַר רָבָא: לֹא שָׁנוּ אֶלָּא כְּשֶׁלֹּא יָשֵׁן. [2]אֲבָל יָשֵׁן, אֵינוֹ אוֹכֵל.
[3]אֵיתִיבֵיהּ אַבָּיֵי: [4]״יָשֵׁן וְעָמַד, הֲרֵי זֶה אוֹכֵל״.
[5]הָתָם בְּמִתְנַמְנֵם.
[6]הֵיכִי דָּמֵי מִתְנַמְנֵם?
[7]אָמַר רַב אַשִׁי: [12B] [8]נִים וְלָא נִים; [9]תִּיר וְלָא תִּיר. [10]דְּקָרוּ לֵיהּ וְעָנֵי. [11]וְלָא יָדַע אַהֲדוּרֵי סְבָרָא, [12]וְכִי מַדְכְּרִי לֵיהּ, מִדְכַּר.
[13]אָמַר רַב כָּהֲנָא אָמַר רַב: יָחִיד שֶׁקִּיבֵּל עָלָיו תַּעֲנִית אָסוּר בִּנְעִילַת הַסַּנְדָּל. [14]חָיְישִׁינַן שֶׁמָּא תַּעֲנִית צִבּוּר קִיבֵּל עָלָיו.
[15]הֵיכִי לִיעֲבֵד?
[16]אָמַר רַבָּה בַּר רַב שֵׁילָא: [17]לֵימָא הָכִי: ״לְמָחָר אֱהֵא לְפָנֶיךָ בְּתַעֲנִית יָחִיד״.
[18]אֲמַרוּ לֵיהּ רַבָּנַן לְרַב שֵׁשֶׁת: [19]״הָא קָא חָזֵינַן רַבָּנַן דְּמְסַיְּימֵי

LITERAL TRANSLATION

[1]There are [some] who say [that] Rava said: They only taught [this] if he did not sleep. [2]But [if] he slept, he may not eat.

[3]Abaye raised an objection against him: [4]"[If] he slept and stood [up], he may eat."

[5]There it is where he was dozing.

[6]How do we visualize the case of dozing?

[7]Rav Ashi said: [12B] [8]He is asleep, but he is not asleep; [9]he is awake, but he is not awake. [10]When they call him, he answers. [11]And he does not know to answer intelligently, [12]but when they remind him, he remembers.

[13]Rav Kahana said in the name of Rav: An individual who accepted a fast upon himself is forbidden to wear shoes. [14]We are concerned that perhaps he accepted a public fast upon himself.

[15]How should he act?

[16]Rabbah bar Rav Shela said: [17]He should say this: "Tomorrow I shall be before You in an individual fast."

[18]The Rabbis said to Rav Sheshet: [19]"Surely we see Rabbis

TRANSLATION AND COMMENTARY

אִיכָּא דְּאָמְרִי [1]The Gemara now gives another version of the difference of opinion between Abaye and Rava. **There are some who say that Rava said: This** ruling, that on the less stringent fasts a person may eat all night, **applies only if he did not** go to **sleep** after finishing his evening meal. [2]**But if he has** already **gone to sleep, he may not eat** anything else, for once a person has gone to sleep for the night, he has it in mind to eat nothing more until morning."

אֵיתִיבֵיהּ אַבָּיֵי [3]**Abaye raised an objection against** the distinction proposed by Rava from the following Baraita, which stated: [4]**"If** a person intending to fast the next day **goes to sleep** after he has finished his evening meal, and later **rises** from his sleep sometime during the night, **he may** continue to **eat** until the morning."

הָתָם בְּמִתְנַמְנֵם [5]The Gemara explains: **There** the Baraita **is** referring to a case **where** the person planning to fast the next day **was** only **dozing.** A person who dozes off may resume eating when he wakes up, and may continue to eat until morning or until he finally retires for the night and sleeps deeply.

הֵיכִי דָּמֵי מִתְנַמְנֵם [6]The Gemara asks: **How** precisely **do we visualize the case of dozing,** as opposed to the case of being fully asleep?

אָמַר רַב אַשִׁי [7]**Rav Ashi said:** [12B] [8]A person is regarded as being half-asleep if **he is asleep, but not** really **asleep;** [9]if **he is awake, but not** really **awake.** [10]**When** such a person **is called** by name, **he answers.** When he is asked a question requiring careful thought, [11]he is so drowsy that **he does not know how to answer** the question **intelligently.** [12]**But when he is reminded** of certain events, **he remembers** them.

אָמַר רַב כָּהֲנָא [13]The Gemara continues: **Rav Kahana said in the name of Rav:** If **an individual takes a fast upon himself** without specifying what kind, he **is forbidden to wear** leather **shoes,** to bathe for pleasure, to anoint himself with oil, or to engage in sexual intercourse, [14]because **we are concerned that he may have taken it upon himself** to observe the stringencies of **a** severe **public fast.**

הֵיכִי לִיעֲבֵד [15]The Gemara asks: **How should a person act** if he wishes to undertake a fast without having to observe all the stringencies connected with a severe public fast?

אָמַר רַבָּה בַּר רַב שֵׁילָא [16]**Rabbah bar Rav Shela said** in reply: When he commits himself to fast, **he should say as follows:** [17]**"Tomorrow I shall observe an individual fast."** If he says so explicitly, there is no concern that he may have meant to accept a more stringent public fast.

אֲמַרוּ לֵיהּ רַבָּנַן [18]**The Rabbis said to Rav Sheshet:** [19]**"Surely we see** that even on public fasts there are **Rabbis**

RASHI

איכא דאמרי אמר רבא כו׳ — והלכה כאיכא דאמרי: אוכל ושותה עד שיישן קבע, ועד שיעלה עמוד השחר, כרבי. **אבל ישן** — הפסקה היא, ושוב אינו אוכל. **התם** — לאו ישן ממש, אלא מתנמנם — *שומיליי״ר בלעז. **תיר** — ער, כדמתרגמינן (בראשית מא) ״ויקץ״ = ואיתער. **אהדורי סברא** — אם צריך ממנו דבר שצריך הרהור — אינו יודע לומר בעוד שמתנמנם. **וכי מדכרו ליה מדכר** — ״כזה שמעת״ — מדכר. **יחיד שקבל עליו תענית** — סתם, ואינו יודע איזה תענית קבל עליו, אם של יחיד אם של צבור. **ואסור בנעילת כו׳** — שמא תענית צבור, כשלש ראשונות

apparently entered the Mishnah anonymously. Rabbi Elazar was therefore referred to as "Rabbi Elazar the son of Rabbi Shimon — the Anonymous Ruler" (סְתִימְתָּאָה). Some of his teachings — which were also quoted by the early Amoraim — are cited in the Tosefta and in the Halakhic Midrashim.

LANGUAGE (RASHI)

שומיליי״ר* From the Old French *someillier,* which means "to doze."

TRANSLATION AND COMMENTARY

who wear their leather **shoes when they go to the house of** prayer during **the fast!"** If Rabbis do not refrain from wearing their shoes even on public fasts, then a person observing an individual fast should certainly be permitted to wear shoes.

אִיקְפַּד [1]Rav Sheshet **became angry** with the Rabbis who made this observation to him, **and he said to them:** [2]**"Perhaps** those **Rabbis also eat** on public fasts, withdrawing themselves from the community in its time of distress." Thus nothing can be inferred from the behavior of Rabbis who wear shoes on fast days.

אַבַּיֵי וְרָבָא [3]It is further related that **Abaye and Rava would enter the synagogue** on fast days **wearing** only the **upper part of their shoes,** thus complying with the prohibition against wearing shoes on fast days. [4]Similarly, **Maremar and Mar Zutra would change their right** shoes **with their left, and their left** shoes **with their right.** By making a significant change in the way they wore their shoes, they avoided violating the prohibition against wearing shoes on public fasts. [5]But **the Rabbis of the academy of Rav Ashi would go out** on public fasts wearing their shoes **in their usual way.** [6]This was because they **agreed with what Shmuel said** — that **there are no** fully stringent **public fasts** imposed by the Rabbis **in Babylonia, except the Ninth of Av alone.** In Babylonia, even when the Rabbis decreed public fasts, they did not impose on them the stringencies of the severe public fasts, except on the Ninth of Av. Thus the Rabbis of the academy of Rav Ashi in Babylonia wore their shoes on public fasts in the ordinary way.

אָמַר רַב יְהוּדָה [7]The Gemara now proceeds to a new topic of discussion. **Rav Yehudah said in the name of Rav:** If **a person** undertakes to observe a fast, and during the course of the fast he sees that he will not be able to complete it, he **may "borrow" the fast** by suspending it, **and he may repay** his debt at some later date by fasting on another day. [8]Rav Yehudah continued: **When I repeated this** ruling **before Shmuel, he said to me:** Why did Rav say that a person who breaks his fast must fast on some other day? [9]**Did he** go so far as to **take a vow** not to eat for a day, **so that it will not suffice** for him **if he does not repay** his debt by fasting

מְסָנַיְיהוּ וְאָתוּ לְבֵי תַעֲנִיתָא״!
[1]אִיקְפַּד וַאֲמַר לְהוּ: [2]״דִּלְמָא מֵיכַל נַמִי אֲכוּל״.
[3]אַבַּיֵי וְרָבָא מְעַיְּילִי כִּי מְסַיְּימִי אַפַּנְתָּא. [4]מָרֵימָר וּמָר זוּטְרָא מְחַלְּפִי דִּימִינָא לִשְׂמָאלָא, וְדִשְׂמָאלָא לִימִינָא. [5]רַבָּנַן דְּבֵי רַב אַשִׁי נָפְקִי כִּי אוֹרְחַיְיהוּ.
[6]סָבְרִי כִּי הָא דְּאָמַר שְׁמוּאֵל: אֵין תַּעֲנִית צִבּוּר בְּבָבֶל אֶלָּא תִּשְׁעָה בְּאָב בִּלְבַד.
[7]אָמַר רַב יְהוּדָה אָמַר רַב: לֹוֶה אָדָם תַּעֲנִיתוֹ וּפוֹרֵעַ. [8]כִּי אָמְרִיתָהּ קַמֵּיהּ דִּשְׁמוּאֵל, [9]אֲמַר לִי: וְכִי נֶדֶר קִבֵּל עֲלֵיהּ דְּלָא סַגִּי דְּלָא מְשַׁלֵּם?

LITERAL TRANSLATION

who wear their shoes and come to the house of the fast!"

[1]He was angry and said to them: [2]"Perhaps they also ate."

[3]Abaye and Rava would enter [the synagogue] while wearing the upper part [of their shoes]. [4]Maremar and Mar Zutra would change the right for the left, and the left for the right. [5]The Rabbis of the academy of Rav Ashi would go out in their usual way. [6]They agreed with what Shmuel said: There is no public fast in Babylonia except the Ninth of Av alone.

[7]Rav Yehudah said in the name of Rav: A man may borrow his fast and repay [it]. [8]When I said this before Shmuel, he said to me: [9]Did he accept a vow upon himself, so that it does not suffice if he does not repay [it]?

RASHI

[האמצעיות] או כשבע האחרונות, קיבל עליו. קאתו רבנן לתעניתא כו' — בתענית צבור, וסברי לה כשמואל, דאמר: אין תענית צבור בבבל בפרק "מקום שנהגו" (פסחים נד,ב) לאסור בנעילת הסנדל ובכל הני. איקפד רב ששת דלמא מיכל נמי אכלי — ופורשים מדרכי צבור, ולית ליה דשמואל, ואנן האידנא נהגינן כשמואל. אפנתא — *אישקריפי"ט. מחלפי — ביומא דתעניתא.

LANGUAGE

אַפַּנְתָּא The upper part of their shoes. This word means the piece of leather of a shoe which covers the foot. In Syriac, פַּנְתָּא means "the back of the hand," or "the skin covering the foot."

LANGUAGE (RASHI)

אישקריפי"ט* From the Old French *escharpet,* which means "a soft shoe."

SAGES

מָרֵימָר Maremar. A Babylonian Amora of the sixth generation, Maremar was a colleague of Rav Ashi. After Rav Ashi's death, Maremar is said to have taken his place as head of the Sura Yeshivah. The Sages of the following generation were his pupils, especially Ravina the younger, who was his close disciple. It is possible that the prefix "Mar" placed before his name is an indication that he belonged to the family of the Exilarch. Maremar's son, Rav Yehudah bar Maremar, was a Sage of the following generation.

מָר זוּטְרָא Mar Zutra. A colleague of Rav Ashi, Mar Zutra was one of the leading Sages of his generation, and his teachers, Rav Pappa and Rav Naḥman bar Yitzḥak, accepted him as their equal.

Apart from his greatness in Halakhah and Aggadah, Mar Zutra was noted as a preacher, and his sermons are cited throughout the Talmud. He apparently held an official position as scholar-in-residence and preacher in the House of the Exilarch. In his old age, he was appointed head of the Pumbedita Yeshivah.

Meetings between Mar Zutra, Amemar, and Rav Ashi are frequently mentioned in the Talmud, and some of these meetings may well have been formal conferences of the leaders of Babylonian Jewry of that generation.

NOTES

כִּי מְסַיְּימִי אַפַּנְתָּא While wearing the upper part of their shoes. The Rishonim disagree about the precise meaning of the term (אַפַּנְתָּא), though they all seem to agree that such shoes do not have leather soles. Our commentary follows *Tosafot,* who explains that the term *apanta* refers to a type of footwear consisting only of the upper portion of a shoe and not having a sole. *Rashi* and *Shittah* explain that *apanta* is a soft slipper. Others maintain that when the Gemara speaks of those who wore *apanta,* it refers to people who turned their shoes upside-down and walked on the upper portions rather than on the soles.

לֹוֶה אָדָם תַּעֲנִיתוֹ וּפוֹרֵעַ A man may borrow his fast and repay it. According to *Rambam* (*Hilkhot Nedarim* 4:15) and a number of other Rishonim, this regulation allowing a

HALAKHAH

לֹוֶה אָדָם תַּעֲנִיתוֹ וּפוֹרֵעַ A man may borrow his fast and repay it. "If a person made a vow to observe a fast on a particular day, but then forgot his vow and ate on the day on which he was to fast, he must refrain from eating for

TRANSLATION AND COMMENTARY

on another day? [1]What **he took upon himself** was **to cause himself distress** by observing a fast. [2]**If he is able** to abstain from food the entire day, **he must cause himself distress** and observe the fast throughout the day. [3]But **if he is unable** to complete the fast, it is enough that he caused himself distress during the part of the day that he observed the fast, and **he is not required to cause himself** additional **distress** by fasting on another day.

אִיכָּא דְּאָמְרִי [4]The Gemara now cites a different version of the previous passage. **There are some** authorities **who say that Rav Yehudah said in the name of Rav**: [5]If **a person** undertakes to observe a fast, and during the course of the fast he sees that he will not be able to complete it, he **may "borrow" the fast** and cancel the fast he is observing on that day, **and may repay** his debt on some day in the future. [6]Rav Yehudah continued: **When I repeated this** ruling **before Shmuel, he said to me:** Why was it necessary for Rav to issue this ruling? [7]Surely **it is obvious!** [8]**Let** his acceptance of the fast **be** regarded as **nothing else than a vow** not to eat! [9]And since his acceptance of the fast is regarded as **a vow,** if he is unable to complete his fast, **is** it **not** obvious that **he is required to repay** his debt **on the next day or on some other day?**

רַב יְהוֹשֻׁעַ בְּרֵיהּ דְּרַב אִידִי [10]It is related that **Rav Yehoshua the son of Rav Idi happened to visit the home of Rav Assi,** [11]where **they prepared a one-third grown calf** in his honor. When the members of Rav Assi's household saw that Rav Yehoshua the son of Rav Idi was not eating, [12]**they said to him: "Taste something** of the food we have prepared for you, **Sir."** [13]**He said to them: "I am observing a fast."**

[1]לְצַעוּרֵי נַפְשֵׁיהּ קַבֵּיל עֲלֵיהּ. [2]אִי מָצֵי, מְצַעֵר נַפְשֵׁיהּ; [3]אִי לָא מָצֵי, לָא מְצַעֵר נַפְשֵׁיהּ.
[4]אִיכָּא דְּאָמְרִי אָמַר רַב יְהוּדָה אָמַר רַב: [5]לֹוֶה אָדָם תַּעֲנִיתוֹ וּפוֹרֵעַ. [6]כִּי אֲמַרִיתָהּ קַמֵּיהּ דִּשְׁמוּאֵל, אָמַר לִי: [7]פְּשִׁיטָא! [8]לֹא יְהֵא אֶלָּא נֶדֶר! [9]נֶדֶר מִי לָא מָצֵי בָּעֵי לְשַׁלּוּמֵי וּמֵיזַל לְמָחָר וּלְיוֹמָא אַחֲרִינָא?
[10]רַב יְהוֹשֻׁעַ בְּרֵיהּ דְּרַב אִידִי אִיקְלַע לְבֵי רַב אַסִּי. [11]עֲבַדוּ לֵיהּ עֶגְלָא תִּילְתָּא. [12]אֲמַרוּ לֵיהּ: לִיטְעוֹם מָר מִידֵי". [13]אֲמַר לְהוּ: "בְּתַעֲנִיתָא יָתֵיבְנָא".

LITERAL TRANSLATION

[1]He accepted upon himself to distress himself. [2]If he is able, he distresses himself; [3]if he is unable, he does not distress himself.

[4]There are [some] who say [that] Rav Yehudah said in the name of Rav: [5]A man may borrow his fast and repay [it]. [6]When I said this before Shmuel, he said to me: [7]It is obvious! [8]Let it be nothing but a vow! [9]Is he not required to repay a vow on the next day or on some other day?

[10]Rav Yehoshua the son of Rav Idi happened to visit the home of Rav Assi. [11]They made him a calf one-third grown. [12]They said to him: "Taste something, Sir." [13]He said to them: "I am fasting."

RASHI

לצעורי בעלמא – אי מצי מצער נפשיה, ואי לא – לא יהא אלא [כיומא] אחרינא.

SAGES

רַב יְהוֹשֻׁעַ בְּרֵיהּ דְּרַב אִידִי Rav Yehoshua the son of Rav Idi. A Babylonian Amora of the fifth and sixth generations, Rav Yehoshua was the son of Rav Idi bar Avin, and he was one of the most important Sages of the period of Rav Ashi. He was apparently the younger brother of Rav Shesha the son of Rav Idi. His teachings are mentioned in several places in the Talmud.

BACKGROUND

עֶגְלָא תִּילְתָּא A calf one-third grown. The expression עֶגְלָא תִּילְתָּא is interpreted in several ways. *Rashi* (*Eruvin* 63a) explains it as meaning a calf one-third grown. He also gives another explanation — that it is a cow's third-born calf, which provides the most select veal. Other commentators explain that it means a calf in the third year of its life.

NOTES

person to "borrow" his fast and repay his debt later applies only if he did not specify the date when he first undertook to observe a fast. But if he undertook to observe a fast on a specific day, he cannot later move his fast to a different date. But most Rishonim (*Ra'avad, Rashba, Ritva*, and others) maintain that this regulation applies even if a person undertook to observe a fast on a specific day. Support for this view is brought from the anecdote cited in our Gemara regarding Rav Yehoshua the son of Rav Idi, for when Rav Yehoshua explained that he was declining to eat because he was observing a fast, the members of Rav Assi's household suggested to him that he observe the fast on some other day, without first asking him whether he had specified a day for his fast.

The Rishonim also disagree about the circumstances under which a person may cancel his fast and observe it on another day. *Rabbenu Ḥananel* maintains that this regulation applies only if the person would suffer great distress if he were to continue fasting. *Rif* and *Rambam* explain that the ruling allowing a person to "borrow" a fast and repay the debt later applies also in a case where the person fasting is invited to a meal that can be characterized as a religious celebration, or where he must take part in a meal in order to show honor to an important person or to maintain good social relations with his friends. *Ritva* argues that the anecdote regarding Rav Yehoshua the son of Rav Idi proves that a person may cancel his fast and observe it on another day, even if he cannot offer any special reason for doing so.

HALAKHAH

the remainder of the day. But if he made a vow to observe a fast without specifying the date of his proposed fast, and then, after beginning to fast, he forgot about his fast and ate, he loses that day of fasting and is required to observe a fast on another day. If a person made a vow to observe a number of fasts without specifying the days on which he was to fast, and after having started to fast on a particular day he wished to cancel the fast on account of some other religious obligation, or in honor of some important person, or because he was in distress (*Rema*), he is permitted to break his fast and 'repay' it on some other day." (*Shulḥan Arukh, Oraḥ Ḥayyim* 568:1-2.)

CONCEPTS

תַּעֲנִית חֲלוֹם **A fast for a dream.** The Sages explained that a bad dream, containing events or symbols that bode ill, must serve as a warning, a kind of "minor prophecy." Therefore the person who has had the dream should immediately repent, in order in some way to repair what he has done. Since the fast prevents the fulfillment of the dream, if someone has a bad dream on Shabbat, it is better for his peace of mind for him to fast and not eat. In such a case, eating will not be a pleasure for him. On the contrary, by fasting he increases his pleasure, because he frees himself of the apprehension resulting from the dream.

SAGES

רַבָּה בַּר מְחַסְיָא **Rabbah [or Rava] bar Meḥasya.** A Babylonian Amora of the second and third generations. The statements found in his name in the Talmud (*Shabbat* 10b-11a) are teachings transmitted in the name of Rav by Rav Ḥama bar Gurya.

רַב חָמָא בַּר גּוּרְיָא **Rav Ḥama bar Gurya** A Babylonian Amora of the second generation, Rav Ḥama bar Gurya was one of the greatest of Rav's students and was closely associated with him, being among those who transmitted his most important teachings. He also studied with Shmuel, apparently after Rav's death. Many of the Sages of the following generation received teachings from him. He is known as "רַבּוֹתֵינוּ הַבְּקִיאִין בְּדִבְרֵי הֲלָכָה" — "our Rabbis who are experts in Halakhah." His teachings are found mainly in the Babylonian Talmud, but some are found also in the Jerusalem Talmud.

TRANSLATION AND COMMENTARY

[1]The members of Rav Assi's household **suggested** a solution **to** Rav Yehoshua's problem: "**'Borrow' this fast, Sir, and repay** your debt by fasting on another day. [2]**Do you not agree, Sir, with what Rav Yehudah said in the name of Rav:** [3]If **a person** undertakes to observe a fast and sees that he is unable to complete it, he **may 'borrow' the fast and repay** the debt by fasting on some other day?" [4]Rav Yehoshua the son of Rav Idi **said to them:** "I agree with Rav's ruling, but I am observing **a fast** to nullify the effect **of a** bad **dream.**" If a person has a disturbing dream at night, it is possible to undo its bad effects by fasting the following day, [5]as **Rabbah bar Meḥasya said in the name of Rav Ḥama bar Gurya, who said in the name of Rav:** A bad dream is often a sign sent from Heaven that a decree has been issued against the dreamer, unless he immediately mends his ways. [6]**A fast is effective** in nullifying the bad effects of a disturbing **dream,** just **as fire** is effective in totally destroying **the waste of flax.**

אָמַר רַב חִסְדָּא [7]**Rav Ḥisda said:** A fast for a dream should be observed **on the very** same **day** that the person had the dream.

וְאָמַר רַב יוֹסֵף [8]The Gemara concludes its discussion with another ruling regarding a fast for a dream. **Rav Yosef said:** [9]A fast for a dream may **even** be observed **on Shabbat** or on a Festival. It is usually forbidden to fast on Shabbat and on Festivals, for on those days one is obligated to experience joy and pleasure. But if a person has a disturbing dream on Shabbat or on a Festival, he is permitted to observe a fast on that day, in order to undo the bad effects of his dream.

מַאי תַּקַּנְתֵּיהּ [10]The Gemara asks: **What remedy** may be offered to a person who observes a fast for a dream on a Shabbat or on a Festival? Surely a person who observes such a fast requires atonement for failing to fulfill his obligation to experience joy and pleasure on that day!

לֵיתִיב תַּעֲנִיתָא לְתַעֲנִיתָא [11]The Gemara answers: If a person observes a fast for a dream on a Shabbat or on a Festival, **he should observe** another **fast** on another day to atone **for the fast** that he observed on a day when fasting is forbidden.

[1]אָמְרוּ לֵיהּ: "וְלוֹזִיף מָר וְלִיפְרַע. [2]לָא סָבַר מָר לְהָא דְּאָמַר רַב יְהוּדָה אָמַר רַב: [3]לֹוֶה אָדָם תַּעֲנִיתוֹ וּפוֹרֵעַ?" [4]אָמַר לְהוּ: "תַּעֲנִית חֲלוֹם הוּא". [5]וְאָמַר רַבָּה בַּר מְחַסְיָא אָמַר רַב חָמָא בַּר גּוּרְיָא אָמַר רַב: [6]יָפָה תַּעֲנִית לַחֲלוֹם כְּאֵשׁ לִנְעוֹרֶת.
[7]אָמַר רַב חִסְדָּא: וּבוֹ בַּיּוֹם.
[8]וְאָמַר רַב יוֹסֵף: [9]וַאֲפִילּוּ בְּשַׁבָּת.
[10]מַאי תַּקַּנְתֵּיהּ?
[11]לֵיתִיב תַּעֲנִיתָא לְתַעֲנִיתָא.

LITERAL TRANSLATION

[1]They said to him: "But, Sir, borrow [this fast] and repay [it]. [2]Do you not agree, Sir, with what Rav Yehudah said in the name of Rav: [3]A man may borrow his fast and repay [it]?" [4]He said to them: "It is a fast for a dream." [5]And Rabbah bar Meḥasya said in the name of Rav Ḥama bar Gurya who said in the name of Rav: [6]A fast is good for a dream as fire is for the waste of flax.

[7]Rav Ḥisda said: And on the very day.

[8]And Rav Yosef said: [9]And even on Shabbat.

[10]What is his remedy?

[11]Let him fast [again] for the fast.

RASHI

ואפילו בשבת — יכול להתענות, כדי שיתבטל לער גופו.

NOTES

תַּעֲנִית חֲלוֹם **A fast for a dream.** *Ritva* discusses at length this issue of observing a fast for a disturbing dream, noting that elsewhere (*Sanhedrin* 30a) the Gemara states that dreams do not have any particular significance (לא מַעֲלִין

HALAKHAH

תַּעֲנִית חֲלוֹם **A fast for a dream.** "A fast is beneficial for undoing the bad effects of a disturbing dream, like fire is effective against the waste of flax. Thus a person who has had a bad dream should observe a fast and do penance (*Magen Avraham*) on the day following the dream. Fasts for dreams are not obligatory but optional (*Rashba*). In recent times, many authorities have ruled leniently on questions regarding fasting for dreams." (*Shulḥan Arukh, Oraḥ Ḥayyim* 220:2.)

וַאֲפִילּוּ בְּשַׁבָּת **And even on Shabbat.** "If a person is distressed by a disturbing dream, he is permitted to observe a fast in order to undo the bad effects of the dream even on Shabbat. According to some authorities, there are only three kinds of dream for which one may observe a fast on Shabbat; others add other types of dream to the list. *Rivash* writes that a person should not fast if the distress caused by his fasting will be greater than that caused by the dream. There are certain authorities who maintain that one should never observe on Shabbat a fast for a disturbing dream (*Rav Amram Gaon, Tur,* and others). If a person has observed a fast for a dream on Shabbat, he is required to observe an additional fast the next day, to atone for fasting on Shabbat. If he is unable to fast on two successive days, or if the Sunday is a day on which fasting is forbidden, he must observe a fast on some other day." (Ibid., 288:4.)

TRANSLATION AND COMMENTARY

MISHNAH **עָבְרוּ אֵלּוּ** [1]This Mishnah continues the discussion of the fasts that are imposed on the community during periods of drought. **If** the first three fasts decreed by the court upon the community at the beginning of the month of Kislev **have passed and** the community's prayers **have** still **not been answered** with rain, [2]**the court** then **decrees another three fasts** to be observed by **the** entire **community** on the third Monday after the first of Kislev, on the following Thursday, and on the following Monday. The restrictions imposed during this second series of three communal fasts are more severe than those that apply to the first series of fasts. As we learned in the previous Mishnah (above, 10a), the three individual fasts and the first three communal fasts are daytime fasts only. [3]The second three communal fasts begin in the evening, so that those fasting are permitted to **eat and drink** on the day before the fast, **while it is still day** — i.e., until nightfall. In addition to the prohibition against eating and drinking, [4]those fasting **are forbidden** to **work,** to **bathe** for pleasure, to **anoint** themselves with oil, to **wear** leather **shoes** for pleasure, **or** to engage in **sexual relations.** [5]On these fasts **the bathhouses are locked** so that nobody can enter for the purpose of bathing in hot water.

עָבְרוּ אֵלּוּ [6]**If** the second series of communal fasts **has passed and** the community's prayers **have** still **not been answered** with rain, [7]**the court decrees an additional seven fasts upon** the community, to be observed on the next four Mondays and the next three Thursdays. [8]**Thus,** together with the first two series of three communal fasts, **there are thirteen fasts** that the court imposes **upon the community** in times of drought. All the stringencies that apply to the second series of communal fasts — the length of the fast, as well as the activities that are forbidden on account of it — also apply to the third series of communal fasts. [9]These last seven fasts **are** in fact **more severe than the** three **preceding ones, for on these** last seven fasts **they sound the alarm** (by blowing the shofar or by a special fast-day supplication inserted into the prayers, as will be explained in the Gemara) **and lock the shops** so that all commerce comes to a halt. [10]**On Mondays** the doors of the shops where food is sold **may be opened for a short period** at the end of the day **when it is** already **getting dark,** so that those fasting can buy food with which to break their fast. [11]**On Thursdays** such shops **are permitted to** remain **open** all day, to allow preparations **in honor of Shabbat.**

עָבְרוּ אֵלּוּ [12]**If** these last seven fasts **have passed and** the community's prayers **have** still **not been answered,** and the drought continues deep into the winter months, the court does not impose any additional fasts on the community. Other measures are taken to elicit God's compassion so that the rains will fall and the drought will come to an end. The entire community must adopt certain customs that are ordinarily associated

משנה [1]עָבְרוּ אֵלּוּ וְלֹא נַעֲנוּ, [2]בֵּית דִּין גּוֹזְרִין שָׁלֹשׁ תַּעֲנִיּוֹת אֲחֵרוֹת עַל הַצִּבּוּר. [3]אוֹכְלִין וְשׁוֹתִין מִבְּעוֹד יוֹם, [4]וַאֲסוּרִין בִּמְלָאכָה, וּבִרְחִיצָה, וּבְסִיכָה, וּבִנְעִילַת הַסַּנְדָּל, וּבְתַשְׁמִישׁ הַמִּטָּה, [5]וְנוֹעֲלִין אֶת הַמֶּרְחֲצָאוֹת. [6]עָבְרוּ אֵלּוּ וְלֹא נַעֲנוּ, [7]בֵּית דִּין גּוֹזְרִין עֲלֵיהֶן עוֹד שֶׁבַע, [8]שֶׁהֵן שְׁלֹשׁ עֶשְׂרֵה תַּעֲנִיּוֹת עַל הַצִּבּוּר. [9]הֲרֵי אֵלּוּ יְתֵרוֹת עַל הָרִאשׁוֹנוֹת, שֶׁבְּאֵלּוּ מַתְרִיעִין, וְנוֹעֲלִין אֶת הַחֲנוּיוֹת. [10]בַּשֵּׁנִי מַטִּין עִם חֲשֵׁיכָה, [11]וּבַחֲמִישִׁי מוּתָּרִין מִפְּנֵי כְּבוֹד הַשַּׁבָּת. [12]עָבְרוּ אֵלּוּ וְלֹא נַעֲנוּ,

LITERAL TRANSLATION

MISHNAH [1][If] these have passed and they have not been answered, [2]the court decrees three other fasts on the community. [3]They eat and drink while it is still day, [4]and they are forbidden work, and bathing, and anointing, and wearing shoes, and marital relations, [5]and they lock the bathhouses.

[6][If] these have passed and they have not been answered, [7]the court decrees on them an additional seven [fasts], [8]so that they are thirteen fasts on the community. [9]These are more severe than the first ones, for on these they sound the alarm, and they lock the shops. [10]On Monday they open [them] a little when it is dark, [11]and on Thursday they are permitted [to open] in honor of Shabbat.

[12][If] these have passed and they have not been answered,

BACKGROUND

וְנוֹעֲלִין אֶת הַמֶּרְחֲצָאוֹת And they lock the bathhouses. In the Talmudic period, public bathhouses (where the means of heating the water were generally very sophisticated) were used not only for washing the body but also as clubs of a sort, where men would bathe and spend time together. Locking the bathhouses was thus a sign of public mourning, not only because it prevented people from washing, but also because bathhouses were places of public entertainment.

NOTES

(ולא מורידין). He explains that if a person has experienced a disturbing dream, he should take it as a sign from Heaven that he should examine his ways and repent. Observing a fast is one measure that facilitates true repentance. One should observe the fast on the very same day that one has had the dream, because then it is still vivid and most likely to lead to repentance, and the fast should be observed even on Shabbat. Ordinarily, the obligation to experience joy and pleasure on Shabbat bars a person from fasting on that day. But someone who has a disturbing dream is permitted to fast on Shabbat, because he would not enjoy his food anyway. On the contrary, he takes pleasure in fasting, for by fasting he can begin to mend his ways and thus diminish the anxiety caused by the dream.

TRANSLATION AND COMMENTARY

with mourning. [1]People **must reduce** their **business activities,** the **building** of houses, the **planting** of trees, **betrothals, marriages, and greetings between one person and another,** [2]and members of the community must act **like people who have received a reprimand from God.** [3]At the same time, pious **individuals once again** begin to **fast** on Mondays and Thursdays, and continue to do so **until the end of Nisan.** These fasts are similar in their severity to the fasts observed by the pious individuals at the beginning of the season, when the signs of drought first began to appear. Thus these fasts are observed only during the daylight hours, and only eating and drinking are forbidden. No additional measures are taken to bring about an end to the drought once the month of Nisan is over, [4]for **if Nisan ends** without any rain having fallen in Eretz Israel throughout the winter, **and** only afterwards does **rain** begin to **fall** there, this late rain **is** regarded as **a sign of a curse,** [5]**as it is said** (I Samuel 12:17): **"Is it not the wheat harvest today?"** I will call unto the Lord, and He will send thunder and rain, and you will know and you will see that your evil is great, which you have done in the sight of the Lord, in asking for a king for yourselves." When the people of Israel asked the Prophet Samuel for a king to rule over them, he admonished them, declaring that the rain that would fall that day during the wheat harvest would testify to God's anger with the people's request.

GEMARA בִּשְׁלָמָא כּוּלְּהוּ [6]The defining feature of a fast is that one does not eat or drink for a specified period of time. As our Mishnah explained, on the more severe communal fasts other activities are prohibited as well. The Gemara opens with a discussion of these other prohibitions. **Granted** that **all the** other activities mentioned in the Mishnah **are forbidden** on the more severe communal fasts; we understand that, [7]**because** the essential feature of all these activities is that **they give pleasure.** It stands to reason that **bathing** for pleasure, **anointing** oneself with oil, wearing leather shoes for pleasure, **and** engaging in **sexual relations** are all forbidden on the more severe communal fasts, because it is inappropriate to engage in pleasurable activities on days dedicated to penance and supplication. [8]**But** why is one forbidden to work on a communal fast? Surely **work is** an activity that causes **distress,** and it is therefore in keeping with the spirit of the fast!

אָמַר רַב חִסְדָּא [9]**Rav Ḥisda said in the name of Rav Yirmeyah bar Abba:** The prohibition against working on a communal fast is derived from **the** following **verse** (Joel 1:14) which **says:** [10]**"Sanctify a fast, call a solemn assembly, gather the elders."** The verse draws an analogy between a fast and a solemn assembly (עֲצָרָה — *atzeret*), thereby alluding to Shemini Atzeret (the day following the Festival of Sukkot), which is called "*atzeret*" in the Torah (Leviticus 23:36 and Numbers 29:35), as well as to Shavuot, which is known as "*atzeret*" in Rabbinic literature. [11]A fast day is **likened to a day of assembly,** Shemini Atzeret and Shavuot. [12]Just **as on a day of assembly doing work is forbidden,** [13]**so too is doing work forbidden on a fast.**

אִי מָה עֲצֶרֶת מֵאוּרְתָּא [14]The Gemara asks: If this is a valid argument, then **perhaps** we should take the analogy one step further and say: **Just as on the day of assembly** work is already forbidden **from the** previous

---

[1]מְמַעֲטִין בְּמַשָּׂא וּמַתָּן, בְּבִנְיָן וּבִנְטִיעָה, בְּאֵירוּסִין וּבְנִישּׂוּאִין, וּבִשְׁאִילַת שָׁלוֹם בֵּין אָדָם לַחֲבֵירוֹ, [2]כִּבְנֵי אָדָם הַנְּזוּפִין לַמָּקוֹם. [3]הַיְּחִידִים חוֹזְרִין וּמִתְעַנִּין עַד שֶׁיֵּצֵא נִיסָן. [4]יָצָא נִיסָן וְיָרְדוּ גְּשָׁמִים, סִימַן קְלָלָה, [5]שֶׁנֶּאֱמַר: ״הֲלוֹא קְצִיר חִטִּים הַיּוֹם, וגו׳?״.

גמרא [6]בִּשְׁלָמָא כּוּלְּהוּ, [7]אִית בְּהוּ תַּעֲנוּג – רְחִיצָה, וְסִיכָה, וְתַשְׁמִישׁ הַמִּטָּה. [8]אֲבָל מְלָאכָה צַעַר הוּא!

[9]אָמַר רַב חִסְדָּא אָמַר רַב יִרְמְיָה בַּר אַבָּא: אָמַר קְרָא: [10]״קַדְּשׁוּ צוֹם, קִרְאוּ עֲצָרָה, אִסְפוּ זְקֵנִים״. [11]כַּעֲצֶרֶת. [12]מָה עֲצֶרֶת אָסוּר בַּעֲשִׂיַּית מְלָאכָה, [13]אַף תַּעֲנִית אָסוּר בַּעֲשִׂיַּית מְלָאכָה.

[14]אִי מָה עֲצֶרֶת מֵאוּרְתָּא,

LITERAL TRANSLATION

[1]they reduce business transactions, building and planting, betrothals and marriages, and greetings between one person and his fellow, [2]like people who are reprimanded by God (lit., "the place"). [3]The individuals fast again until Nisan ends. [4][If] Nisan has ended and rains fall, it is a sign of a curse, [5]for it is said: "Is it not the wheat harvest today, etc?"

GEMARA [6]Granted all of them [are forbidden, [7]because] they give pleasure — bathing, and anointing, and marital relations. [8]But work is distress!

[9]Rav Ḥisda said in the name of Rav Yirmeyah bar Abba: [10]The verse says: "Sanctify a fast, call a solemn assembly, gather the elders. [11]"It is like the [day of] assembly. [12]Just as the [day of] assembly is forbidden for doing work, [13]so is a fast forbidden for doing work.

[14]Or [we can say that] just as the [day of] assembly is from the evening,

RASHI

״קדשו צום קראו עצרה אספו זקנים כל יושבי הארץ בית ה׳ אלהיכם וזעקו אל ה׳״. **מה עצרת** — שבועות ושמיני עצרת. **אי מה עצרת** — איסור מלאכתו מאורתא.

TRANSLATION AND COMMENTARY

evening, because the Festival begins at sundown, [1]**so too** should work be forbidden **from the** previous **evening on a** communal **fast!**

אֲמַר רַבִּי זֵירָא [2]**Rabbi Zera said: I myself personally heard Rabbi Yirmeyah bar Abba explain** his position as follows: [3]**The verse** (Joel 1:14) **says:** "Sanctify a fast, call a solemn assembly, **gather the elders** and all the inhabitants of the land into the house of the Lord your God." The prohibition against working on a fast day, which is derived from the reference to a solemn assembly, [4]is **similar to the gathering of elders** on the day of a fast. [5]**Just as the gathering of elders** on a fast **is** only **by day,** [6]**so too does** the prohibition against working on **a fast apply** only **by day.**

וְאֵימָא [7]The Gemara asks: **But** why should we not **say** that the gathering of the elders on the day of a fast begins **at midday?** And therefore work, too, should be forbidden only from then on!

אֲמַר רַב שֵׁישָׁא בְּרֵיהּ דְּרַב אִידִי [8]**Rav Shesha the son of Rav Idi said:** Rabbi Yirmeyah bar Abba's assumption that the elders begin to gather on the morning of a fast, and not later in the day, [9]**supports** the statement of **Rav Huna, who said that** on communal fasts people begin to **gather** together in the synagogues **from the morning,** and the community leaders examine the conduct of the townspeople and admonish those whose behavior is found wanting.

הֵיכִי עָבְדִי [10]The Gemara asks: **What is done** at the public assemblies that take place on communal fasts?

אֲמַר אַבַּיֵי [11]**Abaye said** in reply: **From the morning until the middle of the day** the community leaders gather together in the synagogues to **examine the affairs of the town.** They investigate the people's conduct and morals, and they right the wrongs they discover, in the hope that these improvements will bring about

[1]אַף תַּעֲנִית נַמִי מֵאוּרְתָּא! [2]אֲמַר רַבִּי זֵירָא: לְדִידִי מִיפַּרְשָׁא לִי מִינֵּיהּ דְּרַבִּי יִרְמְיָה בַּר אַבָּא: [3]אָמַר קְרָא: "אִסְפוּ זְקֵנִים". [4]דּוּמְיָא דַּאֲסִיפַת זְקֵנִים. [5]מָה אֲסִיפַת זְקֵנִים בַּיּוֹם, [6]אַף צוֹם נַמִי בַּיּוֹם.

[7]וְאֵימָא: מִטִּיהֲרָא!

[8]אֲמַר רַב שֵׁישָׁא בְּרֵיהּ דְּרַב אִידִי: [9]מְסַיֵּיעַ לֵיהּ לְרַב הוּנָא, דְּאָמַר מִצַּפְרָא כִּינּוּפְיָא.

[10]הֵיכִי עָבְדִי?

[11]אֲמַר אַבַּיֵי: מִצַּפְרָא עַד פַּלְגָא דְּיוֹמָא מְעַיְּינִינַן בְּמִילֵּי דְּמָתָא.

LITERAL TRANSLATION

[1]so too is a fast from the evening!

[2]Rabbi Zera said: It was explained to me personally by Rabbi Yirmeyah bar Abba: [3]The verse says: "Gather the elders." [4]It is similar to the gathering of elders. [5]Just as the gathering of elders is by day, [6]so too is a fast by day.

[7]But say: From midday!

[8]Rav Shesha the son of Rav Idi said: [9]This supports Rav Huna, who said [that] the gathering is from the morning.

[10]How do they act?

[11]Abaye said: From the morning until the middle of the day we examine the affairs of the town.

RASHI

דומיא דאסיפת זקנים ביום — דבלילה כל אחד בביתו, ואין נאספין. **מסייע ליה לרב הונא** — הא דפשיטא לך דאסיפת זקנים ביום. **דאמר מצפרא כינופיא** — ביום תענית צבור מתקבצין ובאין לבית הכנסת מן הבקר. **מעיינין במילי דמתא** — דרישה וחקירה, לבדוק במעשיהם בעסקי בני העיר, אם גזל וחמס ביניהן, ומפייסין אותן. **היכי עבדי** — מאי עבדי בכינופיא דמצפרא ובכוליה יומא דתעניתא. **ריבעא דיומא** — מאלות ואילך עושין שני חלקים. **בפלגא** — דהיינו ריבעא דיומא, קרו "ויחל משה" ומפטירין "דרשו את ה' בהמצאו".

SAGES

רַב שֵׁישָׁא בְּרֵיהּ דְּרַב אִידִי Rav Shesha the son of Rav Idi. A Babylonian Amora of the fourth and fifth generations, Rav Shesha (or, as he is sometimes called, Rav Sheshet) was the son of the Sage Rav Idi bar Avin, who belonged to the third generation of Babylonian Amoraim. Rav Shesha discusses Halakhic issues with Abaye and Rava and also with the greatest of their students.

TERMINOLOGY

מְסַיֵּיעַ לֵיהּ לְ.... This supports [the opinion of] Rabbi X. When the Gemara wishes to explore the possibility that the Mishnah it is analyzing offers support for the view of a scholar mentioned elsewhere, it often asks נֵימָא מְסַיֵּיעַ לֵיהּ...? — "May we say that the following expression in our Mishnah supports the opinion of Rabbi X?"

NOTES

מְעַיְּינִינַן בְּמִילֵּי דְּמָתָא We examine the affairs of the town. *Gra* (notes to *Shulḥan Arukh, Oraḥ Ḥayyim* 576:16) derives this from the following Biblical verses (Isaiah 58:6-7): "Is not this the fast that I have chosen? To loosen the chains of wickedness, to undo the bands of the yoke, and to let the oppressed go free, and that you break every yoke? Is it not to share your bread with the hungry and that you bring the poor that are cast out to your house? When you see the naked, that you cover him; and that you do not hide yourself from your own flesh?" These verses teach us that God looks favorably at those fasts on which the people examine their behavior and attend to the social injustices they find in their community. *Rabbenu Elyakim.* writes that, on public fast days, the community leaders gather to attend to the community's problems and needs, as well as to right the wrongs that the community as a whole may have done to individuals.

HALAKHAH

מִצַּפְרָא עַד פַּלְגָא דְּיוֹמָא From the morning until the middle of the day. "On those public fast days that are decreed in order to avert an impending calamity, the Rabbinical Court judges and the community leaders gather in the synagogues from the time that the morning prayers are completed until noon and examine the conduct of the townspeople. They attempt to rectify any flaws in behavior that they find. They admonish the wrongdoers and put to shame those who use violence to get their way. During the third quarter of the day, the appropriate portion of the Torah is read, as well as the haftarah connected with the occasion. During the last quarter of the day, the people say the afternoon prayer and offer special petitions and supplications. These practices have not been observed in recent generations, either because the courts no longer have the authority to correct the wrongs they find (*Arukh HaShulḥan*), or because in general the customs regarding public fasts are no longer observed in their entirety." (*Shulḥan Arukh, Oraḥ Ḥayyim* 576:16.)

LANGUAGE (RASHI)

אישתורדי״ן* (The correct reading is אישטורדי״ץ.) From the Old French *estordiz,* which means "confused" or "flustered."

TRANSLATION AND COMMENTARY

divine forgiveness. [1]**From** midday **onwards, they spend a quarter of the day reading from the Torah** a portion that is appropriate for the day, **as well as the haftarah,** a portion from the Prophets which is connected to the occasion. [2]**From then on,** during the final quarter of the day, the people say the afternoon prayer, confess their sins, and **petition for mercy,** pouring out their hearts with special supplications. [3]These customs follow a Biblical precedent, **as the verse says** (Nehemiah 9:3): **"And they stood up in their place, and they read in the book of the Torah of the Lord their God one-fourth part of the day, and another fourth part they confessed, and they prostrated themselves before the Lord their God."**

אֵיפּוּךְ אֲנָא [13A] [4]The Gemara objects: The verse in Nehemiah supports the custom of devoting a quarter of a public fast to the reading of the Torah and a quarter to prayer and supplication, but it does not state explicitly that these activities take place in the afternoon. If the order followed on a public fast is derived from this verse, **we can** just as well **reverse** the order and argue that the first half of the day should be spent reading from the Torah and petitioning for mercy, and that the second half of the day should be spent examining the affairs of the townspeople!

לָא סָלְקָא דַּעֲתָךְ [5]The Gemara rejects this argument: **It cannot enter your mind** to think that the examination of the public's behavior should be delayed until the afternoon of the fast, [6]**for it is written** in another context (Ezra 9:4): **"Then everyone who trembled at the words of the God of Israel because of the transgression of the exiles gathered around me** and I sat appalled until the evening sacrifice." [7]**And it is written** in the next verse (verse 5): **"And at the evening sacrifice I arose from my fast,** and having rent my garment and my mantle I fell on my knees **and I spread out my hands to the Lord."** Those who trembled at the words of God gathered around Ezra, and they spent the morning attending to the most pressing issue of the day — increased intermarriage between the Jews who had returned to Eretz Israel from exile and the other peoples whom they found living in the land. Then the time arrived for the evening sacrifice, which is usually offered in the afternoon, and only then did Ezra fall on his knees and spread out his hands in prayer. Thus we see that the first half of a public fast should be dedicated to an inspection of the community's behavior, and the rest of the day should be devoted to prayer.

[1]מִכָּאן וְאֵילָךְ, רִבְעָא דְּיוֹמָא קָרֵינַן בְּסִפְרָא וְאַפְטַרְתָּא. [2]מִכָּאן וְאֵילָךְ, בָּעֵינַן רַחֲמֵי, [3]שֶׁנֶּאֱמַר: "וַיָּקוּמוּ עַל עָמְדָם, וַיִּקְרְאוּ בְּסֵפֶר תּוֹרַת ה׳ אֱלֹהֵיהֶם רְבִעִית הַיּוֹם, וּרְבִעִית מִתְוַדִּים, וּמִשְׁתַּחֲוִים לַה׳ אֱלֹהֵיהֶם".

[13A] [4]אֵיפּוּךְ אֲנָא!

[5]לָא סָלְקָא דַּעֲתָךְ, [6]דִּכְתִיב: "וְאֵלַי יֵאָסְפוּ כֹּל חָרֵד בְּדִבְרֵי אֱלֹהֵי יִשְׂרָאֵל עַל מַעַל הַגּוֹלָה, וגו׳". [7]וּכְתִיב: "וּבְמִנְחַת הָעֶרֶב קַמְתִּי מִתַּעֲנִיתִי... וָאֶפְרְשָׂה כַפַּי אֶל ה׳".

LITERAL TRANSLATION

[1]From then on, for a quarter of the day we read from the book [of the Torah] and the haftarah. [2]From then on, we petition for mercy, [3]as it is said: "And they stood up in their place, and they read in the book of the Torah of the Lord their God one-fourth part of the day, and another fourth part they confessed, and they prostrated themselves before the Lord their God."

[13A] [4]Let me reverse [it]!

[5]This cannot enter your mind, [6]for it is written: "Then everyone who trembled at the words of the God of Israel because of the transgression of the exiles gathered around me, etc." [7]And it is written: "And at the evening sacrifice I arose from my fast.... and I spread out my hands to the Lord."

RASHI

איפוך אנא — דפלגא דיומא קמא הוו קרו ומפטרי ובעו רחמי, ובאידך פלגא מעייני. **"על מעל הגולה** ואני יושב משומם עד מנחת הערב. ובמנחת הערב קמתי מתעניתי ובקרעי בגדי ומעילי ואכרעה על ברכי ואפרשה כפי אל ה׳ אלהי". **ובמנחת הערב קמתי** — אלמא באידך פלגא בעו רחמי עד פניא, מכלל דפלגא קמא — מעייני במילי דמתא, בנחמיה בן חכליה כתיב בעזרא **"ואלי יאספו"** — לי היו מתאספין ובאין טובים שבהן, להגיד לפני על מעל וחטא הגולה, להפריסם. **משומם** = *אישתורדי"ן בלעז. על מעלם שמתוודין עד מנחת הערב מחצות ואילך, שהצל נוטה, כדאמרינן במסכת יומא (כח,ב): כלותיה דאברהם מכי משחרי כותלי.

NOTES

אֵיפּוּךְ אֲנָא **Let me reverse it.** *Ramat Shmuel* observes: Although it stands to reason that the people should first correct their ways and only then petition for mercy, the Gemara argues that there is good reason to reverse the order, because many of the laws regarding fasting and penance are derived from the Bible's description of the repentance of the people of Nineveh. And we find that the people of Nineveh first petitioned for mercy, and only then attended to the wrongs committed in their community, as the verse says (Jonah 3:8): "But let man and beast be covered with sackcloth, and cry mightily to God; and let them turn every one from his evil way, and from the violence that is in their hands."

TRANSLATION AND COMMENTARY

אָמַר רַפְרָם בַּר פַּפָּא [1]The Gemara now begins a new topic of discussion — the scope of the prohibition against bathing on a communal fast. **Rafram bar Pappa said in the name of Rav Ḥisda: Whenever bathing is forbidden on account of mourning, such as** on **the Ninth of Av,** the day of national mourning for the destruction of the First and Second Temples, **or** on a day of **private mourning** for a close relative, [2]**it is forbidden both in hot water and in cold water.** [3]But **whenever** bathing is forbidden **on account of** the **pleasure** that it provides, **such as** on **a public fast** when pleasurable activities are prohibited, [4]only **bathing in hot water is forbidden,** because it is a pleasurable activity, **but** bathing **in cold water is permitted.**

אָמַר רַב אִידִי בַּר אָבִין [5]The Gemara now considers Rav Ḥisda's ruling in the light of our Mishnah and other Tannaitic sources. **Rav Idi bar Avin said: We too have learned** in our Mishnah that bathing in cold water is permitted on a communal fast, for the Mishnah states: [6]"On the second series of communal fasts, **the bathhouses are locked,** so that nobody can enter for the purpose of bathing." This corroborates Rav Ḥisda's ruling, because bathhouses provide hot water.

אָמַר לֵיהּ אַבַּיֵי [7]**Abaye said to** Rav Idi bar Avin: Your argument, that the Mishnah's formulation proves that bathing in cold water is permitted on a communal fast, is not convincing. If we assume that bathing **is forbidden** even **in cold water,** [8]**how should** the Tanna **have taught** the Mishnah? Should he have said: "On communal fasts, **they dam the rivers,** so that there will be no water available for bathing"? Abaye's objection is directed at a flaw in Rav Idi bar Avin's logic: the fact that our Mishnah speaks only of locking the bathhouses merely shows that other bathing facilities cannot be locked.

[1]אָמַר רַפְרָם בַּר פַּפָּא אָמַר רַב חִסְדָּא: כָּל שֶׁהוּא מִשּׁוּם אֵבֶל, כְּגוֹן תִּשְׁעָה בְּאָב, וְאָבֵל, [2]אָסוּר בֵּין בְּחַמִּין בֵּין בְּצוֹנֵן. [3]כָּל שֶׁהוּא מִשּׁוּם תַּעֲנוּג, כְּגוֹן תַּעֲנִית צִבּוּר, [4]בְּחַמִּין אָסוּר, בְּצוֹנֵן מוּתָּר.

[5]אֲמַר רַב אִידִי בַּר אָבִין: אַף אֲנַן נַמִי תָּנֵינָא: [6]"וְנוֹעֲלִין אֶת הַמֶּרְחֲצָאוֹת".

[7]אֲמַר לֵיהּ אַבַּיֵי: וְאִי בְּצוֹנֵן אָסוּר, [8]"סוֹכְרִין אֶת הַנְּהָרוֹת" מִבָּעֵי לֵיהּ לְמִיתְנֵי?

LITERAL TRANSLATION

[1]Rafram bar Pappa said in the name of Rav Ḥisda: [Bathing on] any [day] that is on account of mourning, such as the Ninth of Av, or [the case of] a mourner, [2]is forbidden both in hot water and in cold water. [3][On] any [day] that is on account of pleasure, such as a public fast, [4][bathing] in hot water is forbidden, [but] in cold water it is permitted.

[5]Rav Idi bar Avin said: We too have also learned [thus]: [6]"And they lock the bathhouses."

[7]Abaye said to him: And if it were forbidden in cold water, [8]should it have taught: "They dam the rivers"?

RASHI

קמתי מתעניתי — לא שמתענה עד המנחה ואחר כך אוכל, אלא כלומר מצער נפשיה. "ובקרעי" — ואם שאני קורע בגדי ומעילי הייתי מתפלל, כדי שאתרצה. **כל שהוא משום אבל** — כל תענית שאסרו חכמים רחיצה משום אבל, כגון תשעה באב שהוא משום אבילות חורבן, וכל שכן אבל ממש שמתו לפניו, דאית ליה צערא טובא — אסור בין בחמין וכו׳. **משום תענוג** — שמצטערין, ואוסרין עצמן בתענוג. הכי גרסינן. **אמר רב אידי בר אבין אף אנן נמי תנינא ונועלין את המרחצאות. ואמר ליה אביי: ואי בצונן אסור, סוכרין את הנהרות מיבעי ליה למיתני** — בתמיה. אף אנן נמי תנינא במתניתין, דקתני גבי תענית צבור: ונועלין את המרחצאות — דהיינו חמין, אבל צונן מותר. אמר ליה אביי: כלומר, ואי הוה סבירא ליה לתנא דידן דצונן אסור — היכי הוה בעי למיתני "סוכרין את הנהרות", היכי מצי למיסכרינהו?

SAGES

רַפְרָם בַּר פַּפָּא Rafram bar Pappa. Rafram bar Pappa was an Amora of the third and fourth generations in Babylonia. According to the Geonic tradition, the name "Rafram" is a shortened form of "Rav Efrayim," and several Sages bore it. Rafram bar Pappa was a close disciple of Rav Ḥisda, and he is principally mentioned as transmitting the teachings of his great master. Rafram bar Pappa also knew Rav Huna and told Rava about Rav Huna's great deeds.

רַב אִידִי בַּר אָבִין Rav Idi bar Avin. He belonged to the third and fourth generations of Babylonian Amoraim. Of Rav Idi's father, Rav Avin Nagara ("the carpenter"), it is told that he was especially punctilious in the ceremony of lighting the Sabbath candles, and Rav Huna predicted that Rav Avin would be privileged to have sons who were eminent scholars. Indeed, his sons were Rav Ḥiyya bar Avin and Rav Idi bar Avin.

Rav Idi was a student of Rav Ḥisda, but he also quotes other Sages of the second generation of Babylonian Amoraim. He was one of the greatest authorities of his generation, and many of his Halakhic discussions with Abaye are recorded in the Talmud. Rav Idi was the chief Rabbinic authority in his city, Shekanzib, where he apparently had a yeshivah. He lived to a great age, and the most eminent scholars of the next generation — Rav Pappa and Rav Huna the son of Rav Yehoshua — were his students. In his old age he called his students דַּרְדְּקֵי — "infants."

We know little of his deeds or the story of his life, except that he had two sons who were Sages.

NOTES

אָסוּר בֵּין בְּחַמִּין בֵּין בְּצוֹנֵן Is forbidden both in hot water and in cold water. Elsewhere (*Pesaḥim* 54b), Rabbi Elazar rules that on the Ninth of Av a person may not even put his finger into cold water, just as he may not do so on Yom Kippur. *Ritva* maintains that Rav Ḥisda agrees with that ruling, so that when he says that bathing in cold water

HALAKHAH

תִּשְׁעָה בְּאָב...אָסוּר בֵּין בְּחַמִּין בֵּין בְּצוֹנֵן On the Ninth of Av... it is forbidden both in hot water and in cold water. "Bathing on the Ninth of Av is forbidden, both in hot water and in cold water, following Rav Ḥisda. It is not permitted even to put one's finger into water for the purpose of washing." (*Shulḥan Arukh, Oraḥ Ḥayyim* 554:7.)

וְאָבֵל, אָסוּר בֵּין בְּחַמִּין בֵּין בְּצוֹנֵן And in the case of a mourner it is forbidden both in hot water and in cold water. "A mourner is forbidden to bathe his entire body even in cold water. He may not wash his face, hands, or feet in hot water, but he may wash them in cold water. If he is particularly dirty, he is permitted to wash himself in the ordinary manner, following Rav Ḥisda (according to the Gemara's conclusion below). *Rema* notes that these prohibitions apply strictly speaking only during the first seven days of mourning, but it is customary for mourners to refrain from bathing for thirty days. In places where this custom prevails, one should not deviate from it." (Ibid., *Yoreh De'ah* 381:1.)

תַּעֲנִית צִבּוּר, בְּחַמִּין אָסוּר, בְּצוֹנֵן מוּתָּר On a public fast, bathing in hot water is forbidden, but in cold water it is permitted. "On the more severe communal fasts that are

TERMINOLOGY

אַף אֲנַן נַמִי תָּנֵינָא We too have also learned thus. This expression is used in the Gemara when proof is adduced for the ruling of an Amora from the words of a Mishnah or a Baraita. In general, the Tannaitic quotation does not deal directly with the subject at hand (for it would be surprising to have an Amora make a Halakhic ruling that

had already appeared in a Mishnah); but the proof is usually more complex, stating that if one examined the matter closely one would reach the conclusion reached by the Amora, although he did not base his ruling on the Mishnah.

BACKGROUND

כָּל חַיָּבֵי טְבִילוֹת All who require ritual immersion. There are various reasons why a person must purify himself. In Temple times, anyone who wished to enter the Temple or to eat from the sacrifices was required to immerse himself, as were priests who wished to eat terumah or ḥallah. More commonly, a wife must purify herself by ritual immersion from the impurity of menstruation or of childbirth in order that marital relations may be resumed. Furthermore, for many generations, during the Second Temple period and thereafter, anyone who had not ritually purified himself was forbidden to recite the *Shema,* to pray, or to study Torah.

TRANSLATION AND COMMENTARY

אָמַר רַב שֵׁישָׁא בְּרֵיהּ דְּרַב אִידִי [1]**Rav Shesha the son of Rav Idi explained** his father's position: My **father,** Rav Idi bar Avin, **had** the following **difficulty** with the Mishnah, which led him to the conclusion that it corroborates Rav Ḥisda's ruling that bathing in cold water is permitted on a communal fast: [2]**Since we have** already **learned** in the Mishnah that on the second series of communal fasts **"bathing is forbidden,"** [3]**why was it necessary** for the Mishnah to state in the very next clause: "On these fasts **the bathhouses are locked"**? What does the second clause add? [4]**Is it not correct to conclude from this** that the purpose of the second clause is to limit the scope of the prohibition mentioned in the first clause and to inform us that bathing **in hot water is forbidden,** [5]but bathing **in cold water is permitted?**

לֵימָא מְסַיַּיע לֵיהּ [6]The Gemara now seeks to adduce support for the first part of Rav Ḥisda's ruling — that whenever bathing is forbidden on account of mourning, it is forbidden both in hot water and in cold. **Shall we say that** the following Baraita **supports** Rav Ḥisda: [7]**"All who** are ritually impure and **require ritual immersion** on a particular day — for example, a woman who has experienced menstrual bleeding, or a woman who has given birth — **may immerse themselves in their usual manner, even** if the day designated for immersion falls **on the Ninth of Av or on Yom Kippur,** when bathing is otherwise forbidden"? Before explaining how it supports the ruling of Rav Ḥisda, the Gemara first clarifies the Baraita itself: [8]**In what** type of water may ritually impure people immerse themselves on the Ninth of Av and Yom Kippur? [9]**If we say** that the Baraita means that they may immerse themselves **in hot water,** this explanation poses a serious difficulty, [10]for **is there** such a thing as **ritual immersion in hot water?** [11]Surely, heated water **is drawn water,** and drawn water is not suitable for ritual immersion! By Torah law, a ritually impure person can be purified only through immersion in naturally flowing water or in a body of stationary water that collected naturally, but not in a body of stationary water collected through human effort. Hot water is drawn in containers and placed on a fire, which is why it cannot be used for ritual immersion. [12]**Rather, does not** the Baraita

LITERAL TRANSLATION

[1]Rav Shesha the son of Rav Idi said: Father had this difficulty: [2]Since we have learned: "They are forbidden bathing," [3]why do I need: "They lock the bathhouses"? [4]Rather is it not [correct] to conclude from this: In hot water it is forbidden; [5]in cold water it is permitted?

[6]Shall we say [that this] supports him: [7]"All who require ritual immersion immerse themselves in their usual manner, both on the Ninth of Av and on Yom Kippur"? [8]In what? [9]If we say in hot water, [10]is there ritual immersion in hot water? [11]It is drawn [water]! [12]Rather, is it not

[1]אָמַר רַב שֵׁישָׁא בְּרֵיהּ דְּרַב אִידִי: אַבָּא הָכִי קַשְׁיָא לֵיהּ: [2]מִכְּדִי תְּנַן: "אָסוּר בִּרְחִיצָה", [3]"נוֹעֲלִין אֶת הַמֶּרְחֲצָאוֹת" לָמָּה לִי? [4]אֶלָּא לָאו שְׁמַע מִינָּהּ: בְּחַמִּין אָסוּר; [5]בְּצוֹנֵן מוּתָּר? [6]לֵימָא מְסַיַּיע לֵיהּ: [7]"כָּל חַיָּיבֵי טְבִילוֹת טוֹבְלִין כְּדַרְכָּן, בֵּין בְּתִשְׁעָה בְּאָב בֵּין בְּיוֹם הַכִּפּוּרִים". [8]בְּמַאי? [9]אִילֵימָא בְּחַמִּין, [10]טְבִילָה בְּחַמִּין מִי אִיכָּא? [11]שְׁאוּבִין! [12]אֶלָּא לָאו

RASHI

אבא — רב אידי, הכי קא קשיא ליה במתניתין, דקאמר: שמע מינה דלא אסר אלא חמין. מכדי קתני מתניתין "אסורין ברחיצה", וסתם רחיצה בין חמין בין צונן — למה לי תו למיהדר ומיתנא "ונועלין"? אלא למימרא דוקא חמין וכו'. **לימא מסייע ליה** — לרב חסדא, דאמר: כל שהוא משום אבל — אסור אפילו בצונן. **כל חייבי טבילות** — נדה ויולדת טובלים כדרכן. **טבילה בחמין מי איכא** — חמי האור, הא שאובין נינהו. **אלא לאו בצונן** — **וחייבי טבילות** — אין, משום דטבילה בזמנה מצוה, שממהר לטהר עצמו.

NOTES

is forbidden on the Ninth of Av and to a mourner, he means that a person may not even wash his face, hands, or feet in cold water. *Talmid HaRamban* argues that, according to Rav Ḥisda, it is only forbidden to bathe the entire body in cold water on the Ninth of Av and during the mourning period, but washing one's face, hands, and feet in cold water is permitted. This dispute has ramifications regarding how to understand the Gemara's objections to Rav Ḥisda's viewpoint below (see next note).

HALAKHAH

decreed in times of drought, on which eating is forbidden from sundown, bathing the entire body in hot water is prohibited. But it is permitted to wash one's face, hands, and feet even in hot water, and it is likewise permitted to wash one's entire body in cold water, following Rav Ḥisda." (*Shulḥan Arukh, Oraḥ Ḥayyim* 575:3.)

כָּל חַיָּבֵי טְבִילוֹת טוֹבְלִין כְּדַרְכָּן All who require ritual immersion immerse themselves in their usual manner. "If the day designated for a person's ritual immersion falls on the Ninth of Av or on Yom Kippur, he is permitted to immerse himself on that day. Today, however, ritual immersion is never practiced on the day designated for immersion by Torah law, and therefore one may not immerse oneself on the Ninth of Av or on Yom Kippur." (Ibid., 554:8.)

טְבִילָה בְּחַמִּין Ritual immersion in hot water. "There are some authorities who forbid pouring hot water into a mikveh in order to heat the water, whereas others maintain

LITERAL TRANSLATION

in cold water [1]and those who require ritual immersion, yes, [2][but] another person, no?

[3]Rav Ḥana bar Ketina said: It is needed because of the hot springs of Tiberias.

[4]If so, read (lit., "say") the last clause: [5]"Rabbi Ḥanina the deputy of the High Priest (lit., 'of the priests') said: The house of our God is worth losing a ritual immersion on its account once in a year." [6]And if you say: In cold water it is permitted, [7]let him bathe in cold water!

[8]Rav Pappa said: [9]It refers] to a place where cold water is not available.

בְּצוֹנֵן, [1]וְחַיָּיבֵי טְבִילוֹת, אִין, [2]אִינִישׁ אַחֲרִינָא, לָא?
[3]אֲמַר רַב חָנָא בַּר קְטִינָא: לֹא נִצְרְכָה אֶלָּא לְחַמֵּי טְבֶרְיָא.
[4]אִי הָכִי, אֵימָא סֵיפָא: [5]״אָמַר רַבִּי חֲנִינָא סְגַן הַכֹּהֲנִים: כְּדַי הוּא בֵּית אֱלֹהֵינוּ לְאַבֵּד עָלָיו טְבִילָה פַּעַם אַחַת בַּשָּׁנָה״. [6]וְאִי אָמְרַתְּ: בְּצוֹנֵן מוּתָּר, [7]יִרְחַץ בְּצוֹנֵן!
[8]אֲמַר רַב פַּפָּא: [9]בְּאַתְרָא דְּלָא שְׁכִיחַ צוֹנֵן.

RASHI

הכי גרסינן: כולי עלמא לא בחמין ולא בצונן. לא נצרכה אלא לחמי טבריא — והלכך: חייבי טבילות — אין, כולי עלמא — לא, אבל בצונן — שרו. **כדי** — ראוי הוא בית אלהינו כו׳. **ואם איתא** — כדמוקמת לה דבצונן שרי, מאי קא מהדר ליה רבי חנינא לתנא קמא מאיבוד טבילה? נהי דלא טבלי בחמין משום כבוד בית אלהינו, הא מצו טבלי בצונן! אלא לאו — בצונן נמי אסירי, והיינו דאמר ״לאבד״. **אמר רב פפא** — לעולם בחמי טבריא, והיינו דקאמרינן חייבי טבילות — אין, כולי עלמא — לא, ובצונן כולי עלמא שרי, ומאי ״לאבד״ דקאמר רבי חנינא, כגון באתרא דלא שכיח צונן.

TRANSLATION AND COMMENTARY

mean that on the Ninth of Av and on Yom Kippur ritually impure people may immerse themselves **in cold water?** [1]**And** is it not the case, therefore, that only **those who require ritual immersion** on the Ninth of Av or on Yom Kippur are **indeed** permitted to immerse themselves in cold water, because it is a meritorious deed to rid oneself of ritual impurity, [2]**but another person,** who is not in need of ritual immersion, may **not** bathe on those days, not even in cold water? Thus the Baraita supports Rav Ḥisda, who ruled that on a day like the Ninth of Av bathing is forbidden even in cold water.

אֲמַר רַב חָנָא בַּר קְטִינָא [3]**Rav Ḥana bar Ketina said:** The Baraita just quoted cannot be used as support for the ruling of Rav Ḥisda, because it is possible that the Baraita's ruling **is applicable only** in a case similar to that of **the hot springs of Tiberias.** Water that is heated naturally does not come into the category of drawn water, and it is therefore suitable for ritual immersion. The Baraita may be understood as saying that those who require ritual immersion may immerse themselves in hot springs even on the Ninth of Av or on Yom Kippur. It follows from this reading of the Baraita that someone who does not require ritual immersion may not bathe in hot water on those days, even if the water was heated naturally. But it is possible that bathing in cold water is permitted to all, even on the Ninth of Av, and this would contradict Rav Ḥisda's ruling.

אִי הָכִי [4]The Gemara raises an objection: **If** this is **so,** and bathing in cold water is permitted even on the Ninth of Av, a difficulty arises with regard to what is **said in the next clause** of the Baraita under discussion: [5]**"Rabbi Ḥanina, the Deputy High Priest, said:** The mourning for the loss of **God's Temple warrants that once a year,** on the Ninth of Av, **ritual immersion is delayed** to commemorate the destruction of the Temple." Thus those whose time for ritual immersion falls on the Ninth of Av must wait another day to complete their purification process. [6]**Now, if you are right in saying** that bathing **in cold water is permitted** on the Ninth of Av, even for those who do not require ritual immersion, what could Rabbi Ḥanina have meant when he said that ritual immersion must be delayed a day in order to commemorate the destruction of the Temple? [7]**Let** those who require ritual immersion **bathe in cold water!** In that way they will be able to purify themselves without infringing the prohibitions imposed to commemorate the Temple's destruction. We must conclude, therefore, that bathing is forbidden on the Ninth of Av even in cold water.

אֲמַר רַב פַּפָּא [8]**Rav Pappa said:** In fact, as was argued above, the Baraita can be understood as referring to immersion in naturally heated water like the hot springs of Tiberias. When Rabbi Ḥanina said that those who require ritual immersion must delay their purification for a day, [9]he was referring to **a place where there** are only hot springs, and **no cold water is available** for ritual immersion. In such a place, the ritually impure must put off immersion for a day in commemoration of the destruction of the Temple. But if cold water *is* available, even Rabbi Ḥanina may agree that ritual immersion is permitted on the Ninth of Av, because bathing in cold water is permitted to all on that day, contrary to the ruling of Rav Ḥisda.

SAGES

רַב חָנָא בַּר קְטִינָא Rav Ḥana bar Ketina. A Babylonian Amora of the third generation His father was an important Amora, Rav Ketina. Rav Ḥana was a disciple of Rav Huna, and is also associated with other important Amoraim of the second and third generations. His Halakhic and Aggadic teachings are mentioned in several places in the Babylonian Talmud.

רַבִּי חֲנִינָא סְגַן הַכֹּהֲנִים Rabbi Ḥanina the deputy of the High Priest. He lived during the period before and after the destruction of the Second Temple and apparently served as deputy to several High Priests. He lived for many years after the destruction of the Temple and many teachings and Halakhot are transmitted in his name, especially matters concerning Temple customs. It seems that the Tanna Rabbi Shimon the son of the Deputy High Priest was Rabbi Ḥanina's son.

BACKGROUND

חַמֵּי טְבֶרְיָא The hot springs of Tiberias. These were baths built around the natural hot springs near the Sea of Galilee, some of which are near the city of Tiberias. These hot springs were known for their curative powers. Since Tiberias is on the Sea of Galilee, it was possible to immerse oneself in its cold water, too; but in other places, such as near the Dead Sea, only hot springs were available.

HALAKHAH

that heating a mikveh is permitted. In Europe, with its severe winters, it was customary to rule leniently on this matter — in particular if hot water was not poured into the mikveh, but the mikveh water itself was heated." (*Shulḥan Arukh, Yoreh De'ah* 201:75.)

BACKGROUND

מְנוּדֶּה **A person under a ban.** Excommunication is a coercive measure employed by the community or the court against people who refuse to obey orders and carry out various responsibilities. There used to be three stages of excommunication: נִידּוּי (ostracism); שַׁמְתָּא (excommunication); and חֵרֶם (ban). נִידּוּי was the first and most lenient stage. It was forbidden to come closer than four cubits to the ostracized person, and he himself followed some of the customs of mourning — he did not cut his hair, wash in hot water, or wear leather shoes. The other stages increased the severity with which the community shunned the transgressor, thereby exerting greater social and economic pressure.

TRANSLATION AND COMMENTARY

תָּא שְׁמַע [1]The Gemara now seeks to disprove the second part of Rav Ḥisda's ruling — that bathing in cold water is permitted on a communal fast. **Come and hear** the following Baraita, which throws light on this point: **"When** the Sages **said that work is forbidden** on a communal fast, **they meant that** work is forbidden **only during the day** of the fast, **but during the night** of the fast **it is permitted.** [2]**And when** the Sages **said that wearing** leather **shoes is forbidden** on a communal fast, **they meant only** that a person may not wear shoes while he is walking about **in town, but** if he sets out to travel **on the road,** wearing shoes **is permitted.** [3]**How** does a traveler act on a communal fast? [4]**When he sets out on the road, he may put on his shoes.** [5]But as soon as **he enters a town** once again, **he must take off** his shoes and continue barefoot. [6]**And when** the Sages **said that bathing is forbidden** on a communal fast, **they meant only** that a person may not wash **his entire body, but washing his face, his hands, and his feet** alone **is permitted.** [7]**And you apply** this rule **similarly with respect to a person** who was placed **under a ban and** with respect to **a mourner,** both of whom are forbidden to bathe, to anoint themselves and to wear leather shoes." This Baraita is difficult to reconcile with the ruling of Rav Ḥisda, for when it compares the law that applies to a mourner with the law that applies on a communal fast, [8]**is it not with regard to all of** the regulations mentioned here, including the prohibition against bathing? Thus a mourner is permitted to wash his face, hands, and feet. [9]**And with what** issue **are we dealing** here? [10]**If we say** that the Baraita is dealing with washing **with hot water, is** a mourner **permitted** to wash **his face, hands, and feet** with hot water? [11]**Surely Rav Sheshet said: A mourner is** absolutely **forbidden** even **to put his finger into hot water!** [12]**Rather,** we are forced to conclude that the Baraita **must be** dealing with washing **with cold water.** Thus the Baraita teaches us that a mourner may not bathe his entire body even in cold water, but may indeed wash his face, hands, and feet with cold water. And since the Baraita compares the law applying to a mourner with the law applying on a communal fast, it follows that on a communal fast washing one's face, hands, and feet with cold water is permitted, but bathing one's entire body is forbidden even in cold water, and this contradicts the ruling of Rav Ḥisda!

[1]תָּא שְׁמַע: ״כְּשֶׁאָמְרוּ אָסוּר בִּמְלָאכָה, לֹא אָמְרוּ אֶלָּא בַּיּוֹם, אֲבָל בַּלַּיְלָה מוּתָּר. [2]וּכְשֶׁאָמְרוּ אָסוּר בִּנְעִילַת הַסַּנְדָּל, לֹא אָמְרוּ אֶלָּא בָּעִיר, אֲבָל בַּדֶּרֶךְ מוּתָּר. [3]הָא כֵּיצַד? [4]יוֹצֵא לַדֶּרֶךְ, נוֹעֵל; [5]נִכְנָס לָעִיר, חוֹלֵץ. [6]וּכְשֶׁאָמְרוּ אָסוּר בִּרְחִיצָה, לֹא אָמְרוּ אֶלָּא כָּל גּוּפוֹ, אֲבָל פָּנָיו, יָדָיו, וְרַגְלָיו מוּתָּר. [7]וְכֵן אַתָּה מוֹצֵא בִּמְנוּדֶּה וּבְאָבֵל״. [8]מַאי לָאו אַכּוּלְּהוּ? [9]וּבְמַאי עָסְקִינַן? [10]אִילֵימָא בְּחַמִּין, פָּנָיו, יָדָיו, וְרַגְלָיו מִי שָׁרוּ? [11]וְהָאָמַר רַב שֵׁשֶׁת: אָבֵל אָסוּר לְהוֹשִׁיט אֶצְבָּעוֹ בְּחַמִּין. [12]אֶלָּא לָאו בְּצוֹנֵן?

LITERAL TRANSLATION

[1]Come [and] hear: "When they said that work is forbidden, they only said during the day, but at night it is permitted. [2]And when they said [that] wearing shoes is forbidden, they only said in town, but on the road it is permitted. [3]How so? [4][When] he goes out on the road, he puts on shoes; [5][when] he enters the town, he takes [them] off. [6]And when they said [that] bathing is forbidden, they only said his entire body, but [to wash] his face, his hands, and his feet is permitted. [7]And similarly you find concerning a person under a ban and concerning a mourner." [8]Is it not with regard to all of them? [9]And with what are we dealing? [10]If we say with hot water, are his face, his hands, and his feet permitted? [11]But surely Rav Sheshet said: A mourner is forbidden to put his finger into hot water. [12]Rather, is it not with cold water?

RASHI

כשאמרו אסור [במלאכה] — גבי תענית צבור לא אמרו אלא ביום, אבל בלילה — מותר. מהכא משמע דלילי תשעה באב מותר במלאכה ואין ביטול אלא ביום, אבל אין מפרסמין הדבר. **יצא לדרך** — חוץ לעיר. **וכן אתה מוצא במנודה ואבל** — הכי גרסינן: במאי? אילימא בחמין — מי שרי, והאמר רב ששת: אבל אסור להושיט אצבעו בחמין, אלא לאו — בצונן. **מאי לאו אכולהו כו׳ הא דקתני וכן אתה מוצא במנודה ואָבֵל** — אכל הני קאי, ואפילו ארחיצה. ושמע מינה דבתענית צבור אסור לרחוץ כל גופו, ואפילו בצונן, ותיובתא לרפרם בר פפא.

NOTES

מַאי לָאו אַכּוּלְּהוּ **Is it not with regard to all of them.** The Rishonim disagree about how to understand the objection raised here. *Rabbenu Gershom, Tosafot, Ritva,* and others explain that the Gemara is citing this Baraita as an objection to Rav Ḥisda's first ruling — that bathing is forbidden on the Ninth of Av and to a mourner, both in hot water and in cold water. For the Baraita states that a mourner is governed by the same laws that apply on a public fast, when bathing the entire body is forbidden, but washing one's face, hands or feet is permitted. But the

TRANSLATION AND COMMENTARY

לָא [1]The Gemara rejects this argument and says: **No,** this Baraita does not contradict the ruling of Rav Ḥisda. **In fact, it is** discussing bathing **in hot water.** On a communal fast, bathing the entire body in hot water is forbidden, but washing the face, hands, and feet with such water is permitted. But one is permitted to bathe even the entire body in cold water, as argued by Rav Ḥisda. [2]**And that** clause of the Baraita which **you** thought presented **a difficulty** according to Rav Ḥisda, **"And similarly you find with respect to a person** who was placed **under a ban and** with respect to **a mourner,"** is not problematic. The comparison between a communal fast and private mourning does not apply to the prohibition against bathing, and therefore it does not prove that the Baraita must be discussing the question of washing in cold water. [3]The comparison in fact **refers to the rest** of the prohibitions common to a communal fast and to a mourner, such as the prohibition against anointing oneself with oil or wearing leather shoes.

תָּא שְׁמַע [4]The Gemara continues by citing an Amoraic ruling that at first glance seems to contradict the position of Rav Ḥisda. **Come and hear** the following statement: **Rabbi Abba the Priest said in the name of Rabbi Yose the Priest:** [5]**It once happened that the sons of Rabbi Yose the son of Rabbi Ḥanina died, and he bathed in cold water throughout the seven-day period of mourning."** Thus we see that a mourner is permitted to bathe in cold water, and this contradicts the ruling of Rav Ḥisda.

הָתָם [6]The Gemara now reconciles this ruling with the viewpoint of Rav Ḥisda. Ordinarily, a mourner is forbidden to bathe even in cold water, as was argued by Rav Ḥisda. But **there**, in the case of Rabbi Yose the son of Rabbi Ḥanina, there were special circumstances that allowed him to bathe in cold water, even though he was in mourning. Rabbi Yose the son of Rabbi Ḥanina was observing two **periods of mourning, the one immediately following the other.** His two sons died within a short time of each other, so that as soon as he completed the mourning period for the one son, he had to observe another period of mourning for the other. In such a case, there is room for certain leniencies that do not apply in ordinary cases, [7]**as it was taught** in a Baraita: "If someone is observing two **periods of mourning** on account of the death of

[1]לָא. לְעוֹלָם בְּחַמִּין. [2]וּדְקָא קַשְׁיָא לָךְ, ״וְכֵן אַתָּה מוֹצֵא בִּמְנוּדֶּה וּבְאָבֵל״, [3]אַשְּׁאָרָא קָאֵי.

[4]תָּא שְׁמַע, דְּאָמַר רַבִּי אַבָּא הַכֹּהֵן מִשּׁוּם רַבִּי יוֹסֵי הַכֹּהֵן: [5]מַעֲשֶׂה וּמֵתוּ בָּנָיו שֶׁל רַבִּי יוֹסֵי בֶּן רַבִּי חֲנִינָא, וְרָחַץ בְּצוֹנֵן כָּל שִׁבְעָה!

[6]הָתָם כְּשֶׁתְּכָפוּהוּ אֲבָלָיו הֲוָה. [7]דְּתַנְיָא: ״תְּכָפוּהוּ אֲבָלָיו בָּזֶה

LITERAL TRANSLATION

[1]No. In fact [it is] with hot water. [2]And as to your difficulty, "And similarly, you find concerning a person under a ban and concerning a mourner," [3][this] refers to the rest [of the laws].

[4]Come [and] hear; for Rabbi Abba the Priest said in the name of Rabbi Yose the Priest: [5]It once happened that the sons of Rabbi Yose the son of Rabbi Ḥanina died, and he bathed in cold water all seven [days of mourning]!"

[6]There it was his mourning periods immediately succeeded [each other]. [7]For it was taught: "[If] his mourning periods immediately succeeded each

RASHI

אשארא קאי — אנעילה וסיכה, לעולם הך רחיצה — בחמין היא, אבל בצונן — שרי לרחוץ כל גופו. והשתא דאמרת במנודה ואבל, לאו ארחיצה קיימי — ליכא לאקשויי כדפרכת לעיל: אי לימא בחמין מי שרי. **ורחץ בצונן בתוך שבעה** — גרסינן, אלמא: בצונן שרי. **שתכפוהו אבליו** — בזה אחר זה, כדקתני: שמתו בניו, שניהם, ולפיכך התירו לו, כדאשכחן גבי שיער.

SAGES

רַבִּי אַבָּא הַכֹּהֵן Rabbi Abba the Priest. A Palestinian Amora of the fourth generation, he is mentioned a few times in the Talmud as the disciple of Rabbi Yose the Priest.

רַבִּי יוֹסֵי הַכֹּהֵן Rabbi Yose the Priest. A Palestinian Amora of the third generation, he was apparently one of the youngest of Rabbi Yoḥanan's disciples; he also studied Torah under other Palestinian Amoraim who were Rabbi Yoḥanan's colleagues and students. There was an earlier Rabbi Yose the Priest, one of the first Tannaim.

רַבִּי יוֹסֵי בֶּן רַבִּי חֲנִינָא Rabbi Yose the son of Rabbi Ḥanina. A Palestinian Amora of the second generation, Rabbi Yose bar Ḥanina was a younger contemporary of Rabbi Yoḥanan and one of his first students. Rabbi Yoḥanan ordained him, and he grew in knowledge of Torah until he came to be regarded as Rabbi Yoḥanan's colleague. Many differences of opinion between the two are recorded (see *Bava Kamma* 39a). Rabbi Yose was also closely associated with Resh Lakish and Rabbi Elazar. Some of Rabbi Yoḥanan's pupils also studied with him. Many of them, especially Rabbi Abbahu and Rabbi Ḥama bar Ukva, transmitted teachings in his name. He is known to have had sons who died during his lifetime.

NOTES

Rishonim disagree as to why the Baraita contradicts Rav Ḥisda's ruling. Some argue that it is because the term used in the Baraita, רְחִיצָה, denotes bathing in hot water, thereby implying that a mourner is permitted to bathe in cold water (*Rabbenu Gershom*). But it could also be because the Baraita states that washing one's face, hands and feet is permitted, whereas Rav Ḥisda maintains that this, too, is forbidden (*Ritva*; see previous note).

Contrary to the foregoing opinions, our commentary follows *Rashi*, *Shittah*, and *Rabbi Akiva Eger*, who explain that the Baraita is cited to disprove Rav Ḥisda's second ruling — that on communal fasts bathing is forbidden only in hot water, but is permitted in cold water. This difference in interpretation depends in part on variant readings of our passage, as well as on the different understandings of the position of Rav Ḥisda.

HALAKHAH

כְּשֶׁתְּכָפוּהוּ אֲבָלָיו Where his mourning periods immediately succeeded each other. "If someone is observing two periods of mourning, the one immediately succeeding the other, he is permitted to bathe his entire body in cold water, as did Rabbi Yose the son of Rabbi Ḥanina." (*Shulḥan Arukh, Yoreh De'ah* 381:4.)

LITERAL TRANSLATION

other, [1] [and] his hair became heavy, [2] he may lighten [it] with a razor, and he may wash his garment in water."

[3] Rav Ḥisda said: "With a razor," but not with scissors. [4] "In water," but not with natron and not with sand.

[5] Rava said: A mourner is permitted to bathe in cold water all seven [days of mourning], [6] as it is with meat and wine.

[7] They raised an objection: [13B] [8] "A *bogeret* is not permitted to make herself unattractive during the days of

אַחַר זֶה, [1] הִכְבִּיד שְׂעָרוֹ, [2] מֵיקֵל בְּתַעַר, וּמְכַבֵּס כְּסוּתוֹ בְּמַיִם״.
[3] אָמַר רַב חִסְדָּא: ״בְּתַעַר״, אֲבָל לֹא בְּמִסְפָּרַיִם. [4] ״בְּמַיִם״, וְלֹא בְּנֶתֶר וְלֹא בְּחוֹל.
[5] אָמַר רָבָא: אָבֵל מוּתָּר לִרְחוֹץ בְּצוֹנֵן כָּל שִׁבְעָה, [6] מִידֵי דַּהֲוָה אַבִּשְׂרָא וְחַמְרָא.
[7] מֵיתִיבִי: [13B] [8] ״אֵין הַבּוֹגֶרֶת רַשָּׁאָה לְנַוֵּול אֶת עַצְמָהּ בִּימֵי

TRANSLATION AND COMMENTARY

two close relatives, **the one** mourning period **immediately following the other,** [1] **and** because of the extended period during which he is in mourning **his hair grows too long,** [2] **he may thin it out with a razor, and he may wash his** soiled **clothes in water."** Just as the Rabbis were lenient with respect to the prohibitions against cutting hair or doing laundry, they were likewise lenient with respect to the prohibition against bathing and allowed the mourner to wash his entire body in cold water.

אָמַר רַב חִסְדָּא [3] The Gemara now adds a note of clarification to the Baraita that has just been cited. **Rav Ḥisda said:** A person who is observing two successive periods of mourning may thin out his hair in an unusual manner **"with a razor,"** as the Baraita said, **but** he may **not** cut his hair in the ordinary way **with** a pair of **scissors.** [4] Such a person may do his laundry **"with water,"** as the Baraita said, **but** he may **not** use **soap or sand** or any other cleaning agent.

אָמַר רָבָא [5] **Rava** disagreed with Rav Ḥisda and **said: A mourner is permitted to bathe in cold water throughout the seven-day period of mourning,** although he derives a certain degree of enjoyment from the cold bath, [6] just **as** he is permitted to eat **meat and wine,** even though he derives a certain measure of enjoyment from them.

מֵיתִיבִי [7] **An objection was raised** against the viewpoint of Rava from a Baraita, in which it was taught: [13B] [8] **"A *bogeret*** [a girl over the age of twelve-and-a-half] **is not** required or even **permitted to make herself unattractive during the mourning period** that she must observe upon the death **of her**

RASHI

מיקל בתער — דשקיל פורתא מינייהו. **ובתער** — דרך שינוי. **נתר** — קרקע הוא, או אבן, כעין שקורין *קרי״א בלעז. **בנתר וחול** — דרך לכבס שיתלבן. **מידי דהוה אבשרא וחמרא** — דתענוג הן כלון. **אין הבוגרת** — שהביאה שתי שערות, רשאה לנוול את עצמה, אלא מתקשטת כדי שיקפצו עליה. הא נערה, שאינה ראויה להינשא עדיין עד שתבגר — רשאה, דבת חיוב אבילות היא. וקטנה אינה חייבת ולא כלום. **בימי אבל אביה** — אפילו אירע אבילות לאביה, שמת בנו. אי נמי: שמת אביה ממש, אף על פי שהיא בת חיוב אבילות — אינה רשאה לנוול.

BACKGROUND

נֶתֶר Natron. The word נֶתֶר apparently means sodium carbonate (Na_2CO_3). It is found in nature in desert areas in colorless crystals containing large amounts of crystallized water. In ancient times נֶתֶר was obtained from the remains of seaweed. It dissolves easily in water, and the solution gives a strongly alkaline reaction. For this reason it is effective in dissolving many types of oil and grease, and has served as a cleaning agent since Biblical times.

LANGUAGE (RASHI)

קרי״א* From the Old French *craie,* which means "chalk" or "limestone."

CONCEPTS

בּוֹגֶרֶת A *bogeret*. When a girl reaches puberty, generally at the age of twelve, she is legally considered a *na'arah*, to distinguish her from a קְטַנָּה — "a minor." After a further six months, she is legally considered a *bogeret*. From this time onward she is considered an independent adult, and her father no longer has the authority to make decisions on her behalf.

NOTES

מִידֵי דַּהֲוָה אַבִּשְׂרָא וְחַמְרָא As it is with meat and wine. During the period of acute mourning known as *aninut* (אֲנִינוּת), from the time of the death of a close relative until after the funeral, a mourner is forbidden to eat meat or drink wine. But during the period of mourning known as *avelut* (אֲבֵילוּת) following the funeral, meat and wine are permitted to the mourner. Likewise, argues Rava, bathing in cold water is permitted during the seven-day period of mourning following burial, even though it is forbidden during the period of acute mourning preceding burial (*Rabbenu Elyakim*).

אֵין הַבּוֹגֶרֶת רַשָּׁאָה A *bogeret* is not permitted. *Tosafot* explains that the term רַשָּׁאָה, which usually means "permitted," is used here in the sense of "obligated." Thus the Baraita is informing us that a *bogeret* is not required to make herself unattractive when she is in mourning, and from this it follows that a *na'arah* is indeed required to make herself unattractive. *Gevurat Ari* cites other examples in the Talmud where the word רַשַּׁאי is used to mean "obligated" rather than "permitted."

Meiri and others maintain that here, too, the word is used in the sense of "permitted." A *bogeret* is not permitted to make herself unattractive when she is in mourning, lest she repel potential suitors; and if she makes herself unattractive, she must be admonished.

HALAKHAH

הִכְבִּיד שְׂעָרוֹ, מֵיקֵל בְּתַעַר If his hair became heavy, he may lighten it with a razor. "If someone is observing two periods of mourning, one immediately after the other, and his hair grows long, he may thin it out with a razor, but not with scissors (and only in private; *Rema*)." (*Shulḥan Arukh, Yoreh De'ah* 390:3.)

וּמְכַבֵּס כְּסוּתוֹ בְּמַיִם And he may wash his garment in water. "If someone is observing two periods of mourning, the one immediately following the other, he may unobtrusively wash his clothes in water, but he may not use any soap or sand, following Rav Ḥisda." (Ibid., 389:1.)

אֵין הַבּוֹגֶרֶת רַשָּׁאָה A *bogeret* is not permitted. "A *bogeret* is permitted to use mascara and to dye her hair when she is in mourning (even during the first seven days of her mourning; *Arukh HaShulḥan*). But a *na'arah* is forbidden to use mascara or to dye her hair while she is in mourning. (Ibid., 381:6.)

TRANSLATION AND COMMENTARY

father." Since she has already reached the age that qualifies her as being fit for marriage, she must maintain an attractive appearance, so as not to deter potential suitors. It may be inferred from this Baraita that this applies only to a *bogeret*, [1]**but a *na'arah*** (a girl aged between twelve and twelve-and-a-half), who is required to observe the laws of mourning but is not yet ready for marriage, **would be permitted** and even required to observe the mourning customs. Now, when the Baraita states that a *bogeret* may not make herself unattractive, [2]**is it not** saying that she must not refrain from **bathing?** [3]**And in what** water? [4]**If we say** that the Baraita is dealing with the issue of bathing **in hot water, is** a *bogeret* really **not permitted** to make herself unattractive by refraining from bathing in hot water? [5]**But surely Rav Ḥisda said: A mourner is** absolutely **forbidden to** wash in hot water, so that he may not even **put his finger into hot water!** This being the case, a *bogeret* in mourning should certainly not be allowed to bathe her entire body in hot water. [6]**Rather,** the Baraita **must be** dealing with bathing **in cold water.** Thus it follows that a *na'arah* is obligated to refrain from bathing even in cold water, and this contradicts Rava's ruling!

אֲבֶל אָבִיהָ״. [1]הָא נַעֲרָה רַשָּׁאָה. [2]מַאי לָאו בִּרְחִיצָה? [3]וּבְמַאי? [4]אִילֵימָא בְּחַמִּין, אֵין הַבּוֹגֶרֶת רַשָּׁאָה? [5]וְהָאָמַר רַב חִסְדָּא: אָבֵל אָסוּר לְהוֹשִׁיט אֶצְבָּעוֹ בְּחַמִּין! [6]אֶלָּא לָאו בְּצוֹנֵן? [7]לָא. אַכִּיחוּל וּפִירְכּוּס. [8]לֵימָא מְסַיֵּיע לֵיהּ: [9]דְּאָמַר רַבִּי אַבָּא הַכֹּהֵן מִשּׁוּם רַבִּי יוֹסֵי הַכֹּהֵן: מַעֲשֶׂה וּמֵתוּ בָּנָיו שֶׁל רַבִּי יוֹסֵי בַּר חֲנִינָא, [10]וְרָחַץ בְּצוֹנֵן כָּל שִׁבְעָה! [11]אָמְרִי: הָתָם בְּשֶׁתְּכָפוּהוּ אֲבָלָיו זֶה אַחַר זֶה. [12]דְּתַנְיָא: ״תְּכָפוּהוּ אֲבָלָיו בָּזֶה אַחַר זֶה, הִכְבִּיד שְׂעָרוֹ, [13]מֵיקֵל בְּתַעַר, וּמְכַבֵּס כְּסוּתוֹ בְּמַיִם״.

LITERAL TRANSLATION

mourning of her father." [1]But a *na'arah* is permitted. [2]Is it not with respect to bathing? [3]And in what? [4]If we say in hot water, is a *bogeret* not permitted? [5]But surely Rav Ḥisda said: A mourner is forbidden to put his finger into hot water! [6]Rather, is it not in cold water?

[7]No. [It refers] to painting [the eyes] and dyeing [the hair].

[8]Shall we say [that this] supports him: [9]For Rabbi Abba the Priest said in the name of Rabbi Yose the Priest: It once happened that the sons of Rabbi Yose bar Ḥanina died, [10]and he bathed in cold water all seven [days of mourning]!

[11]They say: There [it was] where his mourning periods immediately succeeded each other. [12]For it was taught: "[If] his mourning periods immediately succeeded each other, [and] his hair became heavy, [13]he may lighten [it] with a razor, and he may wash his garment in water."

RASHI

אלא לאו בצונן — ואפילו הכי נערה אינה רוחצת בצונן, אלמא: דאבל אף בצונן אסור. **אביחול ואפירכוס** — ולא קא איירי ברחיצה כלל. פירכוס — בשיער, כבוס — בבגדים, רחיצה — בגוף.

לָא [7]The Gemara replies: **No,** when the Baraita states that a *bogeret* may not make herself unattractive when she is in mourning, bathing is not the matter under discussion. The Baraita **is referring to** the issue of whether or not she may **paint her eyes** with mascara **and dye her hair.** A *bogeret* may use makeup, whereas a *na'arah* may not do so. And neither is required to refrain from bathing in cold water, for bathing in cold water is permitted to a mourner, in accordance with Rava's ruling.

לֵימָא מְסַיֵּיע לֵיהּ [8]The Gemara now tries to adduce support for the viewpoint of Rava from the statement it cited earlier to seek to disprove the viewpoint of Rav Ḥisda. **Shall we say that** the following Amoraic statement **supports** Rava: **Rabbi Abba the Priest said in the name of Rabbi Yose the Priest: [9]It once happened that the sons of Rabbi Yose bar Ḥanina died, [10]and he bathed in cold water throughout the seven-day period of mourning.** This ruling indicates that a mourner is permitted to bathe in cold water, and offers support for Rava's ruling.

אָמְרִי [11]The Gemara now **says** that this statement cannot be brought as support for the position of Rava because **there,** in the case of Rabbi Yose the son of Rabbi Ḥanina, there were special circumstances. Rabbi Yose the son of Rabbi Ḥanina was observing two **periods of mourning, the one immediately following the other,** and in such cases certain leniencies are allowed, [12]**as it was taught** in a Baraita: "If someone is observing two **periods of mourning** on account of the death of two close relatives, **the one** mourning period **immediately following the other, and** because of the extended period during which he is in mourning **his hair grows long, [13]he may thin it out with a razor, and he may wash his** soiled **clothes in water."** Just as the Rabbis allowed a person observing two successive periods of mourning to cut his hair and do his laundry, they likewise allowed such a person to bathe in cold water. In ordinary circumstances, however, a mourner may be forbidden to bathe even in cold water, and this contradicts Rava's ruling.

CONCEPTS

נַעֲרָה **A *na'arah*.** A young woman between twelve and twelve-and-a-half years old, who has reached puberty (as evidenced by her having grown at least two pubic hairs), but not full Halakhic maturity. During this period, special laws apply to her. She is no longer considered a minor, nor is she yet an adult. Accordingly, her father retains certain authority over her.

BACKGROUND

כִּיחוּל **Painting the eyes.** The cosmetic used as eye makeup was apparently a blue-black substance made in antiquity from antimony trisulfide (Sb_2S_3). The crystals were ground and women would paint the substance around their eyes to make them stand out and look larger.

LANGUAGE

פִּרְכּוּס **Dyeing the hair.** The origin of this word is uncertain. Some scholars are of the opinion that it comes from the Greek root περκάζω, *perkazo,* meaning to darken, in the sense of "to darken hair."

[1] אֲמַר רַב חִסְדָּא: ״בְּתַעַר״, [2] אֲבָל לֹא בְּמִסְפָּרַיִם. [3] ״בְּמַיִם״, וְלֹא בְּנֶתֶר וְלֹא בְּחוֹל וְלֹא בְּאָהָל.

[4] אִיכָּא דְּאָמְרִי אָמַר רָבָא: [5] אָבֵל אָסוּר בְּצוֹנֵן כָּל שִׁבְעָה.

[6] מַאי שְׁנָא מִבָּשָׂר וְיַיִן?

[7] הָתָם לְפַכּוּחֵי פַּחְדֵּיהּ הוּא דְּעָבֵיד.

[8] לֵימָא מְסַיַּיע לֵיהּ: ״אֵין הַבּוֹגֶרֶת רַשָּׁאָה לְנַוּוֹל עַצְמָהּ״. [9] הָא נַעֲרָה רַשָּׁאָה. [10] בְּמַאי? אִילֵימָא בְּחַמִּין, אֵין הַבּוֹגֶרֶת רַשָּׁאָה? [11] וְהָאָמַר רַב חִסְדָּא: אָבֵל אָסוּר לְהוֹשִׁיט אֶצְבָּעוֹ בְּחַמִּין! [12] אֶלָּא לָאו בְּצוֹנֵן?

LITERAL TRANSLATION

[1] Rav Hisda said: "With a razor," [2] but not with scissors. [3] "In water," but not with natron and not with sand and not with aloe.

[4] There are [some] who say [that] Rava said: [5] A mourner is forbidden [to bathe] in cold water all seven [days of mourning].

[6] How is it different from meat and wine?

[7] There he does [it] to relieve his fear.

[8] Shall we say [that this] supports him: "A *bogeret* is not permitted to make herself unattractive." [9] But a *na'arah* is permitted. [10] In what? If we say in hot water, is a *bogeret* not permitted? [11] But surely Rav Ḥisda said: A mourner is forbidden to put his finger into hot water! [12] Rather, is it not in cold water?

TRANSLATION AND COMMENTARY

אֲמַר רַב חִסְדָּא [1] Having cited the Baraita dealing with a person who is observing two successive periods of mourning, the Gemara adds a note that the Baraita's formulation is precise. **Rav Ḥisda said:** A person observing two successive mourning periods may thin out his hair in an unusual manner **"with a razor,"** as the Baraita said, [2] **but** he may **not** cut his hair in the ordinary way **with** a pair of **scissors.** [3] Such a person may do his laundry **"with water,"** as the Baraita said, **but** he may **not** use **soap or sand or aloe** or any other cleaning agent.

אִיכָּא דְּאָמְרִי [4] All that has been said until now regarding Rava's viewpoint is based on the assumption that according to Rava a mourner is permitted to bathe in cold water. The Gemara now cites a different version of Rava's ruling: **There are some who say that Rava said** as follows: [5] **A mourner is forbidden to bathe in cold water during the entire seven-day period of mourning.**

מַאי שְׁנָא [6] The Gemara asks: According to this version of Rava's ruling, **why is** bathing in cold water **different from** eating **meat and** drinking **wine,** in that the first is forbidden whereas the second two are permitted? The degree of pleasure derived from a cold bath is no greater than that derived from eating meat and drinking wine, and if the latter two are permitted to a mourner, the former should be permitted to him as well!

הָתָם [7] The Gemara answers: **There** the mourner eats meat and drinks wine **in order to allay his fear** of death. A person who loses a close relative is often stricken with the fear that his own day of reckoning may be close at hand. Consequently, the Rabbis allowed a mourner to eat meat and drink wine, and thereby maintain his physical strength so as to overcome that fear. But as for bathing for pleasure, there was no reason for the Rabbis to permit the mourner to bathe even in cold water.

לֵימָא מְסַיַּיע לֵיהּ [8] The Gemara now attempts to support the second version of Rava's statement by means of the Baraita cited earlier to disprove the first version of that statement. **Shall we say that** the following Baraita **supports** the second version of Rava's statement: **"A *bogeret*** [a girl over the age of twelve-and-a-half] **is not** required or even **permitted to make herself unattractive** during the mourning period that she must observe upon the death of her father." [9] We may infer from this Baraita that **nevertheless *a na'arah*** (a girl aged between twelve and twelve-and-a-half) **is** indeed **permitted,** and even required, to observe all the mourning customs. And it stands to reason that when the Baraita says that a *bogeret* may not make herself unattractive, even when she is in mourning, it means that she must not refrain from bathing. [10] **In what** water? **If we say** that the Baraita is dealing with bathing **in hot water, is a** *bogeret* really **not permitted** to make herself unattractive by refraining from bathing in hot water? [11] **But surely Rav Ḥisda said: A mourner is** absolutely **forbidden to** wash in hot water, so that he may not even **put his finger into hot water!** If, in general, a mourner may not even put his finger into hot water, then surely a *bogeret* who is in mourning should not be allowed to bathe her entire body in hot water, even to avoid deterring a potential suitor. [12] **Rather,** the Baraita **must be** dealing with bathing **in cold water.** A *bogeret* is

BACKGROUND

לְפַכּוּחֵי פַּחְדֵּיהּ **To relieve his fear.** When one is mourning for a close relative and is aware of the frightening proximity of death, one is naturally filled with anxiety and feelings of guilt. The result is likely to be an extended period of severe depression. Therefore the Sages permitted the mourner to eat meat and drink wine, for they have a high calorific value and act quickly on the body, thus improving one's mood.

HALAKHAH

מַאי שְׁנָא מִבָּשָׂר וְיַיִן **How is it different from meat and wine.** "After the deceased is buried, the mourner is permitted to eat meat and to drink a small amount of wine during his meal, but he should not drink heavily." (*Shulḥan Arukh, Yoreh De'ah* 378:8.)

TRANSLATION AND COMMENTARY

is permitted to bathe in cold water while she is mourning, but a *na'arah* may not. Thus the Baraita appears to support the second version of Rava's statement, according to which a mourner is forbidden to bathe even in cold water.

לָא [1]The Gemara replies: **No,** the Baraita does not support the second version of Rava's ruling, because it is not talking about bathing at all. [2]**It is referring to** the issue of whether or not the girl may **paint her eyes** with mascara **and dye her hair.** A *bogeret* may use mascara and dye her hair while in mourning, but a *na'arah* may not. But neither is required to refrain from bathing in cold water, and this contradicts the second version of Rava's ruling.

אָמַר רַב חִסְדָּא [3]Referring back to the Baraita dealing with a person who is observing two successive periods of mourning, **Rav Ḥisda said:** From this Baraita, which rules that a person observing two successive periods of mourning may launder his soiled clothing in water, **it follows** [4]**that** in general **a mourner is forbidden to do** his **laundry during the entire seven-day period of mourning.**

וְהִלְכְתָא [5]The Gemara now concludes this discussion by giving decisions about the issues that were left unresolved. **The Halakhah is: A mourner is forbidden to bathe his entire body either in hot water or in cold water during the entire seven-day period of mourning.** [6]**But** as for **his face, his hands, and his feet, washing them in hot water is forbidden, but** washing them **in cold water is permitted.** [7]**Even the smallest amount of anointing is** strictly **forbidden** to a mourner, when it is done for pleasure. [8]**But if** the mourner applies oil to his skin **in order to remove filth** from his body, **it is permitted.**

צְלוֹתָא דְּתַעֲנִיתָא [9]The Gemara now takes up an entirely different topic. It was mentioned earlier (above, 11b) that a special prayer, beginning with the word *anenu* (עֲנֵנוּ — "answer us"), is inserted into the Amidah prayer on fast days. The Gemara asks: When a person observing an individual fast adds **the fast-day** prayer of *anenu* into his prayers, **where** precisely **does he insert it?**

[1]לָא. [2]אַכְּיחוּל וּפִירְכּוּס.

[3]אָמַר רַב חִסְדָּא: זֹאת אוֹמֶרֶת: [4]אָבֵל אָסוּר בְּתִכְבּוֹסֶת כָּל שִׁבְעָה.

[5]וְהִלְכְתָא: אָבֵל אָסוּר לִרְחוֹץ כָּל גּוּפוֹ בֵּין בְּחַמִּין וּבֵין בְּצוֹנֵן כָּל שִׁבְעָה. [6]אֲבָל פָּנָיו, יָדָיו, וְרַגְלָיו בְּחַמִּין אָסוּר, בְּצוֹנֵן מוּתָּר. [7]אֲבָל לָסוּךְ, אֲפִילּוּ כָּל שֶׁהוּא אָסוּר. [8]וְאִם לְעַבֵּר אֶת הַזּוּהֲמָא, מוּתָּר.

[9]צְלוֹתָא דְּתַעֲנִיתָא הֵיכִי מַדְכְּרִינַן?

LITERAL TRANSLATION

[1]No. [2][It refers] to painting [the eyes] and dyeing [the hair].

[3]Rav Ḥisda said: This teaches: [4]A mourner is forbidden [to do] laundry all seven [days of mourning].

[5]And the Halakhah is: A mourner is forbidden to bathe his entire body both in hot water and in cold water all seven [days of mourning]. [6]But [to wash] his face, his hands, and his feet in hot water is forbidden, [but] in cold water it is permitted. [7]But to anoint, even the slightest amount is forbidden. [8]But if [it is] to remove the filth, it is permitted.

[9]How do we mention the fast-day prayer?

RASHI

זאת אומרת — מדמוקמינן לה בכיחול ופירכוס, הוא הדין לתכבוסת. **תפלת תענית** — "עננו".

BACKGROUND

לְעַבֵּר אֶת הַזּוּהֲמָא To remove the filth. For many generations it was common to remove dirt from the body by anointing it with oil, sometimes with the addition of certain types of soap. A mourner is permitted to anoint himself with materials that remove dirt.

NOTES

זֹאת אוֹמֶרֶת: אָבֵל אָסוּר בְּתִכְבּוֹסֶת כָּל שִׁבְעָה This means: A mourner is forbidden to do laundry all seven days of mourning. *Rashi* connects Rav Ḥisda's statement that "this" teaches us that a mourner is forbidden to do his laundry during the entire seven-day period of mourning with what was said immediately previously regarding the use of mascara and hair dye by a girl in mourning. (See *Gilyon HaShas*, who points out several difficulties with this explanation.)

Other commentators connect Rav Ḥisda's statement with the Baraita cited earlier regarding a person who is observing two periods of mourning, the one mourning period immediately following the other. Since the Baraita allows such a person to launder his soiled clothing in water, it follows that under ordinary circumstances a mourner is forbidden to do his laundry. Some transpose Rav Ḥisda's statement so that it comes immediately after that Baraita. Others argue that it is common for the Gemara to conclude its discussion regarding a particular topic, and then return to one of the sources cited in the course of that discussion and draw from that source inferences which are not directly related to the discussion (see *Divrei Shlomo*, *Rabbi Akiva Eger*, and *Rashash*).

HALAKHAH

אָבֵל אָסוּר בְּתִכְבּוֹסֶת A mourner is forbidden to do laundry. "During the seven-day period of mourning, a mourner is forbidden to do his laundry (both during the day and at night; *Rema*)," following Rav Ḥisda. (*Shulḥan Arukh, Yoreh De'ah* 380:1.)

לָסוּךְ אֲפִילּוּ כָּל שֶׁהוּא אָסוּר To anoint, even the slightest amount is forbidden. "During the seven-day period of mourning, a mourner is forbidden to anoint even the smallest amount of his body with oil, if the anointing is done for pleasure. But if the mourner applies oil to his body in order to remove filth or for some medicinal purpose, it is permitted." (Ibid., 381:2.)

¹אַדְבְּרֵיהּ רַב יְהוּדָה לְרַב יִצְחָק בְּרֵיהּ, וְדָרַשׁ: ²יָחִיד שֶׁקִּיבֵּל עָלָיו תַּעֲנִית מִתְפַּלֵּל שֶׁל תַּעֲנִית. ³וְהֵיכָן אוֹמְרָהּ? ⁴בֵּין "גּוֹאֵל" לְ"רוֹפֵא".

⁵מַתְקִיף לָהּ רַב יִצְחָק: וְכִי יָחִיד קוֹבֵעַ בְּרָכָה לְעַצְמוֹ? ⁶אֶלָּא אָמַר רַב יִצְחָק: בְּ"שׁוֹמֵעַ תְּפִלָּה". ⁷וְכֵן אָמַר רַב שֵׁשֶׁת: בְּ"שׁוֹמֵעַ תְּפִלָּה".

⁸מֵיתִיבִי: "אֵין בֵּין יָחִיד לְצִבּוּר אֶלָּא שֶׁזֶּה מִתְפַּלֵּל שְׁמוֹנֶה עֶשְׂרֵה ⁹וְזֶה מִתְפַּלֵּל תְּשַׁע

LITERAL TRANSLATION

¹Rav Yehudah took Rav Yitzḥak his son for a walk, and expounded: ²An individual who accepted a fast upon himself prays [the prayer] of a fast. ³And where does he say it? ⁴Between [the blessing] "Who redeems" and [the blessing] "Who heals."

⁵Rav Yitzḥak objected to this: But does an individual establish a blessing for himself?

⁶Rather, Rav Yitzḥak said: [He inserts the prayer] in [the blessing] "Who hearkens unto prayer." ⁷And similarly Rav Sheshet said: In [the blessing] "Who hearkens unto prayer."

⁸They raised an objection: "There is no [difference] between an individual and the community except that the one prays eighteen blessings ⁹and the other prays nineteen

TRANSLATION AND COMMENTARY

אַדְבְּרֵיהּ רַב יְהוּדָה ¹The Gemara relates that **Rav Yehudah** once **took Rav Yitzḥak his son for a walk and delivered** the following **exposition**: ²If **an individual has imposed a fast upon himself**, he **must insert the fast day** *anenu* **prayer into** his Amidah **prayer**. ³**Where** precisely in the Amidah **does** the individual **say** the added prayer? He recites the *anenu* prayer as an independent blessing with its own separate concluding formula ⁴and inserts it **between** the seventh blessing of the Amidah, which concludes with the words **"Who redeems** Israel," **and** the eighth blessing of the Amidah, which concludes with the words **"Who heals** the sick of His people Israel."

מַתְקִיף לָהּ רַב יִצְחָק ⁵**Rav Yitzḥak objected to** his father's exposition: **Is it possible that an individual's** prayer is so highly regarded by the Rabbis that they would have **established an** independent **blessing for him** to insert into the Amidah prayer when he is fasting?

אֶלָּא אָמַר רַב יִצְחָק ⁶**Rather, Rav Yitzḥak said**: A person who has undertaken a private fast recites the fast-day prayer **in** the middle of the sixteenth blessing of the Amidah, which concludes with the words **"Who hearkens unto prayer."** Though the text of the Amidah is fixed, the blessing "Who hearkens unto prayer" is a general plea that one's prayers be accepted, and an individual may insert into it his own private requests. ⁷**And similarly Rav Sheshet said**: An individual who is fasting recites the fast-day prayer **in** the middle of the blessing **"Who hearkens unto prayer."**

מֵיתִיבִי ⁸An objection was raised against the viewpoint of Rav Yitzḥak and Rav Sheshet from a Baraita, which stated: **"There is no difference** with respect to a fast **between an individual and the community except that** an individual **recites eighteen blessings** in his Amidah prayer and inserts the fast-day prayer of *anenu* into the sixteenth blessing, which concludes with the words "Who hearkens unto prayer," ⁹whereas the community **recites nineteen blessings,** the fast-day prayer being recited as an independent blessing, with its

RASHI

בין גואל לרופא — ברכה בפני עצמה. **וכי יחיד** — חשוב כל כך שיהו מתקנין לו ברכה בפני עצמה, להוסיף בתפלתו? **בשומע תפלה** — שכוללה בתוך הברכה, וחותם ב"שומע תפלה", דאותה ברכה וחתימתה משמע בין אתענית בין אכל מילי. **אין בין יחיד לצבור** — גבי תענית. **שזה** — יחיד מתפלל ביום תעניתו שמונה עשרה, וכולל תפלת תענית ב"שומע תפלה".

LANGUAGE

אַדְבְּרֵיהּ He took him for a walk. This translation follows the interpretation of *Rashi* (*Betzah* 29a). *Rabbenu Ḥananel* (ibid.) explains it as meaning "he instructed him," "he gave him the right to speak," and refers to a situation in which an important Sage permits someone under his protection, his son or his student, to speak in public on his own.

SAGES

רַב יִצְחָק בְּרֵיהּ (דְרַב יְהוּדָה) Rav Yitzḥak the son of Rav Yehudah. A Babylonian Amora of the third generation, Rav Yitzḥak was the son of the famous Amora Rav Yehudah (bar Yeḥezkel). Rav Yitzḥak was his father's disciple, though with Rav Yehudah's consent and encouragement he also studied with the other great Amoraim of that generation. After his father's death he studied Torah in Rabbah's yeshivah, and his other teachers were Rav Sheshet and Rami bar Ḥama. His Halakhic and Aggadic teachings are recorded in various places in the Talmud. His granddaughter Ḥomah was married successively to several Sages, the last being the important Amora Abaye.

NOTES

שֶׁזֶּה מִתְפַּלֵּל שְׁמוֹנֶה עֶשְׂרֵה That the one recites eighteen blessings. *Rashi* notes that the Amidah prayer, the main element of the daily service, is called the *Shemoneh Esreh* ("Eighteen"), even though it consists of nineteen blessings, because originally only eighteen blessings were included in the prayer, the nineteenth blessing — the blessing against heretics — having been added later by Shmuel HaKatan.

Rid discusses the issue at length, pointing out that Shmuel HaKatan added the blessing against heretics in the period soon after the destruction of the Second Temple, and the later Tannaitic sources should therefore reflect the fact that the ordinary Amidah prayer is made up of nineteen blessings. Basing himself on the Tosefta and the Jerusalem Talmud, he argues that, according to the original custom observed in Eretz Israel, the Amidah prayer consisted of only eighteen blessings even after the blessing against the heretics had been added, because the request for the reestablishment of the Davidic Kingdom and the prayer for the rebuilding of Jerusalem were originally included in one blessing.

HALAKHAH

אֵין בֵּין יָחִיד לְצִבּוּר There is no difference between an individual and the community. "An individual who is fasting, whether he is observing an individual fast or is fasting together with the community, inserts the *anenu* prayer in the blessing 'Who hearkens unto prayer.' *Rema* notes that even when a person is observing an individual fast, he should say 'on the day of *our* fast' [בְּיוֹם צוֹם תַּעֲנִיתֵנוּ]. It is the common practice on communal fasts that an individual who is not observing the fast does not recite the *anenu* prayer (*Arukh HaShulḥan*, *Mishnah Berurah*)." (*Shulḥan Arukh*, *Oraḥ Ḥayyim* 565:1.)

TRANSLATION AND COMMENTARY

own concluding formula, between the seventh and eighth blessings of the Amidah." The Gemara first clarifies the meaning of the Baraita: When the Baraita speaks here of an individual and the community, [1]**what** exactly **is meant by** the term **"individual" and what is meant** by the term **"community"?** [2]**If we say** that **"individual"** should be understood **literally,** as referring to an individual who is fasting, and that **"community"** refers to the representative of the community who serves as **prayer leader,** this leads to a certain difficulty, for does the prayer leader really recite only **nineteen blessings** when he repeats the Amidah on a fast day? [3]Surely **there are twenty-four blessings** in the fast-day Amidah of the prayer leader, the eighteen regular blessings of the daily Amidah and six additional blessings occasioned by the fast, as is explained below (15a)!

עֶשְׂרֵה". [1]מַאי "יָחִיד" וּמַאי "צִבּוּר"? [2]אִילֵימָא: "יָחִיד" מַמָּשׁ, וְ"צִבּוּר" שְׁלִיחַ צִבּוּר, הָנֵי תְּשַׁע עֶשְׂרֵה? [3]עֶשְׂרִין וְאַרְבַּע הָווּ!

[4]אֶלָּא לָאו הָכִי קָאָמַר: [5]אֵין בֵּין יָחִיד דְּקִבֵּל עָלָיו תַּעֲנִית יָחִיד לְיָחִיד שֶׁקִּבֵּל עָלָיו תַּעֲנִית צִבּוּר, [6]אֶלָּא שֶׁזֶּה מִתְפַּלֵּל שְׁמוֹנֶה עֶשְׂרֵה [7]וְזֶה מִתְפַּלֵּל תְּשַׁע עֶשְׂרֵה. [8]שְׁמַע מִינָּהּ: יָחִיד קוֹבֵעַ בְּרָכָה לְעַצְמוֹ!

[9]לָא. לְעוֹלָם אֵימָא לָךְ שְׁלִיחַ צִבּוּר. [10]וּדְקָא קַשְׁיָא לָךְ שְׁלִיחַ צִבּוּר עֶשְׂרִין וְאַרְבַּע מְצַלֵּי, [11]בְּשָׁלֹשׁ תַּעֲנִיּוֹת רִאשׁוֹנוֹת דְּלֵיכָּא עֶשְׂרִים וְאַרְבַּע.

LITERAL TRANSLATION

blessings." [1]What is [meant by] "individual" and what is [meant by] "community"? [2]If we say: "Individual" [is meant] literally, and "community" [means] the prayer leader (lit., "the agent of the community"), are there (lit., "these") nineteen [blessings]? [3]There are twenty-four [blessings]!

[4]Rather, is it not [that] he said as follows: [5]There is no [difference] between an individual who accepted an individual fast upon himself and an individual who accepted a public fast upon himself, [6]except that this one prays eighteen [blessings] [7]and this one prays nineteen [blessings]. [8]Conclude from this: An individual establishes a blessing for himself!

[9]No. In fact I can say to you [that "community" means] the prayer leader. [10]And as to your difficulty [that] the prayer leader recites twenty-four [blessings], [11][it refers] to the first three fasts when there are not twenty-four [blessings].

RASHI

תשע עשרה — דקבע ליה בין "גואל" ל"רופא". סתם תפלה קרי שמונה עשרה, דברכת "ולמלשינים" ביבנה תקנוה, כדאמרינן בברכות (כח,ב). **עשרים וארבע הוין** — בפירקין דלקמן (טו,א) דעשרים וארבע ברכות הוו ביומא דתעניתא, והכא קתני תשע עשרה ותו לא! **וצבור** — יחיד שקיבל עליו תענית צבור. **אלמא:** יחיד קובע ברכה לעצמו כשקיבל תענית צבור. **בקמייתא** — בשלש תעניות ראשונות דליכא עשרים וארבע, כדאמרינן בפרק "סדר תעניות כילד" בגמרא (שם).

BACKGROUND

יָחִיד קוֹבֵעַ בְּרָכָה לְעַצְמוֹ Does an individual establish a blessing for himself? The number and wording of the blessings is ancient and sanctified, and the addition of a blessing is permissible only in special circumstances, on festivals or major public fast days. Although an individual is permitted to add to the wording of a prayer, it is unlikely that he would be permitted to create a special blessing for his own personal needs.

אֶלָּא [4]The Gemara now proposes an alternative explanation of the Baraita. **Rather, the following is** what the Tanna **must have meant:** [5]**There is no difference between an individual who has taken an individual fast upon himself and an individual who has taken a public fast upon himself,** [6]**except that** the individual who undertakes the relatively lenient individual fast **recites eighteen blessings** in his Amidah prayer, inserting the fast-day prayer of *anenu* in the "Who hearkens unto prayer" blessing, [7]**whereas** the individual who undertakes the more severe communal fast **recites nineteen blessings,** reciting the fast-day prayer as a separate blessing. [8]Is it not correct, then, to **conclude from this** that **an individual's** prayer is indeed so highly regarded by the Rabbis that they **established a** separate **blessing for him**, and this contradicts Rav Yitzḥak and Rav Sheshet!

לָא [9]The Gemara rejects this argument and says: **No,** this Baraita can be explained as was proposed originally. **I can in fact say to you that** when the Baraita speaks of an "individual," it is referring to an individual who is fasting, and when it speaks of a **"community,"** it **is referring to** the **prayer leader.** Thus, an individual who is fasting always recites only eighteen blessings in his Amidah prayer, because he inserts the *anenu* prayer into the "Who hearkens unto prayer" blessing, as argued by Rav Yitzḥak and Rav Sheshet. [10]**And as to the difficulty you found** with this understanding of the Baraita, that we have learned elsewhere that **the prayer leader recites twenty-four blessings** when he repeats the Amidah prayer on fast days, [11]this can be explained by saying, that the Baraita **is referring to the first three fasts** imposed by the court on the entire community when the rains are late. On those fasts, the prayer leader does **not** recite **twenty-four blessings** in the repetition of the Amidah, but only nineteen. Those sources that speak of the twenty-four blessings recited by the prayer leader on fast days refer to the later fasts decreed by the court when a drought becomes more severe.

TERMINOLOGY

תָּנָא וְשַׁיֵּיר He taught and left out. An expression used when suggesting that a list given in a Mishnah or a Baraita is incomplete: "The Mishnah taught certain cases, and left other cases to be added."

TRANSLATION AND COMMENTARY

וְלָא [1]The Gemara asks: **But are** the twenty-four blessings really **not** recited on the first series of public fasts? [2]**Surely** the Baraita that compares the first three fasts and the middle three fasts **is formulated** in the style of **"there is no difference between...** except...," for it was taught in a Baraita: [3]**"There is no difference between the first three** public **fasts and the middle three** public **fasts,** [4]**except that during** the first three fasts, which are not so severe, people **are permitted to do work, whereas during** the middle three fasts people **are forbidden to do work."** Thus it may be inferred that the only difference between the two series of fasts is with respect to work, [5]**but regarding the twenty-four blessings** recited by the prayer leader when he repeats the Amidah, [6]**the two** series of fasts **are the same!** At this point the Gemara is assuming that the twenty-four blessings are recited during the middle series of public fasts, and it therefore follows that they should also be recited during the first series of public fasts.

תָּנָא וְשַׁיֵּיר [7]The Gemara rejects this argument: The Baraita presents only a partial listing of the differences between the two series of fasts. It may be suggested that the Tanna **mentioned** one difference **but left out** another. Thus it is possible to argue that the prayer leader begins to recite the twenty-four blessings during the middle three fasts, but during the first three fasts he recites only the eighteen regular blessings and the fast-day *anenu* prayer.

מַאי שַׁיֵּיר [8]The Gemara will not accept the suggestion that a list given in a Mishnah or in a Baraita is incomplete unless it can be shown that at least two items were omitted from the list. Thus the Gemara asks: **What else did** the Tanna who formulated the Baraita **omit** from the Baraita **that** it can justifiably be claimed that **he left out** the matter of the number of blessings recited by the prayer leader when repeating the Amidah on a fast day? [9]**And furthermore, surely** the Baraita **is formulated** in the style of **"there is no difference between**... except..."! Not only does the Baraita make no mention of any difference between the two series of fasts with respect to the number of blessings recited by the prayer leader, but it emphasizes that the only difference between the two series of fasts is the prohibition of work. This being the case, it is difficult to argue that the Tanna mentioned one difference and left out another.

אֶלָּא [10]**Rather,** says the Gemara, the Baraita must be explained in a different manner. **The Tanna** states that the only difference between the two series of fasts is that on the first three fasts working is permitted, whereas on the second three fasts working is forbidden. But this ruling **deals** only **with** differences with respect to the **prohibitions** that are imposed during each series of fasts. [11]But **he does not deal with** differences regarding the **prayers** that are recited on the various fasts.

[1]וְלָא? [2]וְהָא "אֵין בֵּין" קָתָנֵי: [3]"אֵין בֵּין שָׁלֹשׁ רִאשׁוֹנוֹת לְשָׁלֹשׁ אֶמְצָעִיּוֹת, [4]אֶלָּא שֶׁבְּאֵלּוּ מוּתָּרִין בַּעֲשִׂיַּית מְלָאכָה וּבְאֵלּוּ אֲסוּרִין בַּעֲשִׂיַּית מְלָאכָה". [5]הָא לְעֶשְׂרִים וְאַרְבַּע, [6]זֶה וָזֶה שָׁוִין! [7]תָּנָא וְשַׁיֵּיר. [8]מַאי שַׁיֵּיר דְּהַאי שַׁיֵּיר? [9]וְתוּ, וְהָא "אֵין בֵּין" קָתָנֵי! [10]אֶלָּא, תַּנָּא בְּאִיסּוּרֵי קָא מַיְירֵי, [11]בִּתְפִלּוֹת לָא מַיְירֵי.

LITERAL TRANSLATION

[1]But are there not? [2]But surely it teaches: "There is no [difference] between": [3]"There is no [difference] between the first three [fasts] and the middle three [fasts], [4]except that on these they are permitted to do work and on these they are forbidden to do work." [5]But regarding the twenty-four [blessings], [6]this and that are the same!

[7]He taught and left out.

[8]What [else] did he leave out that he left this out? [9]And furthermore, surely it teaches: "There is no [difference] between"!

[10]Rather, the Tanna is dealing with prohibitions, [11]he is not dealing with prayers.

RASHI

דאלו מותרין בעשיית מלאכה וכו׳ — ראשונות דלא חמירי כולי האי. הא לעשרים וארבע ברכות — זה וזה שוין. וקא סלקא דעתך דאיתנהו לעשרים וארבע באמצעיות, מדקמתרין קמייתא דליכא עשרים וארבע — מכלל דבאמצעיתא איתנהו. ולא היא, דליתנהו אלא באחרונות, כדקתני התם. ומשום דהא מילתא קמייתא, משום הכי פריך ליה מעשרים וארבע דליתנהו באמצעיות. **תנא ושייר** — תנא מילי דאיתנהו בין אמצעיות לראשונות, ושייר. "אין בין" לאו דוקא הוא, כדמוכח לקמן גבי אידך. **הכי גרסינן: מאי שייר דהאי שייר, אלא באיסורי קא מיירי בתפלות לא קא מיירי.** ומאן דגרים: שייר תיבה מוציאין את התיבה כו׳ — שיבוש הוא, דאינה אלא באחרונות, כדבסמוך. **ומיפשט** פשיטא ליה דאינה אלא באחרונות. **מאי שייר דהאי שייר** — דלא אורחא דתנא למתני כל מילי ולשיורי חדא, אלא לעולם עשרים וארבע בקמייתא ליתנהו, ולהכי לא חשיב להו, ב"אין בין" דבתפלה לא קמיירי.

NOTES

תָּנָא וְשַׁיֵּיר He taught and left out. Sometimes when it is argued that a conclusion is based on an omission of a certain case or regulation from a list found in a Mishnah or in a Baraita, the Gemara answers that the list given there is not complete, and that the Tanna did not wish to mention all the relevant cases or regulations, and therefore

TRANSLATION AND COMMENTARY

וְאִי בָּעֵית אֵימָא [1]**And if you wish,** continues the Gemara, you can **say** that there are indeed no differences between the first three fasts and the middle three fasts, other than what is mentioned in the Baraita with respect to work. But it can still be argued that the prayer leader does not recite the twenty-four blessings during the first three fasts, [2]for **even during the middle three fasts he does not recite the twenty-four blessings.** The twenty-four blessings are recited by the prayer leader only during the last seven fasts decreed by the court when the drought continues well into the winter.

וְלָא [3]The Gemara now challenges this last suggestion: **But are** the twenty-four blessings really **not** recited during the middle series of public fasts?

וְהָתַנְיָא [4]**Surely it was taught** in a Baraita: **"There is no difference between the second three** public fasts **and the last seven** public fasts, **except that during** the last seven fasts **they sound the alarm and lock the shops."** [5]We can infer from this Baraita that **regarding all other matters,** including the number of blessings recited by the prayer leader when he repeats the Amidah, **the two** series of fasts **are the same!** Since the twenty-four blessings are recited during the last series of public fasts, it follows that they should be recited during the middle series as well.

וְכִי תֵימָא [6]The Gemara suggests an answer, but immediately rejects it: **And if you say that** the two series of fasts do in fact differ with respect to the number of blessings recited by the prayer leader, and that **here too** the Tanna of the Baraita **mentioned** one difference **and left out** another, such an explanation is most problematic. [7]For **surely** the Baraita **is formulated** in the style of **"there is no difference between**...except...," which clearly implies that the only differences are those mentioned explicitly in the Baraita!

וְתִסְבְּרָא [8]The Gemara questions this last argument: **Do you** really **understand that** the expression **"there is no difference between**...except..." **is meant** to be taken **literally**, so that we can infer from it that there are no other differences between the two sets of fasts? [14A] [9]**But surely** the Tanna **left out mention of the ark!** During the last seven fasts, the ark containing the Torah scrolls was taken from the synagogue into the street and was covered with ashes. This procedure was not followed during the first two series of fasts, when the prayer service took place as usual inside the synagogue (see below, 15a-b). Thus we see that the

[1]וְאִי בָּעֵית אֵימָא: [2]בְּאֶמְצָעִיָּיתָא נַמִי לָא מְצַלֵּי עֶשְׂרִים וְאַרְבַּע.
[3]וְלָא?
[4]וְהָתַנְיָא: "אֵין בֵּין שָׁלֹשׁ שְׁנִיּוֹת לְשֶׁבַע אַחֲרוֹנוֹת, אֶלָּא שֶׁבְּאֵלּוּ מַתְרִיעִין וְנוֹעֲלִין אֶת הַחֲנוּיּוֹת".
[5]הָא לְכָל דִּבְרֵיהֶן, זֶה וְזֶה שָׁוִין!
[6]וְכִי תֵימָא הָכָא נַמִי תָּנָא וְשִׁיֵּיר, [7]וְהָא "אֵין בֵּין" קָתָנֵי!
[8]וְתִסְבְּרָא "אֵין בֵּין" דַּוְקָא?
[14A] [9]וְהָא שִׁיֵּיר תֵּיבָה!

LITERAL TRANSLATION

[1]And if you wish, say: [2]On the middle three [fasts] as well he does not pray twenty-four [blessings].
[3]But [does he] not?
[4]But surely it was taught: "There is no [difference] between the second three [fasts] and the last seven [fasts], except that on these they sound the alarm and they lock the shops." [5]But regarding all their [other] matters, this and that are the same!
[6]And if you say [that] here too he taught and left out, but surely it teaches: [7]"There is no [difference] between"!
[8]And do you understand [that] "there is no [difference] between" is [meant] literally? [14A] [9]But surely he left out [mention of] the ark!

RASHI

באמצעיות נמי ליכא עשרים וארבע — אלא באחרונות, כדאמרינן התם. **שבאלו** — האחרונות מתריעים ונועלין, כדתנן נמי במתניתין. **הא לכל דבריהן** — זה וזה שוין, דבתרוייהו איתנהו. **והא שייר תיבה** — דבאחרונות איתא והכא ליתא, כדקתני לקמן (טו,א): סדר תעניות כיצד? מוציאין את התיבה כו'. ומותבינן בגמרא בהדיא מתיבה דליתא אלא באחרונות! ומשני: כי קתני נמי מתניתין — בקמייתא.

NOTES

the inference drawn from the omission of a specific item is invalid. Often the Gemara continues with the question: What else did the Tanna of the Mishnah or the Baraita omit so that it can be claimed that he also left out the case or regulation under discussion? For if it is to be argued that an item that indeed belonged in the Mishnah or in the Baraita was omitted, it must be demonstrated that at least one other item was omitted as well.

A number of commentators point out that there are clearly a number of other differences between the first three fasts and the middle three fasts — for example, the first three fasts begin at dawn and bathing is permitted while they last, whereas the middle three fasts begin the previous evening and bathing is forbidden for the duration of each fast, as we learned in our Mishnah. If so, it is clear that the Tanna of the Baraita taught one difference and left out others! It has been suggested that the Baraita is not cited here in its entirety, and that the differences mentioned in the Mishnah are also mentioned in that portion of the Baraita not cited by the Gemara. Thus it was necessary for the Gemara to find additional differences between the two series of fasts, in order to justify its claim that there is a difference between them regarding the number of blessings that must be recited (*Gevurat Ari*, *Keren Orah*).

LANGUAGE

פַּרְהֶסְיָא Public. This word is derived from the Greek *παρρησία, parresia,* the original meaning of which was "freedom of speech"; it was also used to describe a free political regime. As used by the Sages, the word means "in public," something visible to everyone.

LITERAL TRANSLATION

[1]If because of the ark, that is not an omission. [2]It teaches things [done] in private; [3]it does not teach things [done] in public.

[4]Rav Ashi said: Our Mishnah is also precise, [5]for it teaches: "How are these more severe than the first ones? [6]Except that on these they sound the alarm and they lock the shops." [7]But regarding all their [other] matters, this and that are the same.

[8]And if you say [that] here too he taught and left out, [9]but surely it teaches: "How are these"!

[10]And do you understand [that] "how are these" is [meant] literally? [11]But surely he left out [mention of] the ark!

[12]If because of the ark, that is not an omission,

[1]אִי מִשּׁוּם תֵּיבָה, לָאו שִׁיּוּרָא הוּא. [2]מִילֵּי דְּצִינְעָא קָתָנֵי; [3]מִילֵּי דְּבְפַרְהֶסְיָא לָא קָתָנֵי.

[4]אָמַר רַב אַשִׁי: מַתְנִיתִין נַמִי דַּיְקָא, [5]דְּקָתָנֵי: "מָה אֵלּוּ יְתֵירוֹת עַל הָרִאשׁוֹנוֹת? [6]אֶלָּא שֶׁבְּאֵלּוּ מַתְרִיעִין וְנוֹעֲלִין אֶת הַחֲנוּיּוֹת". [7]אֲבָל בְּכָל דִּבְרֵיהֶן זֶה וָזֶה שָׁוִין.

[8]וְכִי תֵּימָא הָכָא נַמִי תָּנָא וְשַׁיֵּיר, [9]וְהָא "מָה אֵלּוּ" קָתָנֵי! [10]וְתִסְבְּרָא "מָה אֵלּוּ" דַּוְוקָא הוּא? [11]וְהָא שַׁיֵּיר לָהּ תֵּיבָה! [12]אִי מִשּׁוּם תֵּיבָה, לָאו שִׁיּוּרָא

RASHI

מילי דצינעא — מתריעין בבית הכנסת, ועשרים וארבע נמי בבית הכנסת. **בפרהסיא** — תיבה ברחובה של עיר. **דיקא נמי** — דלעשרים וארבע זה וזה שוין, דקתני מתניתין: מה אלו יתירות על הראשונות כו׳, ואלו עשרים וארבע לא קא חשיב גבי אחרונות. **והא מה אלו קתני** — דמשמע דווקא.

TRANSLATION AND COMMENTARY

Baraita did not list all the differences between the second and the third series of fasts. It can therefore be argued that during the last seven fasts the prayer leader recites twenty-four blessings when he repeats the Amidah prayer, whereas during the middle three fasts he recites only nineteen blessings.

אִי מִשּׁוּם תֵּיבָה [1]The Gemara rejects this argument: **If** you wish to conclude that the Baraita is imprecise in its formulation **because** it left out the matter of the **ark, that is not an omission** from which one can draw such a conclusion. [2]The Baraita **is referring** only **to matters that take place inside** the synagogue, [3]but **it does not refer to matters that take place outside** the synagogue. The Baraita does not mention that the ark is taken out into the street only during the last series of fasts because that is a matter that takes place outside the synagogue. Thus it notes that the two series of fasts differ with respect to whether or not the alarm is sounded, for this would be done inside the synagogue. Were there a difference between the two series of fasts regarding the number of blessings to be recited by the prayer leader, this too should have been mentioned in the Baraita, because it takes place inside the synagogue. The Baraita's silence on the matter thus implies that the twenty-four blessings are recited during the middle three fasts as well.

אָמַר רַב אַשִׁי [4]**Rav Ashi said:** The formulation of **our Mishnah is also precise** according to this explanation, [5]**because** the Mishnah **states: "How are these** seven last fasts **more severe than the** three **preceding ones?** [6]**Because on these** last seven fasts **they sound the alarm and lock the shops."** The Mishnah seems to imply that these are the only differences between the two series of fasts, [7]**but regarding all other matters,** including the number of blessings recited by the prayer leader when he repeats the Amidah, **the two** series of fasts **are the same.**

וְכִי תֵּימָא [8]The Gemara continues: **And if you say that** the two series of fasts do in fact differ with respect to the number of blessings recited by the prayer leader, and that **here too** the Tanna of our Mishnah **mentioned** one difference **and left out** another, such an explanation is most problematic. [9]For **surely** the Mishnah **states: "How are these** seven last fasts more severe than the three preceding ones," implying that the Mishnah intends to list all the differences!

וְתִסְבְּרָא [10]The Gemara challenges this last claim: **Do you** really **understand** that the expression **"how are these" is meant** to be taken **literally,** implying that there are no other differences between the two series of fasts? [11]**But surely** the Tanna of our Mishnah **left out mention of** the fact that only during the last seven fasts was **the ark** containing the Torah scrolls taken from the synagogue into the street and covered with ashes, whereas during the earlier fasts this was not done! Thus we see that the Mishnah did not list all the differences between the second and the third series of fasts. It is therefore possible that the two series of fasts also differ with respect to the number of blessings recited by the prayer leader when he repeats the Amidah.

אִי מִשּׁוּם תֵּיבָה [12]The Gemara rejects this argument: **If** you wish to conclude that the Mishnah is imprecise in its formulation **because** it left out the matter of **the ark, that is not an omission** from which we can draw

TRANSLATION AND COMMENTARY

such a conclusion, [1]**because** the Tanna of the Mishnah **deals with** the ark **in the next chapter,** and it was therefore unnecessary for him to address the issue here.

הַשְׁתָּא דְּאָתֵית לְהָכִי [2]The Gemara continues: **Now that you have come to this** solution, a similar one can be suggested with respect to the twenty-four blessings. [3]The Mishnah's failure to mention **the matter of the twenty-four blessings** here **is not an omission,** [4]**for** the Tanna of the Mishnah **deals with** the issue of the twenty-four blessings **in the next chapter.**

מַאי הָוֵי עֲלָהּ [5]The Gemara above discussed at length the question of where an individual who is fasting inserts the fast-day *anenu* prayer in his recital of the Amidah, but was unable to prove or disprove any of the opinions expressed on the matter. The Gemara now asks: **What** conclusion **was reached on the matter?**

אָמַר רַבִּי שְׁמוּאֵל בַּר סַסְרְטַאי [6]The Gemara answers: **Rabbi Shmuel bar Sasretai said, and similarly Rav Ḥiyya bar Ashi said in the name of Rav:** An individual who is fasting recites the fast-day prayer as an independent blessing, [7]and inserts it **between** the blessing that concludes with the words: **"Who redeems** Israel," **and** the blessing that concludes with the words: **"Who heals** the sick of His people Israel." [8]**But Rav Ashi said in the name of Rabbi Yannai the son of Rabbi Yishmael:** The fast-day *anenu* prayer is **recited** by an individual **in** the middle of the blessing that concludes with the words: **"Who hearkens unto prayer."** [9]**And,** concludes the Gemara, **the Halakhah is:** The fast-day prayer is recited **in** the middle of the blessing that concludes with the words: **"Who hearkens unto prayer."**

תָּנֵי חֲדָא [10]The Gemara now addresses another difference between the various series of fasts. **One Baraita taught: "Pregnant and nursing women** must **fast on the first** public **fasts, but they are not** required to **fast on the last fasts."** [11]**And another Baraita taught:** "Pregnant and nursing woman must **fast on the last fasts, but they are not** required to **fast on the first fasts."** [12]And yet **another Baraita taught:** "Pregnant and nursing women **fast neither on the first fasts nor on the last fasts."** How are these seemingly contradictory statements to be reconciled?

אָמַר רַב אַשִׁי [13]**Rav Ashi said: Seize the middle** three **fasts in your hand** as the fasts on which pregnant and

הוּא, [1]מִשּׁוּם דְּקָא חָשֵׁיב לָהּ בְּאִידָךְ פִּרְקָא.
[2]הָשְׁתָּא דְּאָתֵית לְהָכִי, [3]עֶשְׂרִים וְאַרְבָּעָה נַמִי לָאו שִׁיּוּרָא הוּא, [4]דְּקָתָנֵי לָהּ בְּאִידָךְ פִּירְקָא.
[5]מַאי הָוֵי עֲלָהּ?
[6]אָמַר רַבִּי שְׁמוּאֵל בַּר סַסְרְטַאי, וְכֵן אָמַר רַב חִיָּיא בַּר אַשִׁי אָמַר רַב: [7]בֵּין "גּוֹאֵל" לְ"רוֹפֵא". [8]וְרַב אַשִׁי אָמַר מִשְּׁמֵיהּ דְּרַבִּי יַנַּאי בְּרֵיהּ דְּרַבִּי יִשְׁמָעֵאל: בְּ"שׁוֹמֵעַ תְּפִילָּה". [9]וְהִלְכְתָא: בְּ"שׁוֹמֵעַ תְּפִילָּה".
[10]תָּנֵי חֲדָא: "עוּבָּרוֹת וּמֵינִיקוֹת מִתְעַנּוֹת בָּרִאשׁוֹנוֹת, וְאֵין מִתְעַנּוֹת בָּאַחֲרוֹנוֹת". [11]וְתַנְיָא אִידָךְ: מִתְעַנּוֹת בָּאַחֲרוֹנוֹת, וְאֵין מִתְעַנּוֹת בָּרִאשׁוֹנוֹת". [12]וְתַנְיָא אִידָךְ: "אֵין מִתְעַנּוֹת, לֹא בָּרִאשׁוֹנוֹת וְלֹא בָּאַחֲרוֹנוֹת".
[13]אָמַר רַב אַשִׁי: נְקוֹט

LITERAL TRANSLATION

[1]because he considered it in the other chapter.
[2]Now that you have come to this, [3][the matter of] the twenty-four [blessings] is also not an omission, [4]for he taught it in the other chapter.
[5]What was [decided] about it?
[6]Rabbi Shmuel bar Sasretai said, and similarly Rav Ḥiyya bar Ashi said in the name of Rav: [7]Between [the blessing] "Who redeems" and [the blessing] "Who heals." [8]And Rav Ashi said in the name of Rabbi Yannai the son of Rabbi Yishmael: In [the blessing] "Who hearkens unto prayer." [9]And the Halakhah is: In [the blessing] "Who hearkens unto prayer."
[10]One [Baraita] taught: "Pregnant and nursing women fast on the first [fasts], but they do not fast on the last [fasts]." [11]And another [Baraita] taught: "They fast on the last [fasts], but they do not fast on the first [fasts]." [12]And another [Baraita] taught: "They do not fast, neither on the first [fasts] nor on the last [fasts]."
[13]Rav Ashi said: Seize the

RASHI

דהא קתני לה באידך פירקין — דמי ששנה מתניתין דהכא תנא נמי דהתם, והאי דלא תנא בהאי — סמיך אהתם, דקתני: באחרונות מוציאין התיבה, מה שאין כן באמצעיות. **השתא דאתית להכי** — דמשום דקתני לה באידך פירקין דאמרת דלא הוי שיור, עשרים וארבע נמי דאמרת דשוין ניניהו — איכא למימר דלא הוי שוין, דהא אפילו שיורא נמי לא הוי, דבהדיא קתני לה באידך פירקין דבאחרונות איתנהו, באמצעיות לא, ואיכא לתרולי כתירוצא קמא: בקמייתא, דליכא עשרים וארבע. **מאי הוי עלה** — היכן אומרה יחיד.

TERMINOLOGY

הָשְׁתָּא דְּאָתֵית לְהָכִי Now that you have come to this. Sometimes the Rabbis raise a series of objections to a certain viewpoint, and each objection is given a different answer; then a new objection is raised, and someone suggests an answer which resolves not only the new objection but also the previous ones. At that point the Talmud uses this expression, proposing a revision of the solutions first advanced.

מַאי הָוֵי עֲלָהּ What was decided about it? I.e., what conclusion was reached about the matter? Or: What was the final Halakhic ruling in this case? This question is usually asked at the end of a lengthy discussion of a problem, in which different opinions have been expressed without being either proved or dismissed.

SAGES

רַבִּי יַנַּאי בְּרֵיהּ דְּרַבִּי יִשְׁמָעֵאל Rabbi Yannai the son of Rabbi Yishmael. He was a Palestinian Amora of the third generation, and he transmitted teachings of Rabbi Yoḥanan and of Resh Lakish, with whom he may have studied. He is known to have entertained close relations with Rabbi Zera, and he was regarded as a senior judicial authority in his generation. His teachings are quoted in both the Jerusalem and Babylonian Talmuds.

רַבִּי שְׁמוּאֵל בַּר סַסְרְטַאי Rabbi Shmuel bar Sasretai. A Palestinian Amora of the third and fourth generations, Rabbi Shmuel bar Sasretai was probably a disciple of Rabbi Abbahu and transmitted many teachings in his name. The story is told in the Jerusalem Talmud (*Bava Metzia* 2:5) that he went to Rome on one occasion and created a profound impression there by his God-fearing behavior. His statements are recorded in both the Babylonian and Jerusalem Talmuds.

רַב חִיָּיא בַּר אַשִׁי Rav Ḥiyya bar Ashi. A member of the second generation of Babylonian Amoraim, Rav Ḥiyya bar Ashi was a very close disciple

of Rav, and he presents teachings in his master's name in dozens of places in the Talmud. He was one of Rav's older students and was the teacher of Rav's son. However, he also studied with Shmuel and with Ze'iri. He apparently lived in the city of Korkonya, close to Sura, and seems to have been an artisan (a netmaker). His relationship with Rav Huna was that of a colleague. Several Sages of his generation and of the following generation present Halakhic teachings in his name. The Talmud also speaks of his righteousness and great piety.

אֶמְצָעִיָּיתָא בִּידָךְ, [1]דְּמִיתָּרְצוּן כּוּלְּהוּ. [2]״מָה אֵלּוּ יְתֵירוֹת עַל הָרִאשׁוֹנוֹת? [3]אֶלָּא שֶׁבְּאֵלּוּ מַתְרִיעִין וְנוֹעֲלִין אֶת הַחֲנוּיוֹת. [4]בְּמַאי מַתְרִיעִין?

LITERAL TRANSLATION

middle [fasts] in your hand, [1]for [in this way] they are all reconciled.

[2]"How are these more severe than the first ones? [3]Except that on these they sound the alarm and they lock the shops." [4]With what do they sound the alarm?

TRANSLATION AND COMMENTARY

nursing women must fast, [1]**for in that way all** three Baraitot **can be understood** as being in agreement. How so? Pregnant and nursing women are not required to observe the first three fasts, which are less severe than others. They are also not required to observe the final seven fasts, for this would be too taxing. But they must observe the middle three fasts, which is what the first Baraita means by the "first" fasts. They precede the last seven fasts, from which pregnant women are exempt. And when the second Baraita says that these women must fast on the "last" fasts, it is also referring to the middle three fasts, which are last in relation to the first three fasts, from which they are also exempt. The third Baraita should be taken literally: Pregnant and nursing women are not required to fast either on the first three fasts or on the last seven fasts; but by implication it informs us that they must indeed fast on the middle three fasts.

מָה אֵלּוּ [2]We learned in our Mishnah (above, 12b): **"How are these** last seven fasts **more severe than the** three **preceding ones?** [3]**Because on these** last seven fasts **they sound the alarm and they lock the shops."** [4]The Gemara asks: **In what way do they sound the alarm?**

RASHI

נקוט מציעיתא בידך — כלומר: תריץ דבשלש אמצעיות היו מתענין, ומתרצת לכולהו הנך מתנייתא, הא דקתני: בראשונות ולא באחרונות — הנך ראשונות לאו ראשונות ממש נינהו, אלא אמצעיות, דאינהו הוו ראשונות לאחרונות, אבל בשבע אחרונות — לא מיתענו, דכיון דשבע נינהו לא מצו עוברות ומיניקות למיקם בהו. והא דקתני: באחרונות ולא בראשונות — הנך אחרונות אמצעיות נינהו, והראשונות ראשונות ממש. ואין מתענין בהן — דלא תקיף רוגזא כולי האי, ואחות לשון הוא לתנא למיקרי לאמצעיות ראשונות לאחרונות, ואחרונות לראשונות.

NOTES

נְקוֹט אֶמְצָעִיָּיתָא בִּידָךְ **Seize the middle fasts in your hand.** Most Rishonim follow *Rashi* and *Rif,* who explain that Rav Ashi rules that pregnant and nursing women must fast only during the three middle fasts. They are not required to observe the first three fasts because those fasts are not very stringent, and they are not required to observe the last seven fasts because those fasts are too numerous and too stringent. *Rabbenu Yehonatan* adds that pregnant and nursing women are not required to observe the last series of fasts, because certain practices laden with emotion are observed on those days (such as visiting the cemetery, and extreme manifestations of crying) which might prove dangerous for them. *Rambam* (*Hilkhot Ta'aniyyot* 3:5) rules that pregnant and nursing women fast on the last seven fasts, and not on the first or middle series of three fasts. Apparently, he had the reading: נְקוֹט אֶמְצָעִיָּיתָא בִּידָךְ, which he understood to mean: Seize the middle Baraita in your hand — in other words, disregard the first and the last Baraita, and rule in accordance with the middle Baraita, which states that pregnant and nursing women are required to fast on the last fasts, but not on the first ones. *Shittah* follows *Rambam*'s ruling that it is only on the last fasts that pregnant and nursing women must fast, and he suggests a way by which all three Baraitot can be reconciled with that position.

בְּמַאי מַתְרִיעִין **With what do they sound the alarm.** A distinction is drawn between trumpets, made of metal, and shofars, made of animal horn. Elsewhere (*Rosh HaShanah* 27a), a Baraita is cited which teaches that outside the Temple, on those occasions on which trumpets are sounded, shofars are not sounded, and on those occasions when shofars are sounded, trumpets are not sounded. *Rashi* and others explain that when this Baraita speaks of those occasions on which trumpets are sounded, it is referring to communal fast days. Thus it follows that, on public fasts, trumpets, and not shofars, must be blown.

Ba'al Ha Ma'or cites the Geonim who noted that by common practice the shofar, and not the trumpet, is sounded on public fasts (a practice which is also supported by the Jerusalem Talmud), and argues that this practice cannot be reconciled with the Baraita in *Rosh HaShanah*. *Ra'avad* sharpens the difficulty by pointing to our passage, where we find that, according to Rav Yehudah, the alarm is sounded on public fasts by means of shofars. *Ra'avad* himself answers that the Baraita in *Rosh HaShanah* refers to the blasts that follow each of the six additional blessings inserted into the prayer leader's Amidah and which were sounded by trumpets, whereas our Gemara refers to the blasts that were sounded by shofars at the conclusion of the Amidah when the service was extended with additional prayers and supplications.

Ramban and *Ritva* cite a view according to which the term "shofars" mentioned by Rav Yehudah actually refers to trumpets. According to these two approaches, trumpets and

HALAKHAH

נְקוֹט אֶמְצָעִיָּיתָא בִּידָךְ **Seize the middle fasts in your hand.** "Pregnant and nursing women must fast on the middle three fasts imposed upon the community in times of drought, but not on the first three fasts or on the last seven fasts. Even on those fasts that they are not required to observe, they may eat only what is necessary for the well-being of the fetus or the infant. *Rema* adds that a pregnant or nursing woman may not act stringently and observe a fast from which she is exempt." (*Shulḥan Arukh, Oraḥ Ḥayyim* 575:5.)

TRANSLATION AND COMMENTARY

רַב יְהוּדָה אָמַר [1]On this question there is a difference of opinion between Amoraim. **Rav Yehudah said: They sound the alarm with shofars,** animal horns prepared for use as musical instruments, at the conclusion of each of the six additional blessings inserted into the prayer leader's Amidah. [2]**Rav Yehudah the son of Rav Shmuel bar Shilat said in the name of Rav:** They sound the alarm **with** a special prayer beginning with the word ***anenu*** (עֲנֵנוּ — "Answer us"). The people who have assembled for the fast-day service cry out together: "Answer us, O Father, answer us," repeating the prayer many times and substituting a different appellation for God each time the prayer is repeated. The *anenu* prayer referred to here should not be confused with the *anenu* blessing inserted into the Amidah, which was discussed at length above. That prayer is inserted into the Amidah prayer even during the first and middle series of fasts.

קָא סָלְקָא דַּעְתָּךְ [3]The Gemara now seeks to clarify this dispute: **We first thought that** Rav, **who said** that the alarm is sounded **with** the special ***anenu*** prayer, **does not agree** that the alarm is sounded **with shofar** blasts, [4]**and** that Rav Yehudah, **who said** that the alarm is sounded **with shofar** blasts, **does not agree** that the alarm is sounded **with** the ***anenu*** prayer. This being our initial assumption, the following objection was raised: [5]**But surely it was taught** in a Baraita: "If the drought continues deeper into the winter, the court **decrees** as its last step of intervention **no less than seven fasts on the community, on each of which there are eighteen soundings of the alarm.** [6]**And a mnemonic** device to remember **the matter is** the story of the fall of the walls of **Jericho** [Joshua, chapter 6]." Now, if the story of Jericho serves as a reminder regarding the alarm that is sounded

[1]רַב יְהוּדָה אָמַר: בְּשׁוֹפָרוֹת. [2]וְרַב יְהוּדָה בְּרֵיהּ דְּרַב שְׁמוּאֵל בַּר שִׁילַת מִשְּׁמֵיהּ דְּרַב אָמַר: בַּ״עֲנֵנוּ״.
[3]קָא סָלְקָא דַּעְתָּךְ מַאן דְּאָמַר: בַּ״עֲנֵנוּ״, לָא אָמַר: בְּשׁוֹפָרוֹת, [4]וּמַאן דְּאָמַר: בְּשׁוֹפָרוֹת, לָא אָמַר: בַּ״עֲנֵנוּ״. [5]וְהָתַנְיָא: ״אֵין פּוֹחֲתִין מִשֶּׁבַע תַּעֲנִיּוֹת עַל הַצִּבּוּר, שֶׁבָּהֶן שְׁמוֹנֶה עֶשְׂרֵה הַתְרָעוֹת. [6]וְסִימָן לַדָּבָר יְרִיחוֹ״.

LITERAL TRANSLATION

[1]Rav Yehudah said: With shofars. [2]And Rav Yehudah the son of Rav Shmuel bar Shilat said in the name of Rav: With *anenu*.

[3]It entered our mind [that] the one who said: With *anenu*, did not say: With shofars, [4]and the one who said: With shofars, did not say: With *anenu*. [5]But surely it was taught: "We do not decree less than seven fasts on the community, on [each of] which there are eighteen soundings of the alarm. [6]And a sign for the matter [is] Jericho."

RASHI

בשופרות — היו עושין ההתרעות. ולשון התרעה כמו תרועה, וסתם תרועה פשוטה לפניה ולאחריה, במסכת ראש השנה (לד,א). והכי מתריעין בשופרות, כדכתיב (במדבר י) "ותקעתם בחצוצרות", וגו'. תוקעין בשופרות כדי שיכניעו לבם לקול השופר, ויהיו נרתעים מחטאתם, ושש ברכות שהיו מוסיפין ביום התענית היו תוקעין על כל ברכה יבבא אחת, שהן שמונה עשרה התרעות. **רב יהודה אמר** — מתריעין "עננו", בקול רם היו צועקים: עננו אבינו עננו, עננו אלהי אברהם עננו, עננו אלהי יצחק עננו, עננו אלהי יעקב עננו, הכל כפי שאומרים בסוף הסליחות. אבל "עננו" דתפלת תענית — אומר אפילו בראשונות, ואפילו יחיד אוקימנא דאומרה ב"שומע תפלה". ותפלה קרי ליה התרעה, דאי בשופרות — "מריעין" מיבעי ליה. ומאן דמפרש "עננו" של תפלת תענית — משתבש, דהא קתני בסמוך שהן שמונה עשרה התרעות, וקא פריך מן ו"סימן לדבר יריחו", ואם איתא — ליפריך בהדיא: שמונה עשרה תפלות של שמונה עשרה ברכות מי איכא בשבע תעניות? **אין פוחתין משבע תעניות** — באחרונות. **שמונה עשרה התרעות** — שהן מוסיפין שש ברכות משמונה עשרה עד עשרים וארבע, ולכל אחת שלש תרועות. **וסימן לדבר** — שלא תטעה אם התרעה הזו תרועה או תפלה. **יריחו** — דכתיב בה שופרות, לישנא אחרינא: סימן לדבר, כלומר לכך מתריעין — כדי שיענו כדרך שנענו ביריחו על ידי שופרות, דכתיב (יהושע ו) "ויתקעו בשופרות" וגו' וכתיב (שם) "ותפול החומה תחתיה".

SAGES

רַב יְהוּדָה בְּרֵיהּ דְּרַב שְׁמוּאֵל בַּר שִׁילַת **Rav Yehudah the son of Rav Shmuel bar Shilat.** He was a Babylonian Amora of the second and third generations. His father, Rav Shmuel bar Shilat, was a close disciple of Rav, and it seems that his son, Rav Yehudah, also studied with Rav, for he reports many teachings in his name. Rav Yehudah maintained close relations with Rav's important disciples, and the Sages of the following generation report his teachings.

NOTES

not shofars should be sounded on public fasts during the Amidah, contrary to the common practice attested to by the Geonim (see also *Rambam, Hilkhot Ta'aniyyot* 1:4, 4:14).

Ramban, *Rashba*, and *Ritva* suggest a number of ways in which our passage can be understood in its plain sense, that shofars are sounded after each of the additional blessings recited on public fasts, and the common practice of sounding the shofars can be reconciled with the Baraita in *Rosh HaShanah*. (1) When the Baraita speaks of sounding trumpets, it is not referring to public fast-days but rather to times of war when the entire people of Israel gather together for special prayers. (2) Alternatively, the Baraita may indeed be referring to public fasts, but it does not mean to say that only trumpets and not shofars may be sounded. Rather it means to say that if trumpets are sounded, shofars should not be sounded together with them, and vice versa. By common practice, shofars are blown, because they are generally more available.

אֵין פּוֹחֲתִין מִשֶּׁבַע תַּעֲנִיּוֹת עַל הַצִּבּוּר, שֶׁבָּהֶן שְׁמוֹנֶה עֶשְׂרֵה הַתְרָעוֹת **We do not decree less than seven fasts on the community, on each of which there are eighteen soundings of the alarm.** According to the standard text of

HALAKHAH

בְּשׁוֹפָרוֹת **With shofars.** "On the last seven fasts, the shofar is sounded after each of the blessings that are added to the Amidah on account of the fast," following Rav Yehudah. (*Shulḥan Arukh, Oraḥ Ḥayyim* 575:4.)

TRANSLATION AND COMMENTARY

on the final seven fasts, it follows that the alarm is sounded with shofar blasts, [1]for **in Jericho** the collapse of the city walls **was** preceded by the sounding of the **shofar** (see Joshua 6:20). [2]**This appears to be a refutation of** the viewpoint of Rav, **who said** that the alarm is sounded **with** the *anenu* prayer!

אֶלָּא [3]**Rather,** says the Gemara, it is necessary to change our previous assumption. The dispute between Rav and Rav Yehudah must be understood differently: **Both** Rav and Rav Yehudah agree **that the Mishnah calls** the sounding of the **shofar the sounding of an alarm.** [4]**What they disagree about is** whether the reciting of the *anenu* prayer also comes under the category of sounding an alarm. [5]**One scholar** — Rav — **maintains** that the reciting of the *anenu* prayer **is** also **called the sounding of an alarm.** And when mention is made elsewhere of the sounding of an alarm in response to other calamities, it may be referring to the reciting of the *anenu* prayer. [6]**And the other scholar** — Rav Yehudah — **maintains** that the saying of the *anenu* prayer **is not called the sounding of an alarm,** and whenever the sources speak of the sounding of an alarm, they can only mean that shofars are sounded. [7]**According to** Rav, **who says** that the sounding of the alarm can be accomplished **by** reciting the *anenu* prayer, **how much more so** can the sounding of the alarm be accomplished **by the** sounding of the **shofar.** [8]**But according to** Rav Yehudah, **who says** that the sounding of the alarm can be accomplished **by** the sounding of the **shofar,** it can be accomplished only by the shofar, **but not by** reciting the *anenu* prayer.

הָתַנְיָא [9]The Gemara now raises an objection against Rav. **But surely it was taught** in a Baraita: **"But in the case of other types of calamity that break out** in the world, [10]such as **scab,** plagues of **locusts, flies, hornets,**

[1]וִירִיחוֹ שׁוֹפָרוֹת הֲוָה. [2]וּתְיוּבְתָּא לְמַאן דַּאֲמַר: בַּ״עֲנֵנוּ״! [3]אֶלָּא, בְּשׁוֹפָרוֹת דְּכוּלֵּי עָלְמָא לָא פְּלִיגִי דְּקָרֵי לָהּ הַתְרָעָה. [4]כִּי פְּלִיגִי בַּ״עֲנֵנוּ״. [5]מָר סָבַר: קָרֵי לָהּ הַתְרָעָה. [6]וּמָר סָבַר: לָא קָרֵי לָהּ הַתְרָעָה. [7]לְמַאן דַּאֲמַר: בַּ״עֲנֵנוּ״ — כָּל שֶׁכֵּן בְּשׁוֹפָרוֹת. [8]וּלְמַאן דַּאֲמַר: בְּשׁוֹפָרוֹת — אֲבָל בַּ״עֲנֵנוּ״ לָא. [9]וְהָתַנְיָא: ״וּשְׁאָר כָּל מִינֵי פוּרְעָנוּיּוֹת הַמִּתְרַגְּשׁוֹת, [10]כְּגוֹן

LITERAL TRANSLATION

[1]And [in] Jericho there were shofars. [2]And [this is] a refutation of the one who said: With *anenu*! [3]Rather, about shofars, everyone agrees (lit., "the whole world does not disagree") that [the Mishnah] calls this the sounding of an alarm. [4]Where they disagree is about *anenu*. [5]One scholar maintains: This is called the sounding of an alarm. [6]And the other scholar maintains: This is not called the sounding of an alarm. [7]According to the one who says: With *anenu* — all the more so with shofars. [8]And according to the one who says: With shofars — but not with *anenu*. [9]But surely it was taught: "But [for] all other types of calamities that break out, [10]such as

RASHI

אלא בשופרות כולי עלמא וכו׳ — דהא ״מתריעין״ דקתני הכא במתניתין, דעבדינן בתעניות בשופרות. **כי פליגי בעננו** — כי פליגי ב״מתריעין״ דאמרינן בעלמא על שאר פורענויות, מר סבר ״עננו״ נמי התרעה, והאי דקתני בעלמא ״מתריעין״ — ב״עננו״. ומאן דאמר בשופרות — אבל ב״עננו״ לא.

NOTES

the Gemara, the Baraita is informing us that on each of the last seven fasts there are eighteen soundings of the alarm, and as the Gemara demonstrates, the Baraita is referring to shofar blasts. *Rashi* explains that there are eighteen shofar blasts on each of these fasts, because the shofar is sounded three times after each of the six additional blessings inserted into the prayer leader's Amidah prayer. A number of Aharonim point out that there are in fact twenty-one shofar blasts, because the shofar is also sounded three times after the prayer leader recites the expanded "Redeemer of Israel" blessing (see *Leḥem Mishneh, Gevurat Ari,* and *Rashash*), but the Baraita is referring specifically to the blasts accompanying the special blessings added on these fast days. For this reason, *Gra* amends the Baraita so that it reads: "On each of these there are twenty-one soundings of the alarm."

Many Rishonim have the reading: "On which there are seven soundings of the alarm." According to *Ra'avad,* the Baraita is not referring to the blasts sounded after each of the additional blessings inserted into the prayer leader's Amidah, but rather to the blasts that were sounded at the conclusion of the Amidah when the service was extended with additional prayers and supplications, one blast of the shofar on each of the seven fasts (see previous note). Others explain that all the shofar blasts on each of the fasts are called a sounding of the alarm, so that there are seven fasts, on which there are seven soundings of the alarm. Alternatively there are seven soundings of the alarm on each of the seven fasts — one sounding after the expanded "Redeemer of Israel" blessing and one sounding after each of the six additional blessings inserted into the Amidah — each sounding of the alarm consisting of three shofar blasts (see *Ramban*, *Ritva*, and *Hashlamah*).

חִיכּוּךְ, חָגָב, זְבוּב, וְצִירְעָה, וְיַתּוּשִׁין, וְשִׁילּוּחַ נְחָשִׁים וְעַקְרַבִּים, [1]לֹא הָיוּ מַתְרִיעִין, אֶלָּא צוֹעֲקִין״. [2]מִדִּצְעָקָה בְּפֶה, [3]הַתְרָעָה בְּשׁוֹפָרוֹת! [4]תַּנָּאֵי הִיא, [5]דִּתְנַן: ״עַל אֵלּוּ מַתְרִיעִין בְּשַׁבָּת: [6]עַל עִיר שֶׁהִקִּיפוּהָ גַּיִיס אוֹ נָהָר, וְעַל סְפִינָה הַמְּטוֹרֶפֶת בַּיָּם. [7]רַבִּי יוֹסֵי אָמַר: לְעֶזְרָה, אֲבָל לֹא לִצְעָקָה״. [8]בְּמַאי? [9]אִילֵימָא:

LITERAL TRANSLATION

scab, locusts, flies, and hornets, and mosquitoes, and an infestation of snakes and scorpions, [1]they would not sound the alarm, but they would cry out." [2]Since crying out is with the mouth, [3]sounding the alarm [must be] with shofars!

[4]It is [a dispute between] Tannaim, [5]for we have learned: "For these they sound the alarm on Shabbat: [6]For a city that an army or a river has surrounded, and for a ship being tossed about at sea. [7]Rabbi Yose said: For help, but not for crying out." [8]With what? [9]If we say:

TRANSLATION AND COMMENTARY

or **mosquitoes, or visitations of snakes or scorpions,** [1]**they would not sound the alarm, but they would cry out.**" The Baraita contrasts sounding the alarm with crying out. [2]Now, **since** it is clear that **crying out** is a reference to an activity that is done **with the mouth,** and refers to prayer, [3]it follows that the **sounding of an alarm** refers to an activity that is not done with the mouth, and indicates that the alarm **must be** sounded **with shofars!**

תַּנָּאֵי הִיא [4]The Gemara answers: This matter **is** the subject of **a dispute between Tannaim.** One Tanna maintains that reciting the *anenu* prayer is not called the sounding of an alarm, but another Tanna disagrees, [5]**for we have learned** in the following Mishnah (below, 19a): "**For the following** impending calamities **the alarm is sounded** even **on Shabbat:** [6]**For a city that is being surrounded by an** enemy **army, and** for a city that is in danger of being inundated by **a river** that has overflowed its banks, **and for a ship that is being tossed about** in a storm **at sea.** [7]**Rabbi Yose said:** In all these cases an alarm may be sounded even on Shabbat in order **to summon help, but** an alarm may **not** be sounded **as** a means of **crying out** to God in prayer for divine salvation." [8]The Gemara seeks to clarify the meaning of this Mishnah: **By means of what** is the alarm mentioned in this Mishnah sounded? [9]**If we say** that

RASHI

חגב — ארבה, כתרגומו. **צירעה** — עוקצת את האדם. **יתושין** — נכנסין בעיניו ובחוטמו. **חיכוך** — כמו נתחכך בכותל. **הא צעקה בפה היא** — אלמא דצעקת פה לא קרי ליה התרעה. **תנאי היא** — האי תנא דשאר מיני פורעניות סבר: צעקת פה לאו שמה התרעה, ואידך סבר כו׳. **גייס** — וצרין עליה. **נהר** — המתפשט ויוצא לחוץ לשטוף את השדה ואת הבתים. **המטורפת** — כמו ״בילים טרופות״ (חולין סד,א) — שהולכת ונדה, ועתידה להיטבע במים. **לעזרה** — צועקין לבני אדם שיבואו לעזרם. **ולא לצעקה** — תפלה, שאין אנו בטוחין כל כך שתועיל תפלתנו לצעוק עליהן בשבת, אלמא: צעקת פה קרי התרעה, מפי מורי. לשון אחר: לעזרה דקאמר תנא קמא ״מתריעין״, דמשמע בקול רם. ואמר ליה רבי יוסי: ״לעזרה״ — שיהו מתפללין כל אחד בביתו לעזרה בעלמא.

BACKGROUND

חִיכּוּךְ **Scab.** This is an infectious disease. Elsewhere in the Talmud (*Bava Kamma* 80b) a distinction is made between more serious skin diseases, which produce pustules, and scab, which causes an irritation in the upper layers of the epidermis but does not usually lead to more serious health complications.

זְבוּב, צִירְעָה, יַתּוּשִׁין **Flies, hornets, mosquitoes.** These insects can cause serious suffering in certain weather conditions that encourage their multiplication. A plague of flies is in itself a serious disturbance. It is even reported that certain peoples held ceremonies involving a special idol just for ridding the land of flies. Mosquitoes not only cause annoyance, but can also spread malaria. The sting of the hornet (*Vespa orientalis*) is mentioned in the Bible as one of the means by which the Canaanites were driven out of Eretz Israel (Exodus 23:28; Joshua 24:12). Likewise, historians tell of later periods when cities were abandoned as a result of plagues of mosquitoes or hornets.

וְשִׁילּוּחַ נְחָשִׁים **And an infestation of snakes.** The commentators explain that this refers to an infestation by many snakes, most of which are not venomous. For an infestation of venomous snakes would present an immediate danger to the community that would call for sounding the alarm.

NOTES

לְעֶזְרָה, אֲבָל לֹא לִצְעָקָה **For help but not for crying out.** Our commentary follows the first explanation offered by *Rashi*, according to which Rabbi Yose allows the community to cry out in times of danger in order to summon people to assist in their rescue, but he does not allow them to cry out to God in prayer. Since there is no assurance that their prayers will be effective, they should not be permitted to offer them on Shabbat. According to *Rashi*'s second explanation, Rabbi Yose maintains that on Shabbat the people may offer prayers for assistance as individuals, but may not cry out in communal prayer.

Rambam (*Hilkhot Ta'aniyyot* 1:6) explains that when Rabbi Yose permits a community that finds itself in danger to summon people to its rescue, he even permits the shofar to be sounded for that purpose. The anonymous first Tanna agrees with him on this point, for when it comes to saving lives, all the prohibitions of Shabbat are suspended.

HALAKHAH

חִיכּוּךְ **Scab.** "If the majority of the members of the community are suffering from boils that ooze with pus, they must fast and sound the alarm. But if they are suffering from dry scabs, they only cry out in prayer." (*Shulḥan Arukh, Oraḥ Ḥayyim* 576:5.)

חָגָב **Locusts.** "If a community is struck by locusts, the people must fast and sound the alarm. But if it is struck by a type of locust called *hagav*, members of the community do not fast or sound the alarm. Today, however, when we cannot distinguish between the different types of locusts, the alarm is sounded for all locusts." (*Shulḥan Arukh, Oraḥ Ḥayyim* 576:9.)

זְבוּב וְצִירְעָה **Flies and hornets.** "If a place is struck by a plague of flies or hornets, the people living there do not fast or sound the alarm, but only cry out in prayer." (*Shulḥan Arukh, Oraḥ Ḥayyim* 576:7.)

עִיר שֶׁהִקִּיפוּהָ גַּיִיס אוֹ נָהָר **A city that was by an army or a river has surrounded.** If a city is surrounded by an enemy army or is threatened by an overflowing river, or if a boat is being tossed about at sea, or even if a single individual is in mortal danger, the community cry out and offer special supplications on Shabbat, but do not sound the shofar. But they may sound the shofar in order to summon people to help with the rescue," following the anonymous first Tanna who agrees with Rabbi Yose on this point. (*Shulḥan Arukh, Oraḥ Ḥayyim* 576:13.)

TRANSLATION AND COMMENTARY

[1]the Mishnah is referring to an alarm sounded **by shofars,** there is a difficulty, for **is** the sounding of **shofars permitted on Shabbat?** Surely the sounding of a shofar on Shabbat is forbidden by Rabbinic decree. [2]**Rather,** the Mishnah must be dealing **with** the reciting of the ***anenu*** prayer, **and the Mishnah calls this recitation the sounding of an alarm.** The anonymous first Tanna of the Mishnah allows the reciting of the *anenu* prayer even on Shabbat as the proper response to the impending calamities listed in the Mishnah. But Rabbi Yose disagrees, arguing that an alarm may be sounded in order to summon help, but special supplications should not be inserted into the Shabbat prayers. [3]We can therefore **conclude from this** Mishnah that there is indeed a Tanna who maintains that when the sources speak of sounding an alarm, they may be referring to reciting the *anenu* prayer, as argued by Rav Yehudah the son of Rav Shmuel bar Shilat in the name of Rav.

בִּשְׁנֵי [4]The Gemara now relates that **during the years** when **Rabbi Yehudah Nesi'ah** (a grandson of Rabbi Yehudah HaNasi) occupied the office of Nasi **there was a** certain **affliction** that caused widespread public suffering in Eretz Israel. [14B] [5]**He decreed** that the community fast a series of **thirteen fasts** — two series of three fasts and then a third series of seven fasts, as laid down in the Mishnah — in the hope that this communal act of repentance would arouse God's compassion and bring an end to the calamity; **but** the community's prayers **were not answered.** [6]Rabbi Yehudah Nesi'ah then **had in mind to decree more** fasts upon the community and to continue until the suffering was removed. [7]But **Rabbi Ammi** objected to this idea and **said to him:** [8]**Surely** the Rabbis have **said: We do not trouble the community too much.** If thirteen fasts have already been imposed on the community, the court may not impose any additional fasts, because the community cannot bear any more privations.

אָמַר [9]Responding to Rabbi Ammi's argument, **Rabbi Abba the son of Rabbi Ḥiyya bar Abba said:** [10]**When Rabbi Ammi issued** this ruling that no more than thirteen fasts may be imposed on the community, **he issued** it **on his own** authority, but the other Sages disagree with him. [11]**Rather, this is what Rabbi Ḥiyya bar Abba said in the name of Rabbi Yoḥanan:** The Rabbis **only taught this** law — that the number of fasts that may be imposed on a community is limited to thirteen — **with regard to** fasts decreed on account of the absence of **rain.** [12]**But regarding** public fasts decreed because of **other types of calamities,** the community **continues to fast** an unlimited number of fasts **until it receives an answer from Heaven.** Thus Rabbi Yehudah Nesi'ah was indeed authorized to impose additional fasts.

[1]בְּשׁוֹפָרוֹת, שׁוֹפָרוֹת בְּשַׁבָּת מִי שָׁרֵי? [2]אֶלָּא לָאו בַּ״עֲנֵנוּ״, וְקָרֵי לָהּ הַתְרָעָה. [3]שְׁמַע מִינָּהּ.
[4]בִּשְׁנֵי דְּרַבִּי יְהוּדָה נְשִׂיאָה הֲוָה צַעֲרָא. [14B] [5]גָּזַר תְּלַת עֶשְׂרֵה תַּעֲנִיּוֹת, וְלָא אִיעֲנִי. [6]סָבַר לְמִיגְזַר טְפֵי. [7]אֲמַר לֵיהּ רַבִּי אַמִי: [8]הֲרֵי אָמְרוּ: אֵין מַטְרִיחִין אֶת הַצִּבּוּר יוֹתֵר מִדַּאי.
[9]אֲמַר רַבִּי אַבָּא בְּרֵיהּ דְּרַבִּי חִיָּיא בַּר אַבָּא: [10]רַבִּי אַמִי דַּעֲבַד, לְגַרְמֵיהּ הוּא דַּעֲבַד. [11]אֶלָּא הָכִי אָמַר רַבִּי חִיָּיא בַּר אַבָּא אָמַר רַבִּי יוֹחָנָן: לֹא שָׁנוּ אֶלָּא לִגְשָׁמִים, [12]אֲבָל לִשְׁאָר מִינֵי פּוּרְעָנוּיּוֹת מִתְעַנִּין וְהוֹלְכִין עַד שֶׁיֵּעָנוּ מִן הַשָּׁמַיִם.

LITERAL TRANSLATION

[1]With shofars, are shofars permitted on Shabbat? [2]Rather, is it not with *anenu*, and [the Mishnah] calls it sounding the alarm. [3]Conclude from this.

[4]In the years of Rabbi Yehudah Nesi'ah there was distress. [14B] [5]He decreed thirteen fasts, but he was not answered. [6]He thought to decree more. [7]Rabbi Ammi said to him: [8]Surely they said: We do not trouble the community too much.

[9]Rabbi Abba the son of Rabbi Ḥiyya bar Abba said: [10]When Rabbi Ammi acted, he acted for himself. [11]Rather, Rabbi Ḥiyya bar Abba said thus in the name of Rabbi Yoḥanan: They only taught [this] regarding rain, [12]but regarding other types of calamities they continue to fast until they are answered from Heaven.

RASHI

גזר תליסר תעניתא – כדאמרינן במתניתין (טו,ב): שלש ראשונות ושלש אמצעיות ושבע אחרונות. ולשאר פורעניות עביד להו ולא לגשמים. **לגרמיה** – לעצמו דרש, שלא אמר אלא לפי שהוא לא היה רוצה להתענות. **לא שנו** – דאין גוזרים יותר משלש עשרה.

SAGES

רַבִּי יְהוּדָה נְשִׂיאָה Rabbi Yehudah Nesi'ah. He was the son of Rabban Gamliel, the son of Rabbi Yehudah HaNasi, and he was called "Nesi'ah" to distinguish him from his eminent grandfather, the editor of the Mishnah. Rabbi Yehudah Nesi'ah was among the foremost Palestinian Amoraim, and the greatest disciples of Rabbi Yehudah HaNasi were his colleagues, including Rabbi Yoḥanan and Resh Lakish.

The court of Rabbi Yehudah Nesi'ah introduced various ordinances and was regarded as the greatest Torah center in the Jewish world, to the extent that even Rav, the great Amora, revised his opinions to conform with that court.

Rabbi Yehudah Nesi'ah served for many years as Nasi, and he seems to have been the last Nasi who was a great Torah scholar and head of the Sanhedrin. His place as Nasi, though not as head of the Sanhedrin, was taken by his son, Rabban Gamliel.

רַבִּי אַבָּא בְּרֵיהּ דְּרַבִּי חִיָּיא בַּר אַבָּא Rabbi Abba the son of Rabbi Ḥiyya bar Abba. He was a Palestinian Amora of the fourth generation. His father, Rabbi Ḥiyya bar Abba, was a Babylonian who immigrated to Eretz Israel, where he became a disciple of Rabbi Yoḥanan. His son, Rabbi Abba, was privileged to see Rabbi Yoḥanan in his extreme old age, but he mainly studied Torah with his own father. He also seems to have studied Torah with Rabbi Ammi and Rabbi Abbahu. He was a colleague of Rabbi Zera and Rabbi Yirmeyah and is regarded as one of the important Sages of his generation.

BACKGROUND

לְגַרְמֵיהּ For himself. This word means "for himself," and some commentators interpret it to mean that his opinion is a single one, that only he maintains it, and that it is not accepted. Others interpret לְגַרְמֵיהּ as meaning "for his own purposes," for reasons that apply only to himself.

NOTES

לְגַרְמֵיהּ הוּא דַּעֲבַד He acted for himself. Our translation and commentary follows *Rashi*'s understanding of this phrase in *Berakhot* 48a. Here, however, *Rashi* and *Rabbenu Ḥananel* offer a different explanation: Rabbi Ammi, who issued the ruling that no more than thirteen fasts may be imposed on the community, was acting *on his own behalf.* He issued this lenient ruling that no more than thirteen fasts should be decreed, because it was difficult for him to fast and he did not want to place himself in a situation where he would be required to do so.

LITERAL TRANSLATION

1 It was also taught thus: "When they said three and when they said seven, 2 they spoke only about rain. 3 But regarding other types of calamities, they continue to fast until they are answered."

4 Shall we say [that] this is a refutation of Rabbi Ammi?

5 Rabbi Ammi can say to you: It is [a dispute between] Tannaim, 6 for it was taught: "We do not decree more than thirteen fasts on the community, for we do not trouble the community too much. 7 [These are] the words of Rabbi. 8 Rabban Shimon ben Gamliel says: It is not for this reason (lit., 'this is not from the [same] name'), 9 but rather because the time of the rainfall has [already] passed."

1 תַּנְיָא נַמִי הָכִי: "כְּשֶׁאָמְרוּ שָׁלֹשׁ וּכְשֶׁאָמְרוּ שֶׁבַע, 2 לֹא אָמְרוּ אֶלָּא לִגְשָׁמִים. 3 אֲבָל לִשְׁאָר מִינֵי פוּרְעָנוּיּוֹת, מִתְעַנִּין וְהוֹלְכִין עַד שֶׁיֵּעָנוּ."

4 לֵימָא תֶּיהֱוֵי תְּיוּבְתֵּיהּ דְּרַבִּי אַמִי?

5 אָמַר לָךְ רַבִּי אַמִי: תַּנָּאֵי הִיא, 6 דְּתַנְיָא: "אֵין גּוֹזְרִין יוֹתֵר מִשְּׁלֹשׁ עֶשְׂרֵה תַּעֲנִיּוֹת עַל הַצִּבּוּר, לְפִי שֶׁאֵין מַטְרִיחִין אֶת הַצִּבּוּר יוֹתֵר מִדַּאי. 7 דִּבְרֵי רַבִּי. 8 רַבָּן שִׁמְעוֹן בֶּן גַּמְלִיאֵל אוֹמֵר: לֹא מִן הַשֵּׁם הוּא זֶה, 9 אֶלָּא מִפְּנֵי שֶׁיָּצָא זְמַנָּהּ שֶׁל רְבִיעָה".

TRANSLATION AND COMMENTARY

תַּנְיָא נַמִי הָכִי 1 The Gemara now cites a Baraita that supports Rabbi Ḥiyya bar Abba's statement. **The same** thing **was also taught** in a Baraita, which stated: **"When** the Rabbis **said** that a series of **three** fasts is imposed on the community, and then another series of three fasts is imposed, and then a series of **seven** fasts is imposed, 2 **they spoke only about** the measures that are taken on account of the absence of **rain.** 3 **But regarding** fasts that are imposed because of **other types of calamities,** the community **continues to fast** an unlimited number of fasts **until it is answered** from Heaven."

לֵימָא 4 The Gemara now seeks to use this Baraita as a refutation of the viewpoint of Rabbi Ammi: **Shall we say that this** Baraita, which states explicitly that there is no limit to the number of fasts that may be imposed on the community when it is faced with a calamity other than drought, **is a refutation of** the ruling of **Rabbi Ammi** that under no circumstances may more than thirteen fasts be decreed upon the community?

אָמַר לָךְ 5 The Gemara answers: **Rabbi Ammi can say to you:** The question of the number of fasts that may be imposed on the community **is** the subject of **a dispute between Tannaim**. Although though the statement of the anonymous Tanna in the Baraita quoted above contradicts the viewpoint of Rabbi Ammi, there is another Tanna who supports Rabbi Ammi and is of the opinion that no more than thirteen fasts may ever be imposed on the community. 6 The Gemara explains: **For it was taught** in the following Baraita: **"We do not decree more than thirteen fasts on the community,** even if the calamity on account of which the fasts were imposed still exists, **for we do not trouble the community too much.** 7 **This is the viewpoint of Rabbi** Yehudah HaNasi. 8 **Rabban Shimon ben Gamliel** disagrees and **says: It is not for this reason** that the Rabbis limited the number of fasts to thirteen. 9 **On the contrary,** they limited the number of fasts in times of drought **because** when the thirteen fasts are over, **the time** that is appropriate **for the** first **rainfall has already passed.** The fasts for drought start at the beginning of the month of Kislev and continue until the end of the month of Tevet. By then the first rainfall is no longer appropriate, for most of the annual rainfall should already have fallen." According to Rabban Shimon ben Gamliel, if the community is faced with a type of calamity other than drought, the fasts may continue indefinitely until the calamity is ended. But according to Rabbi Yehudah HaNasi no more than thirteen fasts may ever be imposed on the community. Rabbi Ammi, who objected to Rabbi Yehudah Nesi'ah's plan to decree more than thirteen fasts, follows the opinion of Rabbi Yehudah HaNasi.

RASHI

כשאמרו — להתענות שלש ראשונות ושלש אמצעיות ושבע אחרונות. **לא מן השם הוא זה** — שאין זה טעם, שאין מניחין בשביל טורח, אלא שכבר יצא זמנה של רביעה של יורה, שהרי מרחשון עבר על כולן לסוף התעניות, שמקצתן היו בכסליו, כדקתני מתניתין. ואיכא למשמע מדברי שמעון דבשאר מיני פורעניות, דכל שעתא הוי זימנייהו למיבטלי — אפילו טפי גוזרין. ורבי דאמר אין מטריחין — סתמא אכולהו קאמר, ואנא דאמרי כרבי.

HALAKHAH

אֵין גּוֹזְרִין יוֹתֵר מִשְּׁלֹשׁ עֶשְׂרֵה תַּעֲנִיּוֹת עַל הַצִּבּוּר We do not decree more than thirteen fasts on the community. "If after thirteen fasts the community's prayers have still not been answered, the court may not impose additional fasts on the community. This ruling applies only if the fasts were imposed on account of drought. But if they were imposed on account of some other calamity, the court may continue to decree fasts until the calamity has passed." (*Shulḥan Arukh, Oraḥ Ḥayyim* 575:6.)

TRANSLATION AND COMMENTARY

שָׁלְחוּ לֵיהּ [1]The Gemara now raises a new topic. **The people of Nineveh sent** the following question **to Rabbi** Yehudah HaNasi: [2]**People like us, who** live in an area where **rain is needed even during the summer, how should we act** with regard to the prayer for rain inserted into the Amidah prayer, when we suffer a drought in the summer? It is clear that we must insert into our prayers the expression: "And give dew and rain for a blessing on the face of the earth." But we are in doubt as to the place in our prayers where this petition should be inserted. [3]**Are we regarded as** a group of **individuals,** each of whom is asking that his own personal needs be met, **or are we regarded as a community** petitioning for a collective need? The Gemara explains how these two ways of viewing the residents of Nineveh differ: [4]**Are we regarded as** a group of **individuals,** each of whom is asking that his own personal needs be met, in which case the prayer for rain should be inserted **into the blessing: "Who hearkens unto prayer,"** for it is into that blessing that an individual inserts his private petitions? [5]**Or are we regarded as a community** putting forward a collective request, in which case the prayer for rain should be inserted **into** the ninth blessing, **the blessing of the years,** for it is into that blessing that the prayer for rain is inserted during the winter, when rain is needed by the entire community?

שְׁלַח לְהוּ [6]Rabbi Yehudah HaNasi **sent** his answer back **to** the people of Nineveh: **You are regarded as individuals,** [7]**and** therefore your prayer for rain must be inserted **into the blessing: "Who hearkens unto prayer."**

מֵיתִיבִי [8]**An objection** against Rabbi Yehudah HaNasi's ruling **was raised** from the following Baraita, which stated: [9]**"Rabbi Yehudah said: When** do the rules laid down in the Mishnah, about the times during which the prayer for rain is said apply? [10]They apply **at a time when the years are as they ought to be,** with sowing taking place in Marḥeshvan and the harvest beginning in Nisan, **and** when **the Jewish people are living in**

[1]שָׁלְחוּ לֵיהּ בְּנֵי נִינְוֵה לְרַבִּי: [2]כְּגוֹן אֲנַן, דַּאֲפִילּוּ בִּתְקוּפַת תַּמּוּז בָּעֵינַן מִטְרָא, הֵיכִי נַעֲבֵיד? [3]כִּיחִידִים דָּמֵינַן אוֹ כְּרַבִּים דָּמֵינַן? [4]כִּיחִידִים דָּמֵינַן, וּבְ״שׁוֹמֵעַ תְּפִלָּה״? [5]אוֹ כְּרַבִּים דָּמֵינַן, וּבְבִרְכַּת הַשָּׁנִים? [6]שְׁלַח לְהוּ: כִּיחִידִים דָּמֵיתוּ, [7]וּבְ״שׁוֹמֵעַ תְּפִלָּה״. [8]מֵיתִיבִי: [9]״אָמַר רַבִּי יְהוּדָה: אֵימָתַי? [10]בִּזְמַן שֶׁהַשָּׁנִים כְּתִיקְנָן וְיִשְׂרָאֵל שְׁרוּיִן עַל

LITERAL TRANSLATION

[1]The people of Nineveh sent to Rabbi: [2][People] like us, who need rain even during the Tammuz period, how should we act? [3]Are we like individuals or are we like many? [4]Are we like individuals, and [we pray for rain] in the blessing "Who hearkens unto prayer"? [5]Or are we like many, and [we pray for rain] in the blessing of the years?

[6]He sent to them: You are like individuals, [7]and [you pray for rain] in [the blessing] "Who hearkens unto prayer."

[8]They raised an objection: [9]"Rabbi Yehudah said: When? [10]At a time when the years are as they ought to be and Israel are living in

RASHI

ובשומע תפלה – אמרינן לשאילת מטר כיחיד השואל צרכיו ב״שומע תפלה״. דהא דאמרינן שאלה בברכת השנים אפילו ביחיד – משום דזמן צבור הוא, אבל במילתא אחריתי, דהוי ליחיד ולא לצבור, כהכא דבתקופת תמוז לאו זמן שאילת צבור הוא – ב״שומע תפלה״ הוא דמדכר ליה, ולא בברכת השנים, כדאמרינן במסכת עבודה זרה (ח,א) ובברכות (לא,א): אם היה לו חולה בתוך ביתו – מזכיר עליו בברכת החולים. ולבסוף מוקמינן: והלכתא ב״שומע תפלה״, כך שמעתי. **אימתי** – הוא סדר תעניות. **בזמן שהשנים כתיקנן** – שהיא קציר בניסן, וזריעה במרחשון, ואין סדר השנים משתנה.

BACKGROUND

בְּנֵי נִינְוֵה The people of Nineveh. Ancient Nineveh was located in the vicinity of present-day Mosul, on the Tigris River in northwest Iraq. Rainfall in the area is low (about 400 millimeters a year) and the summers are extremely dry. Thus it is surprising that the inhabitants of Nineveh would pray for rain in summer. There are alternative readings of our passage which have other cities (Naveh, etc.) in place of Nineveh. It is likely that the Gemara is speaking here of a place other than Nineveh, with a climate that usually included rain in summer.

בִּזְמַן שֶׁהַשָּׁנִים כְּתִיקְנָן At a time when the years are as they ought to be. In Rabbi Yehudah's opinion, the dates when one begins and ceases to pray for rain depend on two factors: (1) The years must be ordinary — in other words, the climate in general, including the time and frequency of rainfall, has been stable for a long time; and (2) the Jews must be on their land — in other words, a majority of the Jewish people must be living in Eretz Israel, according to whose seasons the dates for praying for rain were set.

NOTES

אֵימָתַי? בִּזְמַן שֶׁהַשָּׁנִים כְּתִיקְנָן When? At a time when the years are as they ought to be. *Rashi* explains that this Baraita is referring to the order of fasts described in our chapter. The rules laid down in the Mishnah about the fasts that are decreed during years of drought apply only when the years are as they ought to be, and the Jewish people are living in their land. But outside Eretz Israel, and when times are not as they ought to be, fasts are decreed in accordance with the needs of the community in a particular place at a particular time. But most Rishonim, followed by our commentary, maintain that the Baraita is referring to the prayer for rain in the "Who hearkens unto prayer" blessing. *Rambam* (see *Commentary to Mishnah, Ta'anit* 1:3; *Hilkhot Ta'aniyyot* 3:10) may have understood the Baraita as referring both to the prayer for rain as well as to the order of fasts decreed in times of drought (see *Gevurat Ari, Keren Orah, Sfat Emet*).

HALAKHAH

בְּנֵי נִינְוֵה The people of Nineveh. "Individuals who are in need of rain during the summer months may not insert the prayer for rain into the blessing of the years, but must insert the prayer into the blessing 'Who hearkens unto prayer.' Even if an entire city or an entire country is in need of rain, the city's or the country's inhabitants are treated as individuals, and must insert their prayer for rain into the blessing "Who hearkens unto prayer," following Rabbi Yehudah HaNasi. *Taz* argues that it is only in the congregation's silent Amidah that the prayer for rain is inserted into the blessing 'Who hearkens unto prayer,' but the prayer leader does not recite that prayer when he repeats the Amidah aloud. In some places it is customary not to use the usual formula, 'give dew and rain,' in the

TRANSLATION AND COMMENTARY

their own **land,** Eretz Israel, where the agricultural cycle follows this pattern. [1]**But nowadays,** when the years are not always as they ought to be, and the Jewish people are dispersed, **all** questions regarding the prayer for rain **are** decided **in accordance with the** climatic conditions prevailing in that particular **year** — whether it is dry or rainy — [2]and **in accordance with the** particular **place** — whether rain is needed only during the winter, as in Eretz Israel, or not — and **in accordance with the time** — whether or not rain is needed at that particular time." Thus we see that the prayer for rain is recited whenever and wherever there is a need for rain to fall; and even during the summer the people of Nineveh should insert their prayer for rain in its usual place, the blessing of the years, because rain is needed in Nineveh even during the summer months. Thus this Baraita contradicts Rabbi Yehudah HaNasi's ruling.

אָמַר לֵיהּ [3]The Gemara answers: **The following was said to** the scholar who raised the objection against Rabbi Yehudah HaNasi: **Do you seek to contradict** a ruling of **Rabbi** Yehudah HaNasi, [4]on the basis of **a Baraita? Rabbi** Yehudah HaNasi **is** himself **a Tanna,** and as such he has the authority to **disagree** with the rulings found in a Baraita!

מַאי הָוֵי עֲלָהּ [5]The Gemara ends the discussion with an inquiry regarding the final Halakhic ruling in the case. **What conclusion was reached about** the matter?

רַב נַחְמָן אָמַר [6]There is a disagreement between Amoraim on this point. **Rav Naḥman said:** In times of drought in places where rain is needed during the summer months, the prayer for rain is inserted **into the blessing of the years.** [7]**Rav Sheshet said:** In such cases, the prayer for rain is inserted **into the blessing: "Who hearkens unto prayer."** [8]The Gemara now gives a clear Halakhic decision: **And the Halakhah is:** In such cases, the prayer for rain is inserted **into the blessing: "Who hearkens unto prayer."**

בַּשֵּׁנִי [9]We learned in the Mishnah (above, 12b): **"On Mondays** food stores **may be opened for a short period** at the end of the day **when it is** already **getting dark,** so that those who are fasting can buy food with which to break their fast. [10]**On Thursdays** food stores may remain open **all day,** so that preparations may be made **in honor of Shabbat."**

אַדְמָתָן. [1]אֲבָל בַּזְּמַן הַזֶּה, [2]הַכֹּל לְפִי הַשָּׁנִים, הַכֹּל לְפִי הַמְּקוֹמוֹת, הַכֹּל לְפִי הַזְּמַן.

[3]אֲמַר לֵיהּ: מַתְנִיתָא רָמֵית עֲלֵיהּ דְּרַבִּי? [4]רַבִּי תַּנָּא הוּא וּפָלֵיג.

[5]מַאי הָוֵי עֲלַהּ?

[6]רַב נַחְמָן אָמַר: בְּבִרְכַּת הַשָּׁנִים. [7]רַב שֵׁשֶׁת אָמַר: בְּ״שׁוֹמֵעַ תְּפִלָּה״. [8]וְהִלְכְתָא: בְּ״שׁוֹמֵעַ תְּפִלָּה״.

[9]״בַּשֵּׁנִי מַטִּין עִם חֲשֵׁיכָה, [10]וּבַחֲמִישִׁי כָּל הַיּוֹם מִפְּנֵי כְבוֹד הַשַּׁבָּת״.

LITERAL TRANSLATION

their land. [1]But at this time, all is in accordance with the years, all is in accordance with the places, [2]all is in accordance with the time."

[3]He said to him: You raise a contradiction (lit., "cast") [from] a Baraita against Rabbi? [4]Rabbi is a Tanna, and disagrees.

[5]What was [decided] about it?

[6]Rav Naḥman said: In the blessing of the years. [7]Rav Sheshet said: In [the blessing] "Who hearkens unto prayer." [8]And the Halakhah is: In [the blessing] "Who hearkens unto prayer."

[9]"On Monday they open [them] a little when it is getting dark, [10]and on Thursday all day because of the honor of Shabbat."

RASHI

וישראל שרוין על אדמתן — שמנהג ארץ ישראל בכך. **הכל לפי השנים** — אם צריכה אותה שנה למטר, כגון שנה שחונה שצריכה לגשמים הרבה. **לפי המקומות** — כגון נינוה, דאפילו בתקופת תמוז בעו מטרא — לא גרסינן לפי הזמן, שלא ירדו עדיין גשמים. **בשני מטין עם חשיכה** — ולא נועלין ולא פותחין, הואיל ולאו לכבוד שבת הוה, ובחמישי מותרין לפתוח לגמרי. **מטין** — שלא יראו בני אדם ויצטערו, אלא לעת ערב פותחין מקצתן, כדי שיהא להם מה לאכול בלילה.

NOTES

וְהִלְכְתָא: בְּ״שׁוֹמֵעַ תְּפִלָּה״ And the Halakhah is: In the blessing "Who hearkens unto prayer." Elsewhere (*Avodah Zarah* 8a), the Gemara states that if an individual wishes to offer a private prayer for financial assistance, he should insert his petition in the blessing of the years. Why, then, should those who are in need of rain during the summer

HALAKHAH

blessing 'Who hearkens unto prayer,' but to use other formulations to petition for rain (see *Ba'er Hetev*)." (*Shulḥan Arukh, Oraḥ Ḥayyim* 117:2)

אֲבָל בַּזְּמַן הַזֶּה But at this time. "In places where the rainy season does not parallel the rainy season of Eretz Israel, if it has arrived (whenever that may be) but rain has not fallen, individuals embark on a series of three fasts, and then the court imposes a series of up to thirteen fasts upon the community (following Rabbi Yehudah, that all is in accordance with the particular place). Any public fast decreed outside Eretz Israel is treated as an individual fast, and therefore these fasts begin only at dawn (following Shmuel, that there are no communal fasts outside Eretz Israel other than the Ninth of Av)." (*Shulḥan Arukh, Oraḥ Ḥayyim* 575:9-10.)

TRANSLATION AND COMMENTARY

אִיבַּעְיָא לְהוּ [1]The Gemara notes that **the following problem arose** in discussion among the Sages: **What does** the Mishnah mean to **teach** us here? [2]Does it mean to say that **on Mondays** the doors of the food shops **may be opened a little** for a short while at the end of the day **when it is** already **getting dark,** [3]**whereas on Thursdays** the doors of these shops may be opened a little **all day,** so that adequate preparations may be made **in honor of Shabbat?** If the Mishnah is understood in this way, the only difference between Mondays and Thursdays is the number of hours during which the shopkeepers may conduct their business in this limited manner, opening the doors of their shops a little, but keeping all their merchandise inside. [4]**Or does** the Mishnah **perhaps** mean to say that **on Mondays** the doors of the grocery stores **may be opened a little** for a short while at the end of the day, [5]**whereas on Thursdays** the shopkeepers **may open** their shops fully **the entire day?** If the Mishnah is understood in this way, on Thursdays the shops may be opened all day long in the ordinary manner.

[1]אִיבַּעְיָא לְהוּ: הֵיכִי קָתָנֵי? [2]בַּשֵּׁנִי מַטִּין עִם חֲשֵׁיכָה, [3]וּבַחֲמִישִׁי כָּל הַיּוֹם מִפְּנֵי כְבוֹד הַשַּׁבָּת? [4]אוֹ דִּילְמָא, בַּשֵּׁנִי מַטִּין, [5]וּבַחֲמִישִׁי פּוֹתְחִין כָּל הַיּוֹם כּוּלּוֹ?

[6]תָּא שְׁמַע, דְּתַנְיָא: [7]"בַּשֵּׁנִי מַטִּין עַד הָעֶרֶב, וּבַחֲמִישִׁי פּוֹתְחִין כָּל הַיּוֹם כּוּלּוֹ מִפְּנֵי כְבוֹד הַשַּׁבָּת. [8]הָיוּ לוֹ שְׁנֵי פְתָחִים, פּוֹתֵחַ אֶחָד וְנוֹעֵל אֶחָד. [9]הָיָה לוֹ אִצְטַבָּא כְּנֶגֶד פִּתְחוֹ, פּוֹתֵחַ כְּדַרְכּוֹ וְאֵינוֹ חוֹשֵׁשׁ.

[10]"עָבְרוּ אֵלּוּ וְלֹא נַעֲנוּ, [11]מְמַעֲטִין בְּמַשָּׂא וּמַתָּן, בְּבִנְיָן

LITERAL TRANSLATION

[1]It was asked of them: How does it teach? [2]On Monday they open [them] a little when it is getting dark, [3]and on Thursday all day because of the honor of Shabbat? [4]Or perhaps, on Monday they open [them] a little, [5]and on Thursday they open [them] the entire day?

[6]Come [and] hear, for it was taught: [7]"On Monday they open [them] a little until the evening, and on Thursday they open [them] the entire day because of the honor of Shabbat. [8][If] he had two doors, he opens one and locks one. [9][If] he had a bench outside his door, he opens in his normal way and is not concerned."

[10]"[If these passed and they were not answered, [11]they reduce business transactions, building,

RASHI

או דילמא — פותחין כל היום, והכי משמע מתניתין: בשני מטין ובחמישי היה פתוח כדרכו כל היום לגמרי, מפני כבוד השבת. **איצטבא** — כסא, דהשתא אין החנות פתוחה לרשות הרבים, ואם הוא פתוח — אינו נראה כל כך. **פותח כדרכו** — אפילו בשני.

תָּא שְׁמַע [6]The Gemara answers: **Come and hear** the solution to this problem, **for it was taught** in a Baraita: [7]**"On Mondays** the shopkeepers **may open** the doors of their shops a **little in the evening** when it is getting dark, **and on Thursdays they may open** their shops fully **the entire day,** so that adequate preparations may be made **in honor of Shabbat.** [8]**If** a shop **has two doors,** the shopkeeper **may open one** of the doors fully even on Mondays, provided that **he keeps the other locked,** in order to show that he is not conducting his business in the ordinary manner. [9]And **if there is a bench outside the door of the shop,** the shopkeeper **may open** his shop **in the ordinary manner** even on Mondays, **and he need not be concerned** that he is violating a restriction imposed on account of the fast."

עָבְרוּ אֵלּוּ [10]The Gemara now proceeds to analyze the next clause of the Mishnah, which stated: **"If these** last seven fasts **have passed and** the community's prayers **have** still **not been answered,** the court does not impose any additional fasts on the community. But other measures are taken to elicit God's compassion so that the rains may fall and the drought come to an end. [11]People **must reduce** their **business transactions,**

NOTES

months insert the prayer for rain in the "Who hearkens unto prayer" blessing, and not in the blessing of the years?

Ra'avad answers that an individual may insert his prayer for financial well-being in the blessing of the years, because his well-being will not cause others to suffer. But individuals should not say the prayer for rain during the summer months when they recite that blessing, because rain during the summer months, while necessary for those individuals, is a curse for others. Alternatively, the insertion of a private prayer for financial well-being is not regarded as a fundamental change in the text of the blessing of the years, but the addition of a private prayer for rain when it is not needed by the entire community is indeed considered a deviation from the text of the blessing.

הָיָה לוֹ אִצְטַבָּא כְּנֶגֶד פִּתְחוֹ **If he had a bench outside his door.** *Rashi* explains that if there is a bench outside the

HALAKHAH

עָבְרוּ אֵלּוּ וְלֹא נַעֲנוּ, מְמַעֲטִין בְּמַשָּׂא וּמַתָּן **If these passed and they were not answered, they reduce business transactions.** "If the thirteen fasts have passed and it has still not rained, no additional fasts are imposed on the community, but business transactions (of a joyous nature; *Magen Avraham*) and construction of a joyous nature must be reduced. Likewise, a person is forbidden to enter into betrothal or marriage, unless he has not yet fulfilled his obligation of bringing children into the world. Greetings between one person and another must be reduced. Torah

TRANSLATION AND COMMENTARY

the building of houses, **the planting** of trees, betrothals, marriages and greetings between one person and another." [1]**A Tanna taught** the following Baraita: "When the Rabbis said that **building** must be reduced, they were not referring to the construction of homes for people who have nowhere to live, but rather to **building of a joyous nature.** [2]And when they said that **planting** must be reduced, they were not referring to the planting of food crops, but rather to **planting of a joyous nature.** [3]**What is meant by building of a joyous nature?** [4]**It** refers to **someone who builds a wedding chamber for his son.** [5]And **what is meant by planting of a joyous nature?** [6]**It** refers to **someone who plants trees** for shade and pleasure such as one might find in **a royal garden."**

וּבִשְׁאֵילַת שָׁלוֹם [7]We learned in the Mishnah: "If the thirteen fasts have passed and rain has still not fallen, **greetings** between one person and another must be reduced." [8]**Our Rabbis taught** a Baraita, which stated: **"Observant people do not extend greetings to each other** at all. [9]If **ignorant people,** who are unaware that greetings are to be avoided, **extend greetings,** they **may be answered in low and solemn tones,** for if their greetings are left unanswered, feelings of ill-will will arise. [10]**And they** all **wrap their** heads with their garments **and sit as mourners and as** people who are **under a ban, as people who are** being **reprimanded by God,** [11]**until they are shown mercy from Heaven** and rain begins to fall."

אָמַר רַבִּי אֶלְעָזָר [12]The Gemara continues: **Rabbi Elazar said: An important person is not permitted to fall on his face** in prayer and penance and thus humble

וּבִנְטִיעָה״. [1]תָּנָא: ״בְּבִנְיָן בִּנְיָן שֶׁל שִׂמְחָה. [2]נְטִיעָה נְטִיעָה שֶׁל שִׂמְחָה. [3]אֵי זֶהוּ בִּנְיָן שֶׁל שִׂמְחָה? [4]זֶה הַבּוֹנֶה בֵּית חֲתָנוּת לִבְנוֹ. [5]אֵי זוֹ הִיא נְטִיעָה שֶׁל שִׂמְחָה? [6]זֶה הַנּוֹטֵעַ אַבְוַורְנָקִי שֶׁל מְלָכִים״.
[7]״וּבִשְׁאֵילַת שָׁלוֹם״. [8]תָּנוּ רַבָּנַן: ״חֲבֵרִים אֵין שְׁאֵילַת שָׁלוֹם בֵּינֵיהֶן. [9]עַמֵּי הָאָרֶץ שֶׁשּׁוֹאֲלִין מַחֲזִירִין לָהֶם בְּשָׂפָה רָפָה וּבְכוֹבֶד רֹאשׁ. [10]וְהֵן מִתְעַטְּפִין וְיוֹשְׁבִין כַּאֲבֵלִים וְכִמְנוּדִּין, כִּבְנֵי אָדָם הַנְּזוּפִין לַמָּקוֹם, [11]עַד שֶׁיְּרַחֲמוּ עֲלֵיהֶם מִן הַשָּׁמַיִם״.
[12]אָמַר רַבִּי אֶלְעָזָר: אֵין אָדָם חָשׁוּב רַשַּׁאי לִיפּוֹל עַל פָּנָיו

LITERAL TRANSLATION

and planting." [1][A Tanna] taught: "Building [means] joyful building. [2]Planting [means] joyful planting. [3]What is joyful building? [4]Someone who builds a wedding chamber for his son. [5]What is joyful planting? [6]Someone who plants a tree of kings."

[7]"And greetings." [8]Our Rabbis taught: "Observant people (lit., 'colleagues') do not extend greetings among themselves. [9]Ignorant people who extend greetings are answered in an undertone (lit., 'with a soft lip') and in a solemn manner (lit., 'with heaviness of head'). [10]And they wrap themselves and sit as mourners and as under a ban, as people who are reprimanded by God, [11]until they are shown mercy from Heaven."

[12]Rabbi Elazar said: An important person is not permitted to fall on his face

RASHI

הכי גרסינן: תנא בנין בנין של שמחה נטיעה נטיעה של שמחה — ״בנין״ דקתני מתניתין לא בנין הצריך לו, אלא בנין הצריך לשמחה, דבדבר שמחה ממעטין. **בית חתנות** — לעשות חופתו. **אבוורנקי של מלכים** — שכך היו נוהגין: כשנולד בן למלך היו נוטעין אילן לשמו, ויום שממליכין אותו עושין לו כסא ממנו. לישנא אחרינא: אילן גדול המיסך על הארץ לטייל המלך תחתיו, ודומה לו בעירובין (כה,ב): ההוא אבוורנקא דהוה ליה לריש גלותא בבוסתניה. **של מלכים** — דרך מלכים נוטעין אותו לצל, הוא נוטעו כמו כן לצל, היא והיא נטיעה של שמחה. **ששאל בשלום** — תלמיד חכם מחזיר לו משום איבה, ובשפה רפה. **אבל ומנודה חייבין בעטיפה** — דכתיב ״ועל שפם יעטה״ במועד קטן (טו,א). **רשאי ליפול על פניו** — לבזות עצמו בפני הצבור, שאם לא יענה יחרפוהו, כך שמעתי, אלא אם כן יודעין בו שהוא חשוב כיהושע, שאמר לו

NOTES

shop door, the shopkeeper may open his shop in the ordinary manner even on Mondays, because when a bench stands in front of the door, the shop is not fully open to the public domain, and it is not immediately apparent to passersby that business is being conducted there as usual. *Shittah* argues that ordinarily the shopkeeper displays his wares on the bench that stands in front of his shop. Thus the shopkeeper may open his shop fully even on Mondays, if a bench stands outside his shop and he refrains from placing his merchandise on that bench, for in that way he demonstrates, that on account of the fast, he is not conducting his business in the ordinary manner.

אֵין אָדָם חָשׁוּב רַשַּׁאי לִיפּוֹל עַל פָּנָיו An important person is not permitted to fall on his face. The Jerusalem Talmud

HALAKHAH

scholars may not extend greetings to each other at all. If an uneducated person greets a Torah scholar, the scholar may answer him in a low and solemn tone. Torah scholars once again fast on Mondays and Thursdays, and continue to do so until the end of the month of Nisan." (*Shulḥan Arukh, Oraḥ Ḥayyim* 575:7.)

אֵין אָדָם חָשׁוּב רַשַּׁאי לִיפּוֹל עַל פָּנָיו An important person is not permitted to fall on his face. "An important person

CONCEPTS

חֲבֵרִים Observant people (lit., associates, colleagues). In the Talmudic period, the reference was to people who became members of a group dedicated to the precise observance of mitzvot. A person who wished to enter such a society had formally to accept its practices in the presence of three other members. The main stress of these groups was the strict observance of the laws of terumah and tithes and careful adherence to ritual purity, so much so that they would eat even nonsacrificial food (חוּלִּין) in a state of ritual purity. In practice, all Torah scholars were חֲבֵרִים. However, many of the common people (עַמֵּי הָאָרֶץ) and even some Samaritans (כּוּתִים) were included in this category. Acceptance as a חָבֵר removed an individual from the category of an עַם הָאָרֶץ, and his statements regarding tithes and ritual purity were accepted as true and were relied upon. In later generations, the term חָבֵר took on a more restricted meaning and was used to refer only to an important scholar.

LANGUAGE

אַבְוַורְנָקִי Abvarnaki. The meaning of this word and its correct reading are not clear. *Arukh* and many manuscripts read *Akurnaki* (or *Kurnaki*), which is similar to a Pahlavi or Persian word denoting a small decorative booth that was commonly erected in royal gardens.

Arukh states that on the birth of a prince a tree was planted, from which his throne was later made.

BACKGROUND

בֵּית חֲתָנוּת A wedding chamber. This seems to have been a special structure erected for the wedding feast. Sometimes such a structure continued to be used as a dwelling by the young couple for some time.

לִיפּוֹל עַל פָּנָיו To fall on his face. In this manner of prayer, a person lies on the ground with his face pressed against it, and utters petitions and requests. In some places prostration of this kind used to be customary in the prayer of petition (תַּחֲנוּן — *taḥanun*) recited after the Amidah. But

in most places, to some degree reflecting what is written in the Gemara here, the act of prostration is performed symbolically, and the person praying merely rests his head on his arm.

[1] אֶלָּא אִם כֵּן נַעֲנֶה כִּיהוֹשֻׁעַ בִּן נוּן, [2] שֶׁנֶּאֱמַר: ״וַיֹּאמֶר ה׳ אֶל יְהוֹשֻׁעַ קֻם לָךְ, לָמָּה זֶּה אַתָּה נֹפֵל עַל פָּנֶיךָ?״
[3] וְאָמַר רַבִּי אֶלְעָזָר: אֵין אָדָם חָשׁוּב רַשַּׁאי לַחֲגוֹר שַׂק אֶלָּא אִם כֵּן נַעֲנֶה כִּיהוֹרָם בֶּן אַחְאָב, [4] שֶׁנֶּאֱמַר: ״וַיְהִי, כִשְׁמֹעַ הַמֶּלֶךְ אֶת דִּבְרֵי הָאִשָּׁה, וַיִּקְרַע אֶת בְּגָדָיו, וְהוּא עֹבֵר עַל הַחֹמָה, וַיַּרְא הָעָם, וְהִנֵּה, הַשַּׂק עַל בְּשָׂרוֹ, וגו׳.״
[5] וְאָמַר רַבִּי אֶלְעָזָר: לֹא הַכֹּל בִּקְרִיעָה וְלֹא הַכֹּל בִּנְפִילָה. [6] מֹשֶׁה וְאַהֲרוֹן בִּנְפִילָה; [7] יְהוֹשֻׁעַ וְכָלֵב בִּקְרִיעָה. [8] מֹשֶׁה וְאַהֲרֹן בִּנְפִילָה, דִּכְתִיב: ״וַיִּפּוֹל מֹשֶׁה וְאַהֲרֹן עַל פְּנֵיהֶם״.

LITERAL TRANSLATION

[1] unless he is answered like Joshua the son of Nun, [2] as it is said: "And the Lord said to Joshua, Get up, why do you fall thus on your face?" [3] And Rabbi Elazar said: An important person is not permitted to gird [himself in] sackcloth unless he is answered like Jehoram the son of Ahab, [4] as it is said: "And it came to pass, when the king heard the words of the woman, that he rent his clothes, and he passed by upon the wall, and the people looked, and behold, he had sackcloth upon his flesh, etc." [5] And Rabbi Elazar said: Not all are [answered] by rending, and not all are [answered] by falling. [6] Moses and Aaron [were answered] by falling; [7] Joshua and Caleb [were answered] by rending. [8] Moses and Aaron [were answered] by falling, as it is written: "And Moses and Aaron fell on their faces."

TRANSLATION AND COMMENTARY

himself in public, [1] **unless** it is certain that **he merits to be answered like Joshua the son of Nun,** [2] **as it is said** (Joshua 7:10): **"And the Lord said to Joshua, Get up, why do you fall thus on your face?"** Someone who might not be answered may not fall on his face in public, for if he fails to be answered he will become the object of derision.

וְאָמַר רַבִּי אֶלְעָזָר [3] **And** similarly **Rabbi Elazar said: An important person is not permitted to gird himself in sackcloth** as a sign of mourning and penitence **unless it is** certain that **he will be answered like Jehoram the son of Ahab,** [4] **as it is said** (II Kings 6:30): **"And it came to pass, when the king heard the words of the woman, that he rent his clothes, and he passed by upon the wall, and the people looked, and behold, he had sackcloth upon his flesh."** Even though Jehoram was a wicked king, he repented and girded himself in sackcloth in order to bring an end to the famine that was afflicting his people. And Jehoram's act of penitence was answered, as the verse says (II Kings 7:16): "So a measure of fine flour was sold for a shekel, and two measures of barley for a shekel."

וְאָמַר רַבִּי אֶלְעָזָר [5] **And** similarly **Rabbi Elazar said: Not everybody is answered if he rends** his garments in times of distress in order to elicit divine compassion, **and** likewise **not everybody is answered if he falls** on his face in order to elicit divine compassion. [6] **Moses and Aaron were answered when they fell** on their faces in prayer, but it would not have been right for them to disgrace themselves and rend their garments. [7] **Joshua and Caleb were answered when they rent** their garments, but it would not have been right for them to act pretentiously and fall on their faces in prayer. [8] **Moses and Aaron were answered when they fell** on their faces in prayer, **as it is written** (Numbers 14:5): **"And Moses and Aaron fell on their faces** before all the assembly of the congregation of the children of Israel."

RASHI

הקדוש ברוך הוא: ״קום לך למה זה אתה נופל על פניך״. **אלא אם כן נענה** – שיודעין הן שנענה כיהורם. יהורם רשע היה, אלא שהתענה על רעב שהיה בימיו ונענה, דכתיב (מלכים ב ז) ״ויהי סאה סולת בשקל וסאתים שעורים בשקל״. **לא הכל** – נענין [בנפילה] ולא הכל נענין בקריעה, דיהושע וכלב שלא היו חשובין כמשה ואהרן לא זכו ליענות אלא בקריעה, ומקרא בעלמא קא דריש.

NOTES

(*Ta'anit* 2:6) limits this regulation that a person is not permitted to fall on his face in prayer unless it is certain that his prayer will be answered to a case where the individual wishes to pray on behalf of the community. According to a variant reading (see *Ra'avad, Hilkhot Tefillah* 5:14), the regulation applies only when the individual is praying in public. But if the person is praying in private or on his own behalf, he is permitted to fall on his face (see *Tosafot, Megillah* 22b). A number of explanations have been offered for this regulation. *Rashi* explains that a person may not fall on his face in prayer in public unless it is certain that he merits to be answered, so that he may not be put to shame if in fact his prayer is not answered. *Meiri* (following the Jerusalem Talmud) suggests that he may not pray in that manner, so that he not cause a desecration of God's Name if his prayer is not answered. *Shittah* and *Talmid HaRamban* maintain that he may not fall on his face in public, to avoid seeming pretentious.

לֹא הַכֹּל בִּקְרִיעָה Not all are answered by rending. To illustrate his point, that not everybody is fit to fall on his

HALAKHAH

is not permitted to fall on his face when he prays (in public; *Taz,* in the name of *Rosh*) on behalf of the community, unless he is certain that he will be answered like Joshua the son of Nun. According to *Pri Ḥadash,* he may not fall on his face, even if he is praying on his own behalf. According to *Arukh HaShulḥan,* he may not fall on his face when he prays on behalf of the community, even if he is praying in private." (*Shulḥan Arukh, Oraḥ Ḥayyim* 131:8.)

[1]יְהוֹשֻׁעַ וְכָלֵב בִּקְרִיעָה, דִּכְתִיב: "וִיהוֹשֻׁעַ בִּן נוּן, וְכָלֵב בֶּן יְפֻנֶּה... קָרְעוּ בִּגְדֵיהֶם". [2]מַתְקִיף לָהּ רַבִּי זֵירָא, וְאִיתֵּימָא רַבִּי שְׁמוּאֵל בַּר נַחְמָנִי: [3]אִי הֲוָה כְּתִיב, "יְהוֹשֻׁעַ", [4]כִּדְקָאָמְרַתְּ. [5]הָשְׁתָּא דִּכְתִיב, "וִיהוֹשֻׁעַ", [6]הָא וְהָא עֲבִיד.

[7]וְאָמַר רַבִּי אֶלְעָזָר: לֹא הַכֹּל בְּקִימָה, וְלֹא הַכֹּל בְּהִשְׁתַּחֲוָיָה. [8]מְלָכִים בְּקִימָה, וְשָׂרִים בְּהִשְׁתַּחֲוָיָה. [9]מְלָכִים בְּקִימָה, [10]דִּכְתִיב: "כֹּה אָמַר ה׳, גֹּאֵל יִשְׂרָאֵל, קְדוֹשׁוֹ, [15A] לִבְזֹה נֶפֶשׁ, לִמְתָעֵב גּוֹי, לְעֶבֶד מֹשְׁלִים, מְלָכִים יִרְאוּ וָקָמוּ". [11]וְשָׂרִים בְּהִשְׁתַּחֲוָיָה, [12]דִּכְתִיב: "שָׂרִים וְיִשְׁתַּחֲווּ".

[13]מַתְקִיף לָהּ רַבִּי זֵירָא, וְאִיתֵּימָא רַבִּי שְׁמוּאֵל בַּר

LITERAL TRANSLATION

[1]Joshua and Caleb [were answered] by rending, as it is written: "And Joshua the son of Nun, and Caleb the son of Jephunneh... rent their clothes."

[2]Rabbi Zera and some say [it was] Rabbi Shmuel bar Naḥmani, objected to this: [3]If it had been written, "Joshua," [4][it would have been] as you said. [5]Now that it is written, "*And* Joshua," [6]he did this and that.

[7]And Rabbi Elazar said: Not all [will act] by rising, and not all [will act] by prostrating themselves. [8]Kings [will act] by rising, and princes [will act] by prostrating themselves. [9]Kings [will act] by rising, [10]as it is written: "Thus says the Lord, the redeemer of Israel, his Holy One, [15A] to him whom man despises, to him whom the nation abhors, to a servant of rulers, kings shall see and arise." [11]And princes [will act] by prostrating themselves, [12]as it is written: "Princes also shall prostrate themselves."

[13]Rabbi Zera and some say [it was] Rabbi Shmuel bar Naḥmani, objected to this:

TRANSLATION AND COMMENTARY

[1]**Joshua and Caleb were answered when they rent** their garments, **as the verse says** (Numbers 14:6): **"And Joshua the son of Nun, and Caleb the son of Jephunneh,** of those who spied out the land, **rent their clothes."**

מַתְקִיף לָהּ [2]The Gemara now questions the proof texts cited to support Rabbi Elazar's statement. **Rabbi Zera, and some say it was Rabbi Shmuel bar Naḥmani, objected to** the use of the verses describing the behavior of Moses and Aaron, Joshua and Caleb, as support for Rabbi Elazar's statement: [3]**If the verse had read: "Joshua** the son of Nun, and Caleb the son of Jephunneh... rent their clothes," [4]**it would have been** legitimate to argue **as you did** that Moses and Aaron only fell on their faces, and Joshua and Caleb only rent their garments. [5]But **now that the verse says, "*And* Joshua** the son of Nun, and Caleb the son of Jephunneh," this argument can no longer be made. The Hebrew letter vav ("and") preceding the word Joshua connects this verse to the previous verse describing the actions of Moses and Aaron. The sense of the passage is as follows: Moses and Aaron fell on their faces but did not rend their garments, [6]but Joshua and Caleb **did both.** In addition to falling on their faces, Joshua and Caleb also rent their clothing.

וְאָמַר רַבִּי אֶלְעָזָר [7]**And** similarly **Rabbi Elazar said: Not everybody will stand up** before the Jewish people in the Messianic age, **and** likewise **not all will prostrate themselves** before them. [8]**Kings will stand up** before the Jewish people, **and princes will prostrate themselves** before them. [9]**Kings will stand up** before the Jewish people, [10]**as the verse says** (Isaiah 49:7): **"Thus says the Lord, the redeemer of Israel, his Holy One,** [15A] **to him whom man despises, to him whom the nation abhors, to a servant of rulers, kings shall see and arise."** In the Messianic age, kings will stand up before those who were previously despised and abhorred — the Jewish people. [11]**And princes will prostrate themselves** before them, [12]**as the** same **verse continues: "Princes also shall prostrate themselves."**

מַתְקִיף לָהּ [13]The Gemara now points out a problem with Rabbi Elazar's interpretation of the verse in Isaiah. **Rabbi Zera, and some say it was Rabbi Shmuel bar Naḥmani, strongly objected to this** understanding

RASHI

ויהושע בן נון — כתיב בתריה דההוא ד"ויפל", וי"ו מוסיף על ענין ראשון. **לבזה נפש למתעב גוי לעבד מושלים** — לישראל הבזוים ומתועבים ועבדים מושלין בהן. **ולא הכל בקימה** — לקראת ישראל לעתיד לבא "מלכים יראו וקמו שרים וישתחוו".

NOTES

face in order to elicit divine compassion, Rabbi Elazar cites the example of Joshua and Caleb, who were fit to rend their garments but not to fall on their faces in prayer. *Maharsha* notes that we do in fact find that Joshua was answered when he fell on his face in prayer, as Rabbi Elazar himself stated above. *Maharsha* explains that Joshua was not fit to fall on his face in prayer during the lifetime of Moses and Aaron, for he was not of their stature, and falling on his face would have been regarded as an act of pretentiousness. But after their death, when Joshua enjoyed the status of king, it was appropriate for him to fall on his face in prayer, and at that time it would have been inappropriate for him to rend his garments.

TRANSLATION AND COMMENTARY

of the verse: [1]**If the verse had read: "And princes shall prostrate themselves** [וְשָׂרִים יִשְׁתַּחֲווּ]," [2]**it would have been** legitimate to say **as you did** that the kings will stand up and the princes will prostrate themselves. [3]But **now that the verse says: "Princes *also* shall prostrate themselves** [שָׂרִים וְיִשְׁתַּחֲווּ]," this argument can no longer be made. The Hebrew letter vav ("also") preceding the words "shall prostrate themselves" implies that the princes will also do something else. The kings will stand up before the Jewish people, but they will not prostrate themselves before them. [4]But the princes **will do both.** They will stand up and also prostrate themselves.

אָמַר רַב נַחְמָן בַּר יִצְחָק [5]This chapter concludes with a similar exposition of a Biblical verse: **Rav Naḥman bar Yitzḥak said: I too can make** such a **statement:** [6]**Not everybody is fit** to be rewarded **with light** in the World to Come, **and not everybody is fit** to be rewarded **with gladness.** [7]**The righteous are fit** to be rewarded **with light, and the upright are fit** to be rewarded **with gladness.** [8]**The righteous are fit** to be rewarded **with light, as the verse says** (Psalms 97:11): **"Light is sown for the righteous."** [9]**And the upright are fit** to be rewarded **with gladness, as the** same **verse continues: "And gladness for the upright in heart."**

נַחְמָנִי: [1]אִי הֲוָה כְּתִיב, "וְשָׂרִים יִשְׁתַּחֲווּ", [2]כִּדְקָאָמְרַתְּ. [3]הָשְׁתָּא דִּכְתִיב, "שָׂרִים וְיִשְׁתַּחֲווּ", [4]הָא וְהָא עֲבוּד.

[5]אָמַר רַב נַחְמָן בַּר יִצְחָק: אַף אֲנִי אוֹמֵר: [6]לֹא הַכֹּל לְאוֹרָה, וְלֹא הַכֹּל לְשִׂמְחָה, צַדִּיקִים לְאוֹרָה, [7]וִישָׁרִים לְשִׂמְחָה. [8]צַדִּיקִים לְאוֹרָה, דִּכְתִיב: "אוֹר זָרֻעַ לַצַּדִּיק", [9]וְלִישָׁרִים שִׂמְחָה, דִּכְתִיב: "וּלְיִשְׁרֵי לֵב שִׂמְחָה".

הדרן עלך מאימתי

LITERAL TRANSLATION

[1]If it had been written, "And princes shall prostrate themselves," [2][it would have been] as you said. [3]Now that it is written, "Princes *also* shall prostrate themselves," [4]they did this and that.

[5]Rav Naḥman bar Yitzḥak said: I too say: [6]Not all are [fit] for light, and not all are [fit] for gladness. [7]The righteous are [fit] for light, and the upright are [fit] for gladness. [8]The righteous are [fit] for light, as it is written: "Light is sown for the righteous," [9]and the upright are [fit] for gladness, as it is written: "And gladness for the upright in heart."

RASHI

הכי גרסינן: לא הכל לאורה ולא הכל לשמחה דכתיב אור זרוע לצדיק ולישרי לב שמחה - ישרים לשמחה, דישרים עדיפי מלדיקים.

הדרן עלך מאימתי

NOTES

"אוֹר זָרֻעַ לַצַּדִּיק" **"Light is sown for the righteous."** *Rashi* explains that the upright are superior to the righteous, and they will therefore merit gladness, which is a greater reward than light. *Rashba* maintains that the righteous are superior to the upright. The righteous will be rewarded with light, and certainly with gladness, whereas the reward of the upright will be limited to gladness.

Maharsha argues that the structural similarity between Rav Naḥman bar Yitzḥak's statement and Rabbi Elazar's statements cited above proves that the righteous and the upright will receive different rewards. The righteous, who are superior to the upright, will be rewarded with light — spiritual pleasure in the World to Come; whereas the upright will be rewarded with gladness — physical pleasure.

Conclusion to Chapter One

There are two prayers relating to rain that are inserted into the Amidah prayer during the rainy season. Mention is made of rain ("Who causes the wind to blow and the rain to fall") in the second blessing of the Amidah prayer beginning on the last day of the Sukkot Festival. But the more explicit prayer for rain ("And give dew and rain for a blessing"), which is inserted into the ninth blessing of the Amidah, is not yet recited on that date. In Eretz Israel the prayer for rain is first recited on the seventh of Marḥeshvan, whereas in Babylonia it is first said on the night of the sixtieth day after the autumnal equinox. The custom prevailing in most Diaspora communities follows the practice of Babylonia, even in those places where the rainy season is very different from that of Babylonia.

The rainy season is assumed to begin shortly after the time that the prayer for rain is first inserted into the Amidah. If the time when the first rainfall is expected passes without any rain falling, Torah scholars begin to observe individual fasts on behalf of the community. If these fasts pass and it has still not rained, the entire community must observe a series of three fasts which start at dawn. If these fasts pass and rain has still not fallen, the court imposes another series of three fasts upon the community. The second three communal fasts are more stringent than the first. These fasts begin on the previous evening, and in addition to the prohibitions against eating and drinking, other types of bodily pleasure — for example, wearing leather shoes, bathing, and engaging in sexual relations — are also forbidden. If these fasts pass and it has still not rained, the community observes seven more fasts, which are even more stringent

than the second series. A number of public acts of mourning are observed on those days in order to arouse the community to repentance.

In the course of the discussions regarding the topics mentioned above, the Gemara also considers the issue of individual fasts. If an individual wishes to observe a fast, he must take the fast upon himself on the afternoon prior to his proposed fast. If an individual takes it upon himself to observe a fast, without specifying whether he is taking upon himself a fast with the leniencies of an individual fast or a fast with the stringencies of a public fast, he is required to observe an individual fast that begins in the morning. If a person takes a vow to observe a fast, there are certain cases where he is required to refrain from eating even if he forgot about his fast in the middle of the day and ate, and there are other cases in which he "loses" that day and is required to observe a fast on another day. In certain situations, a person may decide to cancel the fast that he has accepted upon himself and observe it on another day.

List of Sources

Aḥaronim, lit., "the last," meaning Rabbinical authorities from the time of the publication of Rabbi Yosef Caro's code of Halakhah, *Shulḥan Arukh* (1555).

Aggadot Bereshit, collection of Aggadot from the Talmud with commentary, by an author whose name is not known.

Ahavat Eitan, novellae on Aggadot in the Talmud, by Rabbi Avraham Maskileison, Byelorussia (1788-1848).

Arba'ah Turim, code of Halakhah by Rabbi Ya'akov ben Asher, b. Germany, active in Spain (c. 1270-1343).

Arukh, first Talmudic dictionary, by Rabbi Natan of Rome, 11th century.

Arukh HaShulḥan, commentary on *Shulḥan Arukh*, by Rabbi Yeḥiel Mikhel Epstein, Byelorussia (1829-1908).

Ba'al HaMa'or, Rabbi Zeraḥyah ben Yitzḥak HaLevi, Spain, 12th century. *HaMa'or*, Halakhic commentary on *Hilkhot HaRif*.

Ba'er Hetev, commentary on *Shulḥan Arukh*, by Rabbi Zeḥaryah Mendel of Belz, Poland (18th century).

Baḥ (Bayit Ḥadash), commentary on *Arba'ah Turim*, by Rabbi Yoel Sirkes, Poland (1561-1640).

Bereshit Rabbah, Midrash on the Book of Genesis.

Bet Yosef, Halakhic commentary on *Arba'ah Turim*, by Rabbi Yosef Caro (1488-1575), which is the basis of his authoritative Halakhic code, the *Shulḥan Arukh*.

Darkhei Moshe, commentary on *Tur*, by Rabbi Moshe ben Yisrael Isserles, Poland (1525-1572).

Derishah and *Perishah*, commentaries on *Tur*, by Rabbi Yehoshua Falk Katz, Poland (c. 1555-1614).

Dikkdukei Soferim, a collection of variant readings on tractates of the Talmud, by Rabbi Raphael Natan Nata Rabbinovicz, Russia (1835-1888).

Divrei Shlomo, glosses on the Talmud, by Rabbi Zalman Rivlin, Poland, 19th century.

Ein Ya'akov, collection of Aggadot from the Babylonian Talmud by Rabbi Ya'akov ben Shlomo Ḥabib, Spain and Salonika (c. 1445-1515).

Eliyah Rabbah, commentary on *Shulḥan Arukh, Orah Ḥayyim*, by Rabbi Eliyahu Shapira, Prague (1660-1712).

Eshel Avraham, novellae on the Talmud, by Rabbi Avraham Ya'akov Neimark, Israel (20th century).

Eshkol, Halakhic compendium, by Rabbi Avraham ben Yitzḥak of Narbonne, France (c. 1110-1179).

Even HaEzer, section of *Shulḥan Arukh* dealing with marriage, divorce, and related topics.

Geonim, heads of the academies of Sura and Pumbedita in Babylonia from the late 6th century to the mid-11th century.

Gevurat Ari, novellae on the Talmud, by Rabbi Aryeh Leib ben Asher, Lithuania, 18th century.

Gilyon HaShas, glosses on the Talmud, by Rabbi Akiva Eger, Posen, Germany (1761-1837).

Gra, Rabbi Eliyahu ben Shlomo Zalman (1720-1797), the Gaon of Vilna. Novellae on the Talmud and *Shulḥan Arukh*.

Hashlamah, see *Sefer HaHashlamah*.

Ḥokhmat Manoaḥ, commentary on the Talmud, by Rabbi Manoaḥ ben Shemaryah, Poland, 16th century.

Iyyun Ya'akov, commentary on *Ein Ya'akov*, by Rabbi Ya'akov bar Yosef Riesher, Prague, Poland and France (d. 1773)

Keren Orah, novellae on the Talmud, by Rabbi Yitzhak Karlin, Poland, 19th century.

Leḥem Mishneh, commentary on *Mishneh Torah*, by Rabbi Avraham di Boton, Salonica (1560-1609).

Magen Avraham, commentary on *Shulḥan Arukh, Oraḥ Ḥayyim*, by Rabbi Avraham HaLevi Gombiner, Poland (d. 1683).

Maggid Mishneh, commentary on *Mishneh Torah*, by Rabbi Vidal de Tolosa, Spain, 14th century.

Maharsha, Rabbi Shmuel Eliezer ben Yehudah HaLevi Edels,

Poland (1555-1631). Novellae on the Talmud.

Meiri, commentary on the Talmud (called *Bet HaBeḥirah*), by Rabbi Menaḥem ben Shlomo, Provence (1249-1316).

Melekhet Shlomo, commentary on the Mishnah, by Rabbi Shlomo Adeni, Yemen and Eretz Israel (1567-1626).

Midrash Shoḥer Tov, Aggadic Midrash on the Book of Psalms.

Mishnah Berurah, commentary on *Shulḥan Arukh, Oraḥ Ḥayyim,* by Rabbi Yisrael Meir HaKohen, Poland (1837-1933).

Mordekhai, compendium of Halakhic decisions, by Rabbi Mordekhai ben Hillel HaKohen, Germany (1240?-1298).

Nefesh HaḤayyim, treatise on ethics and Kabbalah, by Rabbi Ḥayyim of Volozhin, Lithuania (1749-1821).

Oraḥ Ḥayyim, section of *Shulḥan Arukh* dealing with daily religious observances, prayers, and the laws of the Sabbath and Festivals.

Otzar HaKavod, commentary on Aggadah in the Talmud, by Rabbi Todros Abulafiya, Spain (1234-c. 1304).

Perishah, see *Derishah.*

Pesikta DeRav Kahana, Aggadic Midrash.

Pri Ḥadash, novellae on *Shulḥan Arukh,* by Rabbi Ḥizkiyah Da Silva, Livorno, Italy and Eretz Israel (1659-1698).

Pri Megadim, super-commentary to commentaries on *Shulḥan Arukh,* by Rabbi Yosef Te'omim, Lvov, Ukraine, and Germany (1727-1793).

Ra'avad, Rabbi Avraham ben David, commentator and Halakhic authority. Wrote comments on *Mishneh Torah.* Provence (c. 1125-1198?).

Rabbenu Efraim, Efraim Ibn Avi Alragan, Halakhist, North Africa, late 11th-early 12th century.

Rabbenu Elyakim, German Talmudist, 11th century.

Rabbenu Gershom, commentator and Halakhic authority, France (960-1040).

Rabbenu Ḥananel (ben Ḥushiel), commentator on Talmud, North Africa (990-1055).

Rabbenu Tam, commentator on Talmud, Tosafist, France (1100-1171).

Rabbi Ya'akov of Orleans, French Tosafist, died London, 1189.

Rabbenu Yehonatan, Yehonatan ben David HaKohen of Lunel, Provence, Talmudic scholar (c. 1135-after 1210).

Rabbi Akiva Eger, Talmudist and Halakhic authority, Posen, Germany (1761-1837).

Rabbi Ya'akov Emden,, Talmudist and Halakhic authority, Germany (1697-1776).

Ramat Shmuel, novellae on the Talmud, by Rabbi Shmuel HaLevi, 16th century.

Rambam, Rabbi Moshe ben Maimon, Rabbi and philosopher, known also as Maimonides. Author of *Mishneh Torah*, Spain and Egypt (1135-1204).

Ramban, Rabbi Moshe ben Naḥman, commentator on Bible and Talmud, known also as Naḥmanides, Spain and Eretz Israel (1194-1270).

Ran, Rabbi Nissim ben Reuven Gerondi, Spanish Talmudist (1310?-1375?).

Rash, Rabbenu Shimshon of Sens. Commentary on the Mishnah on the Order of *Zeraim.* France and Eretz Israel (died c. 1230).

Rashash, Rabbi Shmuel ben Yosef Shtrashun, Lithuanian Talmudic scholar (1794-1872).

Rashba, Rabbi Shlomo ben Avraham Adret, Spanish Rabbi famous for his commentaries on the Talmud and his responsa (c. 1235-c. 1314).

Rashi, Rabbi Shlomo ben Yitzḥak, the paramount commentator on the Bible and the Talmud, France (1040-1105).

Rav Amram Gaon, Amram ben Sheshna, Gaon of Sura (died c. 875).

Rav Hai Gaon, Babylonian Rabbi, head of Pumbedita Yeshivah, 10th century.

Rema, Rabbi Moshe ben Yisrael Isserles, Halakhic authority, Cracow, Poland (1525-1572).

Ri, Rabbi Yitzḥak ben Shmuel of Dampierre, Tosafist, France (died c. 1185).

Ri of Lunel, see *Rabbenu Yehonatan.*

Riaf, Rabbi Yoshiyah ben Yosef Pinto, Eretz Israel and Syria (1565-1648). Commentary on *Ein Ya'akov.*

Rid, see *Tosefot Rid.*

Rif, Rabbi Yitzḥak Alfasi, Halakhist, author of *Hilkhot HaRif,* North Africa (1013-1103).

Rishon LeTzion, novellae on the Talmud, by Rabbi Ḥayyim Ibn Attar, Italy and Eretz Israel (1696-1743).

Rishonim, lit., "the first," meaning Rabbinical authorities active between the end of the Geonic period (mid-11th century) and the publication of the *Shulḥan Arukh* (1555).

Ritva, novellae and commentary on the Talmud, by Rabbi Yom Tov ben Avraham Ishbili, Spain (c. 1250-1330).

Rivash, Rabbi Yitzḥak ben Sheshet, Spain and North Africa (1326-1408). Novellae on the Talmud mentioned in *Shittah Mekubbetzet.*

Rosh, Rabbi Asher ben Yeḥiel, also known as Asheri, commentator and Halakhist, Germany and Spain (c. 1250-1327).

Rosh Yosef, novellae on the Talmud, by Rabbi Yosef ben Ya'akov of Pinczow, Lithuania, 17th century.

Sha'ar HaGemul, treatise on resurrection and reward and punishment, by *Ramban.* See *Ramban.*

Sefer HaHashlamah, supplement to *Hilkhot HaRif,* by Rabbi Meshullam ben Moshe, Provence, early 13th century.

Sfat Emet, novellae on the Talmud, by Rabbi Yehudah Leib Alter, Poland, 19th century.

Sha'arei Teshuvah, commentary and responsa on *Shulḥan Arukh,* by Rabbi Ḥayyim Mordekhai Margoliyot, Poland, 18th-19th century.)

Shelah (Shenei Luḥot HaBrit), an extensive work on Halakhah, ethics and Kabbalah, by Rabbi Yeshayahu ben Avraham HaLevi Horowitz. Prague, Poland and Eretz Israel (c. 1565-1630).

Shittah, commentary on tractate *Ta'anit,* attributed to Rabbenu Ḥayyim ben Rabbi Shmuel ben David of Toledo, Spain, 13th-14th century.

Shulḥan Arukh, code of Halakhah by Rabbi Yosef Caro, b. Spain, active in Eretz Israel (1488-1575).

Smag (Sefer Mitzvot Gadol), an extensive work on the positive

and negative commandments by Rabbi Moshe ben Ya'akov of Coucy, 13th century.

Talmid HaRamban, commentary on *Hilkhot HaRif* on tractate *Ta'anit,* by a student of *Ramban,* 13th century.

Targum Onkelos, Aramaic translation of the Five Books of Moses, attributed to the proselyte Onkelos, Eretz Israel, 2nd century C.E.

Taz, abbreviation for *Turei Zahav.* See *Turei Zahav.*

Teshuvot HaRamban, responsa literature, by *Ramban* (see *Ramban*).

Tiferet Israel, commentary on the Mishnah, by Rabbi Yisrael Lipshitz, Germany (1782-1860).

Torat Ḥayyim, novellae on the Talmud, by Rabbi Avraham Ḥayyim Shor, Galicia (d.1632).

Tosafot, collection of commentaries and novellae on the Talmud, expanding on Rashi's commentary, by the French-German Tosafists (12th-13th centuries).

Tosefot Rid, commentary on the Talmud by Rabbi Yeshayahu ben Mali di Trani, Italian Halakhist (c. 1200-before 1260).

Tosefot Yom Tov, commentary on the Mishnah by Rabbi Yom Tov Lipman HaLevi Heller, Prague and Poland (1579-1654).

Tur, abbreviation of *Arba'ah Turim*, Halakhic code by Rabbi Ya'akov ben Asher, b. Germany, active in Spain (c. 1270-1343).

Yalkut Shimoni, Aggadic Midrash on the Bible.

Ya'akov Castro, Rabbinic authority, Egypt and Eretz Israel (1525-1610).

Yoreh De'ah, section of *Shulḥan Arukh* dealing with dietary laws, interest, ritual purity, and mourning.

About the Type

This book was set in Leawood, a contemporary typeface designed by Leslie Usherwood. His staff completed the design upon Usherwood's death in 1984. It is a friendly, inviting face that goes particularly well with sans serif type.